COMM 1010
SALT LAKE COMMUNITY COLLEGE

COMMUNICATING AT WORK
STRATEGIES FOR SUCCESS IN BUSINESS AND THE PROFESSIONS

ELEVENTH EDITION

RONALD B. ADLER
Santa Barbara City College, Emeritus

JEANNE MARQUARDT ELMHORST
Central New Mexico Community College

Mc Graw Hill **Learning Solutions**

Boston   Burr Ridge, IL   Dubuque, IA   New York   San Francisco   St. Louis
Bangkok   Bogotá   Caracas   Lisbon   London   Madrid
Mexico City   Milan   New Delhi   Seoul   Singapore   Sydney   Taipei   Toronto

The McGraw·Hill Companies

COMM 1010 | Salt Lake Community College
Communicating at Work: Strategies for Success in Business and the Professions

1 2 3 4 5 6 7 8 9 0 DIG DIG 14 13 12

ISBN-13: 978-0-07-780404-6
ISBN-10: 0-07-780404-X

Learning Solutions Consultant: Darlene Bahr
Project Manager: Heather Ervolino
Cover Designer: Felicia Cornish
Printer/Binder: Digital Impressions
Cover Photo Credits: © 2012 JupiterImages Corporation

Ronald B. Adler is professor emeritus at Santa Barbara City College. Throughout his career, he has specialized in the study of organizational and interpersonal communication. He is the author of *Confidence in Communication: A Guide to Assertive and Social Skills* and coauthor of *Understanding Human Communication, Interplay: The Process of Interpersonal Communication,* as well as the widely used text *Looking Out/Looking In.* Professor Adler is a consultant for a number of corporate, professional, and government clients and leads workshops in such areas as conflict resolution, presentational speaking, team building, and interviewing.

Jeanne Elmhorst is an instructor in communication studies at Central New Mexico Community College in Albuquerque, New Mexico. Her courses reflect the variety in the communication discipline: business and professional, public speaking, listening, intercultural, and interpersonal. Jeanne lived and taught in Asia for three years and continues to find opportunities to travel, study, and volunteer in other countries. She enjoys designing and presenting communication training for business and not-for-profit clients.

Kristen Lucas is an assistant professor in the Department of Management at University of Louisville, where she directs the business communication program. She teaches courses, conducts research, and facilitates management training sessions on organizational communication, workplace dignity, and careers. Her research has appeared in *Journal of Business Ethics, Management Communication Quarterly,* and *Journal of Applied Communication Research.*

The eleventh edition enhances the strategic approach, real-world practicality, and reader-friendly voice that have made *Communicating at Work* the market leader for three decades. On every page, students learn how to communicate in ways that enhance their own career success and help their organization operate effectively.

This edition retains the features that have been praised by faculty and students: a strong emphasis on ethical communication, focus on cultural diversity, discussions of evolving communication technologies, self-assessment tools to help users analyze their own communication strengths and shortcomings, and coverage of communication in face-to-face and mediated contexts.

Highlights of the Eleventh Edition

- **NEW Connect Communication.** *Communicating at Work* is available to instructors and students in traditional print format, as well as online within an integrated assignment and assessment platform. These online tools, collectively called Connect Communication, make managing assignments easier for instructors—and make learning and studying more motivating and efficient for students.
- **NEW LearnSmart.** No two students are alike. McGraw-Hill LearnSmart™ is an intelligent learning system that uses a series of adaptive questions to pinpoint each student's knowledge gaps. LearnSmart then provides an optimal learning path for each student, so less time is spent in areas the student already knows and more time in areas the student doesn't know. The result is LearnSmart's adaptive learning path helps students retain more knowledge, learn faster, and study more efficiently.

NEW Speech Prep App

McGraw-Hill's new Speech Prep App is a mobile tool designed to help users build confidence in their public speaking skills through practice. Users can view sample speech clips; create and organize note cards; and time, record, and review their own speeches. Students can continue to use the app after they complete their public speaking course—it will come in handy for any speech they have to give in their personal and professional life. Go to **www.mhhe.com/speechprep** to purchase the App for Apple or Android devices.

- **Enhanced speech capture.** Designed for use in face-to-face, real-time classrooms, as well as online courses, enhanced speech capture in Connect Communication allows instructors to evaluate student speeches using fully customizable rubrics. Instructors can also create and manage true peer review assignments and upload videos on behalf of students for optimal flexibility.
- **Enhanced strategic focus.** The new subtitle of this edition reflects an enhanced focus on communicating strategically. Every chapter offers specific tips on how to craft messages and relate to others in ways that achieve desired results. Each part is introduced with a *Strategic Case* that provides an example from the business world to illustrate chapter concepts. Connect activities based around the feature allow for further analysis.

CULTURE **at work** ◄ ···

Collaboration in Cyberspace: Geography Makes a Difference

How important is communication when members from across the country and around the world meet in cyberspace? To answer this question, corporate giants Verizon and Microsoft commissioned a study to determine how virtual teams in a variety of industries and countries collaborate.

The study revealed that the importance of collaboration on performance was consistent across various industries (e.g., health care, government, financial services, manufacturing) and around the world. As one member of the Verizon/Microsoft study remarked, "global companies that collaborate better, perform better. Those that collaborate less, do not perform as well. It's just that simple."

Researchers discovered cultural differences in workers' communication preferences. For example, Americans were more likely to enjoy working alone. They expressed a preference for using e-mail rather than the telephone. They were more comfortable with audio, video, and web conferencing technologies than people of other regions of the world, and they were more likely to multitask when on conference calls.

Europeans expressed a preference for communicating in real time with colleagues. They felt more obligated to answer the phone, and they expected others to call them back rather than leave a voice mail message. Professionals in the Asia-Pacific region, more than anywhere else, expressed a desire to keep in touch throughout the workday. As a result they found the phone an indispensable tool and preferred instant messaging to e-mail. Differences like these show teams are more productive when members take cultural differences into account when planning to communicate.

Source: Frost & Sullivan. (2006). *Meetings around the world: The impact of collaboration on business performance.* Retrieved from http://newscenter.verizon.com/kit/collaboration/MAW_WP.pdf

Throughout the text, these boxes highlight the ways which culture applies to every aspect of business and professional communication. Topics covered include the risks of poor translations, negotiating styles in Asia and the West, how teamwork differs in individualistic and collectivist cultures, and adapting presentations to culturally diverse audiences.

New cases from large corporations, small businesses, world of business, and the professions offer compelling examples of how the principles in the book operate in everyday life.

►**case** STUDY

Device-Free Meetings

It's no surprise that meeting-goers in high-tech environments like California's Silicon Valley often bring along and use digital communication devices—laptops, smartphones, tablets, and a host of other gadgets that keep attendees in touch with the outside world.

Multitasking device users suffer from what one observer calls "continual partial attention." An industry insider describes the problem: "One of my biggest frustrations when I was an engineer at Google was being summoned to an executive meeting only to find three-quarters of the executives too busy with their laptops. I'd spend hours preparing a summary of my project status, a briefing on a new strategy area, or a review of staffing assignments. Nothing communicates disrespect to your reports like ignoring them when they're with you."

In an effort to stem this problem, a growing number of firms in the information economy and beyond have declared a ban on mobile devices in meetings. For example, San Francisco design firm Adaptive Path encourages staffers to leave their laptops and other devices behind when they attend meetings. John Vars, cofounder of San Francisco's Dogster.com, explains the logic of his company's policy on device-free meetings: "Even if people are just taking notes, they are not giving the natural human signals that they are listening to the person who is speaking. It builds up resentment. It can become something that inhibits good teamwork."

The results of these device-free meetings are encouraging. Dogster's Vars reports, "Meetings go quicker and there is also just a shared experience. People are communicating better, the flow is faster."

Sources: Guynn, J. (2008, March 31). Silicon meetings go 'topless'. *Los Angeles Times*, p. A1; Rands. (2007, August 31). The laptop herring [Web log post]. *Rands in repose*. Retrieved from http://www.randsinrepose.com/archives/2007/08/31/the_laptop_herring.html

- **NEW Interviewing Materials Appendix.** A new section on interviewing materials (Appendix I) prepares students for informational and employment interviews with sample strategies, questions, and responses for a positive interviewing experience.

- **The latest coverage of communication technology.** Both the text and *Technology Tip* sidebars show students how to use the latest communication technology to enhance career success. For additional coverage, a new module on using computer-mediated communication in a business environment is available in McGraw-Hill Create. Visit **www.mcgrawhillcreate.com.**

- **Streamlined chapters for improved teaching and learning.** With thoughtful edits and a reorganized chapter structure, the eleventh edition is designed to provide optimal coverage of material in fewer chapters.

- **Added coverage of important topics.** Throughout the text, new research is cited to demonstrate that the principles and strategies covered are based on far more than just "common sense." Coverage has been added or expanded on a variety of important topics, including dignity in the workplace, incivility and workplace bullying, effective meeting management, listening styles, and more.

Hallmark Features

- **Practical, real-world guidance.** Loaded with practical, real-world examples, *Communicating at Work* is known for its accessible and no-nonsense writing style and features that help students consider the application of the concepts and skills they are learning.

Career Guidance ......

CAREER **tip** ◄ ....

Successfully Navigating Job Fairs

Job fairs offer the chance to network with employers and to secure job interviews, sometimes on the spot. In this respect, job fairs serve as initial interviews.

Some job fairs are set on college and university campuses, where employers look for graduating students. Community fairs are open to the public at large. Some target a specific field such as health care or engineering, while others offer a diverse array of organizations and fields.

Before you go

- Ask yourself what will make you stand out from the hundred people a recruiter might see in a day.
- Gain a competitive edge by learning about the employers that interest you. Learn what positions they are hiring for and what qualifications are required. If possible, discover whether companies will be conducting job interviews at the fair or soon thereafter. You may be able to discover this sort of information from the career fair. Contact the company and you may be able to find out whether the person at the table is doing the hiring or if a human resources representative screens for quality candidates to recommend.
- Rehearse your "elevator" speech so you can present yourself clearly and professionally. (See Chapter 1, p. 21.) Bring copies of both your generic résumé and customized versions for positions you will be seeking. Dress conservatively and professionally.
- Carry a briefcase (a shoulder strap leaves your hands free for handshakes and writing notes) with a professional portfolio that you can easily pull out to retrieve résumés and letters of recommendation. Pack tissues and breath mints.

At the fair

- Arrive early. Spend a few minutes getting a feel for the way the fair operates. Is the atmosphere formal or informal?
- Don't ever ASK what an employer does. KNOW before you go.
- Manage your time efficiently: Approach your second-tier choices first to "warm up" so you are confident when approaching your first choices. Some employers pack up an hour or so before the designated closing time, so don't wait until the last minute.
- If you must stand in line, use that time to talk with other candidates: Find out what they've found about employers and positions.
- Approach the company's representative with confidence: "Hello. I'm Janya Greer. I'm a journalism and English major, and I'm interested in the writing positions." Remember, you are being evaluated from the moment you make contact.
- Always think about how your career objectives and qualifications meet the employer's needs. Have specific questions that show you've done your homework.
- Ask for the business card of anyone you speak with.

After the fair

- For employers who look like a good match, follow up with a phone call or e-mail to express thanks and confirm your interest.
- Remind the person where you met, what you talked about, and about your skills and qualifications. Add any information you neglected to mention at the job fair. Express your interest in learning more about the fit between you and the organization.

Source: University of New Mexico Career Center. Retrieved from http://www.collegegrad.com and www.career.unm.edu

Career Guidance

Career Tip boxes give practical advice on how to be more successful in work-related situations. Topics include getting recognized by your bosses, cubicle etiquette, difference as advantage, and using a telephone log.

- **Appendices on business presentations and business writing.** An appendix with sample presentations (Appendix II) covers both informative and persuasive speeches with exemplary outlines, visuals, and helpful annotations. An appendix on business writing (Appendix III) includes tips for writing well in a business environment, as well as information on choosing the best format for résumés and job applications.

Evolving Technology

Technology Tip boxes show readers how to use a variety of communication tools to achieve their goals. New topics include professional networking services such as LinkedIn, when it can be best to go offline, using smartphones to rehearse presentations, valuable communication software, and tips on working in virtual teams.

TECHNOLOGY **tip**

Avoiding Computer Catastrophes in Presentations

When you use computers as presentational aids, you can count on an equipment failure sooner or later. The following tips can minimize the chances that hardware or software glitches will scuttle your performance.

- *Set up in advance.* Give yourself lots of time to set up and test your equipment before the presentation is scheduled to begin. The last thing you want your audience to see is you frantically rebooting the computer, swapping cables, and trying to troubleshoot software.
- *Always bring two of everything.* Assume your equipment will fail because it certainly will at some time. Borrow backups for laptop computers, display panels or projectors, modems, and any other hardware you plan to use.

- *Back up your programs.* Having your work saved on a CD, flash drive, or some other storage medium can salvage a catastrophe. You might also want to e-mail a copy of your files to yourself as another form of backup.
- *Have backup technical support available.* Line up an expert you can call if something doesn't work.
- *Beware of the Web.* Real-time use of the Internet is an invitation to disaster. Connections can be slow, and websites can go down without notice. Whenever possible, it's best to store images of sites you will use on your hard drive and/or on a backup medium: CD, DVD, or flash drive.
- *Have a contingency plan.* Be prepared for the possibility your equipment will fail. Have copies of key exhibits prepared as handouts. They may not be as glamorous as high-tech displays, but they're far better than nothing.

Self-Assessment

Self-Assessment features help students see how well they are applying concepts and identify their own communication strengths and weaknesses.

Self-Assessment   Persuasive Strategies

Rate your presentation on the following items using this scale: 3 = accomplished excellently, 2 = accomplished competently, 1 = needs improvement.

1. I maximized my credibility by
   a. Demonstrating my competence through knowledge of the topic and sharing my credentials.   1   2   3
   b. Earning the trust of my audience via honesty and impartiality.   1   2   3
2. I structured my arguments logically by
   a. Using the most effective organization plan for my goal and audience (problem–solution, criteria satisfaction, comparative advantages, motivated sequence).   1   2   3
   b. Avoiding the use of logical fallacies *(ad hominem, post hoc, etc.)*.   1   2   3
3. I used appropriate psychological strategies such as
   a. Appealing to my audience's needs.   1   2   3
   b. Structuring a realistic goal.   1   2   3
   c. Focusing my appeals on my critical audience segment. 1   2   3
   d. Deferring my thesis with a hostile audience.   1   2   3
   e. Presenting ample evidence to support my claims.   1   2   3
   f. Citing opposing ideas when appropriate.   1   2   3
   g. Adapting to the cultural style of my audience.   1   2   3

Ethical Considerations

Throughout the text and in *Ethical Challenge* boxes, students are invited to consider ways of incorporating ethical considerations into day-to-day work contexts.

ETHICAL **challenge**

Asking Hard Questions about Ethical Behavior

Among its core values, electronics manufacturer Texas Instruments (TI) includes a respect for individuals, a commitment to long-term relationships, a concern for the environment, and a sense of duty to the communities where it does business.

TI encourages employees to use the following guidelines whenever they have a concern about whether a business action is consistent with the company's values. This information is provided to TI employees on a business-card-size minipamphlet to carry with them. You can use the same

guidelines when faced with ethical challenges of your own.

Is the action legal?

Does it comply with our values?

If you do it, will you feel bad?

How will it look in the newspaper?

If you know it's wrong, don't do it!

If you're not sure, ask.

Keep asking until you get an answer.

Source: Texas Instruments, Inc. (2011). *Corporate social responsibility: The TI ethics quick test.* Retrieved from http://www.ti.com/corp/docs/company/citizen/ethics/quicktest.shtml

- **Diversity.** Working with people from different backgrounds is more important and more common than ever. *Communicating at Work* encourages cultural understanding by exploring issues of diversity throughout the text.

Chapter-by-Chapter Changes

Chapter 1
New focus on personal networking and cultural networking differences; new *Technology Tip* and *Case Study* boxes.

Chapter 2
Streamlined and updated section on corporate culture; enhanced coverage of categories of diversity.

Chapter 3
Updated content on listening styles; updated *Self-Assessment* feature based on cutting-edge research.

Chapter 4
Enhanced section on language and identity management; new *Career Tip* features on touch and swearing; new *Case Study* on language and catastrophe.

Chapter 5
New sections on workplace dignity, bullying, and incivility; restructured section on sexual harassment that focuses on avoiding and responding to those issues.

Chapter 6
New streamlined chapter on interviewing; updated coverage of responding to illegal interview questions.

Chapter 7
New section on leader–member relations and Leader–Member Exchange (LMX) theory; new *Case Study* on teamwork.

Chapter 8
Updated and revised section on agendas, including coordinated samples of goals, agendas, and minutes; revised discussion of problem solving and brainstorming.

Chapter 9
New examples of opening statements; revised discussion of speech analysis to include cultural factors.

Chapter 10
Updated examples of support materials; new *Culture at Work* feature.

Chapter 11
Updated *Technology Tip* on using smartphones to analyze speech delivery; revised tips for using notes in a speech.

Chapter 12
New *Case Study* about online training; enhanced coverage of ethical persuasion.

Teaching and Learning with *Communicating at Work*

An array of resources makes teaching and learning both more efficient and more effective.

Create

Design your ideal course materials with McGraw-Hill's *Create*—**www.mcgrawhillcreate.com!** Rearrange or omit chapters, combine material from other sources,  and/or upload your syllabus, or any other content you have written, to make the perfect resources for your students. Search thousands of leading McGraw-Hill textbooks to find the best content for your students, and then arrange it to fit your teaching style. You can even personalize your book's appearance by selecting the cover and adding your name, school, and course information. When you order a *Create* book, you receive a complimentary review copy. Get a printed copy in 3 to 5 business days or an electronic copy (eComp) via e-mail in about an hour.

Register today at **www.mcgrawhillcreate.com** and craft your course resources to match the way you teach.

Tegrity Campus

Tegrity Campus is a service that makes class time available all the time by automatically capturing every lecture in a searchable format for students to  review when they study and complete assignments. With a simple one-click start and stop process, you can capture all computer screens and corresponding audio. Students replay any part of any class with easy-to-use browser-based viewing on a PC or Mac.

Educators know that the more students can see, hear, and experience class resources, the better they learn. With Tegrity Campus, students quickly recall key moments by using Tegrity Campus's unique search feature. This search helps students efficiently find what they need, when they need it, across an entire semester of class recordings. Help turn all your students' study time into learning moments immediately supported by your lecture.

To learn more about Tegrity, watch a two-minute Flash demo at **http://tegrity campus.mhhe.com.**

Online Learning Center

The Online Learning Center at **www.mhhe.com/adler11e** has been thoroughly updated and improved by Carolyn Clark of Salt Lake Community College. The site provides instructors with additional resources, including:

- The **Instructor's Manual** incorporates tools for both new and experienced instructors including: learning objectives, chapter summaries, discussion launchers, classroom activities, and additional resources.
- **PowerPoint Slides** for each chapter.
- The **Test Bank** offers multiple-choice, true or false, and essay questions for each chapter. McGraw-Hill's computerized **EZ Test** allows the instructor to create customized exams using the publisher's supplied test items or the instructor's own questions. A version of the test bank is also provided in Microsoft Word files for instructors who prefer that format.

CourseSmart

CourseSmart is a new way for faculty to find and review eTextbooks. It's also a great option for students who are interested in accessing their course materials digitally and saving money. CourseSmart offers thousands of the most commonly adopted textbooks across hundreds of courses from a wide variety of higher education publishers. It is the only place for faculty to review and compare the full text of a textbook online, providing immediate access without the environmental impact of requesting a print exam copy. At CourseSmart, students can save up to 50 percent off the cost of a print book, reduce their impact on the environment, and gain access to powerful Web tools for learning, including full text search, notes and highlighting, and e-mail tools for sharing notes between classmates.

McGraw-Hill Campus

McGraw-Hill Campus is the first of its kind institutional service providing faculty with true single sign-on access to all of McGraw-Hill's course content, digital tools, and other high-quality learning resources from any learning management system (LMS). This innovative offering allows for secure and deep integration and seamless access to any of our course solutions such as McGraw-Hill Connect®, McGraw-Hill Create™, McGraw-Hill LearnSmart™, or Tegrity®. McGraw-Hill Campus includes access to our entire content library, including eBooks, assessment tools, presentation slides, and multimedia content, among other resources, providing faculty open and unlimited access to prepare for class, create tests/quizzes, develop lecture material, integrate interactive content, and much more.

acknowledgments

We are grateful for the suggestions from colleagues whose thoughts helped guide us in preparing this new edition:

Allen R. Bean, Southeast Community College

Graham D. Bodie, Louisiana State University

Carol Brennan, South Plains College

Robert N. Burns, Salt Lake Community College

Katherine M. Castle, University of Nebraska-Lincoln

Carolyn Clark, Salt Lake Community College

Kandice N. Diaz, El Paso Community College

Cyndi Dunn, Sierra Community College

Richard I. Falvo, El Paso Community College

Stacy Gresell, Lone Star College-CyFair

Daria S. Heinemann, Florida State College at Jacksonville

Pamela Hopkins, East Carolina University

Mary S. Lynch, Waukesha County Technical College

Gordon McLean, Florida State College at Jacksonville

Jorge D. Mota, San Jacinto College, Central Campus

Angela Niedermyer, Austin Community College

Jan Poppenga, Southeast Community College

Christina Ross, Tarrant County College Northwest

Michael J. Scrivens, Finger Lakes Community College

Katherine Taylor, University of Louisville

Blair Thompson, Western Kentucky University

Susan Tomasovic, George Mason University

J.D. Wallace, Abilene Christian University

Robert Zetocha, Southeast Community College

Our heartfelt thanks go to Em Griffin, Wheaton College, for his suggestions on showing the connection between communication theories and the practical skills and strategies in this book. His advice supports Kurt Lewin's observation that there is nothing so practical as a good theory. We continue to be grateful to Carolyn Clark for her ongoing role in updating the instructor materials and new end-of-chapter activities, as well as for many other insightful suggestions.

We also acknowledge the people at McGraw-Hill whose efforts have helped bring *Communicating at Work* to market: Susan Gouijnstook, Briana Porco, Clare Cashen, Suzie Flores, Rhona Robbin, Carey Eisner, Jamie Daron, Karyn Morrison, and Matthew Baldwin. As this edition goes to press, we bid farewell to our longtime marketing manager Leslie Oberhuber. We will miss her talents and congeniality.

A hardworking and skilled group of freelance professionals also contributed to this edition. Deborah Kopka's copyediting transformed a less-than-perfect manuscript into the book you are holding. Kay Mikel proofread every word of the page proofs to make sure the book is error-free. As always, Sherri Adler's selection of photos contributed to the appealing design of this edition.

Ronald B. Alder
Jeanne Elmhorst
Kristen Lucas

brief contents

table of contents

part three

Working in Groups
Strategic Case: Museum of Springfield 182

part four

Making Effective Presentations
Strategic Case: Fresh Air Sports 244

12 Types of Business Presentations 338

Communicating
at Work

Strategies for Success in Business and the Professions

PART ONE

Sundown Bakery

When Carol Teinchek and Bruce Marshall first started Sundown Bakery, the business was fairly simple. Carol ran the shop up front, while Bruce ran the bakery and ordered supplies. When the business began to grow, Carol hired two part-time clerks to help out in the shop. Marina had moved to the country two years ago from El Salvador, and Kim was a newly arrived Korean working his way through college. Bruce hired Maurice, a French Canadian, as an assistant.

The ovens were soon running 24 hours a day, supervised by Maurice, who was now master baker, and two assistants on each of three shifts. Marina and Kim supervised the shop because Carol was usually too busy managing general sales distribution to spend much time with customers. Bruce still spent 3 or 4 hours a day in the bakery whenever he could get out of his office, but he spent most of that time coordinating production and solving problems with Maurice.

Within the next year, Sundown expanded from its original location, adding two new shops as well as two kiosks in local malls. Carol and Bruce hired a new operations manager, Hans Mikelson, formerly a regional manager of a national chain of coffee shops. Hans had plenty of new ideas about how to operate an expanding business: He launched a website, added an extensive range of drinks and meal items to the menu, and instituted two dress codes—one for all counter help and another for kitchen employees. He also put together an employee manual to save time orienting new employees. Hans announced all of these changes by memos, which store managers distributed to the employees.

Sundown's expanding size led to a change in the company. The family feeling that was strong when Sundown was a small operation was less noticeable. The new employees barely knew Bruce and Carol; as a result, there was less give-and-take of ideas between the owners and workers.

Hans' memos on the dress code and the employee manual created a crisis. Old-time employees were furious about receiving orders from "the bureaucrats," as management came to be called. Bruce and Carol recognized the problem and wanted to keep the lines of communication open, but they weren't sure how to do so. "I'm just a baker," Bruce confessed in exasperation. "I don't know how to run a big company."

Another set of challenges grew out of the changing character of the employees. In the original location alone, Sundown now employed workers from seven different countries. José, who was born in Brazil, confessed to Bruce that he felt uncomfortable being managed by Carol. "It's nothing personal," he said, "but where I come from, a man doesn't take orders from a woman." The Sundown employee profile was different in other ways. Two of the assistant bakers were openly gay; one of the sales clerks got around by wheelchair.

Carol, Bruce, and Hans know that good products alone aren't enough to guarantee Sundown Bakery's continuing success. They need to improve the quality of communication among the growing team who make and sell their products.

Basics of Business and Professional Communication

As you read the chapters in this unit, consider the following questions:

chapter 1

1. Apply the Communication Model (see Figure 1.1) to analyze Hans' communication to employees regarding the employee manual and uniforms. Consider the impact of the sender, message, decoding, feedback, context, and probable sources of noise. What elements seem to contribute most to the apparent lack of shared understanding?
2. Identify the changes in communication channels between employees and management as Sundown has grown. Suggest alternative communication strategies that might have reduced employee resentment. Explain why these channels could help improve management's communication about workplace changes. How might an organization's culture affect choice of communication channels?
3. Identify the instrumental, relational, and identity messages employees seem to have received from management as Sundown's business grew. What functions of downward communication do you notice? Can you find examples of upward and horizontal communication in this case study? How could Sundown improve its upward communication flow?

4. How have Sundown's formal and informal communication networks changed as the company expanded? In what ways have both the formal and informal networks contributed to Sundown's growing pains? In what ways can these networks be used to improve the relationships between management and employees?

chapter 2

1. How do changes in the demographic makeup of Sundown Bakery reflect transformation of the larger workforce as described in Communication in a Diverse Society on pp. 33–38?
2. Reflect on the six parts of the Customs and Behavior section, pp. 38–41. Cite a specific instance or predict the impact of three of these customs and behaviors in this workplace.
3. Consider the following hidden dimensions of culture as you describe the impact of culture on communication within the company: high- and low-context styles, individualism and collectivism, power distance, uncertainty avoidance, masculinity/femininity, and long-term orientation.
4. Using the guidelines on pp. 48–52 (Communicating across Diversity), what specific advice would you give to Sundown's management team about how to communicate most effectively in the face of the company's growth?

Chapter One
Communicating at Work

chapter outline

chapter objectives

After reading this chapter you should be able to:

1. Explain the role of communication in career success, providing examples to support your claims.

2. Apply the key principles of communication, knowledge of the basic elements of the communication model, and considerations of effective communication channel use to a specific situation, showing how each one affects the outcome of the interaction.

3. Describe how formal and informal communication networks operate in a given situation in your career field; then create a strategic plan of personal networking to accomplish your goals within an organization.

4. Apply the concepts of ethical communication discussed here to one or more ethically challenging situations.

• Communication and Career Success

The next time you look for job postings online, read the help wanted section of the newspaper, or check out internship opportunities at your college's career services office, look a little closer. No matter what kind of position you're seeking—from entry-level jobs to highly technical professional positions—chances are you will see "excellent communication skills" listed as a job requirement.

Regardless of occupation, people spend a staggering amount of time communicating on the job. Engineers spend most of their professional lives speaking and listening, mostly in one-to-one and small group settings.[1] Accountants may crunch numbers, but they also need to communicate effectively to serve their clients. That's why CPAs and the firms that hire them consistently cite effective communication as essential for career success.[2] One study based on responses from more than 1,000 employees at Fortune 1000 companies found that workers send and receive an average of 178 messages each day via telephone, e-mail, faxes, text messages, blogs, instant messages, and face-to-face communication.[3] Some experts have estimated that the average business executive spends 75 to 80 percent of his or her time communicating—more than 45 minutes of every hour.[4]

When it comes to communication, quality matters in virtually every career,[5] not just those traditionally regarded as people oriented. On-the-job communication skills can even make the difference between life and death. The Los Angeles Police Department cited "bad communication" among the most common reasons for errors in shooting by its officers.[6] Communication skills are essential for doctors, nurses, and other medical professionals too.[7] Researchers discovered that "poor communication" was the root of more than 60 percent of reported medical errors—including death, serious physical injury, and psychological trauma.[8] A survey by a major hospital accreditation group found communication woes to be among the leading causes of medical errors, which cause as many as 98,000 deaths each year.[9] Research published in the *Journal of the American Medical Association* and elsewhere revealed a significant difference between the communication skills of physicians who had no malpractice claims against them and doctors with previous claims.[10]

CAREER tip

Careers in Communication

Communication plays an important role in every job, but it is the primary focus of many careers. While a degree in communication may not be mandatory for jobs like these, academic study of the field is excellent preparation.

Advertising/Marketing: advertising or marketing specialist, copywriter, account executive, sales manager, media planner, media buyer, creative director, media sales representative, sales and marketing manager, media manager.

Electronic Media/Radio-Television/Broadcasting: program director, community relations director, film editor, news director, reporter, sales associate/manager, web designer, audience/market researcher, media buyer, announcer/news anchor, comedy writer, casting director, producer, business manager, floor manager, talk show host.

Health Communication: health educator, school health care administrator, medical grant writer, clinic public relations director, health communication analyst, medical training supervisor, communication manager for federal health agencies, medical center publications editor, hospice manager, health care counselor, health facility fundraiser.

Journalism (Print or Electronic): reporter, editor, newscaster, copywriter, script writer, publisher, news service researcher, technical writer, acquisitions editor, media interviewer.

New Media and Technology: digital graphic designer, web publisher, e-zine writer and editor, game designer, app developer, social media marketing specialist, website designer and administrator, new media researcher.

Organizational Communication: human resources/training/internal communication specialist, meeting manager, labor negotiator, recruiter, industrial media producer/director, technical writer, community/government affairs coordinator, research/knowledge manager.

Political Communication: press secretary, speech writer, political campaign consultant, elected official, political reporter, diplomat, lobbyist, lawyer, legislative assistant, communication director.

Public Relations: publicity manager, press agent, lobbyist, public affairs specialist, development officer, fundraiser, membership recruiter, sales manager, media analyst, media planner, creative director, audience analyst, community relations specialist, internal communications director, public opinion researcher.

Risk and Crisis Communication: public relations officer, corporate spokesperson, corporate trainer, communication consultant, spokesperson for government agencies.

Source: Adapted from National Communication Association. (2011). *Pathways to communication careers in the 21st century.* Washington, DC: National Communication Association.

Communication skills are essential to personal career success too. Technical people with good communication skills earn more, and those who are weak communicators suffer.[11] A survey of corporate recruiters revealed that good communication skills and the ability to work with others are the main factors contributing to job success. People with MBAs reported that the skills they valued most were the ability to work with others, listening skills, the ability to influence others, and communicating with diplomacy and tact.[12] William Schaffer, international business development manager for computer giant Sun Microsystems, made the point emphatically: "If there's one skill that's required for success in this industry, it's communication skills."[13] Executive coach and pharmaceutical recruiter Jim Richman echoes this sentiment: "If I give any advice, it is that you can never do enough training around your overall communication skills."[14]

Table 1-1	Top Qualities/Skills Employers Want

1. Ability to work in a team
2. Verbal communication skills
3. Ability to make decisions and problem solve
4. Ability to obtain and process information
5. Ability to plan, organize, and prioritize work

Source: Reprinted from *Job Outlook 2011,* from JobWeb (http://www.jobweb.com), with permission of the National Association of Colleges and Employers, copyright holder.

Table 1-1 summarizes the results of one annual survey in which employers list the skills and qualities for their ideal candidate. Communication skills always are near the top of the list.[15]

Many people don't appreciate the crucial role communication plays in career success. One survey revealed that students were half as likely as employers to recognize the role communication skills play in becoming an effective professional.[16] Just as disturbing was the finding that students are more likely than employers to believe they are good communicators. In other words, many students underestimate the importance of good communication while overstating their own abilities. This is not a recipe for success.

Because communication skills are an essential ingredient in professional and organizational accomplishment, this book is dedicated to helping you hone your talents in this important area.

• The Nature of Communication

Communication looks simple and almost effortless, especially when it goes smoothly. But every communicative exchange is affected by principles that aren't always apparent. Understanding this process better can help you make strategic choices that help achieve both personal and organizational goals.

Communication Principles

A more sophisticated understanding of how communication operates begins with some fundamental principles.

Communication Is Unavoidable
A fundamental axiom of communication is "One cannot not communicate."[17] As you will learn in Chapter 4, facial expression, posture, gesture, clothing, and a host of other behaviors offer cues about our attitudes. The impossibility of not communicating means we send messages even by our absence. Failing to show up at an event or leaving the room suggests meanings to others. Because communication is unavoidable, it is essential to consider the unintentional messages you send.

Communication Is Strategic Virtually all communication is aimed at achieving goals. On the job, the most obvious type is what scholars call **instrumental communication**—messages aimed at accomplishing the task at hand. Your manager is communicating instrumentally when she says, "I need that report by noon," and you are pursuing instrumental goals when you ask, "How long does it need to be?" People don't always state their instrumental goals outright. Saying, "Wow—look at the time!" could be code for "I'd like to wrap up this conversation." And in a negotiation, your "final offer" may actually be a bargaining ploy to get a better deal.

A second set of goals involves **relational communication**—messages that shape and reflect the way people regard one another. Building positive relationships isn't just about being sociable; a positive climate helps achieve instrumental goals. Conversely, a negative relationship can make it difficult, or even impossible, to accomplish them.

Virtually all messages contain both instrumental and relational dimensions. When a customer service rep asks, "How can I help you?" the instrumental nature of this question is obvious. But the *way* the question is asked shapes the tenor of the relationship between the rep and customer—rushed or deliberate, sincere or phony, friendly or unfriendly.[18]

A third, less obvious reason we communicate involves **identity management,** which is the practice of presenting yourself in ways that produce a preferred image and distinctive sense of self. To understand this concept, take a moment to make a list of 10 words or phrases that describe the way you would like others to see you on the job. Your list probably includes terms such as *competent, trustworthy,* and *efficient.* (Be sure to complete your own list before reading on.) Taken together, the attributes on this list (and many others) make up the professional identity you want to create. Next, think about the ways you communicate, both verbally and nonverbally, to get others to accept your identity. If being calm under pressure is part of your preferred identity, what do you say or do to project that quality? If you want others to see you as knowledgeable, how do you communicate to create that impression?

As these examples show, communication is often *strategic;* we craft messages to achieve instrumental, relational, and identity goals. Sometimes our strategizing operates subconsciously. When meeting a new person, you probably don't think, Must look confident and friendly! Firm handshake! Direct eye contact! At other times, though, crafting a thoughtful strategy to achieve your goals can boost the odds you will succeed.

A major focus of this book is to suggest communication strategies you can use to achieve your goals and the goals of the organizations with which you're involved. Many of these strategies will focus on specific work-related contexts, such as interviews, meetings, and presentations. Others will be useful in virtually every professional context where you want to enhance your professional identity, manage relationships, and get the job at hand done most effectively.

At first, the notion of strategic communication might seem unethical. But communicating purposefully isn't necessarily dishonest. The guidelines on pp. 25–26 show that it's possible to be strategic while still respecting others' rights and needs.

Communication Is Irreversible At one time or another, everybody has wished they could take back words they regretted uttering. Unfortunately, this isn't possible. Our words and deeds are recorded in others' memories, and we can't erase them. As the old saying goes, people may forgive, but they don't forget. In fact, often the more vigorously you try to erase an act, the more vividly it stands out.

Communication Is a Process It isn't accurate to talk about an "act" of communication as if sending or receiving a message were an isolated event. Rather, every

Derogatory E-mails Lead to Firings

Three employees of the Iowa Civil Rights Commission learned the hard way that digital gossip can be costly. They were fired after supervisors found they had used the state's e-mail system to disparage and ridicule coworkers. The culprits referred to colleagues by offensive nicknames, such as Monster, Psycho, Stoned Intern, Roid Rage, Extreme Makeover, Where's My Car?, and Albino. A representative message read, "Where's My Car and Psycho are talking about food—a match made in stoner/fatty heaven!"

The workers called their e-mails harmless office chatter. "It was just talk, water cooler chat," one protested. An administrative law judge disagreed, characterizing their messages as "misconduct" that disqualified them for unemployment insurance benefits.

Source: Foley, R. J. (2011, August 22). Email exchanges gets three Iowa civil rights investigators fired. *Cedar Rapids Gazette.* Retrieved from http://thegazette.com/2011/08/22/email-exchanges-get-three-iowa-civil-rights-investigators-fired

communication event needs to be examined as part of its communication context. Suppose, for example, your boss responds to your request for a raise by saying, "I was going to ask you to take a *cut* in pay!" How would you react? The answer probably depends on several factors: Is your boss a joker or a serious person? How does the comment fit into the history of your relationship—have your boss's remarks been critical or supportive in the past? How does the message fit with ones you have received from other people? What mood are you in today? All these questions show that the meaning of a message depends in part on what has happened before the message. Each message is part of a process: It doesn't occur in isolation.

Communication Is Not a Panacea   Although communication can smooth out the bumps and straighten the road to success, it won't always get you what you want. Misunderstandings and ill feelings can arise even when people communicate carefully,[19] and they can increase even more dramatically when people communicate badly. This helps explain why some problems grow worse the longer they are discussed. Even effective communication won't solve all problems. There are some situations in which the parties understand one another perfectly and still disagree. These limitations are important to understand as you begin to study communication on the job. Boosting your communication skills can increase your effectiveness, but it isn't a cure-all.

Basics of the Communication Model

No matter the setting or the number of people involved, all communication consists of the same elements. Understanding them can help explain what happens when one person tries to express an idea to others. It can also offer clues about why some attempts succeed and others fail.

The communication process begins with a **sender,** the person who transmits a **message.**[20] Some messages are deliberate, while others (such as sighs and yawns) may be unintentional. The sender must choose certain words or nonverbal methods to send an intentional message. This activity is called **encoding.** The **channel** (sometimes called the *medium*) is the method used to deliver a message. You will read much more about channels in the next section.

Even when a message gets to its intended receiver intact, there's no guarantee it will be understood as the sender intended it to be.[21] The **receiver** must still attach meaning to the words or behavior. Receivers don't just absorb messages like passive sponges. Instead, they actively interpret and respond to them. The process of a receiver attaching meaning to a message is called **decoding.**

Misunderstandings often arise because messages can be decoded in more than one way. Consider a situation when a customer responds to a slip-up by saying, "Don't worry about it." Perhaps the literal statement is accurate: "There's absolutely no need to worry." Or perhaps the customer means, "It isn't perfect, but I can tolerate the mistake." On the other hand, the customer could be annoyed but doesn't want to say bluntly, "I'm really unhappy." In the coming chapters, you'll learn a variety of strategies for reaching a shared understanding in these situations.

The receiver's discernible response to a sender's message is called **feedback.** Some feedback is nonverbal—smiles, sighs, and so on. Sometimes it is oral, as when you react to a colleague's ideas with questions or comments. Feedback can also be written, as when you respond by writing your coworker an e-mail. In many cases, no message can be a type of feedback. Failure to answer a letter or to return a phone call can suggest how the noncommunicative person feels about the sender.

Even though we've described sending and receiving as discrete roles, communication is actually a two-way process. Especially when communication is instantaneous—in face-to-face settings, phone conversations, and online chat—people are simultaneously senders and receivers. While you're pitching an idea to your manager (sending a message), she is receiving information. But at the same time, she is sending verbal and nonverbal feedback for you to interpret. When she voices a concern about part of your idea and you respond defensively, both of you are sending and receiving. Because sending and receiving are simultaneous and connected, these two roles are combined into the "communicator" positions represented on both sides of the model pictured in Figure 1.1 below.

Once you understand that receiving and sending are simultaneous and connected, you start to recognize that successful communication isn't something active senders do to passive receivers. Rather, it's a collaborative process in which the participants create a

FIGURE 1.1
Communication
Model

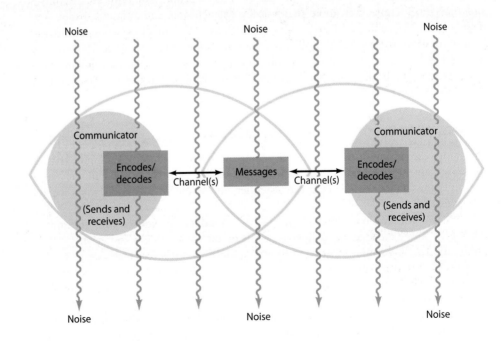

shared understanding through the exchange of messages. In other words, communication isn't something we do *to* others; it's a process we do *with* them. An effective way to build shared meaning is to practice other-orientation—that is, trying to understand the other person's viewpoint, whether or not we agree with it. Feedback helps us in this process of building shared meaning.

One of the greatest barriers to effective communication is **noise**—factors that interfere with the exchange of messages. The most obvious type of noise is *environmental*—for example, the babble of voices in the next room, the annoying ring of someone's cell phone in a meeting, or a smelly cigar. A second type of noise is *physiological*—hearing disorders, illnesses, disabilities, and other factors all make it difficult to send or receive messages. To appreciate the impact of physiological noise, recall how hard it is to process messages when you're recovering from a late-night study session or have a headache. The third type of noise is *psychological*—forces within the sender or receiver that interfere with understanding, such as egotism, defensiveness, assumptions, stereotypes, biases, prejudices, hostility, preoccupation, and fear. If you were thinking strategically about communicating with someone at work, what steps could you take to reduce noise in your environment before delivering your message?

Communication Channels

As a business communicator, the channel you choose to deliver a message can have a big influence on your effectiveness. Should you express your ideas in a phone call? Put them into a text message or e-mail? Send them via fax or in hard copy? Or should you express yourself in person? Deciding which communication channel to use isn't a trivial matter; communication researchers have studied extensively the factors that lead to good channel choice.[22] As you choose the best channel, you should consider several factors.

Consider Channel Characteristics
New technologies have given businesspeople a wider range of choices for communication than ever before. It wasn't that long ago when the choices were in-person, telephone, or written memo. But today, there also are e-mail messages, voice mail, faxes, instant messaging, video conferencing, web conferencing, Facebook, Twitter, cell phones, pagers, texting, and more. One way to start evaluating these choices is to consider each channel's different characteristics and how those characteristics match your communication goals.

- *Richness.* Richness refers to the amount of information available in a given channel: facial expression, tone of voice, eye and body movement. In rich channels— such as face-to-face settings and, to a lesser extent, in video chats—a wide array of nonverbal cues help you better understand another person. Is the customer in a hurry? Is your boss angry? Is a colleague joking or serious? Seeing and hearing others can help you answer questions like these. In contrast, lean channels have much less information. So while a lean e-mail channel is good for exchanging information efficiently, it isn't as effective when factors such as tone and emotion are important. Even emoticons like the smiley face haven't prevented e-mail misunderstandings.[23]

- *Speed.* Speed of the channel refers to how quickly the exchange of messages occurs. High-speed or instantaneous channels are called **synchronous communication.** These include face-to-face conversations, video chat, and telephone conversations. A key benefit of synchronous channels is that there's no time lag between the transmission and reception of messages, so they permit immediate feedback. You can respond to questions as soon as they arise and rephrase or elaborate as necessary. If you need a price quote *now* or if you need to discuss a complex idea that will need a lot of elaboration, a high-speed channel is probably the best choice. But high-speed, synchronous communication isn't always desirable. Another option is **asynchronous communication.** Asynchronous channels include e-mail, interoffice memos, and voice mail. In these "low-speed" channels there is a lag between the transmission and reception of messages. These channels can be effective for less urgent requests. In addition, if you want to avoid a knee-jerk reaction and encourage careful thought, you might be better off choosing an asynchronous method to deliver your message.

- *Control.* Control refers to the degree to which you can manage the communication process. Of course, because communication is a two-way process, you can never have complete control. However, different channels offer different types of control. In written channels (like writing an e-mail), you can have more control over how you encode a message because you will be able to write, proofread, and edit it as many times as you need until you get it exactly the way you want. If you have something highly sensitive to say, this might be a good channel to choose. But there are also some trade-offs to this channel; even though you might spend hours drafting a memo, letter, or report, the recipient may scan it superficially or not read it at all. In contrast, in a face-to-face channel, you have much more control over the receiver's attention. You can reduce noise, interpret nonverbal signals of understanding, or even explicitly ask the sender to pay more attention to your message.

Consider the Desired Tone of Your Message

In general, oral communication is best for messages that require a personal dimension. One corporate manager, whose company spends more than $4 million annually on employee travel, makes the case for face-to-face contact: "Nothing takes the place of a handshake, going to lunch, seeing their eyes."[24] Oral channels are also best for ideas that have a strong need for visual support—demonstration, photos or slides, and so on. Spoken communication is also especially useful when there is a need for immediate feedback, such as question-and-answer sessions or a quick reply to your ideas.

Written communication works well when you want to create a relatively formal tone. Writing is almost always the best medium when you must choose your words carefully. Writing is also better than speaking when you want to convey complicated ideas likely to require much study and thought by the receiver. It's also smart to put your message in writing when you want it to be the final word, with no feedback or discussion. Finally, writing is best for *any* message if you want a record to exist. In business and the professions, sending confirming letters and e-mails is common practice, as is keeping meeting minutes. These steps guarantee that what is said will be a matter of record, useful in case of later misunderstandings or disputes and in case anyone wants to review the history of an issue. Handwritten notes of thanks or sympathy express thoughtfulness and add a personal touch that electronic messages lose.

Consider the Organization's Culture

Besides message-related considerations, the culture of the organization in which you work may favor some communication channels over others.[25] For example, Microsoft Corporation is so e-mail intensive that some voice mail greetings include the directive, "If you're from Microsoft, please try to send electronic mail." In other organizations, voice mail is the preferred channel. Kirk Froggatt, a vice president at Silicon Graphics, offers one explanation: "There's something fundamentally more personal about voice mail. You can get the tone of voice, the

The Virtues of Going Offline

Today's array of communication technologies makes it possible to be connected to others virtually all the time. This connectivity has led to a dramatic growth in teleworking and telecommuting—flexible work arrangements in which employees do their jobs outside the office. Along with their benefits, the technologies that keep workers connected have a downside. When your boss, colleagues, and customers can reach you any time, you can become too distracted to tackle necessary parts of your job.

Communication researchers have discovered that remote workers have developed two strategies for reducing contact and thereby increasing their efficiency.[26] The first simply involved disconnecting from time to time: logging off the computer, forwarding the phone call to voice mail, or simply ignoring incoming messages. The researchers labeled the second strategy *dissimulation*. Teleworkers discourage contact by disguising their activities, for example, changing their instant message status to "in a meeting" or posting a fake "out of the office" message online.

It's important to note that these strategies weren't typically used to avoid work but to get more done. These findings show that too much connectivity is similar to many aspects of life; more isn't always better.

---

passion. People like that."[27] A recent study even indicated that employees who followed corporate norms for e-mail and instant messaging received higher performance evaluations.[28] Along with an organization's overall preference for some channels, it's important to consider the preferences of departments or even individuals. For example, the computer support staff members in some organizations respond to e-mails, while in other companies a phone call to the help desk is the best way to get a quick response. And, if you know a coworker or your boss responds only to face-to-face reminders, your best bet is to use that approach.

Consider Using Multiple Channels   In some cases, it's wise to send a message using more than one channel. For example, you could:

- Distribute a written text or outline that parallels your presentation.
- Follow a letter, fax, or e-mail message with a phone call, or call first and then write.
- Send a report or proposal and then make appointments with your readers to discuss it.

This redundancy capitalizes on the diverse strengths of each channel and boosts the odds of getting your desired message across. One study revealed that following-up a face-to-face exchange with an e-mail that included supplemental information was more persuasive than the single channel approach. The dual-channel approach also enhanced the sender's credibility.[29]

Sometimes channel selection involves trade-offs. For example, face-to-face communication is rich, fast, and allows you to have a lot of control over the receiver's attention. It also has the potential to create personal bonds that are more difficult to create in other types of communication. On the other hand, personal contacts can be difficult to schedule, even when people work in the same building. A cross-town trip for a half-hour meeting can take most of the morning or afternoon.

Ultimately, the question isn't which communication channel to use, but when to use each one most effectively.[30] Knowing how to choose the optimal channel can have a strong impact on your career. In one survey, managers who were identified as "media

Table 1-2	Considerations in Choosing a Communication Channel					
	Richness	**Speed**	**Control over Message**	**Control over Attention**	**Tone**	**Level of Detail**
Face-to-Face	High	Synchronous	Low	High	Personal	Moderate
Telephone Teleconferencing and Videoconferencing	Moderate	Synchronous	Low	Moderate	Personal	Moderate
Voice Mail	Moderate	Asynchronous	Moderate	Low	Moderate	Low
E-mail	Low	Asynchronous	High	Low	Impersonal-Moderate	High
Instant Messaging	Low	Asynchronous but potentially quick	Moderate	Moderate	Moderate	Low
Text Messaging	Low	Asynchronous but potentially quick	High	Low	Impersonal-Moderate	Low
Hard Copy (e.g., handwritten or typed message)	Low	Asynchronous	High	Low	Depends on writer's style	High

sensitive"—those who matched the channel to the message—were almost twice as likely to receive top ratings in their performance reviews when compared with less-media-sensitive peers.[31] Table 1-2 presents some guidelines that will help you decide how to deliver your message most effectively.

• Communicating in and beyond Organizations

For most of us, work is collaborative. It's the rare person who creates, markets, and sells goods or services alone. Whether the people we work with are in adjacent cubicles or on the other side of the planet, we are members of **communication networks**—patterns of contact created by the flow of messages among communicators through time and space.[32] Two kinds of networks exist: formal and informal.

Formal Communication Networks

Formal communication networks are systems designed by management to dictate who should talk to whom to get a job done. In small organizations, networks are so simple they may hardly be noticeable. In larger organizations, they become more intricate. The most common way of describing formal communication networks is with **organizational charts** like the one in Figure 1.2. Organizational charts are more than a bureaucrat's toy; they provide a clear guideline of who is responsible for a given task and which employees are responsible for others' performance. They also depict optimal flows of communication, including downward, upward, and horizontal communication.

Organizational Chart

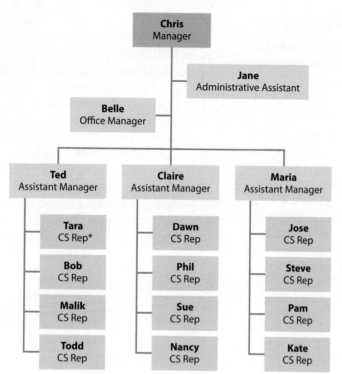

FIGURE 1.2

A Formal Communication Network

*CS Rep = Customer-Service Representative

Downward Communication **Downward communication** occurs whenever superiors initiate messages to their subordinates. There are several types of downward communication:

- *Job instructions:* "Bring in receipts for items under $20 that you pay for with cash. Anything over $20, charge to the company credit card."
- *Job rationale:* "We rotate the stock like that so the customers won't wind up with outdated merchandise."
- *Feedback:* "Backing up the files on your flash drive was a great idea. That saved us a lot of grief when the laptop didn't work."
- *Indoctrination:* "People can buy the stuff we sell at other places, but we can bring them in here by giving them what they want quickly and pleasantly. If we do that, we'll all come out ahead."

Most managers would agree—at least in principle—that downward communication is important. It's hard to argue with the need for giving instructions, describing procedures, explaining rationale, and so on. Like their bosses, employees recognize the importance of downward communication. A study at General Electric (GE) revealed that "clear communication between boss and worker" was the most important factor in job satisfaction for most people. GE was so impressed with the findings of this study it launched a program to encourage managers to communicate more, and more directly, with their employees, including holding informal meetings to encourage interaction.[33]

Getting Recognized by Your Bosses

According to Muriel Solomon, "The big secret to getting recognized is to give creative thinking a priority." She and other career advisers recommend you can showcase your talent, create interest in your work, and display your potential in several ways:

- **Present proposals to your boss.** Learn the history of a challenge, develop a specific plan that shows creativity and understanding of the company's needs. Don't wait for someone to recognize you or choose you for a prime assignment.

- **Volunteer for committees, to chair a committee, or to sponsor a workshop, hearing, or sports event.** Create opportunities to enlarge your working relationships with people at many levels of your organization. Prepare concise summaries and submit reports to your boss.

- **Get your thoughts printed.** Contribute quality writing to company publications, department newsletters, or association or professional journals. Distribute copies to your manager, and post on bulletin boards and company blogs.

- **Use thoughtful gestures to build bridges.** Devote 5 minutes a day to raising your visibility by thanking people who worked on your project, calling or sending thank-you notes to the supervisors of those who helped you (with a blind copy to the one whose help you received), and feeding your gratitude into the grapevine.

- **Be ready to share a story about your accomplishments.** Without bragging, be prepared to weave your accomplishments (be sure to include recent ones) into an interesting story you can tell whenever the opportunity arises: "Something like that happened to us last week. . . ."

Source: Klaus, P. (2007). *The hard truth about soft skills.* New York, NY: Collins Business; Solomon, M. (1993). *Getting praised, raised and recognized.* Englewood Cliffs, NJ: Prentice-Hall.

The desire for feedback is probably so strong among most employees because supervisors rarely provide enough of it. As two leading researchers put it: "The frequent complaint . . . by the individual is that he [sic] does not know where he stands with his superiors."[34] Many companies do take a more enlightened approach to feedback. Ed Carlson, former president of United Airlines, is generally credited with turning the company from a loser into a winner during his tenure. Part of his success was due to keeping United's employees—all of them—aware of how the company was doing. "Nothing is worse for morale than a lack of information down in the ranks," he said. "I call it NETMA—Nobody Ever Tells Me Anything—and I have tried hard to minimize that problem."[35] True to his word, Carlson passed along to the field staff information on United's operations that was previously considered too important to circulate.

Upward Communication Messages flowing from subordinates to superiors are labeled **upward communication.** Virtually every organization *claims* to seek upward messages, but many aren't as open to employee opinions as they claim. In some organizations, questioning the boss can be a recipe for professional suicide. "The disconnect between rhetoric and reality is why Scott Adams [creator of the 'Dilbert' comic strip] is a millionaire," says management expert Warren Bennis.[36]

Businesses that really are open to upward communication can profit from the opinions of employees.[37] Sam Walton, founder of Wal-Mart, the largest retailer in the United States, claimed that "our best ideas come from clerks and stockboys."[38] Industry observers credit the dramatic turnaround of Mattel Corporation to CEO John Aberman's openness to employee suggestions.[39] Upward communication can convey four types of messages:[40]

- *What subordinates are doing:* "We'll have that job done by closing time today."
- *Unsolved work problems:* "We're still having trouble with the air conditioner in the accounting office."
- *Suggestions for improvement:* "I think I've figured a way to give people the vacation schedules they want and still keep our staffing up." As the Career Tip on p. 16 suggests, getting recognized by your boss can pave the way to career advancement.
- *How subordinates feel about each other and the job:* "I'm having a hard time working with Louie. He seems to think I'm mad at him." Or, "I'm getting frustrated. I've been in the same job for over a year now, and I'd like more responsibility."

These messages can benefit both subordinates and superiors, and this explains why the most satisfied employees feel free to express dissent to their bosses.[41] Bennis emphasizes the critical role upward communication plays in the success of an organization:

> The longer I study effective leaders, the more I am convinced of the underappreciated importance of effective followers. What makes a good follower? The single most important characteristic may well be a willingness to tell the truth. In a world of growing complexity, leaders are increasingly dependent on their subordinates for good information, whether the leaders want to or not. Followers who tell the truth, and leaders who listen, are an unbeatable combination.[42]

Despite its importance, upward communication isn't always easy. Being frank with superiors can be both important and risky, especially when the news isn't what the boss wants to hear.[43] One executive gives an example:

> In my first C.E.O. job, a young woman who worked for me walked in one day and said, "Do you know that the gossip in the office is that the way for a woman to get ahead is to wear frilly spring dresses?" And I just looked at her and asked, "Where did this come from?" She said, "Well, you said, 'pretty dress' to four women who happened to be dressed that way. And so now it's considered policy."[44]

Some organizations have developed systems to promote upward communication in the face of potential challenges. Pillsbury Corporation employees can voice their messages on an anonymous voice mail system. An independent company creates transcripts of all calls and forwards them to Pillsbury's CEO.[45]

DILBERT © Scott Adams/Dist. By Universal Uclick.

Most of the responsibility for improving upward communication rests with managers. One recent study showed the likelihood of reporting bad news was highest when employees trusted supervisors and when there was a history in the organization of leaders resolving problems.[46] They can begin the process by announcing their willingness to hear from subordinates. A number of vehicles facilitate upward messages: an open-door policy, grievance procedures, periodic interviews, group meetings, and the suggestion box, to name a few. Formal channels aren't the only way to promote upward messages. Informal contacts can often be most effective. Chats during breaks, in the elevator, or at social gatherings can sometimes tell more than planned sessions. But no method will be effective unless a manager is sincerely interested in hearing from subordinates and genuinely values their ideas. Just talking about this isn't enough. Employees have to see evidence of a willingness to hear upward messages—both good and bad—before they will really open up.

Horizontal Communication   A third type of organizational interaction is **horizontal communication** (sometimes called *lateral communication*). It consists of messages between members of an organization with equal power.[47] The most obvious type of horizontal communication goes on between members of the same division of an organization: office workers in the same department, coworkers on a construction project, and so on. In other cases, lateral communication occurs between people from different areas: accounting calls maintenance to get a machine repaired, hospital admissions calls intensive care to reserve a bed, and so on. Horizontal communication serves five purposes:[48]

- *Task coordination:* "Let's get together this afternoon and set up a production schedule."
- *Problem solving:* "It takes three days for my department to get reports from yours. How can we speed things up?"
- *Sharing information:* "I just found out a big convention is coming to town next week, so we ought to get ready for lots of business."
- *Conflict resolution:* "I've heard you were complaining about my work to the boss. If you're not happy, I wish you would tell me first."
- *Building rapport:* "I appreciate the way you got that rush job done on time. I'd like to say thanks by buying you lunch."

Research suggests that people in most organizations communicate horizontally, but the reasons for doing so in high-performing groups are different from those in less effective ones.[49] Low-performing groups are likely to reach out to different parts of

the organization to get information on how to follow existing procedures. For example, an engineer might contact the purchasing department to check on the status of an equipment order. By contrast, lateral contacts in high-performing organizations are used to get the information needed to solve complex and difficult work problems. For instance, before starting design work on a new product, the same engineer might contact the sales manager to find out what features customers want most. Top-performing organizations encourage people from different areas to get together and share ideas. At Hewlett-Packard, Worldwide Personnel Manager Barbara Waugh and her colleagues spent five years improving horizontal communication. "My role is to create mirrors that show the whole what the parts are doing—through coffee talks and small meetings, through building a net-work, through bringing people together who have similar or complementary ideas."[50]

Despite the importance of good horizontal communication, several forces work to discourage communication between peers.[51] *Rivalry* is one. People who feel threatened by one another aren't likely to be cooperative. The threat can come from competition for a promotion, raise, or other scarce resource. Sometimes rivalry occurs over an informal role. For example, two office comedians might feel threatened each time the other gets a laugh; that could inhibit their cooperation. Another challenge is the *specialization* that makes it hard for people with different technical specialties to understand one another. *Information overload* can also discourage employees from reaching out to others in different areas, and a simple *lack of motivation* is another problem. Finally, *physical barriers,* such as having offices scattered throughout different buildings, can interfere with horizontal connections.

Informal Communication Networks

So far, we have focused on networks within organizations that are created by man-agement. Alongside the formal networks, every organization also has **informal communication networks**—patterns of interaction based on friendships, shared personal or career interests, and proximity. One business writer described the value of informal networks:

> A firm's organizational chart will tell you about authority. It doesn't always show how things get done or created. You know the rules, but you don't know the ropes. For that, you need a map to the network, the corresponding informal structure that is usually invisible.[52]

Informal relationships within organizations operate in ways that have little to do with the formal relationships laid out in organizational charts.[53] Figure 1.3 shows how the actual flow of information in one firm is quite different from its formal structure. And beyond any sort of organizational connection, people are connected with one another through informal personal networks—with friends, neighbors, family members, and all sorts of other relationships.

Some informal networks arise because of personal interests. Two colleagues who are avid basketball fans or share a fascination with rare books are more likely to swap information on work than coworkers who have no such bonds. Personal friendships also create connections that can lead to increased communication. Finally, physical proximity increases the chances for interaction. Shared office space or frequent meetings around the copying machine make it likely that people will exchange information. Even sharing restrooms can lead to networking, as public relations executive James E. Lukaszewski observes in describing one anatomical difference that has benefited men.

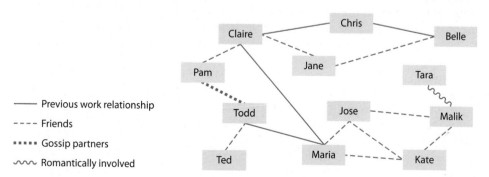

FIGURE 1.3

An Informal Communication Network

Source: Adapted from Orbe, M. P., & Bruess, C. J. (2007). *Contemporary issues in interpersonal communication.* New York, NY: Oxford University Press.

This may sound facetious, even silly, but when these meetings break, where are the women and where are the men? The guys go to the porcelain in that little room with M-E-N on the door. . . . The guys are standing there, facing the wall, talking and deciding things. It's a critical opportunity for important verbal communication to take place during times of decision making.[54]

As this quote suggests, informal networks are often a source of important job-related information, organizational resources, career advice, and social connections that help workers successfully navigate their careers. When someone is excluded from that network—even unintentionally—he or she is placed at a major disadvantage. For example, research has shown that women often are cut off from informal communication networks, and this has a real impact on their ultimate career success.[55] The difference is even more pronounced for minority women, who face "concrete walls" that isolate them from informal relationships with superiors and peers.[56] It's important to identify the informal networks in your organization and try to get as involved as possible—especially if you are a woman or a minority.

Functions of Informal Networks within Organizations

Not all informal messages are idle rumors. Informal communication can serve several useful functions:

- *Confirming formal messages:* "The boss is really serious this time about cutting down on overnight travel. I heard him yelling about it when I walked past his office."

- *Expanding on formal messages:* "The invitation to the office party says 'casual dress,' but don't make it too informal."

- *Expediting official messages:* You might learn about openings within an organization from people in your network long before the vacancies are published.

- *Contradicting official messages:* You might learn from a friend in accounting that the deadline for purchases on this year's budget isn't as firm as it sounded in the comptroller's recent memo.

- *Circumventing formal channels:* Your tennis partner who works in duplicating might sneak in an occasional rush job for you instead of putting it at the end of the line.

Many companies elevate informal communication to an official policy by encouraging open, unstructured contacts between people from various parts of the organization. For example, Hewlett-Packard's approach to problem solving has been termed MBWA, "management by wandering around."

Some observers consider informal contacts to be the primary means of communication within an organization. In one survey, 57 percent of the respondents said that the grapevine is "the only way to find out what's really happening" in their organizations.[57] A decade of research shows engineers and scientists were five times more likely to turn to a person for information than to impersonal sources like the databases or files.[58] Two well-known analysts flatly assert that as much as 90 percent of what goes on in a company has nothing to do with formal events.[59] Writing in the *Harvard Business Review*, David Krackhardt and Jeffrey Hanson capture the difference between formal and informal networks: "If the formal organization is the skeleton of a company, the informal is the central nervous system."[60]

Like the human nervous system, informal networks are faster, and often more dependable, than formal channels.[61] They also provide a shortcut (and sometimes a way around) for the slower and more cumbersome formal channels, making innovation easier.[62] This fact helps explain why organizational decision makers tend to rely on verbal information from trusted associates.[63] Smart communicators don't just rely on informal contacts with peers for information; they take advantage of sources throughout the organization. One study revealed that general managers spent a great deal of time with people who were not direct subordinates, superiors, or peers—people with whom, according to the official chain of command, they had no need to deal. Although many

Your Elevator Speech

Often the chance to present yourself and your ideas lasts less than a minute. You meet a prospective customer at a party. You run into your boss on the street. You are introduced to a potential employer in a hallway. Whether networking opportunities like these turn out well or not may depend on your foresight and preparation.

When the opportunity arises, you can make a good impression by delivering what is called an "elevator speech." (This type of communication gets its name because it should be brief enough to deliver in the length of an elevator ride.) Elevator speeches can accomplish a variety of goals. Besides serving as introductions, they can be a tool for seeking help, establishing a relationship, gaining visibility, marketing yourself or your organization, getting feedback, expanding your personal network, and doing an end-run around someone who is blocking your progress.

Practice your skill at presenting yourself briefly and effectively by planning and delivering an elevator speech to your classmates. Your speech should contain four parts and take less than a minute to deliver.

1. State your name and your current job title or position.
   "Hi. I'm Claire Yoder. I'm a senior, graduating in December."

2. Describe some personal strengths or distinguishing information.

"I'm completing my accounting major this semester with a 3.8 GPA, and I've developed additional skills in tax preparation through volunteer work with Tax-Help USA."

3. Depending on your audience, state what you can do for others *or* ask for their help.
   "If you or someone you know needs help with tax preparation, I can help," *or* "If you know of any openings in accounting, I'd like to hear about them."

4. Indicate how the person can get in touch with you or how you plan to contact this person.
   "Here's my card with my e-mail address. I'd like to hear from you."

While modesty is a virtue, don't be bashful about presenting yourself as an interesting and competent person. Whether or not you want to, you are always presenting yourself to others. Brevity and sincerity are the keys to an elevator speech. Don't overwhelm your audience with information; present enough to make sure you create a positive impression and, ideally, to be asked for more information.

Sources: Wallace, M. (1998, July 1). The elevator speech: It's there for you. *Law Library Resource Exchange.* Retrieved from http://www.llrx.com/columns/guide18.htm. See also Brown, J. G. (2009, October 8). 3 ways to pitch yourself in 30 seconds. *Harvard Business Review* Blog Network. Retrieved from http://blogs.harvardbusiness.org/cs/2009/10/nail_your_elevator_pitch.html?cm_mmc=npv-_-WEEKLY_HOTLIST-_-OCT_2009-_-HOTLIST1013

---

of these people—administrative assistants, lower-level subordinates, and supervisors with little power—seemed relatively unimportant to outsiders, successful managers all seemed to cultivate such contacts.[64]

Enlightened organizations do everything possible to encourage constructive, informal interaction. Siemens leaves overhead projectors and empty pads of paper in its factory lunchrooms to facilitate informal meetings.[65] Corning Glass deliberately installed escalators in its new engineering building to boost the kind of face-to-face contacts less likely in elevators. 3M sponsors clubs for any group of employees that requests them, realizing this sort of employee interaction is likely to encourage new ideas that will help the company. Other firms mingle workers from different departments in the same office, convinced that people who rub elbows will swap ideas and see themselves as part of a companywide team.

Informal networks don't just operate within organizations. Friends, neighbors, and community members increase their effectiveness by sharing information. In some cities, chambers of commerce host networking events to encourage these ties among community businesses. Even without these organized contacts, most people are surprised to realize just how many people they know who can offer useful information.

TECHNOLOGY **tip**

Your Professional LinkedIn Profile

The social networking website LinkedIn (http://www.linkedin.com) has been called "Facebook for professionals." More than 120 million members around the world use this service to advance their careers. Used appropriately, LinkedIn can help you manage your professional identity, expand your network of contacts, and enhance career opportunities. The following guidelines can help you use LinkedIn effectively.

Manage Your Professional Identity

- Adjust settings to display the optimal amount of information about yourself. For example, if you're unemployed, you might want to display all of your "moves" so prospective employers can appreciate your initiative. On the other hand, if you're discretely looking for another job, you may not want your manager and colleagues to see your flurry of searches of companies and requests for recommendations.
- Use LinkedIn for professional messages only. Don't link your page to your Facebook or Twitter identity if you use those tools to share nonprofessional information.
- Use LinkedIn's multimedia capabilities to showcase your work (and yourself).
- Request 360-degree feedback from professors, colleagues, supervisors, and clients who can comment on your work, attitude, skills, achievements, professionalism, and integrity.
- Create personal and powerful headlines and summaries. Avoid cutting and pasting your resume into your summary.
- Proofread everything you post. A single error can demolish your credibility.

Learn from Others

- Join, contribute to, and use groups. Begin by searching for groups in your career field. Focus on trends, glean advice, and garner news and tips particular to your field. Connect with national and international groups as well as local groups to explore employment, training, and networking opportunities virtually and in person. When you understand the culture of different groups, contribute your knowledge, links to pertinent articles, upcoming events, or book reviews.
- Use the Answers Forum to discover what types of questions others are asking and to learn from the answers. Browse by topic and subtopic (e.g., résumé writing, start-ups and small business, nonprofit, work-life balance, mentoring, finance) or by language.

Source: Serdula, D. (n.d.) *LinkedIn makeover: Professional secrets to a powerful LinkedIn profile.* Retrieved from http://www.linkedin-makeover.com/blog

Personal Networking

While all of us have personal contacts, **networking,** as the term is usually used, has a strategic dimension that goes beyond being sociable. It is the process of deliberately meeting people and maintaining contacts to get career information, advice, and leads—and in turn to help others. Some professionals use social networks such as Facebook for business contacts, while others are networking at sites like LinkedIn, which are designed expressly for business purposes. As you explore and expand your network, keep the following tips in mind.[66]

People with highly developed personal networks are more successful in their careers.[67] Over their lifetimes, they earn more raises, are promoted more often, and are generally more satisfied with their jobs. This isn't surprising. With better networks, people have more access to career sponsorship, resources, and information. But membership in any one network probably won't accomplish these goals. The key is to have a wide and diverse network with all kinds of people. You can create and benefit from personal networks by following these tips.

View Everyone as a Networking Prospect   Consider all the networks to which you already belong: family members, friends, neighbors, social acquaintances, fellow workers, members of your religious community, professionals (doctors, dentists, accountants, attorneys, etc.), and school contacts (faculty, fellow students, counselors, etc.). Beyond the people you already know, almost everyone you meet has the potential to be a source of useful information. The passenger seated next to you on a plane or train might be acquainted with people who can help you. The neighbor who chats with you at a block party might have the knowledge or skill to help you solve a problem. Within an organization, the best informants are often people you might overlook. Administrative assistants are exposed to most of the information addressed to their managers, and they usually serve as gatekeepers who can give or deny access to them. Custodial and maintenance people travel around the building and, in their rounds, see and hear many interesting things.

Be Sensitive to Personal and Cultural Factors   While everyone you meet is a potential networking prospect, it's important to think of each person as an individual. Some welcome the chance to share information, whereas others may object to more than occasional contacts. It's also important to recognize culture plays a role in networking practices.

Treat Your Contacts with Gratitude and Respect   Don't make the mistake of equating networking with being dishonest or exploitive. As long as you express a genuine desire for information openly, there's nothing to be ashamed of. Furthermore, seeking information doesn't mean you have to stop enjoying others' company for social reasons. When others do give you information, be sure to express your appreciation. At the very least, a "thank-you" is in order. Even better, let your networking contacts know exactly *how* the information they gave you was helpful.

Help Others   Don't just be an information-seeker. Whenever possible, make an effort to put people who will benefit from contact in touch with one another: "You're looking for a new bookkeeper? I know someone who might be right for you!" Besides being the right thing to do, helping others will earn you a reputation for generosity that can serve you well.[68]

Get Referrals to Secondary Sources   The benefits of personal networks don't stop with your personal acquaintances. Each person you know has his or her own connections, some of whom could be useful to you. Researchers have demonstrated the "small world" phenomenon: A study on the "six degrees of separation" hypothesis involving more than 45,000 messages and more than 150 countries has demonstrated that the average number of links separating any two people in the world is indeed a half-dozen.[69] You can apply this principle to your own information by only seeking people removed from your personal network by one degree: If you ask 10 people for referrals and each of them knows 10 others who might be able to help, you have the potential of support from 100 information-givers.

Secondary sources are so valuable that some online networking group sites exist to help users find the contacts they need. Having a network of people who can refer you to others can be especially helpful in today's workforce, where people often stay in a job for only a year or two.

Seek a Mentor   A mentor is a person who acts as a guide, trainer, coach, and counselor; who teaches you the informal rules of an organization or a field; and who imparts the kinds of wisdom that come from firsthand experience. Many organizations have formal

CULTURE **at work**

Guanxi: **Networking Chinese-Style**

Any savvy businessperson in China knows the value of *guanxi* (pronounced *gwan-shee*)—the web of social relationships that help get a job done through the granting of favors. It takes *guanxi* to get a good job, find a good apartment, overcome bureaucratic hurdles, line up suppliers and distributors. In other words, it's required to accomplish almost any transaction. As one observer put it, "In the West, relationships grow out of deals. In China, deals grow out of relationships."[70]

It may be tempting to think of *guanxi* as the Chinese equivalent of Western networking, but the concept has far more cultural and practical significance. The unwritten code of *guanxi* is rooted in the Chinese national character, reflecting the Confucian emphasis on loyalty, obligation, order, and social harmony.

Guanxi operates on three levels.[71] The strongest bond is with immediate family. In relationships linked by blood and marriage, higher-status members are obligated to perform favors for their lower-status relatives. In return, lower-status family members are obliged to demonstrate fierce loyalty. To a lesser extent, *guanxi* connects extended family members, friends, neighbors, classmates, and people with other strong commonalities. Unlike the closest form of *guanxi*, obligations in these relationships are usually reciprocal; receiving help creates an obligation to return the favor. The least powerful level of *guanxi* is between people who know one another but have no strong relational history. At this level, *guanxi* is similar to networking connections in the West. These relationships lack the history, trust, and power of stronger bonds.

Developing *guanxi* can be challenging for foreigners who want to do business in China, but it isn't impossible. One strategy is to rely on intermediaries to make initial connections. This practice is widespread among native Chinese, so a foreigner won't stand out for using it. Once introduced, be prepared to socialize. Even more so than in the West, important business is often conducted outside of the workplace. When socializing, look for the chance to emphasize commonalties—business experiences, education, and mutual acquaintances are a few examples. After enough trust has developed to seek favors, be indirect. As you will read in Chapter 2, Asian cultures consider oblique, "high-context" communication as a sign of sensitivity and skill. Finally, remember that *guanxi* is reciprocal. Accepting help from others obliges you to assist them in the future.

programs that match new employees with experienced ones. Other mentor–protégé relationships develop informally and unofficially. However you find one, a mentor can be invaluable. This is especially true for women, minorities, and people trying to break into nontraditional fields where "good old boy" networks can be hard to penetrate.[72]

A successful mentoring relationship isn't a one-time affair. Instead, it passes through several stages.[73] In the initial phase, the parties get to know one another and gain confidence in each other's commitment to the relationship. After the initial stage, a period of cultivation occurs in which the mentor guides his or her protégé through a series of conversations and tasks with the goal of building knowledge, confidence, and skill. By the third phase of the relationship, the protégé can function mostly on his or her own, with occasional guidance from the mentor. Finally, the fourth stage involves either separation or a redefinition of the relationship as one of peers. Not all mentoring relationships are this involved or long-lasting; but whether they are relatively brief or ongoing, they can provide great value and satisfaction for both mentor and protégé.

Whatever the relationship, some rules guide mentoring relationships.[74] Look for someone with a position in a field that interests you. Don't be bashful about aiming high: You may be surprised by successful people's willingness to give back by helping aspiring newcomers. Approach your mentor professionally, showing you are serious about growing in your career. See The Career Research Interview in Chapter 6 for guidelines on how to handle this process.

Once you have found a mentor, show respect for his or her time by keeping most of your contacts to regularly scheduled times. Be sure to follow up on your mentor's suggestions about reading, checking websites, and attending activities.

Realize that a mentoring relationship should be primarily professional. If you have serious personal problems, turn to a counselor. A mentor may be able to help you with some personal problems as they affect your work life, but a mentor should not become an emotional crutch. Remember that any personal insights mentors and protégés share should be kept confidential. Finally, don't expect a mentor to grant you special favors, intervene on your behalf with your boss, or boost your chances for promotion. The advice you receive should be reward enough.

Network throughout Your Career   Networking isn't just for job-seekers. It can be just as important once you start climbing the career ladder. In an era when changing jobs and even changing careers is common, expanding your options is always a smart move.

• Ethical Dimensions of Communication

Some cynics have noted the trouble with business ethics is that the phrase is an oxymoron. Despite this attitude, there is a growing recognition that behaving ethically is an essential part of being an effective, promotable employee. Scandalous business practices led to the downfall of major corporations like Enron and WorldCom and have cost others millions of dollars. As a result of these ethical lapses, sensitivity to communicating in a principled way has grown, and several hundred corporations and organizations now include an ethics officer in their organizational chart who reports directly to the chairman.[75] Employees share this concern for ethics. One survey of 800 recent MBA graduates revealed that virtually all were willing to forgo some money to work for an organization with a better reputation for corporate social responsibility (CSR) and ethics.[76]

Doing the ethical thing isn't always easy. On a personal level, you are likely to face conflicts between what you believe is right and what is practical. For instance, you might have to deal with a customer or colleague whose business or approval you want, but who is behaving badly—perhaps making sexist or racist remarks. After a trip together, coworkers turn in inflated expenses and expect you to do the same. Your team is under pressure to finish a project, but you recognize potential safety issues being shortcut. Besides personal challenges, sooner or later you are likely to experience situations like these where others in your organization behave in ethically questionable ways. Do you speak up when a colleague makes promises to clients that you know the company can't keep? Should you challenge your boss when he or she treats other employees unfairly or illegally?

It has been said that ethics centers on a sense of responsibility for someone other than yourself.[77] A blanket obligation to communicate ethically can be too vague to be helpful in specific situations. Five philosophical principles offer standards that can help you decide how to behave in a principled manner.[78] There is no single "right" approach to ethics; these competing ethical perspectives often lead to conflicting actions. For example, what one group perceives as "virtuous" might not bring good to the greatest number; or what one group considers moral might be considered immoral to another group. When

ETHICAL **challenge**

Ethical Communication Choices

Descriptions for these seven guidelines for judging ethical communication are provided in the text:

- Utilitarian Approach
- Rights Approach
- Fairness or Justice Approach
- Common-Good Approach
- Virtue Approach
- Professional Ethic
- Publicity Test

Outline the range of ways you could handle each situation below. Use two or more of the ethical guidelines to compare courses of action. Then decide on a course of action you believe to be both principled and realistic. Justify your decision.

1. A coworker tells you he's about to buy an expensive car that will strain his budget to the maximum. You recently learned he is slated to be laid off at the end of the month but were told to keep this information in strictest confidence. What do you do?

2. Your friend is applying for a job and has given you as a reference. A questionnaire sent by the employer asks if there is any reason you cannot recommend the applicant. You know that your friend is struggling with an alcohol problem, which led to dismissal from a previous job. Do you mention this problem on the reference form? If so, how?

3. Your manager calls you into her office and praises you for doing excellent work on a recent project. She suggests that this level of performance is likely to earn you a promotion and a raise. In truth, a colleague made a far greater contribution to the project. How do you respond to your manager's praise?

4. As part of your job, you learn that some damaged equipment can be repaired for $15,000. Your supervisor tells you to claim the damage is much greater so the insurance company will pay closer to $100,000. What do you do?

5. While you are entertaining a customer, he makes a blatantly offensive joke. How do you respond?

Sources: Adapted from Richardson, J. E. (Ed.). (2003). *Business ethics 03/04* (15th ed.). Guilford, CT: McGraw-Hill/Dushkin; Soeken, D. (2008). On witnessing a fraud. In J. E. Richardson (Ed.), *Business ethics 07/08* (19th ed.). Dubuque, IA: McGraw-Hill/Dushkin.

faced with a decision about how to communicate ethically, it's helpful to ponder the situation from several viewpoints before proceeding.

Utilitarian Approach (Jeremy Bentham and John Stuart Mill): Does this action provide the greatest good for the greatest number?

Rights Approach (Immanuel Kant): Does this action respect the moral rights (truth, privacy, noninjury, promises) of everyone?

Fairness or Justice Approach (Aristotle, John Rawls): Is this action fair and free of discrimination or favoritism?

Common-Good Approach (Plato, Aristotle, Cicero, John Rawls): Does the action further the common or community good?

Virtue Approach: Does this action promote the development of moral virtue (character) in me and my community?

Two additional guidelines can help you evaluate whether you are behaving ethically:

Professional Ethic: How would an impartial jury of your professional peers judge this action?

Publicity Test: Would you be comfortable having the public learn about your behavior in the broadcast or print media?[79]

review points

- Communication is important for career success.
- Communication is unavoidable, strategic, and irreversible. It is a process that involves instrumental and relational communication and identity management. It isn't a panacea that will solve all problems.
- The communication model demonstrates how senders and receivers encode and decode messages in the process of developing a shared meaning. To improve communication, consider the characteristics of various channels, the desired tone of the message, the organization's culture, and the use of multiple channels.
- Noise can interfere with exchange of a message. It can be environmental, physiologic, or psychological and can be present in the sender, receiver, message, or channel. Good communicators reduce noise as much as possible.
- Formal communication networks (organizational charts) represent management's view of organizational relationships: upward, downward, and horizontal/lateral.
- Informal networks, based on proximity, shared interests, or friendships, serve to confirm, expand, expedite, contradict, or circumvent formal communication.
- Effective communicators cultivate and use personal networking for career success.
- Professional success necessitates an understanding of and ability to apply various ethical frameworks (utilitarian, rights, fairness/justice, common good, virtue, professional ethic, publicity test) to consistently make principled decisions around ethical challenges.

key terms

asynchronous communication   12
channel   9
communication networks   14
decoding   10
downward communication   15
encoding   9
feedback   10
formal communication networks   14
horizontal (lateral) communication   18
identity management   8
informal communication networks   19

instrumental communication   8
message   9
networking   22
noise   11
organizational charts   14
receiver   9
relational communication   8
sender   9
synchronous communication   11
upward communication   16

activities

1. Invitation to Insight

Keep a log of your work-related (or school-related) communication over a three-day period. Include who you have communicated with (superior, subordinate, peer, external) and your level of satisfaction with the communication. Based on your findings, analyze the following:

a. How much time you spend communicating.
b. With whom you communicate. (Identify each example as downward, upward, or horizontal flow of communication.)
c. Which channels of communication you tend to use most frequently.
d. Your level of satisfaction.
e. Areas where improving your communication skills would be desirable.

2. Invitation to Insight

Think about a situation you have experienced in which communication went wrong. Diagnose the problem by finding the parts of the communication process that contributed to the trouble. Suggest a remedy for each problem you identify:

a. Sender: Did the wrong person send the message?
b. Encoding: Did the sender use words or non-verbal cues that were confusing, inappropriate, or irrelevant?
c. Message: Was the message too short or too long? Were there too many messages? Was the timing wrong?
d. Channel: Was the most appropriate channel chosen?
e. Receiver: Was there no receiver at all? Was the message poorly formulated for the person(s) at whom it was aimed? Was it received by the wrong person?
f. Decoding: Did the receiver read in meanings that were not intended?

g. Feedback: What impact did the feedback have on the sender? Did the feedback help or hinder shared understanding?
h. Noise: In what ways did environmental, physiological, or psychological noise distort the message? Provide specific examples.

3. Invitation to Insight

Learn about upward communication in the workplace by asking several employees what types of information they share with their supervisors. What types of information do they avoid sharing with their supervisors? How does the organization encourage or discourage accurate upward communication?

4. Skill Builder

Develop your skill at cultivating informal communication networks by following these instructions:

a. Choose one of the following information goals, or identify a school-related or work-related goal of your own.

1. Decide which instructors and/or courses in an academic department of your institution are worth seeking out and which you might want to avoid.
2. Identify the qualities that would help you get the job of your dreams.
3. Locate an organization where you could gain job experience as a volunteer or intern.

b. Identify the people who can help you acquire the information you are seeking. Locate people from a variety of positions within the organization so you will gain a complete perspective. For each person, decide which channel you could use to begin to develop your network.

5. Skill Builder

With your group members, formulate a hypothetical context for each message below. Then use the information on pp. 101–114 to decide which communication channel would be best for each message. Use the criteria from Table 1-2 to explain your choice:

a. Informing your supervisor about difficulties with a coworker.
b. Asking for a few days of leave from work to attend a special reunion.
c. Training a new employee to operate a complicated computer program.
d. Notifying the manager of a local business that you still haven't received the refund you were promised.
e. Reminding your busy boss about a long overdue reimbursement for out-of-pocket expenses.
f. Apologizing to a customer for a mistake your company made.
g. Getting your boss's reaction to the idea of giving you more responsibility.

6. Invitation to Insight

Ask a few of your acquaintances to describe an ethical dilemma they've encountered in the workplace or in their personal lives. How did they handle the situation? What factors influenced them?

With a group of classmates, determine which ethical perspectives your informants seemed to rely on as they decided how to act. Apply various ethical perspectives to the same situations. Would you have followed the same course of action your informants did? Why or why not?

Mc Graw Hill LearnSmart™

For further review, go to the LearnSmart study module for this chapter.

Chapter Two

Communication, Culture, and Work

chapter outline

chapter objectives

After reading this chapter you should be able to:

1. Define culture and co-culture.

2. Identify ways in which race or ethnicity, class, generation, region, and disability can influence business communication.

3. Describe two key intercultural differences in formality, social customs, dress, time, tolerance for conflict, and gender roles.

4. Explain how the hidden dimensions of culture (context, individualism/collectivism, power distance, uncertainty avoidance, masculinity/femininity, long-term and short-term orientations) affect communication in a culturally diverse workforce.

5. Describe additional factors of ethical communication.

6. Apply the guidelines in Communicating across Diversity on pp. 48–52 to describe six specific ways you and others can communicate more effectively in your workplace.

7. Describe the cultural challenges in a specific organization or career and identify specific approaches to communicate most effectively within this culture.

Diversity is a fact of life in today's working world. The population of Miami is two-thirds Hispanic;[1] more than half of Washington, DC, residents are black; and one-third of San Franciscans are Asian Americans.[2] As Figure 2.1 on page 32 shows, the trend toward diversity will continue for the foreseeable future. According to the U.S. Census Bureau, the nation's Hispanic and Asian populations will triple over the next half-century, and non-Hispanic whites will represent about one-half of the total population by 2050.[3]

With the increase in international trade and immigration, the likelihood of working with people from different parts of the world is greater than ever. More than 10,000 foreign companies and their subsidiaries operate in the United States.[4] Some 300 Japanese companies operate in Michigan alone; German, British, and Dutch companies also have many U.S. sites. Immigrants accounted for more than half of the growth in the U.S. labor force at the turn of the twenty-first century.[5] In 2010, nearly 25 million workers, or 15 percent of the total U.S. labor force, were born outside of the United States.[6]

Given figures like these, it's no surprise that intercultural competence has been identified as one of the top skills for the work force in 2020,[7] and that more than 80 percent of the human resources executives surveyed say that global talent is a priority.[8] For companies and individuals who can take advantage of the trend toward increasing cultural diversity, the opportunities are great. DuPont has a policy of hiring men and women of a variety of ages and cultures because "diversity of experience and perspective gives DuPont a competitive edge."[9] Stona Fitch, vice president of manufacturing for Procter & Gamble, says, "Diversity provides a much richer environment, a variety of viewpoints, greater productivity. And, not unimportantly, it makes work more fun and interesting."[10] A spokesperson for the American Society of Civil Engineers states, "Without embracing diversity, the engineering profession will be unable to compete effectively in the global marketplace."[11] Whether you are working abroad, for

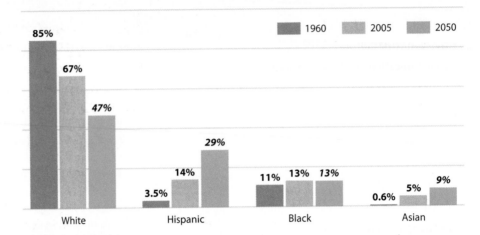

or with foreign nationals at home, or with native-born people from different backgrounds, understanding cultural differences is an essential part of being an effective communicator.

• The Nature of Culture

When most people use the word *culture,* they think of people from different national backgrounds. National cultures certainly do exist, and they play an important role in shaping the way people communicate. In addition, differences such as race/ethnicity, socioeconomic class, gender, and age play a role. Taking all these factors into account, we can define **culture** as a learned set of shared interpretations about beliefs, values, and norms that affect the behaviors of a relatively large group of people.[12]

It's important to realize that culture is learned, not innate. A Korean-born infant adopted soon after birth by non-Korean parents and raised in the United States will think and act differently from his or her cousins who grew up in Seoul. An African American may view the world differently depending on the region in which she was raised—or, more dramatically, if she finds herself working abroad in a country like France or Zaire, where African heritage has a different significance from that in the United States. The overwhelming influence of culture on communication led famous anthropologist Edward Hall to assert that "culture is communication and communication is culture."[13]

Cultures are invisible to the people used to inhabiting them. But to people from different backgrounds, the power of dominant norms is obvious. One account of a corporate training session illustrates this point:

> [The trainer] would run a little experiment when she was talking to corporate audiences that were mixed—including white men, women, and minorities. She would ask the audience to do a simple task: "Please list," she would request, "the rules needed to be successful in a white male society." Immediately the women and the minorities would begin to write down all the things they had to do to "fit in." Meanwhile, the white males in the audience just sat there, doing nothing, looking around at the women and the minorities writing for all they were worth.[14]

The author describing this experiment explains the important truth it reveals:

> [Cultural] paradigms are like water to fish. They are invisible in many situations because it is "just the way we do things." Often they operate at an unconscious level. Yet they determine, to a large extent, our behavior. As a white male, I cannot write down all those rules. My wife can. My minority friends can.[15]

Organizations Are Cultures Too

Every organization has its own way of doing business. Anyone who has worked for more than one restaurant or retail store, attended more than one college or university, belonged to more than one team, or volunteered for more than one worthy cause knows that even when the same job is being performed, the *way* it's done can be radically different. Theorists use the term **organizational culture** to describe these unique traits. An organization's culture is a relatively stable, shared set of rules about how to behave and set of values about what is important. In everyday language, culture is the insiders' view of "the way things are around here."

Organizational culture can affect you in many ways, large and small. Among other things, your organization's culture can determine where and how long you will work. It can shape the emotional environment, including the degree of cooperation or competition, and notions of how much and what kinds of fun are appropriate. Culture will surely influence the way you and others dress and the physical environment in which you'll spend your time. Organizational culture will govern the amount and type of interaction you have (both on and off the job) with other employees, both coworkers and management.[16]

Your fit with an organization's culture can make all the difference between a satisfying and a disappointing job. Research shows that employees are more satisfied and committed to their jobs when their values match those of their supervisors and the organization.[17] They are also more successful. Harvard Business School professors John Kotter and James Heskett flatly claim that people who conform to the norms of their organization's culture will be rewarded, while those who do not will be penalized.[18]

You can get a sense of a company's culture by talking with people who work there. Besides asking about culture in a formal job interview, off-the-record conversations with potential colleagues can provide valuable insights about the way the company operates. For example, ask how employees spend their time. A surprising amount of effort might go into activities only remotely related to getting the job done: dealing with paperwork, playing office politics, struggling with balky equipment, or attending one unproductive meeting after another. Even if you don't learn much about the organization as a whole, you'll get a good picture of the kind of people you will be working with.

You can also get clues about an organization's culture from observing how it operates. Communication practices are a good place to begin. How are you treated when you visit a company or deal with its employees? Do e-mails and other written correspondence suggest a welcoming culture?[19] An organization's physical presence also says something about its culture. Are workers' areas personalized or standardized? Is the workplace clean or dirty? Does the organization seem prosperous, or is it operating on a shoestring?

You're likely to spend more waking hours on the job than anywhere else, so thinking about the "personality" of an organization where you work can be just as important as choosing the culture where you live or the kind of person you choose as a mate.

• Communication in a Diverse Society

When you think about different cultures, you might visualize people living in faraway, even exotic locations. But you don't have to travel abroad to find cultural difference; American society is a cross-section of many people and cultures. Society in general is made up of a variety of **co-cultures**—groups that have a clear identity within the majority culture. Race, ethnicity, social class, gender, generation, and regional affiliation are a few examples of co-cultural markers that can make a difference in how we view ourselves and the people we work with.

Understanding how culture shapes communication can help you avoid mistaken conclusions about what a certain message means. It also might help you understand more about how *you* communicate.

Race and Ethnicity

It's an oversimplification to describe a single Hispanic, Asian, white, or black style of communication, just as it's dangerous to claim that all young people, women, or New Yorkers are alike. Each person's communication style is a combination of individual and cultural traits. Keeping in mind the risks of over-generalizing, researchers have found some patterns of communication that are common for many members of various races and ethnicities.

The amount of talk and silence that is appropriate can differ from one co-culture to another.[20] For example, most Native American and many Asian American cultures value silence more than mainstream U.S. culture does. By contrast, African American and Euro-American cultures place a high value on verbal skills, and their members tend to speak more. It's easy to imagine how the silence of, say, a Japanese American or Native American employee could be viewed by an African American or Euro-American colleague as a sign of dislike.

Attitudes toward conflict also differ from one ethnic co-culture to another. Because Asian cultures place a high value on saving face, some Asian Americans can display a preference for avoiding clear expressions of disagreement. Native Americans may prefer to deal with conflict through silence rather than direct confrontation. By contrast, many (though certainly not all) people with a Greek, Israeli, Italian, French, or South American background may prefer a direct, open conflict style.[21]

Even when communicators from different backgrounds speak roughly the same amount, the degree of personal information they reveal can differ dramatically. For example, Euro-Americans disclose more than African Americans or Puerto Ricans, who in turn reveal more than Mexican Americans.[22] (Of course, varying social and cultural contexts may create different disclosure patterns.)

Nonverbal standards also vary by co-culture. Most communicators unconsciously assume that their rules for behaviors such as eye contact are universal. Researchers, however, have found that eye behavior can vary significantly. One study found that widely opened eyes are often interpreted in mainstream U.S. culture as a sign of surprise or wonder and in Hispanic culture as a call for help, signifying "I don't understand." To some African Americans, the same kind of gaze is often regarded as a measure of innocence.[23] Chapter 4 has more to say about cultural differences in nonverbal behavior.

Because Euro-Americans often associate eye contact with honesty and respect, it is easy to misjudge others for whom steady eye contact would be a sign of disrespect. There are many cases where attempts by Puerto Ricans and Native Americans to show respect to persons in authority by not looking at them have been interpreted as dishonesty or disrespect by those accustomed to greater eye contact. Traditionally, Hopi and Navajo people generally avoid steady eye contact, as it is considered offensive, disrespectful, and rude. Blacks tend to make more eye contact when speaking but will not have such a steady gaze at someone they are listening to. Whites tend to make more continuous eye contact while listening to someone.[24]

Social Class

Even in egalitarian societies like the United States and Canada, social class can have a major impact on how people communicate on the job. Research demonstrates that parents tend to raise their children with the social class values of their own workplaces.[25] For example, children raised in working-class families typically learn to be obedient, follow

Generational Preferences in Communication Technology

Age often matters when choosing the best technology for exchanging messages on the job. The channels that communicators prefer are often a function of the era in which they came of age.

When Baby Boomers entered the workforce, typewriters and telephones were the principal communication technologies. About three-quarters of them now use the Internet in one way or another, and most have embraced e-mail. But Baby Boomers are less likely than younger communicators to use or appreciate the value of e-commerce and social networking. Differences even exist between Gen Xers and their Millennial counterparts. For example, Millennials are much more preoccupied with their gadgets. Rather than simply making phone calls, they use phones for sending e-mail and text messages, playing games and music, and recording videos.

Beyond technology, generational differences also arise in communication style. Millennial workers are used to the speed and brevity of texting and instant messaging. As a consequence, they often aren't sticklers for correct spelling and syntax. By contrast, Baby Boomers and Gen Xers grew up learning that accuracy is essential. They are likely to regard careless writing as a sign of incompetence.

Keeping differences like these in mind can help you choose the communication channel and style that best suit the people you are trying to reach. As always, generalizations don't apply to every person: Some Baby Boomers are avid users of all technologies, and some Millennials resemble their grandparents when it comes to using digital media. Despite exceptions to the rule, it often pays to be mindful of generational differences when communicating strategically.

Source: Zickuhr, K. (2011, February 3). *Generations and their gadgets. Pew Internet & American Life Project.* Retrieved from http://pewinternet.org/Reports/2011/Generations-and-gadgets/Report.aspx?view=all

rules, and defer to authority. By contrast, those raised in middle- and upper-class households are taught how to make convincing arguments, think critically, and solve problems creatively.

These lessons have consequences later in life. College professors often find that working-class and first-generation college students who are raised not to challenge authority can have a difficult time speaking up, thinking critically, and arguing persuasively.[26] The effects of social class continue into business and professional life, where skills like assertiveness and persuasiveness are career-enhancers. People who come from working-class families and attain middle- or upper-class careers face special challenges. New speech and language, clothing, and nonverbal patterns are often necessary to gain acceptance.[27] Many of these individuals must also cope with emotional ambivalence related to their career success.[28]

Generational Differences

The era in which people have been raised can shape the way they communicate. More than just a function of getting older over time, the historical period in which people live can affect their values, expectations, and as a result, their communication. Three generations compose most of today's workforce: Baby Boomers, Gen Xers, and Millennials.[29]

Baby Boomers (born 1945–1964) are the generation that typically has the most seniority in organizations today. Born following World War II, this generation was brought up to be independent and to believe they have the power to effect meaningful changes. They witnessed and participated in an era of social reform and upheaval that included

the Civil Rights movement and the Vietnam War, leading many Boomers to question the claims of authority figures—an ironic position now that they have become the authorities. In the workplace, Baby Boomers receive gratification from winning and achieving. They appreciate challenges, and enjoy pressure to perform.[30]

Generation Xers (born 1965–1980) hold many of the mid-career positions in today's organizations, including middle management and experienced technical work. In the workplace, Gen Xers are adept with technology, skeptical, independent, and possess a strong desire for work–life balance. They also place a high priority on fun, informality, and creativity on the job. They respect performance over tenure and are loyal to people, not organizations. The Pew Research Center found that Gen Xers believe their technology use, work ethic, conservative/traditional values, intelligence, and respectfulness distinguish them from other generations.[31]

Millennials (born 1980–2000) also have been labeled Generation Y, Net Generation, and Digital Natives. They occupy most entry-level positions in organizations and are starting to make their way into leadership roles. They also compose most of the current college student population. When the youngest members of this generation are old enough to get full-time jobs, Millennials will become the largest generation in the workplace. As a group, Millennials are technologically adept, ambitious, confident, hopeful, determined, and entrepreneurial. In the United States, Millennials are the most ethnically diverse generation in history. They have an international worldview; more than half have passports and one-quarter expect to work outside the United States.[32]

Problems can arise when members of different generations work together. For example, Millennials tend to have a much stronger need for affirming feedback than previous generations.[33] Because of their strong desire for achievement, they want clear guidance on how to do a job correctly—but not be micromanaged when they do it. After finishing the task, they have an equally strong desire for praise. To a Baby Boomer boss, that type of guidance and feedback may feel more like a nuisance. In the boss's experience, "no news is good news" and not being told you screwed up should be praise enough. Neither perspective is wrong. But when these co-cultures have different expectations, miscommunication can occur.

Regional Differences

Even in an age of great mobility, regional differences in communication styles persist. For example, your manner of speaking can have a strong effect on how you are perceived. Speakers of standard dialect are rated higher than nonstandard speakers in a variety of ways: They are perceived as more competent and more self-confident, and the content of their messages is rated more favorably.[34] In one experiment, researchers asked human resource professionals to rate job applicants' intelligence, initiative, and personality after hearing a 45-second recording of their voices. The speakers with identifiable regional accents—a Southern or New Jersey accent, for example—were recommended for lower-level jobs, while those with less pronounced speech styles were tagged for higher-level jobs that involved more public contact.[35] The judgments attached to identifiable accents is a key reason why many call centers for U.S. companies are located in Midwestern states. Gallup, the national telephone research agency, uses call centers in Nebraska because of the neutral accents of many of the people who live there.

A $48 Million Misunderstanding?

Jockey Jose Santos filed a libel claim against the Miami *Herald,* seeking $48 million in damages over a reporter's misunderstanding of his accented English. The *Herald* published a photograph showing Santos apparently holding an object in his hand as he rode thoroughbred Funny Cide across the finish line in the 2003 Kentucky Derby. In the accompanying story, reporter Frank Carlson misquoted the jockey as stating the object was an illegal "cue ring." The item turned out to be a Q-Ray, an ionized bracelet the jockey wore to help with his arthritis. As a result of the story, the Kentucky Racing Commission launched an investigation into what one official called "very suspicious" behavior.

The newspaper later printed a correction, but Santos maintained the story caused him emotional distress. The horse's owners were co-parties in the lawsuit, claiming the article's allegation of underhanded racing tactics cost them potential business.

Santos's attorney said that the misunderstanding would never have happened if the *Herald* had chosen a Spanish-speaking reporter. In the same vein, the editor of Miami's alternative paper, *New Times,* commented: "Let me get this straight: In Miami, the most Hispanic city in the country, the newspaper of record screwed up because someone misunderstood a Spanish speaker?"

Source: Photo of Kentucky Derby winner leads to investigation. (2003, May 10). *Sports Illustrated.com.* Retrieved from http:// sportsillustrated.cnn.com/horse_racing/news/2003/05/10/derby_ photo_ap/; Prince, R. (2005, February 11). $48 million misunderstanding: Latino jockey's case against Herald to proceed. *Maynard Institute.* Retrieved from http://www.maynardije.org/richardprince/ 48-million-misunderstanding; Sa ntos, Sackatoga sue Miami Herald for libel. (2004, May 9). *Thoroughbred Times.* Retrieved from http:// www.thoroughbredtimes.com/national-news/2004/may/09/santos- sackatoga-sue-miami-herald-for-libel.aspx

The effect of non-native accents is even more powerful. In one study, jurors in the United States found testimony less believable when delivered by witnesses speaking with German, Mexican, or Middle Eastern accents.[36] Not surprisingly, other research shows speakers with non-native accents feel stigmatized by the bias against them, often leading to a lower sense of belonging and more communication problems.[37]

Beyond accent, regional differences in communication can be significant. In the United States, for example, the unwritten rules about smiling differ from one part of the country to another. One communication researcher found Midwesterners from Ohio, Indiana, and Illinois smiled more than New Englanders from Massachusetts, New Hampshire, and Maine. None of those people smiled as much as people from southern and border states like Georgia, Kentucky, and Tennessee.[38] Given these differences, it is easy to imagine how a manufacturer from Memphis might regard a banker from Boston as unfriendly, and how the New Englander might view the southerner as overly demonstrative.

Disabilities

Belonging to a co-culture based on ethnicity or nationality requires years of immersion. By contrast, "Disability is a club anyone can join, anytime. It's very easy. Have a stroke and be paralyzed. . . . Be in a car wreck and never walk again."[39]

The Americans with Disabilities Act of 1990 (ADA) guarantees that people with disabilities receive reasonable accommodations and equal access to employment, buildings, transportation, and services. These legal guarantees are important, but they don't change the fact that, in many ways, having a disability may change how one is regarded. While there are no hard-and-fast rules about communicating with people who have disabilities, these guidelines apply to virtually all encounters:[40]

1. *Be naturally cordial.* When introduced to a person with a disability, offer to shake hands. People with limited hand use or who wear an artificial limb can usually shake hands. (Shaking hands with the left hand is an acceptable greeting.)

2. *Offer the same level of respect that you would to any other person.* For example, speak directly to people with disabilities rather than looking at and talking to their companion. Address people who have disabilities by their first names only when extending the same familiarity to all others. Realize that leaning on or hanging on to a person's wheelchair is similar to leaning or hanging on to the person using it.

3. *Don't be pushy.* If you offer assistance, wait until your offer is accepted. Then listen to the answers or ask, "How can I help?"

4. *Accommodate to the disability.* For example, when meeting a person who is visually impaired, identify yourself and others who may be with you. When speaking with a person who uses a wheelchair or a person who uses crutches, place yourself at eye level.

5. *Be patient.* When you're talking with someone who has difficulty speaking, wait for him or her to finish rather than correcting. If necessary, ask short questions that require short answers, a nod, or shake of the head. Never pretend to understand if you are having difficulty doing so. Instead, repeat what you have understood and allow the person to respond. The response will clue you in and guide your understanding.

6. *Relax.* Don't be embarrassed if you happen to use accepted, common expressions such as "See you later" or "Did you hear about that?" that seem to relate to a person's disability. Don't be afraid to ask questions when you're unsure of what to do.[41]

● Cultural Differences in International Business

Browse the travel and business sections of any bookseller or library, and you're likely to find many volumes detailing the cultures and business practices around the world. Some cultural differences in customs and behavior are obvious. For example, your work life will be simpler once you understand that punctuality is important in Switzerland and Germany but less important in most parts of Africa. As Table 2-1 on p. 43 shows, other differences are much subtler. We begin this section by looking at the more obvious differences in customs and behavior that distinguish cultures. Next, we explore some fundamental dimensions of diversity that are less obvious but at least as important. The following categories are not an exhaustive list of differences between countries, but they suggest the importance of learning rules of the cultures in which you will operate.

Customs and Behavior

Before cataloging differences in communication around the world, it's important to note that people from varied backgrounds also share many similarities. For example, computer engineers from Singapore, Lima, Tel Aviv, and Vancouver would find plenty of mutual interests and perspectives due to their shared occupational and socioeconomic backgrounds.

Even when we acknowledge cultural variation, the fact remains that not everyone in a culture behaves identically. Figure 2.2 shows both the overlap in communication practices and the range of behavior within each one. Furthermore, within every

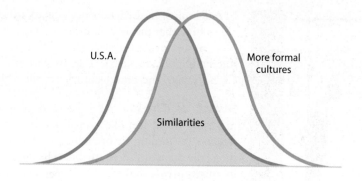

FIGURE 2.2

Differences and Similarities within and between Cultures

Source: Adapted from Bond, M. H. (1991). *Beyond the Chinese face*. New York, NY: Oxford University Press; Trompenaars, F. (1994). *Riding the waves of culture*. New York, NY: McGraw-Hill/Irwin.

culture, members display a wide range of communication styles. Ignoring *inter*cultural similarities and *intra*cultural variations can lead to stereotyping people from different backgrounds.

Formality   Americans take pleasure in their informality and their quickness in getting on a first-name basis with others. With the exception of a few countries, including Thailand and Australia, business exchanges with persons from other countries tend to be much more formal, especially at the beginning of a relationship.[42] In the United States and Canada, first names are seen as friendly and indicative of fondness and attachment. In many other countries—Mexico, Germany, and Egypt, for example—titles are an important way of showing respect, and it's best to use them until you are invited to move to a first-name basis.[43]

Names and titles aren't the only way to express degrees of formality. The way people do—or don't—converse with strangers varies from one culture to another. In North America, it's not uncommon to strike up a conversation with a stranger. But this custom isn't universal. The U.S. retail giant Wal-Mart made the strategic decision not to hire greeters at its German stores for reasons expressed by a public relations expert from that country: "As a German, I find the idea of being greeted at the door uncomfortable. I would feel astonished if someone I didn't know started talking to me."[44]

Social Customs   Cultural differences begin as soon as communicators encounter one another. Greetings range from the bow (lower is more respectful) in Japan, to the *wai* (pressed palms with a head bow) in Thailand, to the handshake in Europe and South America.

In many countries, exchanging business cards is an important ritual. In Japan, especially, cards are given and received with care: The recipient should use two hands and study the card carefully, treating it with the same respect he or she would give its owner.[45] One U.S. businessperson lost a deal in Japan because his inattention to the Japanese businessmen's cards was taken as a measure of the lack of attention he would give to their business.[46]

In many cultures, gift giving is a part of business protocol. Knowing the details of a specific culture can be important. For example, in India, where cows are sacred, gifts of leather are to be avoided. In China, avoid giving white flowers (associated with death) or gifts in sets of four because the sound of that number is the same as the word for death. Lavish gifts may put your host in an awkward position, so learn cultural specifics and choose carefully.

Another variable is the degree of overlap between doing business and socializing. While entertaining is part of business in virtually all cultures, socializing after business hours is a central part of building a working relationship in many parts of the world.

In much of eastern Asia, drinking is regarded as a way of bonding that carries over into working relationships. One consultant alerts travelers to be prepared for a turn singing in the karaoke bars that are part of the scene in China, Japan, and other countries in the region.[47]

Styles of Dress   As travel and communication make the world feel like a smaller place, regional differences in clothing are becoming less pronounced. For men, the standard Western business suit is common in many urban settings. For both men and women abroad, conservative dress will take you much further than the latest fad or fashion. In Muslim countries, women can show respect with modest dress, including longer sleeves and lower hemlines than may be fashionable elsewhere. And women doing business in these countries might consider covering their hair, even if veiling is not part of their personal religion.

Even in an era of international business, local differences exist. For example, when United Parcel Service entered the German market, it belatedly discovered the firm's signature brown uniforms evoked unpleasant memories of brown-shirted Nazi storm troopers. In Indonesia, the company had to modify its usual business suit dress rule and allow executives to wear more casual attire common in that hot and humid climate.[48]

Time   In international business, the first shock for travelers from the United States may be the way members of other cultures understand and use time. North Americans, like most northern Europeans, have what anthropologists term a **monochronic** view of time, seeing it as an almost tangible substance. American speech reflects this attitude when people talk about saving time, making time, having time, wasting time, using time, and taking time. In U.S. culture, time is money, so it is rationed carefully. People schedule appointments and rigidly adhere to them. Tasks are performed in a scheduled order, one at a time.

This monochronic orientation is not universal. Cultures with a **polychronic** orientation see time as more fluid. Meetings go on for as long as they take; they don't abruptly end because "it's time." Most Latin American cultures, as well as southern European and Middle Eastern cultures, have a polychronic orientation. In Mexico, for example, "you make friends first and do business later," according to R. C. Schrader, who heads California's trade office in Mexico City.[49]

Members of polychronic cultures are less concerned with punctuality than those raised with monochronic standards. It is not that being punctual is unimportant; it is just that other relational factors may take priority. This fact helps explain why the notion of being "on time" varies. Extremely monochronic cultures view even small delays as an offense. In polychronic cultures, varying degrees of lateness are acceptable—from roughly 15 minutes in southern Europe to part, or sometimes even all, of the day in the Middle East and Africa.[50]

Tolerance for Conflict   In some cultures, each person is responsible for helping to maintain harmony of a group and of society. The maintenance and pursuit of harmony is expressed in the Japanese term *wa*. In Chinese, a similar term is *zhong he*.[51] In other places—the Middle East and southern Europe, for example—harmony takes a backseat to emotional expression. Figure 2.3 illustrates how the rules for expressing emotions vary around the world.

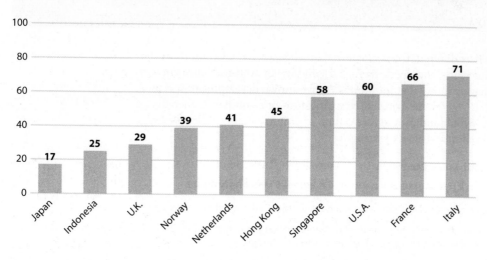

FIGURE 2.3
Percentage of
Employees Who
Would Openly
Express Feeling
Upset at Work

Source: Trompenaars, F.
(1994). *Riding the waves
of culture.* New York, NY:
McGraw-Hill/Irwin.

The cultural avoidance of conflict means most Asian businesspeople will probably not say no directly to you, fearing you will lose face and suffer embarrassment. To help you maintain harmony and save face, they might spare you unpleasant news or information; it will be softened so you don't suffer disgrace or shame, especially in front of others. You may be told they will consider the matter or that it would be very difficult. Mexican business culture also values harmony and discourages confrontation. This attitude creates problems when it clashes with more aggressive standards that U.S. businesspeople usually bring to transactions. As president of Black & Decker Latin America, José Maria Gonzales is used to working with colleagues and suppliers from north of the border. Despite that fact, he says coping with the difference between U.S. and Mexican approaches to conflict doesn't come easily:

> In a meeting Americans can argue, hit the table and leave as if nothing happened, while a Mexican might not forgive you for three months. I have to make sure not to personalize things sometimes.[52]

This sort of accommodation works both ways. People from cultures that seek harmony can learn to adapt to and accept conflict; communicators from more aggressive societies like the United States can learn to appreciate the importance of harmony when communicating cross culturally. Once communicators learn to appreciate different sets of rules about how to express and handle disagreements, conducting business becomes much easier.

Gender Roles   Women from North America, Western Europe, and Australia/New Zealand who travel internationally are likely to be astonished and chagrined by the way they are regarded in some overseas cultures, where ideas of appropriate feminine behavior can be quite different. In some countries, a woman who outranks a man may not be treated that way by hosts; the hosts may still speak to and prefer to negotiate with the male, assuming he is the woman's superior. In Asian countries and Muslim countries, women may find they are excluded from substantive conversation or overlooked in negotiations because of designated gender roles. Sometimes, a woman can establish greater credibility by clarifying her title, role, and responsibilities in writing before a personal visit, but even this step won't guarantee the desired effect.

The differences described here can present challenges when workers from different cultures work together. Table 2-1 illustrates some of these challenges by listing differences between Chinese and Western businesspeople in both concerns and communication styles.

These statements reflect different facets of cultural intelligence, or "CQ" for short. For each set, add up your scores and divide by four to produce an average. Our work with large groups of managers shows that for purposes of your own development, it is most useful to think about your three scores in comparison to one another. Generally, an average of less than 3 would indicate an area calling for improvement, while an average of greater than 4–5 reflects a true CQ strength.

Rate the extent to which you agree with each statement, using the scale:

1 = strongly disagree, 2 = disagree, 3 = neutral, 4 = agree, 5 = strongly agree.

_____ Before I interact with people from a new culture, I ask myself what I hope to achieve.

_____ If I encounter something unexpected while working in a new culture, I use this experience to figure out new ways to approach *other* cultures in the future.

_____ I plan how I'm going to relate to people from a different culture before I meet them.

+_____ When I come into a new cultural situation, I can immediately sense whether something is going well or something is wrong.

Total _____ ÷ 4 = [____] **Cognitive CQ**

_____ It's easy for me to change my body language (for example, eye contact or posture) to suit people from a different culture.

_____ I can alter my expression when a cultural encounter requires it.

_____ I modify my speech style (for example, accent or tone) to suit people from a different culture.

+_____ I easily change the way I act when a cross-cultural encounter seems to require it.

Total _____ ÷ 4 = [____] **Physical CQ**

_____ I have confidence I can deal well with people from a different culture.

_____ I am certain I can befriend people whose cultural backgrounds are different from mine.

_____ I can adapt to the lifestyle of a different culture with relative ease.

+_____ I am confident I can deal with a cultural situation that's unfamiliar.

Total _____ ÷ 4 = [____] **Emotional/ motivational CQ**

Source: Earley, P. C., & Mosakowski, E. (2004, October). Cultural intelligence. *Harvard Business Review, 82*(10), 139–146.

Fundamental Dimensions of Cultural Diversity

So far we have discussed obvious differences between cultures. As important as customs and norms are, they are only the tip of the cultural iceberg. Underlying what might appear to be idiosyncrasies in behavior are a number of fundamental values that shape the way members of a culture think, feel, and act. In the following pages, we look at some of these fundamental differences. Once you appreciate them, you will understand how and why

Table 2-1	Contrasting Chinese–Western Concerns and Communication Practices	
	Chinese	**Western**
Concerns	Saving face	Frankness, "honesty"
	Respect, politeness	Assertiveness
	Compromise, flexibility	Self-assurance
	General feeling, "spirit"	Specific terms
	Social status	Task at hand
	Patience	Time efficiency
Communication practices	Reserved	Extroverted
	Tentative	Firm
	Personal	Less personal
	No body contact	Hugging, backslapping acceptable
	No pointing	Index finger used to point

Source: Chen, M. (2001). *Inside Chinese business: A guide for managers worldwide.* Boston, MA: Harvard Business School Press.

people from different backgrounds behave as they do, and you will have ideas of how you can adapt to improve the quality of your communication with others.

High- and Low-Context   Anthropologist Edward Hall identified two distinct ways in which members of various cultures deliver messages.[53] A **low-context culture** uses language primarily to express thoughts, feelings, and ideas as clearly and logically as possible. To low-context communicators, the meaning of a statement is in the words spoken. By contrast, a **high-context culture** relies heavily on subtle, often nonverbal cues to convey meaning, save face, and maintain social harmony. Communicators in these societies learn to discover meaning from the context in which a message is delivered: the speaker's nonverbal behaviors, the history of the relationship, and the general social rules that govern interaction between people. When delivering difficult or awkward messages, high-context speakers often convey meaning through context rather than plainly stated words to avoid upsetting their listeners. Consider a few differences between how a low-context Westerner and a high-context Chinese person might express the same idea:[54]

Western	Chinese
Do you understand? *(Responsibility placed on other.)*	Am I being clear? *(Speaker takes responsibility for understanding.)*
Is the project acceptable? *(Requires direct yes or no answer.)*	What do you think of the project? *(Gives respondent latitude to reply diplomatically.)*
We can't do that. *(Clear refusal could be perceived as harsh.)*	This may be a little difficult for us to do. *(Context makes it clear that the answer is still no.)*

Mainstream culture in the United States and Canada falls toward the low-context end of the scale. Long-time residents generally value straight talk and grow impatient with beating around the bush. By contrast, most Middle Eastern and Asian cultures fit the high-context pattern. In many Asian societies, for example, maintaining harmony is important, so communicators avoid speaking directly if that would threaten another person's dignity. One U.S. project manager describes how her insensitivity to high-context communication almost derailed an international team in developing a Japanese-language version of an Internet search service:

> As an American project manager, I was expecting that if I was proposing something stupid, I would hear it from the people on the team. In reality, I had a plan with a fatal flaw, and the Japanese team members knew it, but it was not their style of communication to embarrass me by telling me.[55]

Even within a single country, co-cultures can have different notions about the value of direct speech. For example, Puerto Rican language style resembles high-context Japanese or Korean more than low-context English. As a group, Puerto Ricans value social harmony and avoid confrontation, which leads them to speak in indirect ways to avoid offending.[56] The same holds true for Mexican Americans, as communication researcher Don Locke explains:

> Whereas members of the dominant culture of the United States are taught to value openness, frankness, and directness, the traditional Mexican-American approach requires the use of much diplomacy and tact when communicating with another individual. Concern and respect for the feelings of others dictate that a screen be provided behind which an individual may preserve dignity. . . . The manner of expression is likely to be elaborate and indirect, since the aim is to make the personal relationship at least appear harmonious, to show respect for the other's individuality. To the Mexican-American, direct argument or contradiction appears rude and disrespectful.[57]

A preference for high- or low-context communication isn't the only factor that distinguishes one culture from another. One survey of 160,000 employees in 60 countries revealed several other ways in which the worldviews of one national culture can differ from those of another.[58] Table 2-2 lists those dimensions and the styles that are most common in some countries. We will look at those differences now.

Individualism   Members of **individualistic cultures** are inclined to put their own interests and those of their immediate family ahead of social concerns. Individualistic cultures offer their members a great deal of freedom in the belief that this freedom makes it possible for each person to achieve personal success. **Collectivist cultures,** however, have tight social frameworks in which members of a group (such as an organization) feel primary loyalty toward one another and the group to which they belong. China, like most East Asian cultures, is highly collective.

In collectivist societies, members are expected to believe the welfare of the organization is as important as or even *more important* than their own.[59] Workers are less likely to strive to become organizational "stars," because that approach would dishonor other team members. "You seldom see an individual Japanese executive who stands above the rest until he is the most senior individual in the company," says international corporate recruiter Richard M. Ferry.[60] The power of collectivist beliefs was illustrated when PepsiCo rewarded one of its managers in China with a sizable cash bonus that he divided equally among his subordinates.[61]

Table 2-2	Cultural Values in Selected Countries

Long-Term Orientation	Short-Term Orientation
China	Pakistan
Hong Kong	Philippines
Taiwan	Norway
Japan	Canada
South Korea	East Africa*

Individualistic	**Collectivistic**
United States	Guatemala
Australia	Ecuador
United Kingdom	Panama
Canada	Venezuela
New Zealand	Pakistan, Indonesia

Avoid Uncertainty	**Tolerate Uncertainty**
Greece	Singapore
Portugal	Jamaica
Uruguay	Denmark
Guatemala	Sweden
Belgium and El Salvador	Hong Kong

High Power Distance	**Low Power Distance**
Malaysia	Austria
Philippines	Israel
Mexico	Denmark
Arab world**	New Zealand
China	Ireland

Masculine	**Feminine**
Japan	Sweden
Hungary	Norway
Austria	Netherlands
Italy	Denmark
Switzerland	Costa Rica

*Ethiopia, Kenya, Tanzania, Zambia.
**Egypt, Iraq, Kuwait, Lebanon, Libya, Saudi Arabia, United Arab Emirates.
Source: Adapted from Hofstede, G., Hofstede, G. J., & Minkov, M. (1997). *Cultures and organizations: Software of the mind* (3rd ed.). New York, NY: McGraw-Hill. Retrieved from http://www.geert-hofstede.com

Power Distance   The term **power distance** refers to attitudes toward differences in authority. Cultures with high power distance, such as Mexico and the Philippines, accept the fact that power is distributed unequally—that some members have greater resources and influence than others. In these cultures, differences in organizational status and rank are expected, routine, and clear-cut. Employees respect those in high positions. Other cultures, such as the United States, downplay differences in power. Employees are more comfortable approaching—and even challenging—their superiors and may expect to gain greater power.

Colleagues with different notions of power distance might find it difficult to work together. Imagine, for example, how a young business school graduate from a U.S. firm might grow frustrated after being transferred to the Guadalajara branch office, where the same relentless questioning that marked her as a free thinker in school is regarded as overly aggressive troublemaking.

Uncertainty Avoidance
The world is an uncertain place. International politics, economic trends, and the forces of nature make it impossible to predict the future with accuracy. **Uncertainty avoidance** is a measure of how accepting a culture is of a lack of predictability. Some cultures (e.g., Singapore and Hong Kong) are comfortable with this fact. Their acceptance of uncertainty allows them to take risks, and they are relatively tolerant of behavior that differs from the norm. Other cultures (e.g., Japan, Greece, and Portugal) are less comfortable with change. They value tradition and formal rules, and show less tolerance for different ideas.

Masculinity
In the context of intercultural research, masculinity doesn't refer to biological traits. Instead, it addresses a culture's values, expressed in terms of stereotypical gender roles. Cultures in which gender roles are highly differentiated are termed **masculine.** Those in which the gender roles are more similar are called **feminine.**

More masculine cultures (e.g., Japan, Austria, and Switzerland) tend to focus on getting the job done. By contrast, more feminine cultures (Scandinavian countries, Chile, Portugal, and Thailand, and much of Latin America) are more likely to be concerned about members' feelings and their smooth functioning as a team. When compared to other countries, the United States falls slightly toward the masculine end of the spectrum, and Canada is almost exactly in the middle, balanced between task and social concerns.[62]

Masculine societies focus on making the team more competent through training and use of up-to-date methods and are highly concerned with individual success: advancing to more responsible jobs, better training, and so on. By contrast, groups in feminine societies focus more on collective concerns: cooperative problem solving, maintaining a friendly atmosphere, and good physical working conditions.

Future Orientation
Cultures with a **long-term orientation** defer gratification in pursuit of long-range goals, while those with a **short-term orientation** look for quick payoffs. The willingness to work hard today for a future payoff is especially common in East Asian cultures, while Western industrialized cultures are much more focused on short-term results.

As long as employees and employers share the same orientation toward payoffs, the chances for harmony are good. When some people push for a quick fix while others urge patience, conflicts are likely to arise.

It's easy to see how a society's task or social orientation, attitudes toward uncertainty, individuality, power distance, and short-term or long-term results can make a tremendous difference in how work situations evolve. Cultural values shape what people communicate about and how they interact. Cultural differences don't account for every aspect of workplace functioning, of course, but they do provide a set of assumptions that exert a subtle yet powerful effect on each person's workplace communication.

Asking Hard Questions about Ethical Behavior

Among its core values, electronics manufacturer Texas Instruments (TI) includes a respect for individuals, a commitment to long-term relationships, a concern for the environment, and a sense of duty to the communities where it does business.

TI encourages employees to use the following guidelines whenever they have a concern about whether a business action is consistent with the company's values. This information is provided to TI employees on a business-card-size mini-pamphlet to carry with them. You can use the same guidelines when faced with ethical challenges of your own.

Is the action legal?

Does it comply with our values?

If you do it, will you feel bad?

How will it look in the newspaper?

If you know it's wrong, don't do it!

If you're not sure, ask.

Keep asking until you get an answer.

Source: Texas Instruments, Inc. (2011). *Corporate social responsibility: The TI ethics quick test.* Retrieved from http://www.ti.com/corp/docs/company/citizen/ethics/quicktest.shtml

• Diversity and Ethical Issues

Some cultural differences may challenge your sense of what is normal or proper behavior without raising ethical questions. For example, you probably could readjust your sense of promptness or what to wear to a business meeting without facing any sort of moral dilemma. In other cases, though, doing business in an unfamiliar culture might challenge your fundamental sense of right and wrong. You might be offended by differing notions of gender equality. You could be shocked to learn that bribes or payoffs are considered a normal part of doing business. You could encounter favoritism toward friends and family members that offends your sense of fair play. You might see a profound disregard for the environment.

There is growing recognition that businesses that operate in a worldwide economy need a universal code of business ethics. Toward that end, a collaboration of business leaders in Japan, Europe, and the United States have developed a code of ethics based on ideals from both East Asia and the West. Called the Caux Round Table Principles for Business, this code includes many communication-related principles, such as treating all employees with honesty and dignity, listening to employee suggestions, avoiding discriminatory practices, dealing with all customers fairly, and avoiding industrial espionage and other dishonest means of acquiring commercial information.[63]

Despite this admirable effort, you may encounter ethical challenges arising out of cultural differences. In cases like these, you can respond in a variety of ways:

Avoiding: You might refuse to do business in cultures that operate according to ethical principles different from yours.

Accommodating: You could accept the different ethical system and conform to practices fundamentally different from yours.

Forcing: You could insist on doing business in a way you believe is ethically proper.

Educating–Persuading: You could try to convince the people with whom you want to do business why your set of ethical principles is more appropriate.

Negotiating–Compromising: You and the other party could each give up something to negotiate a settlement.

Collaboration–Problem Solving: You could work with the other party to confront the conflict directly and develop a mutually satisfying solution.[64]

All of these approaches have obvious drawbacks. It's easy to imagine a situation in which you may have to choose between compromising your principles to please your bosses and customers or being true to yourself and risking your career.

Facing ethical dilemmas you never anticipated can be especially hard. You can begin to prepare by grounding yourself in ethical principles and learning about a new culture's ethical practices. When you do encounter new situations, ask yourself the following questions to help you make the best possible decision:

- *How morally significant is this situation?* Not all ethical conflicts have the same moral significance. For example, while giving contracts to friends or family members may offend the sensibilities of a businessperson used to awarding jobs on the basis of merit, the practice may not be as morally offensive as one exploiting child labor or damaging the environment.[65]

- *Is there home culture consensus regarding the issue?* If there is not widespread agreement in your home culture about the ethical principle, you justifiably may have more latitude about how to act. For example, corporations in the United States have a wide range of policies about supporting employees' families, so there might be less obligation for a company to provide family benefits in a host country.[66]

• Communicating across Diversity

By now it should be clear that communicating with others from different backgrounds isn't always easy. Matters including culture, ethnicity, and gender may have made others' experiences quite different from yours.[67] Some of the responsibility for building bridges rests with management, and a growing number of businesses are taking this job seriously. But you don't need to join a corporate training program to benefit from cultural diversity.

Three ways to enhance your intercultural competency are to improve your knowledge, attitudes, and behaviors. These principles can be summarized in the five categories on the following pages. Adopting a more perceptive attitude can go a long way toward opening the door to more rewarding and productive communication.

Become Culturally Literate

Many cultural problems are caused not by malice, but by a lack of knowledge. Trainers in cultural sensitivity cite examples of how mistaken assumptions can lead to trouble.[68] Lack of knowledge is most apparent in international settings. One engineer gives an embarrassing example:

> I was in a meeting with some Korean clients, and I had a red marker in my hand to make some corrections to a blueprint. . . . I used my red marker to write the name of one of the Korean guys that I was meeting with. The room got very silent, and everyone looked at me completely stunned.
>
> One of the clients took pity on me and whispered that writing a living person's name in red is a bad idea. Apparently, in Korean culture, red is used to record a deceased person's name. Since my client was alive, I was wishing him dead.[69]

Lack of cultural knowledge can lead to similar problems closer to home. In one West Coast bank, officials were dismayed when Filipino female employees didn't cooperate

Difference as Advantage

Historically, being different from the norm was a disadvantage for many career-minded people. For that reason, job-seekers often tried to downplay differences such as being born abroad, speaking differently, or appearing visibly different from the mainstream. But as society becomes more diverse, tolerance grows, and world trade expands, diversity can be a career-enhancer.

Here are some tips that can help you use your unique background in your career.

1. If you are skilled at speaking other languages, feature that information in your résumé. Being bilingual or multilingual can make you a very attractive candidate. If you are already employed, show your bosses how fluency can help the organization.

2. If English isn't your first language, make sure your literacy skills and accent reduction are up to par.

Most communities offer classes in English, public speaking, and writing where you can sharpen these skills.

3. Identify ways your cultural background will help you be an asset in marketing, sales, client support, management, and other areas. Make sure your bosses understand these advantages.

4. Don't overplay your unique identity and risk being pigeonholed as a "token minority employee." Career success depends on a variety of factors, including your personal background, but performance is the best measure of your value.

Source: Prasad, C. (2009). *Difference as advantage: Maximize the benefits of your cultural identity on the job.* Retrieved from http://www.imdiversity .com/villages/asian/careers_workplace_employment/prasad_ difference_in_workplace.asp

---

with the new "friendly teller" program. Management failed to realize that, in Filipino culture, overtly friendly women can be taken for prostitutes. A Taiwanese executive who was transferred to the Midwestern U.S. offices of a large company was viewed as aloof and autocratic by his peers, who did not understand that Asian culture encourages a more distant managerial style.

Misunderstandings like these are less likely to cause problems when workers understand each other's cultural backgrounds. As Paulette Williams, former senior manager at Weyerhauser's nurseries in Southern California, put it, "If you don't learn how other people feel, you can hurt them unintentionally."[70]

Timothy Weiss, a U.S. professor who spent a year teaching at the Chinese University of Hong Kong, illustrates the kind of open-minded, inquiring attitude that can make communicators more effective when they encounter different cultural practices.

> Why, in a culture that so dearly values every second and minute saved, will meetings and conversations last for what Americans would consider such inordinately long periods? . . . In these departmental meetings—which I find excruciating—I suspect that something else is going on that a Westerner such as myself will understand sooner or later. Although I certainly am not ready to abandon my American sense of how departmental meetings should be conducted, in allowing myself to remain open-minded about other ways of conducting these meetings, I begin to learn something about other ways of approaching departmental issues and of communicating messages within a group.[71]

Develop Constructive Attitudes

It's easy to think of cultural differences as an annoyance that makes it harder to take care of business. Dealing with others who have different attitudes or customs takes patience and time—both scarce commodities in a busy work schedule. But with the right attitude,

CULTURE **at work**

Gender as a Co-Culture

As you will read in Chapter 4, characteristically male and female communication styles differ in some significant ways. These differences have led some observers to suggest that the two sexes belong to two distinct co-cultures. This position was most memorably captured in John Gray's best-selling book *Men Are from Mars, Women Are from Venus.*[72] Research has confirmed there are some differences between the way men and women communicate.[73] For example, sociolinguist Deborah Tannen has described men and women as expressing "different words from different worlds," and being "tuned to different frequencies."[74]

If you accept the "different cultures" argument, then the guidelines for intercultural communication in these pages offer useful tips for dealing with members of the opposite sex. Rather than "ethnocentrically" finding fault with the way they communicate, a more productive approach might be to think that members of the opposite sex are speaking a different language to some degree. As Tannen puts it, "Understanding style differences for what they are takes the sting out of them."[75]

---

cultural diversity can stop being just a necessary cost of doing business and can become an opportunity.[76] Figure 2.4 shows the range of attitudes about cultural differences. It's easy to see which mindsets do and do not lead to productive relationships.

View Diversity as an Opportunity

People with differing backgrounds can bring new strengths to a business. Women, for instance, are generally more skilled than men at reading nonverbal cues.[77] This makes them ideal members of a negotiating team, where they may be especially skilled at interpreting how the other people are feeling. Workers from diverse ethnic groups can offer new insights into how customers or other workers with similar backgrounds can be reached. A Hispanic supervisor, for example, may be especially effective at motivating and training other Hispanics, and a Korean team member can give new insights into how a Korean-managed competitor operates.

Avoid Ethnocentrism

Ethnocentrism is the inclination to see all events from the perspective of your own culture and to evaluate your own culture as superior. Ethnocentrism is evident when you judge someone to be less intelligent or less important because he or she doesn't keep up with your national teams, critique others as less sophisticated because their dress doesn't match your culture's notion of fashion, or assume others have less business acumen because they communicate differently. Taking advantage of intercultural communication training and opportunities for multicultural interactions may help reduce your ethnocentrism.[78]

Denial	**Defense**	**Minimization**	**Acceptance**	**Adaptation**	**Integration**
No perception of differences	Hostility toward other cultures	Belief that cultural differences are superficial	Recognition and exploration of differences	Ability to empathize, shift frame of reference	Recognizing and embracing differences

Self-centered ⟨⟨⟨   ⟩⟩⟩ **Other-centered**

FIGURE 2.4 Stages of Intercultural Sensitivity

MASTER the chapter

review points

- Society is increasingly diverse, making communicating with people from many cultures a business necessity.

- Co-cultures are groups with a clear identity within a major culture, e.g., race and ethnicity, social class, generation, region, disability, and gender. Understanding co-cultures can improve workplace perceptions and behaviors.

- Employees need to be aware of the important international differences in formality, social customs, dress, time, tolerance for conflict, and gender roles as well as "hidden" cultural dimensions of high- and low-context, individualism

and collectivism, power distance, uncertainty avoidance, masculinity and femininity, and future orientations.

- Business success requires consideration of the complexity of multicultural ethical factors.

- Astute business communicators strive to be culturally literate, develop constructive attitudes (such as seeing diversity as an opportunity and avoiding ethnocentrism), and adapt their behaviors for a diverse work environment by avoiding condescension and developing dialogue.

key terms

Baby Boomers   35
co-culture   33
collectivist cultures   44
culture   32
ethnocentrism   50
feminine culture   46
Generation Xers   36
high-context culture   43
individualistic culture   44
long-term orientation   46

low-context culture   43
masculine culture   46
Millennials   36
monochronic time orientation   40
organizational culture   33
polychronic time orientation   40
power distance   45
short-term orientation   46
uncertainty avoidance   46

activities

1. Invitation to Insight

a. Either through personal interviews or research, identify several differences in communication practices between your own culture and another culture that interests you.

b. If you were interacting with a person from that culture, how would you bridge the differences?

2. Invitation to Insight

Choose one set of cultural values summarized on pp. 42–46 and identify the characteristic that is not representative of your own culture. For example, if you are used to a low-context culture, you might focus on high-context communication. Now consider both the advantages and the disadvantages of working in an environment in which this unfamiliar norm is the dominant one. For instance, how might interaction be more effective or otherwise desirable if most people communicated in a high-context manner?

3. Skill Builder

Select one form of disability. Collaborate with several of your classmates to create two role plays, illustrating effective and ineffective communication with a person who is challenged by the disability. Act out your role plays in front of the class.

4. Skill Builder

Develop your ability to identify and communicate effectively within an organization's culture. Choose an organization in a field that interests you, or focus on an organization to which you already belong. By analyzing the organization's physical setting and literature, interviewing others, and making your own observations, construct a description of the organizational culture that addresses the dimensions listed on pp. 48–52. On the basis of your findings, describe an optimal way to communicate in the following areas:

a. Introducing new ideas.
b. Interacting with superiors.
c. Dealing with conflict.
d. Managing time.
e. Socializing with fellow workers.
f. Using preferred methods of exchanging information (e.g., telephone, e-mail, face-to-face interaction).

5. Skill Builder

Choose three cultures around the world with which you might interact in the course of your career. To discover the keys to effective intercultural communication in your three chosen cultures, find some reputable sources on the Internet. For each of the three cultures describe:

a. The culture in general.
b. Business protocol for that culture.
c. The language(s).
d. Sources you could go to for additional training and/or e-mail contacts.

6. Skill Builder

Representatives from Japan, the United States, and European nations collaborated in an attempt to create an international code of business ethics. Read about the Caux Round Table by using a search engine to find articles on this process begun in 1994. Read the document at http://www.cauxroundtable .org, then:

a. List the seven principles found in the document.
b. Describe how these seven principles relate to the ethical standards on p. 26 of Chapter 1.
c. Write a short essay describing how your own personal sense of ethics corresponds to each of the seven principles.

7. Invitation to Insight

Choose one of the following options to better understand the importance of organizational culture. In each case, use the most relevant dimensions of communication described on pp. 33–38 to structure your analysis and description.

a. Interview someone familiar with an organization or field that interests you to learn about its culture. Identify the kinds of communication that shape this culture and how the culture shapes the way communication operates in the organization or field.
b. Assume the administration of your college or university has asked you to brief newly hired faculty members about your school's academic culture from an undergraduate student's perspective. Describe how communication practices at your school both shape and reflect its culture. You can make your remarks more clear and interesting by including one or more brief examples to illustrate how the culture operates.

8. Invitation to Insight

Find a video clip that demonstrates intercultural communication. With a group of classmates, analyze the video. Identify examples of assumptions and behaviors that block or promote authentic relations. For those behaviors that block authentic relations, suggest ways to improve communication. Share your analysis with the class.

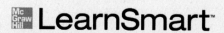

For further review, go to the LearnSmart study module for this chapter.

PART TWO

Omnicom Marketing

Mark's career at the marketing firm Omnicom is off to a good start. After a year as a rookie account representative, he was promoted to his first management position, supervising a team of reps. His group is mostly terrific; they work hard, get along well, and help one another. This is especially good news for Mark because his immediate compensation and his future at the firm depend on the team generating a significant number of billable hours.

Mark's only serious problem is with Kate. She was hired in an entry-level position with great expectations for growth. But after a few months on the job, Kate's performance has slipped dramatically. She missed two important deadlines, and now some of the account reps are starting to complain about having to pick up her slack. She comes in late to the office, and she makes what are obviously social phone calls during work. Yesterday, Mark saw her checking Facebook several times. Mark knows he can't ignore the situation anymore. He has to confront Kate and get her to improve her performance, or else. Fortunately, Kate's upcoming performance review offers a good chance to discuss the problems.

Kate sees the situation very differently. After taking the job with great enthusiasm, she has come to believe that her contributions don't count for anything. "I suggest ideas," she says, "and they all get shot down." She feels overqualified for the job. "I'm ready to do serious work, but all they want me to do is take notes at meetings, make coffee, and run errands." Kate is also discouraged on the relational front. "I try to reach out to the rest of the team, but they're all men, and I just don't fit in. In fact, some of their little jokes about women make me feel really uncomfortable. If I wanted, I could probably file a sexual harassment complaint." She has just about given up hope about things getting better. "If that's the way they want it, fine. I'll do my job, collect my pay, and look for a better place to work."

Personal Skills

As you read the chapters in this unit, consider the following questions:

chapter 3

1. Which barriers to listening described in Chapter 3 might make it difficult for Mark and Kate to hear one another's perspectives when they meet to discuss this situation?
2. Consider the listening styles discussed in Chapter 3. Present evidence that indicates each person's style, and then describe how this knowledge might have created a different communication outcome for Kate and Mark.
3. Describe how Mark might have used the guidelines in Chapter 3 to deal more effectively with their disagreements.

chapter 4

1. Describe a series of messages, ranging from highly ambiguous to highly specific, that Mark and Kate could use to express their concerns to one another. Which approach(es) might have the best chance of success?
2. What specific advice would you give Kate and Mark if they wanted to improve their professional identities through using positive language and an optimal level of powerful language?
3. Give an example of how Mark and Kate might resort to each type of inflammatory language described in this chapter to confront each other. For each statement, provide a noninflammatory alternative.
4. What problematic nonverbal messages might Kate and her colleagues have been sending that contributed to the problem? Suggest alternative nonverbal messages that could help each of them communicate more effectively.

chapter 5

1. How does the need to be treated with dignity affect Kate's perceptions and behaviors?
2. How might Kate use the guidelines about raising delicate issues on pp. 113–116 to express her dissatisfaction to Mark?
3. Are there any ways Mark might have praised Kate that would have minimized her dissatisfaction and enhanced her performance?
4. How might Kate use the skills introduced on pp. 66–71 to respond when Mark raises the issue of her apparent lack of motivation?
5. Describe likely scenarios if Mark and Kate used each of the following approaches to dealing with their conflict: win–lose, compromise, win–win.
6. How might Kate deal with her discomfort over her coworkers' jokes? How might Mark respond?

chapter 6

1. In hindsight, what questions might Kate have asked to explore the nature of her work environment and clarify her expectations during her employment interview?
2. How can Mark frame the opening of his interview to protect Kate's dignity and set a tone that will help him get the information he needs?
3. If Kate does wind up seeking another job, how can she use the information in Chapter 6 to prepare for the interviews associated with her search?

Chapter Three
Listening

chapter outline

chapter objectives

After reading this chapter you should be able to:

1. Describe how effective listening can contribute to your career success, and how false assumptions about listening could impede your career.

2. Identify three major barriers to listening effectively, and outline strategies for overcoming each barrier.

3. Analyze your listening style(s), and explain how you might use this knowledge to understand others better.

4. Apply the six guidelines for listening to understand and be able to create appropriate paraphrasing responses in given situations; apply guidelines with regard to evidence and appeals when listening to evaluate.

5. Evaluate various listening approaches you could use in a specific situation and describe the best approach to accomplish your goals and enhance your career relationships with others.

• Listening at Work

"I told her we were meeting *this* Tuesday, not next Tuesday. Now we have to reschedule the meeting, and we may not make the deadline."

"He said he was listening, but he didn't give me a minute to talk before he started interrupting. That's the last time I'll try to present a better way to do anything around here!"

"Something went wrong down the line. I warned those people to watch the temperature carefully, but they don't listen. Now a whole batch is spoiled. What does it take to get them to understand?"

Situations like these are disturbingly common in business. They show how frequent listening failures are and how costly they can be. You may not be able to make others listen better, but you can boost your own ability to listen carefully to the scores of important messages you are likely to hear every day.

As you will learn in the following pages, listening effectively is hard work. It involves far more than sitting passively and absorbing others' words. It occurs far more frequently than speaking, reading, or writing and is just as demanding and important.

The Importance of Listening

In his best-selling book, Stephen Covey identifies listening—understanding others' messages before making one's own understood—as one of the "seven habits of highly effective people."[1] Former Chrysler chairman Lee Iacocca endorsed this belief:

> You have to be able to listen well if you're going to motivate the people who work for you. Right there, that's the difference between a mediocre company and a great company. The most fulfilling thing for me as a manager is to watch someone the system has labeled as just average or mediocre really come into his own, all because someone has listened to his problems and helped him solve them.[2]

Dennis Hastert, former Speaker of the U.S. House of Representatives, echoed that sentiment about the value of paying attention when describing how he spent most of his time: "They call me the Speaker, but they ought to call me the Listener."[3]

Research backs up these claims. In numerous studies, listening proves to be the most important communication skill throughout one's career in terms of job and career success, productivity, upward mobility, and organizational effectiveness.[4]

Listening is valuable even before your career gets started. Job-hunters can respond best in employment interviews by keeping their ears open.[5] Once you have found a new job, listening can help you learn the ropes. Career consultant Andrea Sutcliffe puts it this way: "If you had to choose one interpersonal skill to work on in your first year on the job, pick listening. It will be the single most important tool you will have for getting along and getting ahead."[6]

Listening remains important throughout your career. When 1,000 executives were asked to list the ideal manager's skills, listening ranked number one.[7] Another study asked business executives what skills were most important on the job. Listening was mentioned more than any other skill or talent, including technical competence, computer knowledge, administrative talent, and creativity.[8]

Along with promoting individual success, effective listening is vital to organizations. It can improve quality, boost productivity, and save money. Poor listening can have the opposite effect. As one consultant put it:

> With more than 100 million workers in this country, a simple $10 listening mistake by each of them, as a result of poor listening, would add up to a cost of a billion dollars. And most people make numerous listening mistakes every week.
>
> Because of listening mistakes, letters have to be rewritten, appointments rescheduled, shipments rerouted. Productivity is affected and profits suffer.[9]

Assumptions about Listening

When it comes to communication, most people pay more attention to sending messages than to receiving them. This imbalance comes from several mistaken assumptions.

Faulty Assumption 1: Effective Communication Is the Sender's Responsibility
Management expert Peter Drucker recognized that communication depends on the receiver as well as the sender when he wrote, "It is the recipient who communicates. The so-called communicator, the person who emits the communication, does not communicate. He utters. Unless there is someone who hears . . . there is only noise."[10]

As Drucker suggests, even the most thoughtful, well-expressed idea is wasted if the intended receiver fails to listen. Both the speaker *and* the listener share the burden of responsibility in reaching an understanding.

Careless Listening Leads to Ridicule

On the first day of her social studies class, York University student Sarah Grunfeld was outraged when she heard Professor Cameron Johnston say that "All Jews should be sterilized." Grunfeld immediately reported her account of the lecture to a campus advocacy group, accused Johnston of being a bigot, and called for him to be fired. Within a few hours, the story went viral and Johnston came under immediate pressure and scrutiny.

The university's investigation found that Grunfeld missed an important point in Johnston's comment—one understood clearly by several hundred other students in the class. Johnston had explained that the belief that "all Jews should be sterilized" is an example of an unacceptable and dangerous opinion. So when it was publicized that Professor Johnston (who is Jewish) did not make an anti-Semitic statement in class, it was Grunfeld who came under attack. She was publicly ridiculed by bloggers and mainstream media for her poor listening skills, hair-trigger reaction, and unwillingness to accept even partial responsibility for the misunderstanding.

Source: Kennedy, B. (2011, September 14). Jewish prof forced to defend himself against anti-Semitism claims. *Toronto Star.* Retrieved from http://www.thestar.com/news/article/1053247—jewish-prof-forced-to-defend-himself-against-anti-semitism-claims.

Faulty Assumption 2: Listening Is Passive Some communicators mistakenly assume that listening is basically a passive activity in which the receiver is a sponge, quietly absorbing the speaker's thoughts. In fact, good listening is hard work. Sometimes you have to speak while listening—to ask questions or paraphrase the sender's ideas, making sure you have understood them.

Even when they remain silent, good listeners are far from passive. Famous attorney Louis Nizer described how he would often emerge dripping with sweat from a day in court spent mostly listening. Sperry executive Del Kennedy, commenting on his company's well-known listening training program, says, "Most people don't know how exhausting listening can be."[11] A good listener is an active communicator.

Faulty Assumption 3: Talking Has More Advantages At first glance, it seems that speakers control conversations while listeners are the followers. The people who do the talking are the ones who capture everyone's attention, so it's easy to understand how talking can be viewed as the pathway to success.

Talking instead of listening can lead professionals to miss important information. One analysis of physician–patient interviews revealed that the more doctors talked, the more they got off track and failed to address concerns raised by the patients.[12]

Despite the value of talking, savvy businesspeople understand that listening is equally important. Consider the advice of communication consultant Bill Acheson: "For every minute a salesperson spends listening, he or she will save four minutes overcoming objections."[13]

Communication expert Susan Peterson reinforces the value of superior listening skills:

> Too many times, whether it's with e-mail, voice mail or Internet, we are concentrating on the art of telling, not listening. Yet good listening, in my opinion, is 80 to 90 percent of being a good manager and an effective leader. . . . Listening is one of the best ways to keep high touch in your organization. In your day-to-day meetings with customers, clients, or employees, if you listen—really listen with full eye contact and attention—you can own the keys to the communication kingdom.[14]

Faulty Assumption 4: Listening Is a Natural Ability Listening may seem like a natural ability—like breathing. "After all," you might say, "I've been listening since I was a child." We could all say the same thing about talking; but even though almost everyone does it, this doesn't mean most people do it well.

ETHICAL challenge

Golden and Platinum Rules

The Golden Rule tells us to treat others the way we would like to be treated, and the Platinum Rule is to treat others the way *they* would like to be treated. The best way to honor the Platinum Rule is to listen to others, discovering what they want. On the other hand, realists acknowledge it is impossible to give equal attention to every message and still accomplish the multitude of tasks that occupy every workday.

How can you, as a busy worker, respond to non-essential messages without alienating the people who deliver them?

Evidence suggests that most people overestimate their ability to listen well. In one study, a group of managers rated their listening skills. Astonishingly, not one of them described himself or herself as a "poor" or "very poor" listener, while 94 percent rated themselves as "good" or "very good." The favorable self-ratings contrasted sharply with the perceptions of the managers' subordinates, many of whom said their bosses' listening skills were weak.[15]

Most organizations, including major corporations such as 3M, AT&T, General Electric, and Dun and Bradstreet, have invested in developing their employees' listening skills.[16] Xerox Corporation's program for improving listening has been used by more than 1.5 million employees in 71,000 companies, and Sperry Corporation invested more than $4 million to advertise its message: "We know how important it is to listen." In addition, Sperry set up listening seminars for its 87,000 employees to make its advertising campaign more than a string of empty slogans.

• Barriers to Effective Listening

Despite the importance of understanding others, research suggests that misunderstandings are the rule rather than the exception. Conversational partners typically achieve no more than 25 to 50 percent accuracy in interpreting each other's remarks.[17] Research shows that immediately after a 10-minute presentation, a normal listener can recall only 50 percent of the information presented. After 48 hours, the recall level drops to 25 percent.[18] As you read in Chapter 1, three kinds of "noise" get in the way of receiving messages: environmental, physiological, and psychological.

Environmental Barriers

The racket on a factory floor or the conversational buzz in a crowded room can make it hard to hear and process messages. Not all environmental barriers are about sound. An overheated office or uncomfortable chairs can also make listening difficult. Ironically, some environmental distractions come from the very tools we use to communicate. Incoming phone calls, text messages, and e-mails can distract us from focusing on a conversational partner.

You can't eliminate all environmental barriers, but you can often manage them. Suggest moving your conversation to a quieter location. Eliminate distractions and

"This requires both ears."

annoyances ("That perfume at the table next to us is getting to me. Can we move?"). Choose more reliable communication channels ("Let me call you back on a landline.").

Physiological Barriers

For some people, poor listening results from actual hearing deficiencies. Once recognized, they can usually be treated. Other hearing problems, such as earaches and headaches, are temporary. Whether the problem is short-term or permanent, the effects can be problematic. Hearing isn't the only physiological barrier to listening. Processing difficulties, such as auditory discrimination, sequencing, or memory can create the appearance of not listening or paying attention when the real problem is physiological.

Another physiological challenge comes from the difference between the relatively slow rate of most speech and the brain's ability to process messages more quickly. Listeners can process information at a rate of about 500 words per minute, while most speakers talk at around 125 words per minute. This difference leaves us with a great deal of mental spare time. While it's possible to use this time to explore the speaker's ideas, it's easy to let your mind wander.

Psychological Barriers

Some of the most pervasive and daunting barriers to effective listening are psychological. These are the issues that interfere with people's willingness to listen as well as their mental capacity for effective listening.

Preoccupation   Business and personal concerns can make it difficult to keep your mind on the subject at hand. Even when your current conversation is important, other unfinished business can divert your attention: the call to an angry customer, the questions your boss asked about your schedule delays, the new supplier you heard about and want to interview, and the problems you have with the babysitter or the auto mechanic. Figure 3.1 illustrates several ways in which preoccupation can cause listeners to lose focus on understanding a speaker.

Message Overload   In a world of smartphones, laptops, and other devices, "multicommunicating" is a challenge previous generations never faced.[19] It's hard to listen carefully when people keep dropping in to give you quick messages; a coworker has just

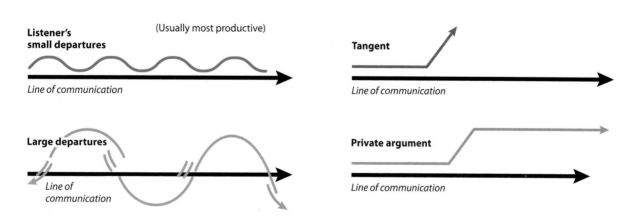

FIGURE 3.1 Thought Patterns

Source: Wolvin, A. D., & Coakley, G. (1993). *Perspectives on listening.* Norwood, NJ: Ablex.

CULTURE **at work**

Gender Differences in Listening

Popular magazines are fond of asking, "Who listens better, men or women?" This question isn't as helpful as asking, "In what ways do men and women listen *differently?*"

For one, women and men tend to use and interpret "listening noises"—vocalizations such as "uh-huh" and "hmmm"—differently.[20] Women may use them to signal attention; men, to signal agreement. Thus, a woman who says "uh-huh" may mean, "I'm listening," while a man hearing this utterance would think she agrees. Once communicators are aware of differences like these, they can clarify the meaning of ambiguous vocal cues: "You seem interested in the idea I'm presenting. Do you agree that we should get started on it?"

Other research shows men and women may hear different parts of a message because they listen for different purposes. They suggest women are more likely to listen for the feelings behind a speaker's words, while men tend to listen for the facts.[21] For example, at a committee meeting, a colleague is asked to redo a report. He says, "Sure." After the meeting, a female colleague may comment on how upset the person was and his reluctance to redo the report. She "heard" the feelings. A male colleague may respond, "What's the problem? He said he'd do it."

handed you cost estimates on a new product line; and your smartphone continuously beeps to let you know you have incoming calls, mail, text messages, and appointments. Coping with a deluge of information is like juggling—you can keep only a few things going at one time.[22] Many students pride themselves in their ability to multitask, but according to neurological evidence, people simply aren't very good at doing multiple tasks at the same time.[23] Human brains waste lag time each time we switch gears. That means we are much more effective and efficient when we complete one task at a time—and pay attention to one message at a time.

Egocentrism   One common reason for listening poorly is the belief—usually mistaken—that your own ideas are more important or valuable than those of others. Besides preventing you from learning useful new information, this egocentric attitude is likely to alienate the very people with whom you need to work. Self-centered listeners are rated lower on social attractiveness than communicators open to others' ideas.[24] As an old saying puts it, Nobody ever listened themselves out of a job.

Ethnocentrism   Cultural ignorance or prejudices can create psychological noise that interferes with understanding others. Consider accents; some communicators mistakenly assume accented speakers are less intelligent and less able to understand spoken words.[25] More subtle attitudes can shape perceptions of proper and improper ways of listening. For example, African Americans and Euro-Americans tend to value speaking over listening and talk over silence.[26] Westerners often feel uncomfortable with long silences and want to fill them in with speech. By contrast, Native Americans and Japanese and other Asians regard silence as an important part of communication.[27] It's easy to imagine how a Westerner, uncomfortable with an Asian's silence, would fill in a conversational gap that seemed perfectly normal to a Korean or Navajo. In the same way, an Asian who wants to communicate successfully with a Euro-American would need to spend more time vocalizing.

Fear of Appearing Ignorant   Some businesspeople think asking for clarification is a sign of ignorance. Rather than seek clarification, they pretend to understand—often with unfortunate consequences. In truth, a sincere desire to seek clarification can pay dividends, as management guru Tom Peters explains:

> My first boss . . . is one of the smartest people I know. He was smart enough and comfortable enough with himself to ask really elementary (some would say dumb) questions. The rest of us were scared stiff; we assumed that since we were being paid an exorbitant fee, we shouldn't ask dumb questions. But the result was we'd lose 90 percent of the strategic value of the interview because we were afraid to display our ignorance.
>
> Mostly, it's the "dumb," elementary questions, followed up by a dozen more elementary questions, that yield the pay dirt.[28]

• Listening Styles

Not everyone listens the same way. Research has identified that people have a general listening style, or a particular motivation for listening. You can identify your own preferences by completing the Self-Assessment on p. 67. Each style has its own advantages, so after you identify your preferred style, try to develop skills in the listening styles that don't come naturally to you. An effective listener is a flexible listener.

Relational Listening

People who are primarily focused on **relational listening** are most concerned with emotionally connecting with others. They listen to understand how others feel, are aware of their emotions, and are highly responsive to those individuals. Relational listeners are usually nonjudgmental about what others have to say. They are more interested in understanding and supporting people than in evaluating them.

A key strength of this listening style is that the people getting "listened to" are more satisfied with relationships and life. So when a relational listener attends to a subordinate or even a peer at work, there can be a positive benefit. Research also has shown that the listener also gets benefits from listening. But there are also drawbacks. It is easy to become overly involved with others' feelings, and even to internalize and adopt them. In an effort to be congenial and supportive, relational listeners may lose their ability to assess the quality of information others are giving. They also risk being perceived as overly expressive and even intrusive by speakers who don't want to connect on a personal level.

Analytical Listening

People who are most interested in **analytical listening** are concerned about attending to the full message before coming to judgment. They want to hear details and analyze an issue from a variety of perspectives. More than just enjoying complex information, these listeners have a tendency to engage in systematic thinking.

Analytical listeners can be a big help when the goal is to thoroughly assess the quality of ideas, and when there is value in looking at issues from a wide range of perspectives. They are especially valuable when the issues at hand are complicated. On the other hand, their thorough approach can be time consuming. It may take them a long time to come to a conclusion. So when a deadline is approaching, they may not respond as quickly as desired.

Task-Oriented Listening

People who are inclined to **task-oriented listening** are most interested in getting the job done. Efficiency is their biggest concern; they expect speakers to get their point across quickly and to stay on topic. Not surprisingly, task-oriented listeners are often impatient.

In a fast-paced business environment, task-oriented listeners can help keep things functioning efficiently. On the other hand, their impatience can sometimes strain relationships because task-oriented listeners are generally not good at responding empathetically and have a tendency toward verbal aggressiveness. Also, an excessive focus on time can hamper the kind of thoughtful deliberation that some jobs require.

Critical Listening

People engaged in **critical listening** have a strong desire to evaluate messages. They may or may not apply the tools of analytical listening, but in either case, they go beyond trying to understand the topic at hand and try to assess its quality. Not surprisingly, critical listeners tend to focus on the accuracy and consistency of a message.

Critical listening can be especially helpful when the goal is to investigate a problem, as in a police interview or an accounting audit. However, people who are critical listeners can also frustrate others who may think that they nit-pick everything others say.

• Listening More Effectively

Social scientists have identified two levels of listening—mindless and mindful.[29] **Mindless listening** occurs when we react to others' messages automatically and routinely, without much mental investment. The term *mindless* sounds negative, but sometimes this sort of low-level processing can be useful because it frees us to focus our minds on messages that require our careful attention.[30] The challenge, of course, is to pay enough attention to decide which messages need more careful attention. By contrast, **mindful listening** involves giving careful and thoughtful attention and responses to the messages we receive.

You might imagine the value of mindful listening is so obvious it hardly needs mentioning. But business and professional communicators recognize that thoughtful listening is difficult and needs cultivating. At General Mills, for example, employees at all levels—including more than 80 vice presidents and directors—have voluntarily signed up for mindfulness programs ranging from a half-day to seven weeks.[31]

One important step toward mindful listening is to be clear about your goal in a given situation. Are you listening to *understand* the other person, or listening critically to *evaluate* the message? Once you've answered this fundamental question, the following tips can help you do a good job.

Listening to Understand

Most of us would claim we always aim to understand what others are saying, but a little introspection will show we're often focused on other tasks: mentally (or overtly) arguing with the speaker, daydreaming, thinking about other tasks, and so on. Following the advice here can boost your accuracy in listening mindfully to the message.

Withhold Judgment   In his study of highly effective people, Stephen Covey said it best: "Seek first to understand, then to be understood."[32] It is often difficult to try to understand another person's ideas before judging him or her, especially when you hold strong opinions on the matter under discussion. For example, you might ask for a

Research has revealed that everyone has default styles of listening. To discover your listening tendencies, fill in the survey below. Use 1 as "strongly disagree" and 7 as "strongly agree." The section(s) where you indicated the strongest agreement (5, 6, or 7) suggests your typical listening style(s).

Relational Listening

When listening to others, it is important to understand the feelings of the speaker.	1	2	3	4	5	6	7
When listening to others, I am mainly concerned with how they are feeling.	1	2	3	4	5	6	7
I listen to understand the emotions and mood of the speaker.	1	2	3	4	5	6	7
I listen primarily to build and maintain relationships with others.	1	2	3	4	5	6	7
I enjoy listening to others because it allows me to connect with them.	1	2	3	4	5	6	7
When listening to others, I focus on understanding the feelings behind words.	1	2	3	4	5	6	7

Analytical Listening

I wait until all the facts are presented before forming judgments and opinions.	1	2	3	4	5	6	7
I tend to withhold judgment about others' ideas until I have heard everything they have to say.	1	2	3	4	5	6	7
When listening to others, I attempt to withhold making an opinion until I've heard their entire message.	1	2	3	4	5	6	7
When listening to others, I consider all sides of the issue before responding.	1	2	3	4	5	6	7
I fully listen to what a person has to say before forming any opinions.	1	2	3	4	5	6	7
To be fair to others, I fully listen to what they have to say before making judgments.	1	2	3	4	5	6	7

Task-Oriented Listening

I am impatient with people who ramble on during conversations.	1	2	3	4	5	6	7
I get frustrated when people get off topic during a conversation.	1	2	3	4	5	6	7
When listening to others, I become impatient when they appear to be wasting time.	1	2	3	4	5	6	7
I prefer speakers who quickly get to the point.	1	2	3	4	5	6	7
I find it difficult to listen to people who take too long to get their ideas across.	1	2	3	4	5	6	7
When listening to others, I appreciate speakers who give brief, to-the-point presentations.	1	2	3	4	5	6	7

Critical Listening

When listening to others, I focus on any inconsistencies and/or errors in what is being said.	1	2	3	4	5	6	7
I often catch errors in other speakers' logic.	1	2	3	4	5	6	7
I tend to naturally notice errors in what speakers say.	1	2	3	4	5	6	7
I have a talent for catching inconsistencies in what speakers say.	1	2	3	4	5	6	7
When listening to others, I notice contradictions in what they say.	1	2	3	4	5	6	7
Good listeners catch discrepancies in what people say.	1	2	3	4	5	6	7

Source: Adapted from Bodie, G. (2011). *The listening styles profile-revised (LSP-R): A scale revision and validation.* Used with permission of the author.

Listening to Voice Mail

Hearing problems aren't just an issue for communicators with physical impairments. The racket of background noise often makes it difficult to hear and understand messages—especially those played back on tinny speakers in most telephones. A variety of products overcome the limitations of trying to discern voice mail messages by transcribing the caller's spoken words into text that can be viewed on the display of a smartphone or computer. Besides saving you the time it takes to replay voice mail, these services allow you to check for calls in a noisy environment, do it unobtrusively, and have a text record of what callers said.

Transcription apps aren't foolproof. They don't capture the vocal qualities that can affect the meaning of a message, and they often bungle specific words. So when in doubt, it's smart to listen to the voice mail version of a message before jumping to conclusions.

You can read about these services by typing the words "convert voice mail to text" into your favorite Internet search engine. Many of the companies providing voice-to-text service offer free trials.

---

customer's reaction to your company's product or service and then spend your mental energy judging the answer instead of trying to understand it. ("Doesn't this guy have anything better to do than make petty complaints?" "Yeah, sure, he'd like us to deliver on a tighter schedule, but he'd scream his head off if we billed him for the overtime.") Or you might find yourself judging the ideas of a boss, coworker, or subordinate before he or she has finished explaining them. ("Uh-oh. I hope this doesn't mean I have to spend a week in the field, trying to get market information." "These college kids come in and want to take over right away.") Listen first. Make sure you understand. Then evaluate.

Talk and Interrupt Less Sometimes the best approach to listening is to stay out of the way and encourage the other person to talk. One marketing expert explained how, even in selling, silence can be more effective than talking:

> The 20/80 rule is a standard in small-business principles. Twenty percent of your customers account for 80 percent of your business. Here's a variation of the theme. . . . When meeting with prospective customers for the first time, listen 80 percent of the time and talk the other 20 percent. Your job is to listen attentively and determine what your prospects require. Before they are prepared to listen to your pitch, they want to tell you what they're looking for.[33]

If you are normally a talkative person, consider rationing your comments when trying to listen. Imagine you have only a finite number of words available so that you speak only when it is absolutely necessary. You may be surprised at how the quality of your conversations and your level of understanding improve.

Ask Questions **Sincere questions** are genuine requests for information. They can be a terrific way to gather facts and details, clarify meanings, and encourage a speaker to elaborate. Former University of Kentucky basketball coach Rick Pitino learned the importance of asking questions after he lost a key recruit by trying to sell the virtues of his program instead of listening to what concerned his prospect. Later, when he courted another potential star (Tony Delk), he used a more effective approach:

> This time, instead of trumpeting Kentucky's virtues, he asked questions: what Delk wanted from a coach, what the family wanted for their son in college. For an hour, he just asked questions and nodded a lot, listening to their answers. . . .

Not only did Pitino get Delk, but four years later, Delk helped lead Kentucky to its sixth national championship and Pitino's first. "That's one of my favorites," Pitino says. "That's one I like to tell business groups because it illustrates how important it is to listen to people."[34]

While sincere, focused questions can be a powerful tool, **counterfeit questions** are really disguised forms of advice or subtle traps: "Have you ever considered offering more money to get experienced people?" or "Why haven't you told me about this?" Counterfeit questions like these can pollute a communication climate just as quickly as any direct attack.[35]

"You haven't been listening. I keep telling you that I don't want a product fit for a king."

© Ted Goff/The New Yorker Collection/www.cartoonbank.com.

Paraphrase   **Paraphrasing** involves restating a speaker's ideas in your own words to make sure you have understood them correctly and to show the other person that fact. Paraphrasing is often preceded by phrases such as, "Let me make sure I understand what you're saying. . . ." or "In other words, you're saying. . . ." When you are paraphrasing, it is important *not* to become a parrot, repeating the speaker's statements word for word. Understanding comes from translating the speaker's thoughts into your own language and then playing them back to ensure their accuracy. After paraphrasing, it is important that you invite the speaker to *verify* your paraphrase so you know if you accurately understood him or her or to *clarify* your paraphrase and clear up what you have misunderstood.

The following conversations illustrate the difference between effective and ineffective paraphrasing:

Ineffective

Print Supervisor:	I'm having trouble getting the paper to run that job. That's why I'm behind schedule.
Plant Manager:	I see. You can't get the paper to run the job, so you're running behind schedule.
Print Supervisor:	Yeah. That's what I said.

After this exchange, the plant manager still doesn't have a clear idea of the problem—why the print supervisor can't get the paper, or what he means when he says he can't get it. Effective paraphrasing, however, could help get to the root of the problem:

Effective

Print Supervisor:	I'm having trouble getting the paper to run that job. That's why I'm running behind schedule.
Plant Manager:	In other words, your paper supplier hasn't shipped the paper you need for this job.
Print Supervisor:	No, they shipped it, but it's full of flaws.
Plant Manager:	So the whole shipment is bad?
Print Supervisor:	No, only about a third of it. But I've got to get the whole batch replaced, or the dye lots won't match—the paper won't be exactly the same color.

Plant Manager:	No problem—the colors can be a little off. But I have to have at least half of that order by Tuesday; the rest can wait a couple of weeks. Can you print on the good paper you have now, then do the rest when the new paper comes in?
Print Supervisor:	Sure.

At first glance, questioning and paraphrasing may seem identical, but a closer look reveals they are different tools. Questions seek new, additional information ("How far behind are we?" "When did it begin?"), whereas paraphrasing clarifies what a speaker has said. This is an important difference.

There are three types of paraphrasing. Although each of them reflects the speaker's message, each focuses on a different part of that statement.

Paraphrasing content   The example above illustrates this most basic kind of paraphrasing, which plays back the receiver's understanding of the explicit message. It is easy to think you understand another person only to find later that you were wrong. At its most basic level, paraphrasing is a kind of safety check that can highlight and clarify misunderstandings. People who practice paraphrasing are astonished to find out how many times a speaker will correct or add information to a message that had seemed perfectly clear.

Paraphrasing intent   Besides helping you understand *what* others are saying, paraphrasing can help you learn *why* they have spoken up. Imagine that, at a staff meeting, the boss announces, "Next week, we'll start using this display board to show when we're out of the office and where we've gone." It's easy to imagine two quite different reasons for setting up this procedure: (1) to help keep customers and colleagues informed about where each person is and when he or she will return, or (2) to keep track of employees because the boss suspects some are slacking off on company time. Paraphrasing intent can help you understand what people mean when they make statements that can be interpreted in more than one way.

Paraphrasing feeling   Often, the speaker's feelings are the most important part of a message.[36] Despite this fact, most people don't express—or even recognize—their emotions. Ask yourself which emotions might be contained in these statements:

> "That's the third time he canceled an appointment on me—who does he think he is?"

> "Whenever a deadline comes, I get excuses instead of results—this can't go on much longer."

"One minute she says we have to spend money to make money, and the next
    minute she talks about cutting costs—I can't figure out what she really wants."

In each example there are at least two or three possible emotions:

Anger, hurt, and self-doubt.

Anger, frustration, and worry.

Anger and confusion.

Paraphrasing the apparent emotion can give the speaker a chance to agree with or
contradict your interpretation: "Yeah, I guess it did hurt my feelings," or "I'm more worried than mad." In either case, this sort of response can help the other person to clarify
how he or she is feeling and to deal with the emotions.

Attend to Nonverbal Cues   Focusing on a speaker's nonverbal cues may tell you
more than his or her words. Watch for the "iceberg tips" that let you know if the speaker
might say more, especially if encouraged to do so.[37] Chapter 4 explains in detail the
wealth of nonverbal cues that are always available to you: gestures, postures, vocal tones,
facial expression, and more.

Nonverbal cues can be especially useful in figuring out another person's feelings and
attitudes. You can get a sense of how emotions are communicated nonverbally by imagining all the different messages that might be conveyed by the following statements. How
many different ways can you imagine each could be expressed? What different meaning
might each set of nonverbal cues convey?

"No, nothing's the matter."

"We should get together one of these days."

"I would like to talk with you in my office."

"Nobody's ever had that idea before."

Besides attending to others' nonverbal cues, it's also useful to pay attention to your own.
To understand why, visualize how a conversational partner would react depending on how
you behaved in a discussion. What signals would you be sending if you leaned back in your
chair, gazed around the room, or yawned? By contrast, what messages would you be sending
if you sat forward, kept eye contact, and occasionally nodded or uttered "mm hmm"? You
may *say* you're listening, but how you behave nonverbally will create a stronger impression.

Take Notes   When the conversation involves details or ideas you need to remember,
notes can be essential. Note-taking can also signal to speakers that you care enough to
write down what they're saying. It can even cause speakers to consider their words more
carefully. And if a question ever arises about the details of a conversation, you can say with
confidence "Let me check my notes. . . ."

Listening to Evaluate

Once you are sure you understand a message, you are ready to evaluate its quality. Most
evaluations are based on two levels of analysis: evidence and emotion.

Analyze the Speaker's Evidence   As a good critical listener, you need to ask
yourself several questions about the evidence a speaker gives to support his or her statements. What evidence does the order fulfillment manager give that the current computer
system is causing problems or that a new one will be better? Does a sales representative
back up the claim that a product will pay for itself in less than a year?

Use a Telephone Log

E-mail provides a virtually automatic record of your correspondence, but telephone conversations are ephemeral. Keeping a simple written log can help you maintain your records, prevent false claims, and reestablish contacts. For example, a log can remind you of the name of the agent you spoke to, the date and time of an appointment you've set up, or the model number of a product you're researching. Weeks later it may be important to tell a client, coworker, or supervisor of all the attempts (successful and unsuccessful) you made to contact them.

You can also rely on your notes to remind others about information and commitments they have made, such as a reservation, promised delivery date, or a price quote: "The job won't be ready until November 15? But last Friday, Rose in your office promised me it would be done by the first of the month." A log can even remind people about what they *didn't* say or do. For example, you might respond to a complaint that you haven't kept a customer informed by explaining, "Actually I've phoned three times before today: On April 4, 11, and 18. Each time your voice mail picked up, and I left a message telling you the job was ready."

For most purposes, a phone log doesn't have to be elaborate, but it should usually include the following:

- Date and time the call was placed
- Subject of the call
- Phone number called
- Whether this call is a part of a series (i.e., a follow-up or response to an earlier call)
- Unsuccessful attempts to contact (busy signal, no answer, malfunctioning voice mail)
- Messages left on voice mail or with another person
- Name of person you spoke with
- Key points you and the other person made

Once you've identified the evidence, you need to make sure it is valid. The success of the flexible-hours program instituted in the New York office doesn't mean the same program will work as well in the factory in West Virginia, where a certain number of people have to be operating the machinery at any given time. The two or three employees unhappy with the new office furniture might be the exceptions rather than the majority, while the one or two satisfied customers you hear about could be the only happy ones. Carefully researched statistics that look at more than a few isolated cases are a much stronger form of proof than a few random examples.

The following questions can help you to examine the overall validity of supporting material:

Is the evidence given true?

Are enough cases cited?

Are the cited cases representative of the whole being considered?

Are there any exceptions to the points the speaker is making?

Do these exceptions need to be considered?

Examine Emotional Appeals   Sometimes emotional reactions are a valid basis for action. The sympathy we feel for underprivileged children is a good reason for donating money to their welfare. The desire to cut down on your own fatigue may be a good reason to hire an assistant.

"I'm not convinced that's the best strategy.
Then again, I wasn't listening."

Used by permission of Marc Tyler Nobleman.

In some cases, though, emotional appeals can obscure important logical considerations that might dissuade you from accepting a proposal. We can see this by thinking about fund-raisers who seek money for underprivileged children. Your sympathy might not justify allowing a fund-raiser to wander around your building soliciting funds from employees: Your employees could resent being asked to give money to *your* favorite cause rather than one of theirs, especially if they have just been asked to donate to another cause. The particular agency asking for your donation might not be the best vehicle for helping underprivileged children: It may have excessive overhead so that much of your contribution never reaches any children, or other organizations might serve needier people.

MASTER **the chapter**

review points

- Listening is the most frequent communication activity at work. Listening effectively helps the organization and also helps you achieve your personal goals.
- A number of faulty assumptions about listening can impede effective understanding.
- Environmental, physiological, and psychological barriers (preoccupation, overload, egocentrism, ethnocentrism, and fear of appearing ignorant) interfere with effective listening.
- Knowing and understanding the characteristics of your default listening style (relational, analytical, task-oriented, critical) and others' listening styles helps you adapt to any given situation.

- Listening to understand requires withholding judgment, talking and interrupting less, seeking feedback by asking sincere (not counterfeit) questions, paraphrasing, attending to nonverbal cues, and taking notes.
- Evaluative listening involves analyzing both a speaker's evidence and emotional appeals.

key terms

analytical listening   65
counterfeit question   69
critical listening   66
mindful listening   66
mindless listening   66

paraphrasing   69
relational listening   65
sincere question   68
task-oriented listening   66

activities

1. Invitation to Insight

a. Recall three on-the-job incidents in which you had difficulty listening effectively. For each incident, describe which of the following factors interfered with your listening effectiveness:

1. Environmental barriers
2. Physiological barriers
3. Psychological factors

b. Develop a list of ways you could overcome the greatest barriers that prevent you from listening more effectively.

2. Invitation to Insight

Read several articles about multitasking. For example, you might want to consult the following:

- "Myths about Effective Student Multitasking Exposed": http://www.westernherald.com/news/campus/myths-about-effective-student-multitasking-exposed/?utm_source=rss&utm_medium=rss&utm_campaign=myths-about-effective-student-multitasking-exposed
- "Is Multitasking More Efficient? Shifting Mental Gears Costs Time, Especially When Shifting to Less Familiar Tasks": http://www.apa.org/news/press/releases/2001/08/multitasking.aspx
- "Think You're Multitasking? Think Again": http://www.npr.org/templates/story/story.php?storyId=95256794

Write a short summary of what you learned about multitasking. Next, identify all the tasks you try to attend to while you are studying. Create a realistic time schedule for the next week, setting aside adequate time for studying. Set aside separate times for the other activities you typically try to do during study time. Try to stick to this schedule for the next week. Then, share your results with classmates. What did you learn about multitasking? How did this affect your studying? Your relationships? Your other tasks? What did you learn about prioritizing? How do the things you learned about multitasking and prioritizing apply in the work environment?

3. Invitation to Insight

Survey several people from various careers to gather their opinions. Ask them to answer the following questions and to provide an example to support their answer.

a. Who do you think is more responsible for effective communication, the speaker or the listener?
b. Would you say listening is easier or harder than speaking?
c. Which do you think has more advantages—speaking or listening?
d. Do you think listening is a natural ability, or would it be a good idea to take classes in listening?

In a small group, compare your respondents' answers with other classmates' results. With your group, create an explanation you could give to people who believe those faulty assumptions about listening, as identified in your text.

4. Invitation to Insight

For each of the listening styles listed below (see pp. 65–66), describe a specific work situation in which this style would be effective and one situation in which the style would probably not be appropriate. Defend your answers.

Relational

Analytical

Task-Oriented

Critical

5. Skill Builder

Explore the difference between genuine and counterfeit questions by answering the following questions:

a. How can you differentiate between sincere questions and counterfeit questions?
b. What impact do counterfeit questions have on the receiver? On the interaction?
c. Write three examples of counterfeit questions. Supply a context that explains why the questions are counterfeit.
d. Convert the counterfeit questions to sincere questions.

6. Skill Builder

Practice your skill at questioning and paraphrasing in groups of four. Each group member should assume one of the following roles: speaker, listener 1, listener 2, and observer.

a. The **speaker** will talk about a problem he or she has recently experienced. If you can't think of a problem, talk about *one* of the following topics: how to perform a task you are familiar with, how to improve your chances for landing the job you want, or how to talk politely to a coworker about a problematic behavior.
b. The **listeners** should use vocalizations, sincere questions, and paraphrasing to *understand* the speaker's content, intent, and feeling.
c. After the conversation ends, the speaker will describe the degree to which he or she feels satisfied that the paraphrasing reflected his or her meaning accurately. This is the measure of success of the interaction.
d. The **observer** should point out specific examples of effective and ineffective techniques used by the listeners.
e. Listeners should answer the following questions:

1. Was paraphrasing difficult or awkward? Why?
2. How does this type of listening compare to your typical manner of responding?
3. What types of useful information did you gain from the conversations? Would you be likely to gain the same quality of information by responding in your more usual manner?
4. How could you use paraphrasing and sincere questioning to help in your everyday work?

7. Skill Builder

Practice your evaluative listening skills by following these steps:

a. Listen to a short persuasive presentation. Identify what the speaker is asking the listeners to believe or do.
b. Evaluate the speaker's evidence by answering the following questions.

1. Does the speaker support the claim with evidence?
2. Does the speaker cite references for the evidence?
3. How accurate is the evidence? Explain.
4. Does the speaker represent opposing evidence fairly?

c. Identify at least two emotional appeals used by the speaker.

1. Do any of the emotional appeals obscure important logical considerations?
2. Do the emotional appeals stretch the truth? Why or why not?

d. Based on this analysis, do you believe the speaker's argument is trustworthy?

LearnSmart™

For further review, go to the LearnSmart study module for this chapter.

Chapter Four
Verbal and Nonverbal Messages

chapter outline

Verbal Messages
Clarity and Ambiguity
Inflammatory Language
Language and Identity Management
Feminine and Masculine Language Use

Nonverbal Communication
Characteristics of Nonverbal Communication
Types of Nonverbal Communication
Improving Nonverbal Effectiveness

chapter objectives

After reading this chapter you should be able to:

1. Describe business situations in which ambiguous or specific language is preferable, giving an example of each type of statement.

2. Define, identify, and remedy examples of each type of inflammatory language described in this chapter.

3. Apply concepts of powerful and positive language to specific examples from your career field.

4. Compare and contrast characteristically feminine and masculine language use and describe the potential benefits and problems arising from differences.

5. Describe how you can apply the information on nonverbal behavior in this chapter to your own career.

6. Define and give examples of seven categories of nonverbal behavior and summarize the importance of each in a specific organization or career field.

Although they are neighbors and see each other almost every day, Bob and Carolyn rarely speak to each other. Ever since their partnership broke up, the hard feelings have made even casual conversation painful.

"We both should have known better," Bob lamented. "It was such a simple misunderstanding. We went into the partnership agreeing that we would be 'equal partners,' but now I can see that we had different ideas about what being 'equals' meant. I saw each of us taking charge of the areas that we did best: I'm good at marketing and sales, and Carolyn knows product design and production backward and forward. So it made sense to me that, while we were each equally responsible for the business and deserving an equal share of the profits, we would each make the final decisions in the areas where we were experts."

"That's not what I meant by 'equal partners,'" stated Carolyn flatly. "Bob wasn't willing to take responsibility for the hard work of production. He kept saying, 'That's where you're the expert.' And he didn't have any faith in my ideas about sales and marketing. He wanted to make those decisions himself, whether or not I agreed. To me, being equal means you have just as much say as the other person in every part of the business."

In hindsight, both Bob and Carolyn realize there had been signs of trouble from the beginning of their partnership. "Even before we opened for business, I could tell that Carolyn was unhappy," sighs Bob. "I always saw the venture as a chance to make a fortune. But whenever I'd get excited and talk about how much money we could make, Carolyn would clam up and get this grim look on her face."

Carolyn also remembers early, unspoken signs of trouble. "I've always wanted to have a business that my kids could be proud of," she said. "But when I'd talk about that, Bob wouldn't have much to say. Even though he never said so, at times I got the feeling that he was laughing at my high ideals."

This story illustrates the importance of paying close attention to verbal and nonverbal messages. The ill-fated partnership between Bob and Carolyn could have been avoided if they had paid more attention to the unspoken but powerful nonverbal clues that warned of trouble. Examining more carefully just what an equal partnership meant also could have helped them avoid the clash that finally led to their breakup.

This chapter looks at the two channels by which you communicate: Your words and your nonverbal behavior. By the time you have finished it, you will recognize that significant problems can lurk in even the simplest statements, and you will have discovered some ways to avoid or overcome such problems. You will also become more aware of the wordless messages each of us constantly sends and receives.

• Verbal Messages

Misunderstandings are a fact of life; the process of encoding and decoding described in Chapter 1 is inherently imperfect. As Table 4-1 shows, a listener can understand the meaning of every word perfectly and still interpret a message completely differently from its intended meaning. In fact, most people vastly overestimate how well their explanations get through and how well they understand others.[1]

Table 4-1	Even Simple Messages Can Be Misunderstood

What the Manager Said	What the Manager Meant	What the Subordinate Heard
I'll look into hiring another person for your department as soon as I complete my budget review.	We'll start interviewing for that job in about three weeks.	I'm tied up with more important things. Let's forget about hiring for the indefinite future.
Your performance was below par last quarter. I really expected more out of you.	You're going to have to try harder, but I know you can do it.	If you screw up one more time, you're out.
I'd like that report as soon as you can get to it.	Drop that rush order you're working on, and fill out that report today.	I need that report within the next week or so.
I talked to the boss, but at the present time, due to budget problems, we'll be unable to fully match your competitive salary offer.	We can give you 95 percent of that offer.	If I were you, I'd take that competitive offer. We're certainly not going to pay that kind of salary to a person with your credentials.
We have a job opening in Los Angeles that we think would be just your cup of tea. We'd like you to go out there and look it over.	If you'd like the job, it's yours. If not, of course you can stay here in Denver. You be the judge.	You don't have to go out to L.A. if you don't want to. However, if you don't you can kiss your career with this firm good-bye.
Your people seem to be having some problems getting their work out on time. I want you to look into this situation and straighten it out.	I don't care how many heads you bust, just get me that output. I've got enough problems around here without you screwing things up too.	Talk to your people and find out what the problem is. Then get together with them and jointly solve it.

Source: Adapted from Altman, S., Valenzi, E., & Hodgetts, R. M. (1985). *Organizational behavior: Theory and practice*. Waltham, MA: Academic Press.

Online Translation Services

In the age of global business, sooner or later you will need to communicate with someone who speaks an unfamiliar language. If you type "online translation" into your Internet search engine, you will find a variety of services available to help you bridge the language gap. One excellent—and free—option is Google Translate (http://www.translate.google.com).

A good test of a computerized translation is to convert a message from one language to another, and then back to the original one. Because idioms don't rely on word-for-word meanings, they provide an especially tough challenge. Google Translate did a surprisingly

effective job at this task. It retained the meanings of expressions such as "cross your fingers," "start from scratch," and "blessing in disguise" when those phrases were translated from English to Arabic and back again.

Even Google Translate wasn't perfect, though: It translated the phrase "from rags to riches" into "of the flags of wealth," and it mistakenly converted the idiom "go for broke" to "broken leg."

While computerized services can't match the talents of a skilled human translator, the better ones are a good start for basic messages and are useful tools in the global village.

Clarity and Ambiguity

Because the most basic language problems involve misunderstandings, we begin our study of language by examining how to prevent this sort of miscommunication. We also look at times when a lack of clarity can actually be desirable.

Use Unequivocal Terms to Avoid Misunderstandings   **Equivocal terms** are those with two different, but equally acceptable or common, meanings. Some examples include:

Plane tickets and hotel reservations for a business meeting in Portland are booked for Oregon instead of Maine.

A client asks a contractor for a mid-project change: "Can you move that door from here to there?" The contractor replies, "No problem." Later, the client is astonished to find that she has been charged for the change order.

You agree to call on a client at home at "dinner time" in a part of the country where "dinner" is midday and "supper" is in the evening. When you appear at 6:00 PM, the client asks why you didn't arrive at the promised time.

Most equivocal misunderstandings arise in casual conversation, where statements seem perfectly clear until you discover that others can interpret them differently.[2] Sometimes equivocal problems arise because communicators from different fields use the same term in specialized ways. Hollywood agent Jerry Katzman describes just such a situation. In a meeting with representatives of a Silicon Valley software publisher, he used the phrase *in development* to mean a project that was at the rough-idea stage. By contrast, the software people were used to using that phrase to describe a project that had been funded and was being created. Katzman reported, "It was like when the Japanese first came to Hollywood. They had to use interpreters, and we did too."[3]

Equivocation sometimes comes from different cultural values. Compared with Americans, Mexicans are less inclined to express conflict and are more polychronic and

case STUDY

Misunderstandings Lead to Airline Catastrophe

The worst accident in aviation history occurred March 27, 1977—in large part due to a tragic misunderstanding. The lessons from that disaster are just as important today as they were almost four decades ago.

The airport on the Spanish island of Tenerife was shrouded in fog as two jumbo jets lumbered toward departure—one at each end of the single runway. As one plane headed into position, the second was pointed straight at it, hidden by the fog. The copilot of that plane radioed the control tower, saying, "We're now at take-off," to which the controller replied, "OK." The crew meant they were ready to begin take-off, while the controller assumed the plane was awaiting final clearance. He added, "Stand by for take-off, I will call you," but interference from another transmission blocked this critical part of the message.

Unaware the runway was occupied, the pilots of the doomed plane began their rush toward disaster. By the time the two aircraft were visible to one another, it was too late to avert impact. In the ensuing collision and fire, 583 lives were lost.

As a result of this catastrophe, aviation authorities now require the use of standard phrases to identify flight operations. The phrase *take-off* is only used when actual lift-off is due to take place. In all other cases, controllers and aircrews use the term *departure*. This simple change has helped prevent anymore fatal misunderstandings like the one in Tenerife. But the clarification came too late for almost 600 innocent travelers.

Sources: Subsecretaria de Aviacion Civil, Spain. (1978). *Official report of the investigation translated into English.* Retrieved from http://www.skybrary.aero/bookshelf/books/809.pdf; Tenerife Information Centre. (2009). *The Tenerife Airport disaster.* Retrieved from http://www.tenerife-information-centre.com/tenerife-airport-disaster.html

---

relaxed about managing time. The Spanish word *ahorita* means "right now" or "immediately" in English. Despite its dictionary meaning, North Americans have found their Mexican counterparts use the term quite differently:

When are those photocopies going to be ready?

"*Ahorita*," answers the secretary who knows the copy machine is broken.

When will that delivery be made?

"*Ahorita*," answers the salesman who has no truck.

One U.S. financial officer sheepishly admits he finally prohibited his Mexican staff from giving him *ahorita* as an answer.[4]

At least some equivocation problems can be avoided if you double-check your understanding of terms that might be interpreted more than one way. When you agree to meet "Wednesday" with someone, mention the date to be sure you're both thinking of the same week. When your supervisor says your ideas are "OK," make sure the term means "well done" and not just "adequate." And beware of the ubiquitous ASAP, which stands for As Soon As Possible. What is considered soon by one person's standard is not always shared by others in the office.

Use Lower-Level Abstractions When Clarity Is Essential   Any object or idea can be described at various levels, some very general and others quite specific. **Low-level abstractions** are specific, concrete statements that refer directly to objects or events that can be observed. By contrast, **high-level abstractions** cover a broader range of possible objects or events without describing them in much detail. High-level abstractions

Poor Translations Create Marketing Blunders

When international firms fail to understand the culture of a new international market, word-for-word translations of product names can range from humorous to offensive. Here are a few examples:

- Scandinavian vacuum manufacturer Electrolux didn't help sales in the United States when it used the slogan, "Nothing Sucks like an Electrolux."

- Clairol introduced the curling iron "Mist Stick" into Germany, only to find out that "mist" is slang for manure.

- Pepsi lost market share in parts of Southeast Asia when it painted vending machines light blue—a color associated with death and mourning.

- Gerber's baby food sales suffered in rural Africa when the company used the same packaging as in the United States with a smiling baby on the label. Later, the company discovered that in areas where many customers can't read, product labels contain pictures of what's inside the package.

- Colgate introduced a toothpaste in France called Cue, the name of a notorious porn magazine.

- Ford's marketing of its Pinto cars flopped in Brazil, where that word is slang for "tiny male genitals."

can create problems because they are often subject to a wide variety of interpretations, such as the following examples:

Statement	Clarification
The job will take a little longer.	How much longer: Hours? Days? Weeks?
Straighten up the area.	A quick cleanup or a spit-and-polish job?
We need some market research.	A short questionnaire for a few customers or lengthy personal interviews and detailed surveys?
Give me your honest opinion.	Be diplomatic or blunt?

Because both abstract language and specific language have their advantages, it is often best to use both. One way to achieve maximum clarity is to begin explaining your proposal, problem, request, or appreciation with an abstract statement, which you then qualify with specifics:

"I'm worried about the amount of time we seem to be spending on relatively unimportant matters [abstract]. In our last meeting, for instance, we talked for 20 minutes about when to schedule the company picnic and then had only 15 minutes to discuss our hiring needs [specific]."

"I'd like to take on more responsibility [abstract]. Until now, the only decisions I've been involved in are about small matters [still abstract], such as daily schedules and customer refunds [more specific]. I'd like a chance to help decide issues such as buying and advertising [specific requests]."

Another type of ambiguous language that causes problems is the use of **relative words** such as *soon, often, large,* and *short* that have meaning only in relation to other (unspecified) terms. Telling your supervisor you'll have the memo done *soon* or agreeing to do a *short* report can cause problems. If *soon* means "in a few weeks" to you, but it means "in a few days" to your boss, a conflict is brewing. Replacing relative words with numeric words can eliminate most of these problems. Use "in two days" rather than *soon* and "two paragraphs" rather than *short,* for example.

Use Slang with Caution
Casual, slang-laden speech may be fine off the job, but it can create the wrong impression with bosses, clients, and even colleagues. Some slang simply won't be understandable to others. For example, the British term "gobsmacked" is likely to draw a blank stare when used in conversation with someone outside the United Kingdom ("I was gobsmacked when they gave me that assignment"). And to compliment a colleague's presentation by calling it "sick" runs the risk of being interpreted as a deep insult. Other slang terms are also likely to cast you in an unprofessional light. You may call your friends "dude," but it's smart to talk more professionally in professional settings.

Use Jargon Judiciously
Every profession has its own specialized vocabulary, called **jargon.** For example, people who work in social media may talk about "SEO," "clickthrough rates," "crowdsourcing," and "enterprise 2.0." In many cases, jargon serves a useful purpose. First, it can save time. It's quicker to use a short term in place of the longer definition of a complex idea. For example, accountants use the term *liquidity* instead of saying "the degree to which an asset can be converted into cash." *Acronyms* are a special kind of jargon that also save time. These abbreviations give people a shorthand way to refer to common things, such as CEO referring to an organization's Chief Executive Officer. Second, jargon can be used to evaluate people's expertise on a subject. That's usually why some job interview questions are peppered with jargon. The interviewer is trying to determine if the job candidate knows the insider language. If the candidate can "talk the talk," it is more likely that he or she possesses the skills to do the job.

A certain amount of jargon has its value for outsiders as well. Speakers who sprinkle their comments with jargon will appear more credible to some listeners.[5] While incomprehensible language may *impress* listeners, it doesn't help them to *understand* an idea. Thus, if your goal is to explain yourself (and not merely to build your image), the ideal mixture may be a combination of clear language sprinkled with a bit of professional jargon.

Use Ambiguous Language When It Is Strategically Desirable
In low-context cultures like the United States and Canada, speaking directly is valued. "Don't beat around the bush" is a common phrase. Vague language can be seen as a sign of deliberate deception, as an old joke shows: A reporter warned a state senator, "Sir, your constituents were confused by today's speech." "Good," the senator replied. "It took me two days to write it that way."

Despite its bad reputation, ambiguous language does have its place. High-context cultures have made an art of *strategic ambiguity,*[6] finding ways to express difficult messages indirectly. One U.S. author describes how indirectness works:

> Instead of criticizing a report, the manager asks for more information. . . . When they say "I'd like to reflect on your proposal a while," when the decision must be [made] soon, it means "You are dead wrong,

"O.K. What part of 'malignant regression and pathogenic reintrojection as a defense against psychic decompensation' don't you understand?"

© Robert Mankoff/The New Yorker Collection/www.cartoonbank.com.

Strategic Ambiguity

A. Develop strategically ambiguous ways to rephrase each of the following statements:

    I. You've done a sloppy job here.

    II. I can't understand what you're trying to say in this letter.

    III. Nobody likes your idea.

    IV. Would you hurry up and get to the point?

B. On the basis of your responses here, decide how honest strategically ambiguous statements are. If they are not completely honest, can they be considered ethical?

Problems arise when insiders use their specialized vocabulary without explaining it to the uninitiated. According to one survey, people in computer support industries are the worst offenders when it comes to jargon.[7] A customer shopping for a computer might be mystified by a dealer's talk about bus speed, onboard circuitry, and data transfer rates. When the same information is translated into language the buyer can understand—the length of time it takes to download a file, for example—a sale is more likely.

Certain words are used so often that they become clichés.[8] As one communication expert says, they "are brief and snappy, roll off the tongue easily, and can fool us into thinking that we know what we're talking about."[9] If you overuse buzzwords like "mission focused," "paradigm shift," and "out of the box," you run the risk of not clarifying your ideas in your own mind and not being clear to others.[10]

and you'd better come up with a better idea very soon. But I don't tell you so, because you should know that yourself!"

It seems to me that such indirectness in interpersonal communication is a virtue; it is just as efficient, and it is certainly more mature and polite than the affront, "You are dead wrong." We need not talk to one another as if we were children (or characters out of the pages of pulp fiction)—yes, children need clarity—but adults can deal with indirectness and multiple meanings.[11]

Even in the normally low-context cultures like the United States, Canada, Israel, and Germany, there are many times when indirect speech helps communicators achieve two useful goals.[12] The first is *to promote harmony.* A group of workers who have been feuding over everything from next year's budget to funding the office coffee supply can at least reach consensus on an abstraction like "the need to reduce waste," a small but important start toward more cooperation.

A second function of ambiguous speech is *to soften the blow of difficult messages.* Business communicators face the constant challenge of delivering difficult messages: "This work isn't good enough." "We don't want to do business with you anymore." While statements like these may be honest, they can also be brutal. Ambiguous language provides a way to deliver difficult messages that softens their blow and makes it possible to work smoothly with the recipients in the future. For example:

Brute Honesty	Strategic Ambiguity
This work isn't good enough.	I think the boss will want us to back up these predictions with some figures.
I don't want to work with you.	Right now I don't see any projects on the horizon.

A final function of strategic ambiguity is to make a *point indirectly that can't be expressed overtly.* In the current litigation-prone environment, business communicators often use strategic ambiguity to communicate critical messages without exposing them-selves to lawsuits.[13] For example, consider this humorous letter of reference "endorsing" a former employee who was fired for being a slow, lazy, unmotivated worker with an inflated ego and who lacked qualifications, causing the company to lose money:

> I am pleased to say John Doe is a former colleague of mine. John left this job the same way he came, fired with enthusiasm. We are deeply indebted for the services he has given our firm over the years.
>
> John will do nothing which will lower your high regard for him. His job requires few skills which he lacks. I honestly don't think he could have done a better job for us if he had tried. I most enthusiastically recommend John Doe with no qualifications whatsoever. It will not take John long to get up to speed. No salary would be too much for him. You won't find many people like John.[14]

One problem with strategic ambiguity, of course, is that it can easily be misunder-stood. This problem can be especially acute in medical settings, when health care provid-ers try to deliver bad news to patients in a way that softens its impact. For example:

> [A surgeon] took one look at a patient's badly infected foot and recognized that it would have to be amputated. "I don't think we're going to be able to deal with this with local treatments," he told the patient.
>
> When the surgeon left the examining room, the woman turned to the doctor and asked: "Does that mean I'm going to have to go to Los Angeles for treatment?"[15]

And even when misunderstandings aren't a problem, strategic ambiguity works only when both sender and receiver are willing to tolerate a deliberate lack of clarity. Without that understanding, the result can be confusion, and often feelings of being betrayed or manipulated.

Inflammatory Language

Language has the power to stir intense emotions. It can motivate, inspire, and amuse audiences. Unfortunately, it can also generate negative feelings: antagonism, defensive-ness, and prejudice. You can prevent these negative outcomes by following two guidelines.

Avoid Biased Language   Emotional problems arise when speakers intentionally or unintentionally use **biased language**—terms that seem to be objective but actually con-ceal an emotional bias. Consider, for example, the range of words you could use to refer to a 25-year-old man who disagrees with your proposal: *man, fellow, guy, young man,* or *dude.* Each one paints a different picture in the listener's mind. None of them is neutral.

When faced with biased language, it's wise to recognize the speaker is editorializing. Tactfully restate the term in language that doesn't contain an evaluation, paraphrase with neutral language, or use terms that quantify:

Speaker Biased Language	Listener's Restatement
It's a *gamble.*	So you don't think the idea is a reason-able risk. Is that it? (paraphrase)
He's *long-winded.*	Bill *has* been talking for a half hour. (quantify)
She's so *wishy-washy.*	You think Susan isn't willing to make a decision? (rephrase in nonbiased language)

Strategic Swearing

Swearing serves a variety of communication functions.[16] It's a way to express emotions and to let others know how strongly you feel. It can be a compliment ("that was #$&@ing terrific!") or the worst of insults. Swearing can build solidarity and be a term of endearment, but it can offend and alienate too.

Swearing on the job can have dire consequences. It has been identified as the leading cause of employee terminations.[17] And some types of language can lead to complaints of sexual harassment, even when it isn't directed at a particular employee.[18] Communication researchers have investigated the effects of swearing in work settings.[19] Not surprisingly, they have found that the more formal the situation, the more negative the appraisal. The chosen swear word also made a difference. "F-bombs" are judged to be more inappropriate than other, less-volatile terms. Perhaps most important, when listeners are caught by surprise by a speaker's swearing, they are likely to deem the person incompetent.

Despite these findings, Stanford University professor Robert Sutton notes that choosing *not* to swear can sometimes violate the norms of some organizations.[20] Moreover, he maintains that swearing on rare occasions can be effective for the shock value. (The fact that Sutton authored a book called *The No Asshole Rule* suggests he practices what he preaches.)

But even Sutton adds a cautionary note about swearing on the job: "If you are not sure, don't do it." This advice is especially important for workers who are new to the organization or whose position is not secure. The rules of communication competence apply: Analyze and adapt to your audience; pay attention to both verbal and nonverbal feedback; and when in doubt, err on the side of restraint.

Beware of Trigger Words   Some terms have such strong emotional associations they act almost like a trigger, setting off an intense emotional reaction in certain listeners. These **trigger words** can refer to specific people (your boss, the president), groups or categories of individuals (union stewards, the Human Resources department, customers with complaints), issues (affirmative action, flexible scheduling), or other topics (imports, downsizing).

What is the best way to deal with trigger words? The first thing to realize is that, like others, you almost certainly have your own trigger words. Therefore, you ought to begin by recognizing them, so when one comes up you'll at least be aware of your sensitivity and avoid overreacting. If, for example, your parents are farmers and you are sensitive about people speaking condescendingly about farmers, you might catch yourself before you overreact when a coworker refers to someone on Casual Friday as "dressed like a farmer." It could be an innocent or uninformed remark.

Sometimes, however, you will discover too late that a term that seems innocuous to you is a trigger word for others. After the other person vents his or her strong feelings, you can acknowledge the misunderstanding, apologize, choose a more agreeable term, and proceed with the discussion.

Language and Identity Management

The way you speak can shape how others perceive you. There are several speech habits that can help you create a professional image.

Choose the Optimal Degree of Powerful Language   Some types of language make a speaker sound less powerful, while other types create an air of power and confidence.

85

Less Powerful Speech	More Powerful Speech
Tag questions "This report is good, *isn't it?*"	"This report is good."
Hesitations "I, *uh,* think we should, *um,* use the newer format."	"I think we should use the newer format."
Qualifiers "*I don't know if you'll like this idea, but* we could hire an outside consultant."	"We could hire an outside consultant."
Intensifiers "That was *such* a good job!"	"That was a good job!"
Questions "*Do you think we* should shorten the report?"	"I think we should shorten the report."

Speakers who use more powerful speech are rated as more competent, dynamic, and attractive than speakers who sound powerless.[21] One study revealed that even a single powerless speech mannerism can make a person appear less authoritative.[22] So, when your goal is to create an impression of power and conviction, it's best to use more powerful speech.

On the other hand, there are times when powerful individuals might intentionally use less powerful language to avoid throwing their weight around. In some situations less powerful forms of speech can even enhance a speaker's effectiveness.[23] For example, a boss might say to her assistant, "Would you mind making copies of these files before you go home?" Both the boss and the assistant know this is an order and not a request, but the questioning form is more considerate and leaves the assistant feeling better about the boss.[24] The importance of achieving both task and relational goals helps explain why a mixture of powerful and polite speech is usually most effective.[25]

Use Positive Language   One strategic way to enhance a professional identity is through positive language. Imagine your boss comes to you at 4:45 PM and asks you to do a job as soon as possible. You could say, "I can't get to that tonight. It'll have to wait until tomorrow." Or instead, you could reply "I'll get to that first thing in the morning." It's easy to imagine which response would be viewed more favorably.

Unintentionally negative language habits can subtly damage a positive image. When someone asks, "*How are you?*" a typical response is, "Not bad." When you're asked, "*What's new?*" it's easy to reply, "Not much." Negativity is often a reflex in other simple exchanges: "*Can you handle this?*" "No problem." *Thanks.* "No big deal." Instead of using negative language, it's better to give quick, *positive* responses. "I'm fine." "Yes, I can." "You're welcome."

Limit Disfluencies   **Disfluencies** are utterances that add no meaning to a statement. Interjections like "umm," "you know," and "like" can make a smart idea sound less persuasive. Prospective senatorial candidate Caroline Kennedy's disfluency habit may have helped sabotage her credibility. One critic reported counting more than 200 "you know's" in a single interview.[26] Another filler word often viewed negatively, especially by older generations, is "like." In fact, personal branding strategist Sylwia Dziedzic names "like" as one of the top filler words that can get in your way of getting hired.[27] Nobody expects colloquial speech to be flawless. In fact, perfect utterances would sound artificial and strange. But practice can help keep the number of disfluences under control.

Feminine and Masculine Language Use

Chapter 2 described how culture affects communication. Some social scientists have suggested that conversation between men and women is a kind of cross-cultural communication in which members of each sex are not speaking different dialects but **"genderlects."**[28] They have argued that these different approaches affect the way men and women interact with one another in ways that are powerful but usually unnoticed.

As you read about differences in male and female speech, understand that the descriptions don't characterize all men and women. The relationship between gender and language is like the one between gender and height: Men are generally taller than women, but some women are taller than some men. In fact, the difference between the tallest man and the shortest man (or the tallest woman and the shortest woman) is greater than the difference between the average man and the average woman. For this reason, the words "masculine" and "feminine" are actually better adjectives to describe language differences since they refer to traits characteristically linked to each gender and not to biological sex. Remember also that gender isn't the only factor that influences conversational style. Cultural, geographical, and occupational influences also play a role. Finally, understand that the differences outlined in this section reflect past communication patterns. As the roles of men and women in society evolve, speech styles may change as well.

Feminine Language Use   From childhood, females learn to use speech for what some researchers refer to as **rapport talk:** talk used to create connections, establish goodwill, show support, and build community.

For many women an important part of building rapport is using language as an *expressive tool:* to articulate emotions ("I'm worried about finishing those reports today"; "I'm glad everybody had a chance to speak") and clarify relationships ("We don't seem to be working well together").

Characteristically feminine speech often goes beyond just expressing emotions; it also is *supportive.* Women are most likely to listen and respond to spoken and unspoken conversational clues about the other person's feelings. A characteristically feminine reply to a description of difficulties at work is, "I know what that's like. Last year I had so much

"Sorry, Chief, but of course I didn't mean 'bimbo' in the pejorative sense."

© Lee Lorenz/The New Yorker Collection/www.cartoonbank.com.

trouble with a client on the Bustos case. . . ." This response lets the speaker know that she is not alone, that she is understood.

Another characteristic of feminine conversational style is its *tentative* nature. This is reflected in questioning forms ("Could we go now?" "Would you type that for me?"), hedges and disclaimers ("I'm not sure about these figures. . . ."; "This might not be a good time to bring this up, but. . . ."), and tag questions ("The report is due today, isn't it?"). While these forms exhibit the less powerful characteristics described earlier in this chapter on pp. 85–86, linguist Deborah Tannen describes them more as a bid for solidarity than a sign of weakness:

> Many women are frequently told, "Don't apologize" or "You're always apologizing." The reason "apologizing" is seen as something they should stop doing is that it seems synonymous with putting oneself down. But for many women, and a fair number of men, saying "I'm sorry" isn't literally an apology; it is a ritual way of restoring balance to a conversation. "I'm sorry," spoken in this spirit, if it has any literal meaning at all, does not mean "I apologize," which would be tantamount to accepting blame, but rather "I'm sorry that happened."[29]

Speech forms such as apologizing, especially when used by women, can create the impression of less authority, status, certainty, accuracy, or credibility. However, tentative speech doesn't have to be regarded as weak.[30] Another interpretation is that it builds rapport by avoiding dogmatism and supporting equality.

Conversational initiation and maintenance are also characteristic of feminine speech. Women have long been taught to ask questions to get a conversation going, to find out what others are interested in, and to show interest in a conversational partner. So, many women ask questions to start and maintain conversations: "Did you hear about . . . ?" "Are you going to . . . ?" "Did you know that . . . ?" In addition, women use "listening noises" ("uh, huh," "yeah," "mmhmm") to show interest. If women do interrupt, it is often to support or affirm the speaker, not to challenge or threaten.

Masculine Language Use   Whereas women use talk to build rapport, men are more comfortable with what linguists have labeled **report talk**—speech that focuses less on feelings and relationships and more on information, facts, knowledge, and competence. Men are more inclined to use language to claim attention, assert a position, establish status, and show independence. Research shows men need to be just as sensitive as women, but they may use that awareness differently. In one study, male managers who were more accurate at emotion perception received higher satisfaction ratings if they used the information to be more persuasive. By contrast, more emotionally perceptive female managers received higher satisfaction ratings when they demonstrated more supportiveness.[31]

Characteristically masculine speech uses language *instrumentally* (as opposed to expressively) to get things done: report information, solve visible problems, achieve, accomplish, attain, execute, and perform. The results are often tangible and the reward is visible: "Fax these reports to accounting"; "I'll make reservations at Sara's"; "Finish that proposal by Monday." Men often use language to define status.

When dealing with personal problems, a characteristically masculine approach is to offer *advice* that will lead to a solution. Empathizing to show sympathy and establish solidarity just doesn't seem helpful or appropriate to many men.

Characteristically masculine speech is more *assertive, certain, direct,* and *authoritative*. Men often use statements of fact rather than opinion: "That deduction belongs on Schedule C" rather than "I think that's a Schedule C deduction." Declarative sentences and dropped pitch at the end create a sense of sureness and authority. Men are more likely to speak directly, giving clear and unambiguous commands or directions rather than couching requests in the form of questions.

Men's speech style typically includes several characteristics of conversational *dominance* or *control:* verbosity, topic control, and interruptions. Most research supports the statement that in public conversations between men and women, men talk at greater length.[32] Often in response to questions from women, men decide which topic of conversation to pursue and talk longer than the women in the same conversation. Research on interruptions is mixed regarding who interrupts more, but it appears that the purpose of men's interruptions is often to gain control of the conversational topic or the conversation itself. Table 4-2 below summarizes research findings on characteristics of feminine and masculine speech styles.

Meeting Gender-Related Language Challenges

Problems can arise when stereotypically masculine and feminine language styles clash on the job—often without anyone knowing exactly why. For instance, a woman who says, "I'm having difficulty with the Garcia account," may want to hear her concerns acknowledged and know that others have experienced similar problems. Her goal may be to gain support, establish connection, and seek rapport. Or she may just want to talk about the situation. A man, conditioned to use speech to solve problems, might respond with advice: "Here's one way you could handle it . . ." If the woman wanted support and connection, being given advice might produce an effect just the opposite of the rapport she was looking for: The woman might feel her male colleague was trying to appear "one-up," coming across as a superior. From his frame of reference, the man *was* being helpful: He offered useful information at the request of someone in need.

Another gender-related problem can arise when a man pays attention to the content of a message while a woman focuses on the relational dimension of the words. If a male supervisor says, "I can't do anything about your hours; the boss says they're set and can't be changed," a woman may hear a relational message of "I don't care" or "I don't want to be bothered." The man, used to dealing with communication at the task level, isn't being unsympathetic; he is just responding to a request.

Both masculine and feminine language styles work well—as long as listeners use the same rules. Frustrations result when people expect others to use the same style as theirs.[33] The following suggestions can help communicators understand and adapt to one another's differing uses of language:

- *Be aware of different styles.* Once you are aware that men and women have been taught to use language differently, there's less likelihood of being dismayed at a style that doesn't match yours. The cultural analogy is apt here: If you were traveling in another country, you wouldn't be offended by the inhabitants' customs, even if they were different from yours. In the same way, accepting gender differences can lead to smoother relationships—even if members of the other sex behave differently from you.

Table 4-2	Characteristics of Feminine and Masculine Speech Styles
Characteristically Feminine Speech	**Characteristically Masculine Speech**
Builds rapport	Reports facts
Is expressive	Is instrumental
Offers support	Offers advice
Sounds tentative	Sounds certain
Initiates and maintains conversation	Controls conversation

- *Switch styles when appropriate.* Being bilingual is an obvious advantage in a multi-cultural world. In the same way, using a communication style that is uncharacteristic of you can be useful. If you routinely focus on the content of others' remarks, consider paying more attention to the unstated relational messages behind their words. If you generally focus on the unexpressed-feelings part of a message, consider being more task oriented. If your first instinct is to be supportive, consider the value of offering advice; and if advice is your reflexive way of responding, think about whether offering support and understanding might sometimes be more helpful.

- *Combine styles.* Effective communication may not be an either–or matter of choosing one style. In many situations, you may get the best results by combining typically masculine and feminine approaches. Research confirms what common sense suggests: A "mixed-gender strategy" that balances the traditionally masculine, task-oriented approach with the characteristically feminine, relationship-oriented approach is rated most highly by both male and female respondents.[34] Choosing the right approach for the other communicator and the situation can create satisfaction far greater than an approach that comes from using a single stereotypical style.

Nonverbal Communication

Words are not the only way we communicate. You can appreciate this fact by imagining the following scenes:

- Your boss has told the staff she welcomes any suggestions about how to improve the organization. You take her at her word and schedule an appointment to discuss some ideas you have had. As you begin to outline your proposed changes, she focuses her gaze directly on you, folds her arms across her chest, clenches her jaw muscles, and begins to frown. At the end of your remarks, she rises abruptly from her chair, says, "Thank you for your ideas" in a monotone voice, and gives you a curt handshake.

- Despite the expense, you have decided to have a highly regarded CPA handle your tax matters. While waiting for the accountant to appear, you scan the impressive display of diplomas from prestigious universities and professional associations. The accountant enters, and as the conversation proceeds, he yawns repeatedly.

Most people would find these situations odd and disturbing. This reaction would have nothing to do with the verbal behavior of the people involved. In each case, nonverbal behavior sends messages above and beyond the words being spoken: The boss doesn't really seem to want to hear your suggestions, and you wonder whether the accountant is capable or caring with regard to your taxes.

In the following pages we examine the role of nonverbal communication in the working world. For our purposes, **nonverbal communication** involves messages expressed without words.

Characteristics of Nonverbal Communication

Now that we have defined nonverbal communication and discussed its importance, we need to take a look at its characteristics. Nonverbal communication resembles verbal communication in some ways and is quite different from it in others.

Nonverbal Behavior Always Has Communicative Value   You may not always *intend* to send nonverbal messages, but everything about your appearance, every movement, every facial expression, every nuance of your voice has the potential to convey meaning.[35] You can demonstrate this fact by imagining your boss has "called you on the carpet," claiming you haven't been working hard enough. How could you not send a nonverbal message? Nodding gravely would be a response; so would blushing, avoiding or making direct eye contact, or shaking your head affirmatively or negatively. While you can shut off your linguistic channels of communication by refusing to speak or write, it is impossible to avoid behaving nonverbally.

One writer learned this fact from movie producer Sam Goldwyn while presenting his proposal for a new film. "Mr. Goldwyn," the writer implored, "I'm telling you a sensational story. I'm only asking for your opinion, and you fall asleep." Goldwyn's reply: "Isn't sleeping an opinion?"

Nonverbal communication operates even in mediated communication. Some nonverbal elements are obvious: The use of emoticons, an abundance of exclamation points, and the impression of shouting when a message is typed in ALL CAPITAL LETTERS are clear examples. But even *not* responding to an e-mail, IM, or text message can suggest a put-down.[36]

Nonverbal Communication Is Powerful   Despite folk sayings like "you can't judge a book from its cover," we form impressions of others mostly from nonverbal observations about physical appearance and behavior. Once we form these impressions, they influence our subsequent impressions and judgments. Canadian communication consultant Lee McCoy gives an example:

> If I meet Susan and initially perceive her to be professional, attractive and intelligent, I'm also likely to begin to attribute other positive characteristics to her. I might see her as organized, successful and warm. This is not to suggest that I'll ignore negative characteristics, but it will take me longer to become aware of something negative if my initial perceptions of her are very positive. If, on the other hand, Susan presents herself to me as sloppily dressed, with bitten fingernails and a lack of eye contact, I may begin to attribute equally negative characteristics to her—insecurity, lack of knowledge, coldness.[37]

Even after first impressions have been made, the impact of nonverbal behavior is powerful. In fact, when nonverbal behavior seems to contradict a verbal message, the spoken words carry less weight than the nonverbal cues.[38]

DILBERT © Scott Adams/Dist. By Universal Uclick.

Nonverbal Behavior Is Ambiguous   While nonverbal communication can create powerful impressions, the messages it conveys are ambiguous.[39] You don't have to be as clueless as the boss in the cartoon on page 91 to misinterpret nonverbal cues. Does a customer's yawn signal boredom or fatigue? Are your coworkers laughing with or at you? Does your boss's frown reflect disapproval or preoccupation? Most nonverbal behaviors have a multitude of possible meanings, and it is a serious mistake to assume you can decide which is true in any given case.

Nonverbal Communication Primarily Expresses Attitudes   While it is relatively easy to infer general interest, liking, disagreement, amusement, and so on from another's actions, messages about ideas or concepts don't lend themselves to nonverbal channels. How, for instance, would you express the following messages nonverbally?

> Sales are running 16 percent above last year's.
>
> Management decided to cancel the sales meeting after all.
>
> Let's meet at 2:00 PM to plan the agenda for tomorrow's meeting.

It's apparent that such thoughts are best expressed in speech and writing. It's also apparent, though, that nonverbal behavior will imply how the speaker *feels* about these statements: whether the speaker is pleased sales are up or worried they're not as high as expected, , whether the staff is relieved or frustrated about the cancelled meeting, and so on.

Nonverbal Communication Affects Career Success   Not surprisingly, the ability to manage your nonverbal behavior plays a strong role in communicative success. For example, salespeople who were better at reading potential clients' nonverbal cues make more sales and earn higher income than less astute colleagues.[40] Likewise, successful entrepreneurs owe a great measure of their success to social skills, including the ability to manage their own nonverbal behavior and read that of others.[41] Managers who were good at reading and responding to nonverbal cues received higher performance ratings from both their bosses and their subordinates.[42]

Much Nonverbal Behavior Is Culture-Bound   Certain types of nonverbal behavior seem to be universal. For example, there is strong agreement among members of most literate cultures about which facial expressions represent happiness, fear, surprise, sadness, anger, and disgust or contempt.[43] On the other hand, many nonverbal expressions do vary from culture to culture. (See Table 4-3 for a few examples.)

In this age of international communication in business, it is especially important to understand there are cultural differences in the meaning assigned to nonverbal behaviors. Consider the different rules about what distance is appropriate between speakers. One study revealed that the "proper" space between two speakers varied considerably from one culture to another: To Japanese, a comfortable space was 40 inches; for a U.S. resident, 35 inches; and to Venezuelans, 32 inches.[44] It's easy to see how this could lead to problems for a U.S. native doing business overseas.

Types of Nonverbal Communication

We have already mentioned several types of nonverbal messages. We now discuss each in more detail.

Voice   Your own experience shows the voice communicates in ways that have nothing to do with the words a speaker utters. You may recall, for instance, overhearing two people arguing in an adjoining room or apartment; even though you couldn't make out their words, their emotions and the fact they were arguing were apparent from the sound

Table 4-3	Co-cultural Differences Can Lead to Misunderstandings	

Behaviors that have one meaning for members of the same culture or co-culture can be interpreted differently by members of other groups.

Behavior (in Traditional Co-culture)	Probable In-Group Perception	Possible Out-Group Perception
Avoidance of direct eye contact (Latino/Latina)	Used to communicate attentiveness or respect.	A sign of inattentiveness; direct eye contact is preferred.
Aggressively challenging a point with which one disagrees (African American)	Acceptable means of dialogue; not regarded as verbal abuse or a precursor to violence.	Arguments are viewed as inappropriate and a sign of potential imminent violence.
Use of finger gestures to beckon others (Asian American)	Appropriate if used by adults for children but highly offensive if directed at adults.	Appropriate gesture to use with both children and adults.
Silence (Native American)	A sign of respect, thoughtfulness, and/or uncertainty/ambiguity.	Interpreted as boredom, disagreement, or refusal to participate/respond.
Touch (Latino/Latina)	Normal and appropriate for interpersonal interactions.	Deemed appropriate for some intimate or friendly interactions; otherwise perceived as a violation of personal space.
Public display of intense emotions (African American)	Accepted and valued as measure of expressiveness. Appropriate in most settings.	Violates expectations for self-controlled public behaviors; inappropriate in most public settings.
Touching or holding hands of same-sex friends (Asian American)	Acceptable behavior that signifies closeness in platonic relationships.	Perceived as inappropriate, especially for male friends.

Source: Adapted from Orbe, M. P., & Harris, T. M. (2001). *Interracial communication: Theory into practice.* Belmont, CA: Wadsworth.

of their voices. Similarly, you have probably overheard people talking in a language you didn't understand; yet the speakers' feelings—excitement, delight, exhaustion, boredom, grief—were conveyed by their voices.

The term **paralanguage** describes a wide range of vocal characteristics, each of which helps express an attitude: pitch (high–low), resonance (resonant–thin), range (spread–narrow), tempo (rapid–slow), articulation (precise–imprecise), disfluencies (*um, er,* etc.), rhythm (smooth–jerky), pauses (frequency and duration), and volume (loud–soft).

Not surprisingly, voice contributes dramatically to business and professional communicators' success or failure. For example, surgeons with harsh, impatient voices were more likely to be sued by patients for malpractice than were those with more friendly speech mannerisms.[45] One distinctive vocal trait is "uptalk"—the tendency to end sentences on a rising pitch. This vocal pattern makes assertions sound like questions: "Mr. Chen? It's Eliza Palmer? From Accounts Receivable?" Since uptalk is more common among women, it's easy to imagine how this trait can contribute to perceptions of female unassertiveness. "If women always sound like they're asking for approval or agreement, they seem less sure of themselves," says communication consultant Mary-Ellen Drummond.[46]

Appearance   Appearance plays a tremendous role in determining how a communicator's messages will be received in business and elsewhere.[47] As a rule, people who *look* attractive are considered to be likable and persuasive, and they generally have more

successful careers.[48] For example, research suggests that beginning salaries increase about $2,000 for every 1-point increase on a 5-point attractiveness scale and that more attractive men (but not more attractive women) are given higher starting salaries than their less handsome counterparts.

A number of factors contribute to how attractive a person seems. For instance, potential employers, customers, and coworkers are usually impressed by people who are trim, muscular, and in good shape. One study, in fact, shows that people who are overweight have more trouble getting job offers.[49] Some aspects of physical appearance cannot be changed easily. One significant factor in appearance, though—clothing—is one over which you may have the most control.

The kind of clothing one wears can influence how people react. Boeing Aircraft CEO Philip Condit is aware of this fact. Having discovered that discussions were hard to get going when he appeared in a business suit and tie, Condit routinely dressed down when making trips to the shop floor to talk with the men and women who build Boeing aircraft.[50]

Attitudes about what clothing is acceptable keep changing. By the mid-1990s, even conservative IBM abandoned its decades-long policy of requiring employees to wear a dark business suit, even allowing male workers in some jobs to show up for work without a suit and tie. A spokesperson for IBM explained, "You try to dress like your customers do."[51] But the casual dress trends brought on by the 1990 dot-coms seem to be in decline.[52]

Whether to dress up or dress down depends on several factors, including the industry or field of work. California's outdoor gear clothing manufacturer Patagonia may have one of the most liberal dress codes: Even shoes aren't required.[53] By contrast, financial services and public administration businesses have some of the most conservative dress standards, while high-tech, utilities, and natural resources tend to be the most informal.[54]

Geography also makes a difference in determining an appropriate working wardrobe. In one survey, Washington, DC, proved to have the most conservative attire, with New York and Philadelphia close behind. California and New England—the location of many high-tech companies—had more liberal standards.[55] Knowing an office has a "business casual" dress code isn't enough, as "casual" is itself an ambiguous term. As business etiquette expert Dana Casperson notes, business casual "means one thing on the West Coast, another thing on the East Coast, and no one knows in the middle."[56] An individual organization's culture also makes a difference in how to dress. Two companies in the same field might have quite different appearance codes.

When choosing your wardrobe, consider the following tips:

- *Look around.* The best guide to an appropriate wardrobe is right in front of you. Look at key people in the industry and company where you work. Wearing a conservative, dark business suit in a freewheeling start-up company where everyone else comes to work in jeans would look just as odd as wearing wrinkled Levis in a Wall Street stock brokerage. You may also inquire with Human Resources about company dress codes.

- *Dress for the job you want.* If you are seeking advancement, consider dressing in a way that makes it easy for the people with the power to promote you to visualize you in a position of more responsibility.

- *Err on the side of dressing conservatively.* Standards of dress are always in flux. For example, only a slight majority of respondents in one survey thought exposed underwear is inappropriate. But you can imagine this look would jeopardize success in most fields.[57] If you aren't sure what attire is appropriate in a given situation, choose the more conservative option. It's easier to loosen or remove a tie for a more casual look than it is to dress up a golf shirt.

- *Don't show too much skin.* What might be the norm on a college campus or out with your friends may not be acceptable at your job. If you work with people from older generations, or in a particularly conservative environment such as banking or energy, it will be very important for your career success to dress modestly. Some general guidelines include avoiding plunging necklines, short skirts, shirts that show midriff, and shoes that show toes.[58]

- *Don't confuse "casual" with "sloppy."* A T-shirt and grubby denim jeans send a different message than pressed khakis and a sharp shirt or sweater. Looking good in casual dress can be at least as challenging (and expensive) as a more formal look. And it's never acceptable to have dirty, stained, or wrinkled clothing.

Even though it may be unfair, it is more important for women to dress professionally and conservatively than it is for men—especially if they have high career ambitions. In multiple studies on the effects of clothing choices, participants evaluated the perceived competence of women who were wearing either professional clothes or "sexy" clothes. When the woman was in a low-status position (an administrative assistant), her choice of clothes had no effect on her perceived competence. But when she was in a high-status position (an executive), the sexily dressed woman was rated as significantly less competent.[59]

The Face and Eyes   On an obvious level, a person's face communicates emotions clearly: A subordinate's confused expression indicates the need to continue with an explanation; a customer's smile and nodding signal the time to close a sale; and a colleague's frown indicates that your request for help has come at a bad time. Facial expressions, like other nonverbal signals, are ambiguous (a coworker's frown could come from a headache rather than the timing of your request). Nonetheless, researchers have found that accurate judgments of facial expressions can be made.[60]

The eyes themselves communicate a great deal. A skilled nonverbal communicator, for example, can control an interaction by knowing when and where to look to produce the desired results. Since visual contact is an invitation to speak, a speaker who does not want to be interrupted can avoid looking directly at people until it is time to field questions or get reactions.

Eye contact can be a good indicator of how involved a person is in a situation, although research partially contradicts the advice to always look people straight in

"You have until he rolls his eyes and looks at his watch."

the eye. In most two-person conversations, people seem to look at their partners somewhere between 50 and 60 percent of the time, often alternating short gazes with glances away. Still, a person who makes little or no eye contact may seem to have little involvement in the situation.

The rules for eye contact and facial expressions vary from one culture to another. In some cultures—Diné (Navajo), for example—lack of eye contact may indicate respect for elders, not a lack of interest. In Japan, smiling is less common than in North America, which can confuse visitors who mistakenly perceive formality for unfriendliness. Clerks greet customers with a simple "Irasshaimase"—"Welcome"—but typically don't accompany the greeting with a smile.[61] Some foreign companies, including McDonald's Corp., have created "smile schools" to teach employees how to greet customers in a manner that seems friendlier.

Even among communicators who follow the rules of Euro-American culture, eye contact can be deceptive; some people *can* lie while looking you right in the eye. And even barely perceptible changes in eye contact can send messages that may or may not be accurate. The following story illustrates how eye contact can be misleading—with serious repercussions:

> Discussing his corporation's financial future in front of television cameras, the chief executive officer of a Fortune 500 company lowered his eyes just as he began to mention projected earnings. His downcast eyes gave the impression—on television—that the executive wasn't on the level. Wall Street observers discounted the CEO's optimistic forecast, and the company's stock price dropped four points over the next few trading days. It took two years to build it up again—even though the projection had proved to be accurate.[62]

Posture and Movement   A person's body communicates messages in several ways. The first is through posture. The way you sit at your desk when you're working can reflect your attitude toward your job or how hard you're working to anyone who cares to look. A less obvious set of bodily clues comes from the small gestures and mannerisms every communicator exhibits at one time or another. While most people pay reasonably close attention to their facial expression, they are less aware of hand, leg, and foot motions. Thus, fidgeting hands might signal nervousness; a tapping foot, impatience; and clenched fists or white knuckles, restrained anger. Table 4-4 describes the way others may be likely to interpret some of your gestures.

A study on privacy in the workplace by GF Business Equipment Company describes ways in which such gestures can be used to discourage visits from coworkers. In addition to avoiding eye contact with your visitor, the company suggests you shuffle papers or make notes to indicate a desire to return to work; keep pen or pencil poised, which communicates an aversion to engage in conversation; and, if interrupted when dialing a call, don't hang up the receiver.[63]

Good communicators are sensitive to small cues like this and tailor their behavior accordingly. They will notice a forward-leaning position as an indication their remarks are being well received and will capitalize upon the point that led to this reaction. When a remark results in a pulling back, a smart communicator will uncover the damage and try to remedy it. Awareness of such subtle messages can make the difference between success and failure in a variety of business settings: interviews, presentations, group meetings, and one-on-one interactions.

Body relaxation or tension is a strong indicator of who has the power in one-on-one relationships. As a rule, the more relaxed person in a given situation has the greater status.[64] This is most obvious in job interviews and high-stake situations in which subordinates meet with their superiors—requesting a raise or describing a problem, for example.

Table 4-4	Common Gestures and Their Possible Perceived Meanings	
Gesture	**In Moderate Form**	**When Exaggerated**
Forward lean	Friendly feelings	Hostile feelings
Direct eye contact	Friendly feelings	Hostile feelings
Unique dress and hairstyle	Creativity	Rebelliousness
Upright posture	Expertise; self-confidence	Uptightness; hostility
Variability in voice pitch, rate, and loudness	Lively mind	Nervousness; anxiety; insecurity
Smiling	Friendliness; relaxed and secure composure	Masking hostility; submissiveness
Averting gaze	Shyness; modesty	Guilt; unreliability
Knitted brow	Involvement	Hostility
Nodding and reaching out the hands while talking	Self-confidence	Uncertainty

Source: Adapted from University of Northern Iowa College of Business Administration. (n.d.). *Body language*. Retrieved from http://business.uni.edu/buscomm/nonverbal/body%20Language.htm

The person in control can afford to relax, while the supplicant must be watchful and on guard. While excessive tension does little good for either the sender or receiver, total relaxation can be inappropriate for a subordinate. A job candidate who matched the interviewer's casual sprawl would probably create a poor impression. In superior–subordinate interactions, the best posture for the one-down person is probably one that is slightly more formal than the powerholder's.

Height also affects perceptions of power: Tallness usually equates with dominance. Standing up tall can help you appear more authoritative; whereas, slumped posture or slouched shoulders create an appearance of submissive or passive demeanor. Getting your body at the same level as others is a way of nonverbally diminishing status whether speaking with a colleague in a wheelchair or with others shorter than you. To literally have to look up to someone may make the shorter person feel like a subordinate. Sitting down with someone could signal your desire for collegiality rather than status, while standing over or behind someone signals power or status. Because women and people from some races or ethnicities may not be as tall as the average American male, and because people in wheelchairs interact at a shorter height, your relative height is a factor worth considering in professional interactions. If you are taller than others or are standing when others are sitting, they may be seeing you as an authority figure or higher-status individual, even if you don't wish to appear as one.[65]

Personal Space and Distance   The distance we put between ourselves and others also reflects feelings and attitudes, and thus it affects communication. Anthropologist Edward Hall has identified four distance zones middle-class Americans use: intimate (ranging from physical contact to about 18 inches), casual–personal (18 inches to 4 feet), social–consultative (4 to 12 feet), and public (12 feet and beyond).[66]

In some cases the distance zones don't apply at all—or at least the distances aren't flexible enough to reflect the parties' attitudes. Dentists and barbers, for instance, work within intimate distance—and actual physical contact—yet the relationship between dentist and patient or barber and client may be rather impersonal.

Touch Enhances Success

The old phrase "keeping in touch" takes on new meaning once you understand the relationship between physical contact and career effectiveness. Some of the most pronounced benefits of touching occur in medicine and the health and helping professions. For example, patients are more likely to take their medication when physicians give a slight touch while prescribing.[67] In counseling, touch increases psychiatric patients' self-disclosure and verbalization.

Touch can also enhance success in sales and marketing. Touching customers in a store increases their shopping time, their evaluation of the store, and the amount of shopping.[68] When an offer to try samples of a product is accompanied by a touch, customers are more likely to try the sample and buy the product.[69] Even athletes benefit from touch. One study of the National Basketball Association revealed that the touchiest teams had the most successful records, while the lowest-scoring teams touched each other the least.[70]

Of course, touch has to be culturally appropriate. Furthermore, touching by itself is no guarantee of success, and too much contact can be bothersome, annoying, or even downright creepy. But research confirms that appropriate contact can enhance your success.

In other cases, though, the distance people put between themselves and others is significant. For example, distance can reflect the attitude of the person who does the positioning. Research shows that a person who expects an unpleasant message or views the speaker as unfriendly takes a more distant position than does someone expecting good news or viewing the speaker as friendly.[71] An observant communicator can thus use the distance others choose with respect to him or her as a basis for hunches about their feelings. ("I get the feeling you're worried about something, Harry. Is there anything wrong?")

Besides reflecting attitudes, distance also creates feelings. In one study, subjects rated people who communicated at a greater distance as less friendly and understanding than those who positioned themselves closer.[72] (Closeness has its limits, of course. Intimate distance is rarely appropriate for business dealings.) Thus, an effective communicator will usually choose to operate at a casual–personal distance when a friendly atmosphere is the goal.

Interpersonal distance is another nonverbal indicator of power. One unspoken cultural rule is that the person with higher status generally controls the degree of approach. As one psychologist puts it, "It is easy enough to picture an older person in this culture encouraging a younger business partner by patting him or her on the back; but it is very difficult to visualize this situation reversed; that is, with the younger person patting the older and more senior partner."[73] This principle of distance explains why subordinates rarely question the boss's right to drop in to their work area without invitation but are reluctant to approach their superior's office even when told the door is open.

When a subordinate does wind up in a superior's office, both tension and distance show who is in charge. The less powerful person usually stands until invited to take a seat and, when given the choice, will be reluctant to sit close to the boss. Wise managers often try to minimize the inhibiting factor of this status gap by including a table or comfortable easy chairs in their offices so they can meet with subordinates on a more equal level.

Some managers try to promote informal communication by visiting employees in the employees' own offices. David Ogilvy, head of one of the largest advertising agencies in the country, says, "Do not summon people to your office—it frightens them. Instead, go to see them in *their* offices."[74]

Cubicle Etiquette

As the comic character Dilbert has shown, the world of daily life in a cubicle has its challenges. These tips can help you manage the communication dynamics of cubicle life.

Privacy

Treat others' cubicles as if they were private offices. Don't enter without verbal invitation or eye-contact permission—act as if there were a door. Never read the occupant's computer screens or borrow items from their desks just because you have access. Let others know when you aren't available by a "Do Not Disturb" sign or by your lack of eye contact. Resist the urge to shout out an answer to another cube-dweller's question just because you overheard it. Avoid popping up over the top of cubicles to talk to others; instead, walk over or send an e-mail or instant message. Remember, others can hear whatever you say, so conduct meetings and personal conversations elsewhere. Keep conversations with your banker, family, doctor, and sweetheart out of the cubicle. Be polite enough to not listen to others' conversations, and certainly don't repeat anything overheard. Don't use a speaker phone in a cubicle; it is rude to the person on the other end and to your colleagues.

Noise

Don't add to the noise of a cubicle farm. Keep your voice low. Set your phone ringer on low, and turn it off when you are away from your desk. Don't let your cell phone ring when you are on another call. Use headphones for radios or CDs, and use a screen saver without sounds.

Odors

Your favorite scent, whether it's perfume or a scented candle, may be someone else's allergen, so think about its effect on others. When possible, eat in lunch areas and not at your desk as your colleagues may not appreciate the odor of your food.

Children

In most organizations, children (especially if they are too young for school) are best kept away from work except on special occasions. No matter how well behaved, children may not be welcome or allowed by company policy to a shared cubicle.

Illness

Your determination to work when sick may be commendable, but you aren't doing anyone any favors if you infect everybody in the office. If you wouldn't want someone in your state of health coming to work, try to stay away yourself.

Note: For more information see Lockard, M. (2011, June 16). Cubicle etiquette: Sights, sounds and smells. *Forbes.* Retrieved from http://www.forbes.com/sites/work-in-progress/2011/06/16/cubicle-etiquette-sights-sounds-and-smells/; Smith, G. M. (2000). Cubicle etiquette. *Intercom, 47,* 10–11.

Physical Environment   So far we have discussed how personal behavior sends nonverbal messages. The physical environment in which we operate also suggests how we feel and shapes how we communicate.

Consider the way space is allocated in an organization. Power locations become apparent when we look at the amount and location of existing space given to various employees and groups. In many organizations, for instance, an employee's status may be measured by whether his or her office is next to the boss's or is in a dark alcove. An office with a window or an office on the corner often indicates higher status than an inside office with no window; any office usually signals higher status than a cubicle.

Another way in which environments shape communication is proximity. The distance that separates people is perhaps the most important factor in shaping who talks with whom. Other things being equal, officemates will talk with one another more than with the people next door, and workers in the same area deal with one another more than with similarly employed people in another area. One researcher studied workers in research facilities, medical laboratories, and business schools. He found that the frequency with which a person spoke to colleagues was a direct function of the distance between their desks.[75]

Furniture arrangement also plays a big role in the way people communicate. For example, in one study of a medical office, only 10 percent of the patients were "at ease" when conversing with a doctor seated behind a desk, while the figure rose to 55 percent when the desk was removed.[76] Even when the location of furniture is fixed, choices about seating can influence interaction. Dominant, high-status persons often select the position at a table where they can see and be seen. This allows more interaction and more influence over the interactions at the table. Not surprisingly, the person seated at the head of a table is more often perceived as a leader. Persons who want to diminish their potential for interaction and leadership often seat themselves in less visible spots along the sides of a table.[77]

This sort of information can be useful on the job. You may be able to relocate your work to an area that will give you the interaction you want. Beyond this, realize that several places in your working environment will probably allow you to interact informally with desirable communication partners. Employee lounges, elevators, and dining areas are a few examples. If you are interested in making your bosses more aware of your work, it's important to be visible to them. On the other hand, if you would just as soon be left alone, the old axiom, "Out of sight, out of mind" applies.

If you are a manager, think about arranging your subordinates' working areas to increase communication between people who should interact and to separate those who don't need to talk to one another. You can encourage communication between groups of workers by arranging gathering spots where congregation is easy. A good setting for informal contact needs to meet three criteria.[78] First, it ought to be centrally located so people have to pass through it on their way to other places. Second, it should contain places to sit or rest, to be comfortable. Finally, it must be large enough so the people gathered there won't interfere with others passing through or working nearby. Of course, if you want to discourage contact at a central spot (the copying machine, for example), simply change one or more of these conditions.

When it comes to managing interaction between members of an organization and its public, you can create the most desirable degree of accessibility by use of space and barriers. Proximity and visibility encourage contact, while distance and closure discourage it.

Time   The way we use time provides a number of silent messages.[79] Leonard Berlin, senior financial analyst at ExxonMobil, attributes his reputation as a hard worker to the fact that he routinely arrives at work a half-hour early. "That's a big thing to my boss," he says.

Many business advisers recommend that you be particularly scrupulous about your use of time during the first few months you are on the job:

> If . . . in that first ninety days, you're late or absent frequently, or seen as a clock watcher, you may earn yourself . . . negative scrutiny for a long time thereafter by your superiors. Rather than excusing any "infractions" of the rules, they'll be looking for slip-ups and a reason potentially to discharge you.[80]

In monochronic cultures, speaking within the allotted time generally shows good planning and concern for the audience. Speaking longer inconveniences the listeners and communicates lack of regard for their schedules. But in some polychronic cultures, speaking only for the allotted time would indicate lack of excitement or actual indifference toward the audience or the issue. Getting down to business quickly can be seen as a rude and insulting move on the part of a potential business associate. In many polychronic cultures, the relationship is an important part of the business at hand. If the personal relationship is not established by taking time for dialogue and discussion, the business relationship will be at risk.

Consideration vs. Candor

Part of being professional is acting politely and showing interest even when you may not feel like doing so. What obligation do you have to present yourself as being interested and respectful when you're bored or dislike another person? How do you balance honesty and professionalism?

Improving Nonverbal Effectiveness

Now that you understand the elements of nonverbal communication, you can use the following guidelines to help achieve your professional goals.

Monitor Your Nonverbal Behavior   If you have ever asked yourself, "how am I doing?" you know something about **self-monitoring**—the process of paying close attention to your behavior and using these observations to shape the way you behave.

High self-monitors are good at knowing when to adapt their nonverbal behavior to suit the situation.[81] By contrast, low self-monitors don't even recognize the negative impact of some of their behaviors. One study found low self-monitors were blissfully ignorant of their shortcomings and more likely to overestimate their skill than were better communicators.[82] For example, experimental subjects who scored in the lowest quartile on joke-telling skills were more likely than their funnier counterparts to grossly overestimate their sense of humor.

It's easy to see how self-monitoring can help you manage your nonverbal behavior. In a meeting or delivering a presentation, you might catch yourself droning on and losing your audience. When dealing with a difficult situation, your mental alarm will go off if you are losing your patience and showing irritation. Dealing with an unhappy client or customer, you can monitor and control your defensiveness.

While too much self-monitoring can make you overly self-conscious, keeping an eye on how you may look and sound to others is likely to enhance your image as a professional.

Demonstrate Interest in Others   The term **immediacy** describes verbal and nonverbal behaviors that indicate closeness and liking. Among the nonverbal cues are closer proximity (within social conventions, of course), more direct eye gaze, more forward lean, more relaxed posture, positive facial expression, and warmer vocal qualities.[83]

There's a strong link between high immediacy and career success.[84] For example, supervisors perceived as having high immediacy are regarded by their subordinates as more competent, credible, and attractive than less immediate bosses, and their subordinates are more cooperative. By contrast, low immediacy cues can be a put-off. Recall from your own experience how you reacted when you encountered someone with an unfriendly expression, a flat or hostile voice, and lack of animation.

Immediacy cues are especially important in the beginning stages of a relationship. First impressions are powerful, particularly when strangers don't have much other information available to form opinions of you. Even after you know someone well, there are times when immediacy is especially important.[85]

Indicate in the space at the left of each item the degree to which you believe the statement applies to you, using the following five-point scale:

1 = Never

2 = Rarely

3 = Occasionally

4 = Often

5 = Very often

_____ 1. I use my hands and arms to gesture while talking to people.

_____ 2. I touch others on the shoulder or arm while talking to them.

_____ 3. I use a monotone or dull voice while talking to people.

_____ 4. I look over or away from others while talking to them.

_____ 5. I move away from others when they touch me while we are talking.

_____ 6. I have a relaxed body position when I talk to people.

_____ 7. I frown while talking to people.

_____ 8. I avoid eye contact while talking to people.

_____ 9. I have a tense body position while talking to people.

_____ 10. I sit close or stand close to people while talking with them.

_____ 11. My voice is monotonous or dull when I talk to people.

_____ 12. I use a variety of vocal expressions when I talk to people.

_____ 13. I gesture when I talk to people.

_____ 14. I am animated when I talk to people.

_____ 15. I have a bland facial expression when I talk to people.

_____ 16. I move closer to people when I talk to them.

_____ 17. I look directly at people while talking to them.

_____ 18. I am stiff when I talk to people.

_____ 19. I have a lot of vocal variety when I talk to people.

_____ 20. I avoid gesturing while I am talking to people.

With practice and self-monitoring, you can manage your nonverbal immediacy most effectively. You can begin by evaluating your current level of immediacy using the Self-Assessment inventory above.

Observe Conventions   As you read in Chapter 2, some nonverbal conventions are cultural. For example, in northern Europe you can expect to greet associates with a handshake, while in Mediterranean countries and Latin America, a hug and even a ritual kiss or two might be more appropriate. Likewise, a nonobservant Western woman traveling in an Islamic country probably would dress more conservatively and be more likely to wear a head covering than she would at home.

_____ 21. I lean toward people when I talk to them.

_____ 22. I maintain eye contact with people when I talk to them.

_____ 23. I try not to sit or stand close to people when I talk with them.

_____ 24. I lean away from people when I talk to them.

_____ 25. I smile when I talk to people.

_____ 26. I avoid touching people when I talk to them.

Scoring Procedure:

1. Start with a score of 78. Add to that the scores from the following items: 1, 2, 6, 10, 12, 13, 14, 16, 17, 19, 21, 22, and 25.

2. Add only the scores from the following items: 3, 4, 5, 7, 8, 9, 11, 15, 18, 20, 23, 24, and 26.

3. Subtract your total score in step 2 from your total score in step 1. This is your final score.

When using this instrument it is important to recognize that the difference in these self-reports between females and males is statistically significant and socially significant (that is, substantial variance in the scores on this instrument can be attributed to biological sex). Whether these differences are "real" (that is, females may actually be more nonverbally immediate than males) or a function of social desirability (that is, females think they should be more immediate than males think they should be) or a function of actual behavior has not yet been determined.

Scoring Norms:

Females   Mean = 96.7   S.D. = 16.1   High = >112   Low = <81

Males   Mean = 91.6   S.D. = 15.0   High = >106   Low = <77

Combined Mean = 94.2   S.D. = 15.6   High = >109   Low = <79

Sources: Adapted from Richmond, V. P., McCroskey, J. C., & Johnson, A. D. (2003). Development of the nonverbal immediacy scale (NIS): Measures of self- and other-reported nonverbal immediacy. _Communication Quarterly, 51,_ 505–517; McCroskey, J. C. (n.d.). _Nonverbal immediacy scale: Observer report._ Retrieved from http://www.jamescmccroskey.com/measures

Some nonverbal conventions are just as strong within certain fields or organizations. The style of dress personal trainers or website designers wear would look out of place at a meeting of investment bankers, and the way you would dress or act at a company picnic or weekend retreat would probably differ from the clothes you would wear or the way you would act back in the office on Monday morning.

Actually, violating others' expectations can be effective, as long as your unexpected behavior is judged positively.[86] Dressing better and being more enthusiastic can generate positive reactions—as long as you don't overdo it to the extent that your violation is regarded as negative or phony.

MASTER the chapter

review points

- Verbal messages are clearest when they use unequivocal and concrete language, with limited slang, jargon, and disfluencies. Strategically ambiguous messages are occasionally useful to promote harmony, soften difficult messages, and make a point indirectly.

- Avoiding inflammatory language (biased terms and trigger words that convey speaker attitudes and generate strong listener emotions) will help you be a better communicator as will monitoring your own responses to others' inflammatory words.

- Use language to manage your professional identity by choosing the optimal degree of powerful language, using positive language, and limiting disfluencies.

- Masculine and feminine language differ in some significant ways. Feminine language emphasizes rapport and relationships, while masculine speech focuses on reporting, accomplishing

tasks, and controlling situations. Meet gender challenges by being aware of style differences and switching or combining styles to suit the situation.

- Nonverbal behavior is a part of every communication exchange. It is powerful, ambiguous, expresses attitudes more than ideas, and needs to be interpreted with caution because it affects career success and is culture bound.

- Nonverbal messages can be expressed through the voice, appearance, face and eyes, posture and movement, personal space and distance, physical environment, and use of time.

- Achieve your workplace goals by monitoring your nonverbal behavior. Demonstrate interest in others through immediacy and observing and adapting to nonverbal cultural and organizational conventions.

key terms

biased language   84
disfluency   87
equivocal terms   79
genderlects   87
high-level abstractions   80
immediacy   101
jargon   82
low-level abstractions   80

nonverbal communication   90
paralanguage   93
rapport talk   87
relative words   81
report talk   88
self-monitoring   101
trigger words   85

activities

1. Skill Builder

Practice your skill at using unequivocal language by describing how each of the following sentences is likely to be misunderstood (or not understood at all). Then improve the clarity of each message by introducing your message with a high-level abstraction and qualifying it with low-level abstractions. To invent meaningful low-level abstractions, you will have to imagine a specific scenario.

a. You did a heck of a job on that proposal.
b. There are just a few small problems to clear up.
c. I just need a little more time to finish the job.
d. Your job performance hasn't been good this year.

2. Skill Builder

Practice clarifying your understanding of another person's ambiguous messages. For each sentence below, construct three polite, sincere questions you could ask the speaker to help clarify the meaning.

a. I need this report right away.
b. This presentation has to be perfect.
c. Whenever I leave to go to a meeting, nothing gets done in this office.
d. I'm on my own around here!

3. Invitation to Insight

Identify jargon in your own line of work, or interview a worker in a field that interests you and identify jargon that he or she uses. Then answer the following questions:

a. How does each term make communication more efficient?
b. What confusion might arise from the use of each term with certain listeners?
c. In cases where confusion or misunderstandings might arise, suggest alternative words or phrases that could convey the meaning more clearly.

4. Skill Builder

Describe a former coworker three times. In your first account, use positively biased terms. In the second description, discuss the same person, using words with negative connotations. Finally, describe the coworker in low-level abstractions without using biased language of any sort. With a group of classmates, role-play by saying these descriptions out loud to the coworker in question. How might the coworkers react to each version?

5. Invitation to Insight

Become more aware of your own emotional triggers by following these instructions:

a. In each category shown, identify two words that trigger positive reactions for you and two other words you react to negatively:

1. A person's name.
2. The label for a category of people (e.g., "fanatic").
3. A rule, policy, or issue (e.g., gay marriage).

b. How do you react, both internally and observably, when you hear these terms? Ponder the source of your reactions (the way you were raised? past experiences?). How might your reactions impact your communication?

c. Use the same categories to identify words that trigger positive and negative reactions in a coworker. What are the consequences of using these emotion-laden words with that person? Suggest neutral words you could use to replace the trigger words.

6. Invitation to Insight

Explore the characteristics of nonverbal communication as communicative yet ambiguous.

a. Observe the nonverbal behaviors of a coworker. What interpretations do you attach to your observations? Describe an alternative interpretation for each nonverbal behavior you have noticed. Speculate on which of your interpretations might be more accurate. Verify your perceptions by asking your coworker what the behavior means.
b. Ask a coworker to observe you during a meeting. After the meeting, have your coworker describe some of your nonverbal behaviors and speculate what meanings you intended. Did your coworker's perceptions match your intentions?

7. Skill Builder

Demonstrate the impact of nonverbal communication by describing effective and ineffective examples of behaviors in each of the following categories.

a. Voice
b. Dress
c. Face and eyes
d. Posture and movement
e. Personal space and use of distance

8. Skill Builder

Choose two countries that are likely to be a part of a specific career field or organization you may work for. Find two or more gestures that have different meanings in those countries. Categorize the gestures into those that appear similar to a gesture in your culture but have a different meaning, those that appear unlike any gesture that would be recognized in your culture, and those that are very different from the gestures with the same meaning in your culture (helpful websites to begin with: http://www.kwintessential.co.uk/country-profiles.html; http://www.getcustoms.com/2004GTC/articles.html).

9. Skill Builder

For each of the statements below, indicate whether it is a less powerful or more powerful speech. If it is less powerful, indicate the type of speech it is. Then rewrite the statement, using the opposite type of speech.

a. Thank you so much.
b. You'd rather work late tonight, wouldn't you?
c. I'm not sure if this group will be OK with a new type of presentation, but I want to demonstrate it.
d. I think we need to update the color scheme in our ads.
e. I'm, uh, thinking that . . . well—we should hear the reports before we decide.

10. Invitation to Insight

Explore your present level of nonverbal effectiveness and how you might improve it.

a. Using the form that follows, identify an important business or professional context from your life (e.g., in meetings, with customers, on the phone). If you are not currently working, choose a context from school (e.g., in-class discussions, meeting with professors).

b. Using the information in this chapter, describe in the form below both the aspects of your nonverbal behavior that are effective and those you could improve.

c. Interview someone who has seen you operate in the context you are analyzing (e.g., a colleague, supervisor, professor, fellow student). Explain the types of nonverbal behavior described on pp. 92–100. Then consider your interviewee's opinion of your nonverbal communication in this context, and how you could communicate more effectively.

d. Based on the information you have compiled, develop an action plan that describes how you can improve your nonverbal effectiveness in the context you are analyzing.

WORKPLACE CONTEXT

	Effective Behaviors	Ineffective Behaviors	Suggestions for Improvement
Self-Appraisal			
Self-Appraisal			
Self-Appraisal			
Self-Appraisal			
Other's Appraisal			
Other's Appraisal			
Other's Appraisal			
Other's Appraisal			

Context _____

	Effective	Could Do Better (Describe How)
Self-appraisal		
Other's appraisal		
Action plan	1.	
	2.	
	etc.	

Mc Graw Hill LearnSmart™

For further review, go to the LearnSmart study module for this chapter.

Chapter Five

Interpersonal Strategies and Skills

chapter outline

chapter objectives

After reading this chapter you should be able to:

1. List important guidelines for giving effective praise, raising difficult issues, and offering and responding to criticism in a nondefensive manner.

2. Explain communication behaviors that exacerbate and alleviate workplace incivility and bullying.

3. Predict the outcomes of various verbal and nonverbal behaviors with regard to sexual harassment and explain communication options for targets of harassment.

4. Identify and give examples of key issues that underlie workplace conflicts. Identify five approaches to conflicts, explain the advantages and disadvantages of each in specific situations, and predict likely consequences of each style in those situations.

5. Demonstrate how to plan for and conduct a work-related negotiation.

• Interpersonal Skills and Success

What does it take to succeed in your career? Talent, good ideas, a good education, technical expertise, skills, hard work, motivation, initiative—all of these are important. In addition, because all jobs require you to get things done with other people—coworkers, customers, managers, people in other companies—career success also depends on your ability to build positive relationships, affirm others' dignity, and contribute to a positive organizational climate.

Building Positive Relationships

It's hard to overstate how important communication skills are in a career. In one survey, 1,000 personnel directors in the United States were asked to describe the "ideal management profile." The top characteristic was the "ability to work well with others one-on-one."[1] Even CEOs who manage technical workers need people skills to succeed, and poor interpersonal skills are often blamed for "derailed" CEOs.[2]

The ability to work well with others is just as important for newcomers as it is for managers. A survey of chief executive officers and human resource managers from leading organizations rated the ability to work cooperatively with others as a most desirable quality in college graduates.[3] Good interpersonal communication skills are important in careers as diverse as medicine, engineering, real estate, and franchise management.[4]

Everyone can tell stories about coworkers, bosses, and customers whose communication style made life unpleasant. Table 5-1 details some types of communication that surveys have found are especially unpleasant. You can probably recognize at least some of these behaviors in people you have worked with, and possibly even in yourself.

Table 5-1	Communication Traits of Unpleasant Coworkers

Busybody	**Unprofessional Behavior**
• Butts in to conversations	• Is rude
• Butts in to others' business	• Gossips and bad-mouths others to a third party
• Expresses opinion on matters that don't concern him/her	• Criticizes others
	• Yells or screams
Controlling/Bossy	**Unprofessional Focus of Attention**
• Tries to control, boss others around	• Talks about personal problems at work
• Gives orders without having the proper authority	• Brings personal problems to work
• Is condescending/talks down to others	• Talks about non-work-related issues
• Wants his/her own way	
Self-promoting	**Defensive and Judgmental**
• Competitive, wants to be number one	• Sees others as a threat to his/her job
• Tries to promote himself/herself	• Attacks others' behavior and judgments
• Is self-centered	• Critical rather than constructive
• Tries to make himself/herself look good	
	Distracting
	• Distracts others from work
	• Behaves in irritating ways

Source: Fritz, J. M. H. (2003). How do I dislike thee? Let me count the ways: Constructing impressions of troublesome others at work. *Management Communication Quarterly, 15,* 410–438.

Some researchers have coined the terms **emotional intelligence (EQ)** and **social intelligence** to describe the ability and skills of interacting well with others.[5] According to emerging research, cognitive intelligence quotient (IQ) takes a backseat to social intelligence in determining outstanding job performance.[6] Across the world and across the job spectrum, from copier repair technicians to scientists, IQ accounts for no more than 25 percent of entrepreneurial failure and success. The more difficult the job and the higher it is in an organization's hierarchy, the more important emotional intelligence becomes. Consultant Robert Dilenschneider contrasts emotional intelligence with intellectual aptitude: "Your cognitive IQ could be 145, and you could get a doctorate in business, but you'll never break away from the pack unless your interpersonal skills are top-drawer."[7]

Affirming Dignity

A major ingredient of social intelligence involves showing respect for others. If you ask people to describe a bad communication experience at work, chances are they will tell you stories about being ignored, offended, belittled, and disrespected. Likewise, when you ask about positive experiences, you probably will hear about people feeling appreciated and respected—even in difficult situations.[8] The term **workplace dignity** refers to a person's ability to gain a sense of self-respect and self-esteem from her job and to be treated respectfully by others.[9]

Copyright Grantland Enterprises; www.grantland.net.

Besides enhancing self-esteem and self-respect, dignity creates conditions in the workplace that improve the bottom line: increased job satisfaction, self-confidence, and work efforts.[10] By contrast, the effects of reduced dignity can be disastrous for both employees and organizations. Employees suffer emotionally (increased stress, anxiety, depression) and physically (headaches, ulcers, increased blood pressure).[11] Along with the individual damage, disregard for dignity costs organizations through decreased productivity, higher turnover and absenteeism, employee resistance and sabotage, and even increased risks of lawsuits.[12]

Workplace dignity arises from three kinds of communication: respectful treatment, recognition of competence, and acknowledgment of a worker's value to the organization.[13] This chapter talks about communication skills and strategies you can use to handle even difficult messages while respecting and enhancing each person's dignity.

Enhancing Organizational Climate

The quality of communication in an organization affects the way people feel about their work and about one another. The term **organizational climate** describes the underlying nature of relationships in work groups. The weather metaphor is apt; climates can range from comfortable and pleasant to cold and stormy. Organizations have an overall climate, which can be healthy or polluted. But within that environment, small work groups can have their own microclimates. For example, your interactions with one team might be described as chilly, while you might enjoy a warm relationship with another group.

The climate of an organization doesn't result as much from the specific tasks members perform as from the feelings they have about those tasks and one another. In fact, a positive climate can exist under the worst working conditions: in a cramped and understaffed office; during the graveyard shift in a factory; or even in a road gang cleaning up trash by the highway. Conversely, the most comfortable, prestigious settings can be polluted by a hostile climate.

Organizational climates have a powerful effect on performance. They have been linked to productivity, job satisfaction, and employees' willingness to express dissent.[14] Climates are important in virtually every kind of business and professional setting. For example, positive climates enhance job-related learning in sales organizations,[15] the ability of advertising agencies to win awards,[16] and patients' trust in their doctors.[17]

The rest of this chapter will introduce communication skills and practices that can help create and enhance positive organizational climates as well as help you achieve your personal goals on the job.

• Sharing Feedback

Some kinds of feedback are a pleasure, while other forms are necessary but tough to deliver. Whether feedback is pleasant or difficult, the guidelines below can help you communicate in ways that get the job done respectfully.

Giving Praise

There's truth to the old saying, you can catch more flies with honey than with vinegar. Sincere praise, delivered skillfully, can work wonders. The following tips can help make sure praise gets the desired results.

Praise Promptly   The more quickly you can provide positive feedback, the more meaningful it will be. It doesn't take much time to praise positive behavior, and the results will most likely be well worth the investment.

Make Praise Specific   Almost any sincere praise will be appreciated, but describing exactly *what* you appreciate makes it easier for the other person to continue that behavior. Notice how the following specific compliments add clarity:

Broad	Specific
Good job on handling that complaint.	You really kept cool, calm, and collected when the customer complained.
I appreciate the support you've given me lately.	Thanks for being so flexible with my schedule while I was sick.
You've really been on top of your work lately.	You've finished every job this month within two days.

Being specific doesn't mean you have to avoid giving broad comments like the ones above. But along with giving general praise, consider the value of adding enough particulars to help the other person understand exactly what you appreciate.

Praise Progress, Not Just Perfection   You might wonder whether some people do much of anything that deserves sincere praise. If you look for outstanding performance, the answer may be no. But you can still deliver genuine compliments by looking for progress. Consider a few examples:

"This draft of the report is a lot clearer. Adding a detailed budget really helps explain where the money will go. I think the same level of detail would help make the schedule clearer."

"I know we still see things differently, but I'm glad we were able to work so well together on the Baretti job."

When You Can't Think of Praise

The value of praise is clear, and the guidelines in this section offer advice for when and how to compliment others. But what can you do when you cannot think of anything about another person's performance to praise?

Praise Intermittently   Too much praise can sound insincere, and social scientists have discovered it isn't even as effective as occasional compliments. Praise others from time to time, when your remarks will have the best effect, but don't go overboard.

Relay Praise   If you already believe complimenting someone sincerely can improve the communication climate in your relationship, wait until you see the benefits of singing their praises to others who deserve to know. You will win the gratitude of the person you are complimenting; you will show your own sense of security and team spirit; and you will be informing others about information they will probably find valuable. Praising others takes little time, and it benefits everyone.

You can also become a "praise messenger" by letting people know you've heard others saying complimentary things about them. They will be more likely to continue the behavior, and they will feel better both about the person who praised them and about you for delivering the good news.

Praise Sincerely   Insincere praise is worse than no praise at all. It casts doubt on all your other compliments. It suggests you can't think of anything the other person has done that deserves genuine acknowledgment, and it suggests you think the recipient is naive enough to believe in your phony compliments.

As you consider when and how to praise, it is important to be aware of the cultural rules that may influence both the person receiving compliments and the audience to whom you are delivering them. In some collectivist cultures, it can be embarrassing to be singled out for praise, especially in front of others. In such cases, giving private reinforcement is probably wiser than lavishing compliments publicly.

Raising Difficult Issues

It's usually a pleasure to deliver praise. But in the real world, there are situations when it's necessary to communicate about problematic behavior. A colleague may not be doing his share of the job. Your manager may not have followed through on her promise to change working conditions. A supplier might be late on a promised delivery. Sometimes the list of problematic behavior can seem endless. Communicating about issues like these can be difficult because your message may seem like an attack on the person whose behavior is causing a problem. And perceived attacks can often trigger defensive responses.

More than 60 years ago, psychologist Jack Gibb identified six kinds of messages likely to evoke defensiveness, and six alternative approaches that boost the odds of getting a more positive response (see Table 5.2)—even when the subject has the potential to be perceived as an attack.[18] As you read about these constructive approaches, imagine how you could use them when you need to raise a difficult issue on the job.

Use Descriptive "I" Language   Many communicators unnecessarily attack the other person when delivering a message:

> "Your report is too sloppy. You'll have to clean it up."
>
> "You're always late."
>
> "That was a dumb promise you made. We can never have the job done by the end of the month."

Statements like these are often called **"you" language** because they point a verbal finger of accusation at the receiver: "You're lazy." "You're wrong." By contrast, **descriptive statements** are often termed **"I" language** since they focus on the speaker instead of judging the other person. Notice how each of the evaluative statements above can be rephrased in descriptive "I" language:

> "I'll get in big trouble if we turn in a report with this many errors. We'll get a better reaction if it's reworked."
>
> "Since you've been coming in late, I've made a lot of excuses when people call asking for you. That's why I need you to start showing up on time."
>
> "I'm worried about the promise you made. I don't see how we can get the job done by the end of the month."

Statements like these show it's possible to be nonjudgmental and still say what you want without landing any verbal punches. In fact, descriptive statements like the ones you just read are *more* complete than typical everyday complaints because they express both the speaker's feelings and the reason for bringing up the matter—things most evaluative remarks don't do.

Focus on Solving Problems, Not Controlling Others   Even if you're in charge, others can get defensive if you force them to accept an idea they don't agree with or understand. If you're up against a tight deadline, it's easy to say, "Just do it my way." Because control shows a lack of regard for the other person's needs, interests, or opinions, it can cause problems in the relationship even if it gets you what you want now.

In contrast, **problem-oriented messages** aim at solving both persons' needs. The goal isn't to solve a problem my way or your way but rather to develop a solution that meets everyone's needs. You will learn more about how to achieve problem-oriented solutions when we discuss win–win negotiating strategies later in this chapter.

Table 5-2	Defense-Reducing and Defense-Arousing Messages

Defense-Reducing	Defense-Arousing
Descriptive (Use "I" language)	Evaluative
Problem-oriented	Controlling
Honest	Manipulative
Concerned	Indifferent
Equal	Superior
Open-minded, provisional	Dogmatic, certain

Is Total Honesty Always the Best Policy?

In principle, few people would dispute the ethical principle that honesty is the best policy. At the same time, it is hard to imagine a world in which everyone told the whole truth all the time.

Explore how you can reconcile the need to be honest with other goals by recreating a list of all the opportunities you had to tell the truth during a typical day. Identify each occasion when you chose to either:

1. Tell even a partial lie (e.g., saying "Nothing's wrong" when you are bothered).

2. Hedge the truth by equivocating (e.g., saying, "That's an interesting idea" instead of saying, "I don't think that idea will work").

3. Keep quiet instead of volunteering the truth.

Based on your self-analysis, construct a principled yet pragmatic code of ethics involving honesty.

Be Honest: Don't Manipulate Once people discover they have been manipulated, a defensive reaction is almost guaranteed. As Roger Fisher and Scott Brown explain, "If one statement of mine in a hundred is false, you may choose not to rely on me at all. Unless you can develop a theory of when I am honest and when I am not, your discovery of a small dishonesty will cast doubt over everything I say and do."[19]

By contrast, simple honesty is less likely to generate defensiveness, even when the news isn't welcome. Even though others might sometimes dislike what you have to say, your reputation for candor can earn you the respect of subordinates, coworkers, and management.

Show Concern for Others Indifference—lack of acknowledgment or concern for others—is likely to trigger a defensive reaction. By contrast, a genuine message of interest can do wonders. The customer support agent who takes the time to find the right person to answer your questions can leave you feeling grateful and worthwhile, encouraging you to do business with that company again. The manager who seems genuinely concerned with your opinions—even if she doesn't agree with them—is easier to work with than one who brushes your concerns aside.

Demonstrate an Attitude of Equality Neither talents nor job titles justify arrogance. Al Neuharth, founder of *USA Today,* earned a reputation as a tough, abrasive boss. Comments like the following one suggest why: "When I criticize a female or when I criticize a grossly overweight person or anybody else, it's because, damn it, I think they ought to do better, just as I do."[20]

The essence of a positive attitude is *respect.* Communication expert Kerry Patterson explains that respect is essential, just like the air we breathe: "If you take it away, it's all people can think about. At that point, the conversation is all about defending dignity."[21] Respect often comes from how we construct

"I'll take care of it impersonally."

© Bruce Eric Kaplan/The New Yorker Collection/www.cartoonbank.com.

messages. Consider, for example, the difference between saying, "Could you get me the files?" and demanding, "Get me the files." As this example illustrates, *how* we speak and act can be more important than the words themselves. When expressing yourself, pay close attention not only to what you say, but also to your nonverbal behavior, including your vocal tone and facial expression.

Keep an Open Mind   Listening with an open mind makes good sense. Whether the people you're dealing with are in your department or another, subordinates or customers, they probably have knowledge that you don't. Hearing them out may teach you something useful. Besides providing useful information, listening open mindedly can promote good relationships. Take a moment and reflect on how much more you value people who consider your ideas carefully than those who dismiss them.

A tentative approach also works well when you are bringing up ideas. Paradoxically, you may get a better hearing if you present them as ideas, not facts. As one business newsletter put it, "There's a certain irony here—the more forceful we are, the less influential we're likely to be."[22]

Offering and Responding to Criticism

In the real world of work, criticism is a fact of life. Sometimes you have to deliver a complaint, and other times you are on the receiving end of others' gripes. Either way, criticism can start a cycle of defensiveness that pollutes the communication climate between people or working groups. Despite their risks, critical messages don't have to create problems. With enough skill, you can learn to both deliver and respond to them in ways that can maintain—or even improve—working relationships.

Offering Constructive Feedback   Despite its fault-finding nature, criticism doesn't have to trigger a defensive reaction. As Table 5-3 illustrates, the way you present criticism can make the difference between your comments being accepted and considered or being disputed and rejected.[23] You can maximize the chances by strategically choosing the best sender of the message, carefully framing your message, and paying attention to your delivery.

Who delivers the criticism can make a big difference in how the feedback is received. Two guidelines will help as you choose the sender:

- *Choose the most credible critic.* Sometimes the recipient will be more receptive to one person than to another. If a choice is available, make sure the message comes from whoever can deliver it most effectively.

- *Make sure the criticism is appropriate to the critic's role.* Even accurate criticism is likely to be rejected if you have no business delivering it. For example, most comments about someone's personal life are out of place unless they affect a working relationship. Job-related comments should be appropriate for your relationship to the other person.

Once you've chosen the appropriate sender, you can decide how to frame the message. This involves several considerations:

- *Limit the criticism to one topic.* You may have several complaints, but it is smart to focus on only one at a time. Your respondent may be able to handle a single problem, but he or she could grow understandably defensive if you pile on one gripe after another.

- *Make sure the criticism is accurate.* Be absolutely sure you get the facts straight before speaking out. If even a small detail is out of line, the other person can argue about that, sidetracking the discussion from the real problem at hand.

Table 5-3	Characteristics of Constructive Feedback

1. It is descriptive. . . .

I like your report. The style was clear and concise, and your ideas were organized logically. The documentation you used made the problem credible and vivid.

. . . *not evaluative.*

That was a terrific report.

2. It focuses on behavior . . .

Slow down a little bit, and I think you can reduce the number of errors.

. . . *not on personal characteristics.*

You could be a lot faster on that machine if you were better coordinated.

3. It is specific . . .

I couldn't hear you from where I was sitting.

. . . *not general.*

Your voice isn't effective.

4. It is timed appropriately . . .

Let's get together around 2:00 PM and talk about your progress on the AMF.

. . . *not delayed or left to chance.*

Let's get together sometime.

5. It is offered . . .

Perhaps my reactions to your report would help you in preparing for next week's meeting. Would you like to get together sometime this afternoon?

. . . *not imposed.*

I've got talk with you about that report before you give it at our meeting next week.

Source: Brownell, J. (2006). *Listening: Attitudes, principles, and skills* (3rd ed.). Boston, MA: Pearson Education.

- *Define the problem clearly.* List the facts in enough detail that the recipient knows exactly what you are talking about. Be prepared to give some examples to back up your point, but don't overwhelm the other person with an avalanche of examples.

- *Show how your criticism can benefit the recipient.* Whenever possible, describe the payoffs for responding to your remarks. At the very least, the other person will get you off his or her back by heeding your complaints.

- *Remember to acknowledge the positives.* Let the other person know that your specific criticism doesn't diminish your respect or appreciation for the person in other areas. Sincerely acknowledging the positives can make the negatives easier to accept. It will also go a long way toward maintaining a positive relationship and preserving that person's dignity.

Finally, how you *deliver* criticism can make a big difference in the way it is received. The most effective feedback is delivered respectfully.[24] These guidelines can help:

- *Deliver feedback privately.* Criticizing in front of others is likely to trigger embarrassment and resentment.

- *Allow enough time.* Waiting until the problem turns into a crisis can be a recipe for disaster. It's far better to discuss the problem in depth when there's plenty of time, before things boil over.

- *Avoid sounding and looking judgmental.* Avoid using the kind of emotive language described in Chapter 4. Don't call names or use inflammatory labels, and don't attribute motives to the other person. Try to use the kind of descriptive "I" language described earlier in this chapter instead of defense-arousing "you" statements. Avoid condescending nonverbal behaviors such as shaking your finger, raising your voice, or rolling your eyes.

- *Listen to the other person.* If you want to genuinely solve a performance problem, listening can be as important as talking. Ask what he or she views as the problem. You will make the other person feel appreciated, and you may be able to generate some creative ideas for improving performance.

- *Remain calm and professional.* Even when your criticism is delivered in a face-saving manner, the other person might respond in highly emotional ways—from cursing to crying. Even if such a reaction leaves you feeling angry or defensive, it's important to remain calm. If necessary, you may need to request that the conversation finish at a later time.

Responding to Criticism

When people are faced with criticism, the two most common responses are "fight" and "flight." Fighters react by counterattacking and blaming others: "I'm not the only one who's at fault here." Your own experience probably shows that fighting with your critics seldom persuades them to back down.

Most businesspeople are too mature to run away from a critic, but there are other ways of evading negative remarks. Sometimes you *can* physically avoid critics—steering clear of their offices or not returning their phone calls, for example. Even when you can't escape unpleasant remarks, you can mentally disengage by refusing to listen thoughtfully to the criticism. While keeping quiet can seem to work in the short run, it is seldom a satisfying way to deal with an ongoing relationship in which you are constantly under attack.

Since neither fighting nor fleeing is likely to satisfy your critics or help you understand legitimate criticism, you need alternatives that allow you to listen nondefensively without losing face. Fortunately, three such alternatives exist.

Seek More Information

Asking your critic to explain the problem gives you a constructive option to fighting or fleeing. By asking your critic for more information, you are showing you take the criticism seriously, but at the same time, you aren't accepting blame for the problem. There are several ways to seek more information:

- *Ask for examples or clarification.* "You've said I'm not presenting a good attitude to customers. Can you describe exactly what I'm doing?"

- *Guess about details of the criticism.* Even if the critic isn't willing or able to offer specifics, you can guess: "Was it the way I handled Mr. Tyson when the bank sent back his check for insufficient funds?"

- *Paraphrase the critic.* "When you say I have a bad attitude toward customers, it sounds like you think I'm not giving them the service they deserve."

- *Ask what the critic wants.* "How do you think I should behave differently around customers?"

It can be hard to listen sincerely when you are being criticized. But it's easier to keep your cool if you realize that trying to understand the objections doesn't mean you have to agree with them—at least not at this point. You may find that keeping notes of your critic's comments can give you something to do besides defend yourself. In addition, this approach will show your critic you take his or her comments seriously.

HOW TO WIN AN ARGUMENT WITH A CUSTOMER:

YOU'RE RIGHT.

GOFF

Used by permission of Ted Goff.

The Art of the Apology

When you have made a mistake, nothing is as honest and potentially effective as a genuine apology. Besides being the right thing to do, apologizing can be a smart business strategy. Research suggests that sincerely acknowledging mistakes can drastically reduce both resentment and legal actions by offended parties.[25]

A complete apology contains several elements:

- *Sincere regret.* The fundamental part of an apology is a genuine expression of regret: "I feel bad about not showing up for yesterday's shift. I'm really sorry I let you down."

- *Understanding that the person suffered harm.* Show that you recognize how the other person was affected and that you're sorry: "I know it was busy, and it must have been a nightmare."

- *An explanation of what happened.* Without offering excuses, consider explaining how the offending behavior came to happen: "I got a panicky call from my grandmother and felt like I had to get over there and see what the matter was. It turned out to be nothing, but by the time I got her calmed down, it was too late to call you."

- *Corrective action.* Show that you intend to prevent future problems: "I've asked her to call my sister if anything like this happens again, so unless there's a real emergency there shouldn't be any more problems like this."

- *Restoration.* Do what you can to compensate the other person for the misdeed: "If it would help, I'm happy to cover tomorrow's shift, even though I'm not scheduled."

Source: Kiger, P. J. (2004, October). The art of the apology. *Workforce Management,* pp. 57–62.

Agree with the Criticism   An obvious but often overlooked way of responding is to agree with the criticism. Although this approach might seem like a form of self-punishment, it can be extremely effective. There are three ways to agree with a critic:

- *Agree with the facts.* Sometimes you are confronted with facts that can't be disputed. In these cases, your best approach is probably to face up to the truth: "You're right. I *have* been late three times this week." Notice that agreeing with the facts doesn't mean you are accepting responsibility for every imaginable fault. In the case of being late to work, you might go on to point out your lateness is a fluke in an otherwise spotless work record. But arguing with indisputable information isn't likely to satisfy your critic, and it will probably make you look bad.

- *Agree with the critic's right to his or her own perception.* Sometimes you can't honestly agree with the criticism. For example, a customer might unjustly accuse you of not caring about good service. After asking for more information to find out the basis of the criticism (a shipment didn't arrive on time, for example), you can acknowledge how the other person might view you as being at fault: "I can understand why it might seem that I don't care about your needs. After all, you did tell me you absolutely had to have that shipment by last Friday, and I told you it would be there. I'd be mad too if I were you." Notice that agreeing with the perception doesn't require you to *accept* your critic's evaluation as accurate, although you might indeed find it does have some merit. What you are doing is acknowledging the other person's right to view the issue in a way that may differ from yours; you are agreeing that you can see how their perception makes sense to them, whether or not you see it the same way.

- *Emphasize areas of common ground.* As much as possible, point out areas where you and the other person share the same point of view. For example:

Critic: The customers will never go for this idea.

Response: We *do* have to keep the customers satisfied. What if we test market the idea? If they hate it, of course I'll drop the suggestion.

Even when the criticism is extreme, you can probably find something in the other person's position to agree with:

Hysterical Critic: You're going to ruin the whole job!

Response: I know how important it is to you. (Then let the critic talk about the job's importance, reinforcing your agreement.)

Work for a Cooperative Solution   Once your critic believes you've understood his or her position and acknowledged at least some parts of it, he or she will be as ready as possible to hear your point of view. A few strategies can maximize the chances for a constructive solution.[26]

- *Ask for the chance to state your point of view.* If you push ahead and state your position before the critic is ready to listen, your words probably won't get through. It's far more productive to give your critic a thorough hearing, agree with whatever points you can, and then ask, "May I tell you my perspective?" Doing so won't guarantee you'll get a respectful hearing, but it gives you the best chance of one.

- *Focus on a solution, not on finding fault.* Your own experience will show that playing the blame game rarely works. A far more productive approach is to focus on finding a solution that will work for both you and the critic by asking, "What would make this situation better?" or "How can we handle this situation in a way both of us can accept?"

• Dealing with Difficult People and Situations

So far, this chapter has described ways of creating respectful communication climates. But sometimes others behave badly despite your best efforts. The following section will describe different types of difficult behavior and offer strategies for dealing with them.

Incivility

Incivility is the exchange of seemingly inconsequential, inconsiderate words and deeds that violate the conventional standards of workplace conduct.[27] Incivility can range from insensitive (checking messages during a meeting) to blatantly rude (name calling). As economic pressures mount and working conditions become more difficult, uncivil communication is on the rise.[28]

Sometimes incivility carries a tinge of aggression: casually mocking or belittling others, spreading rumors, talking down, or excluding someone from a meeting. Incivility doesn't even have to be intentional to have an impact.[29] Small discourtesies like interrupting, not expressing thanks, showing up late, and failing to return phone calls can take a toll, especially over time.

Like most types of messages, what counts as uncivil communication can depend more on the receiver's reaction than the sender's intentions. As Chapter 4 explained, swearing can offend certain employees, even though it's an accepted part of the culture in

The Costs of Incivility

It's easy to imagine how a company focused on the bottom line might view civility as an expendable luxury—nice, but not essential. Corporate giant Cisco Systems believes otherwise, and it has research to back up its belief that civility is a key business practice.

Cisco is a multinational corporation that designs and sells communications technologies and services. It has annual revenue of $40 billion and employs more than 70,000 people. *Fortune* magazine consistently rates it one of the "100 Best Companies to Work For." Cisco has a comprehensive policy aimed at assuring respectful communication among all its employees.

Despite its positive reputation and good business practices, Cisco commissioned a study to determine the cost of such rare incidences of incivility. It discovered that, even if only 1 employee in 100 experienced a single act of incivility in an entire year, the cost in lost productivity and employee turnover amounted to nearly $8 million per year. This figure didn't even include ancillary costs such as effects on other employees and customers who observed the uncivil acts, additional health costs related to job stress, and legal expenses. These findings confirm the fact that civility isn't just morally correct: It's also good business.

Source: Pearson, C., & Porath, C. (2009). *The cost of bad behavior: How incivility is damaging your business and what to do about it.* New York, NY: Portfolio.

---

some organizations. Humor is another example of how perceptions are more important than intentions. Here an employee described her boss's attempt at wit:

> When I was out on disability due to a severely broken ankle, my supervisor wrote an obnoxious letter about my injury. He was trying to be funny, but it was very disrespectful. I guess some people got some laughs from it, but I didn't.[30]

As this example illustrates, in many cases the offenders and targets have different amounts of power. About 60 percent of the time, the offender has higher job status than the target.[31] For example, bosses are more likely to interrupt their subordinates than vice versa. Supervisors can use humor as a putdown without the same consequences employees would face if the tables were turned. And if you're in charge, you can lose your temper in ways that would sabotage the career of an underling. Uncivil communication between equals or from subordinates to superiors is likely to be subtle—withholding information, spreading rumors, or anonymously posting criticism online.

Bullying

Whereas incivility can be relatively mild and unintentional, **workplace bullying** is more intense, malicious, ongoing, and damaging.[32] Bullying can come in several forms:[33]

- Aggression: Controlling through fear and intimidation, using aggressive language, making threats, and sometimes even throwing objects.
- Criticism: Nit-picking that destroys the target's confidence and competence by making unreasonable demands for work, such as impossible deadlines and expectations of perfection.
- Deviousness: Exhibiting passive-aggressive, dishonest, and indirect behavior. Sabotaging the victim behind his or her back.
- Gatekeeping: Controlling the resources needed to succeed, including money, staffing, and time.

CAREER tip

Respecting Spirituality in the Workplace

Research shows spiritual practices can increase integrity and purposefulness while decreasing stress and burnout. The challenge, of course, is to respect all employees' and customers' rights and sensibilities.

Here are some guidelines:

1. **Treat all faiths equally.** If an organization creates opportunity for any spiritual practices by its employees, it must welcome all equally. Some organizations create quiet rooms that can be used for prayers or meditation by people of all persuasions.

2. **Draw clear boundaries.** Personal practices and conversations are private matters. It isn't appropriate to make your beliefs an overt part of work. Open proselytizing or pressuring fellow workers to use any practice such as prayer or meditation, even if it has been shown to be useful, is never acceptable. Religious symbols, art, or sayings in public areas can create discomfort.

In personal work spaces, discretion is the best principle.

3. **Don't be judgmental.** Sooner or later you will encounter beliefs that are contrary to yours. If you can't listen respectfully to beliefs that are different from yours, the best approach is to remove yourself from the situation as soon as possible.

4. **Defuse hot-button issues promptly.** Controversies over spiritual beliefs are bound to arise. One person's idea of what is or isn't appropriate can offend someone else. If possible, the best way to resolve matters is via direct problem-solving among the people involved. (See the tips on pp. 132–135 of this chapter for ideas.) If necessary, bringing in management or some other third party to help work out a constructive solution is far better than letting hostility escalate.

Source: Sullivan, P. M. (2008, November 15). Spiritual etiquette at work. *Workforce Management Online.* Retrieved from http://www.workforce.com/article/20081115/NEWS02/311159998

Bullies—especially those in positions of authority—tend to be effective at making their targets look bad to others. So the target's appeals to management for help are often met with skepticism. (Is the complainer a troublemaker?) If higher-ups don't take the complaint seriously, the target is left isolated and silenced. In such cases, the bullying becomes an ongoing cycle, typically ending only after the target quits or is fired. This rarely satisfies the bully, who moves on to a new victim.[34]

Strategies for Dealing with Incivility and Bullying

It's natural to feel helpless and victimized in an uncivil or bullying workplace. But you do have choices. Based on more than a decade of research, management professors Christine Pearson and Christine Porath provide several options.[35]

- *Negotiate with the offender.* Even if you use the best communication practices, this can be a risky approach—especially if the other person has the power to affect the course of your career. Before you decide to take this step, it can be smart to conduct a risk-benefit analysis. Are you prepared to accept the worst outcome if things go badly? Do you have career options if the worst-case scenario comes to pass? If not, it may be wise to consider one or more of the options outlined below.

  If you do decide to approach the offender, consider whether you want to do so one-on-one, or whether a mediator might be able to help manage the meeting. Choose a neutral meeting place—perhaps a semi-public spot like a restaurant where bystanders' presence might moderate the other person's behavior.

Review the strategies in this chapter, as well as the listening skills outlined in Chapter 3. Imagine how you could apply these approaches, and ideally, rehearse the meeting with a trusted partner who can play the role of the person you'll be approaching.

- *Appeal to a third party.* If your risk-benefit analysis argues against speaking directly to the offender, a third party may be able to manage the situation in your best interests. This might be a coworker who can command the offender's attention and respect, or perhaps your boss. If your boss *is* the offender, your situation might be bad enough for you to take the unconventional step of going up the chain of command. Again, this approach has its risks. Your boss almost certainly won't appreciate the move, and it's possible the authority to whom you appeal might support the offender. So be very cautious when considering this high-risk approach.

- *Back off.* You may decide that retreating from the offender is the best approach. Some strategic options include communicating via phone or e-mail whenever possible rather than in person, working at different times and places (perhaps including from home if the job permits), or working with the offender's assistants or associates. It may even be necessary to back off from your workplace physically and emotionally until you can find a better situation. Avoid company social events, take the sick days and vacation time you've earned, and don't serve on committees that put you in uncomfortable settings. This isn't a recommendation to do less than your best work. Rather, it's a strategy for protecting yourself.

- *Reframe your thinking.* When you are the target of demeaning communication, it's easy to start believing you somehow deserve the abuse. But in the world of business and the professions, there's no justification for bullying or consistently acting uncivil. Once you recognize this fact, it's clear that anybody who acts rudely or abusively is at fault for behaving badly.

  Despite this fact, you may feel like less of a victim if you recognize the ways you have contributed to the painful communication pattern. Perhaps you've let uncivil behavior slide in an effort to get along. Or perhaps you've accepted a job working with or for a bully when your gut feeling or other people warned you against doing so.

Sexual Harassment

Sexual harassment on the job has always existed, but in recent decades it has been identified as a problem significant enough to warrant legal prohibitions and penalties. The Civil Rights Act of 1964 and subsequent legislation and court decisions have identified two types of sexual harassment:

- **Quid pro quo** (a Latin term meaning "this for that"). Examples of this form of harassment include directly or indirectly threatening not to promote someone who won't date you or implying employment depends on granting sexual favors.

- **Hostile work environment.** This category includes any verbal or nonverbal behavior that has the intention or effect of interfering with someone's work or creating an intimidating, offensive, or hostile environment. Unwelcome remarks ("babe," "hunk"), humor, stares ("elevator eyes"), hand or body signs, and invasions of physical space all can create a hostile work environment.

Of the two types of harassment, there is less confusion about blatant quid pro quo propositions, and most people agree on what constitutes blatant harassment.[36] There is less agreement, though, on what kinds of behavior create a hostile working environment. One person's harmless joke can be deeply offensive to someone else, and what seems like a sincere compliment to the person who offers it can sound like a come-on to the receiver.

Sexual harassment isn't necessarily restricted to a single individual behaving inappropriately. It can be caused by an organizational culture that, intentionally or not, allows and even encourages perpetrators while dismissing the concerns of targets.[37]

Sexual harassment can occur in a variety of circumstances. It may arise between members of the same sex or between men and women. The harasser can be the target's supervisor, an agent of the employer, a supervisor in another area, or a coworker. Even behavior by nonemployees (e.g., customers or people from other organizations) can be grounds for a harassment claim. The target doesn't have to be the person harassed but could be anyone affected by the offensive conduct. (Situations like this are termed *third-party harassment.*) Unlawful sexual harassment may occur without economic injury to or discharge of the target.[38]

Reports of harassment are widespread. In 2010, a total of 11,717 complaints were filed with the U.S. Equal Opportunity Employment Commission.[39] That figure doesn't take into consideration the countless other cases of harassment filed with local human resources offices or kept under wraps.

Avoiding Sexual Harassment Problems

Beyond the normal precautions and courtesy, it is smart to be especially sensitive in situations where others might take offense at your words or behaviors. Look at the situation from the other person's point of view. Could your language be considered offensive? Could your actions lead to discomfort? Read your company's sexual harassment policies carefully, know the Equal Employment Opportunity Commission (EEOC) guidelines, and be very familiar with any training and other information your human resources professionals provide. If you wonder whether a behavior might be construed as harassment, not engaging in it is probably the safest course of action.

If you have a position of power within your organization—like being a supervisor or working in human resources—you can play an even bigger role in avoiding sexual harassment problems. Some strategies you can employ include implementing and monitoring policies that won't tolerate sexual harassment, providing training to all managers and workers, enlisting male employees who are supportive of stopping harassment, and carefully examining day-to-day interactions to make sure the organizational climate being created is positive.[40]

Responding to Sexual Harassment

Most organizations have written policies prohibiting sexual harassment and procedures for people who believe they are being harassed. Options may include hotlines and human resources representatives. If you believe you have been the target of harassment, be sure you understand the policies and resources available to you.

In addition to company policy, targets of sexual harassment are entitled to legal protection. The EEOC, state and local agencies, and the court system all enforce civil rights acts relating to harassment.

Despite the government's determination to protect employees, fighting sexual harassment through legal channels can take stamina. The process can be time consuming, and targets sometimes experience depression, ridicule, isolation, and reprisal.[41] For these reasons, taking care of harassment at the lowest, most informal level possible may solve the problem in a way that doesn't punish the target. Listed below are several options, in escalating order. They aren't meant as a step-by-step guide for how to respond, but they will help you decide which options may best suit a given situation.

1. *Consider dismissing the incident.* This approach is appropriate only if the remark or behavior doesn't interfere with your ability to perform your job or doesn't cause high stress or anxiety. Pretending to dismiss incidents you believe are important can lead to repetition of the offensive behavior, self-blame, and diminished self-esteem.

2. *Keep a record of the incident for possible future action.* A record of what happened can be important if you later decide to pursue a grievance. Include the date and location where the incident occurred and a detailed log of the problematic behavior and your reaction. Include the names of any observers. You can save this record in an e-mail to yourself or a trusted colleague.

3. *Write a personal letter to the harasser.* A written statement may help the harasser to understand what behavior you find offensive. Just as important, it can show you take the problem seriously. Put the letter in a sealed envelope (keep a copy for yourself). Use information from your diary to detail specifics about what happened, what behavior you want stopped, and how you felt. You may want to include a copy of your organization's sexual harassment policy. Keep a record of when you delivered the letter. If you want to be certain the delivery of the letter will be acknowledged, take a friend along when you present it or send it via certified mail (See sample letters at http://www.colorado.edu/Ombuds/ InformalStrategies.pdf.)

4. *Ask a trusted third party to intervene.* Perhaps a mutual acquaintance can persuade the harasser to stop. The person you choose should be someone who you are convinced understands your discomfort and supports your opinion. Be sure this intermediary is also someone the harasser respects and trusts.

5. *Use company channels.* Report the situation to your supervisor, human resources office, or a committee that has been set up to consider harassment complaints.

6. *File a legal complaint.* You may file a complaint with the federal EEOC or your state agency. You have the right to obtain an attorney's services regarding your legal options. (See http://www.eeoc.gov for detailed explanations of this procedure.)

• Managing Conflict

Like it or not, conflict is part of every job. In one study, human resource managers reported spending up to 60 percent of their time dealing with employee disputes, and more than half of the workers said they lost time at work worrying about past confrontations or fretting about future conflicts.[42]

To most people, the fewer conflicts, the better. But since conflict is unavoidable, an inability or refusal to face problems can lead to job-hopping. Brenda Richard, director of human resources for the Radisson Hotel New Orleans, describes people who fit this pattern: "They don't want to solve problems, they don't want conflict."[43] The problem isn't conflict itself, but rather *the way in which it is handled.* With the right approach, conflict can produce good results. Management consultant and Harvard Medical School psychologist Steven Berglos argues flatly that constructive conflict is an essential ingredient in organizational success:

If you're not looking for ways to promote healthful conflict between people of different backgrounds who cannot possibly see the world the same way, don't be surprised if anarchy ensues or if the best and the brightest abandon you.[44]

In Chinese, the ideogram for the word *crisis* is made up of two characters: danger and opportunity. A poorly handled organizational conflict can certainly be dangerous; relationships suffer, and productivity declines. On the other hand, a skillfully handled conflict can result in several benefits.[45] It can function as a safety valve, letting people vent frustrations that are blocking their effective functioning, and it can lead to solving troublesome problems.

What Are Conflicts About?

Conflicts fall into several categories.[46]

The Topic at Hand   The most obvious source of conflicts is the subject at hand. Topic-related disagreements are a fact of life in the workplace. They involve issues including:

pay and other compensation	level of autonomy
resources	the quality of products and services
scheduling and job assignments	budgeting

The Process   Some disputes are more about *how* to do something than what to do. For example:

A project team might all agree the work at hand needs to be divided up, but they could disagree on how to decide who does what.

Members of a community nonprofit group might decide to hold a fund-raiser but disagree on how to choose the type of event.

Relational Issues   As you read in Chapter 1, along with substantive content issues are *relational* disputes that center on how parties want to be treated by one another. Relational issues can involve control, affinity, and respect.

Are we a big family, or are we a group of professionals who keep our personal lives separate from work? (affinity)

Should the company allow employees to book their own hotels and flights on business trips as long as costs are within the organization's cost guidelines? (respect, control)

Does management really welcome ideas from rank-and-file employees, or is the suggestion box just a prop? (respect, control)

Ego/Identity Issues   Researchers use the term *face* to describe the identity each of us strives to present. In a work context, most people try to present a face of:

competence	honesty
commitment	reasonableness
fairness	professionalism

Relationships do well when others acknowledge our presenting face, and conflicts intensify when others communicate in face-threatening ways.[47] When someone's face is threatened, it can add a whole new dimension to the dispute. Even though the four types of conflicts are listed separately here, most disputes involve a combination of issues. When you deal with a conflict, it's important to explore all of the dimensions on which it operates.

Approaches to Conflict

When faced with a conflict, you have several choices about how to respond. Each of these approaches has different results.[48]

Avoiding One way to deal with conflict is to avoid it whenever possible and withdraw when confronted. In some cases, avoidance is physical: refusing to take phone calls, staying barricaded in the office, and so on. In other cases, however, avoidance can be psychological: denying that a problem exists or is serious, repressing emotional reactions, and so on. In the workplace, a communicator who avoids conflicts might accept constant schedule delays or poor-quality work from a supplier to avoid a confrontation or might pretend not to see a coworker's dishonest behavior. As these examples suggest, avoidance may have the short-term benefit of preventing a confrontation, but there are usually long-term costs, especially in ongoing relationships. "I think it's better to face whatever the conflict is head on and deal with the situation as it comes up and not side-step it or go to someone else about the problem," advises Jean Stefani, a senior operations analyst at Comcast Communication.[49]

Despite its drawbacks, avoidance may sometimes be a wise choice. Table 5-4 on p. 128 lists some circumstances in which keeping quiet may be the most appropriate course of action. For example, when standing up for your rights would be hopeless, silence might be the best policy. You might simply tolerate a superior's unreasonable demands while you look for a new job, or you might steer clear of an angry coworker who is out to get you. In many cases, however, avoidance has unacceptable costs: You lose self-respect, you become frustrated, and the problem may only get worse.

Accommodating Whereas avoiders stay away from conflicts, accommodators give ground as a way of maintaining harmony. Accommodating can be an effective strategy in some circumstances (see Table 5-4). If you are clearly wrong, then giving up your original position can be a sign of strength, not weakness. If harmony is more important than the issue at hand—especially if the issue is minor—then accommodating is probably justified. For example, if you don't care strongly whether the new stationery is printed on cream or gray paper and fighting for one color might be a big concern for others, then giving in is probably smart. Finally, you might accommodate if satisfying the other person is important enough to your welfare. You might, for example, put up with an overly demanding customer to make an important sale.

Accommodating isn't always a good strategy. In some circumstances, it can be equivalent to appeasement, sacrificing your principles, and putting harmony above dealing with important issues. When safety or legality is the issue, accommodating can be downright dangerous.

Competing A competitive approach to conflicts is based on the assumption that the only way for one party to reach its goals is to overcome the other. This zero-sum approach is common in many negotiations, as you will see later in this chapter.

"It's not enough that we succeed, Cats must also fail."

© Leo Cullum/The New Yorker Collection/www.cartoonbank.com.

Table 5-4	**Factors Governing Choice of a Conflict Style**

Consider Avoiding:

1. When an issue is genuinely trivial or when more important issues are pressing.

2. When you have no chance of winning.

3. When the potential for disruption outweighs the benefits of resolution.

4. To let others cool down and regain perspective.

5. When the long-term costs of winning may outweigh short-term gains.

6. When others can resolve the conflict more effectively.

Consider Accommodating:

1. When you find you are wrong.

2. When the issue is important to the other party and not important to you.

3. To build social credits for later issues.

4. To minimize loss when you are outmatched and losing.

5. When harmony and stability are more important than the subject at hand.

6. To allow others to learn by making their own mistakes.

Consider Competing:

1. When quick, decisive action is vital (e.g., emergencies).

2. On important issues where unpopular actions need implementing (e.g., cost-cutting, enforcing unpopular rules).

3. When others will take advantage of your noncompetitive behavior.

Consider Collaborating:

1. To find solutions when both parties' concerns are too important to be compromised.

2. When a long-term relationship between the parties is important.

3. To gain commitment of all parties by building consensus.

4. When the other party is willing to take a collaborative approach.

Consider Compromising:

1. When goals are important but not worth the effort or not worth potential disruption of more assertive modes.

2. When opponents with equal power are committed to mutually exclusive goals.

3. To achieve temporary settlements of complex issues.

4. To arrive at expedient solutions under time pressure.

5. As a backup, when collaboration is unsuccessful.

Source: Thomas, K. W. (1987). Toward multi-dimensional values in teaching: The example of conflict behavior. *Academy of Management Review, 2*, 484–490.

Sometimes competition may be necessary. When an adversary is out to gain at your cost and refuses to cooperate, you probably need to protect your own interests. And where the principle at stake is too important to compromise on, you may need to fight for your position.

In other cases, though, a competitive attitude is unnecessary. As the section of this chapter on win–win negotiating shows, it's often possible for both sides in a conflict to reach their goals (see pp. 131–135). For instance, an employer might find the cost of providing on-site exercise equipment is more than offset by reduced absenteeism and greater appeal when recruiting new employees. Furthermore, a competitive orientation can generate ill will that is both costly and unpleasant. In our physical fitness example, workers whose needs are ignored are likely to resent their employer and act in ways that ultimately wind up costing the company a great deal.

Despite its drawbacks, competition isn't always a bad approach. In some cases, an issue isn't important enough to spend time working it out. In other instances, there isn't time to collaborate on solutions. Finally, if others are determined to gain advantage at your expense, you might compete out of self-defense.

Collaborating   Collaborative communicators are committed to working together to resolve conflicts. Collaboration is based on the assumption that it is possible to meet one's own needs and those of the other person.

Whereas avoiding and accommodating are based on the assumption that conflict should be avoided, and competing is based on the belief that conflict is a struggle, collaboration assumes conflict is a natural part of life and working with the other person will produce the best possible solution. The benefits of collaboration are clear: Not only can the issue at hand be resolved, but the relationship between the parties can also be improved.

Despite its advantages, collaborative conflict resolution isn't a panacea. It takes time to work with others, and a mutually satisfactory outcome isn't always possible. Furthermore, collaboration requires the cooperation of everyone involved. If the other party isn't disposed to work with you, then you may be setting yourself up for exploitation by communicating openly and offering to work cooperatively.

Compromising   In a **compromise,** each party sacrifices something he or she is seeking to gain an agreement. On one hand, this approach is cooperative, recognizing both parties must agree to resolve a conflict. On the other, compromise is self-centered because the parties act in their self-interest to get the best possible deal.

Compromise is a middle-range approach. It is more assertive than avoiding and accommodating yet less aggressive than competing. It is cooperative yet less so than collaboration. While it does not give any party in a dispute everything he or she seeks, it provides an outcome that, by definition, everyone involved can live with. As Table 5-4 shows, compromise may not be the perfect approach, but under many circumstances it produces the best possible outcome.

Handling Conflicts Constructively

When you avoid a conflict or accommodate another's demand, few communication skills are necessary. But if you decide to address an issue directly—either to collaborate, to compete, or to seek a compromise—you will need to negotiate.

Negotiation occurs when two or more parties—either individuals or groups—discuss specific proposals to find a mutually acceptable agreement. Although we don't always use the term, we negotiate every day. As one consultant explains, "Negotiations are seldom

Instructions: Below are 15 statements that describe possible strategies for dealing with a conflict. Use the following scale to describe how you typically behave in conflicts.

1 = Always   2 = Usually   3 = Sometimes   4 = Not very often   5 = Rarely, if ever

____ a. I argue the merits of my position forcefully.

____ b. I try to work out compromises between my position and others.

____ c. I try to meet others' expectations as much as possible.

____ d. I try to explore differences with others to find mutually acceptable solutions.

____ e. I am firm in resolve when it comes to defending my side of the issue.

____ f. I prefer to avoid conflict, keeping disagreements to myself as much as possible.

____ g. I defend my solutions to problems.

____ h. I'm willing to compromise to reach solutions.

____ i. I like to exchange important information with others so our problems can be solved together.

____ j. I avoid discussing my differences with others.

____ k. I try to accommodate the wishes of my peers and colleagues.

____ l. I prefer to bring everyone's concerns into the open to resolve disputes in the best possible way.

____ m. I advocate middle positions in efforts to break deadlocks.

____ n. I accept others' recommendations about how to resolve conflicts.

____ o. I avoid hard feelings by keeping my feelings and ideas to myself.

Scoring

The 15 statements you just read are listed below under five categories. Each category contains the letters of 3 statements. Record the number you placed next to each statement. Calculate the total under each category.

Style				Total
Competing	a. ____	e. ____	g. ____	____
Collaborating	d. ____	i. ____	l. ____	____
Avoiding	f. ____	j. ____	o. ____	____
Accommodating	c. ____	k. ____	n. ____	____
Compromising	b. ____	h. ____	m. ____	____

Results

My dominant style is _____
(your **LOWEST** score)
and my backup style is _____ (your second-lowest score).

Source: Adapted from Falikowski, A. (2007). *Mastering human relations* (4th ed.). Don Mills, ON: Pearson Education; Hamilton, K. (n.d.). *What's your conflict style?* Retrieved from http://webhome.idirect.com/~kehamilt /ipsyconstyle.html

Managing Conflicts in Cyberspace

In a world where communicators are dispersed around the globe, conflicts often unfold online. The following tips can help you avoid unnecessary disagreements in cyberspace and deal with them constructively when they arise.

1. **Reread the troublesome message, and share it with someone you trust.** Your first reaction to a message may be colored by how you're feeling at the time. Rereading it later may give you a different perspective. Sharing a troublesome message with someone whose judgment you trust can bring a new perspective. If you do share the message, use a printed version rather than forwarding any e-mails. This will reduce the chances of the message being forwarded electronically.

2. **Decide whether or not to respond.** The best response to some messages is no response at all. If the message directed at you is accusatory or inflammatory and the sender's style tends to be aggressive or bullying, the best strategy may be to ignore it.

3. **Don't respond right away.** When you are hurt or angry, it's tempting to respond immediately. Because you can't un-send a regrettable message, it's wise to hold on to a draft of your reply for at least 24 hours. The next day, see whether your message needs rewriting before sending.

4. **Compose your reply offline.** If you use the "Reply" function of your e-mail program to compose your response, you risk hitting the "Send" button before your message is complete. You can avoid this problem by composing your reply offline in a word processing program. When you are sure it's ready to send, copy and paste it into an e-mail.

Sources: Adapted from Munro, K. (2002). *Conflict in cyberspace: How to resolve conflict online.* Retrieved from http://www.kalimunro.com/article_conflict_online.html; Suler, J. (2004). The online disinhibition effect. *CyberPsychology and Behavior, 7,* 321–326.

formal, sit-around-the-table affairs. In fact, almost any form of business problem or disagreement—from scheduling work shifts to 'Who's going to pay this $500 expense?'—is resolved by some form of negotiation."[50]

There's nothing magical about negotiation. When poorly handled, it can leave a problem still unsolved and perhaps worse than before. ("I tried to work things out, but he just tried to railroad me. I'm going to file a lawsuit this time.") When negotiation is handled skillfully, though, it can improve the position of one or even both parties. The remainder of this chapter will introduce communication strategies that can produce the best possible outcomes to your negotiations.

Negotiation Strategies and Outcomes

A common negotiating strategy is the competitive **win–lose approach**. It is based on the assumption only one side can reach its goals and any victory by that party will be matched by the other's loss. As Table 5-4 shows, you probably will need to take a competitive win–lose approach to protect your interests if others insist on gaining at your expense or when resources are truly scarce. For example, your company and another might compete for the same customers, and you might compete with another candidate for the same once-in-a-lifetime job.

Nobody seeks out **lose–lose** outcomes, but they can arise when competitors try to gain an advantage at each other's expense. Like armies that take mortal losses while trying to defeat their enemies, disputants who go for a competitive victory often find they have hurt themselves as much as their opponents. For example, if you push for an unrealistically low price, you might antagonize the seller so much that you don't get the product you're seeking and the seller doesn't make the sale. On the job, feuding parties may ruin their own careers by gaining reputations as difficult employees or poor team players.

Sometimes it seems better to *compromise* than to fight battles competitively and risk a lose–lose outcome. There certainly are cases in which compromise is the best obtainable outcome—usually when disputed resources are limited or scarce. If two managers each need a full-time assistant but budget restrictions make this impossible, they may have to compromise by sharing one employee's services. While compromises may be necessary, they are less than ideal because both parties lose at least some of what they were seeking. Buyers, for instance, may pay more than they can afford, while sellers receive less than they need.

When negotiators collaborate, they can often—though not always—achieve a **win–win** outcome in which everybody involved is satisfied. Win–win solutions are easiest when each party's needs are compatible, as in the following example:

> Even though they were paid overtime, teachers at a preschool resented working weekends to keep school equipment clean and organized. A brainstorming session between the teachers and director produced a solution that satisfied everyone's needs: Substitutes covered for the teachers during some school hours while the teachers sorted and cleaned equipment. This approach had several benefits: Teachers' weekends were free, and they got a weekly change-of-pace from child care. Furthermore, the director welcomed the chance to observe the substitutes who were seeking full-time teaching jobs. She was also happy because the substitutes' pay was lower than the teachers' overtime.

This example shows parties working together can often find no-lose solutions to their problems. And, not surprisingly, research shows that a win–win approach is preferred to other problem-solving styles.[51] In one study, researchers compared the problem-solving styles used in six organizations. They found the two highest-performing organizations used a win–win approach to a greater degree than did the less effective companies, while the lowest-performing organizations used that style less than the others.[52]

Win–win outcomes are ideal, but they aren't always realistic. Table 5-5 offers guidelines about when the chances are best for using this approach, as well as others.

Preparing to Negotiate   Successful negotiations begin before you say a word to the other person. You can take several steps to think out your position and approach your negotiating partners in a way that boosts the odds of getting your message across and getting a constructive response.

Clarify your interests and needs   Communicators can doom negotiations by prematurely focusing on means instead of ends. *Ends* are the goals you want, and *means* are ways of achieving those goals. In their best-selling book *Getting to Yes,* Roger Fisher and William Ury show win–win results come from focusing on means instead of ends.[53] To illustrate the difference, we can adapt a story they tell.

Imagine a dispute between two office workers. John wants to open a window, and Mary wants it closed. (This issue may seem trivial, but long-standing feuds have developed over smaller issues.) At this point, the issue seems irreconcilable; but imagine that a colleague asks each worker what he wants. John replies, "To get some fresh air." Mary replies, "To avoid a draft." "I have an idea," the mediating colleague suggests: "What if we open a window in the next room? That would give John the fresh air he needs and prevent the draft Mary wants to avoid."

Table 5-5	When to Use Competitive and Win–Win Negotiating Styles

Consider a Competitive Approach:	Consider a Win–Win Approach:
When your interests and the other party's clearly conflict	When you and the other party have common interests
When the other party insists on taking a win–lose approach	When the other party is willing to consider a win–win approach
When you do not need a long-term harmonious relationship	When a continuing, harmonious relationship is important
When you are powerful enough to prevail	When you are weaker or power is approximately equal
When short-term goals are more important	When long-term goals are more important

This simple example illustrates the difference between means and ends:

Issue	Ends	Means
John	Fresh air	Open window
		or
		Open window in adjoining room
Mary	No draft	Keep window closed
		or
		Open window in adjoining room

If Mary and John stayed focused on the first means that occurred to them, the issue would never be resolved to their satisfaction. But once they identified the ends each was seeking, the pathway to a mutually acceptable means was perfectly clear. It's far better to identify the real end you are seeking and leave a discussion of means for later.

Consider the best time to raise the issue   Timing can have an impact on the quality of your interactions—whether it is the time of day or time of year. Raising a difficult issue when the other person is tired, grumpy, or distracted by other business is likely to threaten the odds of getting the results you are seeking. Asking, "Is this a good time?" or "Would another time be better for you?" can help you boost your chances of negotiating successfully.

Consider cultural differences   As you plan your approach, consider the cultural sensibilities of your negotiating partners. As Chapter 2 explained, the approach that seems comfortable to you may be alien to someone from a different cultural background. For example, the Culture at Work box on p. 134 illustrates some of the differences that could distinguish the approaches of Western and Chinese negotiators.

CULTURE at work

Prepare your statement   Think over how you can best express yourself, following the advice for offering constructive feedback on pp. 113–118 in this chapter. Practicing your message can help make your point quickly and clearly, and it will prevent you from blurting out an angry statement you'll regret later. When planning your remarks, be sure to think about how you can use "I" language instead of delivering defense-arousing "you" messages.

Rehearsing your statement doesn't mean you should memorize your remarks word for word; this approach would sound canned and insincere. Think about your general ideas and perhaps a few key phrases you'll use to make your ideas clear.

Conducting the Negotiation   The win–win approach is most successful when it follows the steps described below.

Identify the ends both parties are seeking   As you read earlier, seemingly irreconcilable conflicts can be resolved if negotiators focus on their needs and not on positions. Consider the example of a parent who has found the traditional work schedule isn't compatible with his child care responsibilities. Here are the ends the employee and the boss identified:

Employee: Make sure the children are cared for after school.

Boss: Make sure employee's productivity doesn't drop.

Both: Keep the employee on the job. Keep a positive relationship.

Brainstorm a list of possible solutions   Once both parties have identified the ends they are seeking, the next step is to develop a list of solutions that might satisfy each party's needs. Recall the problem-oriented approach introduced earlier in this chapter: Instead of working against one another (How can I defeat you?), the parties work together against the problem (How can we beat the problem?).

Consider again the case of the employee trying to have his child cared for after school. In this case, a number of potential win–win solutions are worth exploring:

- The employee could do some work at home during nonbusiness hours.
- The company could offer flexible work hours so employees can get their jobs done when children are at school or being cared for by others.
- The employee could share his full-time position with another worker, giving the boss the coverage the boss needs and the employee the free time. If the employee needs additional income, he could take part-time work that could be done at home at his convenience.
- The boss could subsidize after-school child care on the assumption that productivity would rise and absenteeism decline when employees' children are being cared for.

While not all of the above options are likely to be workable, the key to successful brainstorming is to avoid judging any possible solutions for the time being. Nothing deflates creativity and increases defensiveness as much as saying, "That won't work." You can judge the quality of each idea later; but for now, the key is quantity. Perhaps one person's unworkable idea will spark a productive suggestion.

Evaluate the alternative solutions   After brainstorming as many ideas as possible, decide which ones are most promising. During this stage, it is still critical to work for an answer that meets all parties' important needs. Cooperation will come only if everyone feels satisfied with the solution.

Implement and follow up on the solution   Once the best plan is chosen, make sure everyone understands it; then give it a try. Even the most appealing plans may need revision when put into action. After a reasonable amount of time, plan to meet with the other parties to discuss how the solution is working out. If necessary, identify the needs that are still unmet, and then repeat the problem-solving procedure.

MASTER **the chapter**

review points

- Interpersonal skills are essential for a successful career. They help create positive relationships, improve organizational climates, and affirm others' dignity.
- A key ingredient of social intelligence is the ability to treat others with respect, even when disagreeing.
- Effective praise creates and maintains positive communication climates. Praise is most effective when it recognizes progress, is specific, prompt, and sincere.
- When raising difficult matters, the odds of success are made greater by using descriptive "I" language rather than accusatory "you" language, focusing on solving problems rather than

imposing solutions, being honest, showing concern for others, and reflecting attitudes of equality and open-mindedness.
- Criticism is most likely to be successful when delivered by the most credible sender and framed to benefit the recipient. It should be delivered respectfully, privately, and without judgment.
- Criticism can be handled nondefensively by seeking more information and finding ways to agree with the critic without compromising one's principles.
- Whether unintentional or deliberate, sexual harassment is illegal. The target of harassment can employ a variety of escalating response options, depending on the circumstances.

- On-the-job conflicts can be handled most constructively by exploring the root causes, choosing the best approach (avoiding, accommodating, competing, collaborating, or compromising), and negotiating a mutually acceptable agreement.

- Successful negotiating requires clarifying interests and needs (ends and means), careful timing and preparation, and managing issues respectfully. Parties in a negotiation can employ several strategies, the ideal being a win–win approach in which the best solution that satisfies all parties is implemented.

key terms

compromise   129
descriptive statement   114
emotional intelligence   110
hostile work environment   123
"I" language   114
incivility   120
lose–lose approach   131
negotiation   129
organizational climate   111

problem-oriented messages   114
quid pro quo sexual harassment   123
social intelligence   110
win–lose approach   131
win–win approach   132
workplace bullying   121
workplace dignity   110
"you" language   114

activities

1. Invitation to Insight

Recall two or three instances in which you have enacted troublesome communicative behaviors (see Table 5-1).

a. Identify which types of behaviors you enacted. What circumstances led you to enact these behaviors?
b. What were the results of these behaviors for you and the other people involved?
c. Describe specifically how you could have behaved less defensively.

2. Skill Builder

Convert each of the following defense-arousing messages to a defense-reducing statement. In each

statement, use descriptive "I" language (p. 114) and unequivocal terms (pp. 79–80). Create details about the situation as necessary.

a. "I sure wish I had someone to help me with this project."
b. "Look . . . stop asking questions and just get it done."
c. "You may think you know how to handle the situation, but you really don't have enough experience. I'm the boss, and I know when an assignment is over your head."
d. "What a lame idea. A formal reception with paper plates! I can't believe you'd even suggest that."
e. "If you want to keep your job, you had better round up 10 new accounts by Monday."

3. Invitation to Insight

Familiarize yourself with effective praise by completing the following exercise:

a. Recall three situations in which someone has praised you. Using the guidelines on pp. 112–113, evaluate the praise you received. Was it specific? Sincere? How did the praise impact you?

b. Think of three coworkers or acquaintances you could praise sincerely. How could you deliver the praise effectively? For each, write a short statement or paragraph expressing your praise.

4. Skill Builder

Practice your ability to manage criticism constructively by creating a brief role play with a partner based on one of the scenarios below (or use any critical message you are likely to receive on the job).

A coworker accuses you of trying to ingratiate yourself with (kiss up to) the boss.

A hard-to-please client snaps at you about not returning his phone calls in a timely manner.

You forgot to proofread the budget committee's minutes before you distributed them; you accidentally mistyped several of the budget figures and the boss is upset.

You walk through a coworker's work area on the way to the drinking fountain. She barks, "Can't you give me some space to do my job?"

At a meeting, you present a proposal that angers one of your coworkers. He attacks you verbally, claiming you don't have your facts right.

Your supervisor criticizes you for taking too long to finish a job.

Enact the role play three times as follows:

a. The sender of the message uses judgmental language, and the receiver responds defensively.

b. The sender uses judgmental language. The receiver responds nondefensively, using the skills described on pp. 118–120.

c. The sender delivers the criticism as constructive feedback, using the guidelines on pp. 113–118. The receiver responds nondefensively.

Discuss the impact each approach is likely to have (1) on the relational climate and (2) on future interactions between these employees. Explain your answer by using the communication model in Chapter 1.

5. Invitation to Insight

Recall two conflicts you've been involved in recently.

a. For each, identify the primary source of conflict described on p. 126 (topic, process, relational, ego/identity). Do you think the other party(ies) would agree about the primary source of the conflict? Why or why not?

b. Next, identify any secondary sources of each conflict.

c. How did each dimension affect the way the participants approached the conflict?

6. Skill Builder

Describe an avoiding, accommodating, competing, collaborating, and compromising response to each of the following situations. Then decide which approach you would recommend. Because the meaning of a message varies with the context, you will need to decide on the specifics of the situation to make an informed choice. Explain your choice, using the information on p. 128.

a. At 4:30 PM a boss asks her assistant to work late to retype a 25-page report due the next morning. The assistant has already purchased nonrefundable tickets to attend a concert that evening.

b. The coworker with whom you share a small cubicle habitually leaves papers, files, and books strewn all over her desk. The litter bugs you. Besides, you are concerned it gives your clients a bad impression.

c. The assistant manager of a bookstore is faced with a customer demanding a refund for a book he claims was a gift. The book has several crumpled pages and a torn cover.

d. You are facilitator of a student group writing a research report worth half of your grade for the term. One group member misses two meetings without contacting you. When he returns, he explains he had a family emergency and asks what he can do to make up the work.

7. Skill Builder

Sharpen your skill at knowing when and how to raise difficult issues by following these steps:

a. Develop a defensiveness-reducing message for each of the following situations in your professional life:

1. Making a difficult request.
2. Describing a problem involving the recipient of your message.
3. Offering a suggestion.

b. Practice each message with a partner until you are confident it is organized and delivered as effectively as possible. Recording your rehearsal can provide valuable feedback.

c. Now discuss with your partner the potential benefits and drawbacks of delivering each assertive message.

8. Skill Builder

In the following conflicts, identify the type(s) of conflict (topic, process, relational, ego/identity) and the ends each party desires. For each situation, identify solutions (means to the end) that can satisfy the needs of everyone involved.

a. A landlord and tenant disagree about who should pay for an obviously necessary paint job for the office space.

b. Two coworkers contributed equally to developing a proposal for an important client. They both want to be the one who delivers the final proposal.

c. A sales manager and sales representatives disagree over the quota necessary to earn bonuses.

d. In a company with limited resources to spend on a new project, the marketing manager wants more money to be spent on advertising, while the product development manager wants a greater budget for researching new product lines.

9. Skill Builder

With a partner, select one of the following situations. Plan how you would prepare for and conduct the negotiation, working through each step on pp. 132–135. Provide details as necessary to explain the situation.

a. You want to ask for a raise.
b. You and your coworkers would like your boss to hire an additional worker so you can accomplish all the necessary work in a timely fashion, without burnout.

c. You want to rent office space for your small business at a rate that is 5 to 10 percent less than the advertised price.
d. You need an extra week to complete a long, complex assignment.

10. Invitation to Insight

With your group, refer to the Ethical Challenge titled Is Total Honesty Always the Best Policy? on p. 115. Describe two equivocal statements you (or someone you know) once used purposefully to disguise the blunt truth. Select one statement you believe was ethical and one you believe was not ethical. Explain your reasoning. You may wish to refer to the Ethical Dimensions of Communication presented on p. 26 of your text.

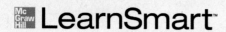

For further review, go to the LearnSmart study module for this chapter.

Chapter Six
Principles of Interviewing

chapter objectives

After reading this chapter you should be able to:

1. Explain how to define interview goals, identify and analyze the other interview party, and choose the best interview structure.

2. Demonstrate knowledge of the uses and limitations of each type of interview question: primary, secondary, closed, open, factual, opinion, direct, indirect, hypothetical, and critical incident.

3. Describe the purpose of and appropriate conduct during each stage of an interview: opening, body, and conclusion.

4. Plan and conduct an information-gathering interview to assist you in a current work or school project; plan and conduct a career research interview that will help you clarify and/ or achieve your career goals.

5. Identify and demonstrate the steps to prepare for, participate in, and follow up after an employment interview.

6. Describe features and common uses of various types of employment interviews and explain ways to prepare for each.

7. Distinguish between legal and illegal employment interview questions and identify advantages and disadvantages of each of four methods of responding to illegal questions.

8. Describe and observe the ethical obligations of interviewers and interviewees.

Before reading further, examine the Case Study on p. 143. Each of the conversations Gina needs to have is an **interview**—a two-party interaction in which at least one party has a specific, serious purpose and that usually involves the asking and answering of questions.[1]

Interviews play a central role in the world of work. Organizations use *employment interviews* (sometimes called *selection interviews*) to identify the best candidates for a job. Supervisors use *performance appraisal interviews* to review employees' performance and help set targets for the future. And when there are problems, they use *disciplinary interviews* to deal with misconduct

or poor performance. Human resources personnel use *exit interviews* to help determine why a person is leaving an organization and to solicit feedback on possible problems in the organization.

Health care providers, attorneys, counselors, and salespeople regularly use *diagnostic interviews* to detect problems and gather information that helps them to respond to their clients' needs. Police officers, journalists, and social workers use *investigative interviews* to help determine the causes of a problem. Businesspeople conduct *research interviews* to gather information upon which to base future decisions. For example, advertising and marketing professionals use *survey interviews* to gather information from a number of people with the intention of using that information to better understand the people they want to reach. Because interviews are important to so many aspects of working life, communication authorities claim interviews are the most common form of planned communication.[2]

Whatever their type, interviews share some common characteristics. First, interviews always involve *two parties*. While there may be several interviewers (as sometimes occurs in employment situations) or multiple respondents (as in a "meet the press" journalistic format), there are always two parties: interviewer and respondent. Second, interviewing is always *purposeful*. Unlike more casual conversations, an interview includes at least one participant who has a serious, predetermined goal. Third, there is a focus on asking and answering *questions*. Questions are the basic "tools" of an interview. They are developed and used to gather information and direct the flow of the exchange.

By now you can begin to see interviews differ from other types of communication exchanges in several ways. Most important, interviews are more *structured* than most conversations. As you will soon learn, every good interview has several distinct phases. Interviews also have an element of *control* not present in more casual interaction. The interviewer's job is to keep the conversation moving toward a predetermined goal. A final difference between interviewing and other conversations involves the *amount of speaking* by each party. While speakers in most informal conversations speak equally, experts suggest participation in most interviews ought to be distributed in roughly a 70 to 30 percent ratio, with the interviewee doing most of the talking.[3]

• Interviewing Strategies

Every good interview shares some common characteristics and communication strategies. The following pages introduce the skills you can use in virtually every interview you face in your career, either as interviewer or interviewee.

Planning the Interview

A successful interview begins before the parties face each other. Whether you are the interviewer or the respondent, doing background work can mean the difference between success and failure.

Define the Goal   Sometimes the purpose of an interview isn't as obvious as it seems at first. In a medical setting, for example, is the goal simply to get information from a patient or is it to build a long-term relationship of trust? Is your goal in a performance appraisal interview to ask for specific changes or simply to have your past concerns acknowledged?

In any interview, you should make your goal as clear as possible:

Vague:	Learn about prospective web designers.
Better:	Evaluate which web designer can do the best job for us.
Best:	Determine which web designer can create and maintain an affordable website that attracts and retains customers.

The interviewee should also have a clear purpose. Notice, for example, the interviewee's purposes with regard to employment interviews:

Vague:	Represent myself well on the job interview.
Better:	Describe my relevant work experience and explain my fit for the position.
Best:	Persuade interviewer I am the best candidate for the position.

The Coffee Bar

Not bad for a 20-year-old, thinks Gina deSilva. I'm the youngest store manager in the history of The Coffee Bar. With this job it will take me a little longer to get my degree, but I won't have to take out student loans and I'll leave school with some real management experience. That should make me much more employable after I graduate.

Gina knows this job won't be easy. As a start, she begins a mental "to do" list of the people she needs to interview.

- *Clarify Marty's expectations of me.* Now that I'm store manager, Marty (the regional manager) will be my boss. I don't know him well, and I need to understand what he wants me to do. What are his priorities? What problems does he see with the store? What does he think of me? Better find out.

- *Hire assistant manager to replace me.* Interview Rashid and Samantha, the top candidates. Rashid is more experienced and sociable, but can I count on him to put the store first when it conflicts with his band? Samantha is serious, but her in-your-face style rubs some clerks the wrong way. Can she learn to be a little less aggressive? Also, I need to be sure whoever I hire is committed to staying with the job for at least a year.

- *Hire two new clerks.* We need to hire two new salesclerks soon. What skills and attitudes are we looking for? How can I handle the interviews to be sure we get the best people?

- *Figure how to cut employee turnover.* We've had to replace 7 out of 10 baristas in the last year. I'm not sure why so many people have left. Training new staff takes a lot of time, and new people don't serve the customers well until they have figured out our routine. I need to talk with the three veteran clerks who are still here and the new ones. I could also track down people who left the store and find out why they quit.

- *Do market research with customers.* Sales have been off since Starbucks opened in the mall. I need to talk with our customers to find out how to keep them here. I also need to track down customers we've lost and find out how to get them back.

Identify and Analyze the Other Party   You can't always choose who you'll interview with, but when you do have options, picking the right person can make your conversation more useful and successful. Mark McCormack, owner of a sports promotion agency, explains:

> One of the biggest problems we have had as a sales organization is figuring out who within another company will be making a decision on what. Very often in our business we don't know if it's the advertising department, the marketing department, or someone in PR, or corporate communications. It may very well turn out to be the chairman and CEO of a multibillion-dollar corporation if the subject is of personal interest to him.[4]

Finding the right interviewee isn't only important in sales. For example, if you want to know more about the safety procedures in a manufacturing area, the plant manager can tell you more about them than, say, the publicity staff—who probably get their information from the plant manager anyway.

Prepare a List of Topics   A list of topics will help you get all the information you need to accomplish your goal. An office manager who is purchasing new tablet computers for the staff might consider the following topics when interviewing sales representatives from different companies.

Objective: To purchase tablet computers that will be affordable, reliable, and compatible with our current setup.

List of Topics:

- Wireless and networking capabilities
- Compatibility with existing software and operating systems
- Pricing and quantity discounts
- Warrantees and tech support

Choose the Best Interview Structure   There are several types of interview structures. As Table 6-1 illustrates, each calls for different levels of planning and produces different results.

A **structured interview** consists of a standardized list of questions that allow only a limited range of answers with no follow-up: "How many televisions do you own?" "Which of the following words best describes your evaluation of the company?" Structured interviews are preferable when the goal is to get standardized responses from a large number of people, as in market research and opinion polls. They are less appropriate in most other situations.

As its name suggests, an **unstructured interview** stands in contrast to its structured counterpart. The interviewer has a goal and perhaps a few topical areas in mind but no list of questions. Unstructured interviews allow considerable flexibility about the amount of time they take and the nature of the questioning. They permit the conversation to flow in whatever direction seems most productive.

Unstructured interviews are usually spur-of-the-moment events. For example, you might meet a useful contact at a party and use the opportunity to explore career options. Or a manager might find herself conducting one when an employee raises a concern. Unstructured interviewing looks easy when it's done with skill, but it's actually difficult. It's easy to lose track of time or to focus too much on one topic and neglect others.

The **moderately structured interview** combines other types of features. The interviewer prepares a list of topics, anticipates their probable order, and designs major questions and possible follow-up probes. The planned questions ensure coverage of important areas, while allowing for examination of important but unforeseen topics. Moderately structured interviews are well suited for most situations because they provide measures of both control and spontaneity.

Table 6-1	Differences between Structured and Unstructured Interviews
Structured Interview	**Unstructured Interview**
Usually takes less time than an unstructured interview	Usually takes more time than a structured interview
Easier for interviewer to control	More difficult for interviewer to control
Provides quantifiable results	Results more difficult to quantify
Requires less interviewer skill	Requires high degree of interviewer skill
Low flexibility in exploring responses	High flexibility in exploring responses

Consider Possible Questions

As you might expect, the type and quality of questions asked are likely to be the biggest factor in determining the success or failure of an interview. As Table 6-2 shows, a question can fit into several categories. For instance, the question "Describe some experiences that demonstrate your leadership abilities" is primary, open, factual, and direct. A question could also be secondary, closed, and hypothetical: "You said you welcome challenges. If the chance arose, would you be interested in handling the next round of layoffs?" A good interviewer considers these question types as tools and chooses the right combination to get the information he or she wants to uncover.

Some questions look legitimate but have no place in most interviews. **Leading questions** suggest the answer the interviewer expects: "You're interested in helping us work on this year's United Way campaign, aren't you?" "You aren't really serious about asking for a raise now, are you?"

Arrange the Setting

The physical setting in which an interview occurs can have a great deal of influence on the results. The first consideration is to arrange a setting free of distractions. Sometimes it's best to choose a spot away from each person's normal habitat. Not only does this lessen the chance of interruptions, but people often speak more freely and think more creatively when in a neutral space, away from familiar settings that trigger habitual ways of responding.

A manager at a major publishing company often interviews subordinates over lunch at a restaurant where company employees frequently eat together. The manager explains:

"Next question: I believe that life is a constant striving for balance, requiring frequent tradeoffs between morality and necessity, within a cyclic pattern of joy and sadness, forging a trail of bittersweet memories until one slips, inevitably, into the jaws of death. Agree or disagree?"

© George Price/The New Yorker Collection/www.cartoonbank.com.

> The advantage of meeting here is we're both relaxed. They can talk about their work without feeling as though they've been called on the carpet to defend themselves. They're also more inclined to ask for help with a problem than if we were in the office, and I can ask for improvements and make suggestions without making it seem like a formal reprimand.

The physical arrangement of the setting can also influence the interview. Generally, the person sitting behind a desk gains power and formality. Sitting together at a table or with no barrier promotes equality and informality. Distance, too, affects the relationship between interviewer and respondent. Other things being equal, two people seated 40 inches apart will have more immediacy in their conversation than those at a distance of 6 or 7 feet.

As with other variables, the degree of formality depends on your goal. A supervisor who wants to assert his authority during a disciplinary interview might increase distance and sit behind a desk. On the other hand, a health care provider who wants to gain a patient's trust may avoid the barrier of a desk.

Table 6-2	Types of Interview Questions

Type	Use
Primary Introduces new topic.	• *To open a new line of discussion:* "Tell me about your past experience . . ."
Secondary Gather additional information on topic under discussion.	• *When a previous answer is incomplete:* "What did she say then?" • *When a previous answer is vague:* "What do you mean you *think* the figures are right?" • *When a previous answer is irrelevant:* "I understand the job interests you. Can you tell me about your training in the field?" • *When a previous answer seems inaccurate:* "You said everyone supports the idea. What about Herb?"
Closed Restrict the interviewee's response.	• *When specific information is needed:* "When do you think the order will be ready?" "How long have you worked here?" • *To maintain control over the conversation:* "I understand you're upset about the delay. What date was the shipment supposed to arrive?" • *When time is short:* "If you had to name one feature you want, what would it be?" • *When a high degree of standardization between interviews is important:* "On a scale of 1 to 10, how would you rate the importance of each of these features. . . ?"
Open Invite broader, more detailed range of responses.	• *To relax the interviewee (if the question is easy to answer and nonthreatening):* "How did you hear about our company?" • *To discover the interviewee's opinions, feelings, and/or values:* "What do you think about. . . ?" • *To evaluate the interviewee's communication skills:* "How would you handle an extremely irate customer?" • *To explore the interviewee's possession of information:* "What do you know about the missing documents?"
Factual Seek concrete information.	• *To seek objective information:* "Can we apply lease payments to the purchase price, if we decide to buy?"
Opinion Explore respondent's viewpoint.	• *To seek respondent's analysis:* "Do you think the investment is worth it?" • *To evaluate the respondent's judgment:* "Which vendor do you think gives the best service?" "Do you think Al is being sincere?"
Direct Straightforward request for information.	• *When respondent is willing and able to provide the information being sought:* "Do you have a list of the employee benefits that come with this position?"
Indirect Elicit information without directly asking for it.	• *When respondent is not in a position to answer direct question (e.g., "Do you understand?"):* "Suppose you had to explain this policy to other people in the department. What would you say?" • *When respondent is unwilling to answer a direct question (e.g., "Are you satisfied with my leadership?"):* How do you think most of your coworkers view my leadership?
Hypothetical Seek answer to a "what if?" question.	• *When respondent lacks experience to answer a direct question:* "If you were manager of this department, what changes would you make?" • *To get input that will help the interviewer make a good decision:* "If you were me, what would you do under these circumstances?"
Critical Incident Ask about a specific account of a real rather than hypothetical situation.	• *To evaluate the respondent's experience:* "Think of a time when you felt you had to break an implicit company policy to achieve the larger company vision. Describe the situation and how you handled it."

Conducting Video Interviews

It isn't always easy to conduct an interview in person, especially when distance separates the parties. In these circumstances video interviews can be a quick, affordable way to conduct a conversation. Besides being inexpensive, video technology boosts the odds an interview can be arranged around busy schedules. Furthermore, it's easy to record a video interview for future analysis and sharing with others.

For all these reasons, journalists increasingly use video interviews. They are also becoming more common when employers want to screen candidates before investing resources in arranging a face-to-face meeting. For example, interviewers at software giant Oracle use the Internet to interview candidates thousands of miles away from its Silicon Valley headquarters. Market researchers can use video to conduct interviews and focus groups, gaining more information than could be gleaned via telephone. Finally, you can use video to conduct informational interviews, both as part of exploring career options and once on the job.

While elaborate options exist for video interviews, affordable technology is easy to use. All you (and the other party) need are an Internet connection, free communication software like Skype or Google Chat, and an inexpensive webcam with a built-in microphone.

The following tips will help make your video interviews a success:

Planning

- Confirm the date and time of your interview in advance.
- Send any necessary background materials before the interview.
- Test your equipment well in advance and again shortly before the interview.
- Arrange an alternate way of contacting the other party (instant messaging, phone) in case you need to communicate while establishing a connection.

During the Interview

- Make sure the field of vision your webcam picks up is clean and neat. (Use the picture-in-picture feature of your webcam to view exactly what the other party can see.)
- Be aware that the microphone picks up background noise as well as your voice. Try to choose a quiet setting, and don't tap your pen or shuffle papers.
- Plan on a shorter interview than you might have if you were in a face-to-face setting. A 15- or 20-minute phone conversation feels much longer than the same encounter would in person.

Sources: Davidson, S. (2008, March) *CNN using Skype for video interviews.* Retrieved from http://share.skype.com/sites/business/2008/03/cnn_using_skype_for_video_inte.html; Doyle, A. (n.d.). *Tips for successful video interviewing.* Retrieved from http://jobsearch.about.com/od/interviewsnetworking/a/videointerview.htm

---

The right time is as important as the place. When you plan an interview, give careful thought to how much time you will need to accomplish your purpose and let the other person know how much time you expect to take. Consider the time of day and people's schedules before and after the interview. For example, you could avoid scheduling an important interview right before lunch so neither person will be more anxious to eat than to accomplish the goal of the interview.

Conducting the Interview

After careful planning, the interview itself takes place. An interview consists of three stages: an opening (or introduction), a body, and a closing. Let's examine each one.

Opening   A good introduction can shape the entire interview. Research suggests people form lasting impressions of each other in the first few minutes of a conversation. Dave

CAREER **tip**

Successfully Navigating Job Fairs

Job fairs offer the chance to network with employers and to secure job interviews, sometimes on the spot. In this respect, job fairs serve as initial interviews.

Some job fairs are set on college and university campuses, where employers look for graduating students. Community fairs are open to the public at large. Some target a specific field such as health care or engineering, while others offer a diverse array of organizations and fields.

Before you go

- Ask yourself what will make you stand out from the hundred people a recruiter might see in a day.
- Gain a competitive edge by learning about the employers that interest you. Learn what positions they are hiring for and what qualifications are required. If possible, discover whether companies will be conducting job interviews at the fair or soon thereafter. You may be able to discover this sort of information from the career fair. Contact the company and you may be able to find out whether the person at the table is doing the hiring or if a human resources representative screens for quality candidates to recommend.
- Rehearse your "elevator" speech so you can present yourself clearly and professionally. (See Chapter 1, p. 21.) Bring copies of both your generic résumé and customized versions for positions you will be seeking. Dress conservatively and professionally.
- Carry a briefcase (a shoulder strap leaves your hands free for handshakes and writing notes) with a professional portfolio that you can easily pull out to retrieve résumés and letters of recommendation. Pack tissues and breath mints.

At the fair

- Arrive early. Spend a few minutes getting a feel for the way the fair operates. Is the atmosphere formal or informal?
- Don't ever ASK what an employer does. KNOW before you go.
- Manage your time efficiently: Approach your second-tier choices first to "warm up" so you are confident when approaching your first choices. Some employers pack up an hour or so before the designated closing time, so don't wait until the last minute.
- If you must stand in line, use that time to talk with other candidates: Find out what they've found about employers and positions.
- Approach the company's representative with confidence: "Hello. I'm Janya Greer. I'm a journalism and English major, and I'm interested in the writing positions." Remember, you are being evaluated from the moment you make contact.
- Always think about how your career objectives and qualifications meet the employer's needs. Have specific questions that show you've done your homework.
- Ask for the business card of anyone you speak with.

After the fair

- For employers who look like a good match, follow up with a phone call or e-mail to express thanks and confirm your interest.
- Remind the person where you met, what you talked about, and about your skills and qualifications. Add any information you neglected to mention at the job fair. Express your interest in learning more about the fit between you and the organization.

Source: University of New Mexico Career Center. Retrieved from http://www.collegegrad.com and www.career.unm.edu

---

Deaver, a national management recruiter, describes the importance of first impressions in a job interview: "The first minute is all-important in an interview. Fifty percent of the decision is made within the first 30 to 60 seconds. About 25 percent of the evaluation is made during the first 15 minutes. It's very difficult to recover the last 25 percent if you've blown the first couple of minutes."[5] These initial impressions shape how a listener regards everything that follows.

A good opening contains two parts: a greeting and an orientation. The opening is also a time for motivating the interviewee to cooperate and giving a sense of what will follow.

Greeting and Building Rapport   The interviewer should begin with a greeting and a self-introduction, if necessary. In formal situations—taking a legal deposition or conducting a structured survey, for example—it is appropriate to get right down to business. But in most situations, building rapport is both appropriate and useful. If the interviewer and interviewee are comfortable with each other, the results are likely to be better for both. Small talk tends to set the emotional tone of the interview—formal or informal, nervous or relaxed, candid or guarded.

The most logical openers involve common ground: shared interests or experiences. "How are you coping with our record snowfall?" "Did you find your way around the airport construction?" Another type of common ground involves job-related topics, though they are usually unrelated to the subject of the interview itself. A manager interviewing employees to help design a new benefits package might start the conversation by asking, "How's the new parking plan working out?"

Orientation   In this stage of the opening, the interviewer gives the respondent a brief overview of what is to follow. This orientation helps put the interviewee at ease by removing a natural apprehension of the unknown and helps establish and strengthen the interviewer's control. In the orientation, be sure to do the following.

Explain the reason for the interview   A description of the interview's purpose can both put the interviewee at ease and motivate him or her to respond. If your boss called you in for a "chat" about "how things are going," curiosity would probably be your mildest response. Are you headed for a promotion or being softened up for a layoff? Sharing the reason for an interview can relieve these concerns: "We're thinking about opening a branch office soon, and we're trying to plan our staffing. I'd like to find out how you feel about your working situation now and what you want so we can consider your needs when we make the changes."

Explain what information is needed and how it will be used   A respondent who knows what the interviewer wants will have a greater likelihood of supplying it. In our example, the boss might be seeking two kinds of information. In one case, a statement of needed information might be, "I'm not interested in having you name names of people you like or dislike. I want to know what parts of the business interest you and what you'd consider to be an ideal job." A quite different request for information might be, "I'd like to hear your feelings about the people you work with. Who would you like to work with in the future, and who do you have trouble with?"

A description of how the information will be used is also important. In our current example, the boss might explain, "I won't be able to tell you today exactly what changes we'll be making, but I promise you this talk will be off the record. Nobody else will hear what you tell me."

Clarify any ground rules   Make sure that you and the other party understand any operating procedures. For example, you might say, "I'd like to record our conversation instead of taking notes."

Mention the approximate length of the interview   An interviewee who knows how long the session will last will feel more comfortable and give better answers.

Motivation   Sometimes you need to give interviewees a reason that will make them feel the interview is worthwhile for them. In some cases, you can simply point out the payoffs: "If we can figure out a better way to handle these orders, it will save us both time." If the

interview won't directly benefit the other person, you might appeal to his or her ego or desire to help other people: "I'd like to try out a new promotional item, and you know more about them than anyone."

Body   Questions and answers are exchanged in the body of an interview. As an interviewer, create a list of questions based on your list of topics. As a respondent, try to anticipate what questions you will be asked and prepare your own list of questions.

Responsibilities of the Interviewer   The interviewer performs several tasks during the question-and-answer phase of the discussion.

Control and focus the conversation   If an interview is a conversation with a purpose, it is the interviewer's job to make sure the discussion focuses on achieving the purpose. A response can be so interesting it pulls the discussion off track: "I see you traveled in Europe after college. Did you make it to Barcelona?" Such discussion about backgrounds might be appropriate for the rapport-building part of the opening, but it can get out of control and use up time that would better be spent achieving the interview's purpose.

A second loss of control occurs when the interviewer spends too much time in one legitimate area of discussion, thereby slighting another. Difficult as it may be, an interviewer needs to allot rough blocks of time to each agenda item and then follow these guidelines.

Listen actively   Some interviewers—especially novices—become so caught up in budgeting time and planning upcoming questions they fail in the most important task: listening carefully to the respondent. Multitasking can present problems. It can be hard to juggle the tasks of asking and answering questions, taking notes, keeping eye contact, and budgeting time. Review Chapter 3 for tips on skillful listening.

Use secondary questions to probe for important information   Sometimes an answer may be incomplete. At other times, it may be evasive or vague. Because it is impossible to know in advance when probes will be needed, the interviewer should be ready to use them as the occasion dictates.

An interviewer sometimes needs to *repeat* a question before getting a satisfactory answer:

Interviewer: You said you attended Arizona State for four years. I'm not clear about whether you earned a degree.

Respondent: I completed the required courses in my major as well as several electives.

Interviewer: I see. Did you earn a degree?

When a primary question doesn't deliver enough information, the interviewer needs to seek *elaboration:*

Interviewer: When we made this appointment, you said Bob has been insulting you. I'd like to hear about that.

Respondent: He treats me like a child. I've been here almost as long as he has, and I know what I'm doing!

Interviewer: Exactly what does he do? Can you give me a few examples?

Sometimes an answer will be complete but unclear. This requires a request for *clarification:*

Respondent: The certificate pays 6.3 percent interest.

Interviewer: Is that rate simple or compounded?

A *paraphrasing* probe restates the answer in different words. It invites the respondent to clarify and elaborate on a previous answer:

Interviewer: You've been with us for a year and have been promoted once. How do you feel about the direction your career is taking?

Respondent: I'm satisfied for now.

Interviewer: So far, so good. Is that how you feel?

Respondent: Not exactly. I was happy to get the promotion, of course. But I don't see many chances for advancement from here.

Often *silence* is the best probe. A pause of up to 10 seconds (which feels like an eternity) lets the respondent know more information is expected. Depending on the interviewer's accompanying nonverbal messages, silence can indicate interest or dissatisfaction with the previous answer. *Prods* ("Uh-huh," "Hmmmm," "Go on," "Tell me more," and so on) accomplish the same purpose. For example:

Respondent: I can't figure out where we can cut costs.

Interviewer: Uh-huh.

Respondent: We've already cut our travel and entertainment budget 5 percent.

Interviewer: I see.

Respondent: Some of our people probably still abuse it, but they'd be offended if we cut back more. They think of expense accounts as a fringe benefit.

Interviewer: (silence)

Respondent: Of course, if we could give them something in return for a cut, we might still be able to cut total costs. Maybe have the sales meeting at a resort—make it something of a vacation.

The Interviewee's Role   The interviewee can do several things to help make the interview a success.

Listen actively and give clear, detailed answers   Careful listening can assure you understand the questions asked, so you do not go off on tangents or give answers unrelated to what is asked. Connecting your answers to what the interviewer has previously said shows both listening and critical thinking skills.

Answer the question the interviewer has asked   An off-the-track answer suggests the respondent hasn't understood the question, is a poor listener, or might even be evading the question.

Correct any misunderstandings   Being human, interviewers sometimes misinterpret comments. Most interviews are important enough for the respondent to want to be sure the message given has been received accurately. Obviously, you can't ask the interviewer, "Were you listening carefully?" but two strategies can help get your message across. First, you can orally restate your message in either the body or conclusion phase of the interview.

For instance, in the body phase, while reporting on a list of exhibit preparations, the interviewee might mention the brochures will have to be hand-carried; the following exchange could come later in the body phase or at the conclusion:

Interviewer: So if we hire you, everything will be at the exhibit booth when we get to the convention, and all we have to do is set up the exhibit?

Interviewee: Not quite. The brochures won't be ready in time to ship to the convention, so you'll have to carry them with you on the plane.

Second, you can *put your ideas in writing*. It's sometimes wise to summarize important ideas in an e-mail so both the recipient and you will have a permanent record of your message.

Cover your own agenda   Interviewees often have their own goals. In a selection interview, the employer's goal is to pick the best candidate, while the applicant's aim is to prove her qualifications make her the best choice. This may involve redefining the concept of best. For instance, a relatively inexperienced candidate might have the goal of showing the employer that experience isn't as important as work ethic, enthusiasm, or networking skills.

Closing   An interview shouldn't end with the last answer to the last question. A good closing will bring the conversation to a satisfactory conclusion.

Review and Clarify the Results of the Interview   Either party can take responsibility for this step, though in different ways. The person with the greater power (usually the interviewer) is most likely to do so in the most forthright manner. For example, in an interview exploring a grievance between employees, a manager might say, "It sounds like you're saying both of you could have handled it better." When the party with less power (usually the interviewee) does the reviewing and clarifying, the summary often takes the form of a question. A sales representative might close by saying, "So the product sounds good to you, but before you make your final decision you'd like to talk to a few of our clients to see how it has worked out for them. Is that right?"

Establish Future Actions   When the relationship between interviewer and respondent is a continuing one, it is important to clarify how the matter under discussion will be handled. A sales representative might close by saying, "I'll put a list of our customers in the mail to you tomorrow. Then why don't I give you a call next week to see what you're thinking?" A manager might clarify the future by saying, "I'd like you to try out the arrangement we discussed today. Then let's all get together in a few weeks to see how things are going. How does the first of next month sound?"

Conclude with Pleasantries   A sociable conclusion needn't be phony. You can express appreciation, concern, or talk about what comes next:

"I appreciate the time you've given me today."

"Good luck with the project."

"We'll follow up on this at the staff meeting tomorrow."

● Types of Interviews

Of all the interview types described at the beginning of this chapter, the ones most essential in almost every occupation involve information-gathering, career research, and employment. The following pages outline the skills required for each of these important types of interview. (Appendix I addresses performance appraisal interviews.)

The Information-Gathering Interview

Many businesspeople owe their success in great part to the lessons they learned in information-gathering interviews. Sam Walton, founder of the Wal-Mart empire, explained how he used this approach early in his career to interview executives who had information that would help him:

> I would just show up and say, "Hi, I'm Sam Walton from Bentonville, Arkansas. We've got a few stores out there, and I'd like to speak with Mr. So-and-So"—whoever the head of the company was—"about his business." And as often as not, they'd let me in, maybe out of curiosity, and I'd ask lots of questions about pricing and distribution, whatever. I learned a lot that way.[6]

Whatever the format, all types of information-gathering interviews follow the same general approach described in the following pages.

View Information-Gathering as a Process

Talking about a single information-gathering interview is really an oversimplification for you will usually conduct several during various stages of a task. Suppose you're interested in proposing a job-sharing plan—a system in which two people would share the responsibilities and salary of one full-time job. Your first step would be to research some basic questions: How common is job sharing? In what industries does it occur? What forms does it take? Has it been tried by any firms in your field? What have the results of such arrangements been?

Once you've collected the necessary background information, you can use this knowledge to plan an intelligent approach to your second round of interviews—perhaps with people your earlier research suggested or with the key decision makers who are your ultimate target.

Define Interview Goals and Questions

As you read earlier, your goal ought to be as specific as possible and worded in a way that will tell you whether you have the answers you were seeking. Here are examples of clear goals for information-gathering interviews:

> What caused the accident, and could it have been prevented?
>
> Will tax-free municipal bonds give me liquidity, appreciation, safety, and tax shelter better than my present investments?
>
> Will a database management system improve our efficiency enough to justify the purchase?

Once you have identified your purpose, you can develop questions that will help you achieve it. For example:

> *Purpose:* To learn what steps I need to take to have a job-sharing arrangement approved by management.
>
> *Questions:*
>
> - Who will be the key decision maker on this issue?
> - Whom should I approach first?
> - Should I present my formal proposal, or should I start by mentioning the subject informally?
> - What objections might management have to the proposal?

- Is anyone else in the company (nonmanagement personnel) likely to oppose or support the idea?
- What arguments (such as precedent, cost savings, employee morale) will most impress management?
- What influential people might support this idea?

Choose the Right Interviewee   Who you interview is likely to shape the value of what you learn. It might be naive to talk with your boss about the job-sharing proposal until you have consulted other sources who could suggest how to broach the subject: Perhaps a politically astute coworker, someone who has experience making proposals to management, or even the boss's administrative assistant, if you have a good working relationship, will be helpful.

After you have established the purpose and the appropriate person to interview, follow the guidelines on pp. 142–154 to plan and conduct the interview.

The Career Research Interview

The **career research interview** is a special type of informational interview in which you meet with someone who can provide information that will help you define and achieve your career goals. It is based on the principle that speaking with the right people can give you valuable ideas and contacts you simply can't find from books, magazines, the Internet, or any other source.

The Value of Personal Contacts   The old phrase, "It isn't what you know, it's who you know" is certainly true when it comes to getting a job. More than 30 years of research confirm the vast majority of people don't find jobs from advertisements, headhunters, or other "formal" means.[7] Like these traditional sources, Web-based services like Monster.com aren't as useful as they might seem: Job-finding expert Richard Bolles cites research suggesting less than 10 percent at best of job-seekers find employment by using the Internet.[8]

Instead of using impersonal means, the majority of new hires get offers for employment through personal contacts. The reverse is also true: Most employers find good employees through their personal networks.[9] One corporate recruiter explained why networking is superior to Web-based employment sites:

> In the rare instances where I actually post a position online, I get résumés from all over the world. Many of them bear no relationship to the job I am trying to fill. It's as though people just "point and shoot."
>
> The last professional position I posted—with extremely explicit qualifications laid out in the posting—received almost 1,000 responses, of whom only 25 or so even met the technical and educational qualifications for the position. My time is much better spent networking personally with people to find good candidates than reviewing and responding to these résumés.[10]

Finding a job is only one goal of career research interviews. These conversations can serve three purposes:

To conduct research that helps you learn more about the field and specific organizations that interest you.

To be remembered by making contacts who will recall you at an appropriate time and either offer you a position, inform you of employment opportunities, or suggest you to a potential employer.

Getting through Gatekeepers

Many potential career research interviewees are guarded by **gatekeepers**—personal assistants, receptionists, secretaries, etc. Even your most carefully crafted request for help may not gain you an interview if the gatekeeper is zealously guarding his or her manager's precious time. Here are some strategies for getting in touch with the person you want to interview.

Make your first request in writing

Your e-mail has a much better chance of getting through to your target than an introductory phone call. Be sure your message follows the approach outlined in these pages and that it is impeccably correct. Be sure to include your e-mail address and phone number so your target can reply.

Phone early or late

If you need to follow your e-mail with a phone call, the best time to reach your potential interviewee may be before or after regular business hours—when the gatekeeper isn't around to screen the boss's phone calls. If you are greeted by voice mail, be prepared to leave a fluent and concise reply: "Hi, Ms. Allen. This is Daniel Mosher [phone number], following up on my e-mail to you from last week. I'm hoping to arrange a time when we can meet so I can get your advice about the best ways to prepare myself for breaking into the field of _____. My professor, Dr. Joy Chen, says you've been very helpful to other

graduating seniors, and I would be very grateful for any ideas you're willing to share. I can be very flexible about when and where to meet. Again, my phone number is _____. I'll look forward to hearing from you at your earliest convenience."

Enlist gatekeepers as allies

If you find yourself speaking to the gatekeeper, begin by confidently asking to be put through to your prospective interviewee: "This is Daniel Mosher calling for Ms. Allen." If the reply is something like, "She's in a meeting now. May I help?" your best approach may be to enlist the gatekeeper's assistance. For example: "I'd appreciate your advice. I'm following up on a letter I sent to Ms. Allen last week, and would like to set up a meeting with her. Could you suggest a time for an appointment, or maybe a time when I could call back and talk to her?" Be sure you get the gatekeeper's name, and address him or her personally from this point on.

Be flexible

Because you are asking for a favor, make yourself available for a meeting whenever it's convenient for your interviewee. Consider offering to conduct your interview over a meal or cup of coffee. One ambitious student even offered to chauffer his interviewee to the airport—a 90-minute drive. He argued that the chance to have an uninterrupted conversation made the effort well worthwhile.

To gain referrals to other people whom you might contact for help in your job search. These referrals can easily lead to meetings with more useful contacts, all of whom might mention you to *their* friends and associates.

Choosing Interviewees
The key to finding the wealth of unadvertised positions is to cultivate a network of contacts who can let you know about job opportunities and pass along your name to potential employers. Chapter 1 (pp. 22–25) offered tips on how to build and nurture a personal network.

There's no doubt the people in your immediate networks can be helpful. But surprisingly, you can benefit even more from more-distant connections who are connected to other, less familiar communication networks that often contain valuable information about new jobs.[11]

You might wonder why the kind of important person you're seeking would be willing to meet with you. There are actually several reasons. First, if you have made contact through a referral, your subject will probably see you in deference to your mutual acquaintance. If you can gain a referral, you're most likely to get a friendly reception. Second, interviewees might be willing to see you for ego gratification. It's flattering to have someone say, "I respect your accomplishments and ideas," and it's difficult for even a busy person to say no to a request that accompanies such a comment. A third reason is simple altruism. Most successful people realize they received help somewhere along the line, and many are willing to do for you what others did for them. Finally, you may get an interview because the person recognizes you as ambitious—someone who might have something to offer his or her organization.

Contacting Prospective Interviewees   When you approach a career research interviewee—especially one you don't know well—it can be smart to make your first contact in writing, sent by e-mail. A telephone call runs the risk of not getting through; even if you do reach the interviewee, your call may come at a bad time. Your first message, like the one in Figure 6.1, should introduce yourself, explain your reason for the interview (stressing that you are *not* seeking employment), state your availability for a meeting, and promise a follow-up telephone call.

Unless you'll be conducting the interview within a day or two of the time your interviewee agrees to meet with you, a second e-mail or phone call should precede the interview and confirm its date, place, and time. This sort of follow-up can save you the frustration of being stood up by a forgetful interviewee. Just as important, it shows that you know how to handle business engagements professionally.

FIGURE 6.1
Request for Informational Interview

From: Emily Park <eprk112@sunnet.net>
Sent: Tuesday, May 25, 2013 12:51 PM
To: Vanessa J. Yoder <v.yoder@DGHattysatlaw.com>
Subject: Seeking your advice

Dear Ms. Yoder:

I am currently a junior at the University of New Mexico, majoring in political science and communication. After graduating from UNM, I plan to attend law school and focus my studies on immigration law.

From several news accounts and also from several of my professors, I've learned that you are an expert in immigration law and have a stellar reputation for representing women when the cases involve both domestic violence and immigration issues. I also heard of your work during my internship at the Women's Workforce Training Center.

I would appreciate the opportunity to meet with you to discuss how I might best prepare myself for an eventual career in immigration law. I would also like to know which law schools you would recommend and hear about the challenges and rewards of this type of practice.

Let me stress that I am not seeking employment at this time. Your advice would be invaluable as I prepare myself for a career in law. I will call your office next week hoping to schedule an appointment. I know you are a busy person and I would be grateful for 30–45 minutes of your time.

I look forward to benefiting from your insights and recommendations.

Sincerely,
Emily Park
9971 Washoe St., NE
Albuquerque, NM 87112
(505) 793-3510

Giving your interviewee an advance list of topic areas and questions you hope to cover will distinguish you as a serious person, worth the interviewee's time and effort. Also, supplying this list will give your interviewee a chance to think about the areas you want to discuss and ideally come to your meeting best prepared to help you. Figure 6.2 illustrates a confirming e-mail with a list of questions.

Following Up   After the meeting, express thanks for the interviewee's time and mention how helpful the information was. Besides demonstrating common courtesy, your message becomes a tangible reminder of you and provides a record of your name and address that will be useful if the interviewee wants to contact you in the future. Of course, all correspondence should be composed with impeccable format, spelling, and grammar.

FIGURE 6.2
Confirming
E-mail with List of
Questions

From: Emily Park <eprk112@sunnet.net>
Sent: Friday, June 11, 2013 8:26 AM
To: Vanessa J. Yoder <v.yoder@DGHattysatlaw.com>
Subject: Interview confirmation and questions

Dear Ms. Yoder:

Thank you again for agreeing to speak with me about how I can best prepare myself for a career in immigration law. I am looking forward to our meeting at your office this coming Thursday, June 17, at 2:00 p.m. I know how busy you must be, and I'm grateful for your giving me 45 minutes of your time.

In order to use our time together most efficiently, here is a list of some questions I hope we can discuss at our meeting:

TRENDS IN IMMIGRATION AND LAW
- What trends do you anticipate in immigration patterns?
- How do you view the field of immigration law changing to reflect these conditions?

EDUCATION
- What law schools do you recommend for someone interested in practicing immigration law?
- Do you recommend any courses I should take in my senior year at the university?

EXPERIENCE
- What types of work experience (paid or volunteer) could help prepare me for law school and eventual employment?
- Can you recommend ways I might pursue positions in these areas?

EMPLOYMENT
- What types of jobs are there for attorneys who specialize in immigration law?
- How easy/difficult do you anticipate it will be to secure employment in these sorts of jobs?
- What, if any, are the pros and cons I might expect as a woman practicing law in this area?

LIFESTYLE
- How would you describe the benefits and challenges of working in the field of immigration law?
- How compatible is a career in this area with being a parent?

OTHER CONTACTS
- Can you recommend other people who might be willing to talk with me about preparing for a career in immigration law?

The Employment Interview

An **employment interview** explores how well a candidate might fit a job. The exploration of fit works both ways: Employers certainly measure prospective candidates during this conversation, and prospective employees can decide whether the job in question is right for them. The Bureau of Labor Statistics reports the typical American worker holds nearly nine different jobs before age 32, so the probability of facing at least one employment interview in the near future is high.[12]

The short time spent in an employment interview can have major consequences. Consider the stakes: Most workers spend the greatest part of their adult lives on the job—roughly 2,000 hours per year or upward of 80,000 hours during a career. The financial difference between a well-paid position and an unrewarding one can also be staggering. Even without considering the effects of inflation, a gap of only $200 per month can amount to almost $100,000 over the course of a career. Finally, the emotional results of having the right job are considerable. A frustrating job not only makes for unhappiness at work, but these dissatisfactions also have a way of leaking into nonworking hours as well.

How important is an interview in getting the right job? The Bureau of National Affairs, a private research firm that serves both government and industry, conducted a survey to answer this question. It polled 196 personnel executives, seeking the factors most important in hiring applicants. The results showed the employment interview is the single most important factor in landing a job.[13] Further research revealed the most important factor during these critically decisive interviews was communication skills. Employers identified the ability to communicate effectively as more important in shaping a hiring decision than grade-point average, work experience, extracurricular activities, appearance, and preference for job location.[14]

Even though interviews can play an important role in hiring, research shows potential employers—at least those who aren't trained in employment interviewing—are not very good at using interviews to choose the best applicant for a job.[15] They fail to recognize the potential in some candidates who would make fine employees, and they are impressed by others who prove to be less than satisfactory as workers. In other words, the best candidate does not necessarily get the job offer.

In many situations, the person who knows the most about getting hired gets the desired position. "Chemistry is the paramount factor in hiring," stated the executive vice president of one New York recruiting firm.[16] While job-getting skills are no guarantee of qualifications once the actual work begins, they are necessary to get hired in the first place.

"You don't look like a Dave."

Pre-Interview Steps   Scanning the Web for openings and then filing a job application is often not the most effective way to find a job. Many employers never advertise jobs, and depending on the salary sought, only 5 to 24 percent of job-seekers find a job solely through local newspaper ads.[17] Employment expert Richard Bolles explains:

I know too many stories about people who have been turned down by a particular company's personnel department, who then went back to square one, found out who, in that very same company, had the power to hire for the position they wanted, went to that woman or man, and got hired—ten floors up from the personnel department that had just rejected them.[18]

Even when a company does advertise, the odds don't favor an applicant who replies with an application and résumé. Since most job announcements attract many more applicants than an employer needs, the job of the human resources department becomes *elimination,* not selection. As career expert Richard Bolles puts it: "Eventually they want to get it down to the "last person standing."[19]

Given this process of elimination, any shortcoming becomes welcome grounds for rejecting the application and the applicant. Many consultants, therefore, suggest identifying and contacting the person who has the power to hire you *before* an opening exists. The process has several steps.

Signs of the social networking times.

Used by permission of Bruce Evans, Geek Culture.

Clean up your online identity   In spite of your best efforts to create a résumé and present yourself as a qualified job applicant, prospective employers have other ways of forming impressions of you, including all of the information available online.[20] "Cybervetting" is increasingly common: Seventy percent of recruiters in the United States have rejected candidates because of information found online—photographs, comments by and about the candidate, and membership in groups.[21] Cleaning up your "digital dirt" can be a challenge, but doing so is well worth the effort.

To discover what others can easily see about you, begin by typing your name into a search engine like Google or Bing. The only hits may be advice you gave about training your Jack Russell terrier or a review you wrote about a great restaurant. On the other hand, you may find comments you made at meetings you attended, information about you in newspaper articles, public hearings, or court actions. You may be able to get site owners to remove things you would rather not have on record. You can learn how to "un-Google" yourself at http://www.wikihow.com/Ungoogle-Yourself.

Review your profile on websites like Facebook and/or websites you have created. Imagine the impression your profiles would make on prospective employers and consider editing references and photos you no longer want to share with the world—or at least change your privacy settings. The photo of you from the Halloween party your sophomore year or the comments others wrote about you might not create the best impression.

Conduct background research   The first step is to explore the types of work and specific organizations that sound appealing to you. This involves reading, researching, taking classes, and talking about jobs you find interesting with anyone who might have useful information. The result of your research should be a list of organizations and names of people who can tell you more about your chosen field.

Besides helping you find organizations where you want to work, your knowledge of a company will distinguish you as a candidate worth considering for a job. Desiree Crips of Salus Media in Carpinteria, California, reflects most potential employers' view: "If someone walks in here and doesn't know anything about our company, that's a real negative. There's just no excuse for not being up to speed on any company you're applying to these days."[22] Doing your homework is just as important in the workforce as in school.

Contact potential employers   At some point, your research and networking will uncover one or more job leads. You might read a newspaper story about a local employer's need for people with interests or training like yours. Perhaps a career research interview subject will say, "I know someone over at _____ who is looking for a person like you." You might learn through a friendly contact that a desirable firm is about to expand its operations. In such a case, it is time to approach the person who has the power to hire you and explore how you can help meet the company's needs.

Whether the job lead comes from a formal announcement or a contact from your personal network, your first step is to let the organization know about your interest in a job. In most cases, the best way to do this is with written correspondence, usually a cover letter and a copy of your résumé. Appendix I has advice for constructing and formatting résumés. A cover letter like the one in Figure 6.3 below that takes the following approach will serve you well.

In the first paragraph, introduce yourself to the reader. Clearly state your purpose for writing (e.g., in response to an advertisement, at the suggestion of a mutual acquaintance, as a result of your research) and describe your ability to meet the company's needs. When appropriate, mention any mutual acquaintances the addressee will recognize. If you are

FIGURE 6.3
Sample Message Requesting Employment Interview

From: Krista Dudley [krista.dudley@rockycast.net]
Sent: Friday, April 16, 2013 5:41 PM
To: John Waldmann [john.waldmann@boulderarts.org]
Subject: Events Coordinator application

Attached: 📄 K Dudley Resume.doc

Dear Mr. Waldmann:

Our mutual friend Marcia Sherwood recently alerted me to the open position of Events Coordinator for the Boulder Arts Council, and I am writing to express my interest in that position.

I would welcome the chance to use skills acquired over the past 12 years planning events for a variety of community organizations in the Denver area to help the Council extend its reach in the community. The attached résumé will help you gain a sense of my experience.

As a person who has coordinated a wide range of community events for nonprofit organizations, I can bring the Arts Council demonstrated ability to motivate and coordinate the work of volunteers and to generate widespread publicity for events on a limited budget. Most recently, I was chairperson for Aurora's Earth Day festival, and I was the public information coordinator for last year's Halloween auction and dance to benefit Denver's Shelter Services for Women. The enclosed résumé details a variety of other activities that have helped prepare me for the position of Events Coordinator.

I would welcome the chance to discuss how I might help the Boulder Arts Council. I will be available any time in the next month, except for the weekend of April 23–24.

I look forward to hearing from you soon.

Sincerely,
Krista Dudley
387 Blythe St.
Aurora, CO 80017
(303) 654-7909

writing to the human resources department of a medium- or large-size organization, be sure to give the job number if there is one; a company that has many job openings won't know which one you're applying for unless you identify it.

In the next paragraph or two, highlight one or two of your most impressive accomplishments that are *relevant to the job at hand*. Don't just say you can help the organization: Offer some objective evidence that backs up your claim.

In the closing paragraph, describe the next step you hope to take—usually requesting an interview. Detail any information about limits on your availability (though you should keep these to an absolute minimum). Supply any other information the prospective employer may have requested. Finally, close with a cordial expression of gratitude.

Most career counselors recommend directing your request for an interview to the person who has the ability to hire you rather than to the company's human resources department. We have already discussed why personnel departments aren't the best avenue for getting hired: Employees there are usually screening large numbers of applicants, so they are looking for reasons to reject as many as possible to arrive at a manageable number of finalists to interview. Also, personnel screeners are usually not familiar with the position, so they may reject candidates for superficial or mistaken reasons.

The mechanical nature of this screening process is best illustrated by the growing use of **scannable résumés**. These documents are "read" by document-scanning devices, not humans. The software searches for keywords and phrases that describe the skills and education required for the position. Applications that contain these words are passed on to a human who evaluates them further. Appendix I offers tips for creating effective scannable résumés; but even the best document may not capture the unique traits you can offer an employer. For this reason, you will maximize your chances at being recognized by developing a relationship with people who know both your talents and the characteristics of the job.

Another screening technique is job interview by computer. Retailers such as Target, Macy's, and Hollywood Video are replacing paper applications and in-person interviews with computer kiosks for initial applicant screening.[23]

Prepare for possible interview formats   The standard one-on-one, question-and-answer interview format isn't the only one you may encounter. Employers use a variety of interview formats. If you are prepared for all of them, you aren't likely to be surprised.

In a **panel interview** (sometimes called a *team* or *group interview*), the candidate is questioned by several people. Panel interviews save the company time and provide the people with whom you may work an opportunity to compare their perceptions of you. When setting up an interview, it is appropriate to ask whether you will be facing a team of questioners. If you are, do your best to learn and use the names of each person. When you answer questions, make sure you look at everyone in the group. Some employers use a **stress interview** to evaluate your behavior under pressure; researching this type of interview and being prepared for such ploys will help you remain calm and in control.

In an **audition interview** you will be asked to demonstrate whatever skills the employer is looking for. You might be asked to create a project, solve a problem, or respond to a typical scenario in the job, such as dealing with a difficult client. The audition shows the potential employer how you are likely to do on the job. The prospect of an audition can be especially helpful if you will be competing against candidates with more experience or stronger credentials. For that reason, you might even volunteer for an audition if you are confident you can handle the job well.[24]

A **behavioral interview** is based on the assumption past experience is the best predictor of future performance. In this approach interviewers explore specifics about the candidate's past accomplishments. John Madigan, a vice president at The Hartford Financial

Services Group, explains the way behavioral interviews work: "We actually ask what you did in specific situations. Concrete examples will demonstrate a person's preferred way of dealing with those situations and give you a better idea of that person and how they're likely to act on the job."[25]

Here are some questions you might hear in a behavioral interview:

- Give me a specific example of when you sold your supervisor or professor on an idea or concept. What was the result?
- Tell me about a time when you came up with an innovative solution to a challenge you or your company was facing. What was the challenge? What role did others play?
- Describe a situation where you faced multiple projects. How did you handle it?[26]

If you have a proven record of accomplishments that will clearly work well in the job you are seeking, a behavioral interview should sound ideal. If you don't have work experience that is clearly relevant to the new position, find ways to demonstrate how things you have done in other contexts apply to the job you are seeking. For example, you might be able to show how experience in retail sales taught you how to deal with difficult customers you'll encounter in a customer service job, or how being a volunteer for a nonprofit charity gave you an appreciation for working with limited resources—an attitude most employers will welcome.

Think constructively   The way you think about an upcoming interview can affect how you feel and act during the session. A research team at Washington State University interviewed both highly anxious and more confident students to discover what causes some people to become especially apprehensive during the process of meeting prospective employers.[27] The differences between the groups were startling. Anxious students avoided thinking about an interview in advance, so they did little research or preparation. When they did think about an upcoming interview, they dwelled on negative self-talk: "I won't do well" or "I don't know why I'm doing this." It's no surprise thoughts like these created negative self-fulfilling prophecies that led to poor interview performances. Students who handled interviews better weren't anxiety-free, but they thought about the upcoming challenge in more productive ways. We can imagine them thinking, "The interviewer isn't trying to trick me or trip me up" and "I'll do a lot better if I prepare."

Dress appropriately and act professionally   Looking good when you meet a potential employer is vitally important. In one survey, recruiters ranked clothing as the leading factor in shaping their initial impressions of applicants (ahead of physical attractiveness and résumé). Furthermore, 79 percent of the recruiters stated their initial impressions influenced the rest of the interview.[28] The best attire to wear will depend on the job you are seeking: The professional business suit appropriate for a banking job would almost certainly look out of place if you were interviewing for a job in the construction industry, and it might look overly formal at many software companies. When in doubt, it is always safest to dress on the conservative side. Of course, cleanliness and personal hygiene are essential.

Be sure to arrive at the interview 5 to 10 minutes early. Be polite to everyone in the office. While you wait, choose reading material about the business or company, not about current TV personalities. When introduced, shake hands firmly, no more than three shakes, avoiding a limp or hand-crushing grip. Smile, make eye contact, and take your lead from the interviewer about how to proceed.

During the Interview

If your fate in the selection process were determined by a skilled, objective interviewer, the need for strategic communication might not be essential. Research shows, however, the rating you are likely to receive from an interviewer can be influenced by a variety of factors as varied as the time of day, the sex of the interviewer and interviewee, whether the candidates before you did well or poorly, and the interviewer's mood.[29] Because the interview is not a scientific measure of your skills, it is especially important to do everything possible to make the best impression. Interviewing expert Anthony Medley describes one memorable job candidate who illustrates the importance of first impressions:

> She was attractive, presentable, and had good references. But after showing up ten minutes late, she called me "Mr. Melody" throughout the interview.
>
> The two things I remembered about her were that she had kept me waiting and constantly mispronounced my name. I finally offered the position to someone whose . . . skills were not nearly so good.[30]

Your background research will pay dividends during the employment interview. One criterion most interviewers use in rating applicants is "knowledge of the position," and a lack of information in this area can be damaging. One example illustrates the advantages that come from knowing even a small amount about a position:

> When I first took a job as a young attorney for Litton Industries, I was interviewing for the position as an assistant division counsel for their Guidance Control Systems Division. That name alone was enough to boggle my mind. A scientist I was not. After a little research, I found that they made something called an inertial navigation system. That was worse than the name of the division. What was an inertial navigation system?
>
> Finally I went to a fraternity brother who had majored in engineering and asked him if he knew what it was all about. He explained to me that inertial navigation was a method of navigating whereby the system allows you, if you know your starting point, to measure speed and distance and therefore know where you are at all times. He also explained the components of the system.
>
> When I went into my interview with the division counsel, I astounded him by my ability to talk the jargon of inertial navigation. . . .
>
> He later told me that I was the first person he had interviewed for the job to whom he did not have to explain inertial navigation. Since he didn't understand it any better than I did, his being relieved of this obligation was a big plus in my favor. Also he said that he knew that it was not an easy task for me to find someone who could explain the subject and understand it well enough to have the confidence to discuss it. My initiative and interest in going to this extent to prepare for the interview had impressed him.[31]

Table 6-3 lists common interviewee mistakes, according to a survey of more than 2,400 hiring managers.

Table 6-3	**Most Frequent Interviewee Mistakes**
Answering cell phone or texting Appearing uninterested Dressing inappropriately Appearing arrogant Talking negatively about current or previous employers	

Source: Careerbuilder.com (2012, February 22). *Hiring managers share the most memorable interview mistakes in annual CareerBuilder Survey.* Retrieved from http://www.careerbuilder.com/share/aboutus/pressreleasesdetail.aspx?id=pr680&sd=2%2f2 2%2f2012&ed=12%2f31%2f2012&siteid=cbpr&sc_cmp1=cb_pr680_

Anticipate key questions   Most employment interviewers ask questions in five areas:

Educational background. Does the candidate possess adequate training for a successful career? Do the candidate's grades and other activities predict success in this organization?

Work experience. Do any previous jobs prepare the candidate for this position? What does the candidate's employment history suggest about his or her work habits and ability to work well with others?

Career goals. Does the candidate have clear goals? Are they compatible with a career in this organization?

Personal traits. Do the candidate's actions and attitudes predict good work habits and good interpersonal skills?

Knowledge of organization and job. Does the candidate know the job and organization well enough to be certain he or she will feel happy in them?

While the specifics of each job are different, many questions are the same for any position. Table 6-4 lists the most common questions interviewers ask. In addition, knowledge of the company and job should suggest other specific questions to you. There's a good chance you will be asked at least some of the common questions listed below. Here are some tips about how to approach them, keeping the focus on what you can do for the organization.

Question	What to Emphasize
Why should we hire you?	Don't give a generic answer: Nearly everyone says they are hardworking and motivated. Briefly list your unique strengths and qualifications, showing **how they will help you perform the job in question.**
Why do you want to work here?	If you have researched the organization, this question gives you an opportunity to explain **how your experience and qualifications match the company's needs.**
Tell me about yourself.	Keep your answer focused on parts of your life that relate to the job. Pick a couple of points that show how you possess skills and/or experiences that **show what you can contribute to this organization.**

You can't anticipate every question a prospective employer will ask. Still, if you go into the interview with a clear sense of yourself—both your strengths and limitations—and the nature of the job you are seeking, you can probably handle almost any question. Consider a few examples of unusual questions and what the interviewers who asked them were seeking.

Table 6-4	Commonly Asked Questions in Employment Interviews

Educational Background

How has your education prepared you for a career?

Why did you choose your college or university?

Describe your greatest success (biggest problem) in college.

What subjects in school did you like best? Why?

What subjects did you like least? Why?

What was your most rewarding college experience?

Work Experience

Tell me about your past jobs. (What did you do in each?)

Which of your past jobs did you enjoy most? Why?

Why did you leave your past jobs?

Describe your greatest accomplishments in your past jobs.

What were your biggest failures? What did you learn from them?

How have your past jobs prepared you for this position?

What were the good and bad features of your last job?

This job requires initiative and hard work. What in your experience demonstrates these qualities?

Have you supervised people in the past? In what capacities? How did you do?

How do you think your present boss (subordinates, coworkers) would describe you?

How do you feel about the way your present company (past companies) is (were) managed?

Career Goals

Why are you interested in this position?

Where do you see yourself in 5 years? 10 years?

What is your career goal?

Why did you choose the career you are now pursuing?

What are your financial goals?

How would you describe the ideal job?

How would you define success?

What things are most important to you in a career?

Self-Assessment

In your own words, how would you describe yourself?

How have you grown in the last years?

What are your greatest strengths? Your greatest weaknesses?

What things give you the greatest satisfaction?

How do you feel about your career up to this point?

What is the biggest mistake you have made in your career?

Do you prefer working alone or with others?

How do you work under pressure?

What are the most important features of your personality?

Are you a leader? (a creative person? a problem solver?) Give examples.

Knowledge of the Job

Why are you interested in this particular job? Our company?

What can you contribute to this job? Our company?

Why should we hire you? What qualifies you for this position?

What do you think about (job-related topic)?

What part of this job do you think would be most difficult?

Other Topics

Do you have any geographical preferences? Why?

Would you be willing to travel? To relocate?

Do you have any questions for me?

Question	What the Interviewer Was Seeking
What's the biggest career mistake you've made so far?	Have you learned from your errors? What mistakes are you not likely to make if you work for us?
If I asked your previous coworkers what I'd better watch out for from you, what would they say?	How aware are you of your own strengths and weaknesses?
Who else are you interviewing with, and how close are you to accepting an offer?	How committed are you to our organization? How do others view your potential as an employee?[32]

Because most employers are untrained in interviewing, you can't expect them to ask every important question.[33] If your interviewer doesn't touch on an important area, look for ways of volunteering information he or she probably would want to have. For instance, you could show your knowledge of the industry and the company when you respond to a question about your past work experience: "As my résumé shows, I've been working in this field for five years, first at Marston-Keenan and then with Evergreen. In both jobs we were constantly trying to keep up with the pace you set here. For example, the VT-17 was our biggest competitor at Evergreen. . . ."

Respond to the employer's needs and concerns   While you may need a job to repay a college loan or finance your new Porsche, these concerns won't impress a potential employer. Companies hire employees to satisfy *their* needs, not yours. Although employers will rarely say so outright, the fundamental question that is *always* being asked in an employment interview is, *"Are you a person who can help this organization?"* That is, *"What can you do for us?"* One career guidance book makes the point clearly:

> It is easy to get the impression during an interview that the subject of the interview, the star (so to speak) of the interview is, well, you. After all, you're the one in the hot seat. You're the one whose life is being dissected. Don't be too flattered. The real subject of the interview is the company. The company is what the interviewer ultimately thinks is important.[34]

Within the broad question of "What can you do for us?" potential employers have three concerns:

1. *Are you qualified to do the job?*
2. *Are you motivated to do the job?*
3. *Will you fit the culture and get along with your colleagues?*[35]

"Will my office be near an ice machine?"

© Leo Cullum/The New Yorker Collection/www.cartoonbank.com.

No matter how the question is worded, these are potential employers' concerns. A smart candidate will answer in ways that address them. Background research will pay off here: If you've spent time learning about what the employer needs, you will be in a good position to show you're motivated and how you can satisfy company needs and concerns. Consider an example:

Interviewer:	What was your major in college?
Poor Answer:	I was a communication major.
Better Answer:	I was a communication major. I'm glad I studied that subject because the skills I learned in school could help me in this job in so many ways: dealing with customers from many cultures, working in the department teams, and creating presentations for the external contractors who are part of the job. . . .
Interviewer:	Tell me about your last job as a sales rep.
Poor Answer:	I handled outside sales. I called on about 35 customers. My job was to keep them supplied and show them new products.
Better Answer:	(elaborating on previous answer) I learned how important it is to provide outstanding customer service. I know the competitive edge comes from making sure the customers get what they want, when they need it. I know this company has a reputation for good service, so I'm really excited about working here.

Just because you respond to the employer's needs doesn't mean you should ignore your own goals; but in an interview, keep in mind you need to demonstrate how you can help the organization or you won't have a job offer to consider.

Because most employers have had bad experiences with some of the people they have hired, they are likely to be concerned about what might go wrong if they hire you. In Richard Bolles's words, employers worry you won't be able to do the job, you lack the skills, you won't work full days regularly, you'll quit unexpectedly, it will take you a long time to master the job, you won't get along with others, you'll do the minimum, you'll need constant supervision, you'll be dishonest, irresponsible, negative, a substance abuser, incompetent, you'll discredit the organization or cost them a lot of money.[36]

You can allay these fears without ever addressing them directly by answering questions in a way that showcases your good work habits:

Interviewer:	What were the biggest challenges in your last job?
Answer:	The work always seemed to come in spurts. When it was busy, we had to work especially hard to stay caught up. I can remember some weeks when we never seemed to leave the office. It was hard, but we did whatever it took to get the job done.
Interviewer:	How did you get along with your last boss?
Answer:	My last manager had a very hands-off approach. That was a little scary at times, but it taught me I can solve problems without a lot of supervision. I was always glad to get guidance, but when it didn't come, I learned I can figure out things for myself.

Be honest   Whatever else an employer may be seeking, honesty is a mandatory job requirement. If an interviewer finds out you have misrepresented yourself by lying or exaggerating about even one answer, then everything else you say will be suspect.[37]

ETHICAL **challenge**

Promoting Yourself with Honesty

Think of a job you are probably capable of handling well but for which you would most likely not be the candidate hired. Develop a list of questions you would probably be asked in an interview for this position. Then develop a list of answers that show you in the best possible light while being honest.

Being honest doesn't mean you have to confess to every self-doubt and shortcoming. As in almost every type of situation, both parties in an employment interview try to create desirable impressions. In fact, some ethicists have noted the ability to "sell" yourself honestly but persuasively is a desirable attribute since it shows you can represent an employer well after being hired.[38] So, highlight your strengths and downplay your weaknesses, but always be honest.

Emphasize the Positive   Although you should always be honest, it is also wise to phrase your answers in a way that casts you in the most positive light. Consider the difference between positive and negative responses to this question:

Interviewer:	I notice you've held several jobs, but you haven't had any experience in the field you've applied for.
Negative Answer:	Uh, that's right. I only decided I wanted to go into this field last year. I wish I had known that earlier.
Positive Answer:	That's right. I've worked in a number of fields, and I've been successful in learning each one quickly. I'd like to think this kind of adaptability will help me learn this job and grow with it as technology changes the way the company does business.

Notice how the second answer converted a potential negative into a positive answer. If you anticipate questions that have the ability to harm you, you can compose honest answers that present you favorably.

Even if you are confronted with comments that cast you negatively, you can recast yourself more positively. Notice how each negative trait below could be reframed as a positive attribute:[39]

Negative Trait	Positive Attribute
Overly detailed	Thorough, reliable
Cautious	Careful, accurate
Intense	Focused
Slow	Methodical, careful
Naive	Open, honest
Aggressive	Assertive

168

Don't misunderstand: Arguing with the interviewer or claiming you have no faults isn't likely to win you a job offer. Still, reframing shortcomings as strengths can shift the employer's view of you:

Employer:	If I were to ask your colleagues to describe your biggest weaknesses, what do you think they'd say?
Candidate:	Well, some might say that I could work faster, especially when things get frantic. On the other hand, I think they would agree I'm very careful about my work and I don't make careless errors.

Another important rule is to avoid criticizing others in an employment interview. Consider the difference between the answers below:

Interviewer:	From your transcript, I notice you graduated with a 2.3 grade-point average. Isn't that a little low?
Negative Answer:	Sure, but it wasn't my fault. I had some terrible teachers during my first two years of college. We had to memorize a lot of useless information that didn't have anything to do with the real world. Besides, professors give you high grades if they like you. If you don't play their game, they grade you down.
Positive Answer:	My low grade-point average came mostly from very bad freshman and sophomore years. I wasn't serious about school then, but you can see my later grades are much higher. I've grown a lot in the past few years, and I'd like to think I can use what I've learned in this job.

Most job candidates have been raised to regard modesty as a virtue, which makes it hard to toot their own horns. Excessive boasting certainly is likely to put off an interviewer, but experts flatly state showcasing your strengths is essential. Florida State University management professor Michele Kacmar found that job-seekers who talked about their good qualities were rated higher than those who focused on the interviewer.[40] Pre-interview rehearsals will help you find ways of saying positive things about yourself in a confident, nonboastful manner.

Back up you answers with evidence   As you read a few pages ago, behavioral interviewers figure the best predictor of a potential employee's performance is what he or she has done in the past. Even if you aren't in a behavioral interview, it is usually effective to back up any claims you make with evidence of your performance.

One good framework for answering questions is the "PAR" approach. These initials stand for the three parts of a good answer: Identifying the *problem,* describing the *action* you took, and stating the *results* your actions produced. You can see the value of this approach by comparing the two answers below:

Interviewer:	What strengths would you bring to this job?
Weak Answer:	I'm a self-starter who can work without close supervision [unsupported claim].
Stronger Answer:	I'm a self-starter who can work without close supervision [claim]. For example, in my last job, my immediate supervisor was away from the office off and on for three months because of some health issues [problem]. We were switching over to a new accounting system during that time, and I worked with the software company to make the change [action]. We made the changeover without losing a single day's work, and without any loss of data [results].

TECHNOLOGY **tip**

Creating a Digital Portfolio

Showing a prospective employer what you can do is much more effective than simply talking about your qualifications. This is especially true for jobs that involve tangible products like graphic design, commercial art, journalism, and technical writing.

Portfolios can also work in less obvious fields. You might, for example, demonstrate your ability to do solid work by sharing a report you helped create, a training program you devised, or a collection of e-mails from satisfied customers praising your work.

The nature of your work may lend itself to a digital portfolio that can be posted online. You can include links to this site in your print material as well as in any electronic correspondence with potential employers and references. To keep a professional appearance, make sure your digital portfolio has its own Web address: Don't embed the portfolio in any social networking sites that include personal information. If you are applying for different types of positions, such as training and marketing, consider creating two different electronic portfolios that showcase your work for each type of position.

You can find extensive guides to constructing portfolios at the career centers of many colleges and universities. For specific tips on creating a digital portfolio, see

- EFolio Minnesota: http://www.efoliomn.com
- Eduscapes: http://eduscapes.com/tap/topic82.htm
- E-portfolios at Penn State: http://www.portfolio.psu.edu
- Quintcareers: http://www.quintcareers.com/QuintZine/archives/20021014.html

Keep your answers brief It is easy to rattle on in an interview out of enthusiasm, a desire to show off your knowledge, or nervousness, but in most cases highly detailed answers are not a good idea. The interviewer probably has a lot of ground to cover, and long-winded answers won't help. A general rule is to keep your responses under 2 minutes. An interviewer who wants additional information can always ask for it.

Be enthusiastic If you are applying for jobs that genuinely excite you, the challenge isn't to manufacture enthusiasm but to show it. This can be difficult when you are nervous during what feels like a make-or-break session. Just remember the interviewer wants to know how you really feel about the job and organization. Sharing your interest and excitement can give you a competitive edge. Career Center director Gregory D. Hayes says, "If I talk to five deadbeat people and have one who is upbeat, that's the one I'm going to hire."[41]

Have your own questions answered After you have answered the interviewer's questions, be prepared to ask a few of your own. Realize that your questions make indirect statements about you just as your answers to the interviewer's inquiries did. Be sure your questions aren't all greedy ones that focus on salary, vacation time, benefits, and so on. Table 6-5 lists some questions to consider asking when you are invited to do so.

Rehearsing an Interview No athlete would expect to win without practicing, and no performer would face an audience without rehearsing. The same principle holds when you are facing an important employment interview. Effective practicing involves several steps:

1. Use your pre-interview research to identify the nature of the job you are seeking. What skills are required? What personal qualities are most desirable for this position? What kind of person will fit best with the organization's culture?

Table 6-5	Questions to Consider Asking the Interviewer during an Employment Interview

Why is this position open?

How often has it been filled during the past five years?

What have been the reasons for people leaving in the past?

Why did the person who most recently held this position leave?

What would you like the next person who holds this job to do differently?

What are the most pressing issues and problems in this position?

What support does this position have (people, budget, equipment, etc.)?

What are the criteria for success in this position?

What might be the next career steps for a person who does well in this position?

What do you see as the future of this position? This organization?

What are the most important qualities you will look for in the person who will occupy this position?

2. Draft a series of questions that explore the job description; use the lists in Table 6-2 on p. 146 as a guide to include each key area.

3. Think about how you can answer each question. Each answer should contain a *claim* ("I have experience making presentations using Apple Keynote") and *evidence* to back it up ("I used it to train customer service reps in my last job"). In every case, make sure your answer shows how you can satisfy the employer's needs.

4. Role-play the interview several times with the help of a friend. Be sure you include the orientation and conclusion phases of the interview and practice the questions you plan to ask the interviewer. If possible, record and review your performance twice: once to evaluate the content of your answers and again to check your appearance and the image you are projecting.

Many colleges have student job placement centers that have tremendous print resources on interviewing as well as a way of scheduling and recording a mock interview with a professional job counselor who will review your video with you and give you constructive advice.

Post-Interview Follow-up   Without exception, every employment interview should be followed immediately by a thank-you note to the person who interviewed you. As Figure 6.4 shows, your thank-you serves several purposes:

- It demonstrates common courtesy.
- It reminds the employer of you.
- It gives you a chance to remind the interviewer of important information about you that came up in the interview and to provide facts you may have omitted.
- It can tactfully remind the interviewer of promises made, such as a second interview or a response by a certain date.
- It can correct any misunderstandings that may have occurred during the interview.[42]

Unlike most business correspondence, a thank-you note can be handwritten. Whatever style you choose—whether a handwritten note card, a formal letter, or an e-mail message—the thank-you should be neat, error free, and carefully composed.

Assess how ready you are to handle employment interviews skillfully by answering the questions below, using the following scale:

5 = strongly agree; 4 = agree; 3 = maybe, not certain; 2 = disagree; 1 = definitely not

Pre-Interview Planning

1. I have conducted background research and understand the organization and the field.   5 4 3 2 1

2. I know the nature of the job (responsibilities, skills, how it fits in the company).   5 4 3 2 1

3. When possible and appropriate, I have asked members of my personal network to give the prospective employer favorable information about me.   5 4 3 2 1

4. I am prepared for any interview format.   5 4 3 2 1

5. I think constructively about the upcoming interview rather than dwell on negative thoughts.   5 4 3 2 1

6. I will dress and groom appropriately for this company and position.   5 4 3 2 1

7. I know how to arrive at the interview site.   5 4 3 2 1

During the Interview

8. I can handle the small talk that arises in the opening phase of the interview.   5 4 3 2 1

9. I nonverbally communicate my interest and enthusiasm for the job.   5 4 3 2 1

10. I am prepared to answer the kinds of questions likely to be asked (see Table 6–2) in a way that shows how I can meet the employer's needs.   5 4 3 2 1

11. I back up all my answers with examples that help clarify and prove what I'm saying.   5 4 3 2 1

12. I give concise answers to the interviewer's questions.   5 4 3 2 1

13. I present myself confidently and enthusiastically.   5 4 3 2 1

14. I am prepared to respond to illegal questions the interviewer might ask.   5 4 3 2 1

15. I know when and how to deal with salary questions.   5 4 3 2 1

16. I have prepared a list of references.   5 4 3 2 1

17. I am prepared to ask my own questions about the job and organization.   5 4 3 2 1

18. I practiced asking and answering questions until I am comfortable and articulate.   5 4 3 2 1

After the Interview

19. I know how to write an effective thank-you letter.   5 4 3 2 1

20. I am prepared to follow up with the interviewer to determine my status, if necessary.   5 4 3 2 1

Scoring

Total the numbers you have circled. If your score is between 80 and 100, you appear to be well-prepared for interviews. If your score is between 60 and 80, you are moderately prepared. If your score is below 60, you would do well to make additional preparations before any employment interviews.

Source: Krannich, C., & Krannich, R. (2002). *Interview for success: A practical guide to increasing job interviews, offers, and salaries (8th ed.).* Manassas Park, VA: Impact Publications.

FIGURE 6.4
Sample Thank-You Message

From: Susan Mineta [stm@comnet.net]
Sent: Tuesday, March 30, 2013 9:14 AM
To: Leslie Thoresen [lesthor@blogsite.com]
Subject: Thank you!
Attached: 📄 S Mineta articles.pdf

Dear Mr. Thoresen:

I left our meeting yesterday full of excitement. Your remarks about the value of my experience as a student journalist and blogger were very encouraging. I also appreciate your suggestion that I speak with Mr. Leo Benadides. Thank you for promising to tell him that I'll be calling within the next week.

Since you expressed interest in the series I wrote on how Asian women are breaking cultural stereotypes, I am attaching copies to this e-mail. I hope you find them interesting.

Your remarks about the dangers of being typecast exclusively as a writer on women's issues were very helpful. Just after we spoke I received an assignment to write a series on identity theft and the elderly. I'll be sure to let you know when these articles appear online.

Thank you again for taking time from your busy day. I will look forward to hearing from you when the job we discussed is officially created.

Sincerely,

Susan Mineta
8975 Santa Clarita Lane
Glendale, CA 90099
(818) 214-0987

If you don't get the job, consider contacting the person who interviewed you and asking what shortcomings kept you from being chosen. Even if the interviewer isn't comfortable sharing this information with you (it might not have anything to do with your personal qualifications), your sincere desire to improve yourself can leave a positive impression that could help you in the future.

Interviewing and the Law   Many laws govern which questions are and are not legal in employment interviews, but the general principle that underlies them all is simple: Questions may not be asked for the purpose of discriminating on the basis of race, color, religion, sex, disabilities, national origin, or age. Employers may still ask about these areas, but the U.S. government's Equal Employment Opportunity Commission (EEOC) permits only questions that investigate a **bona fide occupational qualification (BFOQ)** for a particular job. This means any question asked should be job related. The Supreme Court has said "the touchstone is business necessity."[43] Table 6-6 lists questions that are generally not considered BFOQs as well as those that are legitimate.

The Americans with Disabilities Act of 1990 (ADA) requires equal access to employment and provision of "reasonable accommodations" for persons with disabilities. It defines *disability* as a "physical" or "mental impairment" that "substantially limits" one or more "major life activities." As with any other job-related issue, the key question is what is "reasonable." The law clearly states, however, that disabled candidates can be questioned only about their ability to perform "essential functions" of a job and that employers are obligated to provide accommodations for disabled candidates and employees. If a person indicates a need for reasonable accommodation during the application process, the company is required to provide it. For example, a person who is hearing impaired can request an interpreter at company expense for the interview.[44]

There are several ways to answer an unlawful question:[45]

1. *Answer without objection.* Answer the question, even though you know it is probably unlawful: "I'm 47."

2. *Seek explanation.* Ask the interviewer firmly and respectfully to explain why this question is a BFOQ: "I'm having a hard time seeing how my age relates to my ability to do this job. Can you explain?"

3. *Redirection.* If the interviewer asks, "How old are you?" a candidate might shift the focus toward the position requirements: "What you've said so far suggests age isn't as important as willingness to travel. That isn't a problem for me." Redirection can also involve strategic ambiguity. "I'm old enough to do this job well and young enough to have fresh ideas." Humor can also be a tool for redirecting an inappropriate question: "Hey! You're not supposed to ask a woman her age [laugh]."

4. *Refusal.* Explain politely but firmly that you will not provide the information requested: "I'd rather not talk about my religion. That's a personal matter for me." If you are sure you aren't interested in the job, you could even end the interview immediately: "I'm very uncomfortable with these questions about my personal life, and I don't see a good fit between me and this organization."

Choosing the best response style depends on several factors.[46] First, it is important to consider the interviewer's probable intent. The question may indeed be aimed at collecting information that will allow the employer to discriminate, but it may just as well be a naive inquiry with no harm intended. Some interviewers are unsophisticated at their job. A study reported in *The Wall Street Journal* revealed that more than 70 percent of 200 interviewers in Fortune 500 corporations thought at least 5 of 12 unlawful questions were safe to ask.[47] In another survey, employers at 100 small businesses were presented with five illegal interview questions. All of the respondents said they either would ask or had asked at least one of them.[48] Results like these suggest an illegal question may be the result of ignorance rather than malice. The interviewer who discusses family, nationality, or religion may simply be trying to make conversation. Be careful not to introduce these topics yourself as it may open the door to conversations and questions you would rather not deal with.

A second factor when considering how to respond to an illegal question is your desire for the job at hand. You may be more willing to challenge the interviewer when a position isn't critical to your future. On the other hand, if your career rides on succeeding in a particular interview, you may be willing to swallow your objections. A third factor to consider is your feeling of comfort with the interviewer. For example, a female candidate with school-age children might welcome the chance to discuss child care issues with an interviewer who has identified herself as a single mother who faces the same challenges. A fourth item to consider is your own personal style. If you are comfortable asserting yourself, you may be willing to address an illegal question head-on. If you are less comfortable speaking up, especially to authority figures, you may prefer to respond less directly.

Being interviewed does not mean you are at the interviewer's mercy; laws do govern your rights as a candidate. If you choose to take a more assertive approach to illegal questioning you believe resulted in discrimination, you have the right to file a charge with the EEOC and your state Fair Employment Practices Commission within 180 days of the interview. In practice, the EEOC will withhold its investigation until the state commission has completed its inquiry. Federal and state agencies have a backlog of cases, however, so it may take years to complete an investigation. The commission may mediate the case, file a suit, or issue you a letter to sue.[49] Keep in mind that just because you can file a lawsuit doesn't mean this will always be the best course of action: A suit can take many months, or even years, to be settled, and a ruling in your favor may not result in a large settlement.

Table 6-6 — Questions Interviewers Can and Cannot Legally Ask

Federal law restricts employer interviewer questions and other practices to areas clearly related to job requirements. The following are some questions and practices that are generally considered legitimate and others that are not.

Subject	Unacceptable	Acceptable
Name	What is your maiden name?	What is your name?
	Have you ever changed your name?	"Is there another name I'd need to check on your work and education record?"
Residence	"Do you own or rent your home?"	What is your address?
Age	Age	Statement that hire is subject to verification that applicant meets legal age requirements
	Birth date	
	Dates of attendance or completion of elementary or high school	"If hired, can you show proof of age?"
		"Are you over 18 years of age?"
	Questions that tend to identify applicants over age 40	"If under 18, can you, after employment, submit a work permit?"
Birthplace, citizenship	Birthplace of applicant, applicant's parents, spouse, or other relatives	"Can you, after employment, submit verification of your legal right to work in the United States?" *or* statement such proof may be required after employment
	"Are you a U.S. citizen?" *or* citizenship of applicant, applicant's parents, spouse, or other relatives	
	Requirement that applicant produce naturalization, first papers, or alien card *prior to employment*	
National origin	Questions as to nationality, lineage, ancestry, national origin, descent, or parentage of applicant, applicant's parents, or spouse	Languages applicant reads, speaks, or writes, if use of a language other than English is relevant to the job for which applicant is applying
	"What is your mother tongue?" *or* language commonly used by applicant	
	How applicant acquired ability to read, write, or speak a foreign language	
Sex, marital status, family	Questions that indicate applicant's sex	Name and address of parent or guardian if applicant is a minor, statement of company policy regarding work assignment of employees who are related
	Questions that indicate applicant's marital status	
	Number and/or ages of children or dependents	
	Provisions for child care	
	Questions regarding pregnancy, childbearing, or birth control	
	Name or address of relative, spouse, or children of adult applicant	
	"With whom do you reside?" or "Do you live with your parents?"	
Race, color	Questions as to applicant's race or color	
	Questions regarding applicant's complexion or color of skin, eyes, hair	
Religion	Questions regarding applicant's religion	Statement by employer of regular days, hours, or shifts to be worked
	Religious days observed *or* "Does your religion prevent you from working weekends or holidays?"	

(continued)

Table 6-6	Questions Interviewers Can and Cannot Legally Ask *(Concluded)*

Subject	Unacceptable	Acceptable
Arrest, criminal record	Arrest record *or* "Have you ever been arrested?"	"Have you ever been convicted of a felony?" Such a question must be accompanied by a statement that a conviction will not necessarily disqualify an applicant from employment
Military service	General questions regarding military service such as dates and type of discharge Questions regarding service in a foreign military	Questions regarding relevant skills acquired during applicant's U.S. military service
Organizations	"List all organizations, clubs, societies to which you belong."	"Please list job-related organizations or professional associations to which you belong that you believe enhance your job performance."
References	Questions of applicant's former employers or acquaintances that elicit information specifying the applicant's race, color, religious creed, national origin, ancestry, physical handicap, medical condition, marital status, age, or sex	"By whom were you referred for a position here?" Names of persons willing to provide professional and/or character references for applicant

Sources: Doyle, A. (n.d.). *Illegal interview questions.* Retrieved from http://jobsearchtech.about.com/od/interview/l/aa022403_2.htm; Cobb, L. (2007). *Illegal or inappropriate interview questions.* Retrieved from http://www.gsworkplace.lbl.gov/DocumentArchive/BrownBagLunches/IllegalorInappropriateInterviewQuestions.pdf

Furthermore, knowledge that you've filed a suit is not likely to make you an attractive candidate to other employers who hear of your action. Seeking professional counsel can help you make a decision that balances your personal values and practical considerations.

● The Ethics of Interviewing

Basic ethical guidelines and responsibilities should guide the exchange of information that goes on between interviewer and interviewee.[50] In addition to the moral reasons for following these guidelines, there is often a pragmatic basis for behaving ethically. Because the interview is likely to be part of an ongoing relationship, behaving responsibly and honorably will serve you well in future interactions. Conversely, the costs of developing a poor reputation are usually greater than the benefits of gaining a temporary advantage by behaving unethically or irresponsibly.

Obligations of the Interviewer

A conscientious business communicator will follow several guidelines when conducting an interview.

Make Only Promises You Are Willing and Able to Keep   Don't make offers or claims that may later prove impossible to honor. For example, it's dishonest and unfair for an employer to encourage a job applicant about the chances of receiving an offer until he is sure an offer will be forthcoming. Likewise, a candidate should not indicate a willingness to start work immediately if she cannot begin work until she has sold her home and moved to the town where her new job is located.

Handling Difficult Questions

1. You know an employee has been leaving work early for the past several months. You hope he will volunteer this information without your having to confront him. During a performance appraisal, how can you raise the issue with this employee?

2. You are conducting a series of half-hour interviews with consumers, exploring their attitudes toward a variety of social issues, as part of a market research project for your employer. In the first few minutes of one session, the interviewee makes several racist comments. How do you respond?

3. You are interviewing for a job you really want. The employer asks about your experience with a particular type of database software. You don't know much about this type of program, but you are confident you can teach yourself before the job begins. How do you reply to the interviewer?

Keep Confidences   Interviewers and respondents should not reveal confidential information or disclose any private information gained during a session to people who have no legitimate reason to have it. Be certain to let the interviewee know if you plan to record the session, and make it clear who else may be reviewing the recording.

Allow the Interviewee to Make Free Responses   An interview that coerces the subject into giving unwilling answers is a charade of an honest conversation. For example, a supervisor conducting a performance appraisal who asks a subordinate, "Who do you think is responsible for the problems in your area?" should be willing to accept whatever answer is given and not automatically expect the employee to accept the blame. Trying to *persuade* an interviewee is a normal part of doing business, but coercing one is unethical.

Treat Every Interviewee with Respect   With rare exceptions, the interviewer's job is to help the interviewee do well. This means making sure the interviewee feels comfortable and understands the nature of the session. It also means the interviewer must design clear questions and must help the interviewee answer them as well as possible.

Obligations of the Interviewee

The interviewee is also obliged to behave ethically and responsibly during a session. Several guidelines apply here.

Don't Misrepresent the Facts or Your Position   Whether the setting is an employment interview, a performance review session, or an information-gathering survey, it can be tempting to tell interviewers what they want to hear. The temptation is especially great if your welfare is at stake. But besides being unethical, misrepresenting the facts is likely to catch up with you sooner or later and harm you more than telling the truth in the first place.

Don't Waste the Interviewer's Time   If the choice exists, be sure you are qualified for the interview. For example, it would be a mistake to interview for a job you have little chance of landing or would not accept. Likewise, it would be unethical to volunteer for a customer survey if you aren't a member of the population being studied. If preparation for the interview is necessary, do your homework. Once the interview has begun, stick to the subject to use the time most wisely.

review points

- Interviews are purposeful and structured, use questions as the main tool, and allow one party greater control and the other more speaking time.

- Successful interview participants plan well by defining their goals, identifying and analyzing the other party, listing topics, choosing the best structure and questions, and arranging the setting.

- Interviewers plan primary and secondary questions and should strategically use closed, open, factual, opinion, direct, indirect, and hypothetical questions while avoiding leading questions.

- Interviews consist of three parts: an opening to create rapport, orientation, and motivation; a body to focus conversation with active listening and clear answers; and a closing to review, clarify, and conclude.

- A career research interview helps the interviewer research a career field, be remembered by the interviewee, and gain referrals.

- Employment interviews are an important way to communicate your professional identity. Before an employment interview, clean up your online identity. Then on the interview, put your best foot forward by communicating professionally and dressing appropriately.

- Interviewees need to prepare for key questions, respond to the employer's needs, and support answers with evidence honestly, positively, briefly, and enthusiastically. Interviewees can demonstrate their professionalism by asking pertinent questions and following up with a written thank-you note.

- Laws restrict interviewers from asking questions that are not related to the bona fide occupational qualifications (BFOQs) of a job. Interviewees should know what kinds of questions are legal or illegal and prepare to respond to illegal questions.

- Ethical interviewers treat interviewees respectfully, keep confidences, honor promises, and avoid coercion. Ethical interviewees are sincere and prepared and present themselves honestly.

key terms

audition interview   161
behavioral interview   161
bona fide occupational qualification (BFOQ)   173
career research interview   154
closed question   146
critical incident question   146
direct question   146
employment interview   158
factual question   146
gatekeeper   155
hypothetical question   146
indirect question   146

interview   141
leading question   145
moderately structured interview   144
open question   146
opinion question   146
panel interview   161
primary question   146
scannable résumé   161
secondary question   146
stress interview   161
structured interview   144
unstructured interview   144

activities

1. Skill Builder

Imagine you are conducting a research interview with an employee of a company where you might like to work.

a. Develop a list of topics you will need to cover to get a complete picture of the organization.

b. Decide what structure (structured, moderately structured, unstructured) would be best for this interview. Defend your choice.

c. For each topic, write several appropriate questions.

2. Skill Builder

Become more familiar with types of questions with the following activity.

a. For each of the following situations, describe whether an open or closed question would be more appropriate. Explain your choices. If you think more than one question is necessary to discover the essential information, list each one.

1. You want to find out whether your boss would support your request to attend a convention in a distant city.
2. A manager wants to know whether a project will exceed its projected budget.
3. An insurance sales representative wants to determine whether a customer has adequate coverage.
4. An employer wants to find out why an applicant has held four jobs in five years.

b. For each of the following situations, write one factual and one opinion question. Decide which of these questions is most appropriate for the situation. Then write two secondary questions as follows-ups for the primary question you have chosen:

1. You want to know whether you are justified in asking your boss for a raise, and you decide to question a coworker.
2. A supervisor wants to discover whether an employee's request for a one-month personal leave of absence to visit a sick parent is essential.
3. You are planning to buy a laptop or a desktop PC. You want to decide whether the laptop computer is worth the extra $250 it will cost.

c. For each of the following direct questions, create an indirect question that could elicit the same information:

1. "How hard a worker are you?" (selection)
2. "Do you agree with my evaluation?" (appraisal)
3. "Does the product have any drawbacks?" (diagnostic)
4. "Are you telling me the real reason you're leaving?" (exit)
5. "Do you really believe this idea has merit, or are you just going along?" (research)

3. Skill Builder

With a partner, role-play how you, as an interviewer, could follow the interview guidelines in this section as you conduct the opening stages of each of the following interviews:

a. You are a real estate broker meeting a potential home-buying client for the first time.
b. You are considering opening a new restaurant in town (you choose the kind), and you are interviewing the owner of a similar type of establishment in another city about how you can be successful.
c. You are thinking about taking a specific college course (you choose which one) that will help you in your career, and you are meeting with the professor to get a better idea of what is involved.
d. You are interviewing the manager of an assisted care facility to see if it would be a suitable place for your grandmother.

4. Invitation to Insight

Select a person in your chosen career who plays a role in hiring new employees. Conduct an information-gathering interview to discover the following:

a. What methods are used to identify job candidates?
b. What format is used to interview applicants?
c. What formal and informal criteria are used to hire applicants?
d. What personal qualities of applicants make a positive or negative impression?

5. Skill Builder

For each of the following topics, identify at least two people you could interview to gather information. Write a specific objective for each interview:

a. Learning more about a potential employer. (Name a specific organization.)
b. Deciding whether to enroll in a specific class. (You choose which one.)
c. Deciding which type of personal computer or software application to purchase.
d. Exploring career opportunities in a city of your choice.
e. Determining the best savings or investment vehicle for you at this time.
f. Finding a service activity you would like to participate in.

6. Skill Builder

You can develop your skill and gain appreciation for the value of the informational interview by doing one of the following activities:

a. Conduct an informational interview with a professional in a career field that interests you. Possible goals are to learn more about the field, to learn how to advance in your current job, or to learn what it would take to switch fields. Follow these steps:

1. Identify a promising interviewee.
2. Write an e-mail requesting an interview.
3. Follow up your e-mail with a phone call to arrange a date.
4. Develop a list of questions that will achieve your stated purpose. Be sure that these questions follow the guidelines in Chapter 6.
5. Conduct the interview and report your results. Analyze how well you performed. Suggest how you could improve in conducting future interviews.
6. Write a thank-you letter to your interviewee.

b. Identify a specific organization you would like to work for. Complete the following pre-interview steps:

1. Identify the person—by title and name, if possible—who has the power to hire you.
2. Using research and the results of informational interviews, analyze the requirements for the position you would like to hold.
3. Develop a list of questions a potential boss might ask in a selection interview.
4. Prepare answers to those questions, using the PAR approach.

c. Role-play an actual interview, with a companion filling the role of your potential employer.

1. Videotape the interview.
2. View the interview and analyze your verbal as well as nonverbal performance.

7. Invitation to Insight

Brainstorm 5 to 10 specific actions you have taken (in classes, on the job, or in volunteer activities) that demonstrate your ability to perform well. Include specific evidence for each. Recall the positive results of your actions.

For added practice, team up with a classmate. Use the PAR approach (see p. 169) to role-play asking and answering interview questions. As your classmate asks questions, use your brainstormed accomplishments to answer with actions and results. Then switch roles.

8. Skill Builder

In a group, practice your skill at answering behavioral interview questions using the PAR approach:

a. Describe a time that you needed to work as part of a team.
b. Tell about a time you used creativity and problem-solving skills to solve an important problem.
c. Explain how you handled a situation when you had to make an important ethical decision.
d. Describe a time when you didn't succeed at something you were trying to accomplish.
e. Give an example of a time when you took on a greater share of responsibility or decision making than was required by your job.

9. Skill Builder

a. With your group, consider each of the following questions. Decide whether they would be lawful or unlawful to ask in an interview. Explain your reasoning.

1. "Have you ever been arrested?"
2. "When and where were you born?"
3. "What are your greatest weaknesses?"
4. "Do you own your own car?"
5. "Are you married, divorced, or single?"
6. "What personal qualities do you have that you think would be helpful in working with the teams within our organization?"
7. "You look Vietnamese. Are you?"
8. "Do you own, rent, or lease your home?"
9. "Do you have any handicaps?"
10. "Your address is in an interesting part of town; isn't that the Martineztown section?"
11. "What is your maiden name?"
12. "What do you know about our company?"
13. "Can you show proof of your age if you are hired?"

b. In your group, prepare five more potential job interview questions. Challenge your classmates to determine whether they are lawful or unlawful.

McGraw Hill LearnSmart™

For further review, go to the LearnSmart study module for this chapter.

PART THREE

Museum of Springfield

Paul Georgakis is the new media coordinator at the Museum of Springfield. He is working on the biggest assignment of his career: developing the website for the museum's forthcoming new show "Images of Springfield." Midwestern Industries is underwriting the exhibit, and museum curator Mary Weston has told Paul the board of trustees is counting on the exhibit's success to open the door to more corporate support. "If that happens we'll have a shot at becoming a top-quality regional museum," Mary tells Paul. "I don't have to tell you how important that is to the board of trustees." Mary might as well have said, "I don't have to tell you how important this is to your career."

Along with Paul, the project team for the website includes four other members. Elaine Dorsch is the site's designer. Bringing San Francisco-based Elaine onboard was a coup for Paul. She has created sites for several world-class organizations, and she took the museum job for a deeply discounted fee because she grew up in Springfield and wants to give something back to the community. Roger Chilton, a history professor at the local branch of the state university, is the content expert on the exhibit and the accompanying website. His specialty is the influence of business and government institutions on underprivileged groups in nineteenth-century U.S. society. Julia Winger is the corporate liaison with Midwestern Industries. She has made it clear her company is glad to support the museum and it expects to be recognized for doing so. "Doing good can help Midwestern Industries do well," she told Paul. Mary Weston, Paul's boss, represents the museum's administration and board of trustees.

The website project got off to a good start. But lately, several problems have developed. On a practical level, it has proved almost impossible to get all members to attend the last few meetings. Because Elaine is based in San Francisco and Julia's office is in Minneapolis, it has been difficult for both of them to squeeze in visits to Springfield.

Even more alarming has been the growing tension as it has become clear Roger's exhibit includes some disturbing images and stories. Julia recently sent the team an e-mail saying, "Midwestern Industries isn't contributing several hundred thousand dollars to upset the community." Roger replied, "It isn't a historian's job to make people happy." Paul is growing worried that either Roger or Julia may pull out of the project, and either scenario would be a disaster.

Finally, it has become clear Elaine views any suggestion for revising her design as an assault on her artistic talent. "I don't tell you how to run your museum or Midwestern Industries," she says. "You're the experts in your own fields, and I am in mine. I know what I'm doing, and you just have to trust me." Paul's boss Mary has made it clear she is counting on him to keep the team together and the project on track.

Working in Groups

As you read the chapters in this unit, consider how answers to the following questions might help Paul manage this difficult job:

chapter 7

1. What types of power listed in Chapter 7 does each team member have? How can the members use their power to help the team achieve its goal?
2. What approaches to leadership outlined in Chapter 7 can Paul use to keep the team functioning well?
3. What are each member's personal goals? How do these goals contribute to and/or interfere with the team's job?

chapter 8

1. How can the team use the systematic problem-solving method outlined in Chapter 8 to overcome the challenges it faces?
2. What decision-making method(s) should the members use in deciding how to resolve their disagreements?
3. Are there ways the team can handle some of its tasks without meeting in person?
4. What might an agenda for the team's next meeting look like?
5. What techniques outlined in Chapter 8 can Paul use when he leads face-to-face meetings?

Chapter Seven
Leading and Working in Teams

chapter objectives

After reading this chapter you should be able to:

1. Identify the kinds of communication that distinguish a group from a team.

2. Explain the advantages and disadvantages of face-to-face and virtual teams and describe ways to address the disadvantages.

3. Compare and contrast various approaches to leadership, leader–member relations, and power distribution and explain their impact on teams.

4. Identify and apply guidelines for effective communication in teams with regard to roles, goals, norms, cohesion, conformity, and creativity.

P olitical economist Robert Reich describes the importance of teamwork in an increasingly technological age:

> Rarely do even Big Ideas emerge any longer from the solitary labors of genius. Modern science and technology is too complicated for one brain. It requires groups of astronomers, physicists, and computer programmers to discover new dimensions of the universe, teams of microbiologists, oncologists, and chemists to unravel the mysteries of cancer. With ever more frequency, Nobel prizes are awarded to collections of people. Scientific papers are authored by small platoons of researchers.[1]

Working with others is a vital part of virtually every job.[2] In a national survey of architects and landscape architects, more than 75 percent reported that they "always" or "often" worked in teams.[3] The amount of research done by teams has increased in virtually every scientific field.[4] Even the historically "cowboy" profession of surgery is increasingly becoming a team effort.[5]

In the burgeoning field of multimedia, the ability to work as a team member has been identified as the top nontechnical job skill.[6] Motorola, Ford, USAA Insurance, and 3M have used teams to become leaders in their fields.

Given the prevalence of teams, no matter how talented you are, being a solo player is not an option in today's business world. Gary Kaplan, owner of a Pasadena, California, executive recruiting firm, offers one explanation of why team players are valued over rugged individualists: "The single-combat warrior, that bright, purposeful worker, tends to suck up a lot of oxygen in an organization. And now they're often seen as too innovative and too difficult."[7] As legendary baseball manager Casey Stengel put it, "Gettin' good players is easy. Getting 'em to play together is the hard part."

Teams have several advantages over individuals working alone.[8] One of these advantages is productivity. Research shows that the old saying "Two heads are better than one" can be true: Well-conceived and efficiently operating teams produce more solutions than

individuals working alone, and the solutions are likely to be better. Along with greater productivity, the accuracy of an effective team's work is higher than that of individuals. Consider the task of creating a new product. A team of people from sales, marketing, design, engineering, and manufacturing is likely to consider all the important angles, whereas one or two people without this breadth of perspective would probably miss some important ideas.

Teams not only produce better products but also generate more commitment and enthusiasm from the members who created them. People are usually more committed to a decision if they have had a part in making it. Recognizing this principle, many companies create participatory management programs and quality circles that involve employees in important decisions. For example, William Deardon, chief executive officer of Hershey Foods Corporation, established a corporate planning committee to make the major plans and decisions for the company. "I figured that if we worked it out together," he explained, "the members of the group would feel that it was their plan and our plan—not my plan—and they'd work harder to implement it."[9]

• The Nature of Teams

As Table 7-1 shows, teams play an important role in the world of business and the professions. Project teams work on a specific task, usually for a finite period of time; for example, a team of marketing experts design a publicity program to accompany the rollout of a new software product. Service teams support customers or employees; for example, public utilities have service agents available around the clock to help customers. Management teams work collaboratively on a daily basis within organizations to help them perform their missions. At a university, for example, top officials meet regularly to coordinate their divisions: academic, student support, financial, physical facilities, and so on. Action teams offer immediate responses activated in (typically) emergency situations; for example, community health workers form teams to deal with public health threats.[10]

Table 7-1	Team vs. Individual Performance

Team Superior to Individuals	Individuals Superior to Team
Task requires broad range of talents and knowledge	Task requires limited knowledge, information (that individuals possess)
Complicated task (requires division, coordination of labor)	Simple task (can be done by one person or individuals working separately)
Time available for deliberation	Little time available
Members are motivated to succeed	Members don't care about job
High standards of performance	"Social loafing" is the norm

Sources: Adapted from Rothwell, J. D. (2013). *In mixed company* (8th ed.). Boston, MA: Cengage; Hare, A. P. (2003). Roles, relationships, and groups in organizations: Some conclusions and recommendations. *Small Group Research 34,* 123–154.

Characteristics of Work Groups

The word *group* is often used to refer to any assembly of people—the commuters on the morning train, the sightseers gathering for a walking tour of the downtown area, the rock band at a local nightspot. When we talk about people interacting at work, we use the label differently. But not all collections of people—even people who come together in working settings—are groups.

For our purposes, a **work group** is a small, interdependent collection of people with a common identity who interact with one another, usually face-to-face over time, to reach a goal. Using this definition, we can single out several significant characteristics of work groups that can help you develop ways to work more effectively with others on the job.

Size   Most experts say a twosome is not a group because the partners do not interact in the same way three or more people do. For instance, two people working together can resolve disputes only by persuading each other, giving in, or compromising. In groups, however, members can form alliances and outvote or pressure the minority.

Although less agreement exists about when a collection of people becomes too large to be considered a group, virtually every small group expert argues any collection much larger than 20 people loses many of the properties that define groups—at least effective ones.[11] Research on a number of companies has found 10-person groups and teams often produce better results at a quicker rate and with higher profits than do groups of several hundred.[12] There are several reasons why size doesn't translate into effectiveness: People begin to act in formal ways. Members have fewer chances to participate since a few talkative members are likely to dominate the group; quieter members lose their identity and become less committed to the group. Coalitions can form, leading members to become more concerned with having their side win than with tackling the challenge at hand.

Most communication experts suggest the optimal size for small decision-making groups is either 5 or 7 members.[13] The odd number of participants eliminates the risk of tie votes. Decision-making groups with fewer than 5 members lack the resources to come up with good ideas and to carry them out, while larger groups suffer from the problems of anonymity, domination, and lack of commitment. Recent research suggests 5 to 12 members can succeed, provided the type of task and the group composition are given primary consideration.[14]

Shared Purpose   Guests at a reception or attendees at a convention might talk with one another, but unless they share a collective goal, they won't collectively accomplish anything. One challenge facing anyone leading a newly created group is to give members a clear sense of shared purpose.

Interaction over Time   A collection of people studying in a library or working out at the gym is merely co-acting. Likewise a roomful of trainees at a seminar isn't a group unless and until the individuals start interacting. A group that interacts over a period of time develops particular characteristics. For example, a group will tend to develop shared standards of appropriate behavior members are expected to meet. Typical expectations involve how promptly meetings begin, what contribution each member is expected to make to certain routine tasks, what kind of humor is appropriate, and so on.

Interdependence   Group members don't just interact; they depend on one another. Consider the workers in a restaurant: If the kitchen crew fails to prepare orders promptly or correctly, the servers' tips will decline. If the employees who clear tables don't do their jobs quickly and thoroughly, the servers will hear complaints from their customers. If the waiters fail to take orders accurately, the cooks will have to fix some meals twice.

Learning Teamwork from Firefighters, Comedians, and Musicians

For one action-packed afternoon, a group of corporate workers traded in their office garb for gas masks, heavy boots, and turn-out gear. Coached by New York City firefighters, they assembled in four-person teams to learn about teamwork from first responders.

Dousing fires and staging subway rescues may seem far removed from office life. But the intense demands of performing in an emergency taught the participants a great deal about what it takes for a team to perform successfully.

"Firefighting is very complex and interdependent, and that has obvious applications to the business world," said one program planner. "Since our training puts people into crisis situations, hopefully they will be better prepared to handle any crisis that arises in the workplace."

Firefighting isn't the only nontraditional venue for developing teamwork. Chicago's Second City Communications offers comedy workshops for almost 400 corporate clients who learn that the flexibility and creativity required in an improvisational comedy troupe can transfer to facing business challenges. Music offers another setting to teach collaboration. The Minneapolis firm Jazz Impact has trained workers from Fortune 500 companies. Through improvisational jazz, employees learn from unscripted performing how to integrate solo performances and accompanying others into a successful piece of work.

Whether the setting is a burning building, a nightclub, or an office, the same principles of teamwork apply: Assemble a group of talented and trained members. Be flexible. Forget about personal glory and do whatever it takes to get the job done.

Source: Kranz, G. (2011, May). Corporate leaders train in fire drills and funny skills. *Workforce Management*, pp. 28–30, 32.

Identity   Both members and outsiders view groups as distinct entities. Some groups have a formal title such as "benefits committee" or "accounting department." Others have an informal identity like "lunchtime power walkers" or "those guys who carpool together." In either case, the fact that the group is seen as distinct has important consequences. To a greater or lesser extent, members feel their own image is tied to the way the group is regarded. In addition, the group's identity means the addition or loss of a member feels significant to the people involved, whether the change in membership is cause for celebration or disappointment.

What Makes a Group a Team?

The term **team** appears everywhere in the business world. The positive connotations of a team—spirit, cooperation, hard work—lead some managers to give every collection of workers the team label. You don't have to be an athlete to appreciate the value of teams, and you don't need to be a cynic to know calling a group of people a team doesn't make them one.[15] True teams have all the attributes of a group, but they have other qualities that distinguish them and make them more satisfying to work in and more productive.[16]

Groups	Teams
Members primarily concerned with their own challenges and goals	Members focus primarily on team challenges and goals
Members produce individual products	Members produce collective products
Work shaped by manager	Work shaped collectively by team leader and members

Not all teams are equally effective. Researchers Carl Larson and Frank LaFasto spent nearly three years interviewing members of more than 75 teams that were clearly winners. The teams came from a wide range of enterprises, including a Mount Everest expedition, a cardiac surgery team, the presidential commission that studied the space shuttle Challenger accident, the team that developed the IBM personal computer, and two championship football teams. Although the teams pursued widely different goals, they all shared eight important characteristics.[17] You can understand both why your team functions as it does and how to improve its effectiveness by analyzing how well it fits the profile of these winning teams.

- *Clear and inspiring shared goals.* Members of a winning team know why their team exists, and they believe that purpose is important and worthwhile. Ineffective teams have either lost sight of their purpose or do not believe the goal is truly important.

- *A results-driven structure.* Members of winning teams focus on getting the job done in the most effective manner. Less effective teams either are not organized or are structured inefficiently, and their members don't care enough about the results to do what is necessary to get the job done.

- *Competent team members.* Members of winning teams have the skill necessary to accomplish their goals. Less effective teams lack people possessing one or more key skills.

- *Unified commitment.* People in successful teams put the group's goals above their personal interests. While this commitment might seem like a sacrifice to others, the personal rewards for members of winning teams are worth the effort.

- *Collaborative climate.* Another word for collaboration is *teamwork*. People in successful teams trust and support one another.

- *Standards of excellence.* In winning teams, doing outstanding work is an important norm. Each member is expected to do his or her personal best. In less successful teams, getting by with the minimum amount of effort is the standard.

- *External support and recognition.* Successful teams need an appreciative audience that recognizes their effort and provides the resources necessary to get the job done. The audience may be a boss, or it may be the public the team is created to serve.

- *Principled leadership.* Winning teams usually have leaders who can create a vision of the team's purpose and challenge members to get the job done. Finally, they have the ability to unleash the members' talent.

You may not be able to single-handedly transform your entire organization into a team-friendly environment, but it is still possible to influence the group of people with whom you work. Examine the characteristics of teams listed above and ask yourself whether you are communicating in a manner that makes that small but important leap possible.

Virtual Teams

Virtual teams interact and function without being in the same place at the same time.[18] As one observer put it, virtual team members are "working together apart."[19] Technology permits virtual teams to transcend boundaries of location and time. Barry Caldwell, supervisor of computer-aided industrial design technologies at Ford Motor Company's Corporate Design division, concurs, explaining how Ford's virtual teams span the globe: "We can't change the fact that Europe is five or six hours ahead [of Michigan]," he says. "But virtual teams can be extremely effective if you can have people working in Italy or

TECHNOLOGY **tip**

Working in Virtual Teams

1. Strive for some "face time," especially during the team's formation. Virtual teams are most cohesive, trusting, and successful when members have had a chance to spend time together in person, especially during the team's development.

2. Put communication on the agenda. Agree up front on when and how members should communicate with one another. Consider which channels are most appropriate and agree on response times.

3. Be mindful of time zone differences. When members of a virtual team are dispersed across time zones, it's especially important to schedule meetings so members are inconvenienced as little as possible. Time differences can be especially challenging when groups span several continents. For example, if some members are in California and others in India, they are time shifted by a half-day, the only times that may work for people with normal schedules are early morning and early evening. Remember, Asia is a day ahead of the United States; Europe is five to nine hours ahead.

4. Use time zones to your advantage. Consider handing off tasks that members in other time ~~zones~~ ~~while~~ ~~are~~ ~~off work. For~~ example, a member in Seattle can request information at the end of the workday, and teammates in Florida can respond at the start of their next workday, so an answer will be in the sender's in-box when she or he logs on three hours later.

5. Keep a personal touch. Express some of the same emotions and personal thoughts you would in face-to-face communication. Doing so can build camaraderie and the human feeling virtual teams may lack without face-to-face communication.

6. Consider using "back channels." Use telephone, personal e-mail, and instant messaging to confer directly with one or more team members when you need to deal with issues and relationships personally in a way that will save the team time and effort.

7. Do a trial run of technology. Make sure in advance of meetings that all the technology upon which your team relies is working. It can be frustrating and discouraging to waste meeting time dealing with glitches.

8. Seek input from all team members. Sometimes members who are more comfortable with the technology of the virtual team will "speak" more than those who have more expertise in the team area but not with the technology being used.

9. Be aware of cultural differences in communication style. These exist in cyberspace as well as in face-to-face communication. Remind yourself of style differences in high- and low-context cultures, expectations of leaders and team members, and preferences for direct and indirect means of expression. Learn to read between the lines of ~~communication~~ ~~voicing~~ ~~your~~ ~~ideas~~ or offer advice.

Sources: Duarte, D. L., & Snyder, N. T. (2006). *Mastering virtual teams: Strategies, tools and techniques that succeed* (3rd ed.). San Francisco, CA: Jossey-Bass; Guffey, M. E. (2008). *Business communication: Process and product* (6th ed.). Florence, KY: Southwestern/Cengage; Rothwell, J. D. (2013). *In mixed company: Communicating in small groups and teams* (8th ed.). Boston, MA: Cengage.

Germany—five hours ahead of you—and they can hand work off to Dearborn at the end of their day, and you can carry it further and then pass it back. Instead of an eight-hour day, you can get 14 hours."[20]

Virtual teams aren't always—or even usually—on separate continents. Technology can keep members connected while telecommuting or on the road. Even when people work under the same roof, keeping in e-touch can make work more efficient. It's an oversimplification to suggest teams are either virtual or face-to-face. In truth, many groups are hybrids; members meet from time to time and keep in touch electronically between sessions. The guidelines in the Technology Tip box above can help you make sure the time spent communicating virtually is productive.

Besides being more efficient, in some circumstances virtual teams can be at least as effective as those who meet face-to-face. While newly formed teams do best when members can meet in person, established teams can work equally well in cyberspace.[21] In one study, teams that worked by exchanging e-mails produced better results than individuals and in-person groups.[22]

Virtual teamwork can be just as valuable for busy people who work near one another. Some human resources experts claim that when people work more than 50 feet apart, their likelihood of collaborating more than once a week is less than 10 percent.[23] Given this fact, virtual meetings can boost the efficiency of people who work under the same roof.

Another advantage of virtual teams is the leveling of status differences. On networked teams, rank is much less prominent than in face-to-face groups.[24] In e-mail, the ideas of a new or mid-level worker look identical to those of a senior manager. Back-and-forth dialogue is much less intimidating in mediated format than it might be when you have to face the boss in person.

Sometimes a virtual team needs to communicate in real time. Teleconferencing and instant messaging (IMing) make it easy and inexpensive to conduct synchronous virtual meetings. In other cases, working asynchronously can be more effective. Michael Charnow, vice president at California software developer Ontek Corp., describes the value of asynchronous conferencing for his staff: "We wanted telecommunications capabilities because work such as programming and research is done at all hours of the day and night, and we don't feel that people have to be physically present to do their best work."[25] For asynchronous meetings, Web-based discussion tools provided by Google, Yahoo, and others are simple to set up and manage.

Despite the advantages of virtual teamwork, computer networking can't replace all of the functions of personal contacts. "I go out of my way to ask people about their kids or some other aspect of their personal life," says Annette Suh, a project manager working with a team of U.S. software developers collaborating with developers in Russia.[26]

● Leadership and Influence in Teams

In group endeavors, successes or failures often are attributed to leadership. Coaches of losing sports teams risk being fired, while winning coaches are celebrated. CEOs of bankrupt companies are ousted by their boards of directors, while CEOs of profitable companies earn sizeable bonuses. When ethical lapses occur in an organization, a "lack of leadership" is often cited as the culprit. In this section, we look at the role of communication in effective—and ineffective—leadership.

Perspectives on Leadership

Throughout much of the history of organizations, leadership was considered to be a role held by an individual. More recently, researchers have come to recognize leadership is a process and different team members can take part in providing leadership to the team—with or without an official leadership role. Below is a short summary of several key approaches to understanding leadership.

Trait Approach   The **trait approach** is based on the belief that all leaders possess common traits that lead to their effectiveness. The earliest research sought to identify these traits, and by the mid-1930s scores of studies pursued this goal. Conclusions were contradictory, casting doubt on the approach. Certain traits did seem common in most leaders, including physical attractiveness, sociability, desire for leadership, originality, and intelligence.[27] Despite these similarities, the research also showed these traits were not predictive of leadership. In other words, a person possessing these characteristics would not necessarily become a leader. Another research approach was necessary.

Style Approach   Beginning in the 1940s, researchers began to consider the **style approach.** They asked whether the designated leader could choose a way of communicating that would increase effectiveness. This research identified three managerial styles. Some leaders are **authoritarian,** using the power at their disposal to control members. Others are more **democratic,** inviting members to help make decisions. A third leadership style is **laissez-faire:** The designated leader gives up the power of that position and transforms the group into a leaderless collection of equals.

Early research seemed to suggest the democratic style produced the best results,[28] and contemporary studies suggest members of groups with democratic leadership are slightly more satisfied than those run by autocratic leaders.[29] Still, it is an oversimplification to say that a democratic approach always works best. For instance, groups with autocratic leaders were more productive in stressful situations, while democratically led groups did better when the conditions were nonstressful.[30]

One of the best-known stylistic approaches is the Leadership Grid® by Robert Blake and Jane Mouton (see Figure 7.1),[31] which shows good leadership depends on skillful management of the task and the relationships among group members. The horizontal axis of the grid measures a manager's concern for task or production—getting the job done. The vertical axis measures the leader's concern for people and relationships. Blake and Mouton's grid counteracts the tendency in some naive managers to assume if they focus solely on the task, good results will follow. They argue the most effective leader is one who adopts a 9,9 style, showing high concern for both product *and* people.

Contingency Approaches   Unlike the style approach, **contingency approaches** are based on the idea that the "best" leadership style is flexible—it changes from one situation to the next. For instance, a manager who successfully guides a project team developing an advertising campaign might flop as a trainer or personnel officer.

Psychologist Fred Fiedler conducted extensive research in an attempt to discover when a task-oriented approach works best and when a relationship-oriented style is most effective.[32] He found a decision about whether to emphasize task or relationship issues in a situation depends on three factors: (1) *leader–member relations,* including the manager's attractiveness and the followers' loyalty; (2) *task structure,* involving the degree of simplicity or complexity of the job; and (3) *the leader's power,* including job title and the ability to coerce and reward.

Generally, Fiedler's research suggests a task-oriented approach works best when circumstances are extremely favorable (good leader–member relations, highly structured tasks) or extremely unfavorable (poor leader–member relations, unstructured task, weak leader power). In moderately favorable or unfavorable circumstances, a relationship-oriented approach works best. While these findings are useful, it is important not to overstate them. In most cases, good leadership requires a mixture of relationship and task concerns. The question is not which dimension to choose but which one to emphasize.

Another model of situational leadership is the life-cycle approach developed by Paul Hersey and Kenneth Blanchard.[33] The **life-cycle theory** suggests a leader's concern for tasks and relationships ought to vary. A worker with a low level of readiness to work independently needs a highly directive and task-related style of leadership. As the subordinate becomes able to perform the task without guidance, the manager withdraws the task-related supervision even more. Finally, when the worker's ability to handle a task is

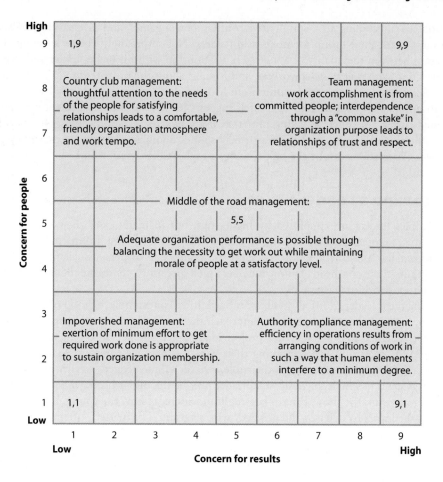

FIGURE 7.1

The Leadership Grid®

Source: From *Leadership Dilemmas—Grid Solutions* by Robert R. Blake and Anne Adams McCanse (formerly the *Managerial Grid* by Robert R. Blake and Jane S. Mouton). Houston: Gulf Publishing Company, p. 29. Copyright 1991 by Scientific Methods, Inc. Reproduced by permission of Grid International Inc.

superior, the boss can cut back the amount of socioemotional support, knowing the worker is functioning at the highest level and any reinforcements are now primarily internal.

Leader–Member Exchange

So far we've been assuming leaders treat all group members equally. But your own experience probably shows leaders have different relationships with each person on their team. Some of these relationships are characterized by positive communication and mutual satisfaction. Others can be more distant or even fraught with dissatisfaction on both sides. Recognizing this fact, **Leader–Member Exchange (LMX)** theory views leadership as a collection of multiple relationships with members, each one unique.

The basic premise of LMX is that leaders—no matter how good they are—have a limited amount of time and energy. As a result, they can't give every member an equal amount of resources. Inevitably, some people get more, and some get less.[34] This "differential distribution" is both the cause and the effect of some leader–member relationships being "high quality" (i.e., more rich and satisfying) and others being lower quality.

Communication in high-quality LMX relationships is typically positive and reinforcing, characterized by support statements, coaching, and joint decision making. When disagreements arise, they are handled respectfully and constructively. This treatment marks certain members as "insiders." Communication in low-quality LMX relationships is dramatically different. There is often less interaction, and what does occur can include more face-threatening acts, competitive conflict, power games, and defensiveness.[35] Such patterns mark these group members as outsiders. Not surprisingly, there's a strong connection between the quality of a member's relationship with his or her leader and overall satisfaction with that boss, coworkers, and feelings about the organization as a whole.[36]

As a member, you can communicate in ways that lead to a high-quality "insider" relationship with your leader.[37] Research suggests leaders are most impressed by "work-related currencies," such as taking initiative, exercising responsibility, and going beyond the official job description.[38] Basic as it may sound, doing a good job and exceeding the leader's expectations can be the best route to a high-quality relationship.

Becoming a Leader

Sometimes leaders are appointed by higher-ups, but in many cases they emerge from a group. **Emergent leaders** may be chosen by the members of a group either officially or informally. An athletic team may elect a captain. The owners' association of a condominium chooses a head. Union members pick a team to represent them in contract negotiations with management.

Emergent leaders don't always have official titles. For example, a group of disgruntled employees might urge one person to approach the boss and ask for a change. A team of students assigned to develop a class project might agree one person is best suited to take the lead in organizing and presenting their work. Sometimes emergent leaders are officially recognized, but other times their role is never acknowledged overtly. In fact, there are often cases in which the designated leader may be the titular head, while an emergent leader really runs the show. Fans of late-night movies recall how the young, inexperienced lieutenant learns to defer to the grizzled, wise sergeant. This pattern often repeats itself in everyday working situations when new managers or supervisors recognize the greater knowledge of old-timers who are subordinates on the organizational chart. In cases like these, the new manager is smart to defer to the unofficial, emergent leader—at least until he or she gains some experience and wisdom.

Communication researcher Ernest Bormann studied how emergent leaders gain influence, especially in newly formed groups.[39] According to Bormann, a group selects a leader by the *method of residues*—a process of elimination in which potential candidates are gradually rejected for one reason or another until only one remains. This process of elimination occurs in two phases. In the first, members who are clearly unsuitable are rejected. The surest path to rejection is being quiet; less talkative members were never chosen as leaders in the groups Bormann studied. Failing to participate verbally in a group's work leaves the impression of indifference and lack of commitment. Another ticket to early rejection is dogmatism: Members who express their opinions in strong, unqualified terms are usually perceived as being too extreme and inflexible to take a leading role. A third cause of elimination as leader is a lack of skill or intelligence: Competence is obviously a necessary condition for successful leadership, and members who lack this quality are rejected early.

Quietness, dogmatism, and incompetence are almost always grounds for disqualification. Beyond these factors, a communication style members find irritating or disturbing is likely to knock a member out of consideration as a leader. A variety of behaviors fall into this category, depending on the composition of the group. In one case being too serious might be grounds for rejection, while in a different situation a joker would earn disapproval. Using inappropriate language could be a disqualifier. In a group with biased members, gender or ethnicity might be grounds for rejection.

After clearly unsuitable members have been eliminated, roughly half of the group's members may still be candidates for leadership. This can be a tense time since the jockeying for a role of influence may pit the remaining candidates against one another. In some

How to Emerge as a Team Leader

If you are interested in seeking a leadership position—and you almost certainly will be at one time or another—research has demonstrated the following types of behavior will help you assert your influence.

- Participate early and often. Talking won't guarantee you will be recognized as a leader, but failing to speak up will almost certainly knock you out of the running.

- Demonstrate your competence. Make sure your comments identify you as someone who can help the team succeed. Demonstrate the kinds of expert, connection, and information power described later in this chapter.

- Don't push too hard. It's fine to be assertive, but don't try to overpower other members. Even if you are right, your dogmatism is likely to alienate others.

- Provide a solution in a time of crisis. How can the team meet a deadline? Gain the sale? Get the necessary equipment? Members who find answers to problems like these are likely to rise to a position of authority.

Source: Hackman, M. A., & Johnson, C. E. (2004). *Leadership: A communication perspective.* Long Grove, IL: Waveland Press. Reprinted by permission of Waveland Press, Inc. All rights reserved. See also Anderson, C., & Kilduff, G. J. (2009). Why do dominant personalities attain influences in face-to-face groups? The competence-signaling effects of trait dominance. Journal of Personality and Social Psychology, 96, 491–503.

groups, the contenders for leader acquire what Bormann calls "lieutenants," who support the contenders' advancement. If only one candidate has a lieutenant, his or her chances of becoming leader are strong. If two or more contenders have supporters, the process of leader emergence can drag out or even reach a stalemate. The Career Tip box above offers advice for the times when you want to take on leadership of a group.

In their book *Getting It Done: How to Lead When You're Not in Charge,* Roger Fisher and Alan Sharp describe "lateral leadership" as a way to avoid the extremes of doing nothing or taking charge and bossing others. They suggest a team member can lead others by doing three things: *asking* thoughtful, sincere questions to get others to think creatively and contribute their ideas; *offering* ideas to help the team while inviting others to challenge your thoughts; and *doing* something constructive needed by the team and modeling the behavior needed.[40]

Power and Influence of Members

Many teams have a **designated leader**—the supervisor, chairperson, coach, or manager who has formal authority and responsibility to supervise the task at hand. Other groups, called **self-directed work teams,** are responsible for managing their own behavior to get a task done.[41] For example, at one General Mills cereal plant, teams schedule, operate, and maintain machinery so effectively the plant runs with no managers present during night shifts. The company reports productivity at plants that rely on self-managed teams is as much as 40 percent higher than at traditional factories. At Federal Express, a team of clerks spotted and solved a billing problem, saving the company $2.1 million in just one year. Harley-Davidson successfully organizes operations at its Kansas City, Missouri, motorcycle assembly plant using self-directed teams.[42]

Whether or not a team has a designated leader, every member has the power to shape events. More than a half-century ago, John French and Bertram Raven identified several forms of power that are usually possessed by one or more members of a group—not necessarily just the designated leader.[43] Depending on how they are used, these forms of power can make or break a team's success.

"Now that you've all put in your two cents' worth, I should like to interject my fifty-one per cent controlling interest."

© Joseph Mirachi/The New Yorker Collection/www.cartoonbank.com.

Position Power

Position power is the ability to influence that comes from the position one holds. We often do things for the boss precisely because he or she holds that title. While position power usually belongs to designated leaders, people in lesser positions sometimes have jobs that involve telling higher-ups what to do. For example, a media expert might have the position power to tell the CEO or board chairman what will and won't work in a presentation to stockholders.

Coercive Power

The power to punish is known as **coercive power** because we often follow another's bidding when failure to do so would lead to unpleasant consequences. Designated leaders have coercive power: They can assign unpleasant tasks, deny pay raises, and even fire people. Other members have coercive power, too, though it is usually subtle. A committee member or officemate who acts as a blocker when things don't go his way is coercing others to take his views into account, implying, "If you don't follow at least some of my suggestions, I'll punish the team by continuing to object to your ideas and refusing to cooperate with you."

Reward Power

The flip side of coercive power is **reward power**—the ability to reward. Designated leaders control the most obvious rewards: pay raises, improved working conditions, and the ability to promote. But, again, other members can give their own rewards. These come in the form of social payoffs, such as increased goodwill, and task-related benefits, like voluntary assistance on a job.

Expert Power

Expert power comes from the group's recognition of a member's expertise in a certain area. There are times when one expert is better suited to make a decision than is an entire team. Designated leaders aren't always the experts in a group. In a manufacturing firm, for example, a relatively low-ranking engineer could influence management to alter a project by using her knowledge to declare a new product won't work. Problems can arise either when management doesn't recognize a knowledgeable member as an expert or when unqualified people are granted expert status.

Referent Power

The term **referent power** alludes to the influence members hold due to the way others in the group feel about them: their respect, attraction, or liking. It is here the greatest difference between designated leaders and members with true influence occurs. An unpopular boss might have to resort to his or her job title and the power to coerce and reward that comes with it to gain compliance, whereas a popular person, with or without a leadership title, can get others to cooperate without threatening or promising.[44] Mike Zugsmith, co-owner of a commercial real estate brokerage, captures the importance of referent power, even for a boss: "When I started this company in 1979, I was 28. I was supervising salespeople who were 20 to 30 years my senior. It readily became apparent that simply because your name is on the door doesn't mean you'll get respect. You have to earn it."[45]

Information Power

Information power is the ability of some members to influence a group because of the information they possess. This information is different from the kind of knowledge that gives rise to expert power. Whereas an expert possesses some form of talent based on training or education, an information-rich group member has access to otherwise obscure knowledge valuable to others in the group. A new employee who was hired away from a competitor, for example, is likely to play a key role in the decisions of how his new company will compete against the old one. Likewise, a member who is well connected to the organizational grapevine can exert a major influence on how the group operates: "Don't bring that up now. Smith is going through a divorce, and he's saying no to everything." "I just heard there's plenty of money in the travel and entertainment budget. Maybe this is the time to propose that reception for the out-of-town distributors we've been thinking about."

Connection Power   In the business world, a member's influence can often come from the connections he or she has with influential or important people inside or outside the organization—hence the term **connection power.** The classic example of connection power is the boss's son or daughter. While the official word from the top may be "Treat my kid just like any other employee," this is easier said than done. Not all connection power is harmful. If one member sees a potential customer socially, he is in a good position to help the business. If another one knows a government official, she can get off-the-record advice about how to handle a government regulation.

If we recognize the influence that comes with connection power, the old saying "It isn't what you know that counts, it's who you know" seems true. If we look at all the types of power described in this section, we can see a more accurate statement is "What counts is whom you know [connection power], what you know [information and expert power], who respects you [referent power], and who you are [position power]." This range of power bases makes it clear that the power to influence a group is truly shared among members, all who have the ability to affect how well a group works as a unit and the quality of the product it turns out.

• Effective Communication in Teams

Whether you are in a team with a powerful leader or one with shared decision-making power, you can communicate in ways that help the team work effectively and make the experience satisfying. For the team to function well, each member must take into account the issues and problems that may arise whenever people try to communicate.

"What we didn't have but obviously needed was an alarmist."

© Leo Cullum/The New Yorker Collection/www.cartoonbank.com.

Fill Functional Roles

One way every member can shape the way a team operates is by acting in whatever way is necessary to help get the job done. This approach has been labeled the "functional perspective" because it defines influence in terms of fulfilling essential functions, not formal titles. These essential contributions have earned the name **functional roles** because they involve functions that are necessary for the team to do its job. Table 7-2 lists these functional roles and notes some dysfunctional behaviors that reduce the effectiveness of a team. As the table shows, there are two types of functional roles. **Task roles** play an important part in accomplishing the job at hand. **Relational roles** help keep the interaction between members running smoothly.[46]

Table 7-2 is a valuable diagnostic tool. When a team isn't operating effectively, you must determine which functions are lacking. For instance, you might note the team has several good ideas but no one is summarizing and coordinating them. Or perhaps the team lacks a crucial piece of information, but no one realizes this fact.

In some cases, your diagnosis of a troubled team might show that all the necessary task functions are being filled but members' social needs aren't being met. Perhaps members need to have their good ideas supported ("That's a terrific idea, Neil!"). Maybe personal conflicts need to be acknowledged and resolved ("I know I sound defensive about this. I've worked on this idea for a month, and I hate to see it dismissed in 5 minutes."). When social needs like these go unfilled, even the best knowledge and talent often aren't enough to guarantee a team's smooth functioning.

Sometimes a team will transform important functional roles into formal ones. For example, at financial services giant Charles Schwab, one person in every meeting serves as an observer-diagnoser.[47] This person doesn't take part in the discussion; instead, he or she creates a list of what went right (e.g., "Good creativity," "Excellent use of time") and what went wrong (e.g., "Lots of digressions," "Personal criticism created defensiveness") in the meeting. This list is included in the minutes, which management reviews. It's easy to imagine how the observer's comments can help a team improve its effectiveness.

Having too many people fill a particular functional role can be just as troublesome as having nobody fill it. For example, you might discover several people are acting as opinion-givers but no one is serving as an opinion-seeker. If two or more people compete for the role of direction-giver, the results can be confusing. Even social roles can be overdone. Too much tension relieving or praise giving can become annoying.

Once you have identified the missing functions, you can fill them. Supplying these missing roles often transforms a stalled, frustrated team into a productive one.[48] Other members probably won't recognize what you're doing, but they will realize you somehow know how to say the right thing at the right time.

Recognize Both Team and Personal Goals

Every team operates to achieve some specific goal: selling a product, providing a service, getting a job done, and so on. In addition to pursuing a team's goals, members usually also have their own individual goals. Sometimes an individual's goal in a team

Table 7-2	Functional Roles of Team Members

Task Functions

1. *Information- or opinion-giver.* Offers facts or opinions relevant to team task.

2. *Information- or opinion-seeker.* Asks others for task-related information or opinions.

3. *Starter or energizer.* Initiates or encourages task-related behavior (e.g., "We'd better get going on this").

4. *Direction-giver.* Provides instructions regarding how to perform task at hand.

5. *Summarizer.* Reviews what has been said, identifying common themes or progress.

6. *Diagnoser.* Offers observations about task-related behavior of team (e.g., "We seem to be spending all of our time discussing the problem without proposing any solutions").

7. *Gatekeeper.* Regulates participation of members.

8. *Reality-tester.* Checks feasibility of ideas against real-world contingencies.

Relational Functions

1. *Participation encourager.* Encourages reticent members to speak, letting them know their contribution will be valued.

2. *Harmonizer.* Resolves interpersonal conflicts between members.

3. *Tension-reliever.* Uses humor or other devices to release members' anxiety and frustration.

4. *Evaluator of emotional climate.* Offers observations about socioemotional relationships between members (e.g., "I think we're all feeling a little defensive now," or "It sounds like you think nobody trusts you, Bill").

5. *Praise-giver.* Reinforces accomplishments and contributions of members.

6. *Empathic listener.* Listens without evaluation to personal concerns of members.

Dysfunctional Roles

1. *Blocker.* Prevents progress by constantly raising objections.

2. *Attacker.* Aggressively questions others' competence or motives.

3. *Recognition-seeker.* Repeatedly and unnecessarily calls attention to self by relating irrelevant experiences, boasting, and seeking sympathy.

4. *Joker.* Engages in joking behavior in excess of tension-relieving needs, distracting members.

5. *Withdrawer.* Refuses to take stand on social or task issues; covers up feelings; does not respond to others' comments.

is identical (or nearly identical) to the group's shared goal. For example, a retailer might join the community Christmas fund-raising campaign out of a sincere desire to help the needy. In most cases, however, people also have more personal motives for joining a team. The retailer, for instance, might realize that working on the fund-raising campaign will improve both his visibility and his image in the community—and ultimately lead to more business. Notice the relationships between some common team and individual goals:

Use the inventory below to identify how well your team is performing these important communication practices.

As a Team, How Well Did You:	Not Well				Very Well
Define or clarify the task	1	2	3	4	5
Exchange and share information	1	2	3	4	5
Encourage expression of various points of view	1	2	3	4	5
Evaluate and analyze data	1	2	3	4	5
Use the best decision-making approach (consensus, majority rule, etc.)	1	2	3	4	5
Focus on tasks, not individuals	1	2	3	4	5
Demonstrate respect for all	1	2	3	4	5
Encourage feedback	1	2	3	4	5
Encourage expression of opinion	1	2	3	4	5
Build on others' ideas	1	2	3	4	5
Ask for clarification of ideas	1	2	3	4	5
Demonstrate equality	1	2	3	4	5
Address disagreements or misunderstandings	1	2	3	4	5
Stay on task	1	2	3	4	5

Team Goal	Individual Goal
Sales department wants to meet annual sales target.	Sales representative wants to earn bonus.
Retailer wants to expand hours to attract new business.	Employees want to avoid working nights and weekends.
Company wants employee to attend a seminar in Minneapolis.	Employee wants to visit family in Minneapolis.

As some of these examples show, personal goals aren't necessarily harmful to a team or an organization if they are compatible with overall objectives. In fact, under these circumstances they can actually help the team to achieve its goals. For instance, sales representatives who want to increase their commissions will try to sell more of the company's products. Similarly, an otherwise reluctant employee might volunteer to attend a January seminar in Minneapolis to see her family during the visit.

Only when an individual's goals conflict with the organization's or team's goals do problems occur. If Lou and Marian hate each other, their arguments could keep the team from getting much done in meetings. If Bill is afraid of losing his job because of a mistake that has been made, he may concentrate on trying to avoid being blamed rather than on solving the problem.

The range of personal goals that can interfere with team effectiveness is surprisingly broad. One or more team members might be concerned with finishing the job quickly and getting away to take care of personal business. Others might be more concerned with being liked or appearing smart than with doing the job as quickly or effectively as possible. Someone else might want to impress the boss. All these goals, as well as dozens of others, can sidetrack or derail a team from doing its job.

As Table 7-3 shows, teams will be harmonious and most efficient when the members are also reaching their personal goals. You can boost your team's effectiveness by doing everything possible to help members satisfy those goals. If the people in your team are looking for fun and companionship, consider ways to tackle the job at hand that also give them what they want. On the other hand, if they are in a hurry because of busy schedules, concentrate on keeping meetings to a minimum. If some members like recognition, stroke their egos by offering compliments whenever you can sincerely do so. The extra effort you spend attending to members' individual needs will pay dividends in terms of the energy and loyalty the team gains from happy members.

In some cases, team members announce their personal goals. In other cases, though, stating a personal goal outright could be embarrassing or counterproductive. A committee member wouldn't confess, "I volunteered to serve on this committee so I could find new people to date." An employee would never say openly, "I'm planning to learn everything I can here and then quit the firm and open my own business." Personal goals that are not made public are called **hidden agendas.**

Table 7-3	Team Process Variables Associated with Productivity

1. Members are clear about and agree with team goals.
2. Tasks are appropriate for team versus individual solutions.
3. Members are clear about and accept their formal roles.
4. Role assignments match members' abilities.
5. Level of leader's direction matches the team's skill level.
6. All team members are encouraged to participate.
7. Team gets, gives, and uses feedback about its effectiveness and productivity.
8. Team spends time defining and discussing problems it must solve or decisions it must make. Members also spend time planning how they will solve problems and make decisions.
9. Team uses effective decision-making strategies that were outlined in advance.
10. Team evaluates its solutions and decisions.
11. Norms encourage high performance and quality, success, and innovation.
12. Subgroups are integrated into the team as a whole.
13. Team contains the smallest number of members necessary to accomplish its goals.
14. Team has enough time to develop cohesiveness and accomplish its goals.
15. Team has cooperative orientation.
16. Disagreements occur frequently but are usually resolved quickly.

Source: Wheelan, S. A., Murphy, D., Tsumura, E., & Kline, S. F. (1998). Member perceptions of internal group dynamics and productivity. *Small Group Research, 29,* 371–393.

Hidden agendas are not necessarily harmful. A member's dating goals need not interfere with team functions. Similarly, many other personal motives are not threatening or even relevant to a team's business. Some hidden agendas may even be beneficial. For instance, an up-and-coming young worker's desire to communicate competence to the boss by volunteering for difficult jobs might help the team. International team consultant Frank Heckman sees that the "bottom line is that we all have personal agendas and to some degree, some are hidden even to us."[49] Other hidden agendas, however, are harmful, and Heckman adds that "the problem will come in if the individual is duplicitous and undermines what the team is trying to achieve."[50] Two feuding members who use meetings to disparage each other can only harm the team, and the person collecting ideas to go into business himself will most likely hurt the organization when he takes its ideas elsewhere.

There is no single best way to deal with harmful hidden agendas. Sometimes the best course is to bring the goal out into the open. For example, a manager might speak to feuding subordinates one at a time, let them know she recognizes their problem, and work with them to solve it directly and constructively (probably using the conflict management skills described in Chapter 5). When you do decide to bring a hidden personal goal into the open, it's almost always better to confront the member privately. The embarrassment of being unveiled publicly is usually so great the person becomes defensive and denies the hidden goal exists.

At other times, it is best to treat a hidden personal goal indirectly. For example, if a member's excessive talking in meetings seems to be a bid for recognition, the best approach might be to make a point of praising his valid contributions more frequently. If two feuding subordinates continue to have trouble working together, the manager can assign them to different projects or transfer one or both of them to different teams.

Promote Desirable Norms

Norms are informal, often unstated rules about what behavior is appropriate.[51] Some norms govern the way tasks are handled, while others shape the social interaction of the team. A team's norms are often shaped by the culture of the organization to which it belongs. For example, 3M's success has been attributed to its "bias for yes": When in doubt, employees are encouraged to take a chance instead of avoiding action for fear of failure.[52] Likewise, Motorola's turnaround has been attributed to its changing norms for conflict. The company's culture now makes it acceptable to disagree strongly (and loudly) in meetings instead of keeping quiet or being overly diplomatic.[53] As Table 7-4 shows, the norms in some teams are constructive, whereas other teams have equally powerful rules that damage their effectiveness.[54]

The challenge of establishing norms is especially great when members come from different cultural backgrounds.[55] For example, team members from a low-context culture (such as the United States or Canada) would be more likely to address conflicts directly, whereas those from high-context backgrounds (East Asia or the Middle East, for example) would be inclined to use indirect approaches. Likewise, members from a background where high power distance is the norm would be less likely to challenge a team's leader than those from a background where low power distance is the norm.

Once norms are established, members who violate them create a crisis for the rest of the team, who respond in a series of escalating steps.[56] Consider, for example, a worker who violates the norm of not following up on her obligations between team meetings. Her teammates might react with increasing pressure:

- *Delaying action.* Members talk among themselves but do not approach the deviant, hoping she will change without pressure.
- *Hinting about the violation.* Members tease the violator about being a "flake" or about being lazy, hoping the message behind the humor will cause her to do her share of work.

Table 7-4	Typical Constructive (and Destructive) Norms for a Team

- Handle (Ignore) business for coworkers who are away from their desks.
- Be willing (Refuse) to admit your mistakes.
- Occasional time off from work for personal reasons is (isn't) okay, as long as the absence won't harm the company.
- Do (Don't) be willing to work overtime without complaining when big, important deadlines approach.
- Say so (Keep quiet) if you disagree. Don't (Do) hint or go behind others' backs.
- Avoid (Hold) side conversations during meetings.
- Don't (Do) interrupt or ignore others' ideas.
- Arrive on time (Be late) for meetings.
- Celebrate (Don't celebrate) successes.
- Honor (Shirk) your commitments.

Source: Baum, J. A. C. (n.d.). Avoiding common team problems. *Rotman School of Management*. Retrieved from http://www.rotman .utoronto.ca/~baum/mgt2003/avoid.html

- *Discussing the problem openly.* Members confront the nonconformist, explaining their concerns about her behavior.
- *Ridiculing and deriding the violator.* Persuasion shifts to demands for a change in behavior; the team's pressure tactics may well trigger a defensive response in the nonconforming member.
- *Rejecting or isolating the deviant.* If all other measures fail, the team member who doesn't conform to team norms is asked to leave the group. If she cannot be expelled, other members can excommunicate her by not inviting her to meetings and by disregarding any attempts at communicating she might make.

There are two ways in which an understanding of norms can help you to function more effectively in a team.

Create Desirable Norms Early   Norms are established early in a team. Once they exist, they are difficult to change. This means when you participate in a team that is just being established, you should do whatever you can to create norms you think will be desirable. For example, if you expect committee members to be punctual at meetings, it's important to begin each session at the appointed time. If you want others to be candid about their feelings, it's important to be frank yourself and encourage honesty in others at the outset.

Comply with Established Norms Whenever Possible   In an established team, you have the best chance of reaching your goals if you handle the task and social relationships in the team's customary manner. If your coworkers are in the habit of exchanging good-natured insults, you shouldn't be offended when you are the target—and you will be accepted as one of them if you dish out a few yourself. In a team in which the norm is never to criticize another member's ideas directly, a blunt approach probably won't get you very far. When you are entering an established team, it's wise to learn the norms by personal observation and by asking knowledgeable members about them before plunging in.

ETHICAL **challenge**

The Unproductive Teammate

You are a member of what was once a dream team of productive workers. Until recently, everyone worked well together to meet the team's goals. When one member took time off to care for a child in the hospital a few months ago, everyone was happy to cover for him. Over the next months the same member began missing more work because of other problems—a spouse needing care, a sports injury, and moving to a new home. The rest of the team has begun to doubt their unproductive colleague will ever contribute his fair share to the team again, and they agree it's time to raise this issue.

Describe how the team can deal with this issue in a way that acknowledges both the unproductive member's legitimate problems and the team's need for the member to do his share.

A national or regional culture can also shape the way team members communicate with one another. Differences in managing conflict are a good example. The straight-talking, low-context style that is accepted in many parts of the English-speaking world is not the norm in other places.[57] It may not always be possible to follow established norms. If a team is in the habit of cracking racist jokes, doing shabby work, or stealing company property, for example, you would probably be unwilling to go along just to be accepted. This sort of conflict between personal values and team norms can lead to a major crisis in values. If the potential for conflict is great enough and the issue is sufficiently important, you may decide to do whatever you can to join a different, more compatible team.

Promote an Optimal Level of Cohesiveness

Cohesiveness can be defined as the degree to which members feel themselves part of a team and want to remain with that team. You can think of cohesiveness as a magnetic force that attracts members to one another, giving them a collective identity. As you might suspect, highly cohesive teams have happier members than less closely knit groups. Workers who belong to cohesive teams are likely to have higher rates of job satisfaction and lower rates of tension, absenteeism, and turnover than those who belong to less cohesive ones.[58] They also make better decisions.[59]

Not all cohesive teams are productive—at least not in terms of the organization's goals. In strikes and slowdowns, for example, highly cohesive workers can actually shut down operations. (Of course, the workers' cohesiveness in such cases may help them to accomplish other team goals, such as higher pay or safer working conditions.) In less dramatic cases, cohesiveness in observing anti-organization norms ("Don't work too hard," "Go ahead and report our lunch as a business expense—we always do that," "If you need some art supplies for your kids, just take them from the supply closet") can leave team members feeling good about each other but raise ethical issues and harm the organization's interests. Finally, too much cohesiveness can lead to the kinds of "groupthink" described on pp. 206–207.

Cohesiveness develops when certain conditions exist in a team. Once you understand these conditions, you can apply them to groups on or off the job. You can also use them to analyze why a team's cohesiveness is high or low and choose ways to reach and maintain a desirable level of cohesiveness. Here are seven factors that promote an optimal level of cohesiveness.[60]

Shared or Compatible Goals   Team members draw closer together when they have a similar aim or when their goals can be mutually satisfied. For instance, the members of a construction crew might have little cohesiveness when their pay is based on individual efforts, but if the entire crew receives a bonus for completing stages of the building ahead of schedule, the members are likely to work together better.

Progress toward Goals   When a team makes progress toward its target, members are drawn together; when progress stops, cohesiveness decreases. Members of the construction crew just mentioned will feel good about each other when they reach their target dates or can reasonably expect to do so. But if they consistently fall short, they are likely to get discouraged and feel less attraction to the team; when talking to their families or friends, there will be less talk about "us" and more about "me."

Shared Norms or Values   Although successful teams tolerate or even thrive on some differences in members' expressed attitudes and behaviors, wide variation in what members consider appropriate behavior reduces cohesiveness. For example, a person who insists on wearing conservative clothes in a business where everyone else dresses casually probably won't fit in with the rest of the group.

Minimal Feelings of Threat among Members   In a cohesive team, members usually feel secure about their status, dignity, and material and social well-being. When conflict arises over these issues, results can be destructive. If all of the junior executives in a division are competing for the same senior position—especially if senior positions rarely open—the team's cohesiveness is likely to suffer, at least until the job is filled.

Interdependence among Members   Teams become more cohesive when members need one another to satisfy team goals. When a job can be done by one person alone, the need for unity decreases. An office team in which each member performs a different aspect or stage of a process will be less cohesive than one in which members rely on one another.

Competition from Outside the Team   When members perceive an external threat to their existence or dignity, they draw closer together. Almost everyone knows of a family whose members seem to fight constantly among themselves until an outsider criticizes one of them. The internal bickering stops for the moment, and the team unites against the common enemy. An uncohesive team could draw together in a similar way when another group competes with it for such things as use of limited company resources or desirable space in a new office building. Many wise managers deliberately set up situations of competition between teams to get tasks accomplished more quickly or to generate more sales.

Shared Team Experiences   When members have been through an experience together, especially an unusual or trying one, they draw closer together. This is why soldiers who have gone through combat together often feel close for the rest of their lives. Teams that have accomplished difficult tasks are also likely to be more cohesive. Some organizations also provide social events such as annual "retreats" for their executives. These retreats might include high-ropes courses, workshops, sports

Devil's Advocate and Other Anti-Conformity Tools

Since medieval times, the Catholic Church has appointed a "Devil's advocate" to present all possible arguments—even seemingly slight ones—against promoting a candidate toward sainthood. The Church recognizes the danger of one-sided enthusiasm and relies on the advocate to make sure decision makers consider all sides of the issue. This approach can serve nonreligious groups just as well, especially when there is an undisputed consensus toward making an important decision. If your team doesn't have the foresight to appoint a devil's advocate, you can take on this role by challenging the majority's thinking.

Other approaches can serve as antidotes to groupthink. If the team has enough members, it can be helpful to set up two (or more) subgroups to consider approaches independently. Another approach is to request the opinions of respected outsiders who haven't been influenced by the collective enthusiasm of members.

events, and parties. Annual sales meetings, although not the most cost-efficient way to distribute sales information, are often partially intended to increase team cohesiveness.

Avoid Excessive Conformity

Bad group decisions can also come about through too much agreement among members. Irving Janis calls this phenomenon **groupthink,** an unwillingness, for the sake of harmony, to examine ideas critically.[61] Janis describes several characteristics of groups that succumb to groupthink:

- *Illusion that the group is invulnerable:* "We can afford to raise the price on our deluxe-model kitchen appliances because they're so much better than anything else on the market. Even if our competitors could develop comparable models, we'd still outdo them on style."

- *Tendency to rationalize or discount negative information:* "I know the market research says people will buy other brands if our prices go up anymore, but you know how unreliable market research is about things like that."

- *Willingness to ignore ethical or moral consequences of the team's decision:* "The waste we're dumping in the river may kill a few fish, but look, this company provides jobs and a living for all the people who live in this town."

- *Stereotyped views of other teams:* "The only thing those people at the head office care about is the bottom line. They don't give a damn about what we think or what we need."

- *Team pressure to conform:* "Come on, none of the rest of us is interested in direct-mail marketing. Why don't you forget that stuff?"

- *Self-censorship:* "Every time I push for an innovative ad campaign, everybody fights it. I might as well drop it."

- *Illusion of unanimity:* "Then we all agree: Cutting prices is the only way to stay competitive."

- *"Mindguards" against threatening information:* "They're talking about running the machines around the clock to meet the schedule. I'd better not bring up what the supervisor said about how her staff feels about working more overtime."

Diversity of voices can serve as an antidote to groupthink by broadening outlooks and enriching discussions. However, one study found multicultural teams might be inclined toward groupthink if their awareness of cultural differences creates a desire to avoid conflict.[62]

A second type of harmful conformity has been labeled **risky shift:** the likelihood of a group to take positions that are more extreme than the members would choose on their own.[63] A risky shift can work in two directions. When members are conservative, their collective decisions are likely to be more cautious than their individual positions. More commonly, teams are prone to taking riskier positions than the choices members would have taken had they been acting separately. Thus, risky shift results either in taking unjustified risks and suffering the costs or in avoiding necessary steps that the team needs to take to survive and prosper.

Paradoxically, cohesive teams are most prone to groupthink and risky shift. When members like and respect one another, the tendency to agree is great. The best way to guard against this sort of collective blindness—especially in very cohesive teams—is to seek the opinions of outsiders who may see things differently. In addition, leaders who are highly influential should avoid stating their opinions early in the discussion.[64]

MASTER **the chapter**

review points

- Small groups share characteristics of size, inter-action, shared purpose, interdependence, regular interaction and communication, and identity.

- Effective teams are productive, competent, and produce member commitment to their decisions.

- Virtual teams transcend time and space boundaries and present both advantages and challenges.

- The best approach to group leadership depends on the circumstances. In groups with a designated leader, the optimal style depends on leader–member relations, the structure of the task, and the leader's power. In groups with no designated leader, a predictable process occurs in which a single leader often emerges.

- Leadership is often shared among members who possess various types of power: position, coercive, reward, expert, referent, information, and connection.

- Members contribute to team effectiveness by enacting functional roles (both task and relational) while avoiding dysfunctional roles.

- Teams can be more successful when members recognize and try to fulfill both personal and team goals, promote desirable norms, promote an optimal level of cohesiveness, avoid excessive conformity, and boost creativity.

key terms

activities

1. Invitation to Insight

Consider an effective team you have observed or participated in. Identify the characteristics that contributed to this team's productivity. Provide an example of how the team enacted each of these characteristics. Then use concepts from this chapter to suggest at least one way the team could have improved.

2. Invitation to Insight

Interview a professional who regularly participates in virtual meetings. Identify what the person likes most and least about virtual meetings. In this person's opinion, what contributes most to the success of virtual meetings?

3. Invitation to Insight

Analyze the types of power that exist in a working group you are familiar with. Which members use each type of power? Who exerts the most influence? What kinds of power do you possess? Which types of power contribute most and least to your group's effectiveness?

4. Skill Builder

Using Table 7-2, identify the role each of these statements represents. Is it a task, relational, or dysfunctional role?

a. "Debby, could you hold on and let Martin speak first?"
b. "So far we have discussed six funding sources. . . ."
c. "Although you seem to disagree, both of you are concerned with. . . ."
d. "I think you're really on to something. That seems like the information we need."
e. "What else do you think we should consider?"
f. "George, that is a really stupid idea."
g. "This is an exciting idea we're considering. Before we commit, let's look at how much it's going to cost to see if we can really do it."
h. "If you ask me, this is just too much work. Let's quit and play a video game instead."
i. "OK. Now that we've finished brainstorming ideas, our next step is to evaluate them."
j. "I spent all yesterday evening making this graph. Why doesn't anyone at least thank me for it?"
k. "I found three websites with research studies we can use in this project."

5. Invitation to Insight

Which of the functional roles in Table 7-2 do you generally fill in groups? Do you fill the same role in most groups at most times, or do you switch roles as circumstances require? Do you tend to fill task roles or relational roles? How could you improve the functioning of one group you belong to by changing your role-related behavior?

6. Invitation to Insight

Although it may be larger than most of the groups discussed in this chapter, your class is a good model of the principles described here. Answer the following questions about your class or about a group you participate in:

a. What are the stated goals of the class or group? Does the group have any unstated, shared goals?

b. What are your individual goals? Which of these goals are compatible with the group's goals, and which are not compatible? Are any of your individual goals hidden agendas?

c. What are your instructor's or the group leader's individual goals? Were these goals stated? If not, how did you deduce them? How compatible are these goals with the official goals of the class or group?

d. How do the other members' individual goals affect the functioning of the group as a whole?

7. Skill Builder

Suggest several norms that would be desirable for each of the following groups. In your list, include norms that address tasks, relationships, and

procedures. How could you promote development of these norms as the group's leader? As a member?

a. A student fund-raising committee to develop scholarships for your major or department.

b. The employees at a new fast-food restaurant.

c. A group of new bank tellers.

d. A company softball team.

8. Skill Builder

Use the skills you learned in Chapter 6 to interview one member of a work-related group. Identify the following:

a. What is the level of the group's cohesiveness? Is this level desirable, too high, or too low?

b. Which of the factors on pp. 204–206 contribute to the level of cohesiveness in this group?

c. On the basis of your findings, develop a report outlining specific steps that might be taken to improve this group's cohesiveness.

9. Skill Builder

Recall a group you've participated in that demonstrated an excessive level of conformity. Identify negative outcomes that resulted from the excessive conformity. Which characteristics of groupthink did the group exhibit? What allowed these characteristics to exist? Write at least three suggestions that might have helped the group prevent over-conformity.

LearnSmart™

For further review, go to the LearnSmart study module for this chapter.

Chapter Eight
Effective Meetings

chapter objectives

After reading this chapter you should be able to:

1. Describe various types and purposes of meetings.

2. Identify reasons to hold (or not hold) a meeting.

3. Construct a complete meeting agenda.

4. Identify methods to balance participation of members, keep discussion on track, and create a positive atmosphere.

5. Effectively bring a meeting to a close and follow up appropriately.

6. Describe the stages and characteristics of each stage of group problem solving.

7. Apply various methods for groups to enhance creativity, solve problems, and make decisions; be able to identify the most appropriate method for specific circumstances.

Meetings are a fact of life on the job. Between 11 million and 20 million business meetings take place each day in the United States.[1] In one corporation alone, managers spend an astonishing 4.4 million hours per year in meetings.[2] But meetings aren't just for managers. According to a survey by Microsoft, the typical American worker spends 5.5 hours per week in meetings. If these meetings were held consecutively, they would fill up more than seven weeks of full-time work per year.[3]

Just because meetings are common doesn't mean they're always worth the time and effort.[4] In fact, hours spent in meetings usually aren't considered well spent; more than 70 percent of people in the Microsoft survey thought their meetings were unproductive. Other surveys show employees consider at least one-third of the gatherings they attend to be unnecessary and/or conducted poorly.[5] While unambitious workers may find meetings break up a busy workday, more-focused employees view unnecessary and inefficient meetings as a frustrating waste of time.[6] It's not surprising, then, that workers cited a lack of team communication and ineffective meetings as the top reasons why organizations aren't more productive.[7]

Poorly run meetings waste time and money. As Table 8-1 shows, the cost of meetings—even for small organizations—is considerable. If you include the time spent planning and following up on face-to-face interaction, the costs are even higher. One estimate put the cost of unproductive meetings in U.S. businesses at as much as $37 billion annually.[8]

Beyond wasting precious time and money, pervasively inefficient meetings also contribute to an overall atmosphere of cynicism. "Meetings matter because that's where an organization's culture perpetuates itself," says William R. Daniels, senior consultant at American Consulting & Training.[9] Meetings—whether they are good or bad—are a sign of an organization's health.

Because meetings are so common and so important, this chapter takes a closer look at them. By the time you have finished it, you should understand some methods for planning and participating in meetings that will produce efficient, satisfying results. In this chapter, we focus specifically on how teams operate in meetings, that is, on those occasions when their members communicate simultaneously to deal with common concerns.

Table 8-1	Hourly Costs of Meetings*				
	Number of People Attending Meeting				
Average Annual Salary of Attendees	**2**	**4**	**6**	**8**	**10**
$100,000	$112	$224	$236	$448	$560
75,000	84	168	252	336	420
62,500	70	140	210	280	350
50,000	56	112	168	224	280
37,500	42	84	126	168	210
25,000	28	56	84	112	140

*Figures do not include cost of employee benefits, facilities, and equipment.

Types of Meetings

People meet for many reasons. Whether they occur in person or online, in most business and professional settings, meetings fall into three categories: information-sharing, problem-solving, and ritual activities. Of course, some meetings may serve more than one purpose.

Information-Sharing Meetings

In many organizations, people meet regularly to exchange information. Police officers and nurses, for example, begin every shift with a meeting in which the people going off duty brief their replacements on what has been happening recently. Members of a medical research team experimenting with a new drug may meet regularly to compare notes on their results. In many office teams, the Monday morning meeting is an important tool for informing members about new developments, emerging trends, and the coming week's tasks. Perkin Elmer Corporation, a producer of scientific measuring instruments and precision optical equipment, is a typical example. The firm schedules a weekly meeting of all corporate and top executives to keep them up to date on the activities of the more than 20 divisions the company has around the world.

© Warren Miller/The New Yorker Collection/www.cartoonbank.com.

Problem-Solving and Decision-Making Meetings

In other meetings, a team may decide to take some action or make a change in existing policies or procedures. Which supplier should we contract? Should we introduce a new product line? Should we delay production so we can work out a design flaw in our new keyboard? Where can we cut costs if sales don't improve this year? How can we best schedule vacations?

Problem solving of one sort or another is the most common reason for a business meeting. Because problem-solving and decision-making meetings are the most challenging types of group activity, the bulk of this chapter discusses how to conduct them effectively.

Ritual Activities

In still other meetings, the social function is far more important than any specific task. In one firm, Friday afternoon "progress review sessions" are a regular fixture. Their apparently serious title is really an insider's tongue-in-cheek joke: The meetings take place in a local bar and to an outsider look like little more than a TGIF party. Despite the setting and apparently un-businesslike activity, these meetings serve several important purposes.[10] First, they reaffirm the members' commitment to one another and to the company. Choosing to socialize with one another instead of rushing home is a sign of belonging and caring. Second, the sessions provide a chance to swap useful ideas and stories that might not be appropriate in the office. Who's in trouble? What does the boss really want? As you read in Chapter 1, this sort of informal communication can be invaluable, and the meetings provide a good setting for it. Finally, ritual meetings can be a kind of perk that confers status on the members. "Progress review committee" members charge expenses to the company and leave work early to attend. Thus, being invited to join the sessions is a sign of having arrived in the company.

Virtual Meetings

The term *meeting* conjures images of people seated around a table, transacting business. But technology has made meetings possible even when the participants are half a world apart. Virtual meetings can take different forms.

Teleconferences are essentially multiparty telephone calls. They are a useful way for distant parties to meet and hash out details that would take much longer via e-mail or a chain of two-person phone conversations. Company phone systems usually have a teleconferencing capability, and most telephone companies and Internet service providers offer a similar feature either free or for a modest fee. Once all parties have connected to the call, they can talk freely with one another.

Videoconferences allow users in distant locations to see one another while they talk. Videoconferencing is especially valuable in organizations with widespread operations. For example, CKE Restaurants of Santa Barbara, California, operates more than 3,400 restaurants, including Hardee's, Carl's Jr., La Salsa, and Timber Lodge Steakhouse. The company uses Web-based conferencing to link members spread across the United States, saving thousands of dollars over the cost of face-to-face meetings.[11]

You don't need an elaborate organizational network to hold a videoconference. With low-cost webcams and microphones, free software, and a high-speed Internet connection, you can hold virtual meetings with people anywhere on Earth. Chapter 12 describes webinars, a special kind of videoconference in which a host presents a product or idea to a group of participants who can comment and ask questions.

CULTURE **at work**

Collaboration in Cyberspace: Geography Makes a Difference

How important is communication when members from across the country and around the world meet in cyberspace? To answer this question, corporate giants Verizon and Microsoft commissioned a study to determine how virtual teams in a variety of industries and countries collaborate.

The study revealed that the importance of collaboration on performance was consistent across various industries (e.g., health care, government, financial services, manufacturing) and around the world. As one member of the Verizon/Microsoft study remarked, "global companies that collaborate better, perform better. Those that collaborate less, do not perform as well. It's just that simple."

Researchers discovered cultural differences in workers' communication preferences. For example, Americans were more likely to enjoy working alone. They expressed a preference for using e-mail rather than the telephone. They were more comfortable with audio, video, and web conferencing technologies than people of other regions of the world, and they were more likely to multitask when on conference calls.

Europeans expressed a preference for communicating in real time with colleagues. They felt more obligated to answer the phone, and they expected others to call them back rather than leave a voice mail message. Professionals in the Asia-Pacific region, more than anywhere else, expressed a desire to keep in touch throughout the workday. As a result they found the phone an indispensable tool and preferred instant messaging to e-mail. Differences like these show teams are more productive when members take cultural differences into account when planning to communicate.

Source: Frost & Sullivan. (2006). *Meetings around the world: The impact of collaboration on business performance.* Retrieved from http://newscenter.verizon.com/kit/collaboration/MAW_WP.pdf

Whether you are having a teleconference or videoconference, following these basic guidelines will help the meeting run smoothly:

- Before the meeting, send your agenda and copies of any documents that will be discussed to all participants. Number pages of longer documents to avoid unnecessary paper shuffling.
- At the beginning of the meeting, have participants introduce themselves and state their location.
- In phone conversations, parties should identify themselves whenever necessary to avoid confusion. ("Ted talking here: I agree with Melissa. . . .")
- Avoid interrupting others or leaving out people simply because you can't see them.
- Keep distractions (ringing phones, slamming doors, etc.) to a minimum.
- Use the best equipment possible. Cheap speakerphones and computer cameras may make it difficult to understand one another.[12]

● Planning a Problem-Solving Meeting

As you read earlier, problem-solving meetings are the most common type of business meeting and the most challenging to do well. By thinking strategically about how to plan for a successful problem-solving meeting, you will be taking an important step in boosting your team performance.

Dealing with Opposing Viewpoints

Your manager has asked you to provide suggestions from your department with regard to the company's policy on flex time. These suggestions will be taken seriously and have a strong chance of being adopted. You are in a position to call a meeting of key people in your department to discuss the issue.

Two of the most vocal members of the department have diametrically opposed positions on flex time. One of them (whose position on the issue is different from yours) will be out of the office for a week, and you could call the meeting while he is gone. What do you do?

When to Hold a Meeting

Given the costs of bringing people together, the most fundamental question is whether to hold a meeting at all. In one survey, middle and upper managers reported that more than 25 percent of the meetings they attended could have been replaced by a memo, e-mail, or phone call.[13] Other experts report that roughly half of all business meetings are unproductive.[14] Not surprisingly, workers believe they attend too many meetings.[15]

There are many times when a meeting probably isn't justified:[16]

- The matter could be handled just as well over the phone.
- You could send a memo, an e-mail, or a fax to achieve the same goal.
- Key people are not available to attend.
- The subject would be considered trivial by many of the participants.
- There isn't enough time to handle the business at hand.
- Members aren't prepared.
- The meeting is routine, and there is no compelling reason to meet.
- The job can be handled just as well by one or more people without the need to consult others.
- Your mind is made up, or you've already made the decision.

Keeping these points in mind, a planner should call a meeting (or appoint a committee) only when the following questions can be answered yes.[17]

Is the Job beyond the Capacity of One Person? A job might be too much for one person to handle for two reasons: First, it might call for more information than any single person possesses. For example, the job of improving health conditions in a food-processing plant would probably require a health professional's medical background, employees' experience, and a manager who knows the resources.

Second, a job might take more time than one person has available. For instance, even if one employee were capable of writing and publishing an employee handbook, it's unlikely the person would be able to handle the task and have much time for other duties.

Are Individuals' Tasks Interdependent? Each member at a committee meeting should have a different role. If each member's share of the task can be completed without input from other members, it's better to have the members co-acting under a manager's supervision.

Consider the job we just mentioned of preparing the employee handbook. If each person on the handbook team is responsible for a separate section, there is little need for them to meet frequently to discuss the task.

There are times when people who do the same job can profit by sharing ideas with a group. Members of the handbook team, for example, might get new ideas about how the book could be made better from talking to one another. Similarly, sales representatives, industrial designers, physicians, or attorneys who work independently might profit by exchanging experiences and ideas. This is part of the purpose of professional conventions. Also, many companies schedule quarterly or annual meetings of people who perform similar job functions but work independently. While this may seem to contradict the requirement for interdependence of members' tasks, there is no real conflict. A group of people who do the same kind of work can often improve their individual performance through meetings by performing some of the complementary functional roles. For example, one colleague might serve as reality tester. ("Writing individual notes to each potential customer in your territory sounds like a good idea, but do you really have time to do that?") Another might take the job of being information-giver. ("You know, there's a printer just outside Boston who can do large jobs like that just as well as your regular printer, but he's cheaper. Call me, and I'll give you the name and address.") Others serve as diagnosers. ("Have you checked the feed mechanism? Sometimes a problem there can throw the whole machine out of whack.") Some can just serve as empathic listeners. ("Yeah, I know. It's tough to get people who can do that kind of work right.")

Is There More than One Decision or Solution?

Questions that have only one right answer aren't well suited to discussion in meetings. Whether the sales force made its quota last year and whether the budget will accommodate paying overtime to meet a schedule, for instance, are questions answered by checking the figures, not by getting the regional sales managers or the department members to reach an agreement.

Tasks that don't have fixed outcomes, however, are appropriate for committee discussion. Consider the job facing the employees of an advertising agency who are planning a campaign for a client. There is no obvious best way to sell products or ideas such as yearly physical examinations, office equipment, or clothing. Tasks such as these call for the kind of creativity a talented, well-chosen group can generate.

Are Misunderstandings or Reservations Likely?

It's easy to see how meetings can be useful when the goal is to generate ideas or solve problems. But meetings are often necessary when confusing or controversial information is being communicated. Suppose, for instance, that changing federal rules and company policy require employees to document their use of company cars in far more detail than previously required. It's easy to imagine how this sort of change would be met with grumbling and resistance. In this sort of situation, simply issuing a memo outlining the new rules might not gain the kind of compliance that is necessary. Only by talking out their complaints and hearing why the new policy is being instituted will employees see a need to go along with the new procedure. "I can write down the vision of the company a thousand times and send it out to people," says Dennis Stamp, chairman of Vancouver's Priority Management Systems, Inc. "But when I sit with them face-to-face and give them the vision, for some reason it is much more accepted."[18]

Setting an Agenda

An **agenda** is a list of topics to be covered in a meeting. A meeting without an agenda is like a ship at sea without a destination or compass: No one aboard knows where it is or where it's headed. Smart organizations appreciate the importance of establishing agendas. At computer chip giant Intel, company policy requires meeting planners to circulate an agenda before every meeting. You can start building an agenda by asking three questions:

1. What do we need to do in the meeting to achieve our objective?
2. What conversations will be important to the people who attend?
3. What information will we need to begin?[19]

Agenda items can come from many sources: the group's leader, minutes from previous meetings, team members, or standing items (e.g., committee reports).[20]

As Figure 8.1 illustrates, a complete agenda contains this information: a list of the attendees (and whoever else needs to see the agenda), the meeting's time and location, necessary background information, and a brief explanation of each item. You might argue such a detailed agenda would take too much time to prepare. But once you realize preparing the attendees with this sort of information will produce better results, you will realize the advance work is well worth the effort. In fact, it's probably wise to follow up your detailed memo with another e-mail or phone call to make sure members are prepared to deal thoughtfully with important items.

MEETING AGENDA

Louisville Design Group
Marketing Advisory Task Force

Meeting time: November 27, 9:00–10:00 a.m.

Location: Conference Room A

Invitees: Frank Brady, Monica Flores, Ted Gross, Scott Hendrickson, Kevin Jessup, Pat Rivera, Carly Woods

---

Call to Order (5 minutes)
- Review and approval of minutes from November 13 meeting (Ted)

Reports (10 minutes)
- Client Appreciation Event (Monica)
- Budget (Ted)

Unfinished Business (20 minutes)
- Website Redesign (Frank)
 Frank will present two design options for the LDG website redesign.

New Business (20 minutes)
- Client Research Project (Carly)
 Please bring ideas for what your team needs to know about our clients and their design needs.

Adjournment

FIGURE 8.1

Format for a Comprehensive Agenda

Time, Length, and Location

To avoid problems, all three of these details need to be on an agenda. Without the starting time, you can expect to hear such comments as, "I thought you said 10, not 9," or "We always started at 3." Unless you announce the length, expect some members to leave early. Failure to note the location results in members' stumbling in late after waiting in the "usual place," wondering why no one showed up.

If your team needs to meet regularly, the best way to schedule meetings may be to build the time and place into everyone's schedule. At the Ritz-Carlton chain of luxury hotels, everyone in the organization starts the workday with a briefing. At company headquarters, top managers meet with the president of the company. Around the world, local employees start their daily shifts by covering the same points addressed in the head-quarters meeting.[21]

Participants

The overall size of the group is important: When attendance grows beyond seven members, the likelihood of some members falling silent increases. If the agenda includes one or more problem-solving items, it's best to keep the group size small so everyone can participate in discussions. If the meeting is primarily informational, a larger group may be acceptable.

Be sure to identify on the agenda the people who will be attending so you alert all members about whom to expect in the meeting. If you have overlooked someone who ought to attend, a member who received the agenda can tell you. It is frustrating and a waste of time to call a meeting and then discover the person with key information isn't there.

Background Information

Sometimes participants will need background information to give them new details or to remind them of things they may have forgotten. Background information can also provide a description of the meeting's significance.

Items and Goals

A good agenda goes beyond just listing topics and describes the goal for the discussion. "Meetings should be outcome- rather than process-driven," says Anita Underwood, Dun and Bradstreet's vice president of organizational management.[22] Most people have at least a vague idea of why they are meeting. Vague ideas, however, often lead to vague meetings. A clear list of topics and goals like those in Figure 8.1 will result in better-informed members and more productive, satisfying meetings.

The best goals are result-oriented, specific, and realistic. Notice the difference between goals that do and don't meet these criteria:

Poorly Worded	Better Worded
Hear the budget report.	Learn whether we are on track to meet this year's budget.
Discuss the website redesign.	Choose the design that best represents our company's image and has the greatest functionality.
Talk about the new client research project.	Finalize topics that should be covered in the upcoming client survey.

Goals like these are useful in at least two ways: First, they help to identify those who ought to attend the meeting. Second, specific goals also help the attendees prepare for the meeting. Third, they help to keep the discussion on track once it begins.

CAREER **tip**

Members Can Be Leaders Too

Good leadership promotes successful meetings, but members can also play an important role in making a meeting successful. Every person involved in a meeting can use the following tips:

- Ask that an agenda be sent out before the meeting or agree on an agenda at the beginning of the meeting.

- Ask for help at the beginning of the meeting. Seek clarification on the meeting's goal. Is it to present information? To make a decision?

- Be tactfully bold and suggest canceling an unnecessary or badly planned meeting. Convene it when there is a need and an agenda.

- Volunteer to be a record-keeper. A written set of minutes reduces the chance for misunderstandings, and keeping notes yourself leads to a record that reflects your perception of events.

- Suggest that a timekeeper be appointed, or volunteer yourself. This person advises the group when time for addressing each issue—and the meeting itself—is nearly over and alerts the group when time runs out.

- Ask for help before the meeting closes: "Exactly what have we decided today?" "What do we need to do before our next meeting?"

Source: Adapted from Keep, A. M. (1994). *Moving meetings.* New York, NY: Irwin.

The person who calls the meeting isn't the only one who can or should set goals. There are many times when other members have important business. The planner is wise to use an "expectations check" to identify members' concerns.[23] Members can be polled before the meeting so their issues can be included in the agenda or at the start of the meeting. The fact that a member wants to discuss something, however, does not mean the topic should automatically be considered. If the issue is inappropriate, the planner may choose to postpone it or handle it outside the meeting.

Pre-Meeting Work   The best meetings occur when people have done all the necessary advance work. The agenda is a good place to tell members how to prepare for the meeting by reading information, developing reports, preparing or duplicating documents, or locating facts or figures. If all members need to prepare in the same way (for example, by reading an article), add that fact to the agenda. If certain members have specific jobs to do, the meeting organizer can jot these tasks on their individual copies: "Sarah, be sure to bring last year's sales figures"; "Wes, please duplicate copies of the annual report for everyone."

The order of agenda items is important. Some experts suggest the difficulty of items should form a bell-shaped curve, with items arranged in order of ascending and descending difficulty (see Figure 8.2). The meeting ought to begin with relatively simple business: minutes, announcements, and the easiest decisions. Once members have hit their stride and a good climate has developed, the team can move on to the most difficult items. Ideally, these should occupy the middle third of the session. Then the final third of the meeting can focus on easier items to allow a period of decompression and goodwill.

• Conducting the Meeting

To the uninitiated observer, a well-run meeting seems almost effortless. Time is used efficiently, the tone is constructive, and the quality of ideas is good. Despite their apparent simplicity, results like this usually don't just happen: They grow from some important communication skills.

FIGURE 8.2
A Bell-Shaped
Agenda Structure

Source: Tropman, J. E.
(1995). *Effective meetings:
Improving group decision
making* (2nd ed.). Thousand
Oaks, CA: Sage. Copyright
© John E. Tropman. Used
with permission.

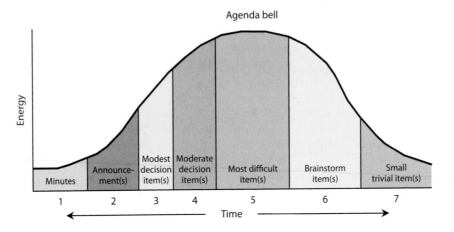

Beginning the Meeting

Effective openings get the meeting off to a good start. First, they give everyone a clear picture of what is to be accomplished. Second, they define how the team will try to reach its goal. Finally, they set the stage for good teamwork and, thus, good results. The first few remarks by the person who called the meeting can set the stage for a constructive session. They should cover the following points.[24]

Identify the Goals of the Meeting   This means repeating the information listed in the agenda, but mentioning it here will remind everyone of the meeting's goals and help to focus the discussion. For example:

> "We're faced with a serious problem. Inventory losses have almost doubled in the last year, from 5 to 9 percent. We need to decide what's causing these losses and come up with some ideas about how to reduce them."

Provide Necessary Background Information   Background information explains the context of the meeting and gives everyone the same picture of the subject being discussed. It prevents misunderstandings and helps members to understand the nature of the information the group will consider. This can range from bringing photocopies of budget information or other key documents to delivering a short informational presentation to the team at the meeting.

Show How the Team Can Help   Outline the contributions members can make during the meeting. Some of these contributions will come from specific people:

> "Tom's going to compare our losses with industry figures, so we can get an idea of how much of the problem is an unavoidable cost of doing business. Chris will talk about his experiences with the problem at Sterling, where he worked until last year. That firm had some good ideas we may be able to use."

Other contributions can be made by everyone present. This is the time to define specifically how each member can help make the meeting a success:

> "We're counting on everybody here to suggest areas where we can cut losses. Once we've come up with ideas, I'll ask each of you to work out a schedule for putting the ideas to work in your department."

Preview the Meeting   Even though members should have reviewed the agenda, it can be smart to spend a few moments previewing the agenda and goals. For instance:

> "We'll begin by hearing the reports from Tom and Chris. Then we'll all work together to brainstorm a list of ways to cut losses. The goal here will be to get as many ideas as possible. Once we've come up with a list, we can decide which ideas to use and how to make them work."

Identify Time Constraints   Clarify how much time is available to prevent wasting time. In some cases, it's only necessary to remind the group of how much time can be spent in the meeting as a whole ("We can develop this list between now and 11 o'clock if we keep on track"). In other cases, it can be useful to preview the time available for each agenda item:

> "Tom and Chris have promised to keep their remarks brief, so by 10 o'clock we should be ready to start brainstorming. If we get our list put together by 10:30, we'll still have a half-hour to talk about which ideas to try and how to put them into action."

Following these guidelines will get your meeting off to a good start. Even if you are not in charge of the meeting, you can still make sure the opening is a good one by asking questions that will get the leader to share the kind of information just listed: "How much time do you expect we'll need?", "How far do you expect we'll get today?", and "What can we do to help solve the problem?"

Conducting Business

No meeting will be successful without committed, talented participants. But even the best attendees do not guarantee success. Someone—either the leader or a responsible member—has to be sure all important business is covered in a way that takes advantage of the talents of everyone present.

Parliamentary Procedure   **Parliamentary procedure** is a set of rules that governs the way groups conduct business and make decisions in meetings.[25] The term may bring up images of legislators using obscure rules to achieve political goals. ("Madam Chairperson, I move we set aside the order of business and refer this motion to the committee of the whole. . . .")

While parliamentary procedure can be a form of gamesmanship, when used sensibly it can be a helpful tool for managing group meetings. This approach can keep discussions clear and efficient while safeguarding the rights of everyone involved in deliberations.

When to use parliamentary procedure   There are several situations when parliamentary procedure is an appropriate way to operate a meeting:

- *When a group's decisions will be of interest to an external audience.* This approach provides a record of the group's operations (the "minutes" of meetings), so interested observers can learn about each member's input and the decisions the group made as a whole.

- *When haste may obscure critical thinking.* Because it slows down the pace of discussions, parliamentary procedure can help groups deliberate before making decisions. Of course, there is no guarantee this approach will help a group avoid making bad decisions, but it might.

- *When emotions are likely to be strong.* Parliamentary procedure gives members with minority viewpoints a chance to speak, and its rules (when properly enforced) discourage uncivil behavior.

Order of business   It's always a good idea to have an agenda. Under the rules of parliamentary procedure, the agenda provides a plan to handle business logically. The standard meeting agenda has the following parts:

1. *Reading of the minutes.* A good set of minutes is more than a formality; it gives everyone involved a chance to make sure the record describes what really happened. It also stands as a lasting record, which the group can consult in the future if there are any questions about what decisions had been made in the past.

2. *Reports.* Teams often use committees to handle specific tasks that don't require the involvement of everyone in the group. Reports function as a place in which these committees, as well as individual members, share information with the rest of the group.

3. *Unfinished business.* If there are any matters from previous meetings that haven't yet been settled or ongoing projects that need attention, this unfinished or "old" business gets covered next.

4. *New business.* This is the time when members can bring up new issues for the group to discuss and decide on.

Motions   When a member wants the group to deliberate, he or she introduces a **motion:** a specific proposal for action.

> "I move we redirect 10 percent of the Annual Fund contributions to the endowment."

> "I move that we send two delegates to the annual convention in Chicago, with the goal of interviewing candidates for the position of associate director."

> "I move we go on record opposing the city's proposal to convert open parkland into parking."

Good motions address a single issue briefly and clearly. Once introduced, a motion must be seconded by someone other than its sponsor. This procedure ensures the group only discusses those motions at least two members deem worthy. Motions can be discussed and amended by other members. Once discussion is complete, a motion is decided by a public vote.

Using parliamentary procedure isn't an all-or-nothing proposition. Many groups use some of its elements without binding themselves to learning and using the full set of rules.

Balancing Participation

Loosely structured, informal meetings may appear to give everyone an equal chance to speak out, but because of personality, gender, culture, and style differences, every member may not have the same access.[26] Unbalanced participation can cause two sorts of problems: First, it discourages people who don't get a chance to talk. Second, it prevents the group from considering potentially useful ideas. There are several ways to improve participation at meetings.

Have members take turns   Another approach is to give every member a turn to speak. While it probably isn't wise to conduct an entire meeting this way, the technique can be useful at the beginning of a meeting to start members off on an equal footing, in the middle if a few people are dominating the discussion, or at the end if some people have not been heard.

Use questions   Questions that draw out listeners are another way to encourage participation. Four types of questions can balance members' contributions.

Overhead questions are directed toward the group as a whole, and anyone is free to answer:

> "Sales have flattened out in the western region. Can anybody suggest what's going on?"

> "We need to find some way of rewarding our top producers. I'd like to hear your ideas."

As long as overhead questions draw a response from all members, it's wise to continue using them. When a few people begin to dominate, however, it's time to switch to one of the following types.

Direct questions are aimed at a particular individual, who is addressed by name:

> "How would that suggestion work for you, Kim?"

> "Greg, how's the new plan working in your department?"

Direct questions are a useful way to draw out quiet members, but they must be used skillfully. Never start a discussion with a direct question. This creates a schoolroom atmosphere and suggests the rule "Don't speak until you're called on"—hardly a desirable norm in most meetings. It's also important to give respondents a way out of potentially embarrassing questions. For example, a chairperson might ask, "Tony, can you give us the figures for your department now, or will you need to check them and get back to us?"

Reverse questions occur when a member asks the leader a question and the leader refers the question back to the person who originally phrased it:

> "Suppose the decision were up to you, Gary. What would you do?"

> "That's a good question, Laurie. Do you think it's a practical idea?"

Reverse questions work well when the leader senses a member really wants to make a statement but is unwilling to do so directly. It's important to use reverse questions with care: The member could be asking for information, in which case a direct answer is appropriate.

Relay questions occur when the leader refers a question one member asks to the entire group:

> "Cynthia has just raised a good question. Who can respond to it?"

> "Can anyone offer a suggestion for Les?"

Relay questions are especially useful when the leader wants to avoid disclosing his or her opinion for fear of inhibiting or influencing the group. Relays should usually be rephrased as overhead questions directed at the entire group. This avoids the suggestion that one member is smarter than the others. Of course, if a particular person does have special expertise, it is appropriate to direct the inquiry to him or her:

> "Didn't you have a problem like that once with a distributor, Britt? How did you work things out?"

Use the nominal group technique   One method for giving every member's ideas an equal chance to be considered is the *nominal group technique* described on p. 235. This approach gives every member an equal chance to participate. Furthermore, the equal input produces better results than traditional discussion.[27]

Keeping Discussions on Track
Sometimes the problem isn't too little discussion but too much. Teams often can talk on and on without moving any closer to accomplishing the goal. When this happens, the leader or some other member needs to get the discussion back on track by using one of the following techniques.

case STUDY

Device-Free Meetings

It's no surprise that meeting-goers in high-tech environments like California's Silicon Valley often bring along and use digital communication devices—laptops, smartphones, tablets, and a host of other gadgets that keep attendees in touch with the outside world.

Multitasking device users suffer from what one observer calls "continual partial attention." An industry insider describes the problem: "One of my biggest frustrations when I was an engineer at Google was being summoned to an executive meeting only to find three-quarters of the executives too busy with their laptops. I'd spend hours preparing a summary of my project status, a briefing on a new strategy area, or a review of staffing assignments. Nothing communicates disrespect to your reports like ignoring them when they're with you."

In an effort to stem this problem, a growing number of firms in the information economy and beyond have declared a ban on mobile devices in meetings. For example, San Francisco design firm Adaptive Path encourages staffers to leave their laptops and other devices behind when they attend meetings. John Vars, cofounder of San Francisco's Dogster.com, explains the logic of his company's policy on device-free meetings: "Even if people are just taking notes, they are not giving the natural human signals that they are listening to the person who is speaking. It builds up resentment. It can become something that inhibits good teamwork."

The results of these device-free meetings are encouraging. Dogster's Vars reports, "Meetings go quicker and there is also just a shared experience. People are communicating better, the flow is faster."

Sources: Guynn, J. (2008, March 31). Silicon meetings go 'topless'. *Los Angeles Times*, p. A1; Rands. (2007, August 31). The laptop herring [Web log post]. *Rands in repose.* Retrieved from http://www.randsinrepose.com/archives/2007/08/31/the_laptop_herring.html

Remind the group of time pressures When the group is handling an urgent topic in a leisurely manner, you can remind everyone about the importance of moving quickly. But when doing so, it is important to acknowledge the value of the comments being made:

> "Radio ads sound good, but for now we'd better stick to the newspaper program. John wanted copy from us by noon, and we'll never make it if we don't get going."

Summarize and redirect the discussion When members ramble on about a topic after the job is done, you can get the discussion moving again by tactfully summarizing what has been accomplished and mentioning the next task:

> "It seems we've come up with a good list of the factors that might be contributing to absenteeism. Can anybody think of more causes? If not, maybe we should move on and try to think of as many solutions as we can."

Use relevancy challenges When a discussion wanders from the business at hand, summarizing won't help. Sometimes the unrelated ideas are good, but just don't apply to the group's immediate job. In other cases, they are not only irrelevant but also worthless. In either situation, you can get the group back on track by questioning the idea's relevancy. In a **relevancy challenge,** the questioner tactfully asks a member to explain how an apparently off-the-track idea relates. Typical relevancy challenges sound like this:

> "I'm confused, Tom. How will leasing new equipment instead of buying it help us to boost productivity?"

> "Fran asked us to decide which word processing package to buy. Does the graphics package you mentioned have something to do with the word processing decision?"

CAREER tip

Opting Out of Meetings

What should you do when you are expected to attend a meeting you know will be a waste of time? There are some occasions when you can't escape worthless meetings: when you are formally obligated to attend, when your absence would damage your reputation, or when your boss insists you show up.

On other occasions, though, you may consider using one of the following strategies to make your nonattendance acceptable:

- Provide written input. If your sole reason for showing up is to provide information, a memo or written report may be a good substitute for your physical presence.

- Suggest a productive alternative. There may be other ways for you—and maybe even other attendees—to achieve objectives without actually having a face-to-face meeting: an exchange of e-mails, teleconferencing, or delegating the job to a smaller group. Suggesting these alternatives may earn you the gratitude of others who don't want to attend the meeting anymore than you do.

- Tell the truth. In some cases you may choose to explain your reasons for not wanting to attend. Of course, you should do so diplomatically. Instead of saying, "These meetings are always a waste of time," you might say, "I'm not sure my attendance would serve any useful purpose."

Source: Adapted from Lippincott, S. M. (1999). *Meetings: Do's, don'ts, and donuts* (2nd ed.). Pittsburgh, PA: Lighthouse Point Press.

At this point the member who made the original remark can either explain its relevance or acknowledge it wasn't germane. In either case, the advantage of this sort of challenge is that it isn't personal. It focuses on the remark and not on the person and thus reduces the chance of a defensive response.

Promise to deal with good ideas later   Another way to keep the goodwill of a member who has brought up an irrelevant idea is to suggest a way of dealing with it at the appropriate time:

> "That equipment-leasing idea sounds promising. Let's bring it up to Jeff after the meeting and see what he thinks of it."

> "A graphics package seems important to you, Lee. Why don't you look into what's available, and we can decide whether the change would be worth the cost."

As with relevancy challenges, your suggestion about dealing with an idea later has to be sincere if the other person is going to accept it. One way to show your sincerity is to mention exactly when you would like to discuss the matter. This might be a specific time ("after lunch"), or it might be when certain conditions are met ("after you've worked up the cost"). Another way to show your sincerity is to inquire about the idea after the meeting: "How's the research going on the graphics package?"

Keeping a Positive Tone   Almost everyone would agree that getting along with people is a vital ingredient in a successful career. In meetings, getting along can be especially tough when others don't cooperate with your efforts to keep the meeting on track—or, even worse, when others attack your ideas. The following suggestions can help you handle these irritating situations in a way that gets the job done and keeps potential enemies as allies.

Reframing Complaints in Meetings

Problem-solving meetings can generate complaints, defensiveness, and even outright hostility. Reframing members' complaints can nudge the discussion toward constructive solutions. Here are some reframing strategies:

Reframe complaints about the past as hopes for the future

Statement: "Why do we always have to drive across town for these meetings?"

Reframe: "From now on, you'd like to find a way to keep everybody's travel time equal, right?"

Reframe negative statements as positive desires or visions

Statement: "I've got work to do! All this long-range planning is a waste of time."

Reframe: "You want to be sure the time we spend planning makes a difference in the long run, right?"

Reframe personal attacks as issues

Statement: "Jaclyn is always butting in when I have a customer, stealing my commissions."

Reframe: "So, we need to make sure we have clear lines about communicating with customers."

Reframe individual concerns as community or team interests

Statement: "I've got kids at home and no child care! I can't keep working weekends on short notice."

Reframe: "All of us have lives outside of work. Let's talk about how we can handle rush jobs without creating personal emergencies or burning out."

Sources: Littlejohn, S., & Domenici, K. (2007). *Communication, conflict, and the management of difference.* Long Grove, IL: Waveland Press. See also Domenici, K., & Littlejohn, S. (2007). The affirmative turn in strategic planning. *OD Practitioner, 39,* 36–39.

Ask questions and paraphrase to clarify understanding   Criticizing an idea—even an apparently stupid one—can result in a defensive reaction that will waste time and generate ill will. It's also important to remember even a seemingly idiotic remark can have some merit. Given these facts, it's often wise to handle apparently bad ideas by asking for some clarification. And the most obvious way to clarify an idea is to ask questions:

> "Why do you think we ought to let Marcia go?"

> "Who would cover the store if you went skiing next week?"

You can also paraphrase to get more information about an apparently hostile or foolish remark:

> "It sounds as if you're saying Marcia's doing a bad job."

> "So you think we could cover the store if you went skiing?"

This sort of paraphrasing accomplishes two things: First, it provides a way to double-check your understanding. If your replay of the speaker's ideas isn't accurate, he or she can correct you: "I don't think Marcia's doing a bad job. I just don't think we need so many people up front." Second, even if your understanding is accurate, paraphrasing is an invitation for the other person to explain the idea in more detail: "If we could find somebody to work a double shift while I am skiing, I'd be willing to do the same thing for him or her later."

Enhance the value of members' comments   It's obvious that you should acknowledge the value of good ideas by praising or thanking the people who contribute them.

Surprisingly, you can use the same method with apparently bad ideas. Most comments have some merit. You can take advantage of such merits by using a three-part response:[28]

1. Acknowledge the merits of the idea.
2. Explain any concerns you have.
3. Improve the usefulness of the idea by building on it or asking others for suggestions.

Notice how this sort of response can enhance the value of apparently worthless comments:

> "I'm glad you're so concerned about the parking problem, Craig [acknowledges merit of comment]. But wouldn't requiring people to carpool generate a lot of resentment [balancing concern]? How could we encourage people to carpool voluntarily [builds on original idea]?"
>
> "You're right, Pat. Your department could use another person [acknowledges merit of comment]. But Mr. Peters is really serious about this hiring freeze [balancing concern]. Let's try to come up with some ways we can get you more help without having to hire a new person [builds on original idea]."

Pay attention to cultural factors   Like every other type of communication, the "rules" for conducting productive, harmonious meetings vary from one culture to another. For example, in Japan problem-solving meetings are usually preceded by a series of one-to-one sessions between participants to iron out issues, a process called *nemawashi*.[29] The practice arises from the Japanese cultural practice that two people may speak candidly to each other, but when a third person enters the discussion, they become a group, requiring communicators to speak indirectly to maintain harmony. By contrast, in countries where emotional expressiveness is the norm, volatile exchanges in meetings are as much the rule as the exception. "I've just come back from a meeting in Milan," stated Canadian management consultant Dennis Stamp. "If people acted the same way in North American meetings you'd think they were coming to blows."[30]

Concluding the Meeting

The way a meeting ends can have a strong influence on how members feel about the group and how well they follow up on any decisions made or instructions given.[31]

When to Close the Meeting   There are three times when a meeting should be closed.

When the scheduled closing time has arrived   Even if the discussion has been good, it's often best to close on schedule to prevent members from drifting off to other commitments one by one or losing attention and becoming resentful. It's wise to press on only if the subject is important and the members indicate willingness to keep working.

When the group lacks resources to continue   If the group lacks the necessary person or facts to continue, adjourn until the resources are available. If you need to get cost figures for a new purchase or someone's approval for a new idea, for example, it is probably a waste of time to proceed until the data or go-ahead has been secured. In these cases, be sure to identify who is responsible for getting the needed information, and set a new meeting date.

Evaluate the effectiveness of your meetings by using this format:

0 = Never; 1 = Rarely; 2 = Sometimes; 3 = Usually; 4 = Often; 5 = Always

Planning the Meeting

_____ 1. Are meetings held when (and only when) necessary?

_____ 2. Is membership well chosen (appropriate size and necessary knowledge and skills)?

_____ 3. Is enough time allotted for tasks, and is the meeting time convenient for most members?

_____ 4. Is the location adequate (size, facilities, free from distractions)?

_____ 5. Is a complete agenda created (date, time, length, location, attendees, background information, goals) and circulated far enough in advance of the meeting?

During the Meeting

_____ 6. Opening the meeting

    a. Are goals, necessary background information, and expectations for members' contributions clear?

    b. Are the sequence of events and time constraints previewed?

_____ 7. Encouraging balanced participation

    a. Do leader and members use questions to draw out quiet members?

    b. Are off-track comments redirected with agenda references and relevancy challenges?

    c. Do leader and members suggest moving on when an agenda item has been dealt with adequately?

When the agenda has been covered   It seems obvious a meeting should adjourn when its business is finished. Nonetheless, any veteran of meetings will testify that some discussions drag on because no one is willing to call a halt. Unless everyone is willing to socialize, it's best to use the techniques that follow to wrap up a meeting when the job is completed.

How to Conclude a Meeting   A good conclusion has three parts. In many discussions, the leader will be responsible for taking these steps. In leaderless groups or in groups with a weak leader, one or more members can take the initiative.

Signal when time is almost up   A warning allows the group to wrap up business and gives everyone a chance to have a final say:

> "We have about 15 minutes before we adjourn. We still need to hear Bob's report on the Kansas City conference, so let's devote the rest of our time to that."

_____ 8. Maintaining a positive tone

    a. Are questioning and paraphrasing used as nondefensive responses to hostile remarks?

    b. Are dubious comments enhanced as much as possible?

    c. Does the meeting reflect attendees' cultural norms?

_____ 9. Solving problems creatively

    a. Is the problem defined clearly (versus too narrowly or broadly)?

    b. Are the causes and effects of the problem analyzed?

    c. Are clear criteria for resolving the problem established?

    d. Are possible solutions brainstormed without being evaluated?

    e. Is a decision made based on the previously established criteria?

    f. Are methods of implementing the solution developed?

Concluding and Follow-up

_____ 10. Concluding the meeting

    a. Does the meeting run the proper length of time with a warning given shortly before conclusion to allow wrap-up of business?

    b. Are a summary of the meeting's results and a preview of future actions given?

    c. Does the leader acknowledge member's contributions and clarify assignments?

_____ 11. Follow-up activities

    a. Are the meeting minutes prepared and distributed to all group members?

    b. Does the leader build an agenda for the next meeting upon results of the previous one?

    c. Do members follow through, and does the leader follow up with member action items?

Summarize the meeting's accomplishments and future actions   For the sake of understanding, review what information has been conveyed and what decisions have been made. Just as important is reminding members of their responsibilities:

> "We'll meet next Tuesday in San Juan. We'll follow the revised schedule we worked up today. Chris will have copies to everyone first thing tomorrow morning. Nick will book the larger meeting room, and Pat will have the awards made up. Let's all plan to meet over dinner at the hotel next Tuesday night."

Thank the group   Acknowledging the group's good work is more than just good manners. This sort of reinforcement shows you appreciate the group's efforts and encourages good performance in the future. Besides acknowledging the group as a whole, be sure to give credit to any members who deserve special mention:

> "We really got a lot done today. Thanks to all of you, we're back on schedule. Bruce, I appreciate the work you did on the specifications. We never would have made it without you."

Following Up the Meeting

It's a mistake to assume that even a satisfying meeting is a success until you follow up to make sure the desired results have really been obtained. A thorough follow-up involves four steps.

Prepare and Distribute Minutes of the Meeting
It may be tempting to think a meeting is over when the group members leave the room or log off of the virtual meeting space. But after the meeting ends, there is still important work to be done. One of the most important follow-up steps to a meeting is to prepare and distribute the **meeting minutes**— a written record of the major discussions held, decisions made, and action items assigned.

A good set of minutes should be complete and concise. This means they should be thorough enough that someone who was not at the meeting should be able to know exactly what happened. But at the same time, they should be short and to the point, omitting irrelevant and play-by-play information. See Figure 8.3 for sample meeting minutes. In addition, a good set of minutes will include **action items,** specific tasks assigned during the course of a meeting. They should include what the specific task is, who is responsible for completing the task, and the deadline. By keeping a very specific record of action items in your group meeting minutes, your team will become more accountable, and your meetings will become more effective.

Build an Agenda for the Next Meeting
Most groups meet frequently, and they rarely conclude their business in one sitting. A smart leader plans the next meeting by noting which items need to be carried over from the preceding one. What unfinished business must be addressed? What progress reports must be shared? What new information should members hear?

Follow Up on Other Members
You can be sure the promised outcomes of a meeting actually occur if you check up on other members. If the meeting provided instructions—such as how to use the new accounting software—see whether the people who attended are actually following the steps outlined. If tasks were assigned, check on whether they're being performed. You don't have to be demanding or snoopy to do this sort of checking. A friendly phone call or personal remark can do the trick: "Is the new phone system working for you?" "How's it going on those sales figures?" "Did you manage to get a hold of Williams yet?"

Take Care of Your Own Action Items
Being a good team member means taking care of your action items. As you participate in the meeting, you should keep track of the tasks you've been assigned and also double-check in the meeting minutes to make sure you didn't miss any. By taking care of your assigned tasks prior to the deadlines, you will solidify your reputation as a valuable team member.

● Problem-Solving Communication

Most of the communication aimed at solving problems and making decisions occurs in meetings. In the past decades, researchers have developed several methods for accomplishing these goals. By taking advantage of these methods, teams can efficiently come up with the highest-quality work.

Stages in Group Problem Solving

When it comes to solving problems and making decisions, groups move more or less regularly through several phases characterized by different types of communication. Aubrey Fisher identified four of these stages: orientation, conflict, emergence, and reinforcement.[32]

MEETING MINUTES

Louisville Design Group
Marketing Advisory Task Force

Meeting date: November 27

Attendees: Frank Brady, Monica Flores, Ted Gross, Kevin Jessup, Pat Rivera, Carly Woods

Absent: Scott Hendrickson

---

1. Ted called the meeting to order. The meeting minutes from the November 13 meeting were approved.

2. Monica reported on the Client Appreciation Event that was held on November 15. We had a great turnout, with 28 clients and their guests attending the invitation-only event. Clients were treated to hors d'oeuvres and cocktails, given a tour of the offices, and had their caricatures sketched by LDG's best cartoonist, Dave Ketchum. Monica received more than a dozen emails after the event thanking her for a terrific time. Based on the success, Monica suggested that we make this an annual event.

3. Ted provided an update on the budget. The committee was allotted $25,000 for marketing expenses during the year, and the total expenditures year-to-date come to $22,500. This leaves a balance of $2,500 that must be used by the end of the year, as the funds will not carry forward to next year.

   Action Item: Everyone must submit all outstanding marketing expense reports to Ted immediately. (Due 11/30)

4. Frank presented the committee with two designs for the LDG website redesign. Design A was a "clean" style with monochromatic colors, sleek fonts, and geometric graphics. Design B was a "splashy" style with a brightly colored palette, bolder fonts, and photos. Both designs incorporated the website navigation hierarchy agreed to by the committee. Ted thanked Frank for his hard work on the project.

   After the initial presentation, the committee debated the pros and cons of each design. They thought that the clean feel of Design A presented a more professional image. But they thought that the colorful palette of Design B showed LDG's fun side. There was no clear favorite.

   Action Item: Frank will create a mock-up of a third design option that will merge the sleek look of Design A with the color palette of Design B for consideration at the next committee meeting. (Due: 12/11)

5. Carly solicited input on the upcoming Client Research Project. The last research project conducted by LDG was five years ago. But with the advent of new social media technologies and the opening of two new firms in town, it is important that LDG get the most up-to-date info available. Carly asked for input into what topics to cover and how to administer the survey.

   The committee brainstormed several areas and agreed to ask about clients' primary design needs, familiarity with social media platforms (Twitter, Facebook), annual budgets for advertising and web design, and relative importance of cost/turnaround time/artistic quality/copywriting quality/firm reputation in selecting a firm for a job.

   There was some discussion on how to administer the surveys. The committee unanimously agreed to use an online survey system. However, Kevin said that it would be valuable information to have clients identified on the surveys, while Monica argued that we might get better quality information if the surveys were anonymous. The majority vote was for anonymous data collection.

   Action Item: Pat and Carly will use committee input to generate a preliminary survey, which will be reviewed and critiqued at the next committee meeting. (Due: 12/11)

FIGURE 8.3 Format for Meeting Minutes

The first stage in a group's development is the **orientation phase,** sometimes called **forming.**[33] This is a time of testing the waters. Members may not know one another very well and so are cautious about making statements that might offend. For this reason, during the orientation stage, group members aren't likely to take strong positions even on

Table 8-2	Characteristics and Guidelines for Problem-Solving Stages		
	Member Behaviors	**Member Concerns**	**For Higher Performance**
Forming	Most comments directed to designated leader	Why am I in this group?	Clarify tasks, roles, and responsibilities
	Direction and clarification frequently sought	Why are the others here?	Provide structure
		Will I be accepted?	
	Status accorded to members based on their roles outside the group	What is my role?	Encourage balanced participation
		What jobs will I have? Will I be able to handle them?	Identify one another's expertise, needs, values, and preferences
	Issues discussed superficially	Who is the leader? Is she or he competent?	
Storming	Some members try to gain disproportionate share of influence	How much autonomy will I have?	Use joint problem solving
		Will I be able to influence others?	Discuss group's problem-solving ideas
	Subgroups and coalitions form		Have members explain how others' ideas are useful and how to improve them
		What is my place in the pecking order?	
	Designated leader may be challenged	Who are my friends and allies?	Establish norm supporting expression of different viewpoints
	Members overzealously judge one another's ideas and personalities	Who are my enemies?	
		Do my ideas get any support here?	Discourage domination by a single person or subgroup
		Why don't some of the others see things my way?	
		Is this aggravation worth the effort?	

issues they regard as important. It is easy to mistake the lack of conflict during this phase as harmony and assume the task will proceed smoothly. Peace and quiet are often a sign of caution, not agreement. Despite the tentative nature of communication, the orientation stage is important because the norms that can govern the group's communication throughout its life are often formed at this time.

After the group members understand the problem and have a feel for one another, the group typically moves to the **conflict phase,** which has been called **storming.** This is the time when members take a strong stand on the issue and defend their positions against others. Disagreement is likely to be greatest during this phase, and the potential for bruised egos is strongest. The norms of politeness formed during orientation may weaken as members debate with one another, and there is a real risk personal feelings will interfere with the kind of rational decision making described in the preceding section. Conflict does not have to be negative, however. If members adopt the kinds of constructive approaches outlined in Chapter 5, they can come up with higher-quality solutions than groups that make harmony a top priority.[34]

Some groups never escape from the conflict stage. Their interaction—at least about the problem at hand—may end when time pressures force a solution almost no one finds satisfactory. The boss may impose a decision from above, or a majority might overrule the minority. Time may even run out without any decision being made. Not all groups suffer from such unhappy outcomes, however. Productive teams manage to work through the conflict phase and move on to the next stage of development.

	Member Behaviors	**Member Concerns**	**For Higher Performance**
Norming	The group establishes and follows rules and procedures	How can we get organized well enough to stay on top of our tasks?	Challenge the group, fight complacency
	Members sometimes openly disagree	How close should I get to other members?	Establish norms of high performance
	The group laughs together, has fun	How can we work in harmony?	Request and provide both positive and constructive feedback on individual and group actions
	Members have a sense of "we-ness"	How do we compare to other groups?	
	The group feels superior to other groups	What is my relationship to the leader?	Encourage open discussions about individual ideas and concerns
	Groupthink may be a risk	How do we keep conflicts and differences under control?	
		How can we structure things to run smoothly?	
High Performing	Members seek honest feedback from one another	How can we continue at this pace?	Jointly set challenging goals
	Roles are clear, yet members cover for one another as needed	How might we share our learnings with one another?	Look for opportunities to increase group's scope
	Members openly discuss and accept differences	What will I do when this process is over?	Question assumptions, norms, and traditional approaches
	Members encourage one another to do better	How will I find another group as good as this one?	Develop mechanism for ongoing self-assessment and group assessment

The **emergence phase** of problem solving, sometimes called **norming,** occurs when the members end their disagreement and solve the problem. Every member may enthusiastically support the final decision. In some cases, though, members may compromise or settle for a proposal they didn't originally prefer. In any case, the key to emergence is acceptance of a decision members can support (even if reluctantly). Communication during the emergence phase is less polarized. Members back off from their previously held firm positions. Comments like "I can live with that" and "Let's give it a try" are common at this point. Even if some people have doubts about the decision, there is a greater likelihood they will keep their concerns to themselves. Harmony is the theme.[35]

The fourth stage of discussion is the **reinforcement phase.** This stage has also been called **performing** because members not only accept the decision but also actively endorse it. Members who found arguments against the decision during the conflict stage now present evidence to support it. In school, the reinforcement stage is apparent when students presenting a team project defend it against any complaints the instructor might have. On the job, the same principle applies: If the boss finds fault with a team's proposals, the tendency is to band together to support them.

In real life, groups don't necessarily follow this four-step process (summarized in Table 8-2) neatly. In an ongoing group, the patterns of communication in the past can influence present and future communication.[36] Teams with a high degree of conflict might have trouble reaching emergence, for example, whereas one that is highly cohesive might experience little disagreement.

FIGURE 8.4
Cyclical Stages
in an Ongoing
Group

Source: Galanes, G. J.,
Adams, K., & Brilhart, J. K.
(2004). *Effective group discussion* (11th ed.). New York,
NY: McGraw-Hill.

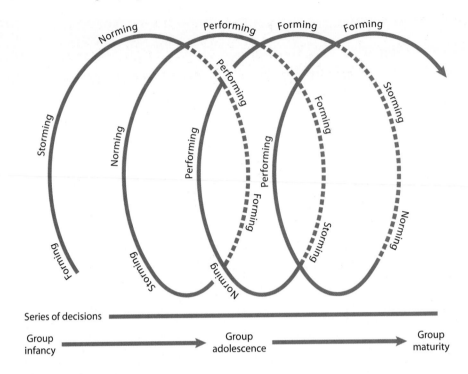

Sometimes a group can become stuck in one phase, never progressing to the phases that follow. Members might never get beyond the superficial, polite interaction of orientation. If they do, they might become mired in conflict. Ongoing groups might move through some or all of the stages each time they tackle a new problem, as pictured in Figure 8.4. In fact, a group that deals with several issues at one time might be in different stages for each problem.

Knowing a team to which you belong is likely to pass through these stages can be reassuring. Your urge to get down to business and quit wasting time during the orientation phase might be tempered if you realize the cautious communication is probably temporary. Likewise, you might be less distressed about conflict if you know the possibility of emergence may be just around the corner.

Enhancing Creativity

One advantage of teams is the greater chance for creativity.[37] As more members bring their different perspectives to a task, the chances of coming up with a winning solution increase. As one executive put it, "innovation is a team sport."[38]

Brainstorming   One way to boost the creativity of the group is through **brainstorming**—an approach that encourages free thinking and minimizes conformity. The term was coined by advertising executive Alex Osborn, who noticed groups were most creative when they let their imaginations run free.[39] As Nobel Prize winner Linus Pauling put it, "The key to creativity is to have lots and lots of ideas, then throw away the bad ones."[40]

Out of these observations came a series of steps that, with variations, are now used widely. The cardinal rules of brainstorming include:

1. All evaluation and criticism of ideas is forbidden during the early phases of the process.

2. Quantity—not quality—of ideas is the goal.

3. New combinations of ideas are sought.

One expert offers several other tips for healthy brainstorming:

- Don't let the boss speak first.
- Encourage members to speak whenever they have an idea. Don't follow a set speaking order.
- Include a variety of members in a session, not just experts.[41]

Brainstorming can be even more effective in virtual groups than in face-to-face meetings.[42] Furthermore, more ideas are generated when brainstorming is anonymous than when members know who is contributing suggestions.

Nominal Group Technique   While brainstorming can generate a large number of ideas, researchers have found a procedure called **nominal group technique (NGT)** generates a greater number of high-quality suggestions.[43] The method's name comes from the fact that, for much of this process, the participants are a group in name only because they are working independently. The NGT method consists of five phases:

1. Each member anonymously writes down his or her ideas, which a discussion leader then collects. This method ensures good ideas from quiet members will have a chance for consideration.

2. All ideas are posted for every member to see. By keeping the authorship of ideas private at this point, consideration is less likely to be based on personal factors such as authority or popularity.

3. Members discuss the ideas to better understand them, but criticism is prohibited. The goal here is to clarify the possibilities, not to evaluate them.

4. Each member privately rank-orders the ideas from most to least promising. Individual ranking again prevents domination by a few talkative or influential members.

5. The group critically and thoroughly discusses items that receive the greatest number of votes. At this point, a decision can be made, using whichever decision-making method described later in this chapter (e.g., consensus, majority rule) is most appropriate.

This approach lends itself nicely to virtual meetings. With most groupware packages, members can anonymously input ideas via computer and have their contributions displayed for everyone's consideration. This anonymity can empower quiet group members, who might otherwise be too intimidated to speak up.

The NGT method is too elaborate for relatively unimportant matters but works well for important issues. Besides reducing the tendency for more talkative members to dominate the discussion, the anonymity of the process lessens the potential for harmful conflicts.

Systematic Problem Solving

The range of problems that groups face on the job is almost endless. How can we cut expenses? Increase market share? Reduce customer complaints? Offer a better employee-benefits program? Not all groups approach problems like these systematically,[44] but most

DILBERT © Scott Adams/Dist. By Universal Uclick.

researchers agree that groups have the best chance of developing high-quality solutions to problems like these when they follow a systematic method for solving problems.[45]

The best-known problem-solving approach is the **reflective-thinking sequence,** developed more than 100 years ago by John Dewey and used in many forms since then.[46] In its most useful form, the reflective-thinking sequence is a seven-step process.

1. *Define the problem.* A group that doesn't understand the problem will have trouble finding a solution. Sometimes the problem facing a group is clear. It doesn't take much deliberation to understand what's necessary when the boss tells you to work out a vacation schedule for the next six months. On the other hand, some problems need rewording because they are too broad as originally presented. The best problem statements are phrased as probative questions that encourage exploratory thinking:

Too Broad	Better
How can we reduce employee turnover?	How can we reduce turnover among new employees? (This suggests where to look for the nature of the problem and solutions.)
How can we boost office staff's morale?	How can we reduce the complaints about too much work?

2. *Analyze the problem.* At this stage, the group tries to discover the causes and extent of the problem, probably by doing some research between meetings. Questions that are usually appropriate in this stage include (a) How bad is that problem? (b) Why does it need to be resolved? and (c) What are its causes? It can be just as useful to focus on the positive aspects of the situation during this phase to consider how they can be strengthened. Questions in this area include (a) What forces are on our side? (b) How do they help us? and (c) How can we strengthen them?

   A team analyzing the question "How can we reduce complaints about too much work?" might find the problem is especially bad for certain staffers. It might discover the problem is worst when staffers have to do a slew of website updates at the last minute. It might learn the major complaint doesn't involve hard work as much as it does resentment at seeing other people apparently having a lighter load. Positive research findings might be that the staffers understand the importance of their role, that they view being chosen to do important jobs as a sign of respect for the quality of their work, and that they don't mind occasional periods of scrambling to meet a deadline.

3. *Establish criteria for a solution.* Rather than rushing to solve the problem, it's best to spend some time identifying criteria (that is, the characteristics of a good solution and the standards you will use to evaluate your proposed solutions). For example, who will have to approve your solution? What are the cost constraints? What schedule needs to be met? Sometimes criteria like these are imposed from outside the group. Other requirements come from the members themselves. Regardless of the source of these requirements, the team needs to make them clear before considering possible solutions. Without defining the criteria of a satisfactory solution, the team may waste time arguing over proposals that have no chance of being accepted.

4. *Generate possible solutions to the problem.* This is the time for using the creative thinking techniques, such as brainstorming. A major hazard of group problem solving is that it may get bogged down in arguing over the merits of one or two proposals without considering other solutions that might exist. Besides limiting the quality of the solution, such squabbling also leads to personal battles among members.[47]

   The most valuable feature of brainstorming is the emphasis on generating many ideas before judging any of them. This sort of criticism-free atmosphere encourages people to volunteer solutions that, in turn, lead to other ideas. A brainstorming list for the overworked staffers might include the following:

   - Cut down on the number of jobs that have to be done over; create a company style book that shows how letters are to be set up, how contract clauses should be phrased, and so on.

   - Have staffers help each other out—someone with too much work to do can ask someone else to take over a project.

   - Invest in scanning technology that digitizes documents so they don't need to be retyped from scratch.

5. *Decide on a solution.* Once the group has considered all possible solutions to a problem, it can go back and find the best answer to the problem. This is done by evaluating each idea against the list of criteria developed earlier by the team. In addition to measuring the solution against its own criteria, team members should judge any potential solutions by asking three questions: First, will the proposal bring about all the desired changes? If it solves only part of the problem, it isn't adequate without some changes. Second, is the solution feasible? If the idea is good but beyond the power of this group to achieve, it needs to be modified or discarded. Finally, does the idea have any serious disadvantages? A plan that solves one set of problems while generating another probably isn't worth adopting.

6. *Implement the solution.* Inventing a solution isn't enough. The group also has to put the plan into action. This probably involves several steps. First, it's necessary to identify the specific tasks that must be accomplished. Second, the group must identify the resources necessary to make the plan work. Third, individual responsibilities must be defined: Who will do what, and when? Finally, the group should plan for emergencies. What will happen if someone is sick? If the project runs over budget? If a job takes longer than expected? Anticipating problems early is far better than being caught by surprise.

7. *Follow up on the solution.* Even the best ideas don't always work out perfectly in practice. For this reason, the group should check up on the implementation of the solution to see whether any adjustments are needed.

Decision-Making Methods

Disagreement may be a healthy, normal part of solving problems on the job, but sooner or later it becomes necessary to make a decision as a group. Whether the issue is who will work over the weekend, how to split the year-end bonus money among members, or which approach to advertising is best, there usually has to be only one answer to a problem. As business instructor Joel Baum puts it, "How you decide is just as important as what you decide. The process you use has a direct impact on how members feel about the decision. It can influence commitment, excitement, and buy-in; or it can create feelings of resentment and exclusion."[48] There are a number of ways to make business decisions like these.

Consensus   **Consensus** is a collective group decision that every member is willing to support. The purest form of consensus is unanimous, unequivocal support: every member's belief that the decision reached is the best possible one. For instance, an entire employee search committee might agree that a particular candidate is perfect for a job. This state of unanimity isn't always possible, however, and it isn't necessary for consensus. Members may support a decision that isn't their first choice, accepting the fact that it is the best one possible for the group at that time. In the case of the new employee, committee members might agree on a candidate who is some members' second choice because the people who will be working most closely with her are her most enthusiastic supporters.

Some cultures value consensus more highly than others. For example, British and Dutch businesspeople value the "group must be aboard" approach. On the other hand, Germans, French, and Spanish communicators depend more on a strong leader's decision and view a desire for consensus as somewhat wishy-washy.[49]

Cultural norms aside, consensus has both advantages and drawbacks. While it has the broadest base of member support, reaching consensus takes time. It requires a spirit of cooperation among team members, a willingness to experience temporary disagreements, a commitment to listening carefully to other ideas, and a win–win attitude. Given these challenges, it's wise to limit consensus decisions to important issues when the need for agreement is high and when the team can dedicate the time and effort necessary to reach agreement.[50]

Majority Vote   Whereas consensus requires the agreement of the entire group, deciding by a **majority vote** needs only the support of most of the members. Thus, majority voting decisions are much quicker and easier to reach. A 10-member staff choosing a decorating scheme for the new office might talk almost endlessly before reaching consensus, but with a majority vote, the decision would require the agreement of only 6 members. While majority vote works well on relatively minor issues, it is usually not the best approach for more important decisions (at least not in small groups) because it can leave a substantial minority unsatisfied and resentful about being railroaded into accepting a plan they don't support.

Minority Decision   In a **minority decision,** a few members make a decision affecting the entire group. This is frequently the case in business situations. For instance, the executive committee of a corporation often acts on behalf of the board of directors, which, in turn, represents the shareholders. Minority decisions are also made in less exalted circumstances. A steering group responsible for planning the company picnic might delegate tasks like publicity, entertainment, and food to smaller committees. As long as the minority has the confidence of the larger group, this method works well for many decisions. While it doesn't take advantage of the entire group's creative thinking, the talents of the subgroup are often perfectly adequate for a task.

Expert Opinion   When a single person has the knowledge or skill to make an informed decision, the group may be best served by relying on his or her **expert opinion.** As one observer puts it, "If you want a track group to win the high jump, you find one person who can jump 7 feet, not seven people who can jump 1 foot." Some team members are experts because of specialized training: a structural engineer working with a design team on a new building, a senior airline mechanic who decides whether a flight can depart safely, or a systems analyst involved in the development of a new data control system. Other people gain their expertise by experience: the purchasing agent who knows how to get the best deals or a labor negotiator seasoned by years of contract deliberations.

Despite the obvious advantages, following an expert's suggestions isn't always as wise an approach as it might seem. First, it isn't always easy to tell who the expert is. Length of experience isn't necessarily a guarantee: The business world abounds with old fools. Even when a member clearly is the expert, the other members must recognize this fact before they will willingly give their support. Unfortunately, some people who are regarded as experts don't deserve the title, while some geniuses may be ignored.

Authority Rule   In many business groups, decision making is often a matter of **authority rule:** The designated leader makes the final decision. This doesn't mean such leaders must be autocratic: They often listen to members' ideas and suggestions before making the decisions themselves. The owner of a family business might invite employees to help choose a new company logo while selecting the final design after hearing their opinions. A store manager might consult with employees about scheduling work hours while reserving the final decisions for herself. The input from team members can help an authority to make higher-quality decisions than would otherwise be possible. One major risk of inviting suggestions from subordinates, however, is the disappointment that might follow if these suggestions aren't accepted.

Choice of a Decision-Making Method   Each decision-making method has its advantages and disadvantages. The choice of which one to use depends on several factors.

What type of decision is being made?   If the decision can best be made by one or more experts, or if it needs to be made by the authorities in charge, then involving other group members isn't appropriate. If, however, the task at hand calls for creativity or requires a large amount of information from many sources, then input from the entire team can make a big difference.

How important is the decision?   Trivial decisions don't require the entire team's involvement. It's a waste of time and money to bring everyone together to make decisions that can easily be made by one or two people.

How much time is available?   If time is short, it simply may not be possible to consult everyone on the team. This is especially true if the members are not all available—if some are away from the office or out of town, for example. Even if everyone is available, the time-consuming deliberations that come with a team discussion may be a luxury you can't afford.

What are the personal relationships among members?   Even important decisions might best be made without convening the whole team if members are on bad terms. If talking things out will improve matters, then a meeting may be worth the emotional wear and tear it will generate. But if a face-to-face discussion will just make matters worse, then the decision might best be made in some other way.

MASTER the chapter

review points

- Meetings are common, often time-consuming, and costly.

- Meetings serve one of these purposes: sharing information, solving problems/making decisions, or engaging in ritual activities.

- Virtual meetings present advantages and challenges for leaders and participants.

- Meetings should be held only when the job at hand is more than one person can handle, requires a division of labor, and has more than one right answer. If misunderstanding or resistance to a decision is likely, it is also wise to hold a meeting to overcome those hazards.

- Well in advance of each meeting, an agenda announces the time, length, and location of the session; those who will attend; background information; goals, and advance work members need to do.

- After a meeting is called to order, the chair announces the goals of the session, reviews necessary background information, shows how members can help, and identifies time constraints.

- Member participation can be balanced by turn-taking and using questions (relay, reverse, direct, overhead).

- The chair and members keep discussion on track by referring to time pressures, summarizing and redirecting remarks of members who have digressed, using relevancy challenges, and arranging to deal with tangential issues after the meeting.

- The tone of meetings stays positive if members make an attempt to understand one another by asking questions and paraphrasing, enhancing the value of one another's comments, and being culturally aware.

- A meeting should close at its scheduled time, when the group lacks resources to continue, or when the agenda has been completed—whichever comes first. The chair should give notice that time is almost up, summarize accomplishments and future actions, and thank group members for their contributions.

- Chairs' duties after a meeting include preparing meeting minutes, building agendas for next sessions, following up with other members, and honoring their own commitments.

- Teams move in and out of stages (forming, storming, norming, and performing).

- Brainstorming and nominal group technique (NGT) are effective ways to generate creative solutions to problems.

- By following a systematic approach to problem solving, teams can maximize their ability to make solid decisions.

- Choosing the best decision-making method (consensus, majority vote, minority decision, expert opinion, or authority rule) ensures the group uses time effectively and generates an outcome members support.

key terms

activities

1. Invitation to Insight

You can gain an appreciation for the importance of meetings by interviewing one or more people in a career field that is of interest to you.

  a. Ask questions such as:

    1. How frequent are meetings in your work?
    2. How long do these meetings typically take?
    3. What kinds of topics are covered in your meetings?
    4. What formats are used (parliamentary procedure, following an agenda, open-ended discussions with no clear agenda, virtual versus face-to-face)?
    5. How effective are meetings? What factors contribute to their effectiveness or ineffectiveness?

  b. Compare your findings with your classmates' findings.

    1. Which types of meetings occur most frequently (informational, problem-solving, ritual)?
    2. Which types of formats occur most frequently?

    3. Are the advantages mentioned by interviewees similar to those identified in the text?
    4. Based on concepts from the text, suggest remedies for the challenges identified by the interviewees.

2. Skill Builder

Use the information in this chapter to decide which of the following tasks would best be handled by a problem-solving group and which should be handled by one or more individuals working separately. Be prepared to explain the reasons for each choice.

  a. Developing procedures for interviewing prospective employees.
  b. Tabulating responses to a customer survey.
  c. Investigating several brands of office machines for possible purchase.
  d. Choosing the most desirable employee health insurance program.
  e. Organizing the company picnic.
  f. Researching the existence and cost of training programs for improving communication among staff members.

3. Invitation to Insight

Ask someone you know to provide you with a copy of an agenda from a workplace meeting, or provide one of your own from a meeting you have attended. With a group of classmates, analyze the agenda.

   a. Which elements of an effective agenda are present? Which are absent?
   b. To what degree does the agenda illustrate result-oriented, specific, and realistic goals?
   c. Suggest improvements for future agendas. If result-oriented goals are missing, write some examples.

4. Skill Builder

You are chairing a meeting in which one member whom everyone dislikes is aggressively promoting an idea. Time is short, and everyone in the group is ready to make a decision that will go against the disliked member's position. You realize the unpopular idea does have real merit, but lending your support and urging further discussion will put the group further behind and leave the other members annoyed with you.

   Suggest three different ways you could handle the situation. For each, write out the specific comments you would make. Using concepts and vocabulary from this chapter, discuss advantages and disadvantages of each scenario.

5. Skill Builder

Use the skills introduced on pp. 222–225 to describe how you would respond to the following comments in a meeting. Identify which skill you are using:

   a. "There's no way people will work Sundays without being paid double overtime."
   b. "No consultant is going to tell me how to be a better manager!"
   c. "I don't think this brainstorming is worth the time. Most of the ideas we come up with are crazy."
   d. "Talking about interest rates reminds me of a time in the 1980s when this story about President Carter was going around. . . ."
   e. "Sorry, but I don't have any ideas about how to cut costs."

6. Skill Builder

With a group of your classmates, simulate a group decision-making process using the nominal group technique. Use one of the following scenarios or create one of your own:

   a. Choosing a topic from this class about which you could deliver a group oral presentation.
   b. Deciding where you and your classmates might go for a field trip.
   c. Selecting the next novel your book club will read and discuss.

   After you complete the role play, discuss advantages and disadvantages of the nominal group technique as a decision-making procedure.

7. Skill Builder

Select seven volunteers to form a circle in the center of the classroom and simulate a group decision-making process using the reflective-thinking sequence. The rest of the class will gather around to the periphery of the group to observe and offer suggestions. Due to time constraints, each step, especially problem analysis, will need to be abbreviated. Use the same topic you used for the NGT skill builder in exercise 6.

After the role play is completed, discuss advantages and disadvantages of the reflective-thinking sequence as a decision-making procedure. Then compare your experiences using the nominal group technique and the reflective-thinking sequence.

8. Skill Builder

With three to six of your classmates, decide which method of decision making would be most effective for your group in each of the following situations:

a. Choosing the safest course of action if you were lost in a dangerous area near your city or town.

b. Deciding whether and how to approach your instructor to propose a change in the grading system of your course.

c. Designing the most effective campaign for your school to recruit minority students.

d. Duplicating for distribution to your instructor and classmates the solutions to this exercise your group developed.

e. Hiring an instructor for your department.

f. Choosing the name for a new brand of breakfast cereal.

g. Selecting a new computer system.

h. Deciding which of three employees gets the desirable vacant office.

i. Planning the weekend work schedule for the upcoming month.

j. Deciding whether the employees should affiliate with a labor union.

For further review, go to the LearnSmart study module for this chapter.

PART FOUR

Fresh Air Sports

Fresh Air Sports Rentals began eight years ago in a southern California beachfront hut where Woody and Sandy Belmont rented out fat-tired cruiser bikes to tourists. Business was good, and within a year Fresh Air customers could also rent a variety of other outdoor gear including surfboards, mountain bikes, and paddleboats.

Over the years Fresh Air has grown into a network of 18 locations throughout the western United States and Canada. The company is big enough now that name recognition is feeding the business: Customers who have rented from Fresh Air in one location look for it in other vacation spots. Woody and Sandy are thinking seriously of expanding the business to resorts on the East Coast, in Mexico, and in Central America.

Next month, Fresh Air is having its first-ever associates' meeting in San Diego. Woody and Sandy need to develop several presentations for that conference:

- A keynote speech, welcoming the employees and building enthusiasm for the company and the upcoming meeting. During this speech, Sandy and Woody will also introduce Fresh Air's new management team.

- An informative program on how to avoid sexual harassment claims. Fresh Air's new human relations director will deliver this talk, but Sandy wants to play a close role in its development.

- A session introducing the company's new incentive plan in which employees will receive bonuses for increasing sales. While the potential for greater compensation is good, base salaries will decline under this arrangement. Woody knows it's important to sell the plan to employees for it to have a chance of succeeding.

- A series of awards presentations at the closing dinner. At this session, employees will be honored for their exceptional service. Woody and Sandy want to include enough employee awards to boost morale, without creating so many awards they appear meaningless.

Making Effective Presentations

As you read the chapters in this unit, consider the following questions for each presentation:

1. What is the general goal for each presentation? Create a specific goal for each one.
2. What factors outlined in Chapter 9 (audience, occasion, speaker) should Sandy and Woody consider for each presentation?
3. Construct an outline for at least one of the presentations, based on your analysis in question 2 above. Include material for the introduction and conclusion and the main points in the body.
4. For each main point in the body of the presentation you developed in question 3, identify at least one type of supporting material you could use to make the point clearer, more interesting, and/or more persuasive.
5. Describe the style of delivery that would be most effective for each of the presentations to be delivered at the San Diego meeting. In addition to the speaker's style, discuss ways in which the speaking environment could be arranged to help achieve the presentation's goal.

Chapter Nine

Developing and Organizing the Presentation

chapter objectives

After reading this chapter you should be able to:

1. Develop an effective strategy for a specific presentation based on a complete analysis of the situation.

2. Identify general and specific goals for a given speaking situation.

3. Construct a clear thesis based on an analysis of a specific speaking situation.

4. Choose and develop an organizational plan for the body of a presentation that best suits its goal and the audience.

5. Create an effective introduction and conclusion for a presentation, following the guidelines in this chapter.

6. Design a presentation that contains effective transitions between the introduction and body, between points in the body, and between the body and conclusion.

W hatever your field, whatever your job, speaking to an audience is a fact of life. Sales representatives and account executives deliver presentations to potential customers. Brand managers propose ideas to management and explain new product lines to the sales force. Department heads and supervisors brief superiors on recent developments and subordinates on new company policies. Computer specialists explain new systems and software to the people who will use them. Presentations are so pervasive some experts have estimated that speakers address audiences an astonishing 33 million times each day.[1] According to one survey, businesspeople give an average of 26 presentations a year.[2] Table 9-1 offers a sample of the kinds of presentations most people deliver sooner or later in their careers. Chapter 12 offers specific advice on planning and delivering various types of business presentations.

While some business and professional presentations are formal, full-dress performances before large audiences, most are comparatively informal talks to a few people or even a single person. If you drop into your boss's office and say, "Do you have a few minutes? I have some information that may help us cut down our travel expenses," you're arranging a presentation. You're also delivering a presentation when you teach the office staff how to use the new database, explain the structure of your department to a new employee, or explain to management why you need a larger budget.

Even when you create a written report, you may be asked to introduce its contents in an oral presentation, and the quality of your spoken remarks may be the measure of your success. In fact, the quality of your presentation may determine whether anyone ever reads your documents. Furthermore, the highly public nature of presentations means your reputation depends on how you handle yourself in front of an audience.

As your career progresses, presentational speaking skills become even more important.[3] One automobile executive explained:

> As an executive rose in management, he had to
> rely less on his technical training and more on his
> ability to sell his ideas and programs to the next

Table 9-1	Common Types of Presentational Speaking

Type of Presentation	Example
Briefing and informational announcements	Announcing new health insurance procedure
Orientation sessions	Providing information on health care benefit plans
Training programs	Explaining how to operate new computer software
Research and technical reports	Describing a market research survey
Progress reports	Giving a status report on monthly sales
Civic and social presentations	Making a speech at a local service club
Convention and conference presentations	Reporting on company's technological breakthroughs
Television and radio interviews	Describing company's position on industrial accident or injury
Introductions	Introducing new employee to other workers
Sales presentations	Demonstrating product to potential customer
Project and policy proposals	Proposing new travel policy to management
Seeking resources	Making loan request to commercial lender
Ceremonial occasions	Speaking at retirement celebration for long-time employee

level of management. When I was just an engineer somewhere down the line working on a technical problem, everything affecting me was in my grasp. All I had to do was solve this particular problem, and I was doing my job. But now, as head of advanced engineering, I have to anticipate and predict product trends and then sell my programs for capitalizing on those trends.[4]

Most people who work in organizations eventually find their effectiveness and success depend on their ability to organize their ideas and present them effectively. Sometimes a written memo or report will do the job, but there are often important reasons for presenting your ideas personally. For example, if people don't understand a point in a proposal, they may put it aside for weeks or simply veto it. Delivering your message personally provides immediate feedback that helps you clarify points and answer questions. Oral presentations are often more persuasive as well. A speaker's knowledge, enthusiasm, and apparent confidence can influence people to accept or reject an idea in a way that a written document cannot.

In practice, you'll rarely get approval for an important idea without explaining it personally. As one executive put it:

The people who have the power and responsibility to say yes or no want a chance to consider and question the proposal in the flesh. Documents merely set up a meeting and record what the meeting decided. Anyone serious about an idea welcomes the chance to present it himself [or herself!]—in person. We wisely discount proposals whose authors are unwilling to be present at the launching.[5]

Presentations aren't delivered only to internal audiences. Many people also give work-related addresses to listeners outside their organizations. Realizing that effective speakers carry their message to the public in ways that print and electronic media can't match, companies send representatives into the community to deliver speeches in a wide variety of settings.[6] Some of the world's biggest corporations sponsor training. Toastmasters International, a group dedicated to helping businesspeople present their ideas effectively,

How Much Time Does It Take to Plan a Presentation?

Mark Twain once said, "It usually takes more than 3 weeks to prepare a good impromptu speech." This humorous observation highlights a truth about virtually every presentation: Success comes from careful planning, and planning takes time.

Almost every inexperienced speaker underestimates the amount of time necessary to create an effective presentation. Most experts use the hour-per-minute principle: Expect to spend about 1 hour of preparation time for every minute you will be speaking. Some professionals suggest a more modest 9-to-1 ratio between preparation and speaking time. "If I'm building a new presentation from scratch, you're probably talking about at least 10 hours of research and development for 1 hour of delivery time," says corporate trainer Bob Pike.

Experts agree the way you spend preparation time is more important than the actual number of hours you spend. Most suggest that analyzing your audience is essential. Even for 1-hour speeches he has delivered many times before, Pike spends at least 2 to 3 hours researching the specific audience he will be addressing. He often asks key clients to fill out questionnaires that identify their specific interests, level of knowledge, requested topics, or even specific words he should avoid.

Speakers are like athletes: Time spent planning and practicing is an investment that produces winning results.

now has more than 270,000 members in 13,000 clubs in 116 countries.[7] Research confirms that speakers can become more effective with training.[8] Even people who seem to work in fairly solitary jobs give speeches to clubs, professional organizations, and community groups.

Different kinds of presentations make different demands on the speaker. For example, a sales presentation to one customer may often seem more like a conversation because the customer may interrupt with questions, while a speaker addressing an audience of several hundred people may delay questions until the end. In spite of the differences, all presentations make many of the same demands on the speaker. The planning, structure, support, and strategy of each of them are very important, and a good speaker follows approximately the same steps in planning and developing almost any presentation. The material in Chapters 9 through 12 applies to almost any presentation you will give in your career.

• Analyzing the Situation

Before you plan even one sentence of the actual presentation, you have to think about the situation in which you'll speak. A presentation that might fascinate you could bore or irritate the audience. You can make sure your approach is on target by considering three factors: the audience, yourself as the speaker, and the occasion.

Analyzing the Audience

The saying "Different strokes for different folks" is never more true than when you are delivering a presentation. Having good ideas isn't enough. You have to present those ideas in a way your listeners will understand and appreciate. One corporate communication expert declared, "Designing a presentation without an audience in mind is like writing a love letter and addressing it 'To Whom It May Concern.'"[9] Former Chrysler president Lee Iacocca pinpointed the value of audience analysis:

It's important to be able to talk to people in their own language. If you do it well, they'll say, "God, he said exactly what I was thinking." And when they begin to respect you, they'll follow you to the death. The reason they're following you is not because you're providing some mysterious leadership. It's because you're following them.[10]

Asking yourself a number of questions about your listeners will shape the way you adapt your material to fit their interests, needs, and backgrounds.

Who Are the Key Audience Members?

Not all audience members are equally important. Sometimes one or two listeners have the power to approve or reject your appeal. For example, if you're making a sales pitch for a new database management system to a workgroup, it is important to know who has the final say. Is it the department supervisor? Is it a senior clerk whose judgment the rest of the team trusts? Whoever the decision makers are, you need to identify their interests, needs, attitudes, and prejudices and then focus your appeal toward them.

Sometimes it's easy to identify the key members. You don't have to be a communications expert to figure out that your boss has more power than the interns who are listening to your presentation. There are times, though, when you will need to do some pre-speaking investigation to identify the opinion leaders and decision makers in your audience.

How Much Do They Know?

A group of experts doesn't need the background information that less informed audiences would require. In fact, these people would probably be bored and offended by your basic explanation. Likewise, people who are familiar with a project don't need to be brought up to date—unless they have missed some late-breaking developments.

It's also important to ask yourself what your listeners do *not* know: Uninformed people or nonexperts will be mystified (as well as bored and resentful) unless you give them background information.

What Do They Want to Know?

People will listen to you if you address *their* interests, not yours. Asking for a promotion because you need the money isn't nearly as effective as demonstrating you can help the company better in the new position. Asking for an assistant because you feel overworked isn't as likely to impress your boss as showing how the help will increase productivity or allow you to take on more business. Perhaps the most important key to effective selling is identifying the prospect's needs and showing how the product can satisfy them.

Your listeners' job titles can give you clues about what they want to know. If audience members are specialists—in engineering, finance, or marketing, for example—they'll probably be interested in the more technical aspects of your talk that pertain to their specialties. On the other hand, an audience of nonexperts would probably be bored by a detailed talk on a subject they don't understand. Surprisingly, most managers fall into this category. "Just give me a quick description, a schedule, and the dollar figures" is a common managerial attitude.

What Are Their Personal Preferences?

Your listeners' personal idiosyncrasies can make all the difference in how your message is received. Does your audience prefer a presentation to be formal or casual? Humorous or straitlaced? Fast-paced or leisurely? Knowing these preferences can make the difference between a presentation's success and failure. One business consultant described how attitudes can vary from one set of listeners to another:

In the same corporation engineers giving reports to different department heads were required to go about it in a totally different manner. One department head wanted every detail covered in the report. He wanted analyses of why the report was being done, complete background on the subject under discussion, and a review of the literature, and he expected the report to run twenty or thirty written pages. In addition, he wanted an oral presentation that covered almost every detail of the report. The man who ran the department right down the hall wanted just the opposite. He wanted short, comprehensive reports discussing only the elements that were new. He said he already knew what was going on in his department. He didn't want an analysis of the situation, and he didn't want any young engineer wasting his time. The reports that got an A in one department got an F in another and vice versa. Therefore, the first rule for anyone giving a report is to ask those who requested the report what form they would like it to take.[11]

Audience attitudes can be hard to anticipate. One architect describes how his firm disguises the use of cost-saving technology to suit some clients' mistaken assumptions.

> When I [used to] prepare a preliminary design for a client, I often sketch[ed] a floor plan "free-hand": meaning that I quickly [drew] the design idea without a lot of detailed measurements. . . . With the advent of computer aided design (CAD), we can produce the same design on the computer . . . faster, more accurately, and at the same cost as before.

Although this approach seems like a win–win scenario for the architect and the client, experience proves this isn't the case.

> Some of our clients have complained that we are spending too much time and money on these preliminaries . . . they want something fast and cheap. They assume that because of how the product looks, we are spending more time (and more of their money) too early in the process. No amount of explanation will appease them.
>
> So, what to do? We just purchased a new software product. It is called Squiggle. It takes the very accurate, crisp, straight lines of a computer design and actually makes it look hand-drawn. Now, the clients will look at a computer drawing, but see hand-drawn.[12]

Which Demographic Characteristics Are Significant?

A number of your listeners' measurable characteristics might suggest ways to develop your remarks. One such characteristic is *gender*. What is the distribution of men and women? Even in this age of relative enlightenment, some topics must be approached differently, depending on your audience's gender.

A second demographic characteristic is *age*. A life insurance salesperson might emphasize retirement benefits to older customers and support for dependent children to younger ones with families.

Cultural background is often an important audience factor. You would use a different approach with blue-collar workers than you would with a group of white-collar professionals. Likewise, the group's ethnic mix might affect your remarks. The points you make, the examples you use, and even the language you speak will probably be shaped by your audience's cultural makeup. At the most basic level, you need to be respectful of your audience. For example, when speaking to people from other countries, avoid chauvinistic remarks like, "That's the way we do it back home."[13]

Another demographic factor is your audience's *economic status*. This factor is especially important in sales, where financial resources "qualify" potential customers as prospects for a product or service as well as suggest which features are likely to interest them.

Not every variable is important in planning every speech. For instance, an engineer speaking about recent advances in the field should consider her audience's level of knowledge (about engineering and those advances) and occupations (that is, what those

CULTURE **at work**

Understanding International Audiences

Here is the partial text of a speech planned by a U.S. executive newly assigned to head an Asia Pacific sales operation:

> I'm very pleased to have the opportunity to work with all of you in our Asian organization. Although I have worked with many Asian companies in the past, it is an exciting opportunity to now become a part of the APAC sales force with you. While I was Director of Sales for the Western region in the United States, we made a strong contribution to the company's earnings. I believe that we now have a great opportunity to build a strong and profitable business together in Asia that will yield outstanding returns for the parent company and our shareholders. My wife and I look forward to living out here and getting to know you better.

This speech may seem to include perfectly good comments if you share the background and expectations of the U.S. manager. But the people in his audience are likely to respond in not-so-favorable ways to this speech and to others like it. Their thoughts may not be voiced in public, and certainly not directly to the foreign manager, but here are some likely interpretations from local employees:

- "He sounds very proud of his accomplishments."
- "It seems like he doesn't recognize all the efforts we have been making here."
- "Why does he have to talk about profit on a formal occasion like this? Of course we recognize profit is necessary, and we're all working hard to make that happen. But he makes it sound as though we are only concerned about our stockholders."
- "Does he think Asia is one place?"
- "Why did he mention his wife?"

Having a group of employees think about their new manager in this way is not an ideal introduction to a working environment. In the initial phase of this person's presence abroad, an image of boastfulness, arrogance, and shortsightedness is being formed that could require considerable time, energy, and goodwill to erase. Even worse, there is a natural reluctance on the part of local employees to cooperate with leaders who are labeled in this way—at times there is passive or even active resistance to their directives. Good intentions and a formula for self-presentation learned in one's home setting can actually become a recipe for trouble in a different setting.

Source: Gundling, E. (2007). Twelve people skills for doing business across borders. *Employee Relations Today, 34,* 29–42.

---

advances have to do with her listeners' work), but matters such as gender, age, and economic status probably wouldn't be as important. On the other hand, a representative from Planned Parenthood speaking to a community organization would have to consider gender, age, and economic status, listeners' religious backgrounds, and their attitudes toward pregnancy planning and the medical profession. The first step to good audience analysis is to recognize which dimensions of your listeners' background are important and to profile those dimensions accurately.

What Size Is the Group?

The number of listeners will govern some very basic speaking plans. How many copies of a handout should you prepare? How large must your visuals be so everyone can see them? How much time should you plan for a question-and-answer session? With a large audience, you usually need to take a wider range of audience concerns into account; your delivery and choice of language will tend to be more formal; and your listeners are less likely to interrupt with questions or comments. A progress report on your current assignment would look ridiculous if you delivered it from behind a podium to four or five people. You would look just as foolish speaking to 100 listeners while reclining in a chair.

What Are the Listeners' Attitudes?   You need to consider two sets of attitudes when planning your presentation. The first is your audience's attitude toward *you as the speaker.* If listeners feel hostile or indifferent ("Charlie is such a bore"), your approach won't be the same as the one taken if they are excited to hear from you ("I'm glad he says he's going to simplify the paperwork; last year, he did a great job of speeding up the process for getting repairs done").

In addition to listeners' feelings about you, the audience's attitude about *your subject* should influence your approach. Do your employees think the new pension plan benefits are too far in the future to be important? Does the sales force think the new product line is exciting or just the same old line in a new package? Do the workers think the new vice president is a genius or just another figurehead? Attitudes such as these should govern your approach.

One way to discover your audience's attitudes—and to gain the audience's approval of your idea—is to meet with listeners before your presentation. One experienced professional explained how he applies this principle:

> Whenever I'm going to make a proposal—to clients or to my own bosses—I make it a practice to sit down with them in advance and test my approach with them. Then I go back and design a presentation that either supports their positive attitudes or provides answers to their questions and objections.

In addition to making personal contacts, you often can research your audience's attitudes online. With almost instant access to a wealth of sources including news stories, blogs, social networking sites, and comments on company websites, you often can find out what your key listeners think about you and your topic before you speak to them. One trial consultant uses this approach to research potential jurors before a big case: "If a juror has an attitude about something, I want to know what that is. . . . Anyone who doesn't make use of [Internet searches] is bordering on malpractice."[14]

Selling to Seniors: Audience Analysis or Audience Deception?

For more than 13 years, entrepreneur Tyrone M. Clark operated "Annuity University." This two-day workshop trained more than 7,000 people to sell annuities to senior citizens. In late 2002, the state of Massachusetts slapped Clark with a cease-and-desist order, accusing his firm of tricking seniors into trading in their investments for expensive and complicated annuity policies.

According to *The Wall Street Journal,* here are some of the practices Clark advocated:

- Oversimplifying the nature of the investments being sold. Clark says, "You'll waste time if you think you can impress them with charts, graphs, printouts or use sophisticated words." Instead, he recommends, "Tell them it's like a CD—it's safe, it's guaranteed."

- Using fear appeals. "[Seniors] thrive on fear, anger, and greed," says Clark. "Show them their finances are all screwed up so that they think, 'Oh, no, I've done it all wrong.'"

- Enticing retirees to attend sales seminars by offering free meals.

- Learning about investors' concerns. At seminars, seniors note their concerns from a list of topics including taxes, Social Security, insurance, and protection of assets. Salespeople are encouraged to refer to these concerns when they call customers to set up a sales appointment.

Sources: Schultz, E. E., & Opdyke, J. D. (2002, July 2). Annuities 101: How to sell to senior citizens. *Wall Street Journal,* pp. C1, C10; Complaint is filed in annuity case. (2002, September 26). *Wall Street Journal,* p. C3.

Analyzing Yourself as the Speaker

No two presentations are alike. While you can learn to speak better by listening to other speakers, a good presentation is rather like a good hairstyle or sense of humor: What suits someone else might not work for you. One of the biggest mistakes you can make is to try to be a carbon copy of some other effective speaker. When developing your presentation, be sure to consider several factors.

Your Goal   The very first question to ask yourself is why you are speaking. Are you especially interested in reaching one person or one subgroup in the audience? What do you want your key listeners to think or do after hearing you? How will you know when you've succeeded?

Your Knowledge   It's best to speak on a subject about which you have considerable knowledge. This is usually the case since you generally speak on a subject precisely because you *are* an authority. Regardless of how well you know your subject, you may need to do some research—sales figures over the past three years, the number of companies that have used the flexible-hours program you're proposing, the actual maintenance costs of the new equipment your company is buying, and so on.

If you do need more information, don't fool yourself into a false sense of security by thinking you know enough. It's better to over-prepare now than to look like a fool later. Kenneth Clarke, Britain's finance minister, embarrassed himself due to faulty knowledge. While visiting the town of Consett in northern England, he praised its success as an industrial center, saying it had "one of the best steelworks in Europe." But the steel mill had closed down 15 years earlier, putting 3,000 employees out of work. To redeem himself for that gaffe, Clarke cited another Consett factory as a major competitor in the world of disposable diapers. The town's diaper plant had closed down two years before.[15]

Your Feelings about the Topic   An old sales axiom says you can't sell a product you don't believe in. Research shows that sincerity is one of the greatest assets a speaker can have.[16] When you are excited about a topic, your delivery improves: Your voice becomes more expressive, your movements are more natural, and your face reflects your enthusiasm. On the other hand, if you don't care much about your topic—whether it's a report on your department's sales, a proposal for a new program, a product you're selling, or a new method you're explaining—the audience will know it and think, "If the speaker doesn't believe in it, why should I?" A good test for your enthusiasm and sincerity is to ask yourself if you really care whether your audience understands or believes what you have to say. If you feel indifferent or only mildly enthusiastic, it's best to search for a new idea for your proposal or a new approach to your subject.

Analyzing the Occasion

Even a complete understanding of your audience won't give you everything you need to plan an effective presentation. You also need to adapt your remarks to fit the circumstances of your presentation. Several factors contribute to the occasion.

Facilities   Figure 9.1 shows how you can adapt the layout of a room to suit the speaking situation. Whatever arrangement you choose, you need to consider some important issues. Will there be enough seating for all the listeners? What type of equipment is available for you to use? Will there be distracting background noises?

When you control the room arrangement where you will speak, consider these options:

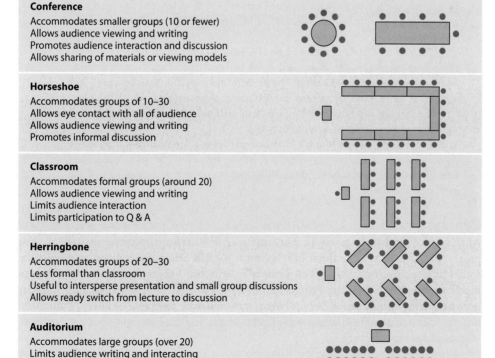

Conference
Accommodates smaller groups (10 or fewer)
Allows audience viewing and writing
Promotes audience interaction and discussion
Allows sharing of materials or viewing models

Horseshoe
Accommodates groups of 10–30
Allows eye contact with all of audience
Allows audience viewing and writing
Promotes informal discussion

Classroom
Accommodates formal groups (around 20)
Allows audience viewing and writing
Limits audience interaction
Limits participation to Q & A

Herringbone
Accommodates groups of 20–30
Less formal than classroom
Useful to intersperse presentation and small group discussions
Allows ready switch from lecture to discussion

Auditorium
Accommodates large groups (over 20)
Limits audience writing and interacting
Limits audience participation to Q & A

FIGURE 9.1

Room Arrangement Options

Source: Morrisey, G. L., Sechrest, T. L., & Warman, W. B. (1997). *Loud and clear: How to prepare and deliver effective business and technical presentations* (4th ed.). Cambridge, MA: Perseus Books.

Answering questions like these is critical, and failure to anticipate facility problems can trip you up. For example, the absence of an easel to hold your charts can turn your well-rehearsed presentation into a fiasco. Lack of a convenient electrical outlet can replace your PowerPoint show with an embarrassing blackout. Even the placement of doorways can make a difference. Most experienced speakers won't settle for others' assurances about facilities; they check out the room in advance and come prepared for every possible disaster.

Time   There are at least two considerations here. The first is the time of day you'll be speaking. A straightforward, factual speech that would work well with an alert, rested audience at 10:00 AM might need to be more entertaining or emphatic to hold everyone's attention just before quitting time.

Besides taking the hour of day into account, you also need to consider the length of time you have to speak. Most business presentations are brief. One director of a Los Angeles shopping mall typically gives prospective vendors 20 minutes to make their pitch: "I automatically x-out anyone who is late or exceeds their time allotment. My experience has shown that people who have trouble adhering to parameters and deadlines are unreliable."[17] Alan Brawn, national sales manager for Hughes-JCC, reinforces the importance of keeping your remarks within the preset time limit: "Typically, if major points aren't made in about six minutes, a person's time in the sun is done."[18]

Sometimes the length of your talk won't be explicitly dictated, but that doesn't mean you should talk as long as you like. Usually, factors in the situation suggest how long it's wise for you to speak. Notice, for example, how well speaker Hugh Marsh adapted his remarks to the after-dinner setting of his summary business report to a group of association members:

> Good evening, ladies and gentlemen. Whenever I get on a podium this late, after a long day at the office, I remind myself of several immutable laws.
>
> First, there is Marsh's First Law of Oratory—on any platform, any speech will grow in length to fill the time available for its delivery. Well, take heart. I only have fifteen minutes.
>
> Then there is Marsh's Second Law of Oratory—the farthest distance between two points is a speech. Or, as we used to say in Texas, speeches too often are like a Longhorn steer—a point here and a point there and a lot of bull in between. Well, again, take heart. I will try to keep my two points close together.
>
> Another law I remind myself of is Marsh's Third Law of Oratory—no speech ever sounds as good at 7:00 PM as it did at noon.
>
> And, finally, there is Marsh's First Law of Meeting Attendance—everybody's gotta be someplace. As long as we're here, let's be friends. I'll be brief. You be attentive. I'll make my few points and get off so we can get back to the fun part of the meeting—socializing.[19]

Context   As Chapter 1 explained, the context of your presentation also influences what you say or how you say it. For example, if others are speaking as part of your program, you need to take them into account. ("I had originally planned to discuss the technical aspects of our new express delivery system, but I think Carol has covered them pretty thoroughly. So let me bring your attention to two things.") Preceding speakers may have left your audience feeling bored or stimulated, receptive or angry, thoughtful or jovial. Since that state of affairs will affect how the audience receives your presentation, you should try to adjust to it.

Current events could also affect what you say or how you say it. For example, if you're presenting your new budget proposal just after the company has suffered a major financial loss, you should be prepared to show how your budget will cut costs.

• Setting Your Goal and Developing the Thesis

An absolutely essential step in planning any presentation is to define your goal—what you want to accomplish. Speaking without a clear goal is a recipe for failure. As speaking coach Sandy Linver put it:

> Giving a presentation without recognizing, focusing on, and remembering your objective is the equivalent of dumping the contents of your briefcase all over your boss's desk. You don't speak to fill time by reeling off fact after unorganized fact, nor to show beautiful pictures that take the breath away, nor to impress the audience with your wit and skill as a dramatic speaker. You don't give speeches to win speech-making awards. You are there to make the best of an opportunity, just as you do in every other aspect of your business activities.[20]

General and Specific Goals

There are two kinds of goals to consider: general and specific. As the name implies, a **general goal** (sometimes called a *general purpose*) is a broad indication of what you're trying to accomplish. There are three general speaking goals: to inform, persuade, and entertain. While one type of goal may be primary, a speaker often attempts to accomplish more than one. For example, a human resources officer would be smart to make an informative session on filing insurance claims as entertaining as possible to keep the audience's attention.

The goal of an *informative* presentation is either to expand your listeners' knowledge or to help them acquire a specific skill. Teaching a group of product managers about new developments in technology, training a new sales representative, or giving a progress report on regional sales to a senior sales manager are all typical examples of informative talks.

Persuasive presentations focus on trying to change what an audience thinks or does. Selling is the most obvious example, but there are others as well. A union organizer will try to persuade a group of employees to vote for a union. An accountant might try to convince management to adopt a different procedure for reporting expenditures. A marketing manager might try to convince sales representatives to be more enthusiastic about a product that has not sold well.

Sometimes a speaker's goal is to *entertain* the audience. The welcoming speaker at a convention might concentrate on getting the participants to relax and look forward to the coming events. After-dinner speakers at company gatherings or awards dinners usually consider themselves successful if their remarks leave the group in a jovial mood.

The **specific goal** (sometimes called the *specific purpose*) of your presentation describes the outcome you are seeking. If you think of a speech as a journey, your specific goal is your destination. Stating the specific goal tells you what you will have accomplished when you have "arrived." A good specific goal statement usually describes *whom* you want to influence; *what* you want them to think or do; and *how, when,* and *where* you want them to do it. Your goal statement should combine the answers to these questions into a single statement: "I want (who) to (do what) (how, when, where)." Here are some good examples of goal statements:

> "I want the people who haven't been participating in the United Way campaign to sign up."

> "I want at least five people in the audience to ask me for my business card after my talk and at least one person to schedule an appointment with me to discuss my company's services."

Keeping Your Goals Private

Sometimes it can be ethical to withhold your goal from an audience, while doing so at other times is unethical. Check your ability to distinguish the difference by identifying three situations for each of the following:

1. When it is legitimate to withhold your goal.
2. When withholding your goal would be unethical.

> "I want at least five people in the department to consider transferring to the new Fort Worth office."
>
> "I want the boss to tell the committee he's in favor of my proposal when they discuss it after my presentation."

Like these examples, your goal statements should do three things: describe the reaction or outcome you are seeking, be as specific as possible, and make your goal realistic.

Describe the Reaction You Are Seeking

Your goal should be worded in terms of the *desired outcome:* the reaction you want from your audience. You can appreciate the importance of specifying the outcome when you consider a statement that doesn't meet this criterion: "I want to show each person in this office how to operate the new voice mail system correctly."

What's wrong with this statement? Most important, it says nothing about the desired audience response. With a goal such as this, you could give a detailed explanation of the whole system without knowing whether anyone learned a thing! Notice the improvement in this statement: "I want everyone in this group to show me that he or she can operate the voice mail system correctly after my talk." With this goal, you can get an idea of how well you've done after delivering your presentation.

Be as Specific as Possible

A good goal statement identifies the *who, what, how, when,* and *where* of your goal as precisely as possible. For instance, your target audience—the who—may not include every listener in the audience. Take one of the statements we mentioned earlier: "I want the boss to tell the committee that he's in favor of my proposal when they discuss it after my presentation." This statement correctly recognizes the boss as the key decision maker. If you've convinced him, your proposal is as good as approved; if not, the support of less influential committee members may not help you. Once you identify your target audience, you can focus your energy on the people who truly count.

The best goal statements describe your goals in *measurable terms.* Consider these examples:

Vague	Specific
I want to collect some donations in this meeting.	I want to collect at least $15 from each person in this meeting.
I want to get my manager's support for my idea.	I want my manager to give me one day per week and the help of a secretary to develop my idea.

Table 9-2	Methods for Defining a Thesis Statement

1. Imagine you met a member of your audience at the elevator and had only a few seconds to explain your idea before the doors closed.

2. Imagine you had to send a one- or two-sentence e-mail that communicated your main ideas.

3. Ask yourself, if my listeners heard only a small portion of my remarks, what is the minimum they should have learned?

4. Suppose someone asked one of your listeners what you said in your presentation. What would you want the audience member to tell that person?

Knowing exactly what you want to accomplish dramatically increases the chances you will reach your goal. Suppose you need to convince a group of subordinates to stay within budget. You already know the following statement is not good: "I want to talk about the importance of our new budget limitations." (If you're not sure why it's not good, take another look at the preceding section on describing reactions.) A more result-oriented goal would be, "I want this group to stay within budget." But even this goal statement has problems. Whom are you going to encourage: people who are already holding the line on expenses or those who look like they might overspend? How many people do you hope to persuade? How will you appeal to them? When do you want them to do it: beginning immediately or when they get around to it? The latter may not be until after the fiscal year is over—too late to save this year's profits in your department. A comprehensive specific goal statement can take care of questions such as these: "I want to convince the four people who had spent more than half their year's budgets by May 1 that the department's solvency depends on their cutting expenses and have them show me a revised plan by the end of the week that demonstrates how they intend to trim costs for the rest of the year." This statement gives you several ideas about how to plan your presentation. Imagine how much more difficult your task would be if you had settled for the first vague goal statement.

Developing the Thesis

The **thesis statement**—sometimes called the *central idea* or *key idea*—is a single sentence that summarizes your message. Some communication coaches even advise boiling down your thesis to two words.[21] Table 9-2 offers some tips for formulating this sort of statement. Once you have a thesis, every other part of your talk should support it. The thesis gives your listeners a clear idea of what you are trying to tell them:

"We're behind schedule, but we can catch up and finish the job on time."

"The credit rating you earn now can help—or hurt—you for decades."

"Investing now in a new system will save us money in the long run."

Presentations without a clear thesis leave the audience asking, What's this person getting at? And while listeners are trying to figure out the answer, they'll be missing much of what you're saying.

The thesis is so important you will repeat it several times during your presentation: at least once in the introduction, probably several times during the body, and again in the conclusion.

Beginning speakers often confuse the thesis of a presentation with its goal. Whereas a goal statement is a note to *yourself* outlining what you hope to accomplish, a thesis statement tells your *audience* your main idea. Sometimes the two can be virtually identical. There are other cases, however, where goal and thesis differ. Consider a few examples:

Goal	Thesis
I want this client to advertise on our website.	Advertising on our website will boost your sales.
Workers will be more careful about conserving.	Energy conservation cuts expenses, which leaves energy money for salaries.
Audience members will be able to respond to sexual harassment instead of accepting it.	You don't have to accept sexual harassment.
I want to acquire new customers seeking this state-of-the-art technology.	Recent advances have dramatically changed industry in the past few years.

It may seem unethical to avoid mentioning your goal to an audience, but sometimes the omission is a matter of common sense and not deception. Real estate clients know that the listing agent wants to sell the property she is showing, but they are most interested in hearing why it's a good one. Similarly, an after-dinner speaker at a local service club might have the goal of getting the audience to relax, but sharing that goal would probably seem out of place.

There are other times, however, when hiding your goal would clearly be unethical. A speaker who began his presentation by saying, "I don't want to sell you anything; I just want to show you some aspects of home safety that every homeowner should know," and then went on to make a hard-sell pitch for his company's home fire alarms would clearly be stepping out of bounds. It usually isn't necessary to state your goal as long as you are willing to share it with your audience, if asked. It's very rare, however, not to state the thesis at the beginning of a presentation.

• Organizing the Body

Inexperienced speakers make the mistake of planning a talk by beginning at the beginning and writing an introduction first. This is like trying to landscape a piece of property before you've put up a building. The body is the place to start organizing, even though it doesn't come first in a presentation. Organizing the body of a talk consists of two steps: identifying the key points that support your thesis and deciding what organizational plan best develops those points.

Brainstorming Ideas

Once you have figured out your thesis, you are ready to start gathering research to support your presentation. The first step is to pull together a list of all the information you might want to include. You'll probably already have some ideas in mind, but finding other possibilities will usually require further research. For example, if you want to sell potential customers on your product, you'll want to find out which competing products they are using and how they feel about them. You'll also want to discover whether they are familiar with your product and what attitudes they have about it. In other cases, the material you'll need to discuss may appear to be obvious. If you're giving a report on last month's sales, the figures might form the bulk of your remarks. If you are explaining how to use a new piece of equipment, the operating steps appear to be the obvious body of your talk.

Your brainstorming and research will produce a list of material from which you'll build your presentation. For example, suppose you have been asked to address a group of employees about why you want them to use Mercury Overnight for letters and packages that need to be delivered quickly. Using your research on Mercury Overnight, you might make up a list that looks something like the one in Figure 9.2.

Notice this list is a random assortment of points. In fact, your own collection of ideas probably won't even be neatly listed on a single piece of paper. More likely it will be scribbled on an assortment of index cards, check stubs, message pads, or whatever you had at hand when you came across a piece of promising information. Once you've assembled what seems like enough raw material, you're ready to organize it.

Basic Organizational Plan

Once you have a list of possible ideas, you are ready to organize them in a clear form that helps achieve your speaking goal. Most people will agree that clarity is important, but few realize just how critical it is. A substantial body of research indicates that organizing your remarks clearly can make your messages more understandable, keep your audience happy, and boost your image as a speaker.[22] Despite the benefits of good organization, most presentations suffer from a variety of problems in this area:

- Taking too long to get to the point
- Including irrelevant material
- Leaving out necessary information
- Getting ideas mixed up[23]

Problems like those above can lead to organizational chaos. Even experienced speakers can get into trouble when they speak without preparing their ideas. Former U.S. president George W. Bush was a more effective speaker when working from prepared notes than when speaking off the cuff. His answer to a question about his proposed Social Security plan illustrates the problem:

> Because the—all which is on the table begins to address the big cost drivers.
> For example, how benefits are calculated, for example, is on the table; whether or not benefits rise based upon wage increases or price increases. There's a series of parts of the formula that are being considered. And when you couple that, those different cost drivers, affecting those—changing those with personal accounts, the idea is to get what has been promised more likely to be—or closer delivered to what has been promised.[24]

- Mercury Overnight will pick up the package at your office instead of you having to go through the mailroom.
- It will also deliver right to your office if the label is marked properly, so you don't have to wait for the mailroom to process and deliver it to you.
- When we experimented with different delivery services, Mercury delivered every single package we gave it within 24 hours.
- Some of the companies we tried took 2 days or more about 25 percent of the time.
- One company we tried got the package in on time about 90 percent of the time.
- Other companies we've tried have held up packages for as much as a week for no good reason.
- Mercury will deliver into the rural areas where many of our customers are, while some of the other companies only deliver in the urban areas.
- Mercury will bill the departmental accounts, saving bookkeeping time.
- Some companies charge a lot of extra money for the odd-sized packages we send sometimes, but Mercury just charges by weight.
- Because we can't always count on overnight delivery with the delivery service we're using now, we often have to take time off to run a package across town.
- Mercury charges less than its competitors for heavy packages.
- If we send several things at once to the same place, Mercury will give us a lower "group rate."
- Mercury will come out at any time to pick up a package.
- Other companies will only make a regular daily stop, which doesn't do you much good if your package isn't ready when they come.
- Mercury will make pickups from 7 in the morning until midnight, which is nice if you're working early or late.
- If you send the package through the post office and don't put enough postage on it, the post office sends it back and the package won't get there in time.
- The packages that we've sent through some other shippers sometimes get so badly damaged that the contents have to be replaced. The shipper will pay for the contents if you insure the package, but that doesn't get it there on time.
- Sometimes you have to ship a one-of-a-kind item, like a prototype for an advertisement, and if it gets lost or damaged it can take weeks to make a new one.
- Mercury's best shipping fee includes insurance.
- It isn't easy to figure out which delivery service is best.
- When the company was smaller, we used to just send things by mail.
- We researched the idea of setting up our own delivery service, but management vetoed it because it cost too much.

FIGURE 9.2 Selling Points Produced by a Brainstorming Session

Most speakers would find that some of their own remarks would look almost as disjointed. The key to avoiding a meaningless stream of ideas is to organize your ideas before speaking.

No matter the subject or the goal, most effective presentations follow a well-known pattern: First, tell them what you're going to tell them; then, tell them; then, tell them what you told them. The format looks like this:

Introduction

- Attention-getter
- Thesis
- Preview

Body (two to five main points)

I.

II.

III.

IV.

V.

Conclusion

- Review
- Closing statement

This linear, logical approach to organization isn't the only way to structure a presentation. Researchers have found it works best with Euro-American audiences or listeners receptive to the Euro-American cultural standard. Listeners from other backgrounds may use less linear patterns, which have been given labels including "star," "wave," and "spiral."[25] Despite the value of these patterns in certain situations, the standard format is probably the safest approach with most business audiences who are part of Euro-American culture.

You have probably encountered this format many times. Despite its familiarity, many speakers act as if they have never heard of it. They launch into their subjects without any opening remarks on what they're about to say. Some finish their main ideas and then stop speaking without any summation or closing. Still others deliver what seems to be a model three-part talk but don't stop there; they continue tacking on new information after audience members have closed their mental files: "Did I mention that. . . .", "We had the same problem, by the way, last year when. . . . ", or "Oh, another thing I should have mentioned. . . . " Even worse, many speakers don't seem to have *any* organizational plan in mind. Their remarks sound as if they had dropped their note cards and shuffled them together in random order before addressing the group.

Identify Main Points and Subpoints

The list of ideas you've compiled by brainstorming and research probably contains more material than you'll be able to use in your talk. So the next step is to figure out which key points best support your thesis and help you achieve your purpose. Your analysis of the speaking situation will also help you to pinpoint your key ideas.

On the basis of this analysis, you might decide these are the major reasons that would convince listeners to sign up to use Mercury:

I. Mercury is more reliable.

II. Mercury is more convenient.

III. Mercury is more economical.

None of these points was on the brainstorming list in Figure 9.2, but they emerge as themes from that list. Each of the points that did appear on that list will fit into one of these categories, so the speech can be organized around these three points.

FIGURE 9.3

A Logic Tree Illustrates the Relationship between the Thesis, Main Points, and Subpoints in a Presentation

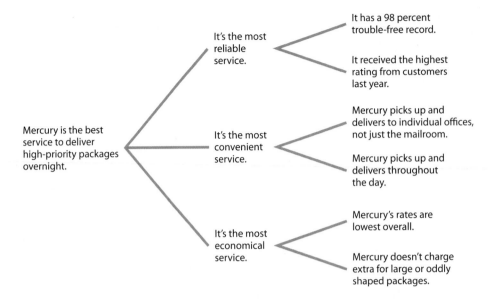

How do you identify your main points? One way is by applying the "one week later" test: Ask yourself what main points you want people to remember one week after the presentation. Since most listeners won't recall much more than a few ideas, your one week later points logically should be emphasized during your talk.

The basic ideas that grow out of your audience analysis or brainstorming list might work well as the main points of your talk, but this doesn't always happen. As with the Mercury delivery service example, there may be better ways to organize your material. Before you can decide, you need to think about the different ways the body of a presentation can be organized.

Once you have identified main points, you can fill in your plan with the subpoints that expand on each of them. These subpoints can be added to a standard outline like the one in Figure 9.4 on p. 280. A more visual way to represent the relationship between a thesis, main points, and subpoints is to draw a logic tree like the one in Figure 9.3.[26]

Choose the Best Organizational Pattern

There are many ways to organize the body of a presentation. Some work best for fundamentally informative subjects, and others are more effective when you want to persuade your listeners. You should choose the one that best develops your thesis and thus helps you to achieve your goal.

Chronological   A **chronological pattern** arranges your points according to their sequence in time. You can use it to explain a process, such as the steps in putting an order through the order fulfillment and shipping departments or the schedule for developing a new product. One of its most common uses is to give instructions:

Thesis: Downloading the software program is easy.

    I. Click *Manual Download.*

    II. When the *File Download* box appears, choose a folder location.

    III. Close all applications including your web browser.

    IV. Double-click on the saved file icon to start the installation process.

Chronological patterns are also useful for discussing events that develop over time:

Thesis: We need to stay on schedule if we're to get the catalog out in time for the holidays.

   I. A product list must be ready by March 1.

  II. Photography and catalog copy have to be completed by May 6.

 III. Page proofs have to be read and corrected by July 30.

 IV. Final proofs have to be reviewed by department heads by August 30.

  V. Catalogs have to be shipped no later than October 5.

Chronological patterns may be used for discussing history:

Thesis: A review of the past five years shows we've been moving toward empowering our entire workforce to make decisions.

   I. Five years ago, management introduced the Employee Advisory Council.

  II. Four years ago, we started project teams with people from every division.

 III. Two years ago, the company started allowing department supervisors to approve purchases.

 IV. Over the past year, the company has made changes in our billing process.

Spatial A **spatial pattern** organizes material according to how it is put together or where it is physically located. You might use a spatial pattern to show the parts in a model for a new product; the location of various departments in your building; or the safety requirements of a piece of equipment, such as where safety shields should be placed, the support required in the floor, and so on. You might sell a piece of real estate with a spatially organized presentation like this:

Thesis: This home provides all the space you need.

   I. The main floor is spacious, with a large living room, a formal dining room, and an eat-in kitchen.

  II. The second floor has enough bedrooms for every member of the family, plus a private study.

 III. The basement has a finished playroom for the children and a utility room.

 IV. The yard has large trees and lots of space for a garden.

You can also show the subject's geographical nature by citing examples from many places:

Thesis: Business is better in some areas than in others.

   I. Northeast regional sales are 50 percent ahead of last year's.

  II. Mid-Atlantic regional sales are 10 percent ahead of last year's.

 III. Southern regional sales are about the same as last year's.

 IV. Midwest regional sales are down about 25 percent from last year's.

Topical   A **topical pattern** groups your ideas around some logical themes or divisions in your subject. For example, you might organize a proposal for simplifying the expense-accounting procedures around the reasons for the change or a sales presentation for photocopiers around the three major types of copiers you think a customer might be interested in. An accountant might organize a proposal for a new inventory system this way:

Thesis: A just-in-time inventory system has three major benefits.

I. It eliminates excess inventory that may result from long-term ordering.
II. It cuts down on waste resulting from supplies becoming outdated or shopworn.
III. It saves on storage and computer records costs.

The topical approach is sometimes termed a *catchall approach* because people occasionally describe a list of points as *topical* if they can't think of another pattern that will work. However, a jumbled list of ideas isn't organized just because you call it topical. A genuine topical approach has elements logically related according to some scheme an audience can easily recognize.

Cause–Effect   A **cause–effect pattern** shows that certain events have happened or will happen as a result of certain circumstances. For example, you might show prospective life insurance customers how certain clauses will provide extra coverage if they are hospitalized or demonstrate how a new advertising program will help a product reach a wider market. You might also use it to demonstrate how certain circumstances are creating a problem:

Thesis: Redecorating the offices before raising salaries *[cause]* will damage morale and affect productivity *[effect]*.

I. When employees see the offices being redecorated without having received a cost-of-living raise over the past year, they'll be discouraged.
II. Discouraged employees aren't as likely to give the company their best efforts during the upcoming season.

An alternative form of the cause-effect structure is an *effect-cause* structure. When you use this structure, you focus more on results: You begin with the result and how it came to pass or how you think it can be made to happen. For example, you might use an effect-cause pattern to explain why a company has a strict policy about absenteeism or to explain how you expect to accomplish a sales goal you have set. It may also be used to explain how a problem has been created:

Thesis: The decline in our profits *[effect]* is the result of several problems *[cause]*.

I. Our profits have decreased 15 percent.
II. Several factors are responsible.
    A. Our competitors are offering better service at lower prices.
    B. Our maintenance costs have nearly doubled.
    C. Our advertising is not effective.

As Table 9-3 shows, chronological, spatial, topical, and cause–effect plans are best suited to informative presentations. While they can be used when your goal is to persuade an audience, you will have better results if you use whichever of the following organizational plans best matches your topic and the speaking situation.

Problem-Solution   A **problem–solution pattern** is the simplest persuasive scheme. As its name suggests, you begin by showing the audience something is wrong with the present situation and then suggest how to remedy it.

Table 9-3	Presentation Styles and Their Corresponding Organizational Patterns	

Informative	**Persuasive**
Chronological	Problem–Solution
Spatial	Criteria Satisfaction
Topical	Comparative Advantages
Cause–Effect	Motivated Sequence

This plan works especially well when your audience doesn't feel a strong need to change from the status quo. Because listeners have to recognize a problem exists before they will be interested in a solution, showing them that the present situation is not satisfactory is essential before you present your idea. For example:

Thesis: Establishing a system of employee incentives can boost productivity.

I. Our level of productivity has been flat for two years while the industry-wide rate has climbed steadily in that period. *[problem]*

II. Establishing an incentive system will give employees a reason to work harder. *[solution]*

A problem–solution pattern might also be used to show how updating a computer system will solve problems with inventory monitoring, why a potential customer needs a personal financial advisor, or why a department needs additional staff.

The problem–solution approach can be effective, but it isn't the best strategy for every persuasive situation. If your listeners already recognize a problem exists, you may not need to spend much time proving the obvious. In such circumstances, you might do better to use one of the following three strategies.

Criteria Satisfaction A **criteria satisfaction** organizational strategy sets up criteria the audience will accept and then shows how your idea or product meets them.

A venture capitalist used a criteria satisfaction plan when seeking investors for a business project. Notice he introduced each criterion and then showed how his project would satisfy it:

Introduction: Being in the right place at the right time can be the key to financial success. I'm here to offer you a chance to reap substantial benefits from an extremely promising project. Like any investment, this project needs to be based on the sound foundation of a solid business plan, a talented management team, and adequate financing. Let me show you how the project meets all of these important requirements.

Body:

I. The first criterion is that the business plan must be solid. Extensive market research shows the need for this product. . . .

II. The second criterion is a talented management team. Let me introduce the key members of this management team and describe their qualifications. . . .

III. The third criterion is a solid, realistic financial plan. The following plan is very conservative yet shows strong potential for a substantial profit. . . .

Conclusion: Because it meets the conditions of a solid business plan, this project is worth
your serious consideration.

In this example, the speaker introduced each criterion and then immediately
showed how his plan satisfied it. A different approach is to present all the criteria first
and then present your proposal. The strategy here is to gain the audience's acceptance
first and boost your credibility. Having done this, you go on to show how your plan
meets the criteria presented. With this approach, the thesis is deferred—which is especially smart when the audience may not be inclined to accept it without some powerful
arguments.

A manager used a criteria satisfaction plan with a deferred thesis to announce a wage
freeze to employees—hardly a popular idea. If she had announced her thesis first ("A wage
freeze is in your best interest"), the employees probably would have been too upset to
listen thoughtfully to her arguments. By leading her audience through the reasons leading
up to the freeze, she increased the chances that the employees would understand management's reasoning. Notice how the thesis is first presented in the middle of the body and
is restated in the conclusion:

Introduction: You know that we've faced declining revenues for the past year. During
these hard times, we need a policy that is best both for the company and for you,
the employees. That's the only way we will be able to survive.

Body:

    I. There are three important criteria for selecting a policy. *[introduces criteria first]*
      A. It should be fair.
      B. It should cause the least harm to employees.
      C. It should allow the company to survive this difficult period without suffering
         permanent damage.

    II. A wage freeze is the best plan to satisfy these criteria. *[satisfaction of criteria]*
      A. It's fair.
      B. It causes minimal harm to employees.
      C. It will enable the company to survive.

Conclusion: A wage freeze is the best plan at this difficult time.

Comparative Advantages   A **comparative advantages** organizational plan puts

several alternatives side-by-side to show why yours is the best. This strategy is especially
useful when the audience is considering an idea that competes with the one you're advocating. In many such cases a head-on comparison that supports your case is far more
effective than ignoring alternative plans. A purchasing agent made the case to her boss for
leasing office equipment instead of borrowing to buy it outright:

Thesis: When we remodel the offices, we can use our budget far more efficiently by leasing equipment and furnishings instead of buying them.

Body:

    I. Our up-front costs will be dramatically lower because there's no down payment.
    II. The application process will be easier. To qualify for a loan, we have to give the
      bank two to three years of financial records. A lease requires us to furnish only six
      months of records.

III. We can keep pace with technology. Short-term leases will cost us less than buying new equipment every few years. We couldn't afford to do that if we buy equipment outright.

IV. We can buy more. Because lease costs are lower, we can get better-quality equipment that will improve our productivity.

Conclusion: When it comes to value for our dollar, leasing is definitely the way to go.

Motivated Sequence

The **motivated sequence** organizational plan is a five-step scheme designed to boost the audience's involvement and interest.[27] Regardless of the topic, the sequence of steps is the same:

1. *Attention.* Capture the audience's attention by introducing the problem in an interesting manner. (This functions as an introduction.)

2. *Need.* Explain the problem clearly and completely. Use a variety of supporting material to back up your claim, proving the problem is serious. Ideally, make your listeners feel the problem affects them in some way. Make them eager to hear a solution.

3. *Satisfaction.* Present your solution to the problem. Provide enough support to prove the solution is workable and that it will, indeed, solve the problem.

4. *Visualization.* Describe clearly what will happen if your proposal is adopted so the audience has a clear mental picture of how your proposal will solve the problem. You may also paint a verbal picture of what will happen if your proposal is *not* adopted. In either case, the key to success in this step is to paint a vivid picture of the outcomes, showing how your proposal will make a real difference.

5. *Action.* Call for a response from your audience. Explain what listeners can do to solve the problem. (This functions as the conclusion.)

The motivated sequence plan provides a step-by-step approach for organizing a speech. It builds on the basic problem–solution plan: Step 1 arouses listeners' interest so they will be more receptive to the topic. Step 4 goes beyond simply providing a solution and helps the audience picture what a difference it will make. Step 5 guides the audience on how to bring the solution about, making it easier for listeners to take the necessary steps and rousing them to act. Unlike most presentations, this approach usually won't require a preview in the opening of your remarks.

The motivated sequence approach works best when the problem you present and the solution you propose are easy to visualize. If your listeners can imagine the problem and see themselves solving it by following your plan, they'll be motivated to accept your reasoning. And because the motivated sequence approach closes with an appeal to action, it is especially well suited to getting an immediate response to your proposal. Recognizing this fact, a fund-raiser used it to generate pledges for an urgent appeal:

[Attention]   Here's a picture of the Myer family. Ted, the father, is a trained stonemason and proud of it. Anne, the mom, is a registered nurse. Little Chris is a normal kid who loves baseball and pizza. His teachers say he has a gift for math and languages.

[Need]   Since this photo was taken, the Myers have had a run of terrible luck. Last year, Ted fell at work and wrenched his back. He's been unable to work ever since, and his disability insurance has almost run out.

Concept Mapping Software

Sometimes the best way to organize ideas is visually. Until recently, the best approach was to write ideas on index cards, spread them out on the table or floor, and rearrange them until a clear plan emerged. Now, computer software makes the task quicker and easier. While no program can substitute for critically analyzing your organizational strategy, "concept mapping" software programs are a useful tool for visualizing your options.

More elaborate programs available online offer free trials so you can see how well they work for you. Here are some notable examples:

"Inspiration" (http://www.inspiration.com) is a suite of visual tools for developing ideas. The program's diagram view provides an easy-to-use equivalent of the index card approach. Each idea you type into the computer appears onscreen inside its own box or circle. You can rearrange these ideas with your mouse until they fall into patterns that seem clear and effective. Then, with a simple command, the visual map is turned into a traditional outline, suitable for conversion into speaker's notes, handouts, or visual aids. Besides serving as an outlining tool, Inspiration makes it easy to create concept maps, process flows, knowledge maps, flowcharts, and other visual diagrams.

Other concept-mapping software programs include Decision Explorer (http://www.banxia.com/dexplore/index.html), Mindjet (http://www.mindjet.com), IHMC's Concept Map (http://cmap.ihmc.us/conceptmap.html), and VisiMap (http://www.visimap.com). Additional resources to try include ActionOutline (http://www.canadiancontent.net/tech/download/ActionOutline.html) and B-liner (http://www.bliner.com).

Three months after Ted's accident, Anne was diagnosed with leukemia. She's undergoing treatment, and the doctors are optimistic; but she can't work now, and there's no telling when she will be able to return to her job. The Myers lived on their savings for six months, but now all the money is gone. Last week they had to move out of their apartment, and they have nowhere else to go. Nowhere, that is, except Transition House.

[Satisfaction]   You can help provide temporary housing for the Myers and other neighbors who are in trouble by contributing to Transition House. Your donations will give these people a safe place to stay while they get back on their feet and save them from life on the street.

[Visualization]   We're hoping to raise enough money tonight to give the Myer family a month at Transition House. During that time, Ted can finish training for a new career as a bookkeeper and get back to work. He hopes to become a CPA. Once he's on the job, the Myers will be able to find a new apartment so Anne can fight for her health and Chris can stay in his same school, where he's doing so well.

[Action]   What we need from you tonight is a donation. We're asking for anything you can afford: the price of an evening on the town or maybe a postponement of that new outfit you were thinking of buying. In just a moment, I'll be passing out pledge cards. . . .

At first glance, the motivated sequence approach seems to depart from the basic introduction-body-conclusion pattern of organizing a presentation. A closer look shows that the plan does follow the same pattern:

Introduction

- Attention

Body

  I. Need

  II. Satisfaction

  III. Visualization

Conclusion

- Action

    Each has an introduction that captures your audience's attention and gives members reasons to listen. Each has a body arranged in a pattern that is easy to follow and helps achieve the presentation's purpose. Each has a conclusion that reinforces the thesis of the talk and leaves the audience motivated to accept it.

Rules for Main Points

Whichever pattern of organization you use, your main points should meet the following criteria.

Main Points Should Be Stated as Claims

A **claim** is a statement asserting a fact or belief. If you state your claims in full, grammatical sentences, they will probably satisfy the one week later test and be remembered by your listeners. Notice how describing main points as claims in complete sentences is clearer and far more effective than using simple three- or four-word statements.

Fragment	Claim
Choosing a physician	It's essential to choose a health care provider from the list of approved doctors.
Sexual and ethnic discrimination	Allowing sexual or ethnic considerations to intrude into our hiring decisions isn't just bad judgment, it's illegal.
Demographic changes in the market	Due to demographic changes, we can expect our market to shrink in the next ten years.

All Points Should Develop the Thesis

Consider the following outline:

Thesis: Allowing employees more latitude in choosing their work hours is good for the company and for the workers.

  I. Flexible scheduling can work in several ways.

  II. Flexible scheduling improves morale.

  III. Flexible scheduling reduces absenteeism.

The first point may be true but doesn't say anything about flexible scheduling's value and, therefore, ought to be dropped.

A Presentation Should Contain No More than Five Main Points   Your main points are, after all, what you want your listeners to remember, and people have difficulty recalling more than five pieces of information presented orally.[28] For that reason, it is imperative that your presentation contain no more than five main points. This requires some discipline. Consider the advice of David Dempsey, a trial attorney and professor of public speaking at Oglethorpe University in Atlanta, about the need to ruthlessly edit your ideas:

> Make three points that stick, rather than 10 quick points that leave no lasting impression. Constantly ask yourself, "Is this the most important issue, the best example, the most compelling way to illustrate my point?"[29]

Even when you have a large amount of material, it's usually possible to organize it into five or fewer categories. For example, if you were preparing an analysis of ways to lower operating expenses in your organization, your brainstorming list might include these ideas:

- Reduce wattage in lighting fixtures
- Hire outside data processing firm to handle seasonal billing rather than expand permanent in-house staff
- Sell surplus equipment
- Reduce nonbusiness use of copying machines
- Reduce temperature in less used parts of the building
- Pay overtime rather than add new employees
- Retrofit old equipment instead of buying new machinery

Your outline could consolidate this list into three areas:

Thesis: We can reduce operating costs in three areas: energy, personnel, and equipment.

   I. We can reduce our energy costs.
     A. Reduce wattage in lighting fixtures
     B. Reduce temperature in less used parts of the building

  II. We can reduce money spent on new personnel.
     A. Hire outside data processing firm for seasonal billing
     B. Encourage overtime instead of adding employees

 III. We can reduce our purchase and maintenance costs on equipment.
     A. Retrofit old equipment
     B. Sell surplus equipment
     C. Reduce personal use of copying machines

This outline contains all the items in your list, but organizing them into three broad categories makes your presentation much easier to comprehend than a seven-point presentation would be.

Main Points Should Be Parallel in Structure Whenever Possible   Parallel wording can reflect your organization and dramatize your points. Consider how the repetition of "We can reduce. . . . " in the outline above helps drive the point home far more forcefully than does the following, less effective wording of your main points:

   I. Managing energy costs can save us money.
  II. Careful hiring practices will reduce overhead.
 III. Equipment purchase and maintenance are controllable costs.

You won't always be able to state your main points using parallel construction, but a look at many of the examples in this chapter shows it can be used often.

Each Main Point Should Contain Only One Idea   Combining ideas or overlapping them will confuse audiences. Consider this outline:

Thesis: Many local businesses boost their effectiveness and serve their communities by seeking a diverse workforce.

   I. Employees from diverse ethnic backgrounds can reach multiple audiences.

  II. Employees with disabilities can function as effectively as other workers.

 III. Age diversity provides a variety of points of view that can help sales, marketing, and operations.

• Planning the Introduction and Conclusion

The body of a presentation is important, but the introduction that precedes it needs just as much attention. Your introduction should take between 10 and 15 percent of the speaking time. During this short time—less than 1 minute of a 5-minute talk—your listeners form their initial impression of you and your topic. That impression, favorable or not, will affect how they react to the rest of your remarks. To be most effective, an introduction should accomplish several purposes.

Functions of the Introduction

As you have already learned, an introduction should have two parts: an attention-getter and a thesis statement and preview. These two parts should accomplish five things.

Capture the Listeners' Attention   As you learned in Chapter 3, audiences don't always approach a presentation ready to listen. The topic may not seem important or interesting to them. Your listeners may have been ordered to attend your presentation. Even when the presentation is obviously important, your listeners will usually have other matters on their minds. It's vital, therefore, to begin by focusing attention on you and your topic if there is any chance the listeners' minds are elsewhere.

Give Your Audience a Reason to Listen   The best way to grab and hold your listeners' attention is to convince them your message will be important or interesting to them. For example, if company employees are generally satisfied with the insurance program the company has been using, they won't be interested in hearing about a new health plan that will be cheaper for the company unless you can begin by enumerating its advantages to them—for instance, that it will provide them with better emergency services. Similarly, management will be more interested in hearing your new ideas if you first say that the plans you're proposing will yield higher profits.

Set the Proper Tone for the Topic and Setting   If you want potential customers to buy more fire insurance, your opening remarks should prepare them to think seriously about the problems they would encounter if they had a fire in the house. If you want to congratulate your subordinates about their recent performance and encourage them to perform even better on the next assignment, your opening remarks should put them in a good mood—not focus on the problems you must face. In any case, your introduction should establish rapport with your listeners. Robert Moran accomplished this goal when he began his remarks to a Japanese audience:

> If I were an American and you were an American audience, I would probably begin my speech with a joke. If I were Japanese speaking to a Japanese audience, I would probably begin with an apology. Since I am neither American nor Japanese, I will begin with an apology for not telling a joke.[30]

Establish Your Qualifications   If the audience already knows you are an expert on the subject, if a previous speaker has given you an impressive introduction, or if your authority makes it clear you're qualified to talk, establishing credibility isn't necessary. In other cases, however, you need to demonstrate your competence quickly so the listeners will take your remarks seriously. Nonverbal behaviors will also help boost (or diminish) your credibility. Recall the information on nonverbal communication in Chapter 4, and see additional advice on building credibility through nonverbal behavior in Chapters 11 and 12.

Introduce Your Thesis and Preview Your Presentation   In most cases, you need to state your main idea clearly at the beginning of your remarks so your listeners know exactly what you're trying to say. In addition to your thesis statement, a preview of your main points tells your listeners where you're headed.

Accomplishing these five goals in less than a minute isn't as difficult as it might seem because you can accomplish several functions at the same time. For example, notice how an insurance agent introduced a 30-minute talk on an admittedly difficult topic:

> Being an insurance agent gives me a lot of sympathy for tax collectors and dog catchers. None of us has an especially popular job. After all, it seems that with life insurance you lose either way: If the policy pays off, you won't be around to enjoy the money. On the other hand, if you don't need the policy, you've spent your hard-earned savings for nothing. Besides, insurance isn't cheap. I'm sure you have plenty of other things you could use your money for: catching up on bills, fixing up your house, buying a new car, or even taking a vacation.
>
> With all those negatives, why should you care about insurance? For that matter, why am I devoting my career to it? For me, the answer is easy: Over the years, I've seen literally hundreds of people—people just like you and me—learn what a difference the right kind of insurance coverage can make. And I've seen hundreds more suffer from learning too late that insurance is necessary.
>
> Well, tonight I want to give you some good news. I'll show you that you can win by buying insurance. You can win by gaining peace of mind, and you can even win by buying insurance that works like an investment, paying dividends that you can use here and now.

Types of Opening Statements

Of all parts of a presentation, the opening words are the hardest for many speakers. You have to be interesting. You have to establish the right tone. Your remarks have to relate to the topic being discussed. And, finally, the opening statement has to feel right for you.

The kind of opening you choose will depend on your analysis of the speaking situation. With familiar topics and audiences, you may even decide to skip the preliminaries and give just a brief background before launching into the thesis and preview:

> "We've made good progress on Mr. Boynton's request to look into cost-cutting steps. We've found it is possible to reduce operating expenses by almost 10 percent without cutting efficiency. We'll be introducing six steps this morning."

DILBERT © Scott Adams/Dist. By Universal Uclick.

In most cases, you will want to preface your remarks with an opening statement. Following are seven of the most common and effective ways to begin a presentation.

Ask a Question
Asking the right question is a good way to involve your listeners in your topic and establish its importance to them.

Many speakers try to capture attention by asking the audience a **rhetorical question:** one with an obvious answer and one that does not really call for a response. For example, a manager who wants to whip up employee enthusiasm for a proposal that will reduce paperwork might ask, "Is it just me, or does anybody else feel like we've spent too much time filling in forms?" Rhetorical questions work well when you can be sure the audience's reaction is the one you want.

When used poorly, rhetorical questions can be risky. Beware of asking questions listeners won't care about: "Have you ever wondered what the Sherman Antitrust Act means to you?" Other rhetorical questions can be so thought-provoking your audience will stop listening to you: "If you had to fire three of the people who report to you, how would you decide which ones to let go?" When you decide to begin with a rhetorical question, be sure to avoid mistakes like these.

Other questions call for an overt response: "How many people here are from out of state?" "Who has had trouble meeting deadlines for sales reports?" "What do you see as the biggest threat facing the company?" If you *are* seeking an overt reaction from your listeners, be sure to let them know: "Let me see a show of hands by the people who. . . ." "Hold up your program if you're among those who. . . ." If you want them to respond mentally, let them know: "Answer this question for yourself. Are you sure all of your expense reports would pass an Internal Revenue audit?"

Tell a Story
Because most people enjoy a good story, beginning with one can be an effective way to get the audience's attention, set the tone, and lead into the topic. Author Kathryn Schulz begins a speech about the value of admitting one's errors by telling a story about one of her own mistakes during a cross-country road trip:

> Somewhere in the middle of South Dakota, I turn to my friend and I ask her a question that's been bothering me for 2,000 miles. "What's up with the Chinese character I keep seeing by the side of the road?" She just stares at me for a few moments, and then she cracks up, because she figures out what I'm talking about . . . Right, the famous Chinese character for picnic area.[31]

Schulz's story of a personal blunder provides a good lead-in to her talk about the importance of acknowledging errors, even when they are

embarrassing. It also illustrates two vital principles about using stories. First, *keep it brief.* Remember, an introduction should take no more than 15 percent of your total speaking time. That means the story has to be even shorter. A second principle is to *establish a clear connection between the story and your topic.* Even though the connection may be clear to you, make sure you describe to your listeners why your story is relevant.

Present a Quotation
Quotations have two advantages: First, someone else has probably already said what you want to say in a very clever way. Second, quotations let you use a source with high credibility to back up your message.

Not every quotation has to come from a distinguished person. As long as the individual you quote is appropriate for the audience and the topic, he or she can be almost anyone—even a fictional character:

> "The comic strip character Pogo once said, 'We have met the enemy, and it's us.' If you think about all the paperwork that keeps us from being more productive, that comment could describe us."

Make a Startling Statement
An excellent way to get listeners' attention is to surprise them. Sales presentations often include startling facts in their openings: "Do you know that half of all business calls never reach the intended party?" This approach will work only if your startling statement bears a clear relationship to your topic. Social networking executive Pamela Meyer used this approach in a speech about the prevalence of deception in everyday life:

> It's just come to my attention that the person to your right is a liar. Also, the person to your left is a liar. Also the person sitting in your very seats is a liar. We're all liars.[32]

Refer to the Audience
Mentioning your listeners' needs, concerns, or interests clarifies the relevance of your topic immediately and shows you understand your listeners. For example: "I know you're all worried by rumors of cutbacks in staff. I called you here today to explain just what the budget cuts will mean to this department."

Former California governor George Deukmejian used the technique of referring to the audience in a talk to the Los Angeles Rotary Club. Deukmejian acknowledged the fact that people who listen to after-lunch speakers—even famous ones—appreciate brevity:

> I promise not to speak for too long this afternoon. It's worth noting that the Lord's Prayer is only 56 words long. The Gettysburg Address is 226. The Ten Commandments are 297. But the U.S. Department of Agriculture's order on the price of cabbage is 15,269 words. I'll try to finish somewhere in between.[33]

Refer to the Occasion
Sometimes the event itself provides a good starting point: "We're here today to recognize some very important people."

Sometimes you can begin by referring to some other aspect of the situation, for example, by relating your remarks to those of a previous speaker: "I was very interested in what Larry had to say about the way our expenses will rise in the next couple of years. Let's look at one way we can keep that increase as small as possible."

In a speech to employees at the U.S. Department of Justice, U.S. Attorney General Eric Holder referred to the occasion that prompted his remarks: "Every year, in February, we attempt to recognize and to appreciate black history. It is a worthwhile endeavor, for the contributions of African Americans to this great nation are numerous and significant."[34]

By referring to the occasion of Black History Month, Holder prepared his audience for the message that Americans reach out to those from different racial backgrounds:

> Black History Month is a perfect vehicle for the beginnings of such a dialogue. And so I urge all of you to use the opportunity of this month to talk with your friends and coworkers on the other side of the divide about racial matters. In this way we can hasten the day when we truly become one America.[35]

Use Humor   The right joke can be an effective way to get attention, make a point, and increase your audience's liking for you. The vice president of an advertising agency, for example, might begin an orientation session for new management trainees with the following tale:

> Maybe you've heard the story about the guy who smells awful all the time. When asked the reason for this he explains that it's because of his job—working in a circus giving enemas to elephants. The listener asks, "Why don't you get another job?" and the guy replies hotly, "What! And get out of show business?"
>
> Well, that story has some truth in our business too. Lots of people view advertising as glamorous: three-hour expense account lunches and big commissions. Advertising is certainly a kind of show business, but along with all the glamour comes a lot of hard, messy work. I want to begin this orientation program by telling you about both the clean, easy parts and the tough, grubby ones. Then you'll have a better idea what to expect in the next months and years.

Jokes aren't the only kind of humorous opener. Sometimes you can make an amusing remark that will set the tone perfectly for your message. For instance:

> Some people say that problems are not problems, but rather, they are opportunities. If that's the case, then given the present situation, we are faced with a hell of a lot of opportunities.[36]

Any humor you use should be appropriate to your topic and to the occasion. Telling a few knock-knock jokes before you launch into your financial report will draw attention—but not to your topic. The tone of your presentation could be ruined by a joke. For instance, you probably shouldn't tell a few jokes about smog and then say, "But seriously, folks, I want to talk about what we're doing to curb air pollution from our own factories."

Your jokes should also be appropriate for your audience. The inside jokes that work well with your office staff, for example, are likely to alienate clients at a contract negotiation because outsiders won't understand them. Jokes that are off-color or in any way make light of sexism, racism, or disabilities are likely to offend or embarrass someone in your audience. The risks of telling them aren't worth the laughs they might generate.

Think twice about using humor cross culturally as jokes rarely translate. Not everyone will have the advantage that former U.S. President Carter recounted about telling a joke during a speech in Japan: "I told my joke, and then the interpreter gave it and the audience collapsed in laughter. It was the best response I have ever had to a joke in my life."

When Carter asked his translator to explain the words he used when repeating the joke in Japanese, he got an evasive response. When the president insisted on knowing, the translator explained: "I told the audience, 'President Carter told a funny story. Everyone must laugh.'"[37]

**"Will your presentation have
a bloopers part at the end?"**

Used by permission of Ted Goff.

Functions of the Conclusion

With the end of your presentation in sight, it can be tempting to wrap things up with a lame comment like, "That's about it." Resist the temptation to close quickly and weakly: Experts agree your final words may create a lasting impression.[38] The conclusion of your presentation should be even shorter than the introduction: not much more than 5 percent of your total speaking time. Within those few moments, though, you must accomplish two important things: review and close. Let's look at each of these parts in detail.

The Review   Your review should contain a restatement of your thesis and a summary of your main points. Sometimes these two elements will be presented almost exactly as they appear on your outline:

> "This afternoon, I've suggested that our merchandising approach needs changing to become more profitable. I've suggested three such changes: first, to increase our newspaper advertising; second, to feature higher-quality merchandise; and third, to expand our product line in all areas."

Your review can also be a subtler rewording of the same information:

> "By now I hope you agree with me that some basic merchandising changes can improve our balance sheet. When people find out we have a broad range of high-quality products, I'm convinced we'll have more customers who will spend more money."

The Closing Statement   A strong closing will help your listeners to remember you favorably; a weak ending can nullify many of your previous gains. Besides creating a favorable impression, the closing statement will give your remarks a sense of completion. You shouldn't leave your audience wondering whether you've finished. Finally, a closing statement ought to incite your listeners, encouraging them to act or think in a way that accomplishes your purpose. Let's look at several varieties of closing statements.

Types of Closing Statements

Several of the techniques used for getting attention in your introduction will also work well as closing statements: ask a question, tell a story, give a quotation, make a startling statement, refer to the audience, refer to the occasion, or use humor. In addition, there are several other types of closing statements you might use.

Return to the Theme of Your Opening Statement   Coming back to where you started gives a sense of completeness to your presentation. With this approach, you should refer to your opening statement but add a new insight, further details, or a different ending:

> "At the beginning of my talk, I asked whether you might not be paying more tax than you need to. I suspect you discovered you've been overly generous with Uncle Sam. I hope I have helped you to understand your real liability and to take advantage of some of the tax shelters available to you."

One way to capture your audience's attention is to split your story. Start, but don't finish it in your introduction. Cut off your narrative at a key point, perhaps just before the climactic finish, promising your audience you will wrap it up in the course of your remarks.

Appeal for Action   When your goal involves getting the audience to act in a certain way, you can sometimes close your presentation by asking for your desired result:

> "So now that you know what these workshops can do, the only question is when you ought to enroll. We have openings on August 19 and on September 23. I'll be available in a moment to sign you up for either date. I'm looking forward to seeing you soon."

End with a Challenge   Whereas an appeal asks for some action, a challenge almost demands it:

> "You can go on as before, not failing completely but not doing the best possible job. Or you can use the ideas you've heard this morning to become more creative, more productive, and more successful. Why be average when you can be superior? Why settle for a few hopes when you can reach your dreams? It's up to you."

• Adding Transitions

Transitions are words or sentences that connect the segments of a presentation. As Figure 9.4 shows, they work like bridges between the major parts of your remarks and tell your listeners how these parts are related. Transitions should occur between the introduction and the body, between the main points within the body, and between the body and the conclusion. The examples below illustrate each of these instances:

> "Those are big promises. Let me talk about how we can deliver on them."

> "Not all the news is bad, however. Let me tell you about some good things that happened at the conference."

> "After hearing about so many features, you may have trouble remembering them all. Let's review them briefly."

Functions of Transitions

Transitions like the preceding examples serve three important purposes.

They Promote Clarity   Clarity in speech—especially in one-way, speech-like presentations—is more difficult to achieve than clarity in writing. The format of a letter, memo, book, or report makes its organization of ideas clear. Paragraphs, headings, bulleted lists, different typefaces, and underlining can all emphasize how ideas are related to one another. In a presentation, however, listeners don't have the benefit of any of these aids to figure out how your ideas are put together. They have only what the verbal cues—transitional words and phrases—provide.

They Emphasize Important Ideas   Transitions within presentations highlight important information the way italics and bold type emphasize it in print:

> "Now let's turn to a third reason—perhaps the most important of all—for equipping your field representatives with electronic pagers."

> "That's what company policy says about the use of expense accounts. Now let's take a look at how things *really* work."

They Keep Listeners Interested   Transitions give momentum to a presentation. They make listeners want to find out what comes next:

> "So we gave them the best dog-and-pony show you've ever seen. And it was perfect—just like we planned. What do you think they said when we were finished?"

> "By now you're probably asking yourself what a product like this will cost. And that's the best news of all. . . . "

Purpose: After hearing this talk, the prospective customer will sign up to use Mercury as its exclusive overnight delivery service.

Thesis: Mercury is the best service to deliver your high-priority packages on time.

INTRODUCTION

  A. Overnight delivery services aren't cheap, but they are worth the expense *if* they do the job of getting important materials into the right hands quickly. [*Attention getter*]

  B. After comparing Mercury with the other delivery services, you'll see that it is the best one to do the job. [*Thesis*]

  C. As I'll explain in the next few minutes, Mercury is more reliable, convenient, and economical than the competition. [*Preview*]

Transition: Let me start by explaining why Mercury is best with the most important feature of any delivery service: reliability.

BODY

  I. Mercury is more reliable than other services.

    A. Mercury's 98 percent trouble-free record beats every other service.

    B. Other services have held up deliveries for as much as 1 week.

    C. Other services have damaged packages.

    D. In some cases, other services have even lost packages.

Transition: Besides being reliable, Mercury is the best service in another important way ...

  II. Mercury is more convenient than other services.

    A. Mercury picks up and delivers items to individual offices, not just to the mailroom like ABC Overnight.

    B. Mercury picks up or delivers packages any time between 7:00 A.M. and midnight, instead of only coming by once a day like International Air Freight.

    C. Mercury is the only service that will bill departmental accounts separately, saving you bookkeeping time.

Transition: Because it's so convenient and reliable, you might think that Mercury is more expensive than other services, but it's not.

  III. Mercury is more economical than other services.

    A. It doesn't charge extra for oddly shaped packages.

    B. It charges less than every other service for heavy packages.

    C. The shipping fee includes insurance.

Transition: By now you can see why it's worth considering Mercury as the provider of your overnight mail service ...

CONCLUSION

  A. Mercury is reliable, convenient, and economical. [*Thesis/Review*].

  B. With Mercury you won't just pay for the best service ... you'll get it.

FIGURE 9.4 A Complete Presentation Outline

Use this list to check how well your presentation is organized.

Does the **introduction**

_____ 1. Capture the attention of your audience?

_____ 2. Give your audience reasons to listen?

_____ 3. Set an appropriate tone?

_____ 4. Establish your qualifications, if necessary?

_____ 5. Introduce your thesis and preview the content?

Does the **body**

_____ 1. Use the most effective organizational pattern?

      a. Chronological

      b. Spatial

      c. Topical

      d. Cause–effect

      e. Problem–solution

      f. Criteria satisfaction

      g. Comparative advantages

      h. Motivated sequence

_____ 2. State your main points in complete sentences?

_____ 3. Use your main points to develop your thesis?

_____ 4. Contain no more than five main points?

_____ 5. Express only one idea in each main point?

_____ 6. State your main points in parallel structure if possible?

Do you have **transitions** that

_____ 1. Refer to both recent and upcoming material, showing relationships between the two?

_____ 2. Emphasize your important ideas?

_____ 3. Clarify the structure of your ideas?

_____ 4. Exist in all necessary parts of presentation?

      a. Between introduction and body

      b. Between main points within body

      c. Between body and conclusion

Does the **conclusion**

_____ 1. Review your thesis and your main points?

_____ 2. Conclude with an effective closing statement?

Characteristics of Effective Transitions

Transitions that promote clarity, emphasize important ideas, and keep listeners interested possess two characteristics. First, they refer to both preceding and upcoming ideas. A transition is like a bridge: To get listeners from one point to another, it must be anchored at both ends. By referring to what you just said and to what you'll say next, you are showing the logical relationship among those ideas. Notice the smooth connections between the ideas in these transitions:

> "Those are the problems. Now let's see what can be done about solving them."

> "Now you see that the change makes sense financially. But how will it be received by the people who have to live with it?"

If you have trouble planning a transition that links preceding and upcoming material smoothly, the reason may be that the ideas aren't logically related or the organizational plan you've chosen is flawed. Review the organizing patterns on pp. 264–271 and the rules for main points on pp. 271–273 to be sure the structure of your presentation's body is logically suited to the topic.

Transitions should also call attention to themselves. You should let listeners know you're moving from one point to another so they will be able to follow the structure of your ideas easily. Notice how the examples you have read so far all make it clear that the presentation is shifting gears. This sort of highlighting is often due to the use of keywords:

> "The *next* important idea is. . . . "

> "*Another* reason we want to make the change. . . . "

> "*Finally,* we need to consider. . . . "

> "To *wrap things up.* . . . "

Phrases like these are not in themselves good transitions because they do not refer to both previous and upcoming material strongly enough. But when used as part of a transition like the ones illustrated in these pages, they do signal listeners that you are moving to a new part of your presentation. A presentation checklist, covering transitions and the other organizational concepts discussed in this chapter, is presented in the Self-Assessment on p. 281.

MASTER the chapter

review points

- Almost everyone makes on-the-job presentations, formal and informal, for external and internal audiences. Career direction and success may depend on a speaker's reputation.

- Speakers should use a three-part analysis: First, analyze the audience. Who are the key listeners; what do they already know; what do they want to know; and what are their preferences, significant demographics, size, reason for being there, and attitudes?

- Second, speakers should analyze themselves as speakers by considering their goal for speaking, their knowledge of the subject, and the sincerity they bring to the topic.

- Finally, speakers should analyze the speaking occasion by considering the facility, the time of day and length of time they will speak, and the context in which their remarks will occur.

- A speaker's next steps are to define both general and specific goals and to create the thesis. Is the general goal to inform or persuade? The specific goal identifies who the speakers want to reach; what they want them to do; and how, when, and where they want them to act. Clear goal statements define the desired audience reaction in a specific and attainable manner.

- After defining the goal, speakers must clearly structure the thesis as a single sentence. It is the central idea and will be repeated throughout the presentation, so it is essential to design it carefully.

- Clearly organized presentations increase audience comprehension and speaker credibility by following a basic structure of introduction, body, and conclusion.

- While brainstorming for ideas, the goal statement and audience analysis serve as devices for choosing items that are appropriate for this specific presentation. These items are then arranged into main points and subpoints and into the most appropriate organizational pattern.

- Common organizational patterns are chronological, spatial, topical, cause–effect, problem–solution, criteria satisfaction, comparative advantages, and motivated sequence.

- After the body of the presentation has been developed, an introduction is created to capture the attention of the audience, give a reason to listen, and state the thesis. The conclusion reviews the thesis and main points and closes with a strong statement.

- Finally, transitions connect the introduction to the body, the main points of the body, and the body to the conclusion. They call attention to themselves to keep listeners oriented and highlight the preceding and following material.

key terms

cause–effect pattern   266
chronological pattern   264
claim   271
comparative advantages pattern   268
criteria satisfaction pattern   267
general goal   257
motivated sequence pattern   269

problem–solution pattern   266
rhetorical question 275
spatial pattern   265
specific goal   257
thesis statement   259
topical pattern   266
transition   279

activities

1. Invitation to Insight

Gain insights about occasion and audience analysis by interviewing a professional who frequently delivers presentations to a variety of audiences in the workplace. Ask your interviewee questions such as:

a. How do you gather information about your potential audience? About the expectations of the occasion?
b. Compare the expectations of some of the various audiences you address.
c. In what ways do you adjust your presentations for these audiences?
d. What do you do if you discover your audience members' knowledge level about your topic will vary widely?
e. How do you appeal to an audience who will probably be bored by or opposed to your topic?
f. What are some strategies for tweaking your presentation so it's appropriate to the occasion?

In class, share answers gleaned from various interviews.

2. Skill Builder

Identify the most important factors about your audience, the occasion, and yourself as a speaker that you should consider when planning a presentation to:

a. Explain what a "tweet" is to a group of senior citizens.
b. Give instructions to a group of trainees.
c. Encourage high school seniors to attend your college.
d. Announce a cost increase in employee health care benefits (you are a human relations representative at your company).
e. Honor a beloved ecology professor during a public ceremony on your college commons, where a tree will be planted in her name.

3. Skill Builder

With your group, imagine you have been asked to speak to one of the audiences below. Your task is to present a 15-minute description of your workplace department's functions. With this audience in mind, answer each of the seven questions listed under the section of your text titled Analyzing the Audience (see pp. 249–254). Because this is a hypothetical scenario, you will need to make your best estimate rather than conducting real audience research. After you have answered each of the seven questions, describe how you could use that information to create an interesting and informative presentation tailored to this specific audience. Each group will then share and compare their analyses.

a. A group of new employees from all over the company.
b. New employees within the department.
c. A group of managers from other departments.
d. Several of your superiors.
e. A supplier who is helping you update equipment.
f. A group of customers touring the company.

4. Skill Builder

Write a specific goal statement for four of the following situations. Then translate your goal into an effective thesis:

a. A farewell speech honoring an unpopular manager at his retirement dinner.
b. A training session introducing a new emergency evacuation plan.
c. A kick-off speech for the United Way payroll deduction campaign.
d. An appeal to the boss to hire an additional employee in your department.
e. A proposal to your department head for changing course requirements for the major.
f. A banker's speech to an economics class on the topic "The Changing Banking Industry."
g. A request to your landlord for new office carpeting.

5. Skill Builder

Write a specific goal and thesis statement for a presentation about the value of learning communication skills introduced in this book. Imagine you will be addressing your presentation to an organization you work for or a college class you're taking. What demographic information would be important to know about your audience? Which demographic information would not be relevant to your presentation? Identify three to five key points you would cover in your presentation.

6. Invitation to Insight

How would you enhance your credibility if you were delivering a presentation to various businesses in your community, asking them to establish internships for communication students?

7. Skill Builder

What kinds of material would you gather for a presentation on each of the following topics? Where would you find your information?

a. How changes in the cellular telephone industry will affect consumers.
b. How to begin an investment program.
c. Changing trends in the popularity of various academic courses over the last 10 years.
d. Why students should (should not) buy an e-book reader.
e. Career opportunities for women in the field of your choice.

8. Skill Builder

With your group, determine which organizational pattern (chronological, spatial, and so on) you would recommend for each of the following presentations. Explain your recommendations.

a. Instructions on how to file a health insurance claim form.
b. A request for time and money to attend an important convention in your field.
c. A comparison of products or services between your organization and a competitor.
d. A report on an industrial accident.
e. Suggestions on reducing employee turnover.

9. Skill Builder

Select two of the following topics (or use topics you are knowledgeable about). For each topic, create a thesis statement. Then apply the rules for main points from this chapter to write two to five main points you would cover in delivering a presentation relevant to your thesis. Express each main point in a complete sentence.

a. When to use small claims court.
b. The importance of creativity in advertising.
c. Renting versus leasing a car.
d. The proper format for a business letter.
e. Types of sexual harassment.
f. The fastest-growing jobs in the twenty-first century.

10. Skill Builder

Prepare an introduction and a conclusion for the topics you developed in the previous exercise, or choose two of the following presentations. Exchange your paper with a classmate. Use the checklists for the introduction and conclusion found on p. 281 (Self-Assessment: Checklist for Organizing a Presentation) to review each other's introductions and conclusions.

a. A talk to employees announcing personnel layoffs.
b. The last in a day-long series of talks to a tired audience on maintaining and operating equipment.
c. An appeal to coworkers for donations to the Community Holiday Relief Fund.
d. A talk, the topic of which is "What Employers Look for in a College Graduate," to your class by the president of the local chamber of commerce. (Plan your concluding remarks to follow a question-and-answer period.)

Mc Graw Hill **LearnSmart**™

For further review, go to the LearnSmart study module for this chapter.

Chapter Ten

Verbal and Visual Support
in Presentations

chapter objectives

After reading this chapter you should be able to:

1. Define and describe guidelines for each type of verbal support; develop and use each type of verbal support as suitable to add interest, clarity, and/or proof to a main point.

2. Discuss whether there is a need for visual aids in various situations; determine the advantages and disadvantages of various types of visual aids for those contexts; then design a visual aid appropriate for a given context.

3. Choose the most effective medium for presenting visual aids in specific contexts.

4. Design and critique a presentation using PowerPoint or other presentation format.

Tom Sutcliffe was frustrated. "I know I deserve that raise," he said firmly to his friend and coworker Tina Agapito. "I laid out all the reasons to the boss as clear as day. I've been doing the work of two people ever since Van left. My productivity is higher than anybody else's in the place. My salary is way behind the industry average. And all my clients are happy. What else does he want?"

Tina tried to be supportive. "I know you deserve the raise, Tom. And I just can't believe the boss doesn't see that too. Did you back up your claims?"

"What do you mean?" Tom asked.

"Did you give him evidence about your productivity or about how your salary compares with the industry? And did you give him some proof about all your happy clients?"

"I guess not," said Tom. "But I shouldn't have to sell myself around here. The boss ought to appreciate a good employee when he has one!"

"Maybe so," Tina answered. "But the boss hears a lot of requests for money and resources. And he's really busy. Maybe if you can make your case clearer and more interesting, you've still got a chance."

Tina's advice to Tom was good. Solid ideas won't always impress an audience. Most listeners are busy and preoccupied, and they usually don't care nearly as much about your message as you do. The kind of clear organization described in Chapter 9 will help make your presentations a success, but you often need to back up your well-organized points in a way that makes your audience take notice, understand you, and accept your message. In other words, you need to use plenty of supporting material.

• Functions of Supporting Material

Supporting material is anything that backs up the claims in a presentation. You can see the relationship between these claims and supporting material in the following examples:

Claim	Support
We could increase sales by staying open until 10 PM on weekday evenings.	An article in *Modern Retailing* cites statistics showing that stores with extended evening hours boost profits by more than 20 percent of the direct overhead involved with the longer business day.
Configuring a wireless network isn't as hard as it might seem.	Here's a video that shows how easy it can be.
Taking the time to help customers will boost their loyalty and increase your commissions.	Let me read you a letter written just last week by one satisfied customer.

As these examples show, a presentation without supporting material would still be logical if it followed the organizational guidelines in Chapter 9. But it probably wouldn't achieve its goal because it would lack the information necessary to develop the ideas in a way the audience would understand or appreciate. Carefully selected supporting material can make a presentation more effective by adding three things: clarity, interest, and proof.

Clarity

Supporting material can make abstract or complicated ideas more understandable. Notice how the following analogy clarifies how computers with point-and-click user interfaces were such a revolutionary improvement over earlier generations that relied on keyboard commands:

Imagine driving a car that has no steering wheel, accelerator, brake pedal, turn signal lever, or gear selector. In place of all the familiar manual controls, you have only a typewriter keyboard.

Any time you want to turn a corner, change lanes, slow down, speed up, honk your horn, or back up, you have to type a command sequence on the keyboard. Unfortunately, the car can't understand English sentences. Instead, you must hold down a special key with one finger and type in some letters and numbers, such as "S20:TL:A35," which means, "Slow to 20, turn left, and accelerate to 35."

If you make typing mistakes, one of three things will happen. If you type an unknown command, the car radio will bleat and you will have to type the command again. If what you type happens to be wrong but is nevertheless a valid command, the car will blindly obey. (Imagine typing A95 instead of A35.) If you type something the manufacturer didn't anticipate, the car will screech to a halt and shut itself off.[1]

Interest

Supporting material can enliven a presentation by making your main points more vivid or meaningful to the audience. Notice how one attorney added interest to a summary aimed at discrediting his opponent's restatement of evidence:

> It seems that when Abe Lincoln was a young trial lawyer in Sangamon County, Illinois, he was arguing a case with a lawyer whose version of the facts came more from his imagination than the testimony. Lincoln, in his argument, turned on him and said:
>   "Tell me, sir, how many legs has a sheep got?" "Why, four, of course," the fellow answered. "And if I called his tail a leg, then how many legs would that sheep have?" Lincoln asked. The answer came, "Then he'd have five." "No!" Lincoln roared, pounding the jury rail, "he'd still have just four legs. Calling his tail a leg won't make it a leg. Now let's look at the actual testimony and see how many tails you've been calling legs."[2]

Proof

Besides adding clarity and interest, supporting material can provide evidence for your claims and make your presentation more convincing. A speaker might use supporting materials this way to back up the claim "Employer-sponsored day care can boost productivity as well as help parents":

> A survey of Union Bank employees in California showed the value of on-site, employer-sponsored day care. Turnover of employees using the bank's on-site center was only 2.2 percent, less than one quarter of the 9.9 percent turnover for workers who used other forms of day care. And that's not all: Employees using the day care center were absent from work an average of 1.7 days a year less than other parents of young children.[3]

Whenever you use others' work to back up your claims, be sure to cite the source. Some sources, of course, are more credible than others. In the preceding paragraph, for example, the claim that employer-sponsored day care is good for employers is strengthened by citing a survey done by a respected bank. The same claim wouldn't be as persuasive coming from a survey of employees who were seeking day care because their motives would be more self-serving.

• Verbal Support

As Table 10-1 shows, many kinds of verbal supporting material can be used to add interest, clarity, or proof to a presentation. The most common supports for business and professional presentations are definitions, examples, stories, statistics, comparisons, and quotations. Consider your audience's preferences when choosing the types of support you'll present.

Definitions

You can appreciate a speaker's need to define unclear terms by recalling times when someone began using unfamiliar language, leaving you confused and unable to understand:

> "SQLite is a software library that implements a self-contained, serverless, zero-configuration, transactional SQL database engine. Content can be stored as INTEGER, REAL, TEXT, BLOB, or as NULL."

Table 10-1	Types of Verbal Support		
Type	**Definition**	**Use**	**Comments**
Definition	Explains meaning of a term	Clarify	Important when terms are unfamiliar to an audience or used in an uncommon way
Example	Brief reference that illustrates a point	Clarify Add interest (if sufficient number given)	Usually best in groups of two or more, if example is brief Often an extended example is most effective
Story	Detailed account of an incident	Clarify Add interest Prove (factual only)	Adapt to audience Must clearly support thesis Tell at appropriate length
Statistics	Numerical representations of point	Clarify Prove Add interest (when combined with other form of support)	Link to audience's frame of reference Use sparingly Round off Supplement with visuals, handout
Comparisons	Examinations or processes that show how one idea resembles another	Clarify Add interest (figurative) Prove (literal)	Tailor familiar item to audience Make sure comparison is valid
Quotations	Opinion of expert or articulate source	Clarify Add interest (sometimes) Prove	Paraphrase lengthy quotes Very short quotes can be read verbatim Cite source Use sources credible to audience Follow up with restatement or explanation

Definitions remove this sort of confusion by explaining the meaning of terms that are unfamiliar to an audience or used in a specialized or uncommon way: Words can be defined by denotation (specific meaning), connotation (associated meanings), etymology (history or origin of the word), or negation (stating what it is not).

"A *smart electrical meter* doesn't just measure how much energy a customer uses. It identifies when you used it and sends that information back to the local utility for monitoring and billing purposes." (denotation)

"*Bollywood* is the informal name of the Hindi language film industry based in Mumbai, India. The term is a combination of the words 'Bombay'—the old name for Mumbai—and 'Hollywood.'" (etymology)

"In the tax code, *a capital gain* is not the same as ordinary income. It is the profit that results when you sell assets like real estate or shares of stock for more than you paid for them. A *capital gains tax* is the amount government charges on that profit." (negation)

Examples

Examples are brief illustrations that back up or explain a point. A speaker arguing for an enhanced package of employee benefits could cite examples of companies that already provide a variety of perks:

- The Microsoft campus includes a shopping mall with 23 shops and restaurants, a spa, bicycle repair shop, and a pub.
- Umpqua Bank employees get 40 hours of paid time off every year to do volunteer work.

- Timberland employees who buy a hybrid vehicle get $3,000 back from the company and a preferred parking spot.
- Cisco employees can leave their cars with mechanics for an oil change while they work.
- SAS Airline benefits include on-site health care, summer camp for employees' children, car cleaning, a beauty salon, and a 66,000-square-foot fitness center.
- Anheuser-Busch employees get a monthly allowance of two free cases of beer.[4]

Likewise, a marketing consultant explaining how the name of a business can attract customers could back up the claim by citing examples of clever names:

- Totally Twisted, a Maryland pretzel company
- Now Showing, a movie theater turned lingerie shop in Oklahoma
- Access/Abilities, a California firm that helps people with disabilities[5]

The same consultant could show how poor names can discourage business:

- Coffin Air Service
- Big Bill's Plumbing
- Bland Farms, a mail-order food company[6]

In many cases you don't need to look outside your own experience for examples to back up a point. Union members claiming that "management cares more about buildings and grounds than employees" might back up their claim by offering examples:

> We keep hearing that "employees are our most important asset," yet we don't see dollars reflecting that philosophy. In the two and a half years since our last pay raise, we have seen the following physical improvements at this site alone: a new irrigation system for the landscaping, renovation of the corporate offices, expansion of the data processing wing, resurfacing of all the parking lots, and a new entrance to the building. Now all those improvements are helpful, but they show that buildings and grounds are more important than people.

When they are used to prove a point, examples are most effective when several are given together. If you are supporting the claim that you are capable of taking on a more challenging job, it is best to remind your boss of several tasks you have handled well. After all, a single example could be an isolated instance or a lucky fluke.

Stories

Stories illustrate a point by describing an incident in some detail. Almost everyone loves to hear a good story. It adds interest and, when well chosen, it can drive home a point better than logic and reasoning alone.[7]

This account of a farmer and his children shows how stories can make a powerful point—in this case, a farmer's contrast between conventional agriculture and an organic approach:

> When I worked for a conventional farm, I would come home and my kids would want to hug me. They couldn't because I had to shower first and my clothes had to be removed and disinfected. Today, I can walk right off the field into the waiting arms of my kids because there's nothing toxic on my body to harm them.[8]

As the consultant who retold this story explained, "While data are obviously important and must support your story, you have to touch hearts before you can influence minds."[9]

CULTURE **at work**

Culture Shapes Support Preferences

Most native English speakers are raised to value arguments in which a clear thesis is backed up by supporting material. But this style isn't preferred in every culture. For example, in Latin America, an inductive approach that begins with multiple pieces of support can be more compelling. Hispanic marketing consultant Miguel Gomez Winebrenner explains:

> When asked a question like "what is your favorite color?" most Americans tend to work down from that question and explain the reasoning behind the answer. So, a typical answer would be "my favorite color is blue, and this is why. . . ."
>
> When asked the same question, many Latin Americans would answer something along the lines of, "when I was a kid I preferred yellow because the flag of my favorite sports team was yellow, but then I started to like black because of the color of my first girlfriend's eyes . . . , etc." until after a rather long a personal dialogue they answer "so my favorite color is blue."
>
> Neither is right nor wrong—they're just different. U.S. Americans expect an answer upfront followed by supporting arguments. Latin Americans might first give the supporting arguments that lead to the answer.

Even the most persuasive type of support can depend on the audience's cultural background. In Latin America, examples and stories that evoke an emotional reaction can be more compelling than data-based arguments.

Culture isn't the only factor that shapes an audience's preferences. Educational background, career focus, and socioeconomic status can also be powerful. A smart speaker will consider all these variables when choosing how to support arguments.

Sources: Jaffee, C. I. (2013). *Public speaking: Concepts and skills for a diverse society* (7th ed.). Boston, MA: Wadsworth; Moran, R. T., Harris, P. R., & Moran, S. V. (2007). *Managing cultural differences: Global leadership strategies for the 21st century* (7th ed.). Amsterdam, NL: Elsevier; Weinbrenner, M. G. (2007, June 13). Building an effective case to Latin American and Hispanic dominant consumers: The inverted triangle dilemma. *Hispanic Marketing and Public Relations*. Retrieved from http://www.hispanicmpr.com/resources/articles/building-an-effective-case-to-latin-american-and-hispanic-dominant-consumers-the-inverted-triangle-dilemma

Research bears out the power of stories to reach an audience. In a study exploring effective ways to persuade listeners, one group of subjects was presented with statistical information like "Food shortages in Malawi are affecting more than 3 million children." A second group was shown the photo of a seven-year-old girl from Malawi named Rokia and told that she is desperately poor and that "her life will be changed for the better by your gift." People in the second group gave significantly more.[10]

Stories come in three categories: fictional, hypothetical, and factual. *Fictional stories* allow you to create material that perfectly illustrates the point you want to make. This fictional story uses humor to help listeners understand the importance of being proactive in business:

> In Greece there is an old monastery perched on top of a high mountain, with steep cliffs on every side. The only way to visit it is to get in a wicker basket and have a monk pull you up by ropes.
>
> One visitor noticed that this rope—the one his life depended on—was old and quite frayed. He asked the monk, "When do you change the rope?" The monk replied, "Whenever it breaks."

After the laughter died down, the speaker used this story to make his point:

> In this company we don't wait until the rope breaks. We don't even let it fray. We fix things before they become hazards.[11]

Other stories are *hypothetical:* "Imagine yourself. . . ." "Think about a typical customer. . . .", and "What would you do if. . . ." Besides being involving, hypothetical stories allow you to create a situation that illustrates exactly the point you are trying to make. You can adjust details, create dialogue, and use figures that support your case. But your account will be effective only if it is believable.

A representative explaining the concept of "Guaranteed Account Value" in a variable annuity investment might use a hypothetical example like this:

> Suppose you were unlucky enough to have a nasty accident that kept you from working for six months. Imagine dealing with the pain and inconvenience of your injuries. Then imagine yourself trying to cope with your loss of income. Would you have enough money saved to support yourself and the people who are counting on you? Would you have enough insurance coverage to make up for your lost income?

Factual stories can also add interest and clarity. The story below, from a frustrated consumer, illustrates the thesis that many businesses are more interested in making a sale than in supporting their products after the deal is closed. Notice how the last sentence restates the main idea so the point of the story is clear:

> Last Tuesday I decided to call the automobile dealership. There were two numbers listed in the phone book, one for "Sales," the other for "Service." I asked the service manager if I could bring my car in the following Saturday. Service managers always have a way of making you feel unwanted, and he seemed pleased to be able to tell me that they were closed Saturday and wouldn't be able to take me until a week from Thursday.
>
> I didn't make a date. Instead I called the other number, under "Sales." "Are you open Saturday?" I asked. "Yes, sir," the cheery voice said at the other end of the phone. "We're here Saturdays from eight in the morning till nine in the evening, and Sundays from noon until six."
>
> Now, if I can buy a car on Saturday, why can't I get one fixed on Saturday? What's going on here anyway? I think I know what's going on, of course. We're selling things better than we're making them, that's what's going on.[12]

While both factual and fictional stories can make a presentation clearer and more interesting, only the factual type can prove a point:

> "Cutting the payroll by using temporary employees sounds like a good idea, but it has problems. Listen to what happened when we tried it at the place I used to work. . . ."
>
> "I'm sure Wes can handle the job. Let me tell you what happened last year when we assigned him to manage the Westco account. . . ."
>
> "You might think life insurance isn't necessary for a young, healthy person like you, but remember Dale Crandall, the linebacker from State? Well, he was about as healthy as they come, but. . . ."

Whether they are fictional or factual, effective stories have several characteristics.[13] First, they should be relatively brief: Don't spin out a 5-minute yarn to make a minor point. They should also be interesting and appropriate for your audience: A story that offends your listeners will be memorable but not in the desired way. Most important, a story must support the point you are trying to make. An amusing story that doesn't support your thesis will just distract your listeners.[14]

DILBERT © Scott Adams/Dist. By Universal Uclick.

Statistics

Statistics are numbers used to represent an idea. Most statistics are collections of examples reduced to numerical form for clarity. If you were arguing that there was a serious manufacturing problem with a new product line, describing one or two dissatisfied customers would not prove that the problem went beyond the usual "acceptable" rate of error in manufacturing. The following statement, though, would constitute proof: "Our return rate on the new line is just over 40 percent—as opposed to the usual rate of 5 percent—and of all those returns, four-fifths are related to a flaw in the gear assembly." Statistics are a common form of support in business presentations. They are used to measure the size of market segments, sales trends, decreasing or increasing profits, changes in costs, and many other aspects of business.

When handled well, statistics are especially strong proof because they are firmly grounded in fact and show that the speaker is well informed.[15] Consider this example:

> The U.S. Census Bureau reports that people with a bachelor's degree earn an average of 62 percent more than those with only a high school diploma. Over a lifetime, the gap in earning potential between a high school grad and someone with a B.A. is more than a million dollars. These figures show that whatever sacrifices you make for a college education in the short term are worth it in the long term.

Despite their potential effectiveness, poorly used statistics can spoil a presentation. One common mistake is to bury an audience under an avalanche of numbers like this speaker did at an annual stockholders' meeting:

> Last year was an exciting one for our company. We earned $6.02 per share on a net income of $450 million, up from $4.63 per share on income of $412 million in the preceding year. This increase came in part from a one-time gain of $13 million from the sale of common stock to New Ventures group, our research and development subsidiary. Excluding this one-time gain, we increased our earnings per share 5.8 percent in the recent year, and we increased our net income 6.5 percent.

These numbers would be very appropriate in a printed annual report, but when a speaker rattles them off one after another, there is little chance that audience members will follow them. Rather than smothering your listeners with detail, you can provide a few key numbers in your presentation, backed up by accompanying written materials if necessary.

> As the report you're holding details, last year was a good one for us. Earnings per share were up almost 6 percent, our net income grew by 6.5 percent, on top of a $13 million one-time gain.

As this example shows, it's usually best to simplify information by rounding off numbers. For example, it's easier to understand "almost two-thirds" than it is to absorb "64.3 percent"; "approximately twice the cost" is easier to grasp than "Item A costs $65.18, while Item B runs $127.15." Hollywood star Angelina Jolie used "over" and "almost" to maximize the comprehensibility of statistics in a speech to United Nations officials:

> Of the over 400,000 Somali refugees [in the Dadaab Refugee Camp in Northeast Kenya], almost 100,000 arrived in the past nine months, fleeing drought, insecurity, and famine conditions.[16]

Besides having too many numbers, statistic-laden presentations are too dry for all but the most dedicated and involved audiences to handle. When you are speaking to a group of nonspecialists, it's important to link your figures to a frame of reference the group will understand. Notice how the following statistics (presented in the form of examples) give new impact to the old principle that time is money:

> For a manager who is earning $30,000 a year, wasting one hour a day costs the company $3,750 a year. . . . And for a $100,000-a-year executive, a two-hour lunch costs the company an extra $12,500 annually.[17]

When a presentation contains more than a few statistics, you will probably need to use visual aids to explain them: Numbers alone are simply too confusing to understand. The material on pp. 299–304 offers guidelines about how to present statistical data graphically.

Comparisons

Comparisons can make a point by showing how one idea resembles another. Some comparisons—called analogies—are *figurative.* They compare items from an unfamiliar area with items from a familiar one. By considering a few examples, you can appreciate the value of figurative comparisons to add clarity and interest to a presentation:

> "The cheap special fares advertised by some airlines are misleading since the 'mouse print' at the bottom of the page lists so many restrictions. No food chain could get away with advertising prime rib at $3 a pound, limited to six roasts per store, available only when bought in pairs Tuesday through Thursday afternoons."[18]

U.S. senator Mitch McConnell used a comparison to illustrate the magnitude of spending in a multitrillion-dollar bill before Congress: "if you had spent a million dollars every day since Jesus was born, you still wouldn't have spent a trillion."[19]

By linking the familiar with the unfamiliar, figurative analogies can also help listeners understand concepts that would otherwise be mystifying. One speaker used a figurative comparison to explain a limitation of cable modem Internet connections in terms easily understandable by nonexperts:

> Remember what happens when you're taking a shower and someone turns on another faucet or flushes the toilet? The flow of water drops for everybody. A similar thing happens with the flow of data over an Internet connection: When more people are using the system, the speed at which data flows is slower.

Other comparisons are *literal,* linking similar items from two categories. An account executive might use this sort of comparison to argue, "We need to spend more of our advertising budget on direct mail. That approach worked wonders on the NBT campaign, and I think it can do the same for us here."

ETHICAL **challenge**

Cherry Picking Support?

Imagine you are planning a sales presentation to a prospective client. To back up your claims that the product or service you are offering is outstanding, you know you need to use examples of outstanding service and testimonials of satisfied customers. You do have a few good examples of each, but sadly they aren't representative of the kind of feedback your organization usually receives. It would be easier to come up with examples and complaints that reflect unhappy clients.

How can you reconcile the need to be honest with the desire to sign up a new customer?

After an explosion killed 12 in a West Virginia coal mine, some observers used a comparison to argue that weak federal laws make it financially worthwhile for mine owners to break safety rules:

> Driving solo in a California carpool lane carries a bigger fine than allowing combustible materials to accumulate in a coal mine.[20]

Whenever you propose adopting a policy or using an idea because it worked well somewhere else, you're also using comparisons as proof. The strength of this proof will depend on how clearly you can establish the similarity between the items you are comparing. Microsoft founder and philanthropist Bill Gates used a vivid statistical comparison to demonstrate misplaced priorities in drug research:

> Ten times as much funding is devoted to research on the prevention of male baldness as malaria, a disease that kills more than 1 million people each year.[21]

Whether their purpose is to add clarity, interest, or proof, comparisons should possess two characteristics: First, the familiar part of comparisons should be well known to the audience. For instance, it would be a mistake to say, "Jumbo certificates of deposit are similar to Treasury bills in several ways" if your listeners don't know anything about Treasury bills. Second, you should be sure your comparisons are valid. You would be stretching a point if you tried to discourage employee abuse of the copying machine by claiming, "Using the machine for personal papers is a crime, just as much as robbery or assault." A closer match is both more valid and effective: "You wouldn't help yourself to spare change from a cash register; everybody with a conscience knows that would be a case of petty theft. But using the copying machine for personal papers costs the company, just as surely as if the money came out of the cash register."

Quotations

Quotations use the words of others who are authoritative or articulate to help you make a point more effectively than you could on your own. Some quotations add clarity and impact. You might, for example, add punch to a talk on the importance of listening to customer complaints by citing a successful businessperson like Bill Gates, founder of Microsoft: "Your most unhappy customers are your greatest source of learning." Likewise, you could emphasize the importance of getting agreements in writing by quoting movie producer Sam Goldwyn: "A verbal contract isn't worth the paper it's written on." Or you might repeat Oprah Winfrey's words about taking responsibility for your own success:

> I don't think of myself as a poor deprived ghetto girl who made good. I think of myself as somebody who from an early age knew I was responsible for myself, and I had to make good.[22]

Mosquitoes Create a Buzz over Bill Gates's Speech

Microsoft founder Bill Gates is passionate about eliminating the scourge of malaria from the world. The disease kills millions of people each year, but Gates told an elite California audience it's hard for Westerners to appreciate the impact of the disease because the majority of deaths occur in the developing world.

Then Gates used a unique strategy to show his listeners the risk so many less fortunate people face in tropical parts of the world. "There's no reason only poor people should have the experience," he calmly remarked as he opened a jar and released a swarm of mosquitoes. Nervous laughter erupted as the tiny insects flew into the audience.

The stir the mosquito stunt caused was immediate and widespread. Audience members tweeted the news into cyberspace, where it spread around the world faster than any infectious disease. Gates's simple strategy of using mosquitoes as props dramatized his point far more effectively than would otherwise have been possible.

Source: Gates, B. (2009, February 4). *How I'm trying to change the world now.* Speech delivered at TED annual conference, Long Beach, CA. Retrieved from http://www.ted.com/talks/bill_gates_unplugged.html

Citing Your Sources

Whether you are quoting someone or using a statistic, it's both proper and effective to cite the source. Showing your ideas are based on authoritative sources boosts your credibility.

Here is a simple four-step method for citing sources without interrupting the flow of your presentation:

1. *State your point:* "The trend of working from home is growing."
2. *Identify the source of your citation:* "In the March 12 edition of *USA Today,* columnist Stephanie Armour states that. . . ."
3. *State the content of your citation:* "Just about anyone with a high-speed Internet connection and a telephone can become a virtual free agent, handling customer service calls for major corporations."
4. *Explain how and why the material is important for members of your audience:* "That means almost everybody in this room has the potential to work from home, whether you are going to school, raising a child, or have limited mobility."

Use the following guidelines to cite sources.

Cite the Source in a Way That Adds to the Credibility of Your Presentation
If necessary, explain why the source is credible: "Here's what the nonpartisan, independent Congressional Budget Office said. . . ."

Cite Sources That Have Credibility with Your Audience
Citing Karl Marx about the abuse of workers won't impress an audience of Republican manufacturers, whereas a similar message from an article in the *Wall Street Journal* might be effective.

Restate the Point of Long Citations
If your citation takes a long time to deliver, summarize the point it makes before moving on:

"After hearing Roberta's figures, you can see that our advertising dollars are well spent."

"You can see from this research there are hidden costs in this proposal."

"Customer letters like those make it clear we need to improve our service."

• Visual Aids

The old cliché is true: A picture often *is* worth a thousand words. That is why charts, diagrams, and other graphic aids are part of most business presentations.

Researchers have verified what good speakers have always known intuitively: Using visual aids makes a presentation more effective. In one study, two groups of business students watched videotaped presentations describing upcoming time-management seminars. One group saw a version of the talk with no visual support, while the other saw the same talk with a number of high-quality visuals. After the presentation, audience members were asked about their willingness to enroll in the time-management course and about their opinion of the speaker they had just viewed.

Audience members who saw the presentation with visuals were clearly more impressed than those who saw the same talk with no visual support. They planned to spend 16.4 percent more time and 26.4 percent more money on the time-management seminar being promoted. They also viewed the speaker as more clear, concise, professional, persuasive, and interesting.[23]

Well-designed graphics are also easier to understand than words alone. A chart listing a point-by-point comparison of two products is easier to follow than a detailed narrative. A plummeting sales curve tells the story more eloquently than any words. Visuals can also boost your image in ways that extend beyond the presentation itself. A professional display of visuals labels you as a professional person—a candidate for recognition in the future by superiors and the public. Finally, visuals can make your information more memorable. Researchers have discovered that audiences recall far more information when it is presented both verbally and visually than when it is presented in only one way:[24]

Visual aids perform many useful functions:

- *Show how things look.* An architect could use a model or an artist's sketch to describe a project to potential clients; an advertising director could use photographs of a new product as part of a campaign.
- *Show how things work.* An engineer could include diagrams as part of the instructions for a piece of equipment; a sales representative could use a model to show how a boat is designed for speed and safety.
- *Show how things relate to one another.* An organizational chart provides a clear picture of the reporting relationships in a company; a flowchart pictures the steps necessary to get a job done.
- *Emphasize important points.* An account representative could use a chart to show customers the features of a new product; an investment consultant could use a graph to display the performance of a stock.

Types of Visual Aids

As a speaker, you can choose from a wide array of visual aids to make your presentations more effective. You won't use them all every time you speak. But sooner or later you will use almost every type described in the following pages.

Objects and Models   As the Case Study on p. 297 shows, there are times when objects can add interest, clarity, and proof to your topic. This is certainly true in training sessions and in some types of selling, where hands-on experience is essential. It's difficult to imagine learning how to operate a piece of equipment without actually giving it a try, and few customers would buy an expensive, unfamiliar piece of merchandise without seeing it demonstrated.

When you do use an object or model for instructional purposes, be sure the item is large enough for everyone to see. Small items like a microchip or a piece of jewelry can work in a one-on-one presentation, but this approach will only frustrate a larger group of listeners. It is almost always a bad idea to pass an object around for the audience to examine. Doing so will probably distract both the person who has the object at a given moment and the other people who are craning their necks to get a preview.

When you use a model or object as part of a demonstration, be sure you have practiced enough to avoid any unpleasant surprises of the sort described by one accountant:

> To try to make taxes more interesting, I thought I'd make a point that people's hard-earned money can go up in smoke if they don't consider the tax consequences. I planned to ignite a piece of paper that magicians use to produce a brilliant flame. When the time came to do the trick, the paper hardly burned, so I put it in an empty coffee can I had brought and grabbed another piece of paper. This one caught fire right away.
>
> It ended up burning my blouse, but the audience didn't seem to notice; instead it was staring at the flames suddenly shooting out of the coffee can. An audience member jumped up and put out the fire, and I somehow got through the rest of the talk. I was never so humiliated.[25]

Photographs   Photographs can be the most effective means of illustrating a variety of images that need literal representation: an architectural firm's best work, a corporation's management team, or a stylish new product. Photographs also provide an excellent form of proof. For instance, an insurance investigator's picture of a wrecked auto may be all that exists of the car months later, when a claim is argued in court.

Diagrams   Diagrams are abstract, two-dimensional drawings that show the important properties of objects without being completely representational. Types of diagrams you might use in presentations include drawings (see Figure 10.1) and maps (see Figure 10.2). Diagrams are excellent for conveying information about size, shape, and structure.

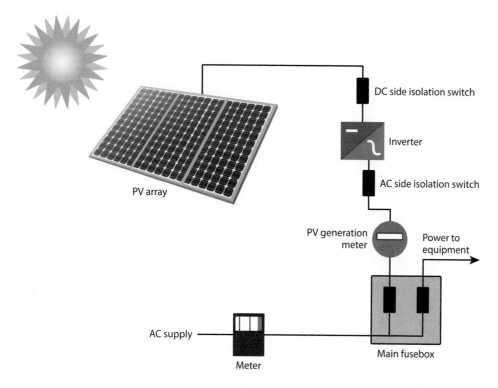

FIGURE 10.1 Diagram

FIGURE 10.2 Map

Sales regions

FIGURE 10.3
Table

College costs, 2002–2012

Year	Private 4-year	Public 4-year	Public 2-year
2002–2003	$18,060	$4,098	$1,674
2005–2006	$21,235	$5,491	$2,191
2008–2009	$25,143	$6,585	$2,402
2011–2012	$28,500	$8,244	$2,963

Lists and Tables   Lists and tables are effective means of highlighting key facts and figures. They are especially effective when you list steps, highlight features, or compare related facts: advantages and disadvantages, current and past performance, your product versus a competitor's, and so on. The table in Figure 10.3 shows how the cost of a college education has increased over time. A sales manager might use a similar chart to compare this year's sales performance and last year's in several regions.

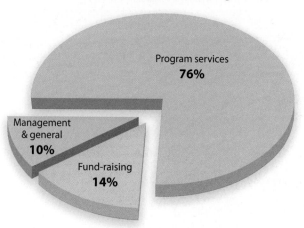

Where does your donation go?

FIGURE 10.4
Pie Chart

Amateur speakers often assume they need only enlarge tables from a written report for an oral presentation. In practice, this approach rarely works. Most written tables are far too detailed and difficult to understand to be useful to a group of listeners. As you design lists and tables for presentation, remember the following points:

- *Keep the visual aid simple.* List only highlights. Use only keywords or phrases, never full sentences.

- *Use numbered and/or bulleted lists to emphasize key points.* Numbered lists suggest ranking or steps in a process, while bulleted lists work best for items that are equally important.

- *Use text sparingly.* If you need more than seven lines of text, create two or more tables. Lines of text should never exceed seven words across.

- *Use large type.* Make sure the words and numbers are large enough to be read by everyone in the audience.

- *Enhance the list's or table's readability.* Careful layout and generous use of white space will make it easy to read.

Pie Charts

Pie charts like the one in Figure 10.4 illustrate component percentages of a single item. Frequently, they are used to show how money is spent. They also can illustrate the allocation of resources. For example, a personnel director might use a pie chart to show the percentage of employees who work in each division of the company.

Follow these guidelines when constructing pie charts:

- *Place the segment you want to emphasize at the top center* (12 o'clock) *position* on the circle. When you are not emphasizing any segments, organize the wedges from largest to smallest, beginning at 12 o'clock with the largest one.

- *Label each segment,* either inside or outside the figure.

- *List the percentage for each segment* as well as its label.

Bar and Column Charts

Bar charts like the one shown in Figure 10.5 compare the value of several items: the productivity of several employees, the relative amount of advertising money spent on different media, and so on. Simple **column charts** reflect changes in a single item over time. Multiple-column charts like the one in Figure 10.6 compare several items over time.

FIGURE 10.5
Bar Chart

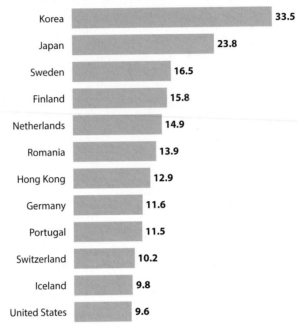

Global download speed (MBps)

FIGURE 10.6
Multiple-Column
Chart

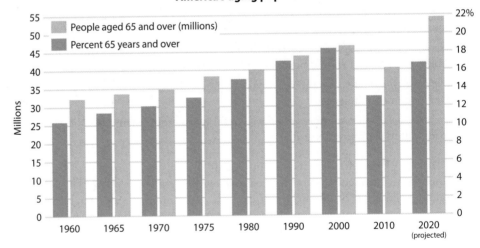

America's aging population

Several tips will help you design effective bar and column charts:

- *Always represent time on the horizontal axis* of your chart, running from left to right.
- *Arrange the bars in a sequence* that best suits your purpose. You might choose to order them from high to low, from low to high, in alphabetical order, or in order of importance.
- *Make sure the numerical values represented are clear.* This may mean putting the numbers next to bars or columns. In other cases, the figures will fit inside the bars. In a few instances, the scale on the axes will make numbering each bar unnecessary.

FIGURE 10.7
Pictogram

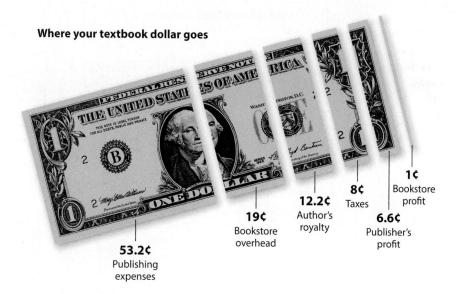

Where your textbook dollar goes

53.2¢
Publishing
expenses

19¢
Bookstore
overhead

12.2¢
Author's
royalty

8¢
Taxes

6.6¢
Publisher's
profit

1¢
Bookstore
profit

Pictograms   **Pictograms** are artistic variations of bar, column, or pie charts. As Figure 10.7 shows, pictograms are more interesting than ordinary bars. This makes them useful in presentations aimed at lay audiences such as the general public. Pictograms are often not mathematically exact, however, which makes them less suited for reports that require precise data.

Graphs   **Graphs** show the correlation between two quantities. They are ideally suited to showing trends, such as growth or decline in sales over time. They can also represent a large amount of data without becoming cluttered. Graphs can chart a single trend, or they can show relationships among two or more trends like the graph in Figure 10.8. Notice in Figure 10.9 how identical data can be manipulated by adjusting the horizontal and vertical axes.

Video   There are times when video support is a plus. If you are illustrating action— the performance of an athletic team or the gestures of a speaker, for example—video may do the job better than any other medium.

Despite the benefits of video, including clips you pull off websites like YouTube or footage you create yourself can be risky. Problems with amateur work include segments that last too long and lack continuity, casting the rest of your message in an unprofessional light.

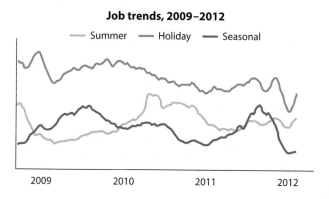

Job trends, 2009–2012

— Summer   — Holiday   — Seasonal

2009   2010   2011   2012

FIGURE 10.8
Multiple-Line
Graph

FIGURE 10.9

FIGURE 10.9
The same data can be distorted by varying the horizontal and vertical size and axes of a graph. These graphs were created using Microsoft PowerPoint.

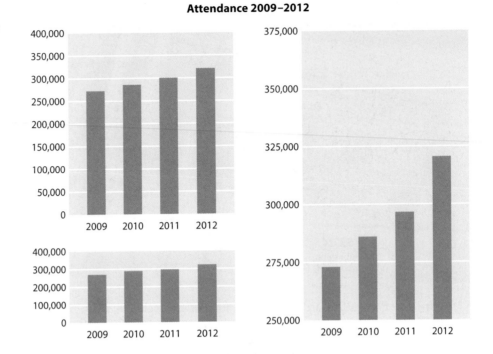

Attendance 2009–2012

Media for Presenting Visual Aids

Choosing the most advantageous way to present your visual aids is just as important as picking the right type. The best photograph, chart, or diagram will flop if it isn't displayed effectively.

Chalk and Dry-Erase Boards   When these boards are available in a presentation room, they can be useful for recording information that comes up on the spot, such as brainstorming ideas or a tally of audience responses to your questions. When you're presenting preplanned visuals, though, it's usually best to use a medium that doesn't require you to turn your back on the audience and write or draw freehand.

Instead of using a chalk or whiteboard, consider large size Post-it notes. This makes it easy for you (or other participants) to recategorize the ideas without having to erase and rewrite them. Also, you can take the sticky notes with you at the end of your talk as a record of the points.

Flip Charts and Poster Board   **Flip charts** consist of a large pad of paper attached to an easel. You reveal visuals on a flip chart one at a time by turning the pages. You can also produce visuals on rigid poster board, which you can display on the same sort of easel.

A major advantage of flip charts and poster displays is that they are relatively simple to prepare and easy to use. Their low-tech nature eliminates the risk of equipment problems. Also, you can create them with familiar materials: pens, rulers, and so on. Most copy shops can also turn computer-generated files into high-quality posters. In addition, flip charts and poster boards are relatively portable (most easels collapse into a carrying case) and easy to set up. Despite these advantages, the size of flip charts and poster boards is a problem: They may be too small for easy viewing and too large to transport easily.

Computer Displays   With a computer and data projector you can present a wealth of material: text photos, charts, graphs, and video. With the right setup, you can even use a computer to create visuals during your presentation: a website demonstration, for example, or a brainstorming list. It's easy to transport the data you want to project on a flash drive or other portable storage device.

With all computer-supported presentations, keep Murphy's Law in mind: Whatever can go wrong with the system probably will. Don't count on having a fast, stable Internet connection. Beware of compatibility problems. Test all parts of the system together, just as you plan to use it, ideally in the place where you will speak. A sophisticated display is useless if it doesn't work when you are standing in front of an expectant audience.

Handouts   **Handouts** provide a permanent record of your ideas. Intricate features of a product, names and phone numbers, or "do's and don'ts" are easier to recall when your listeners have a printed record of them. Handouts also enable you to give your audience more details than you want to talk about in your presentation. You might, for instance, mention the highlights of a sales period or briefly outline a new product's technical features and then refer your listeners to a handout for further information.[26]

You can use handouts to reduce or eliminate your listeners' need to take notes. If you put key ideas and figures on a handout, listeners' attention will be focused on you instead of on their notebooks—and you'll be sure their notes are accurate. Some speakers use an "electronic blackboard," a plastic write-and-wipe board that can produce handout-sized copies of what you've written on the board. Environmentally astute presenters may save paper and boost portability by e-mailing handouts after the presentation or posting them online.

The biggest problem with handouts is that they can be distracting. The activity that accompanies passing around papers interrupts the flow of your presentation. Once the handout is distributed, you'll have to compete with it for your audience's attention. For this reason, it's better to distribute handouts *after* you've finished speaking. If printed material has to be introduced during your presentation, tell your listeners when to begin referring to it and when to stop: "Let's take a look at the budget on the pink sheet in your folders. . . . Now that we've examined the budget, let me direct your attention to the chart up here."

Presentation Software

Presentation software such as Microsoft PowerPoint, Apple Keynote, and Prezi allow anyone with a computer to create and deliver a professional-looking presentation with text and visuals.

Advantages of Presentation Software   Presentation software helps speakers in many ways by enabling them to generate customized materials on an as-needed basis. Listed below are some of the things you can do with a good software program:

- Deliver an onscreen show with special effects such as smooth transitions between screens, animation, and synchronized timing that reveals each point as you raise it.
- Organize a set of speaker's notes for yourself.
- Prepare a variety of handouts for your audience, based on your speaking notes or displays.
- Create "run-time" versions of your displays so you can distribute copies of your presentation to people who may not have seen you speak.
- Create charts, graphs, and tables.

"I need someone well versed in the art of torture—do you know PowerPoint?"

© Alex Gregory/The New Yorker Collection/www.cartoonbank.com.

Although computer-assisted design can be very effective, it isn't foolproof. Even basic presentation software programs—like word processing and spreadsheet programs—take time to learn. If you are using such a program for the first time, prepare to invest an hour or two of study and practice before turning out a finished product. It's even better to get the help of a friend or coworker who is already skilled with a design program. Such help can save you a great deal of the time and frustration you would otherwise experience in trial-and-error experimenting or leafing through an instruction book.

Once you have mastered a program, it is important to resist the temptation to overuse it. In most presentations, simplicity is a virtue. Just because it is *possible* to produce an elaborate visual full of detail doesn't mean that this sort of display will communicate your message effectively. For example, the three-dimensional chart in Figure 10.10 is probably as complex as a visual display should be—at least in an oral presentation. If it were any more complex, the figure would be hard to understand in the limited time available for viewing. Detailed visuals may be appropriate for written reports, but in oral talks simplicity is usually the best approach.

Dangers of Presentation Software   Every competent speaker should be able to use presentation software when the need arises. But, like any form of technology, presentation software programs can cause new problems at the same time they solve old ones.[27] You should avoid several pitfalls of computerized design programs.

Poorly conceived messages   Presentation software makes it relatively easy to create charts and graphs, import images, integrate snappy animation, and wrap them all up in a handsome design; but if the structure of your presentation isn't clear, listeners won't understand your message or believe what you say. For this reason, it is essential that you organize your points clearly and back up your claims before you begin transferring your message to software. Resist the temptation to format your ideas with presentation software before you have a structure that follows one of the organizational plans in Chapter 9, and make sure your points are backed up with the kinds of supporting material described earlier in this chapter.

FIGURE 10.10

Displaying Data

Most presentational software programs can display data in a variety of formats. The best exhibits illustrate a point clearly without becoming too complex.

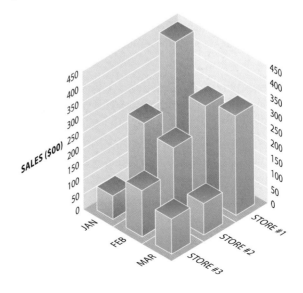

Design over content   A common mistake is to spend more time on the design of a presentation than its content. Even the most handsome slides won't make up for weak ideas. Design expert Edward Tufte says:

> If your numbers are boring, then you've got the wrong numbers. If your words or images are not on point, making them dance in color won't make them relevant. Audience boredom is usually a content failure, not a decoration failure.[28]

There is something seductive about the ease with which you can tinker with fonts, backgrounds, and transitions. Before you know it, you will have spent far too much time without much additional return. As one expert put it:

> We've got highly paid people sitting there formatting slides—spending hours formatting slides—because it's more fun to do that than concentrate on what you're going to say. . . . Millions of executives around the world are sitting there going "Arial? Times Roman? Twenty-four point? Eighteen point?"[29]

Again, the best way to avoid the seduction of favoring form over content is to create at least a rough outline of your material before you start using your presentation software.

Overly complex presentations   Just because you *can* use presentation software to create elaborate computer productions doesn't mean you always *should* use it. A digital display may dazzle your audience, but the spectacle might actually draw attention away from you and your message. It's hardly a success if listeners remember your terrific graphics and elaborate animation but can't recall the points you made.

Another danger of overly elaborate presentations is the possibility they will make material more confusing than it would have been if presented in a simpler way. As Figure 10.11 shows, this has been a problem in the U.S. armed forces, where overzealous presenters are known as "PowerPoint Rangers." Secretary of the Army Louis Caldera acknowledged that some military brass have alienated lawmakers by staging overly elaborate presentations. "People are not listening to us because they are spending so much time trying to understand these incredibly complex slides," he says.[30]

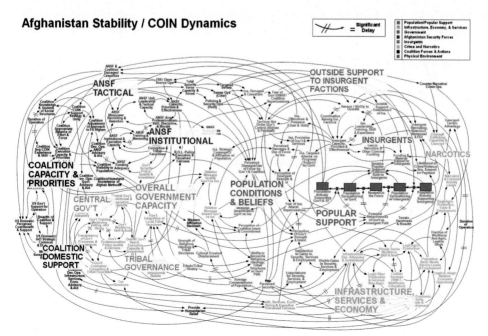

FIGURE 10.11

An Overly Complex Visual Aid

Avoiding Computer Catastrophes in Presentations

When you use computers as presentational aids, you can count on an equipment failure sooner or later. The following tips can minimize the chances that hardware or software glitches will scuttle your performance.

- *Set up in advance.* Give yourself lots of time to set up and test your equipment before the presentation is scheduled to begin. The last thing you want your audience to see is you frantically rebooting the computer, swapping cables, and trying to troubleshoot software.
- *Always bring two of everything.* Assume your equipment will fail because it certainly will at some time. Borrow backups for laptop computers, display panels or projectors, modems, and any other hardware you plan to use.
- *Back up your programs.* Having your work saved on a CD, flash drive, or some other storage medium can salvage a catastrophe. You might also want to e-mail a copy of your files to yourself as another form of backup.
- *Have backup technical support available.* Line up an expert you can call if something doesn't work.
- *Beware of the Web.* Real-time use of the Internet is an invitation to disaster. Connections can be slow, and websites can go down without notice. Whenever possible, it's best to store images of sites you will use on your hard drive and/or on a backup medium: CD, DVD, or flash drive.
- *Have a contingency plan.* Be prepared for the possibility your equipment will fail. Have copies of key exhibits prepared as handouts. They may not be as glamorous as high-tech displays, but they're far better than nothing.

Guidelines for Using Visual Aids

Whether you are using handouts, poster boards, flip charts, slides, chalkboard, or computer displays, be sure to follow the basic rules discussed in this section.[31]

Selection   As with any part of your presentation, visual exhibits must be chosen carefully. Use a visual only when it makes a point better than you could alone.

Be sure you have a reason for using a visual aid   If your image doesn't explain a point better than words alone, don't use it. One professional described the common mistake of using too many visuals:

> The biggest mistake people make is in expecting the visuals to be the presentation when, in reality, you should be the presentation. If the audience is too involved in looking at the screen, they're not looking at you, so your words have less of an impact. The goal of any visual presentation should be to enhance what the speaker says, not distract from it.[32]

Visuals used for their own sake will distract your audience from the point you're trying to make. Douglas Vogel, a professor of management information systems at the University of Arizona, cites an example of how using animation without any purpose can backfire: "If the animation is improperly focused or too clever, people may only remember 'dancing cows' and not 'how milk may be good for you.'"[33]

Keep your slide shows brief   Keep in mind the "less is more" rule. The chances of listeners recalling your points is inversely proportional to the number of slides you show.

Match the sophistication of your visuals to the audience   Presentations to important audiences—top management, bosses, key customers, and so on—usually require polished graphics. There are exceptions, however. For example, financial and scientific professionals are usually receptive to a no-frills approach. Amy Ofsthun, product manager of Polaroid's Digital Palette film recorder, explains: "If they see color and exciting visuals, people feel the data is being massaged somehow. They don't trust the results."[34]

For routine talks, you can probably produce perfectly adequate exhibits on your own. Thanks to advances in computer graphics, you may even be spared the trouble of having to create figures from scratch. In any case, you shouldn't mix informal images with more formal ones anymore than you would wear tennis shoes with a business suit.

Design   Confusing or sloppy exhibits will be counterproductive. The simple guidelines below will help you create clear, neat images.[35]

Make sure the visual is large enough to see   The visual that looks so clear on the desktop in front of you might be almost microscopic from where your listeners are seated. Avoid using items, drawings, or photographs that are so small you have to describe them or pass them around. Remember, a distracting or unclear visual is worse than no support at all.

Keep the design of your visuals simple   Show only one idea per exhibit and avoid unnecessary details. Use simple typefaces.[36]

Use only a few words   Most exhibits are visual images, so you should avoid excessive text. Captions should contain only keywords or phrases, not sentences. Omit subtitles. Follow the "Rule of Seven": Each slide should contain no more than seven lines, and each line should have no more than seven words. If an exhibit needs further explanation, supply it verbally. Remember, you are giving an oral presentation, not showing your audience a written report.

Use only horizontal printing   Avoid vertical or diagonal wording. If necessary, place captions in margins to allow you to use a horizontal format.

Label all items for clear identification   Make sure each exhibit has a descriptive title. Label each axis of a chart, each part of a diagram, and so on.

Display a visual only while you are discussing it   Putting up a visual before discussing it or leaving it up after you've finished talking about it is confusing and distracting. In PowerPoint, for example, you can blank out the screen by pushing either the "B" or period (.) keys. Pushing a second time makes the screen visible again.

Make sure your visuals will work in the meeting room   Double-check the availability of easels, screens, and other equipment you'll need. Be sure electrical outlets are in the right locations and extension cords are available if you will need them. Check sight lines from all audience seats. Be sure you can easily control lighting levels as necessary.

Practice using your visuals   Rehearse setting up and removing visuals smoothly and quickly. Review the comments you'll make with each one. Be sure exhibits are arranged in the right order and lined up properly so you can avoid the embarrassment of mixed-up charts or upside-down slides.

Use the scale below to answer each item. Then focus your efforts on improving your use of supporting material in areas you identified as needing work.

	Excellent 3	Competent 2	Needs Work 1
1. Each point (claim) contains at least one piece of verbal and/or visual support.	3	2	1
2. Each piece of supporting material makes my claims more			
a. Clear	3	2	1
b. Interesting	3	2	1
c. Persuasive	3	2	1
3. I used a variety of verbal support (definitions, examples, stories, statistics, and comparisons) to add impact to my presentation.	3	2	1
4. My visuals (charts, graphs, photos, video, etc.) make my points more clear, interesting, and persuasive.	3	2	1
5. I present visuals in a way that contributes to my effectiveness:			
a. I look at my audience, not at the visuals, while speaking.	3	2	1
b. I display visuals only when discussing them.	3	2	1
c. I practiced using all technology (e.g., computers, projectors) to make sure it operates smoothly in the venue where I will speak.	3	2	1
6. I present information honestly and accurately to support my claims.	3	2	1
7. The complexity and sophistication of the materials I cite are appropriate for my audience and topic.	3	2	1
8. I cite the sources of my supporting material when appropriate. (You don't always cite sources: for hypothetical examples, some definitions, stories you've created, etc.)	3	2	1

MASTER **the chapter**

review points

- Supporting material is vital in any presentation and serves three purposes: to clarify ideas, to make material more interesting, and to offer proof.

- Definitions, examples, stories (fictional, hypothetical, and factual), statistics, comparisons (figurative and literal), and quotations all serve as verbal support.

- Speakers create ethical and credible presentations by knowing when and how to cite their sources.

- In business presentations, well-designed visual aids can make a point more quickly and clearly than words alone, add variety and interest, and boost a speaker's professional image.

- Visuals serve several functions: They highlight important information, show how things look, how they work, or how they relate to one another.

- Speakers can use several types of visual aids: objects, models, photographs, diagrams, lists and tables, pie charts, bar and column charts, pictograms, graphs, and videos.

- Visuals can be presented via a number of media: Chalk and dry-erase marker boards, flip charts and poster boards, computer displays, and handouts.

- Presentation software allows presenters to develop professional-looking visual exhibits. Take care not to overuse features that result in cluttered and overstimulating, but unclear, visuals.

- Successful speakers plan their messages carefully, emphasize content over design, and strive for simplicity and clarity.

- Whatever the medium, all visuals should follow the same basic conventions: easy to understand, purposeful, suited to the point they illustrate and to the audience, and workable in the presentational setting.

- Speakers need to be familiar with their visuals to avoid unpleasant surprises during delivery.

key terms

bar chart   301
column chart   301
comparison   295
definition   290
example   290
flip chart   304
graph   303
handout   305

pictogram   303
pie chart   301
presentation software   305
quotation   296
statistics   294
stories   291
supporting material   288

activities

1. Invitation to Insight

Read a printed version of a speech. You can find sample speeches in your college library or at online sites such as Federal Observer (http://www.federalobserver.com) or Newsmax (http://archive.newsmax.com/hottopics/Great_Speeches.shtml).

Find examples of at least three types of supporting material. For each item, categorize which type of support it is. How well does it follow the guidelines in the text (for example, if it's a citation, does it follow the four-step method)? Then analyze whether the supporting material provides clarity, interest, and/or proof of the thesis. In your analysis, consider the interests and knowledge level of the intended audience.

2. Skill Builder

Which types of support introduced in this chapter (definition, statistics, etc.) would you use to add interest, clarity, and proof to the following points? Provide specific examples.

a. Tuition costs are keeping promising students out of college.
b. Textbooks are (are not) overpriced.
c. Timely payment of bills is in the customer's best interest.
d. Companies are helping themselves as well as employees by sponsoring and subsidizing exercise programs during work hours.
e. A liberal arts education can benefit one's career—better in many ways than technical training.

3. Skill Builder

Practice paraphrasing definitions into your own words by selecting several detailed definitions from an encyclopedia or from an online source such as http://dictionary.law.com or http://www.financial-dictionary.com. First read the definition to the class word for word. Then restate the definition in your own words. Ask your classmates which version of the definition was easier to follow.

4. Skill Builder

Well-chosen and well-told stories can help you make a point in an interesting and compelling way. In a brief presentation of 1 minute or less, use a story to illustrate an important lesson regarding professional communication. The story you tell may be based on your personal experience, something you observed, or something you read or heard about from others.

Organize your presentation in one of two ways: Either state your thesis first and then show how the story supports it, or tell the story first, and then show how it illustrates your thesis. In either case, conclude by showing audience members how your thesis and the story that illustrates it relate to their professional lives.

5. Skill Builder

Practice citing references out loud. Locate interesting facts in a variety of types of sources (newspapers, credible magazines, books, Internet sites, interviews with a professional). In class, cite the facts and references out loud, using the four-step method for citing sources found on p. 297 of your text.

6. Skill Builder

Construct a brief speech about one of the types of supporting material identified in the text. In your mini-speech, present a brief attention-getter, a definition, and a visual aid that illustrates this type of support. Explain potential uses and misuses of this type of support. Close your speech effectively by using one of the types of conclusions discussed in Chapter 9.

7. Skill Builder

Practice your skill at developing visual aids by doing one of the following activities:

a. Develop a chart or graph showing the overall changes in the demographic characteristics (age, sex, and so on) of your student body over the past 10 years.

b. The local chamber of commerce has hired you to compile graphic exhibits that will be used in presentations to encourage people to visit and settle in your area.

Design materials reflecting the following information:

1. Average salaries for typical types of jobs.
2. Types of recreational activities available.
3. Average days per month with sunshine.

If you believe that these figures would *discourage* an audience, choose data that paint an appealing picture of your area.

c. Develop three visual aids that could be used to introduce new employees to benefits offered by your company.

8. Skill Builder

Choose a fact or statistic you can illustrate with visual aids. Develop two different versions of your visual aid that would be effective for two different audiences or occasions (e.g., a group of interns, a workshop at a scientific conference, a formal company dinner, a weekly staff meeting).

9. Skill Builder

Collect examples of each type of verbal and visual support described in this chapter. Comment on how effectively each example follows the guidelines in the text. Describe how each one should be adapted for use in an oral presentation.

10. Invitation to Insight

You can get a sense of how visual aids are used, ignored, overused, or misused by attending a presentation of your choice in the community. Identify the visual supports the speaker uses and evaluate their effectiveness for the intended audience and occasion. If you had been hired as a consultant, what advice would you give the speaker about the effectiveness of his or her visual exhibits?

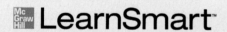

For further review, go to the LearnSmart study module for this chapter.

Chapter Eleven
Delivering the Presentation

chapter objectives

After reading this chapter you should be able to:

1. Evaluate delivery formats and select and use the delivery type best suited for any specified presentation.

2. Create and deliver effective extemporaneous and impromptu presentations.

3. Conduct effective question-and-answer sessions following recommended guidelines.

4. Apply information about communication apprehension in order to speak effectively to others.

No matter how well designed, a presentation has to be well delivered in order to succeed. If you look sloppy, speak in a way that is hard to understand, or seem unenthusiastic, listeners are likely to doubt or even reject your ideas. As communication consultant Roger Ailes puts it, "You become the message. People cannot distinguish between the words and who speaks them."[1]

This chapter offers suggestions to help you deliver your remarks in a way that makes your message clearer, more interesting, and more persuasive. It describes the various styles of delivery, offers tips for improving your visual and vocal performance, explains how to deal with questions from the audience, and gives advice for dealing with the nervousness that often accompanies an important presentation.

• Types of Delivery

The word *presentation* may conjure up images of a speaker standing behind a lectern delivering information to a passive audience. While some business and professional presentations follow this model, many of them are far more interactive.

There are three patterns of presentation style:[2] *Monologues* are one-way speeches, delivered without interruption. These are most appropriate in large settings and on formal occasions. In smaller groups they can feel artificial and create the impression the speaker doesn't care much about the audience. *Guided discussions* are more interactive. A speaker presents information and has a preset idea of what material to cover, but listeners are encouraged to speak up with questions and comments. Managing a guided discussion is more challenging, but the potential for more audience buy-in can be worth the effort. *Interactive presentations,* as their name implies, involve the audience even more. Although the speaker still controls the program, an interactive presentation feels more like a conversation than a speech. Interactive presentations are common in sales settings, where customer interest drives the communication.

Speakers have four options when delivering presentations. However, two of them—extemporaneous and impromptu—will serve you best in most situations.

Manuscript Presentations

In **manuscript presentations,** speakers read their remarks word for word from a prepared statement. Manuscript speaking is common at annual company meetings, conventions, and press conferences. Yet few experiences are as boring as the average manuscript presentation.

Novice speakers often try to conceal their nervousness at facing a large audience by reading from a script—and they turn into lifeless drones. Because most speakers aren't trained at reading aloud, their delivery is halting and jerky. Even worse, a nervous speaker who relies too heavily on a manuscript can make serious mistakes without even knowing it. Management consultant Marilyn Landis describes one such disaster:

> I remember the president of a large corporation who followed his usual pattern of asking his public relations director to write a speech for him. Due to a collating error, the script contained two copies of page five. You guessed it. The president read page five twice—and didn't even realize it.[3]

In legal or legislative testimony, diplomatic speeches, or other situations in which a slight misstatement could have serious consequences, manuscript speaking may be your best means of delivery. Most presentations, however, do not fall into this category. A simple but important rule for most cases, then, is *don't read your presentation.*

Memorized Presentations

If speaking from a script is bad, trying to memorize that script is even worse. You have probably been subjected to a memorized sales pitch from a telemarketer or door-to-door salesperson. If so, you know that the biggest problem of a **memorized presentation**—one recited word for word from memory—is that it *sounds* memorized.

It might seem that memorizing a presentation would help with your nervousness, but memorizing almost guarantees that stage fright will become a serious problem. Speakers who spend great amounts of time simply learning the words of a talk are asking for trouble. During the presentation, they must focus on remembering what comes next instead of getting involved in the meaning of their remarks.

Sometimes it's necessary to memorize parts of a presentation, as referring to notes at a critical moment can diminish your credibility. A salesperson is usually expected to know a product's major features: how much horsepower it has, how much it costs, or how many copies per minute it delivers. A personnel manager might be expected to know, without referring to a brochure, the value of employee life insurance (if each employee's is the same) and how much employees contribute to the premium. A coworker would look foolish at a retirement dinner if she said, "Everybody knows about Charlie's contributions. . . ." and then had to pause to refer to her notes. For such situations, you can memorize essential *parts* of a presentation.

Extemporaneous Presentations

An **extemporaneous presentation** is planned and rehearsed but not memorized word for word. When you speak extemporaneously, you learn your key points and become familiar with the support you'll use to back them up. In other words, you practice the big picture but let the specific words come naturally during your delivery. If you prepare carefully and practice your presentation several times with a friend, a family member, or even a group of coworkers or subordinates, you have a good chance of delivering an extemporaneous talk that seems spontaneous—and maybe even effortless. Virtually every presentation you plan—a sales presentation, a talk at the local high school, a progress report to a

management review board, a training lecture, an annual report to employees or the board of directors—should be delivered extemporaneously.

A good extemporaneous presentation should be carefully rehearsed, but it will never be exactly the same twice because you will be speaking *with* the audience, not *at* them. One speaking coach explained:

> I tell presenters to strive for dialogue behavior in a monologue setting. Dialogue behavior is two people talking across a kitchen table—it's comfortable and natural, and you don't have to think much about it. Monologue behavior is a presenter talking stiffly to his slides.[4]

Extemporaneous speakers use notes for reminders of the order and content of ideas. There is no single best format for these notes. Some speakers prefer abbreviated outlines, while others find that index cards with keywords or phrases work best. One hint if you use note cards: It is a good idea to have them hole-punched and clipped on a ring, so they can't scatter if dropped. If you don't want to put them on a ring, you can number the back of each card, so you can quickly put them in the correct order.

Whatever form you use, your speaking notes should have the following characteristics.

Notes Should Be Brief   Overly detailed notes tempt a speaker to read them. Inexperienced salespeople who rely on a brochure, for instance, often wind up reading to their prospective customers. More experienced salespeople might be able to use the brochure's boldface headings as a guide. If you are using presentation software, the points on your slides may be all you need to guide you.

Notes Should Be Legible   Your words shouldn't turn into meaningless scribbles when you need them. The writing on your notes should be neat and large enough to be read at a glance. Better yet, print them out in an easy-to-read typeface and size. The font size should be large enough for you to read it at a quick glance.

Stand or Sit?

The decision whether to sit or stand during any presentation will be based on your goals for that presentation. Certainly, in a large room without amplification, you'll need to stand to be seen and heard. It would seem awkward and unnecessary to stand when presenting to one other person over coffee. There are other times, however, when the decision to sit or stand could go either way.

Consider standing when you want to:

- Be perceived as taking charge.
- Be able to breathe and project better.

- See and be seen by the audience and maintain eye contact.
- Stand out from other speakers, who may be seated.

Consider sitting when you want to:

- Be seen as building rapport with the group.
- Be considered part of the team.
- Avoid being labeled arrogant or show stealing.

Source: Daly, J. A., & Engleberg, I. N. (2008). *Presentations in everyday life* (3rd ed.). Boston, MA: Allyn & Bacon.

Notes Should Be Unobtrusive   Most audiences won't be offended if you speak from notes as long as they aren't distracting. Flapping a sheet of paper in your hand or shuffling several sheets of paper on a lectern can become a noisy irritation. Some speakers avoid such problems by providing their listeners with a printed handout, which they also use for their own notes. That can be a fine idea as long as the handout is brief enough that it doesn't tempt the audience to read instead of listen.

Impromptu Presentations

Sooner or later you will be asked to give an **impromptu presentation**—an unexpected, off-the-cuff talk. A customer might stop in your office and ask you to describe the new model you'll have next spring. At a celebration dinner, you may be asked to "say a few words." A manager might ask you to "give us some background on the problem" or to "fill us in on your progress." You may suddenly discover at a weekly meeting that your subordinates are unaware of a process they need to know about in order to understand the project you are about to explain.

Giving an impromptu talk needn't be as threatening as it seems. Most of the time, you will be asked to speak about a subject within your expertise—such as a current project, a problem you've solved, or a technical aspect of your training—which means you have thought about it before. Another reassuring fact is that most listeners won't expect perfection in unrehearsed remarks.

Your impromptu presentations will be most effective if you follow these guidelines.[5]

Anticipate When You May Be Asked to Speak   Most impromptu speaking situations won't come as a complete surprise. You may be an "expert" on the subject under discussion or at least one of the people most involved in a situation. Or perhaps your knowledge of the person in charge suggests impromptu remarks are to be expected. Just in case you are asked to speak, your remarks will be better planned and delivered if you prepare yourself.

Focus on Your Audience and the Situation   Think about your audience and the situation in which you'll be speaking. What is on your listeners' minds? What are their attitudes? What are the circumstances in which you are speaking? The more you can ground your remarks in the context, the better.

Accept the Invitation with Assurance   Try to look confident, even if you're less than delighted about speaking. If you stammer, stall, or look unhappy, your audience will doubt the value of your remarks before you say a word. Once asked, you're going to speak whether or not you want to. You might as well handle the situation well.

Organize Your Thoughts   To avoid rambling, use the few moments before you speak to sketch an outline—jotted down if possible. It can follow the introduction-body-conclusion format described in Chapter 9. When you speak, state your thesis in the first moments you are addressing the audience: "I see several problems with that idea," or "From my experience with the Digitech project, I think our cost projections are low." If you aren't sure what your opinion is, present that thesis: "I'm not sure which approach we ought to take. I think we need to look at both of them closely before we decide."

Label each of your main points as you cover it in the body of your remarks: "My first point is that. . . ." Then conclude by restating your thesis.

Present Reasons, Logic, or Facts to Support Your Viewpoint   As with any presentation, your points will be clearer and more persuasive when you back them up with supporting material: statistics, examples, comparisons, and so forth. Of course, this information won't be as detailed as it would be if you had been able to prepare it in advance, but provide some evidence or explanation to support your points: "As I recall, the Digitech job ran 10 percent over estimate on materials and 15 percent over on labor."

Don't Apologize   Nobody expects a set of impromptu remarks to be perfectly polished, so it is a mistake to highlight your lack of knowledge or preparation. Remarks like "You caught me off guard" or "I'm not sure whether this is right" are unnecessary. If you really don't have anything to contribute, say so.

Don't Ramble   Many novice speakers make the mistake of delivering their message and then continuing to talk: "So that's my point: I think the potential gains make the risk worthwhile. Sure, we'll be taking a chance, but look what we stand to win. That's why I think it's not just a matter of chance, but a calculated risk, and one that makes sense. We'll never know unless we try, and. . . ." The speaker needed only one sentence to conclude: "I think the risk is worth taking."

• Guidelines for Delivery

Choosing the best method of delivery will help make your presentations effective, but it is no guarantee of total effectiveness. Your speeches will be better if you also consider the visual and vocal elements of delivery: how you look, what words you use, and how you sound.

Visual Elements

A major part of good delivery is how a speaker looks. You can improve your visual effectiveness by following several guidelines.

CULTURE **at work**

Speaking to International Audiences

Developing a presentation for any audience takes careful planning. When your listeners come from a background different from yours, extra thought is required. The following tips will boost the odds of achieving your goal with a diverse audience.

1. *If in doubt, address listeners more formally than usual.* As a rule, business is conducted more informally in the United States and Canada than in many other parts of the world. What seems friendly in much of North America may be perceived as disrespectful elsewhere.

2. *Make your presentation highly structured.* Be sure to follow the guidelines in this chapter for organizing a presentation. Have a clear introduction in which you identify your thesis and preview your remarks. Highlight key points during the body of your presentation, using a clear organizational pattern. Conclude with a summary of your main ideas.

3. *Use standard English.* Most non-native speakers learned English in school, so avoid idioms and jargon that may be unfamiliar. Whenever possible, use simple words and sentences. Also, use nouns instead of pronouns whenever possible to minimize confusion.

4. *Speak slightly more slowly than usual.* However, don't raise the volume of your voice: Shouting won't make you easier to understand.

5. *Use handouts.* Most non-native audience members will have higher reading than listening comprehension, so printed supporting materials will help them understand and remember your points. Providing listeners with printed information in advance of your presentation will make it easier for them to follow your remarks.

6. *Consult with a local coach.* Share your remarks with someone familiar with your audience before the presentation to make sure your ideas are clear and free of blunders that will undermine your credibility.

Sources: Adapted from Pearson, L. (1996, April). Think globally, present locally. *Presentations, 68,* pp. 20–27; Schmidt, K. (1999, September). How to speak so you're open to interpretation. *Presentations, 68,* pp. 126–127.

Dress Effectively   Appearance is important in any setting. How you dress is even more important when you get up to speak. You may be able to hide a rumpled suit behind your desk or get away with wearing clothes more casual than usual office norms dictate the day you move your office furniture. But that's not the case when you get up to give your financial report at the annual meeting or present your latest proposal to top management. Generally speaking, you should follow the norms of professional dress for your organization and the tips in Chapter 4.

But dressing effectively doesn't always mean dressing up. If the occasion calls for casual attire, an overly formal appearance can be just as harmful as being under dressed. Automotive consultant Barry Isenberg found an informal appearance contributed to his success as a leading speaker. While waiting to speak to an audience of hundreds of auto wreckers at a day-long seminar, Isenberg looked on as an attorney dressed impeccably in a three-piece suit gave an organized talk on warranties. Despite the importance of the topic, the audience was obviously bored silly. Isenberg rushed upstairs to his hotel room and changed out of his business suit and into the attire of his listeners—casual pants and an open-neck shirt. When his turn to speak arrived, Isenberg moved out from behind the lectern and adopted a casual speaking style that matched his outfit. Afterward, a number of listeners told Isenberg he was the first speaker who seemed to understand their business.[6]

Step Up to Speak with Confidence and Authority   Employees are often surprised to discover their forceful, personable superiors completely lose their effectiveness when they have to address a group of people—and show this before they say a word. Speakers who fidget with their hands or their clothing while waiting to speak, approach the podium as if they were about to face a firing squad, and then fumble with their notes and the microphone send the nonverbal message, "I'm not sure about myself or what I have to say." An audience will discount even the best remarks with such a powerful nonverbal preface.

Your presentation begins the moment you come into your listeners' view. Act as if you are a person whose remarks are worth listening to.

Get Set before Speaking   If you need an easel or projection screen, move it into position before you begin. If a lectern needs repositioning, do it before you begin your talk. The same goes for the other details that come with so many presentations: Adjust the microphone, close the door, reset the air conditioner, rearrange the seating.

Just as important, be sure to position yourself physically before beginning. Some speakers blurt out their opening remarks, usually out of nervousness, before they are set in their speaking position. A far better approach is to stand or walk to the position from which you will talk, get set, wait a brief moment (a "power pause") while you connect with your audience, and then begin speaking.

Begin without Looking at Your Notes   Make contact with the audience as you begin speaking. You can't establish a connection if you are reading from notes. You can memorize the precise wording of your opening statement, but it isn't really necessary. Whether you say, "I have a new process that will give you more reliable results at a lower cost" or "My new process is more reliable and costs less" isn't critical: The important thing is to make your point while speaking directly to your listeners.

Establish and Maintain Eye Contact   A speaker who talks directly to an audience will be seen as more involved and sincere. Whether you're proposing an innovative new product line, reassuring your employees about the effects of recent budget cuts, or trying to convince a group of local citizens your company is interested in curbing pollution, your impression on the audience can ultimately determine your success.

This kind of immediacy comes in great part from the degree of eye contact between speaker and listeners. Use the moment before you speak to establish a relationship with your audience. Look around the room. Get in touch with the fact that you are talking to real human beings: people you work with, potential customers who have real problems and concerns you can help with, and so on. Let them know by your glance that you are interested in them. Be sure your glance covers virtually everyone in the room. Look about randomly: A mechanical right-to-left sweep of the group will make you look like a robot. Many speech consultants recommend taking in the whole room as you speak. If the audience is too large for you to make eye contact with each person, choose a few people in different parts of the room, making eye contact with each one for a few seconds.

Stand and Move Effectively   Table 11-1 describes some effective and ineffective ways to stand and move when you are speaking. The best stance for delivering a presentation is relaxed but firm. The speaker's feet are planted firmly on the ground and spaced at shoulder width. The body faces the audience. The head is upright, turning naturally to look at the audience.

Having good posture doesn't mean standing rooted to the ground. Moving about can add life to your presentation and help release nervous energy. You can approach and refer to your visual aids, walk away from and return to your original position, and approach the audience. Your actions should always be purposeful, though. Nervous pacing might make a speaker feel better, but it will turn listeners into distracted wrecks.

Table 11-1	Common Interpretations of Speaker's Body Language

Viewed as dictatorial or arrogant:

- Crossed arms
- Pounding fists
- Hands on hips
- Pointing index finger
- Hands behind back
- Hands in "steeple" position
- Hands on lapel or hem of jacket
- Preening gestures

Viewed as insecure or nervous:

- Gripping the lectern
- Chewing on objects, cuticles, fingernails, lips
- Constant throat clearing
- Playing with hair, beard, jewelry
- Rocking back and forth
- Rubbing or picking at clothes or body
- Clenched fists
- Jingling coins or keys in pockets or hands
- Repeatedly putting glasses on and taking them off
- Slouching
- Standing extremely rigidly

Viewed as open and confident:

- Open hands
- Expansive gestures
- Stepping out from behind the lectern
- Walking toward and into the audience
- Animated facial expressions
- Dramatic pauses
- Confident and consistent eye contact

Source: Bocher, D. (2003). *Speak with confidence: Powerful presentations that inform, inspire and persuade.* New York, NY: McGraw-Hill.

If you're addressing a small group, such as four or five employees or potential customers, it may be more appropriate to sit when you're delivering a presentation. Generally, the same rules apply in such cases. You should sit up straight and lean forward—lounging back in your chair or putting a foot up on the desk indicates indifference or even contempt. Sit naturally; your behavior should be as direct and animated as it would be if you were conversing with these people—which, in a way, you are.

Don't Pack Up Early   Gathering your notes or starting for your seat before concluding is a nonverbal statement you're anxious to get your presentation finished. Even

Cheerleader Sales Reps

Anyone who has spent time in a physician's waiting room has probably noticed pharmaceutical sales representatives seeking the doctor's attention. Observation is likely to show that many, if not most, of those reps are young and attractive. One physician noted, "There's a saying that you'll never meet an ugly drug rep."

A *New York Times* story revealed many of these good-looking salespeople are former university cheerleaders. A Memphis, Tennessee, employment agency named Spirited Sales Leaders (SSL) specializes in providing former cheerleaders to organizations.

Recruiters and industry officials, however, insist that attractiveness isn't the main criterion for choosing good-looking sales reps. "It's the personality," says Lamberto Andreotti, president of worldwide pharmaceuticals for Bristol-Myers Squibb.

Source: Saul, S. (2005, November 28). Gimme an Rx! Cheerleaders pep up drug sales. *New York Times*, p. A1.

---

if you are, advertising the fact will only make your audience see the presentation as less valuable. Keep your attention focused on your topic and the audience until you are actually finished.

Pause, Then Move Out Confidently

Be certain you drop your pitch to end your remarks so you clearly indicate you are finished. A raised pitch sounds questioning and unsure, and it leaves the audience wondering whether you are finished. When you end your remarks (or finish answering questions and recapping your thesis), pause, then move out smartly. Even if you are unhappy with yourself, don't shuffle off dejectedly or stomp away angrily. Most speakers are their own greatest critics, and there is a good chance the audience rated you more favorably than you did. If you advertise your disappointment, however, you might persuade them you really were a flop.

Verbal Elements

The words you choose are an important part of your delivery. As you practice your presentation, keep the following points in mind.

Use an Oral-Speaking Style

Spoken ideas differ in structure and content from written messages. The difference helps explain why speakers who read from a manuscript sound so stuffy and artificial. When addressing your audience, your speech will sound normal and pleasing if it follows these simple guidelines:

- *Keep most sentences short.* Long, complicated sentences may be fine in a written document, where readers can study them until the meaning is clear. But in an oral presentation your ideas will be easiest to understand if they are phrased in brief statements. Complicated sentences can leave your listeners confused: "Members of field staff, who are isolated from one another and work alone most of the time, need better technology for keeping in touch with one another while in the field as well as while working from a home office." The ideas are much clearer when delivered in briefer chunks: "Members of the field staff work alone most of the time. This makes it hard for them to keep in touch with one another and with the home office. They need better means of technology to stay in contact."

- *Use personal pronouns freely.* Speech that contains first-person and second-person pronouns sounds more personal and immediate. Instead of saying, "People often ask," say "You might ask." Likewise, say, "Our sales staff found," not "The sales staff found."

- *Use active voice.* Active voice sounds more personal and less stuffy than passive use of verbs. Saying, "It was decided" isn't as effective as saying, "We decided." Do not say, "The meeting was attended by 10 people"; say "Ten people attended the meeting."

- *Use contractions.* Unless you need the complete word for emphasis, contractions sound much more natural. Instead of saying, "We do not expect many changes," say "We don't expect many changes." Rather than saying. "I do not know; I will find out and give you an answer as soon as possible," say "I don't know; I'll find out and give you an answer as soon as possible."

- *Address your listeners by name.* Using direct forms of address makes it clear you are really speaking to your listeners and not just reading from a set of notes. Personalized statements will help build rapport and keep an audience listening: "Frank, you and your colleagues in the payroll office are probably wondering how these changes will affect you"; "Ms. Diaz, it's a pleasure to have the chance to describe our ideas to you this morning."

Don't Emphasize Mistakes   Even the best speakers forget or bungle a line occasionally. The difference between professionals and amateurs is the way they handle such mistakes. The experts simply go on, adjusting their remarks to make the error less noticeable.

Usually, an audience won't even be aware of a mistake. If listeners don't have a copy of your speaking outline, they won't know about the missing parts. Even if they notice you have skipped a section in a brochure you're going over with them or in a prepared outline you've distributed after your speech for their reference, they'll assume you did it on purpose, perhaps to save time. If you lose your place in your notes, a brief pause will be almost unnoticeable—as long as you don't emphasize it by frantically pawing through your notes.

What about obvious mistakes, such as citing the wrong figures, mispronouncing a name, or trying to use equipment that doesn't work? The best response here is again the least noticeable. "Let me correct that. The totals are for the first quarter of the year, not just for March," you might say and then move on. When technology fails, adapt and move on: "The chart with those figures seems to be missing. Let me summarize it for you."

Finally, don't emphasize what you *didn't* do ("I didn't have time to create a chart like I wanted to"); instead, emphasize what you *did* do ("I researched the sales figures for the past five years").

Use Proper Vocabulary, Enunciation, and Pronunciation   The language of a board of directors' meeting or a formal press conference is different from that of an informal gathering of sales representatives at a resort. Each situation will call for varying amounts of formality in terms of address, jargon, slang, and so forth. It is important to choose language appropriate to the particular setting.

Using Your Smartphone to Analyze Delivery

Seeing yourself from the audience's point of view can be an effective way to analyze and improve your delivery in presentations. A smartphone (or digital camera) that can record video is all you need.

After recording your presentation, view it carefully, taking notes along the way. Make two columns labeled "Liked" and "Didn't Like." Then jot down both your strengths and the areas to improve as you watch the video four times:

- *As Is:* Replay the video in its original form, just as it would appear to an audience.

- *Muted:* Now watch yourself with no audio. Pay attention to your physical presence: posture, gestures, facial expressions, and so on.

- *Audio Only:* Listen to your voice without any video. Are you easy to understand? Fluent? Enthusiastic? Are you pronouncing words correctly and enunciating clearly?

- *Fast Forward:* Finally, speed up the video and see whether any important expressions, mannerisms, or other movements become apparent.

This simple exercise will give you both a sense of your delivery strengths and a list of areas to work on.

It is also important to pronounce your words correctly. Few mistakes will erode your credibility or irritate an audience as quickly as mispronouncing an important term or name: The word is *scenario,* not *screenario,* and the author of this book likes to be called *Adler,* not *Alder.* Enunciation—articulating words clearly and distinctly—is also important. "We are comin' out with a new data processin' system" makes the speaker sound ignorant to many people, even if the ideas are good.

Vocal Elements

How you sound is just as important as what you say and how you look. Speakers' voices are especially effective at communicating their attitudes about themselves, their topics, and their listeners: enthusiasm or disinterest, confidence or nervousness, friendliness or hostility, respect or disdain. The following guidelines are important elements in effective communication.

Speak with Enthusiasm and Sincerity   If you don't appear to feel strongly about the importance of your topic, there's little chance your audience will. Yet professionals often seem indifferent when they present ideas they're deeply committed to.[7]

The best way to generate enthusiasm is to think of your presentation as sharing ideas you truly believe in and speak with conviction, in your own style. Consultant Roger Ailes makes this point emphatically:

> The truth is, no one can manufacture an image for anyone. If you want to improve or enhance yourself in some way, the only thing a consultant can do for you is to advise and guide you. We can point out assets and liabilities in your style and we then offer substitutions and suggestions to aid you. You have to want to improve and work at it. Most importantly, whatever changes you make have to conform to who you really are—at your best. All the grooming suggestions, all the speech coaching, all the knowledge about lighting, staging, and media training—everything popularly associated with "image-making"—won't work if the improvements don't fit comfortably with who you essentially are.[8]

In the stress of making a presentation, you might forget how important your remarks are. To prevent this, remind yourself of why you are speaking in the moments before you speak. Thinking about what you want to say can put life back into your delivery.

Speak Loudly Enough to Be Heard   At the very least, a quiet voice makes it likely that listeners won't hear important information. In addition, listeners often interpret an overly soft voice as a sign of timidity or lack of conviction. ("He just didn't sound very sure of himself.") Shouting is offensive too ("Does she think she can force her product down our throats?"), but a speaker ought to project enough to be heard clearly and to sound confident.

Avoid Disfluencies   **Disfluencies** are those stammers and stutters ("eh," "um," and so forth) that creep into everyone's language at one time or another. Other "filler words" are "ya know," "like," "so," "OK," and so on. A few disfluencies will be virtually unnoticeable in a presentation; in fact, without them, the talk might seem overly rehearsed and stilted. An excess of jumbles, stumbles, and fillers, however, makes a speaker sound disorganized, nervous, and uncertain. In cases where disfluencies are extreme, listeners may stop listening to the content of your ideas and instead start counting the number of times you say "like" or "ya know."

Vary Your Speech   Just as in your best everyday speaking style, the rate, pitch, and volume of your speech in a presentation should vary. Let your genuine enthusiasm for the topic and situation drive your speaking style, just as it does in your everyday conversations. Be sure to slow down and speak slightly louder when you are stating your thesis and your main points, however. Your audience understands such cues to mean, "This is important."

Use Pauses Effectively   Don't be afraid of silence; it can be used for emphasis, to give your audience time to consider what you've presented, to formulate an answer to a question you've posed, or to indicate the importance of what you've just said. Being comfortable with pauses indicates you're comfortable in the role of speaker; every second does not have to be filled in with words.

● Question-and-Answer Sessions

The chance to answer questions on the spot is one of the biggest advantages of oral presentations. Whereas a written report might leave readers confused or unimpressed, your on-the-spot response to questions and concerns can win over an audience.

Audience questions are a part of almost every business and professional talk from sales presentations and training sessions to boardroom meetings. Sometimes question-and-answer sessions are a separate part of the presentation. Other times, they are mingled with the speaker's remarks. In any case, a skillful response to questions is essential.

When to Answer Questions

The first issue to consider is whether you should entertain questions at all. Sometimes you have no choice, of course. If the boss interrupts your talk to ask for some facts or figures, you're not likely to rule the question out of order. But there may be cases when time or the risk of being distracted will lead you to say something like, "Because we only have 10 minutes on the agenda, I won't have time for questions. If any of you do have questions, see me after my presentation or during the break or lunch."[9] If your presentation does call for questions from the audience, you can pretty much control when they are asked.

Use your smartphone, flipcam, or webcam to capture a rehearsal of a presentation you are planning. If possible, present your remarks to at least one or two listeners, who will represent your real audience.

After your presentation, review the recording and note the effectiveness of your delivery in each of the following areas.

Visual Elements

_____ I dressed effectively.

_____ I stepped up with confidence and authority.

_____ I got set before speaking.

_____ I began speaking without looking at notes.

_____ I maintained eye contact throughout my presentation.

_____ I stood and moved effectively.

_____ Upon conclusion, I paused and then moved out confidently.

Verbal Elements

_____ I used an oral-speaking style.

_____ I didn't emphasize my mistakes.

_____ I used proper vocabulary, enunciation, and pronunciation.

Vocal Elements

_____ I spoke with enthusiasm and sincerity.

_____ I spoke loudly enough to be heard.

_____ I avoided disfluencies.

_____ I varied the rate, pitch, and volume of my voice.

_____ I used pauses effectively.

Your first rehearsal will probably reveal things you want to change about your delivery. After noting areas you want to improve, record and review the presentation again. Repeat this process until you are satisfied with the results.

During the Presentation   Speakers often encourage their listeners to ask questions during a talk. This approach lets you respond immediately to your listeners' concerns. If people are confused, you can set them straight by expanding on a point; if they have objections, you can respond to them on the spot.

Dealing with your listeners' questions during a talk does have its drawbacks. Some questions are premature, raising points you plan to discuss later in your talk. Others are irrelevant and waste both your time and other listeners'. If you decide to handle questions during a talk, follow the guidelines below.

Allow for extra time   Answering questions sometimes occupies as much time as your planned talk. A 15-minute report can run 30 minutes or longer with questions. If your time is limited, keep your remarks brief enough to leave time for the audience to respond.

Minimizing Audience Interruptions

A few interruptions can rattle even confident speakers. The following tips can help minimize the chances that deliberate or unintentional interruptions throw you off:

- Post a sign outside the room warning a presentation is in progress, and close the doors to the room before you begin speaking.

- Program telephones in the room to ring elsewhere, or activate voice mail to prevent them from ringing during your talk.

- Ask your audience to turn off their cell phones and laptops for the duration of the presentation.

- Ask that questions and comments be held until the end of your presentation (if you won't be comfortable responding to them during your talk).

- Let the audience know when there will be a break in the presentation.

- Check with service personnel or post notices outside the room to be sure refreshments aren't delivered in the middle of your presentation.

- Be certain that setup for another event isn't about to begin in your room before you are finished. (This is especially important if you are the last speaker in a program.)

Promise to answer premature questions later Don't feel obligated to give detailed responses to every question. If you plan to discuss the information requested by a questioner later in your talk, say, "That's a good question; I'll get to that in a moment."

After the Presentation

Postponing questions until after your prepared remarks lets you control the way your information is revealed. You don't have to worry about someone distracting you with an irrelevant remark or raising an objection you plan to answer. You also have much better control over the length of your talk, lessening the risk you'll run out of time before you run out of information.

On the other hand, when you deny listeners the chance to speak up, they may be so preoccupied with questions or concerns they miss much of what you say. For instance, you might spend half your time talking about product benefits while your listeners keep wondering whether they can afford it. In addition, because most of the information people recall is from the beginning and the end of presentations, you risk having your audience remember the high price you mentioned during the question-and-answer session or the sticky question you couldn't answer rather than the high quality you proved in your presentation.

How to Manage Questions

Whether you handle them during or after a presentation, questions from the audience can be a challenge. Some are confusing. Others are thinly veiled attacks on your position: "How much time have you New York folks spent out here in the Midwest?" Still other questions are off the topic you're discussing: "Your talk about film projectors was very interesting. I wonder, do you ever teach classes on making films?" You can handle questions most effectively by following the suggestions below.

Start the Ball Rolling

Sometimes listeners may be reluctant to ask the first question. You can get a question-and-answer session rolling with your own remarks: "One question you might have is . . . ," or "The other day someone asked whether. . . ." You can also encourage questions nonverbally by leaning forward as you invite the audience to speak up. You might even raise your hand as you ask for questions.

Faking Your Feelings

Every speaker wants to appear confident and enthusiastic. But sometime during the course of your speaking career, you are likely to face an audience when you do not feel self-assured or enthusiastic about your topic. How can you reconcile the ethical demand to be honest with the pragmatic reality that business communicators are sometimes asked to present ideas they do not personally like?

Suppose, for instance, you have been asked to introduce a colleague you dislike and believe is unqualified for his or her job to a group of new employees or customers. How would you handle this challenge? Or imagine your supervisor created a proposal for your department to share certain equipment with another department. You do not favor the proposal because you foresee conflicts in completing work on time. Because you are enthusiastic and well liked in all departments, your supervisor asks you to present the proposal to the other department "with your usual enthusiasm and persuasion." What do you do?

You may choose to use the interviewing skills described in Chapter 6 to ask experienced communicators how they face these challenges. On the basis of their answers and your own thoughts, develop a policy on how accurately your public demeanor should reflect your private misgivings.

Anticipate Likely Questions   Put yourself in your listeners' position. What questions are they likely to ask? Is there a chance they will find parts of your topic hard to understand? Might some points antagonize them? Just as you prepare for an important exam by anticipating the questions likely to be asked, you should prepare responses to the inquiries you're likely to receive.

Clarify Complicated or Confusing Questions   Make sure you understand the question by rephrasing it in your own words: "If I understand you correctly, Tom, you're asking why we can't handle this problem with our present staff. Is that right?" Besides helping you understand what a questioner wants, clarification gives you a few precious moments to frame an answer. Finally, it helps other audience members to understand the question. If the audience is large, rephrase every question to make sure it has been heard: "The gentleman asked whether we have financing terms for the equipment."

Treat Questioners with Respect   There's little to gain by antagonizing or embarrassing even the most hostile questioner. You can keep your dignity and gain the other listeners' support by taking every question seriously or even complimenting the person who asks it: "I don't blame you for thinking the plan is far-fetched, Nora. We thought it was strange at first, too, then the more we examined it, the better it looked."

Even when you are certain you are right, you can't win by arguing with audience members. A "yes-but" reply ("Yes, we did exceed the budget, but it wasn't our fault. . . .") is likely to make you sound argumentative or defensive and antagonize the questioner. Instead, you can use a "yes-and" response: "Yes, we did exceed the budget, and that bothers us too. That's why we included an explanation of the problems in our report."[10]

Keep Answers Focused on Your Goal   Don't let questions draw you off track. Try to frame answers in ways that promote your goal: "This certainly is different from the way we did things in the old days when you and I started out, Steve. For instance, the computerized system we have now will cut both our costs and our errors. Let me review the figures once more."

You can avoid offending questioners by promising to discuss the matter with them in detail after your presentation or to send them further information: "I'd be happy to show you the electrical plans, Peggy. Let's get together this afternoon and go over them."

Buy Time When Necessary   Sometimes you need a few moments to plan an answer to a surprise question. You can buy time in several ways. First, *wait for the questioner to finish speaking*. Besides being courteous, this gives you time to mentally compose an answer. Next, you can *reflect the question back to the person who asked it:* "How would you deal with the situation and still go ahead with the project, Mary?" You can also *turn the question to another audience member:* "Chris, you're the best technical person we have. What's the best way to save energy costs?"

Address Your Answer to the Entire Audience   Look at the person asking the question while he or she is asking it, but address your answer to everybody. This approach is effective for two reasons: First, it keeps all the audience members involved instead of making them feel like bystanders. Second, it can save you from getting trapped into a debate with hostile questioners. Most critics are likely to keep quiet if you address your response to the entire group. You may not persuade the person who has made a critical remark, but you can use your answer to gain credibility with everybody else.

Follow the Last Question with a Summary   Because listeners are likely to remember especially well the last words they hear you speak, always follow the question-and-answer session with a brief restatement of your thesis and perhaps a call for your audience to act in a way that accomplishes your purpose for speaking. A typical summary might sound like this:

> I'm grateful for the chance to answer your questions. Now that we've gone over the cost projections, I think you can see why we're convinced this proposal can help boost productivity and cut overhead by almost 10 percent overnight. We're ready to make these changes immediately. The sooner we hear from you, the sooner we can get started.

• Speaking with Confidence

If the thought of making a presentation leaves you feeling anxious, you are in good company. According to Irving Wallace and David Wallechinsky's *Book of Lists,* a sample of 3,000 Americans identified "speaking before a group" as their greatest fear, greater even than death.[11] This doesn't mean most people would rather die than give a speech, but it does underscore the fact that public speaking can be nerve-wracking.

Stage fright—or **communication apprehension**, as communication specialists call it—is just as much a problem for businesspeople as it is for the general population. Communispond, a New York communications consulting firm, surveyed 500 executives and found that nearly 80 percent listed stage fright as their greatest problem in speaking before a group, putting it ahead of such items as "handling hostile interrogators."[12] Another survey found that roughly a third of the population in one city suffered from more-than-normal anxiety about speaking to an audience.[13]

When the demands of a job include presentational speaking, speech anxiety can jeopardize career success.[14] If you get butterflies in your stomach at the thought of giving a speech, if your hands sweat and your mouth gets dry, if you feel faint or nauseated or have trouble thinking clearly, you might be comforted to know that most people, including famous performers, politicians, and business executives who frequently appear before audiences, experience some degree of nervousness about speaking. Although it is common, communication apprehension doesn't have to present a serious problem.

DILBERT © Scott Adams/Dist. By Universal Uclick.

It is reassuring to know that, however anxious you feel, your apprehension isn't as visible as you might fear. In several studies, communicators have been asked to rate their own level of anxiety.[15] At the same time, other people gave their impression of the speaker's level of nervousness. In every case, the speakers rated themselves as looking much more nervous than the observers thought they were. Even when the anxiety is noticeable, it doesn't result in significantly lower evaluations of the speaker's effectiveness.

These research findings are good news for anxious speakers. It's reassuring to know that, even if you are frightened, your listeners aren't likely to recognize the fact or find it distracting. And knowing the audience isn't bothered by your anxiety can actually reduce a major source of nervousness, leading you to feel more confident.

Accept a Moderate Amount of Nervousness

A certain amount of anxiety is not just normal, it's even desirable. One consultant says, "If I had a way to remove all fear of speaking for you, I wouldn't do it. The day you become casual about speaking is the day you risk falling on your face."[16] The threat of botching your presentation can lead to what Edward R. Murrow once called "the sweat of perfection," spurring you to do your best. And the adrenaline rush that comes as you stand up—your body's response to a threatening situation—can make you appear more energetic, enthusiastic, and forceful than if you were more relaxed and casual.

A proper goal, then, is not to eliminate nervousness but to *control* it. As one experienced speaker put it, "The butterflies never go away; it's just that after a while they begin to fly in formation."

The time of greatest nervousness for most speakers is before they even begin speaking, when they are thinking about an upcoming presentation.[17] Once you get under way, your anxiety will likely decrease. Keeping this fact in mind ("It will only get better once I start speaking") may even help reduce your prespeech nervousness.

Speak More Often

Like many unfamiliar activities—ice skating, learning to drive a car, and interviewing for a job, to mention a few—the first attempts at speaking before a group can be unnerving. One source of anxiety is lack of skill and experience. In addition, the very newness of the act is frightening.[18]

Since newness generates anxiety, one way to become a more confident speaker is to speak more. As with other skills, your first attempts should involve modest challenges with relatively low stakes. Speech courses and workshops taught in colleges, corporations, and some community organizations provide opportunities for a group of novices to practice before one another and a supportive instructor. Once on the job, it's a good idea to make a number of beginning presentations to small, familiar audiences about noncritical matters.

Rehearse Your Presentation

Many presentational catastrophes come from inadequate rehearsal. Missing note cards, excessive length, clumsy wording, and confusing material can all be remedied if you practice in advance. As you add more and more technological aids to your presentation, the need for complete and careful rehearsal increases dramatically. Projector bulbs can burn out, extension cords can be too short, Internet connections and presentation files can crash, and microphones can fail. It's better to find out these facts before you face a real audience.

Computer-assisted presentations can create the ultimate presentational nightmare, as these two examples illustrate:

> Multimedia producer Dave Mandala was scheduled to deliver a sophisticated presentation in Hungary. Just to be safe, he shipped himself 12 monitors instead of the 8 he needed. He was horrified to open his metal-framed, cushioned packing cases to find that each one was filled with water.
>
> Craig O'Connor, a telecommuting consultant, used his own equipment to deliver an important talk. Halfway through the presentation, O'Connor's personal calendar program flashed a message onto the two huge projection screens he was using, reminding him of his wife's request to run errands on the way home.[19]

Rehearsals can minimize catastrophes like these. They will also ensure you are familiar with your material by the time you face your audience. As you practice your talk, follow the guidelines below.

Pay Special Attention to Your Introduction and Conclusion
Audiences remember the opening and closing of a talk most clearly. The first and last moments of your presentation have special importance, so make sure you deliver them effectively in a way that makes every word count.

Rehearse on Your Feet, before an Audience
Mental rehearsal has its place, but you won't know if your ideas sound good or if they fit into the available time until you say them aloud. Rehearse several times in front of live listeners. In fact, the more closely the size of your practice audience resembles the number of people you will face in your real presentation, the more confident you will feel.[20] David Green, a curriculum director for Dale Carnegie & Associates, explains: "That's what rehearsal is for—to get your mind off the content and onto connecting with an audience."[21]

Rehearse in a Real Setting
If possible, rehearse in the room where you will actually speak. Make sure you have all the equipment you will need and that it all works.

Focus on Your Topic and the Audience

Thinking about your feelings—especially difficult ones like anxiety—is understandable. But obsessing about your nervousness will only make you more anxious. It's far more productive to focus your energy on the message you are delivering and on the audience to whom you are delivering it. If you believe in what you're saying and you have a genuine desire to have your audience understand and accept your message, then your natural enthusiasm will take over and your nervousness will shrink to a manageable size.

Confidence-Building Strategies

Sooner or later, even the most confident speakers encounter a situation that generates anxiety. When this happens to you, the following tips can help you keep your feelings under control.

- Rehearse your presentation in front of friends or colleagues. Make sure your test audience tells you honestly what works and what doesn't. It's better to learn while there is plenty of time to adjust your approach.

- Wear clothing that projects a professional image. Putting on a new suit jacket or even a freshly pressed shirt and slacks can give you a quick boost of confidence.

- Avoid alcohol, caffeine, and carbonated beverages before speaking.

- Before the presentation, walk around or stretch to relieve stress and burn off excess nervous energy.

- Before speaking, walk around the room and talk with people who will be listening to your presentation. This will help bridge the speaker–listener gap and help you think of audience members as real people.

- Remember, you are sharing what you know with people who want to know it too. Keep the presentation in perspective, and you will do better.

- During the presentation, seek out friendly faces and establish and maintain eye contact. Once you see that people are on your side, your self-confidence will grow.

- Don't try to be like anyone else. It's fine to observe speakers you admire for pointers, but develop your own approach. Recall how effective you are when you are speaking at your best, and use that as the basis of your speaking style.

Think Rationally about Your Presentation

Some speakers feel more apprehensive because of the way they *think* about the speech than because of the act of speaking.[22] Researchers have identified a number of irrational but powerful beliefs that lead to unnecessary apprehension.[23] Among these mistaken beliefs are the following three myths.

Myth: A Presentation Must Be Perfect   Whether you're addressing a meeting of potential clients worth millions of dollars to your company or a small group of trainees, your presentation must be clearly organized, well documented, and effectively delivered. Expecting it to be perfect, though, is a surefire prescription for nervousness. "Practice only makes you better," says Otis Williams Jr., founder of a professional development and training firm in Cincinnati. He continues, "but perfection doesn't exist. The goal is to become so comfortable with what you're saying, it'll roll off your tongue with minimum effort."[24] A talk can be effective without being flawless. The same principle holds for other types of speaking errors. Most listeners won't notice if you omit a point or rearrange an idea or two.

Myth: It Is Possible to Persuade the Entire Audience   Even the best products don't sell to everyone, and even the most talented people don't win the full support of their audiences. It is unrealistic to expect one presentation will achieve everything you are seeking. If you think of your remarks as one step in a campaign to achieve your long-term goals, you will feel less pressure. Chapter 12 offers more tips on how to gradually move your audience toward your ultimate goal.

Myth: The Worst Will Probably Happen   Some pessimistic speakers make themselves unnecessarily nervous by dwelling on the worst possible outcomes. They imagine themselves tripping on the way to the podium, going blank, or mixing up their ideas. They picture the audience asking unanswerable questions, responding with hostility, or even laughing. Even though such disasters are unlikely, these daydreams take on a life of their own and may create a self-fulfilling prophecy: The fearful thoughts themselves can cause the speaker to bungle a presentation.

Replacing this type of self-defeating thinking with more rational beliefs can result in dramatically increased confidence when you face an audience.[25] One way to overcome the irrational fear of failure is to indulge your catastrophic fantasies. Picture yourself fainting from terror, everyone falling asleep, or the boss firing you on the spot. Then consider the slim likelihood these worst-case scenarios are likely to happen. Next, consider the possibility that you will encounter minor problems, such as being interrupted or encountering a technology glitch. Consider how you can manage these challenges and how little they are likely to affect your presentation's success. Now imagine the best possible outcome, such as receiving a standing ovation or an immediate promotion to vice president. And consider more probable positive outcomes such as keeping the audience's attention and achieving your goal. Realize that catastrophes are unlikely and that, to a great extent, you have the power to determine the outcome of your presentation.

review points

- An extemporaneous style of delivery is usually the most effective of the four types (manuscript, memorized, extemporaneous, impromptu) as it combines the enthusiasm of spontaneity with the accuracy of rehearsal. However, manuscript delivery may be necessary for legal or diplomatic reasons.

- A speaker's notes should be brief, legible, and inconspicuous.

- When an impromptu talk is necessary, it is most effective if the speaker presents a clear thesis; supports it with reasons, logic, or facts; speaks without apologizing; and does not ramble.

- Good delivery involves visual, verbal, and vocal elements. Visually, a speaker needs to look enthusiastic and confident by getting set physically and making eye contact before beginning; by maintaining eye contact and moving naturally; and by ending without rushing away.

- Verbally, a speaker should use an oral style, avoid calling attention to mistakes, and use appropriate vocabulary and pronunciation.

- Vocally, a speaker sounds committed to both the topic and the audience when using enough volume, variety, and pauses without disfluencies.

- Question-and-answer sessions are part of almost every presentation, allowing speakers to respond to audiences quickly. Speakers should decide whether to invite questions during or after the prepared presentation. Handling questions during a talk permits the speaker to clarify points as they arise, although there is a risk of getting sidetracked. Responding to questions after the talk lets the speaker control the timing of information.

- Speakers can improve question-and-answer sessions by asking a question if no one else does, anticipating potential questions, clarifying complex questions, addressing the audience with focus and respect, and providing a summary.

- Communication apprehension is common, and a manageable amount of anxiety contributes to an energetic presentation. Keep anxiety within tolerable limits by accepting it as normal, speaking often, rehearsing, being audience-centered (not self-centered), and thinking rationally.

- Rational thought dispels these myths: the speech needs to be perfect to be effective, everyone at a presentation can be persuaded, and that catastrophes are certain.

key terms

communication apprehension   330
disfluencies   326
extemporaneous presentation   316

impromptu presentation   318
manuscript presentation   316
memorized presentation   316

activities

1. Invitation to Insight

With two or more classmates, try the various styles of delivery for yourself. Follow these steps:

a. Begin by choosing a paragraph of text on an appropriate business or professional topic. You can write the copy yourself or select an article from a newspaper, magazine, or some other publication.

b. Read the text to your listeners verbatim. Pay attention to your feelings as you deliver the comments. Do you feel comfortable and enthusiastic? How do your listeners describe your delivery?

c. Try to memorize and then deliver the segment. How difficult is it to recall the remarks? How effective is your delivery? What do you do if you get stuck and can't remember the rest of the passage?

d. Now deliver the same remarks extemporaneously, rephrasing them in your own words. Create a brief set of speaking notes, written as key phrases rather than as complete sentences. Arrange your notes in outline format with an introduction (attention-getter, thesis, and preview), a body (organized according to main points and supporting points), and a conclusion. See whether this approach leaves you more comfortable and your listeners more favorably impressed.

2. Skill Builder

Practice your ability to speak off the cuff by delivering a brief (approximately 1 minute) talk to your group on a topic your instructor has just presented to you or that you have just drawn out of a hat.

Remember to follow the guidelines for impromptu speaking in this chapter as you plan and deliver your remarks. Take a few minutes to organize your thoughts into an identifiable plan: topical, chronological, problem–solution, and so on. Step up with confidence, pause, then begin to present your talk to your classmates. Make sure your introduction and conclusion contain a clear statement of your thesis.

3. Skill Builder

On a sheet of paper, write a phrase that represents one interesting piece of information about yourself you'd like to share with the class. Take turns with your classmates, so each of you has a chance to walk to the front of the room, notes in hand, and share this information with the class. Heed the guidelines for visual elements of delivery. Arrange your notes before your speak. Establish eye contact and a confident posture before you begin speaking. After you finish speaking, maintain eye contact while the audience applauds. Don't pack up your notes and walk away until the audience has completely finished clapping.

4. Invitation to Insight

Scan a current television guide and select a program in which a speaker is making an oral presentation. The subject matter is not important: The show can be educational, religious, political, or news related.

a. Turn down the volume, and observe the speaker's visual delivery. Notice the effects of dress, posture, gesture, facial expression, and eye contact.

b. What do these aspects of delivery suggest about the speaker's status, enthusiasm, sincerity, and competence?

5. Invitation to Insight

Locate a television program or Internet video that involves an oral presentation on some subject. The content is not important. Interview shows are fine, but don't choose shows in which the characters are acting roles other than themselves. Use the criteria in the Self-Assessment on p. 327 to evaluate the quality of delivery. What lessons can you apply to your speaking from your analysis of this speaker?

6. Skill Builder

Practice using an oral-speaking style. Fill in the empty boxes below with examples of effective oral language. A few examples have been completed for you.

Advice	Poor	Better
Keep sentences short.	"Members of field staff, who are isolated from one another and work alone most of the time, need better technology for keeping in touch with one another while in the field as well as with the home office."	"Members of the field staff work alone most of the time. This makes it hard for them to keep in touch with one another and with the home office. They need better means of technology to stay in contact."
	"The idea I'd like to explain to you is that, although avoiding and accommodating seem like polite ways of interacting, it can sometimes be preferable to employ an assertive linguistic style."	
	"A substantial body of research indicates that organizing your remarks clearly can make your messages more understandable, keep your audience happy, and boost your image as a speaker."	
Use personal pronouns.	"People often ask. . . ."	"You might ask. . . ."
	"Those who attempt to use this strategy don't always succeed at first."	
	"Students would be well advised to learn strategies of effective communication."	
	"Members of the audience might like to try this idea."	
Use the active voice.	"It was decided that. . . ."	"We decided that."
	"It has been pointed out that. . . ."	
	"Memorization was tried by some of the most apprehensive student speakers in the class."	
Use contractions.	"We do not expect many changes."	"We don't expect many changes."
	"I will describe the strategies that I have found to be most effective in conducting interviews."	
	"It is important to ponder how often you have been in this situation."	
Address listeners by name.	"We're pleased to present our ideas this morning."	"Ms. Diaz, it's a pleasure to describe our ideas to you this morning."
	"Last week someone gave a speech about wearing seat belts. Tonight I'll build on that theme."	

7. Invitation to Insight

Gain useful insights about managing communication apprehension by interviewing several professionals who frequently deliver presentations. Inquire whether they have ever felt anxiety about speaking in front of others. If so, how have they managed their stage fright?

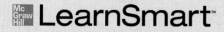

LearnSmart™

For further review, go to the LearnSmart study module for this chapter.

Chapter Twelve
Types of Business Presentations

chapter objectives

After reading this chapter you should be able to:

1. Prepare and deliver the following types of informative presentations: briefing, feasibility report, status report, final report, and training session.

2. Choose the most persuasive organization plan for your topic, audience, and situation.

3. Understand the elements of and be able to construct motivational speeches, goodwill speeches, proposals, and sales presentations.

4. Design a persuasive appeal that is ethical and effective.

5. Distinguish persuasive strategies (problem–solution, comparative advantages, criteria satisfaction, and motivated sequence) and use each in appropriate presentations.

6. Work with others to plan and deliver a group presentation.

7. Prepare and deliver remarks for these special occasions: welcoming remarks, introducing another speaker, honoring a person or institution, giving a toast, and presenting and accepting an award.

After reading this far, you know how to deliver an effective presentation. The information in Chapters 9 through 11 will serve you well, but specific situations call for specific approaches. This chapter offers guidelines for delivering a variety of presentations: informative talks (briefings, reports, training), persuasive talks in various forms, group presentations, and remarks you will make on special occasions (welcoming remarks, introductions, honoring guests or institutions, celebratory toasts, and presenting and accepting awards).

This chapter builds on the skills you have already learned, helping you gain an extra margin of effectiveness that can make your presentations interesting and effective—even outstanding.

• Informative Presentations

Informative presentations are a common feature on the job. You may be called upon to update your boss on the status of your project, to relay information to your teammates you learned from a customer survey, or to teach your coworkers how to use a new software system. In each of these scenarios—whether they are formal or informal—the basic principles of informative presentations will help you organize your remarks. These principles are the building blocks for persuasive presentations too.

Briefings

Briefings are short talks that give already interested and knowledgeable audience members the specific information they need to do their jobs. Some briefings update listeners on what has happened in the past. For example, nurses and police officers attend briefings before each shift to learn what has been happening since their last watch. Other briefings focus on the future. The executive chef of a restaurant might brief waiters about the details of the day's menu specials, and the representative handling an advertising account might brief the agency's team about a client's interests

and quirks before an important meeting. Although used for many purposes, briefings share the following characteristics:

- *Length.* As the name suggests, most briefings are short—usually no more than 2 or 3 minutes on a given subject.
- *Organization.* Because of their brevity, briefings usually don't require the kinds of attention-grabbing introductions or conclusions described in Chapter 9. They are organized simply, usually topically or chronologically.
- *Content.* Briefings may summarize a position ("As you know, we're committed to answering every phone call within 1 minute"), but they usually don't make complex arguments in its favor. Most briefing attendees already know why they are there, and the main focus should be getting them ready to do the job at hand.
- *Presentation aids.* Some briefings may include simple visual aids ("Here's what our new employee ID badges will look like"), but they rarely contain the kind of detail found in longer and more complex presentations.
- *Language and delivery.* Because of their informal nature, briefings are usually quite conversational. Delivery is more matter-of-fact than dramatic.

Here is a sample briefing for a group of representatives who are preparing to staff a start-up company's exhibit booth at a trade show. Notice that the remarks are concise and well organized. They briefly state a thesis ("How we handle ourselves will make a huge difference") and then lay out clear instructions for the sales team.

> This is our first chance to show the public what we've got. The way we handle ourselves the next three days can make a huge difference in our initial year. I know you're up to the job. Here are a couple of last-minute items before we get going.
>
> First, about the brochures: They were supposed to show up today via overnight mail, but they haven't arrived yet. Casey will keep checking with the mail room, and if they aren't here by 9:00, he will head over to the copy shop across the street and print 500 fact sheets we can use until the brochures arrive. So if the brochures are here, we'll use them. If they're not here, we'll hand out the fact sheets.

Technical Reports

There are two types of technical reports: those given to technical audiences (colleagues in your workplace or at technical conferences) and those given to nontechnical audiences (clients and customers with varying levels of expertise or officials in charge of money or decision making who don't share your level of mastery). Follow these guidelines for both types:

- Use language appropriate for your audience. For a nontechnical audience, use understandable language and teach technical terms that are essential to understanding the presentation. For a technical audience that will understand it, use jargon with absolute precision.

- Use analogies to clarify concepts for a nontechnical audience; be certain to point out limits of an analogy.

- Adapt visual aids to the audience. The nontechnical audience needs visuals that make sense to nonexperts; have extra visuals in even simpler formats to use if the audience seems unclear. Knowledgeable audiences appreciate precise data presented in formats common to your field; have extra visuals with more technical data if the audience requires it.

- Watch your audience carefully. If they seem puzzled, try to slow down, reiterate key points, use additional examples, or in a small, interactive group, stop and ask about the puzzled looks. If an audience seems bored or is losing interest, try to become more animated with greater vocal variety and movement.

Source: Hering, L., & Hering, H. (2010). *How to write technical reports: Understandable structure, good design, convincing presentation.* New York, NY: Springer-Verlag.

It's going to get very busy, especially midmorning and midafternoon. You may not have as much time as you'd like to chat with visitors. At the very least, be sure to do three things. First, sign up each person for the drawing for our free Caribbean vacation. The information people give us on the sign-up sheets will help us track who visited our booth.

Second, invite each person to the reception we're giving tomorrow night. Give them one of our printed invitations so they know where and when it is.

Finally—and this is the most important thing—ask them what product they're using and how they like it. If they are happy with their current product, find out what they like about it and show them ways in which they might find ours even easier to use. If they don't like the product they're using, show them the features of ours.

Remember—stay upbeat, and never criticize our competitors. Listen to the customers, and show them how our product can meet their needs. Any questions?

Reports

In a **report,** you give your audience an account of what you or your team has learned or done. Reports come in an almost endless variety. Table 12-1 lists some common types. Some are internal, given to audiences within your organization. Others are external, delivered to outsiders such as clients, agencies, or the general public. Some reports are long and detailed, while others are brief. Some reports are presented formally and others informally. While reports can be delivered either in person or in writing, we'll focus on strategies for organizing those you deliver orally.

An organization's culture determines the manner in which you present a report: brief or elaborate, with or without visual aids and question-and-answer sessions, and so on. Learn the conventions for your audience by watching accomplished colleagues and asking experienced (and successful) coworkers.

Table 12-1	**Common Report Types**

Progress/Status
- Contractor or architect's report to client
- Quarterly financial report to board of directors
- Monthly marketing report to marketing manager
- Annual report to public

Investigative
- Was a customer's complaint justified?
- Why has our overhead increased 15 percent in the last year?
- Is there gender bias in our hiring and promotions?

Feasibility
- Will staying open 24/7 be profitable?
- Can we afford to offer health insurance to part-time staff?

Status Reports   The most common type of informative presentation is the **status report,** sometimes called a *progress report.* In many meetings, you can expect to hear someone ask, "How's the project going?"

The person asking this question usually doesn't want a long-winded blow-by-blow account of everything that has happened since your last report. You will gain your audience's appreciation and boost your credibility by presenting a brief, clear summary of the situation. The following format will serve you well in most situations. Cover each of the points briefly, and expect your listeners to pose questions when they want more information.

1. *Review the project's purpose.*
2. *State the current status of the project.* When relevant, include the people involved (giving credit for their contributions) and the actions you've taken.
3. *Identify any obstacles you have encountered and attempts you have made to overcome those obstacles.* If appropriate, ask for assistance.
4. *Describe your next milestone.* Explain what steps you will take and when they will happen.
5. *Forecast the future of the project.* Focus on your ability to finish the job as planned by the scheduled completion date.

A brief progress report would sound something like this:

On February 3, we were told to come up with an improved website for the company. *[Reviews the project's purpose.]* Paul and I have been exploring the sites of other companies in the field, and we've developed a list of features our site should have. We'll be happy to share it with anybody who is interested. *[Describes the current status of the project. In a longer progress report, the speaker might identify the features and even give examples of them.]*

We know we'll need a website designer soon, and we haven't found anybody locally whose work we like. *[Identifies issues and problems. In a longer report, the speaker might list the shortcomings.]* We welcome any suggestions you might have. If you have some names and contact information, please e-mail them to me.

We plan to pick a designer and have sketches ready by the end of next month. *[Describes next milestone.]* If we can do that, we should be able to have the new website up by the end of March, right on schedule. *[Forecasts the future of the project.]*

Final Reports   As its name suggests, a **final report** is delivered upon completion of an undertaking. The length and formality of a final report will depend on the scope of that undertaking. If you are describing a weekend conference to your colleagues, it would most likely be short and informal. On the other hand, a task force reporting to top management or the general public on a year-long project would most likely deliver a more detailed and formal report. You can adjust the following guidelines to fit your situation:

1. *Introduce the report.* State your name and your role unless everyone in the audience already knows you. Briefly describe the undertaking you are reporting on.

2. *Provide necessary background.* Tell your listeners what they need to know to understand why the project was undertaken, why you and others became involved, and any other factors that affected your approach.

3. *Describe what happened.* Explain what happened during the undertaking. Aim this discussion at the level of interest appropriate for your audience. For example, if others will be following in your footsteps, give details of challenges and how you dealt with them. If other persons were involved, mention them and offer your thanks.

4. *Describe the results.* Report on the outcomes of the undertaking. Include a discussion of successes and failures. Describe any future events related to your topic.

5. *Tell listeners how to get more information.*

An abbreviated final report might sound like this:

Hi, everybody. My name is Betsy Lane, and I'm the chair of our county's United Way campaign. *[Self-introduction.]*

As you know, United Way is dedicated to helping people in our community to help themselves develop healthier, more productive lives. We support more than 50 agencies that provide a multitude of services: promoting wellness for all ages and abilities, making sure all children enter school ready to learn, helping people toward lifetime independence, sustaining safe neighborhoods, and educating young people for responsible adulthood. The need and the opportunities are great, and we set the bar high this year: $3 million. *[Provides necessary background.]*

This has been an especially challenging year for local nonprofits: The economy has been on the weak side, and there are more deserving causes and people needing support than ever. Rather than letting this situation discourage us, it energized the United Way team. This year we were fueled by the efforts of almost 2,500 volunteers at more than 400 organizations, large and small. Every one of them gave generously of their time and talents. *[Describes what happened.]*

I am delighted to tell you that, as of last Friday, we met our goal. The campaign has raised more than $3 million in donations and pledges for the coming year. This means we won't have to say no to a single organization. *[Describes results.]*

There is so much to tell you about this campaign and the work of so many terrific people. We do hope you'll read more about the effort that led to this year's success. Our report will be available in about three weeks, and in the meantime you can read the highlights on the United Way website. *[Tells listeners how to get more information.]*

For now, though, let's celebrate!

Feasibility Reports   A **feasibility report** evaluates one or more potential action steps and recommends how the organization should proceed. Would a bonus system increase profitability and retain employees? Is job-sharing a good idea? Would subsidizing employees who use public transportation solve the parking problem? Feasibility studies help answer questions like these.

Most feasibility reports should contain the following elements.

1. *Introduction.* Briefly define the problem and explain its consequences. Explain why it is important to consider the alternatives you will be discussing. Briefly show the audience you have approached this problem methodically. Consider explaining your conclusions if the audience won't object strongly. If listeners are likely to object to your recommendation, consider postponing it until later in your presentation.

2. *Criteria.* Introduce the standards you used to evaluate alternative courses of action. For example:

   - Will the course of action really do what's wanted?
   - Can we implement it?
   - Will implementation fit within time constraints?
   - Can we afford it?

   Explaining your criteria is especially important if your recommendations are likely to be controversial. It's hard for anyone to argue with criteria like those above, so getting listeners to accept them before they hear your recommendations can be an effective way of selling your conclusions. (See the criteria satisfaction organization plan in Chapter 9.)

3. *Methodology.* Describe the process you used to identify and evaluate the plan(s) under consideration. The amount of detail you supply will depend on the audience and situation. For a relatively minor project, your explanation will probably be brief. For a major feasibility study—especially when it's controversial or when your credibility is in question—you will probably need to describe your approach in detail.

4. *Possible solutions.* Provide a detailed explanation of each solution you considered.

5. *Evaluation of the solutions.* Measure the suitability of each solution against the criteria you listed earlier. Offer whatever supporting material is necessary to show how you arrived at your conclusions.

6. *Recommendations.* Describe the solution that best fits the criteria provided earlier. If you have done a good job evaluating solutions using the criteria already introduced, the recommendation should be relatively brief and straightforward.

7. *Conclusion.* Briefly summarize your findings, showing how they can help solve the problem at hand.

Training

Training teaches listeners how to *do* something: operate a piece of equipment or use software, relate effectively with the public, avoid or deal with sexual harassment—the range of training topics is almost endless. Training can be informal, such as the simple advice an experienced employee gives a newcomer about how to transfer a telephone call. At the other end of the spectrum, some training is extensive and highly organized. Corporations including Disney, Anheuser-Busch, Dell Computer, Harley-Davidson, and General Electric have full-blown institutes dedicated to training their employees.[1]

Successful businesses recognize the value of training. One measure of its importance is the amount of time and money firms invest in training their employees. The average U.S. employee spends 32 hours per year in formal training sessions, and U.S. companies spend an estimated $171 billion per year on training initiatives.[2] The more technical the job, the more time is spent in training. For example, employees at the biotech firm

Adult Learning Styles

Adults in the workplace learn in ways that are different from the ways they learned in educational institutions from primary school through university. Adults learn best when:

- Material is clearly relevant to their personal lives. Show them what personal value the training program will have for them. Encourage learners to explore and explain how they can use the material you present.

- They take an active role in the training process. Don't just lecture. Give them a chance to experience the principles you are introducing.

- Training is aimed at their level of experience. Go over their heads and you will lose them; approach the topic too simplistically and you will insult and bore them.

- The trainer has some control over the pace of learning. Be prepared to speed up or slow down your coverage in response to feedback from your audience.

Sources: Knowles, M. S. (1996). Adult learning. In R. L. Craig (Ed.), *The ASTD training and development handbook.* New York, NY: McGraw-Hill; Scullard, M., & Sugeman, J. (2009, March 5). Everything DiSC pulse: Challenging your assumptions about e-learning. *Training.* Retrieved from http://www.trainingmag.com/article/everything-disc-pulse-challenging-your-assumptions-about-e-learning

CaridianBCT spend an average of 69 hours per year on training, and brand new sales representatives can spend more than a year receiving hands-on training before they are approved to sell high-tech products and demonstrate procedures.[3]

Some training is done by experts. Large organizations have staffers who design and deliver instructional programs. There are also firms and freelancers who create and deliver training on a fee-for-service basis. Despite the existence of a training industry, the U.S. Bureau of Labor Statistics says that almost 75 percent of all work-related training is delivered informally on the job.[4] This fact suggests that, sooner or later, you will be responsible for designing and delivering training no matter what your job may be. The information that follows will help you do a good job.

Planning a Training Program   A successful training presentation begins long before you face your audience, when you use the guidelines in Chapter 9 (pp. 249–253) to analyze the audience, the occasion, and your own goals and knowledge about the topic. Most training experts agree about the importance of each of the following steps.[5]

Define the training goal   Training always aims to change the way your audience acts, so begin by identifying who you want to teach and the results you want to bring about. The more specifically you can identify the target audience and the desired outcome, the more successful your training will be. You can see the difference between vague and specific goals in these examples:

Vague:	Train employees to deal more effectively with customer complaints.
Better:	Everyone in the Sales and Customer Service departments will know how to use the tactics of listening, asking questions, and agreeing to deal more effectively with customer complaints.
Vague:	Train the staff to use our new online purchasing system.
Better:	Employees who are authorized to buy new and replacement equipment will know how to use the new online purchasing system to locate vendors, place orders, track shipments, and check their department's purchasing budget.

See the discussion of Setting Your Goal and Developing the Thesis in Chapter 9 for more guidelines on defining goals.

Develop a schedule and list of resources   Once you have defined your goals and identified the target audience, you are ready to design the training. This step includes:

- Figuring how much time you will need to plan and publicize the training, and the steps you need to take between now and the time you deliver it.
- Identifying the staffing and physical resources you need, and making sure they are available. Line up the facility, and make sure its furnishings and layout suit your design. Identify the materials participants will need (pens, pencils, folders, name tags or name tents, refreshments, etc.) and the equipment you will use (computer, projection system, lectern, charts, etc.).
- Creating and/or purchasing necessary training materials.

Involve the audience   Lecturing to a passive audience has its place, but it isn't the only way to train an audience. Figure 12.1 lists several ways you can present new information. It shows that listeners who are actively involved in a presentation will understand and remember the material far better than a passive audience.[6] People will learn how to operate a particular machine, fill in a certain form, or perform a specified procedure much better with hands-on experience than they will if they are only told what to do. For example, Lever Corporation trains its representatives to sell industrial cleaning equipment by teaching them to operate the machines themselves.[7]

A variety of other tools involve the audience in a way that boosts both understanding and interest: quizzes, contests, and having trainees teach one another. For example, if you plan to give the audience statistics such as the ethnic makeup of the United States, first present them with blank charts listing major ethnic groups and have them try to fill in the correct percentages. This way, when you present the information, they will be more eager to hear the statistics and see how accurate or inaccurate their estimates were. The few minutes you take to let an audience fill in the blanks measurably enhances interest

FIGURE 12.1

Average Retention Rates of Various Training Methods

An important learning principle, supported by extensive research, is that people learn best when they are actively involved in the learning process. The "lower down the cone" you go, the more you learn and retain.

Source: Reprinted by permission of NTL® Institute for Behavioral Sciences.

People generally remember . . .

Read	**10%** of what they read
Hear a lecture	**20%** of what they hear
Look at exhibits, mock-ups, diagrams, displays	**30%** of what they see
Watch live demonstrations, video, or movies, go on a site visit	**50%** of what they hear and see
Complete worksheets, manuals, discussion guides	**70%** of what they say or write
Simulate a real experience (practice, with coaching) do the real thing	**80%** of what they say as they do an activity

case STUDY

Online Training at Cheesecake Factory

How do you deliver affordable and effective training to a geographically dispersed workforce? Cheesecake Factory, the California-based restaurant chain, has found that one answer lies in social media. The company has created Video Café, an interactive portal that lets employees at the company's 150 restaurants around the country create, view, and share video clips on a variety of topics, including customer service and food preparation.

The online medium has many advantages. It saves time. Clips are short—typically only 2 or 3 minutes—and employees can view them whenever they or their managers see fit. The cost is low. Employees create the videos, which saves thousands in consulting and production costs. Because the clips are produced by Cheesecake Factory staff, the content fits with company protocols and procedures. Finally, the social media portal fits with the media consumption habits of a mostly Millennial workforce.

The company still relies on traditional tools like print materials and face-to-face sessions to teach employees. But adding social media is proving to be a smart option for efficient, effective training.

Sources: Kranz, G. (2011, June 20). Online café serves up a heaping helping of training for staff. *Workforce Management.* Retrieved from http://www.workforce.com/article/20110620/NEWS02/306209997; Chrapaty, D. (2011, June 5). Can online training be personal and interactive?" *Training.* Retrieved from http://trainingmag.com/article/can-online-training-be-personal-and-interactive

in your figures. Similarly, you can create worksheets and surveys that mirror information you'll present. You can also involve the audience by letting them practice the skill you are teaching, having volunteers demonstrate a skill, or pausing for an audience to read a passage silently. You can let the whole audience brainstorm or form small groups to brainstorm and then let each group report back.[8]

Listeners are likely to understand and remember a message when you use more than one approach. You can show a diagram, for example, while you describe it. If you're discussing a physical object, you might display photos of it on slides or even bring in the object itself to show your listeners. If you are illustrating a process, you might decide to play a brief video of it. Talking about a new line of clothing or a new food product isn't nearly as effective as giving your audience a firsthand look or taste, for example. Likewise, telling listeners in a training session how to deal with customer objections isn't nearly as effective as demonstrating the procedure for them or letting them handle a situation themselves.

Organize your presentation Use the tips in this section and see Chapter 9 for methods of organizing the overall presentation. The most reliable format is often a problem–solution approach since listeners are most likely to pay attention to the information you provide when they view it as solving a problem they face.

Delivering the Training
When you finally are ready to deliver the training, several tips can help make it most effective.

Link the topic to the audience Sometimes the intrinsic interest of the subject is reason enough to listen. For instance, most people would pay close attention to a session on employee benefits because they know these benefits are worth something to them personally.

What can you do with a subject that isn't intrinsically interesting? One way to boost interest is to show that listening will help the audience avoid punishment. ("Don't try to charge the company for anything you're not entitled to. If you do, you could lose your job.") A more pleasant and effective alternative involves demonstrating the payoffs that come from listening. A financial officer explaining new expense account procedures, for instance, might begin by saying, "We want to make sure you get the company to reimburse you for all expenses you're entitled to. I also don't want you to spend your own money, thinking the company will pay you back, and then find out it won't." Expense reporting might be a tedious subject to many people, but the chance to save money (or to avoid losing money) would interest most listeners.

Start with an overall picture   Every presentation needs an introduction. But when the goal is to inform listeners, a clear preview is especially important. Without an overview, your listeners can become so confused by your information "trees" that they won't be able to see the conceptual "forest." Orient the audience by sketching the highlights of your message in enough detail to help listeners see what they are expected to know and how you will explain it to them:

> This morning, we're going to learn about the new electronic billing system. I'll start by spending a little time explaining how the system works. Then we'll talk about the three main things you will do with the system. First, I'll show you how to track time you've spent working on different client tasks—and I'll show you how to make corrections, too. After that, I will show you how to add a new client into the system when you take on new projects. Finally, I will show you how to compile, approve, and submit your weekly report to the Accounting Department for client billing.
>
> I'll spend about 10 minutes describing each of these steps in detail, and after each description you'll get a chance to try out the system yourself. And, of course, we'll have time for some Q and A. By the time you leave for lunch, you should be able to use the system like a pro and say good-bye to that stack of billing paperwork!

Emphasize the organization of your material   You can use a number of devices to help listeners understand the structure of your material:

- *Number items:* "The first advantage of the new plan is. . . ." or "A second benefit the plan will give us is. . . ."
- *Use signposts:* "We've talked about the benefits of our new health care plan. Now let's talk about who will provide them"; "*Another* important cost to consider is our overhead"; "*Next,* let's look at the production figures"; and "*Finally,* we need to consider changes in customer demand."
- *Use interjections:* "So what we've learned—and this is important—is that it's impossible to control personal use of office telephones."

DILBERT © Scott Adams/Dist. By Universal Uclick.

Poster Presentations

Most presentations have a clearly defined beginning and ending and are delivered to a fixed group of listeners. Poster sessions are different: They present work to conference attendees who are walking around an exhibit area, choosing the topics that interest them. The presenter usually stands next to the poster, allowing for passersby to engage in one-on-one discussions.

Unlike most presentations in which visual aids support the words, in poster sessions a few words support the visuals. At their best, posters are visual representations of ideas, not just papers or slides tacked on a board. Clear titles allow the viewer to locate sections of interest: goals, methods, conclusions.

Practice your skill in this unique form of communication by preparing a brief poster presentation on a topic about which you are familiar. For example, presentations in a typical group might include "How to choose an internet service provider," "How restaurant menus manipulate customers," or "How to choose an internship."

These guidelines will help you conduct effective poster sessions:

- Design your display for eye-catching viewing at arm's length. Use large type to highlight your key points rather than trying to cover everything you would put in a longer paper. Use display elements—bullets, enumeration, tables, clip art, graphs, figures, photos—rather than paragraph style to convey your points clearly and concisely.

- Prepare a brief (less than 1 minute) explanation of your topic that expands on the information your poster describes. You can deliver this explanation to listeners who ask general questions like, "Tell me more about your work."

- Be prepared to speak louder than you usually would to a small audience. Posters are often displayed in noisy, crowded environments without good acoustics.

- Keep your enthusiasm high, remembering each new person will be hearing your explanation for the first time.

- Be prepared to give interested listeners more information on your work. A handout with more details and/or a website or e-mail address can let them follow up.

Sources: Adapted from Coffin, C., & Health Care Communication Group. (2001). Planning and preparing an effective scientific poster. In *Writing, speaking, & communication skills for health professionals.* New Haven, CT: Yale University Press. See also Radel, J. (n.d.). *Developing a poster presentation.* Retrieved from http://www.kumc.edu/SAH/OTEd/jradel/Poster_Presentations/PstrStart.html

- *Use repetition and redundancy:* "Under the old system it took three weeks—that's 15 working days—to get the monthly sales figures. Now we can get the numbers in just two days. That's right, two days."

- *Add internal summaries and previews:* "You can see we've made great progress in switching to the new inventory system. As I've said, the costs were about 10 percent more than we anticipated, but we see that as a one-time expense. I wish I could be as positive about the next item on the agenda—the customer service problems we've been having. Complaints have increased. We do believe we've finally identified the problem, so let me explain it and show you how we plan to deal with it."

Cover only necessary information   You will usually be far more knowledgeable about the topic than your audience is. This knowledge is both a blessing and a potential curse. On the one hand, your command of the subject means you can explain the topic thoroughly. On the other hand, you may be tempted to give listeners more information than they want or need.

If you cover your topic in too much detail, you are likely to bore—or even antagonize—your listeners. One personnel specialist made this mistake when briefing a group of staffers about how to file claims with a new health insurance carrier. Instead of simply explaining what steps to take when they needed care, he launched into a 20-minute explanation of why the company chose the present carrier, how that company processed claims at its home office, and where each copy of the four-part claims form was directed after it was filed. By the time he got to the part of his talk that was truly important to the audience—how to get reimbursed for out-of-pocket expenses—the staffers were so bored and restless they had a hard time sitting still for the information. Don't make a mistake like this in your presentations. As you plan your remarks, ask yourself what your listeners need to know, and tell them just that much. If they want more information, they will probably ask for it.

Avoid Jargon   Sometimes you will be introducing trainees to specialized terms and language. This may be as simple as introducing new employees to your company jargon for departments ("If you need help with your computer, call IRD") or locations ("This is what we call the Annex"). Some jargon is necessary, but don't use more than necessary. If you overwhelm your listeners with too much specialized terminology, you will probably bore them and leave them so confused they'll give up trying to understand the material you are explaining. Don't be a techno-snob: Tell people what they need to know in language they will understand.

Link the Familiar to the Unfamiliar   Research has shown people have the best chance of understanding new material when it bears some relationship to information they already know.[9] Without a familiar reference point, listeners may have trouble understanding even a clear definition. Two examples illustrate how comparisons and contrasts with familiar information help make new ideas more understandable:

Confusing:	Money market funds are mutual funds that buy corporate and government short-term investments. [To understand this definition, the audience needs to be familiar with money market funds and with corporate and government short-term investments.]
More Familiar:	Money market funds are like a collection of IOUs held by a middleman. The funds take cash from investors and lend it to corporations and the government, usually for between 30 and 90 days. These borrowers pay the fund interest on the loan, and that interest is passed along to the investors. [If the listeners understand IOUs and interest, they can follow this definition.]

• Persuasive Presentations

Sooner or later, everyone needs to influence others' thinking or actions. When an issue is especially important, persuasion frequently takes place in a presentation. Even when you have made your case in writing, a good presentation is often essential. Business consultant James Lukaszewski explains:

> We live in a "tell me" world. The last time you presented a plan to your boss to accomplish something—you know—that beautiful 2-inch-thick, tabbed notebook with 150 pages, 31 tabs, and 5,000 well-chosen words? Was it actually read? Or did your boss simply put his hand on it, look you in the eye, and say, "Show me what's in here and tell me how it's going to help us achieve our objectives."[10]

The following discussion shows you how to create presentations that change minds and produce the results you are seeking.

Table 12-2	Considerations for Choosing a Persuasive Organization Pattern

Organization Plan	Considerations
Problem–solution	Most basic persuasive pattern. Most helpful when audience needs convincing that a problem exists.
Comparative advantages	Use when audience is considering alternatives to your proposal. Show how your plan is superior to others. Defer thesis if audience will object to idea before hearing your reasoning.
Criteria satisfaction	Use when audience is not likely to consider alternative plans. Choose criteria important to your audience, and show how your plan meets them. If audience may be hostile to your plan, introduce criteria before discussing the plan.
Motivated sequence	Use when problem and solution are easy to visualize. Effective when seeking immediate audience reaction.

Organizing Persuasive Messages

Credibility may be important, but the way you structure your message also plays a major role in determining how successful you will be at persuading an audience. Chapter 9 discussed several patterns for organizing the body of a presentation. Here we recap the use of problem–solution, comparative advantages, criteria satisfaction, and motivated sequence patterns as they apply to persuasive situations. As Table 12-2 shows, there is no single best plan. The one you choose will depend on the topic and your audience's attitude toward it.

Problem–Solution　　As its name suggests, a problem–solution plan first persuades the audience something is wrong with the present situation and then suggests how to remedy it. This plan works especially well when your audience does not feel a strong need to change from the status quo. Because listeners have to recognize that a problem exists before they will be interested in a solution, it's essential to show them the present situation is not satisfactory before you present your idea. For example:

Problem	Solution
Many employees are arriving late due to increasing congestion.	Offer flexible working hours.
Cost of travel is skyrocketing.	Increase capability to hold some meetings via videoconference.

A problem–solution pattern might also be used to show how updating a computer system will solve problems with inventory monitoring, why a potential customer needs a personal financial advisor, or why a department needs additional staff.

If your listeners already recognize a problem exists, you may not need to spend much time proving the obvious. In such circumstances, you might touch on the problem in the introduction to your talk and devote the entire body to suggesting a solution. If you are competing against other ideas, however, a comparative advantages plan may be a better organization strategy.

Comparative Advantages　　A comparative advantages approach puts several alternatives side by side and shows why yours is the best. This strategy is especially useful when the audience is considering an idea that competes with the one you're advocating.

Under this circumstance, ignoring alternative plans is a bad idea. A head-on comparison that supports your case is a far more effective plan. A health club manager used a comparative advantages approach to encourage new members:

Introduction: When you decide to join a health club, you have several choices in the area. You might be tempted by the special introductory rates at some other clubs in town, but a feature-by-feature look shows that Millennium is your best choice.

Body:

I. The club is open longer every day than any other club in town.

II. The club has more exercise machines than any other in town.

III. The club has a wider variety of activities than any other in town: aerobics classes, swimming, saunas, massage, racquetball, and a snack bar.

IV. The club's staff members are all licensed fitness counselors—a claim no other club in town can make.

Conclusion: When it comes to value for your dollar, Millennium is your best health club choice.

In the preceding example, the manager made her thesis clear at the beginning of her presentation. A comparative advantages approach also works well when you choose to defer your thesis. In this instance, you can build a case showing how your proposal is superior to the alternatives and then present your thesis as a conclusion. An insurance agent used this strategy to convince an audience to buy coverage:

Introduction: How should you spend your discretionary income?

Body: You have several alternatives.

I. Spend it all on recreation, but that won't buy financial security for your family if anything happens to you.

II. Make investments to plan for the future, but there is always the risk of losing that money.

III. Buy more expensive housing, but it risks placing you even more in debt.

IV. Insure your family and guarantee them an income if you die or are disabled.

Conclusion: At least some of your disposable income ought to be devoted to insurance. *[Deferred thesis]*

In this situation, deferring the thesis was a smart idea. If the speaker had started by praising the virtues of buying insurance, most listeners would have tuned out. Because very few people relish the thought of spending their discretionary income on something as intangible as more insurance coverage, they'd probably reject the idea unless they could see the comparisons that led to the conclusion that it is the best choice.

Criteria Satisfaction
A criteria satisfaction strategy sets up criteria for a plan the audience will accept and then shows how your idea or product meets them.

> "When you look for a cell phone carrier, you want one that has a strong signal, low rates, and a good data plan."

After establishing your criteria, show how the product, service, or idea you are presenting will meet the criteria.

> "Let me show you how our company offers the strongest signal coverage across the country, affordable voice plans that include free calls on nights and weekends, and a range of data options."

It can be even more effective to invite the audience to supply the criteria. If you have researched your audience, you should know in advance what they are likely to want, and your appeal will be even more effective:

> "I'd like you to tell me what things you want in a cell phone carrier."

Once your listeners have identified what will satisfy them, you can show how your product or service will meet their needs. Organize criteria in the order of importance to the client, not to you.

Unlike a comparative advantages approach, a criteria satisfaction plan does not consider alternative ideas. For this reason, it is a good approach when your audience isn't likely to think of alternative plans.

Motivated Sequence   As you read in Chapter 9, the motivated sequence organization plan has five steps:

1. Attention
2. Need
3. Satisfaction
4. Visualization
5. Action

The need and satisfaction steps are similar to those in a problem–solution approach, but the visualization and action steps add a new element. The visualization step allows listeners to picture how your solution could work for them. An event planner proposing to organize a wedding or a business meeting might show clients photos of similar occasions she planned or describe in vivid detail the way she proposes to create a memorable occasion for this client. As its name implies, the action step calls for the listeners to go beyond just agreeing with the presenter to take a step toward adopting his or her plan. Salespeople sometimes call this step "closing" because it cements the deal.

Types of Persuasive Presentations

Unlike purely informative presentations that don't advocate a position, persuasive presentations aim to change the way an audience thinks, feels, or acts. The most common types of persuasive presentations are motivational and goodwill speeches, proposals, and sales presentations.

Consider these examples to see how common persuasion is on the job:

- Two partners are convinced they have a winning idea for a new restaurant. They meet with a commercial loan officer from a local bank to seek financing for their project.

- Faced with a wave of injuries, the foreman of a construction crew convinces his team members they need to observe safety practices more carefully.

- As part of a community relations program, the electric company has started a community speakers' bureau. The bureau's director is speaking to a group of employees to recruit them as volunteers for the service.

- A group of employees has grown increasingly disgruntled with the boss's policy on vacation scheduling. They have chosen a three-person delegation to present their grievances.

Motivational Speeches   A **motivational speech** attempts to generate enthusiasm for the topic being presented. When delivered effectively and at the proper time, such presentations can produce excellent results. For example, the organizers of a fund-raising event can generate enthusiasm to recruit and energize volunteers. A team leader can inspire an otherwise skeptical workforce to work extra hard to cut costs. A manager can encourage an unmotivated employee to turn his performance around and become a top producer for the company.

Goodwill Speeches   As its name implies, a **goodwill speech** aims to create a favorable image of the speaker's cause in the minds of the audience. Representatives of organizations frequently speak to audiences to promote interest or support for their organizations. A corporate recruiter addressing graduating seniors and a bank economist explaining economic forecasts are making speeches of goodwill.

These goodwill speeches may seem informative, but they also try to change the listeners' attitudes or behavior. The corporate recruiter is trying to encourage some students to apply for jobs with his company; the economist is trying to build the image of her institution as a leading business bank.

Proposals   In a **proposal** you advocate that your audience take specific action. Some proposals are aimed at external audiences. Others are focused on internal audiences. You might, for example, try to persuade management to support a ride-sharing program or reimburse employees for education costs, or you might try to convince your boss to give you more staffing support or a raise in pay. (See the Career Tip for advice on requesting a raise.)

Whatever the topic and audience, the most straightforward approach for a proposal is the problem–solution approach described in Chapter 9. While the particulars will vary, each section of this two-part approach is likely to include information listed here:

1. *Introduce the problem.*
    a. Demonstrate the nature of the problem in terms the audience will understand.
    b. Show undesirable consequences of the problem.
    c. Highlight ethical dimensions of the situation if the current situation is morally wrong.
    d. Provide causal analysis of the situation. (How did this problem develop?)

2. *Provide a solution (with supporting evidence).*
    a. Describe the positive consequences of your proposal.
    b. Show how your proposal will avoid bad consequences.
    c. Highlight the ethical reasons for your approach. Show why it's the right thing to do.
    d. Address the feasibility of your proposal. Show it can be done: cost, time, motivation, etc. Include an operation timeline to strengthen the proposal.

Here, in outline form, is how the problem–solution plan would look in the body of a presentation proposing an employee wellness program:

I. Health-related problems are hurting our company *[Problem]*

A. Health care costs are increasing
    1. Insurance premiums are increasing
    2. Out-of-pocket expenses for employees are growing

B. Productivity is declining due to employee health problems
    1. Absenteeism is growing
    2. Workers who stay on the job are less productive
    3. Some employees are leaving us due to health problems

How to Request a Raise

Asking for a raise is a kind of proposal, even though you typically will present your arguments informally to your boss. Here are tips that can increase your chances for success:

The best time to seek a raise

- When you or your department have been recognized for doing a good job.

- After you have volunteered to take on additional responsibilities (and have handled them successfully).

- If the organization can't easily replace you or do without your services.

- After you have contributed directly to the company's profitability and success (and you can demonstrate this connection).

- When the organization is in strong financial shape.

- When your relationship with your boss is good.

What to ask for

- Research the compensation range for jobs like yours in the industry. Check with professional associations in your field or web-based salary surveys such as http://www.jobstar.org. Demonstrate your request is reasonable by providing comparative figures.

- Consider asking for noncash benefits. For many people, pay isn't the only kind of compensation. For example, you might also seek more vacation time, a more flexible schedule, discounts on company products, or use of a company vehicle.

Don'ts

- Don't get emotional. Losing your temper is unlikely to be persuasive, and it can damage your long-term relationship with your boss.

- Don't confuse effort with contribution. Working hard is admirable, but effort alone probably won't be enough to earn you a raise. Show your boss the *results* you produce justify better compensation.

- Don't rely on longevity ("I've been here for 8 years") or personal need ("My rent just went up 20 percent"). It's better to demonstrate you *deserve* a raise.

II. A wellness program could reduce the impact of these problems *[Solution]*
   A. Elements of a program
      1. Nutrition education
      2. Exercise education
      3. Substance abuse counseling
   B. Benefits
      1. Healthier employees
      2. More productive employees
      3. Lower health costs (insurance and out-of-pocket)

When circumstances warrant, you might consider organizing your proposal by using one of the other persuasive strategies such as criteria satisfaction, comparative advantages, or motivated sequence.

Sales Presentations   In a **sales presentation,** one party presents remarks aimed at persuading another to purchase a product or service. Unlike the communication in retail settings, sales presentations are planned in advance. Sales presentations range from platform speeches in front of large audiences to less formal sit-down talks with small groups of decision makers.

Whatever their size, sales presentations will adhere to the guidelines that follow.

Establish client relationships before your presentation   Whenever possible, establish relationships with your audience before you make your presentation. Getting to know the people you hope to persuade will give you valuable information on what they want and suggest how you can satisfy their needs. Just as important, preexisting relationships will make your listeners more comfortable with you.

Just before speaking, try to talk informally with the people to whom you'll present. This sort of conversation can help build rapport and give you ideas about how to fine-tune your remarks to address what's on their minds.

Put your clients' needs first   Your clients don't want to hear about you or what you have to offer. They want to hear how to solve their problems. Don't focus on your products, company, services, or needs, but on the buyer's problems and concerns. What isn't working well for the client right now? What does he or she want to happen? Once you know what's missing, you can find out how your product or service can fill that need. As business expert and educator Robert Kiyosaki puts it, "True selling means being *passionate* about your company's product or service and *compassionate* with the wants, dreams, needs of your fellow human beings." He adds that "manipulation, deception, pressure, false sincerity, and phony smiles is *not* selling. *Selling is communication.* True selling is caring, listening, solving problems and serving your fellow human being."[11]

Listen to your clients   Unlike most other presentations, sales-oriented talks call for greater audience involvement. One study of salespeople found that the difference between top and average performers was the willingness to listen. The prospective buyers of top performers spoke between 30 and 70 percent of the time.[12] Rather than viewing questions and comments as interruptions, welcome them as a chance for you to learn what the client wants. Once you hear what's on your listeners' minds, you have the chance to speak directly to their concerns. Remain flexible: If you are interrupted, address the concerns. Then review your last points before moving on. Trainer Kevin Hogan captures this approach: "The great salespeople ask questions and have great listening skills. Poor salespeople get locked into script mode. They focus on the product they have to sell rather than the client who has a need."[13]

Emphasize benefits, not features   **Features** are qualities of a product or service that make it desirable and distinguish it from the competition. Salespeople can understandably get excited about features, and they are often tempted to promote them to prospective customers. But it really isn't features that will impress customers—it's the **benefits** that will flow from those features. So you must "sell the benefit, not the feature."[14]

Here is an example of the difference between some features and benefits of a web-based customer service product. It's obviously important to describe the features, but the benefits will motivate customers to sign on.

Feature	Benefit
100% web-based	You don't have to host the product on your server or maintain it.
"Knowledge base" gives customers answers to frequently asked questions (FAQs)	Your telephone support costs are substantially reduced.
	Your support personnel are relieved from the drudgery of repeatedly answering the same questions.
	Your staff can add new solutions with a single mouse click.
Fully customizable	Lets you create the content, look, and feel just right for your business.

Use an effective closing strategy   In closing, a presenter must be upbeat and optimistic. Clear and realistic goals from the outset help you determine how best to close. An effective close summarizes the primary benefits and the ways in which the benefits meet or exceed clients' needs. It then calls for any action that moves the sale along: agreement to a test or trial run, agreement to another meeting, agreement to attend a demonstration or arrange for your presentation to higher level decision makers. Think long term. As consultant Hans Stennek states, "I've never been a believer in closing because my objective is not to close the sale but to open a relationship."[15]

Strategies for Ethical Persuasion

Persuasion is the act of motivating an audience, through communication, to voluntarily change a particular belief, attitude, or behavior.[16] When you convince an interviewer you're the right person for the job, when you make a pitch to a prospective client for a new business project, and when you sway your team to adopt your great idea, you're engaging in persuasion. In these cases, you most likely are pursuing a goal that has your own and others' best interests in mind. But as you might imagine, not all persuasive efforts are ethical. Think of the unscrupulous salesperson who knowingly misleads you into buying an inferior product. In this section we distinguish ethical persuasion from other kinds of unethical attempts to influence an audience.

To understand the ethical dimensions of persuasion, imagine the City Council has announced its intention to turn a local athletic field and playground into a parking lot. The area's residents are understandably upset and want to influence the City Council to change its mind. There are a few ways the residents could approach the situation. First, they could use **coercion**—the use of force and/or threats of punishment—to force the council against its will to reverse its decision. The group could try to compel a change by invading and disrupting a City Council meeting and demanding that Council members promise to keep the park or face more demonstrations. Threatening to mount a recall campaign against any members who support the parking lot would be another coercive approach. Although coercion can influence behavior, it usually isn't a good approach. The recipient of the threats can counterattack, leading to an escalating cycle of hostility. Threatened parties often dig in their heels and resist changing to save face or as a matter of principle, responding, "I'll be damned if I'll change just because you threaten me." Coercion also makes the instigator look bad.

Second, the residents could get the City Council to change its position through **manipulation**—using deception to trick the other party into thinking or acting in the desired way. A deceptive approach to the park-versus-parking lot problem might be to present the City Council with a petition against the lot containing forged signatures that inflate the petition's size or to gain public sympathy by exaggerating the adverse effects of the project on certain groups—children, the elderly, and small business owners, for example. Manipulation is not a good approach to persuasion either. If the deception is later detected, the influenced parties may feel betrayed, leading to a "boomerang effect" in which people change their attitudes in opposition to the one a speaker advocated.[17] And some forms of manipulation are downright illegal. For example, a financial advisor can't promise that a stock or mutual fund will have the same stellar performance in the future as it has had after a few good years.

Third, the residents could use *ethical persuasion strategies*—honest communication that convinces the other party to act voluntarily in the desired way. Two measures of whether a particular persuasive message is genuinely ethical are (1) whether the recipient feels truly free to make a choice and (2) whether the originator would feel comfortable if he or she were the recipient of the message instead of its sender. In the case of the parking lot debate, the citizens' group could organize an appeal showing the community sees keeping the park as more important than increasing the amount of available parking.

ETHICAL **challenge**

It could describe the benefits of the park, bringing in local residents to testify about its importance to the community. By being honest (avoiding manipulation) and by relying on logical arguments instead of threats (avoiding coercion), ethical communicators can feel good about themselves and their persuasive appeals. And if that isn't benefit enough, they also will build a solid reputation in their workplace and the larger community.

What you'll learn in this section is how to make the best and most ethical case for your position so others will voluntarily choose to accept it.

Maximize Your Credibility

Winston Churchill once said that when it comes to public speaking, what matters most is who you are, then how you say what you want to say, and, finally, what you say. Even without taking this assertion literally, it is true that credibility is a powerful factor in persuasion. **Credibility** is the persuasive force that comes from the audience's belief in and respect for the speaker. When your audience has little time or inclination to examine your evidence and reasoning in detail, it will rely almost exclusively on your credibility to decide whether to accept your claims.[18] Research shows you can enhance your credibility in a variety of ways.[19]

Demonstrate your competence Listeners will be most influenced by a speaker they believe is qualified on the subject. You are more likely to believe career advice from a self-made millionaire than from your neighbor who has been fired from four jobs in three years. Similarly, the department staff is more likely to accept the direction of a new manager who seems knowledgeable about that department's specific work. Management is likely to take a risk on a new manufacturing material if the product manager seems to know the market well. These are all examples of trusting someone's competence.

There are three ways to boost your competence. The first is by demonstrating your *knowledge of the subject.* For example, the product manager might help to establish her credibility by citing statistics ("Our market research showed 85 percent of the potential market is more concerned with maintenance costs than the initial cost of the product"). She could also remember facts ("Dorwald Associates tried something like this, although only in government markets, and it was pretty successful") and recent appropriate examples ("I was checking the records last week, and I realized we could afford to replace the machines every 5 years on what we'd save on maintenance if we used plastic instead of metal").

A second way to demonstrate competence is by making your *credentials* known. These credentials could be academic degrees, awards and honors, or successful experiences ("I helped set up Hinkley's profitable system a few years ago, and I think the same approach we took there could help us now"). To avoid the appearance of egotism, it can be best to have others talk about your credentials ("Clara has a degree in accounting, so her ideas have special value here").

A third way to show your competence is through *demonstration of your ability.* This means speaking effectively during your presentation, of course. But with an audience who already knows you, the reputation you have acquired over time will be even more powerful. If you have a reputation for being talented and hardworking, listeners will be disposed to accept what you have to say. If they regard you as incompetent, you will have a hard time persuading them to accept the ideas in your presentation.

Earn the trust of your audience   The most important ingredient of trustworthiness is *honesty.* If listeners suspect you aren't telling the truth, even the most impressive credentials or grasp of the subject will mean little. For instance, a union leader gets little support from union members if they think he's made a private agreement with management. If your motives will ever be suspect, confess them before others can raise doubts ("I know the compensation plan in this proposal will benefit me, but I hope you can see how it will boost productivity and cut turnover"). Of course, you should never say *anything* that can be considered dishonest.

Impartiality is a second element of trustworthiness. We are more likely to accept the beliefs of impartial speakers than of those who have a vested interest in persuading us. If you have a vested interest in the position you are presenting (e.g., asking for a pay raise or a desired assignment), you can boost your credibility by citing impartial third parties who support your position. With the pay raise, for example, you might cite salary surveys showing the compensation you are seeking is in line with industry standards. If you are asking for a plum assignment, you could get the people with whom you would be working to endorse your request.

Emphasize your similarity to the audience   Audiences are most willing to accept the ideas of a speaker whose attitudes and behaviors are similar to their own. This persuasive ability exists even when the similarities are not directly related to the subject at hand. Thus, a subordinate may get a better hearing from the boss when both are golfers, have children of the same age, come from the same part of the country, or dress similarly. Customer service representatives for farm machinery generally wear casual clothing and open-necked shirts to fit in with the people they visit. Many sales representatives begin conversations with prospects by mentioning a common interest—gardening, baseball, or a recent event that affects the customer's business.

Similarity in areas related to the speaker's topic is even more persuasive. This fact has led to the strategy of establishing *common ground* between speaker and listeners early in a presentation. A speaker who shows he and the audience have similar beliefs will create goodwill that can make listeners willing to consider more controversial ideas later on. Notice, for example, how a business owner seeking a zoning variance based her appeal to the local architectural review board:

> Like you, I'm a strong believer in preserving the character of our town. As a businesswoman and a long-time resident, I realize beauty and lack of crowding are our

Balancing Logic and Emotion

Some presentations are based on highly reasoned arguments backed up by plenty of fact-based supporting material. Others appeal more to the listeners' emotions. What support they offer may have more entertainment value than logical force. Well-told jokes or dramatic stories may not pass a careful analysis, although they can capture some audiences' attention.

Which type of support—logical or emotional—is better? According to the *elaboration likelihood model of persuasion,* the answer depends on your audience. Listeners who are highly involved in a subject and care deeply about it are most likely to look for strong arguments backed up by a wealth of supporting material. By contrast, listeners who are less involved with the subject are more easily persuaded by an engaging speaker who delivers easy-to-digest stories and examples. They also rely more heavily on the speaker's credibility and likability than the content of his or her arguments.

Fortunately, choosing logic versus emotion isn't an either–or matter: Most presentations will contain elements of each approach.

Source: Griffin, E. (2009). *A first look at communication theory* (7th ed.). New York, NY: McGraw-Hill.

greatest assets. Without them, our home would become just another overgrown collection of shopping malls and condominiums.

Also, like you, I believe change isn't always bad. Thanks to your efforts, our downtown is a more interesting and beautiful place now than it was even a few years ago. I think we share the philosophy that we ought to preserve what is worth saving and improve the town in whatever ways we can. I appreciate the chance to show you how this project will make the kind of positive change we all seek.

This speaker's demonstrated support for the principles the board promotes increased her chances of gaining acceptance for her proposal. Of course, the board has to believe the speaker is sincere. If members suspect she is just telling them what they want to hear, her credibility will shrink, not grow.

Use Logical Arguments
An organized presentation isn't necessarily a logical one. Many arguments that sound logical at first are actually flawed by errors in reasoning, or **fallacies.**[20] Fallacious reasoning isn't always intentional: The person making the case might not be aware his or her thinking is flawed. Whether or not they are deliberate, fallacies can weaken your case by casting doubt on the merits of your position. The following sections describe the most common fallacies (by both English and Latin names), so you can avoid using them.[21]

Personal attack (ad hominem)   An ad hominem fallacy attacks a person's integrity in order to weaken the argument he or she is making. Some ad hominem arguments are easy to spot: Calling someone an "idiot" isn't very persuasive. Other ad hominem arguments aren't so obvious, though.

Reduction to the absurd (reductio ad absurdum)   A reductio ad absurdum fallacy attacks an argument by extending it to such extreme lengths that it looks ridiculous. "If we allow developers to build homes in one section of this area, soon we will have no open spaces left." Or, "If we have our after-hours customer service handled by an offshore company, pretty soon we won't have any employees here at home." Far-fetched projections like these call for a closer look: Developing one area doesn't necessarily mean that other areas have to be developed, and hiring some employees from overseas won't necessarily lead to widespread layoffs at home. Either of these policies might be unwise, but the ad absurdum reasoning doesn't prove it.

Either–or   An either–or fallacy sets up false alternatives, suggesting that if the inferior one must be rejected, then the other must be accepted. "If you believe the arts in this community are important, you'll contribute to our fund-raising campaign." This sort of argument ignores the fact that it's possible to support the arts in other ways besides donating to a particular cause.

False cause (post hoc ergo propter hoc)   A post hoc fallacy mistakenly assumes one event causes another because they occur sequentially. Post hoc fallacies aren't always easy to detect without careful research. For example, a critic might blame a drop in productivity on the policy of letting some employees work from home, noting that output began to drop shortly after telecommuting was introduced. A causal link in this case *may* exist, but there might be other reasons for the decline—a change in the nature of work, for example.

Bandwagon appeal (argumentum ad populum)   An argumentum ad populum fallacy is based on the often dubious notion that just because many people favor an idea, you should too. Sometimes, of course, the mass appeal of an idea can be a sign of its merit. If leading companies have adopted a product, there's a good chance it will work for yours. But in other cases widespread acceptance of an idea is no guarantee of its validity. The majority of employees in your company might invest the bulk of their retirement plan dollars in the company's stock, but almost every financial advisor will tell you this is a dangerous idea. The lesson here is simple to comprehend but often difficult to follow: Don't just follow the crowd; consider the facts carefully and make up your own mind.

Use Psychological Appeals
Logical arguments and your own credibility are both strong assets when you're trying to persuade others. In addition, though, a number of strategies for presenting your arguments will boost the odds you can achieve your goal.

Appeal to the needs of your audience   Perhaps the key to effective selling is identifying the prospect's needs and showing how the product can satisfy them. *Fortune* magazine featured one organization's success at implementing this principle:

> [At Lanier] a salesman does not merely sell hardware. He goes into an office, asks to see how the paperwork is handled, makes himself an overnight expert about the business involved, then prepares a plan for increasing its productivity by using a specific Lanier machine. When he gives a demonstration, he programs the machine to churn out that prospect's actual paperwork.[22]

Even if the audience is not interested in or is unsympathetic to an idea, there is usually some way to link a proposal to the listeners' needs or values. A representative of an oil company speaking to residents of a coastal town where offshore drilling is being proposed could defend the move by showing how the local economy would benefit and how drilling platforms increase the abundance of marine life in the oceans, which in turn improves fishing.

Whenever possible, base your appeal on several needs. Listeners who are not reached by one appeal can still be persuaded by another. If you were trying to persuade your fellow workers to use public transportation instead of driving their own cars to work, you could identify several needs and show how your proposal would satisfy each one:

Need	Satisfaction
Save money	Getting out of your car, even for a few days each week, means you'll spend less on gas, parking, and auto maintenance.
More time	On the bus or train, you can read and/or work instead of having to drive yourself.
Less stress	You won't have to deal with the aggravation of traffic congestion and annoying drivers.

Make your goal realistic   Presentational speaking is like most other aspects of life: You usually don't get everything you want. Even the best presentation can't accomplish miracles. Asking audience members to accept an idea they strongly oppose can backfire. Persuasion experts have refined this commonsense principle into *social judgment theory.*[23]

This theory helps speakers decide how to craft their arguments by identifying the range of possible opinions listeners might have about a speaker's arguments. (See Figure 12.2.) A listener's preexisting position is termed an **anchor.** All the arguments a persuader might use to change the listener's mind cluster around this anchor point in three zones. The first area is the listener's **latitude of acceptance.** As its name implies, this zone contains positions the listener would accept with little or no persuasion. By contrast, the **latitude of rejection** contains arguments the listener opposes. Between these areas lies the **latitude of noncommitment,** containing arguments the listener neither accepts nor rejects.

Social judgment theory teaches a very practical lesson about how much to ask from your audience. Arguments in the listeners' latitude of noncommitment may not impress them, and those in the latitude of rejection will just strengthen their opposition. The best chance for success comes when your plea is at the outer edge of the audience's latitude of acceptance. Communication scholar Em Griffin offers a perfect example of this principle:

> A striking story of social judgment theory in action comes from a university development director I know who was making a call on a rich alumnus. He anticipated that the prospective donor would give as much as $10,000. He made his pitch and asked what the wealthy businessman would do. The man protested that it had been a lean year and that times were tough—he couldn't possibly contribute more than $20,000.
>
> The fundraiser figured that he had seriously underestimated the giver's latitude of acceptance and that $20,000 was on the low end of that range. Without missing a beat he replied, "Trevor, do you really think that's enough?" The alumnus wrote a check for $25,000.[24]

FIGURE 12.2

Range of Responses to a Persuasive Appeal

| Latitude of noncommitment | Latitude of acceptance | Latitude of noncommitment | Latitude of rejection |

Social judgment theory teaches that persuasion isn't a one-shot affair. In many cases your persuasive campaign will consist of many messages delivered over time, each one aimed at expanding your listeners' latitude of acceptance. Investors who want to build a new housing development probably shouldn't ask for the local zoning board's support in its first hearing. Rather, it might encourage the board to investigate the company's track record on similar projects in other communities. Assuming the investigation shows the company delivers as promised, the chances of a favorable ruling at a later meeting will increase. Similarly, a sales representative trying to sell furnishings for a new office building should not expect to make a $2 million sale on her first call; she might try only to make an appointment to present her proposal to a planning committee.

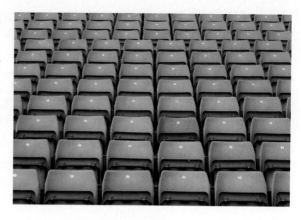

A human resources assistant at a medium-sized company used the lessons of social judgment theory to choose a realistic goal in her campaign to persuade the corporation to set up a day care center for the preschool children of employees. Rather than ask her boss to authorize funds for the center—a goal she knew was unrealistic—she requested approval to conduct a feasibility study in which she would explore the ways that similar companies provided for child care. If the boss responded favorably to the center after seeing the results of this survey, she would present a full-blown proposal. If he still had doubts, her backup proposal was to suggest the company subsidize tuition at a nearby child care center—a plan closer to the boss's anchor point.

Focus appeals on critical audience segments   Sometimes one or two listeners have the power to approve or reject your appeal. In such cases, it is important to identify the key decision makers' interests, needs, attitudes, and prejudices and focus your appeal toward them. For instance, if the office furnishings sales representative finds that most of the members of the planning committee vote with the president, her presentation to the committee will be aimed at his apparent needs and interests. If she finds the president doesn't meet with the planning committee, she might try to get an appointment to speak with the president.

Defer thesis with hostile audience   Usually, you state your thesis during the introduction of a presentation, but this rule may not be effective with skeptical or hostile listeners. If a manager seeking acceptance of changes in staffing thinks the audience will respond favorably to her thesis ("Increased business has led us to open up several new positions, and we'd like you to apply for them"), she'll put the idea in the introduction of the speech. If she believes the thesis will not be received enthusiastically ("Employee contributions to health care premiums will have to increase") or if she believes an audience that hears the news too early will be too upset to accept—or even hear—the rationale behind the decision, she will present the thesis later in the speech.

A presentation with a deferred thesis still needs an introduction to capture the audience's attention, demonstrate the importance of the topic, and orient the listeners to what will follow. In talks with a deferred thesis, the part of the introduction containing the preview carries the extra burden of setting up the thesis without stating it directly:

> It's no secret that increasing health care costs, combined with an industry-wide slump, have hurt the company. Today I want to tell you how management has tried to cope with these problems in a way that will protect our jobs as much as possible.

After the preview, the body of the presentation leads the audience members, step by step, to the point at which they are ready to understand and accept the speaker's thesis:

> Given the problems we've faced, management's choice has been to either lay off personnel, cut wages, or ask all of us to help pay for our own health care. We hope you agree that our decision to ask us to chip in on health costs is the best one under the circumstances and that you'll realize we still consider you valuable members of our team.

Present ample evidence to support claims   Chapter 10 outlined the types of support that can help you prove your claims: examples, stories, statistics, comparisons, and quotations. When your goal is to persuade an audience, the generous use of support is especially important.

Research demonstrates that when an audience hears persuasive evidence backing up a persuasive claim, the chances increase that the influence of the message will last long after the presentation has concluded.[25] Furthermore, evidence supporting a claim makes listeners less likely to accept opposing viewpoints they may hear after you have finished speaking.

The best evidence comes from credible sources. If your credibility on the subject is not high, be sure to cite others whose expertise and impartiality your listeners respect. For example, a prospective customer would expect a sales representative to praise a product he or she is trying to sell. But if the salesperson cites others who know the product and don't have an interest in its sale, the message ("This product is excellent") becomes more persuasive. In this case, the testimony of other customers or of an independent testing service such as Consumers Union would be excellent evidence.

Consider citing opposing ideas   Research indicates it is generally better to mention and then refute ideas that oppose yours than to ignore them.[26] There are three situations when it is especially important to forewarn listeners about opposing ideas.

When the audience disagrees with your position   With hostile listeners, it's wise to compare their position and yours, showing the desirability of your thesis. If management has previously opposed products similar to the one you are about to propose, for instance, you'll need to bring up the managers' objections ("It's too risky, the capital outlay is too big, and the sales force can't sell it") and show how your proposal will meet their objections ("We can minimize the risk and the initial costs by limiting the first production run; if we put extra emphasis on advertising and show the salespeople how other companies have sold similar products very successfully in the last few years, they'll be more enthusiastic and more effective"). Similarly, if you're trying to sell an out-of-the-way plant location to a company planning to build its new plant in a more central location, you might show that transportation is as cheap and available in your location as in the central one or that savings on real estate taxes and labor will allow the company to pay higher transportation costs. If you don't mention arguments already on their minds, your listeners may consider you uninformed.

When the audience knows both sides of the issue   Well-informed listeners, even if they haven't made up their minds about an issue, will find a one-sided appeal less persuasive than a presentation that considers opposing arguments. Discussing these ideas shows you are not trying to avoid them. Even if you refute the competition, considering it at all is more evenhanded than focusing exclusively on your plan and never acknowledging alternatives exist.

An account executive at a full-service stock brokerage showed he respected his listeners' knowledge and judgment at an investment seminar when he discussed the alternatives to using the services of his firm:

> I know most of you are familiar enough with the financial marketplace to be asking yourself, "Why don't I save money and use a discount brokerage?" And that's a fair question. After all, discount firms charge you a much smaller commission for each transaction than full-service houses like mine. I'd like to suggest that the answer to the question of which kind of brokerage to use lies in the old saying "You get what you pay for." If you use a discount firm, you'll get limited service. Now, that may be all you want and all you need. But if you're looking for a source of financial support and attention, you'll get it at a full-service brokerage. Let me explain.

When the audience will soon hear your viewpoint criticized or another one promoted
You will be better off defusing the opponents' thesis by bringing up and refuting their arguments than by letting them attack your position and build up theirs in its place. For example, a union organizer speaking to a group of plant workers might anticipate an argument from management this way:

> The company representative will tell you that after we organized the Oregon plant, the people were out of work, on strike, for four months the next year. That's true. What the company probably won't tell you is that the people got strike pay from the union. The company also won't tell you that the people there were losing money every year before that because their wages weren't keeping up with inflation, and the strike got them guaranteed cost-of-living raises, plus life, health, and disability benefits and improved safety conditions.

Adapt to the cultural background of your audience   Your listeners' cultural background may affect the way they respond to various types of persuasive appeals.[27] The intensity of emotional appeals is a good example. The traditional Euro-American ideal is to communicate without becoming too excited. By contrast, cultures in Latin America and the Middle East are generally more expressive, and their members respond more favorably to displays of emotion. An approach that would seem logical and calm to an audience in Seattle or Toronto might seem cold and lifeless to a group in Mexico City or Istanbul. Conversely, a Mexican or Turkish speaker might seem overly excitable to a group in the United States or Canada.

The types of supporting material regarded as most persuasive also differ from one culture to another. Euro-American culture places a high value on data that can be observed and counted. Statistical data and eyewitness testimony are considered strong evidence. Communicators from other backgrounds are less impressed by these sorts of proofs. Arab speakers commonly rely on religious and national identification. They are more likely to use elaborate language, which would be considered flowery by other cultural standards. In some parts of Africa, for example, the words of a witness would be regarded with suspicion because members of that culture believe people who speak out about a topic have a particular agenda in mind.

As Chapter 9 suggested, acceptable ways of organizing a message also vary. U.S. presenters are used to straightforward messages that introduce a thesis early in the presentation, develop it in the body, and summarize it in the conclusion. Japanese presenters rely less on a strong, direct close. Instead, they stress harmony with the audience, relying on this climate to generate acceptance of an idea.

Differences like these make it important to know your audience's cultural preferences. Just because listeners come from a particular country or belong to a particular ethnic group doesn't mean they can be stereotyped, especially in a shrinking world where

Rate your presentation on the following items using this scale: 3 = accomplished excellently, 2 = accomplished competently, 1 = needs improvement.

1. I maximized my credibility by
   a. Demonstrating my competence through knowledge of the topic and sharing my credentials.   1   2   3
   b. Earning the trust of my audience via honesty and impartiality.   1   2   3
2. I structured my arguments logically by
   a. Using the most effective organization plan for my goal and audience (problem–solution, criteria satisfaction, comparative advantages, motivated sequence).   1   2   3
   b. Avoiding the use of logical fallacies (*ad hominem, post hoc,* etc.).   1   2   3
3. I used appropriate psychological strategies such as
   a. Appealing to my audience's needs.   1   2   3
   b. Structuring a realistic goal.   1   2   3
   c. Focusing my appeals on my critical audience segment.   1   2   3
   d. Deferring my thesis with a hostile audience.   1   2   3
   e. Presenting ample evidence to support my claims.   1   2   3
   f. Citing opposing ideas when appropriate.   1   2   3
   g. Adapting to the cultural style of my audience.   1   2   3

communication and travel blur national boundaries. Nonetheless, being sensitive to your listeners' attitudes can help you avoid delivering a message that antagonizes, rather than persuades, them.

• Group Presentations

Group presentations are common in the working world. Sometimes the members of a group may be asked (or told) to present their information together. Other times team members choose to speak collectively, realizing that several presenters can be more effective than a single person.

Group presentations can be effective for a variety of reasons. Hearing from several speakers can provide the variety that will keep audience members tuned in. In addition, several people's skills and perspectives can give a more complete message than any single speaker could provide. For example, a sales pitch to a potential client would probably be strengthened by the contributions of experts in marketing, customer support, and product design. Finally, team presentations can boost audience receptivity by providing a balance of gender, ethnicity, age, and other factors.

Approaches to Organizing a Group Presentation

There are two ways to decide who will say what in a group presentation: by topic and by task. The approach you take will depend on an analysis of the situation.

Organizing by Topic   In some cases, it makes sense to break the presentation into separate segments, with each speaker addressing one or more topics. Organizing by topic is a logical approach when different parts of the material call for special expertise. For instance, a press conference in which county department heads announce new approaches to cost-cutting almost demands separate information from each person. Likewise, a sales presentation would profit from having topics like customer support, engineering, and production discussed by representatives from each of those departments.

Organizing by Task   Sometimes a presentation doesn't fall neatly into separate topics. In this case, it may make sense to assign speakers separate roles within the discussion of a topic. One role might be "spokesperson," whose job is to introduce the main points. Other members might take the role of "example-givers," offering details to support the spokesperson's claims. For

example, a neighborhood association urging the city council to install a new traffic signal at a busy intersection might use a problem–solution plan. One person's job would be to describe the overall problem and the group's solution. After making each of these main points, that speaker may introduce several individuals to back up the points with a range of supporting details. This plan organizes the material clearly and provides an impressive array of speakers who are more likely to convince the council than a single presenter. A rough outline for this approach would look something like this:

1. *Spokesperson describes the problem:* "Lack of a traffic signal encourages speeding traffic, leading to several accidents and near misses. This situation risks lives and exposes the city to liability suits."

2. *Other speakers offer support:* Neighbor 1 cites police reports on the number of speeding tickets issued in the past year. Neighbor 2 describes hospital reports on injuries from accidents at the intersection. Neighbor 3 describes recent near misses. Neighbor 4 (an attorney) explains the city's exposure to lawsuits.

3. *Spokesperson suggests a solution:* "Installation of a new traffic signal will reduce or eliminate the problem in a cost-effective way."

4. *Other speakers offer support:* Person 1 compares the cost of a new signal to the cost of settling lawsuits arising out of future accidents at the intersection. Person 2 shows that funds are available in the city's street improvement fund. Person 3 presents a petition of neighbors requesting traffic control at the intersection, which demonstrates voter support for the signal.

Planning Introductions, Conclusions, and Transitions in Group Presentations

Along with an introduction and conclusion to the entire presentation, each speaker should provide a mini-introduction and conclusion to his or her segment. These help listeners follow the overall plan and prevent confusion that can come when several speakers share the stage.

This mini-introduction is part of a group presentation by members of an architectural firm seeking to make the short list of candidates for a corporate design job:

Good morning, everybody. As David told you in his introduction, I'm Diana Salazar. I think you'll agree my colleagues have shown you a beautiful design. But beauty alone isn't enough: You need a building that can be constructed on time and on budget. That's why I want to spend a few minutes showing you how we can deliver just that.

Like the introduction, transitions are an especially important way to help listeners follow the structure of a group presentation. Clear transitions help smooth the adjustment listeners need to make as they shift their attention from one speaker to another. There are two ways to handle transitions: A single master of ceremonies (probably the person who introduced the presentation) can make them, or each speaker can introduce the next person after summarizing his or her own section. Whichever method you choose, make sure the relationship between the preceding and following sections is clear.

The same or the final speaker can give the conclusion. If you choose the final speaker, be certain the wrap-up restates the group's overall thesis and main points and doesn't just review the most recent remarks.

Delivering a Group Presentation

The potential for mix-ups and mistakes is especially great in group presentations. The key to minimizing problems is extensive rehearsal. Consider issues like the setup and position of speakers in advance to avoid last-minute bumbling. Will members speak while seated around a table? Will they sit in a row until it is each one's turn? Or will they come up from the audience? Choose the format that helps you make the best possible impression and avoid delays. Waiting for speakers to get from their chairs to the lectern greatly increases lag time, and the larger the room, the greater the distance. Sitting together at a table may provide a better and more cohesive look, as well as minimize delays. If the group does sit around a table, try to angle it so the team members can comfortably see speakers as they present. However you set up the presentation, be sure speakers can rise and sit as necessary without bumping, banging, and clanging into equipment, the table, and each other.

In considering where to position team members when they are not speaking, think about how they will look to the audience. Remember, they will make an impression even when they aren't the principal focus of attention. When it is your turn to speak, be sure to talk to the audience, not your teammates. When you're not speaking, look at the speaker and listen with undivided attention. Even if you are bored because you've heard the remarks so often during rehearsal, or you are nervous about your upcoming turn, act like the ideas are fresh or interesting. Don't review your notes or let your eyes wander from the speaker, or you will encourage the audience to do the same.

• Special-Occasion Speaking

In business settings, there are many special speaking occasions and events, some of which you will quite likely be asked to participate in or be given a chance to volunteer for. You may be asked to give a welcome to guests touring your facility, introduce a speaker at a staff meeting or annual banquet, present an award to an employee, or accept an award you've won. Perhaps you'll present a tribute to a member of a civic organization you belong to or bid farewell to a supervisor who was promoted out of your department. Keep in mind that every context is unique; you will want to adjust to the physical, social, chronological, and cultural context of each occasion. The following guidelines will help you feel confident and achieve your goals when delivering special-occasion remarks.

Welcoming a Guest or Group

When you are **welcoming** someone, your remarks often set the tone for the whole event. Warmth and sincerity in words and behavior are important. Whether you are welcoming

Honoring a Less-than-Honorable Person

Imagine your job is to speak briefly to welcome, introduce, toast, or give an award to someone you know is undeserving of respect. For example, the person about whom you must speak might be manipulative, racist, or lazy. (Feel free to think of a specific person who fits this description, and imagine the circumstances under which you might be required to publicly honor him or her.)

Describe how you would proceed in these circumstances. How could you be true to yourself while dealing with the obligations that often operate in business and professional situations?

a special guest for a two-hour banquet or a group of permanent new employees, try to follow these guidelines:

- Say who you are (if the audience doesn't know) or on whose behalf you are speaking.
- Identify the person or people you are welcoming (unless you are welcoming the entire audience).
- Thank the guest or group for coming (if either had a choice).
- Tell why the occasion is especially important or significant.

As you deliver your remarks, be sure to speak to the person or group you are welcoming. If appropriate, turn to the audience and invite your listeners to participate in the welcome by clearly stating or showing them how you want them to behave. The example below illustrates how this technique can be used with the guidelines to produce effective welcoming remarks:

> All of us at Sizetec USA welcome members of our Japanese plant's team to the ribbon-cutting of our new facility. We are honored you took time to travel so far to be with us today. We have a great deal to learn from one another, and your visit will help all of us make Sizetec an industry leader. This is an exciting day for us, and we extend a warm welcome to you. *[Turn to audience.]* Please join me in a round of applause to welcome our Japanese guests.

Introducing Another Speaker

When handled well, your **speech of introduction,** an introduction of another speaker, will help make his or her remarks a success. Here are some guidelines that will help you deliver an effective introduction. You may choose to switch the order of the information here, but you will almost always need to include it in some way unless the audience is aware of it already.

- *Briefly preview the topic about which the person will speak.* If the speaker's topic is very familiar, you may need only to mention it. If the audience is unfamiliar with the topic, you may need to include more background information about the topic and explain why it is significant for the group.
- *Give the audience reasons to listen to the person you are introducing.* Share interesting and relevant parts of the speaker's background. Whenever possible, show how his or her remarks will have value for the audience.
- *Enhance the credibility of the person you are introducing.* Share information that will showcase his or her qualifications. Select the most interesting biographical

information for your audience to describe the person you are introducing. It is best to give some general information and a few specifics rather than rattling off long lists: "John has done training with many groups, including the Air Force, IBM, and Baxter Healthcare." Don't be vague ("John has done a lot of training for big groups"), but don't burden the audience with too much time-consuming detail either ("John has done training for. . . ." followed by a list of 20 companies).

A good introduction requires that you learn about the person you are introducing in advance. If you can, meet in person or interview the speaker over the phone. If possible, obtain a résumé or biographical information in writing ahead of time. The more you know, the better you can make your introduction.

Make sure all the information in your introduction is accurate. Check and practice the pronunciation of names, cities, and companies you are unsure of. Ask the person how he or she would like to be referred to (title and last name, first and last name, or first name only).

As you plan your introduction, be sensitive to culture and gender differences. For example, members of many cultures prefer to be identified by formal titles (such as "director") that are not commonly used in the United States or Canada. Likewise, the humor that may be appreciated in the United States could easily offend listeners—or the persons being introduced—if they are from cultures with more formal communication styles. Strive for consistency if you are introducing more than one person. A common faux pas is referring to men as "Mr." or "Dr." while calling women by their first names.

Notice how these points have been incorporated in this informative introduction:

> For the last nine months you've heard a great deal about how we will be expanding operations into Mexico. This is a big step for us, and I'm sure everybody has a lot of questions and maybe some concerns.
>
> Today I'm pleased to introduce you to Mr. Dante Gutierrez, who will be managing our Mexican operations. Mr. Gutierrez comes to us with a great amount of experience on both sides of the border. After founding and operating one of northern Mexico's foremost import-export firms, Mr. Gutierrez became executive director of Baja California's Asociación de la Industria, a leading business group. He has lived and worked in both Mexico and the United States. His experience in manufacturing and cross-border trade will be a tremendous help as we expand our operation in Mexico and Central America.
>
> Along with his professional credentials, you'll find that Mr. Gutierrez is a great guy. He's friendly and helpful, and very approachable. I'm sure you will find that Mr. Gutierrez is a terrific resource as we learn more about our new market and its customers.
>
> Please join me in giving Mr. Gutierrez a warm welcome!

The following tips will help your introduction be a success:[28]

- Plan your remarks carefully in advance. Don't take an impromptu approach.

- Your introduction should *appear* spontaneous and natural, even though it is planned. Practice your delivery so you won't have to rely on notes.

- When making your introduction, look at the audience, not at the person being introduced.

- Keep the introduction short. You aren't the main attraction. In most cases a 1- or 2-minute introduction will be enough. If the audience already knows the person you are introducing, it can be even shorter.

Honoring a Person or an Institution

When you are asked to give a speech of **tribute,** both chronological and topical approaches can be effective. You can follow the person's life or career chronologically and pay tribute to achievements and characteristics along the way, or you might choose some themes or traits from the person's life and organize around those topics. If you do choose to pay tribute along theme lines (bravery and commitment, for example), anecdotes and examples can illustrate your points.

Many of the guidelines for tributes parallel those for introductions: accuracy of names and details and sensitivity to culture, gender, and personal desires. Check your information with the person to whom tribute is being paid if possible or practical; if not, check with an extremely authoritative source. A sample tribute to an accountant who is leaving a firm is presented below. Of course, if the speaker had more time, each of the traits selected could be illustrated with more anecdotes that the audience would be familiar with.

> Today is a day of celebration as we pay tribute to Joseph Begay. It is a privilege to speak for the management team here at Contrast Accounts and to honor Joe.
>
> In thinking about Joe's accomplishments here, two words come to mind: commitment and community. Joseph is committed to doing a job well. He commands a tremendous measure of respect and esteem from colleagues in all of our departments. From Betty Murphy in Costs Analysis to Mike Burroughs in Media Relations, Joseph has earned our admiration for his commitment to quality work for our clients. Who else could have persuaded us to redo the entire Simpson account in less than two months? Who else could have enticed us with pizzas to get us to stay late and finish? Joe is committed to our clients and to our colleagues. The focal point of his work has been to help us all better understand the needs of members from various departments who populate our company. Joseph has helped us come together to look at specific ways we could meet the needs of diverse departments, and he has provided us with opportunities to give expression to our common frustrations and concerns which revolve around quality products for our clients.

Giving a Toast

Sooner or later you are likely to be asked to deliver a special type of tribute—a **toast.** Besides honoring the person to whom it refers, a well-crafted toast can boost your visibility and notability in any organization. Remember, toasts usually express appreciation and recognize accomplishments as well as hopes and wishes for the future. Here are some hints to help you choose the right words.

- *Choose the time wisely.* If it is up to you to choose the moment, be sure everyone is present. At a dinner, choose the moment when the group has just been seated or wait until just before dessert. At a stand-around cocktail party or outdoor barbecue, wait until most people have drinks.

- *Be prepared.* Think ahead about the occasion, the attendees, and the person or people you are toasting. Delivering an impromptu toast can be risky. Use some inside information or little-known facts that compliment the person.

- *Look spontaneous.* Even though you have planned your remarks in advance, try to avoid reading notes or sounding memorized.

- *Be brief.* A 30- to 60-second toast is the norm; a 2-minute one is the maximum. If in doubt, say less, not more. End by raising your glass and gently clinking the glass of a person near you and saying, "Cheers," "Salud," or a similar expression.

- *Be visible and audible.* Be sure to stand. If it is an unorganized mill-around affair, look for an elevation: a hillside, a stair (not a chair) to stand on, the step to the stage, the back porch. Be certain you have everyone's attention before speaking, and begin loudly enough to be effective.

- *Be inclusive.* Alternate your gaze between the audience and the person or people you are honoring.

- *Be sober.* Beware of your consumption of alcohol beforehand. You may pay the price for a slurred or inappropriate toast for a long time. The beverage need not be alcoholic; club soda and water are also used for toasts.

- *Be appropriate.* If you are debating whether a remark or story would be humorous or offensive, leave it out. If you think something is funny but aren't sure the honoree and guests will appreciate the humor, leave it unsaid.

Go to the Advanced Public Speaking Institute website at http://www.public-speaking .org and click on "Humor Techniques" for more suggestions for toasts.

Presenting an Award

Sometimes persons may know they are recipients of awards, and at other times the announcement may come as a surprise. Depending on the situation, you will choose whether to let the audience (and winner) know who is receiving the award at the beginning of the speech or save that information until the end. For an effective **award presentation,** follow these tips:

- If everyone knows who is receiving the award, mention the person's name early in your remarks. If the audience doesn't know who is receiving the award, you might want to build suspense by withholding his or her name until the end.
- State the name and nature of the award.
- State the criteria for selection.
- Relate the way (or ways) in which the recipient meets the criteria, using specific examples.
- Make the presentation.
- Be sure the person receiving the award—not you, the presenter—is the center of attention and focus.

As the example below illustrates, this approach can serve as a framework for creating interesting, enthusiastic presentations:

> "Success isn't measured by where you are, but by how far you've come from where you started." These words exemplify the spirit of the Most Improved Player award. Each year, players have the privilege and difficult task of voting for the player they believe is the most improved. The winner of this award must have demonstrated to her teammates spirit and commitment and must have shown improvement and refinement in skills. This is not an easy task. Always spurring others on and never giving up even when we were down 14–7 against the Bulldogs, this year's winner went from being unable to stop a goal to stopping six goals in our last championship game. So, Mary Lee, it is with gratitude and delight that I present to you from your teammates the Most Improved Player award.

Accepting an Award

When you accept an award, a few brief remarks are usually all that are necessary. Recalling the long-winded speeches at the annual Academy Awards ceremony will help you appreciate the sentiment behind Marlene Dietrich's advice to Mikhail Baryshnikov when she sent him to accept her award from the Council of Fashion Designers: "Take the thing, look at it, thank them, and go."[29] This approach is probably too extreme, but brevity is certainly

an important element of most acceptances. So, too, is gratitude. The following plan can help you organize your sincere gratitude in an effective way:[30]

- Express your sincere gratitude (and surprise, if appropriate).
- Acknowledge and show appreciation to contributors.
- Describe how the award will make a difference.
- Say thank you again.

The following thank-you remarks, given by the head of a volunteer committee that had staged a profitable fund-raiser, illustrate how this simple approach can be sincere, easy, and effective:

> You have really surprised me today. When I said I'd help plan the auction, the last thing on my mind was an award. Raising scholarship money was our goal, and breaking last year's fund-raising record was the only reward I'd hoped for. Getting this special thank-you is more than I had ever expected, and I am deeply honored.
>
> I'm also a little embarrassed to be singled out like this. We couldn't have broken that record without a tremendous amount of hard work by everybody. Chris and her committee rounded up an incredible bunch of auction items. Ben and his gang provided food and entertainment that we'll be talking about for years. Darnelle's publicity team brought in the donors. And Leo's talents as an auctioneer squeezed every last dollar out of those items. With wonderful people like this, how could we have gone wrong?
>
> I'm going to put this plaque in my office, right above my desk. Whenever I'm feeling tired and discouraged about human nature, it will remind me how generous and hard working people can be for a good cause. It will also remind me how lucky I am to know you all and to have worked with you.
>
> So thanks again for this wonderful award. You're a great bunch of people, and I can hardly wait until we do it all again next year!

MASTER the chapter

review points

- Informative presentations include briefings, reports (status, feasibility, and final), and training sessions.

- Unlike reports, briefings are short and give the minimum information needed. Status reports review the project's purpose; describe its current state, its obstacles, and the efforts to overcome them; the next milestone; and the project's future. Final reports require introductions, background information, a description of events, results, and directions to get more information. A feasibility report includes an introduction, criteria, methodology, possible solutions, an evaluation of solutions, recommendations, and a conclusion.

- Training sessions necessitate careful planning by defining the desired outcome, scheduling the needed time and resources, choosing the best training method, and organizing all training elements. Effective trainers link the topic to the audience, create an overall picture, emphasize their organization plan, cover only required information, avoid jargon, and link the familiar to the unfamiliar.

- Many business occasions call for persuasive presentations such as motivational and goodwill speeches, proposals, or sales presentations.

- Ethical persuasion differs from both manipulation and coercion. It encourages listeners to make free choices after hearing sound reasoning and accurate information.

- Persuasive presentations may follow several organization plans: problem–solution, comparative advantages, criteria satisfaction, or

motivated sequence. The audience, topic, and goal will determine which of these plans will be the most effective.

- Proposals advocate a specific action and consist of two parts: the problem and the solution. Sales presentations are most successful in the long term when they establish client relationships, consider client needs, listen to and welcome clients' participation, focus on benefits not features, and use effective closings.

- Speakers heighten their credibility by demonstrating competence, trustworthiness, and similarity to the audience. Speakers earn their audience's trust through honesty and impartiality. Successful speakers avoid fallacies or errors in reasoning such as personal attacks, reduction to the absurd, either–or, false cause, and bandwagon appeals.

- Group presentations require special planning and can be organized by topic or by task. Careful analysis of the topic and situation often reveals the best approach. Group presentations need effective introductions and conclusions, and especially well-planned transitions to connect main points and avoid confusion from multiple speakers. Attention to nonverbal communication helps speakers enhance the presentation's flow and create unity and cohesion.

- Business contexts often require special-occasion presentations such as speeches of welcome and introductions, toasts, honoring persons or institutions, and presenting and accepting awards. Effective business communicators know the basics of each of these special presentations.

key terms

activities

1. Skill Builder

Create an approach that will actively involve the audience in each of the following trainings. Demonstrate your technique in class.

a. How to handle phone customer complaints nondefensively.
b. How to insert digital photos to update your website.
c. How to conduct an earthquake preparedness workshop.

2. Skill Builder

Define a specific training goal and a method to link the information to the audience for the following training sessions.

a. Listening skills for student service employees.
b. Presenting a "Dress for Success" seminar for a specific industry or employer (sales, marketing, law).
c. Training volunteer students to lead campus tours for visiting high school students.

d. Using *APA* style to cite sources in term papers for first-year college students.
e. Using a particular campus system (registration, student job placement) or filling out a widely used form (financial, graduation, or internship application).

3. Invitation to Insight

Increase your understanding of adult learning styles by conducting one of the following exercises.

a. Interview a professional who conducts trainings in the workplace. Ask your interviewee to describe successful strategies for motivation, direct involvement, and retention.
b. Attend a workplace training or explanation session. Analyze the presenter's use of goals, motivation, direct involvement of the learners, and techniques to enhance retention.

4. Invitation to Insight

Attend a professional persuasive presentation. Try to identify the speaker's goal and organizational pattern. Based on the descriptions in this text of various types of persuasive presentations, would you consider the presentation successful? Which of the speaker's strategies did you find effective? Which strategies did you find to be ineffective? Did the presentation illustrate ethical persuasion? How did the speaker establish credibility? Explain your answers and provide examples.

5. Skill Builder

Choose a product or service you are familiar with, or choose one of these: off-site archiving of computer files, cell phone pricing plan, deli delivery service for employees, company-supported memberships at a health club.

a. Identify an audience to whom you could sell this product.
b. Create a chart with two columns: features and benefits. List and differentiate between the product's features and benefits.

6. Invitation to Insight

Public service announcements (PSAs) are short pieces aimed at persuading audiences to support nonprofit organizations, issues, or causes. View one of the PSAs posted online at http://saloproductions.com/public-service-announcements/psa-samples.php.

What strategies are used to motivate the audience? Are these strategies ethical? Explain your answer. Why are these strategies successful?

7. Skill Builder

What organizational plan would be best suited to the message in each of the following situations?

a. Showing a customer why leasing a car is a better choice than buying one.
b. Convincing a charitable foundation to grant money to your job-training program for disadvantaged teenagers.
c. Demonstrating the features of an expensive computer system.
d. Persuading the loan officer at a local bank to lend you money for your proposed business venture.
e. Encouraging local businesspeople to join a service club to which you belong.

8. Invitation to Insight

Read a persuasive article in a magazine or newspaper. Try to determine which organizational pattern the article follows. Why do you think the author chose this pattern? Is it effective for the intended audience?

9. Skill Builder

With a small group of your classmates, plan an informative group presentation in which you (a) review the meaning of a communication concept you've learned about in this course, (b) provide examples to illustrate the concept, and (c) explain how students can apply this concept in their own lives.

Decide whether you will organize your presentation by topic or by task. Assign speaking roles, and plan your introduction, transitions, and conclusion. Agree on a set of unobtrusive signals you can use to regulate teammates' delivery. Conduct at least one dress rehearsal of your presentation. When you are ready, deliver and videotape the presentation.

Watch your video. Evaluate your group's organization, content, and delivery, using guidelines from Chapters 9–12 of your text. Discuss your evaluation with your teammates.

10. Skill Builder

Prepare the following special occasion speeches.

a. Welcome. Prepare a speech of welcome for a guest from the community who is visiting your class to better understand your college's opportunities.

b. Introduction. Create an introduction for a guest from a prominent community business who is invited to speak to your class about job interview strategies.

c. Speech to honor. Construct and present a speech that honors one of your classmates or a person or institution in your community whom you believe deserves recognition.

d. Award. Present an award to a classmate (best team member, best listener, best speaker, most improved speaker) that reflects some achievement or activity during the semester.

e. Celebration dinner. Your work team has just met a very important project deadline, and your work received rave reviews from your supervisor.

Mc Graw Hill **LearnSmart™**

For further review, go to the LearnSmart study module for this chapter.

appendix I
Interviewing Materials

● Sample Plan for an Informational Interview

The following plan shows the kind of work that should occur before an interviewer and interviewee sit down to or even schedule a meeting. Every important interview requires the kind of planning exhibited here to achieve its goals. As you read this account, notice that it follows the advice outlined in Chapter 6.

Analysis and research I know I'll never build the kind of financial security I am seeking by relying only on the income I earn from my job. Investing successfully will be the path to financial success. I also know I'm very unsophisticated when it comes to investing, so I want to get a financial advisor who can teach me about the world of finance and help me set up and follow a plan.

Picking a financial advisor is like choosing a doctor. Skill is important, but it's not the only thing that matters. I need to find someone who has a personal style I'm comfortable with and whose philosophy matches mine. I also need to find someone who is willing to devote time to me even though I don't have a great deal of money to invest . . . yet!

I've compiled a list of possible advisors from friends, newspaper articles, and listings in the phone directory. I will call several of the people on this list to set up appointments for interviews.

Goal To identify a financial planner with expertise in the field, whose investment philosophy matches mine, and who has a personal style I am comfortable with.

Interview strategy I will conduct interviews in the offices of each financial planner. Seeing where and how they do business will give me a good idea of my comfort level before asking any questions. For instance, seeing a shabby or disorganized office would cause me to doubt an advisor's competence. On the other hand, a very plush office might make me wonder if I was being charged too much just to support a lavish lifestyle.

I'm also interested in seeing how much time each person gives me for the interview. If the person is rushed when trying to get a new client, this could mean I won't get the time or attention I need once my money is in the planner's hands.

I want to see how much each person lets me explain my concerns and how much each controls the conversation. I'm no financial expert, but I don't like the attitude, "I'm the expert, so don't waste time asking too many questions." Because I would like someone who is willing to explain investing to me in a way I can understand, I'll be looking for a good teacher.

Topics and questions The following list shows the questions I'm planning to ask in each topic area as well as follow-up questions I can anticipate asking. I'm sure there will be a need for other secondary questions, but I can't predict all of them. I'll have to think of them on the spot

Topic A: Expertise in Investments and Financial Planning

[This series of open questions explores the interviewee's qualifications and also provides an opportunity for her to talk about herself.]

1. What credentials do you have that qualify you as a financial planner? How important are credentials? If they aren't important, what is the best measure of a financial planner's qualifications?

[These questions move from a narrow to a broader focus.]

2. Do you have any areas of specialization? How and why did you specialize in this area?

[These indirect questions are a way of finding out whether the advisor's performance has been satisfactory.]

3. How many clients have you served in the last five years? What is the length of the relationship with your clients? How many have you retained, and how many are no longer with you?

[The average portfolio size is one measure of the advisor's expertise.]

4. What's the average amount of money you have managed for your clients?

[A closed question, designed to give interviewer references.]

5. May I see a list of your past and current clients and call some of them for references?

[The first question is a broad, open one. The second, closed question will produce a specific answer that can be compared with those of other potential advisors.]

6. How would you describe your track record in terms of investment advice? Specifically, what has been the ratio of successful to unsuccessful advice?

Topic B: Investment Philosophy

[This broad, open question gives the advisor a chance to describe his or her approach.]

1. How would you describe your investment philosophy?

[This hypothetical question will provide specific information about how a client–advisor relationship might operate.]

2. If I became your client, what steps would you recommend to start and maintain a financial program?

[This sequence of questions moves from specific to broad topics in a logical order.]

3. What kind of products do you like to deal in? Which specific ones might you recommend for me? Why?

[This two-question sequence moves from a narrow to a broader focus. The most important information for the client is contained in the second question.]

4. I've read that some financial advisors make their income from commissions earned when their clients buy and sell investments. Other advisors charge a fee for their time. What approach do you take? Can you explain how this approach is in my interest as well as yours?

[Although this sounds like a closed question, it is likely to generate a long answer.]

5. How much should I expect to pay for your advice?

Topic C: Personal Style

[This indirect question really asks, "Would we work well together?"]

1. What kind of clients do you work well with? What kinds don't you work well with?

[The first question here is really an indirect way of discovering how much attention the advisor has paid to the potential client.]

2. Have you looked over the papers I sent you about my financial condition? What did you think of them?

[This clever hypothetical question has a better chance of generating a useful answer than the more direct "What can you tell me about the kind of service I can expect?"]

3. If I were to call one of your clients at random, what would he or she tell me about the type of service and frequency of communication I can expect with you?

[This is a straightforward, open question.]

4. If we were to develop a relationship, what would you expect of me?

[This hypothetical question anticipates an important issue.]

5. Suppose I were to disagree with your advice. What would you say and do?

• Sample Employment Interview

The following transcript is based on a real interview. As you read it, pay attention to both the interviewer's questions and the applicant's responses. In both cases, notice the strengths and the areas needing improvement. What parts of this interview would you like to incorporate in your style? What parts would you handle differently?

[The interview begins with an exchange of pleasantries]

Interviewer: Monica Hansen? I'm Chris Van Dyke. Welcome.

Applicant: It's good to meet you.

[. . . and small talk.]

Interviewer: Did you have any trouble finding us?

Applicant: The directions were perfect. And thanks for the parking pass.

[The interviewer briefly previews the approach of the interview and the anticipated amount of time.]	**Interviewer:**	Oh, yes. That's a necessity. The garage costs $12 per day if you don't have one. We'll have about a half-hour this morning to talk about the personnel administrator's position you've applied for. I'd like to learn about you. And, of course, I want to answer any questions you have about us.
	Applicant:	Great. I'm looking forward to it.
[Body of interview begins with an open question about employment history.]	**Interviewer:**	Good. Let's begin by having you tell me about your most recent position. Your résumé says you were at ITC in Springfield. Is that right?
[Interviewee uses answer to showcase the skills acquired in past job that could help in the one being offered here.]	**Applicant:**	That's right. My official job title was personnel assistant, but that really doesn't describe very well the work I did. I recruited nonexempt employees, processed the payroll, oriented new employees, and maintained the files.
[Follow-up questions explore areas of interest in the new job.]	**Interviewer:**	Were you involved with insurance?
[The applicant uses this answer to point out another skill that she brings to the job.]	**Applicant:**	Yes. I processed workers' compensation claims and maintained the insurance reports for our health care plans. I learned a lot about dealing with government regulations.
	Interviewer:	And you said you were involved in hiring?
	Applicant:	Yes. I was responsible for recruiting and interviewing all clerical and administrative support people.
[Another open question, this time exploring the applicant's ability to analyze her own performance.]	**Interviewer:**	How did that go?
[The applicant fails to use this answer to showcase her abilities . . .]	**Applicant:**	It was tough in Springfield. There's actually a shortage of talented support people there. It's an expensive town to live in, and there aren't a lot of people who can afford living there on an administrative assistant's salary. It's not like Atlanta, where there's plenty of good help.
[so the interviewer follows up with another question.]	**Interviewer:**	What did you learn about hiring from your experiences at ITC?

| | **Applicant:** | I learned to look further than the résumé. Some people seem great on paper, but you find there's something wrong when you hire them. Other people don't have much experience on paper, but they have a lot of potential. |

[This answer is better because it describes insights and skills the applicant brings to this job.]

Interviewer: How did you get beyond paper screening?

Applicant: Well, if someone looked at all promising, I would phone the former employers and talk to the people the applicant actually worked for. Of course, a lot of former employers are pretty noncommittal, but they usually would give clues about what they really thought about the person I was investigating—giving an indirect opinion without saying it outright.

Interviewer: What would you do if this was the person's first job?

[The applicant demonstrates resourcefulness here, spelling out her skill in the last sentence of her answer.]

Applicant: I found that almost everyone had done some kind of work—part-time or volunteer. And I could check up on that. Or I would even ask for the names of a few teachers and phone them, if the person was just graduating. I learned there's almost always a way to find what you're looking for, if you get creative.

Interviewer: Didn't that take a lot of time?

[This is a subtle way of saying, "I have good judgment."]

Applicant: Yes, it did. But it was worth it in the long run because we got much better employees that way. We almost never had to dismiss someone whom we'd done a phone check on.

Interviewer: You were promoted after a year. Why?

[Again, the applicant's answer introduces a trait that would be valuable in the new job: The desire for self-improvement.]

Applicant: I was lucky to be in the right place. The company was growing, and we were very busy. I tried to take advantage of the situation by offering to do more and by taking classes at night.

Interviewer: What classes did you take?

[Presumably the skills acquired in these courses would be useful if the applicant is hired. In any case, she demonstrates the desire to learn skills useful in the business world.]

Applicant: I took an applied human relations class last spring. And before that, a couple of computer classes: one in database management and one in desktop publishing. Our department was thinking about starting an employee newsletter, and I wanted to see if we could produce it in-house.

Interviewer: It sounds like you've done very well at ITC. Why do you want to leave?

<table>
<tr>
<td>[The response begins with a provocative statement and then goes on to supply a solid reason for seeking a new job.]</td>
<td>Applicant:</td>
<td>In some ways I don't want to leave. The people are great—most of them—and I've enjoyed the work. But I'm looking for more challenges, and there isn't much chance for me to take on more responsibility there.</td>
</tr>
<tr>
<td></td>
<td>Interviewer:</td>
<td>Why not?</td>
</tr>
<tr>
<td></td>
<td>Applicant:</td>
<td>Well, my boss, the personnel director, is very happy in her job and has no plans to leave. She's young, and there's very little chance I'll be able to advance.</td>
</tr>
<tr>
<td>[The interviewer seeks specifics to elaborate on the broad statement "I'm looking for more challenges"]</td>
<td>Interviewer:</td>
<td>I see. Well, that is a problem. And what kind of responsibilities are you looking for?</td>
</tr>
<tr>
<td>[. . . and the candidate supplies answers.]</td>
<td>Applicant:</td>
<td>I'd say the biggest one is the chance to help make policy. In my past jobs, I've been carrying out policies that other people—management—have made. That's been fine, but I'd like to be involved in setting some policies myself.</td>
</tr>
<tr>
<td>[Again, the interviewer follows up by seeking more specifics]</td>
<td>Interviewer:</td>
<td>What kinds of policies?</td>
</tr>
<tr>
<td>[. . . and the candidate is prepared with detailed responses.]</td>
<td>Applicant:</td>
<td>Oh, there are several. Designing benefits packages. Coming up with a performance review system that people will take seriously. Teaching our supervisors how to interview and hire more systematically.</td>
</tr>
<tr>
<td>[The interviewer makes a smooth transition to a new topic.]</td>
<td>Interviewer:</td>
<td>I see. Well, the position you've applied for certainly does have those sorts of responsibilities. Let me ask you another question. What do you enjoy most about personnel work?</td>
</tr>
<tr>
<td>[The stock answer "I like to work with people" is so broad that it has little meaning]</td>
<td>Applicant:</td>
<td>Well, I really enjoy the chance to work so much with people. Of course, there's a lot of paperwork, too, but I especially like the chance to work with people.</td>
</tr>
<tr>
<td>[. . . so the interviewer seeks clarification.]</td>
<td>Interviewer:</td>
<td>When you say "people," what kinds of work are you thinking of?</td>
</tr>
<tr>
<td></td>
<td>Applicant:</td>
<td>I guess the common denominator is making people happy. Lots of employees get involved with the personnel department—once they've been hired, that is—because they have problems. Maybe it's an insurance claim or a problem with their performance</td>
</tr>
</table>

review. It makes me feel good to see them leave feeling satisfied, or at least feeling better after they've come in so upset.

Interviewer: Are you always able to help them?

Applicant: No, of course not. Sometimes a person will want the impossible, and sometimes there just won't be any answer.

[Again, the interviewer uses a situational approach, seeking specifics.]

Interviewer: Can you give examples of these times?

[The applicant does a good job of describing a situation that illustrates her previous answer.]

Applicant: Well, one example of an impossible request comes up a lot with health insurance. At ITC we could choose from two plans. With one plan you could use any doctor you wanted. You had to make a co-payment with that one. With the other plan, you had to choose a doctor from a list of preferred providers, but there was no co-payment. If an employee chose the preferred-provider plan and later decided he or she wanted to use a doctor who wasn't on the list, we just couldn't do anything about it.

Interviewer: We've had that problem here, too. How did you handle it?

Applicant: Being sympathetic helped a little. Even if I couldn't give them what they wanted, at least saying I was sorry might have made it seem less like a total rejection. I also pointed out that they *could* switch plans during the open-enrollment period, which comes every year. I've also suggested to my boss that we do a better job of informing people about the restrictions of the preferred-provider plan before they sign up and maybe even get them to sign a statement that says they understand them. I think that would reduce the surprises that come up later.

[With this new topic, the interviewer shifts from fact to opinion questions.]

Interviewer: That's a good idea. Monica, what qualities do you think are important for a personnel officer?

Applicant: Knowing the job is definitely important, but I'd say getting along with people might be even more important.

Interviewer: And how would you describe your ability to get along?

Applicant: Sometimes I think I deserve an Academy Award for acting the opposite of the way I feel.

Interviewer: Really? Tell me about it.

	Applicant:	Every so often people will come in with an attitude problem, and I try to calm them down by acting more pleasant than I feel. For example, we've had people who think they're entitled to take six months off for a workers' compensation claim, when the doctor has said they're ready to come back after a few weeks. They come in and yell at us, and it's tough to be pleasant at times like those. But I don't think there's any point in being blunt or rude. It just makes them more angry.

[The applicant offers a specific example to illustrate her provocative statement about acting the opposite of the way she feels.]

[This indirect question really asks, "What kind of manager might you be?"]	**Interviewer:**	I see what you mean. Let's shift gears, Monica. If you were to pick a boss, what are the important traits that he or she should have?
	Applicant:	Let me see . . . certainly lots of follow-up—letting people know where they stand. The ability to give criticism constructively and to compliment good work. Giving people a task and then leaving them alone, without nagging.
	Interviewer:	But still being there to help if it's needed, right?
	Applicant:	Sure. But also giving me the space to finish a job without staying *too* close.
	Interviewer:	Anything else?
	Applicant:	Being available for help, as you said. Being consistent. And being willing to train employees in new jobs, letting them grow. And considering employees' personal goals.

[The interviewer turns to a new topic area.]	**Interviewer:**	In personnel work, there's a need for confidentiality. What does that mean to you?
	Applicant:	That's an important area. You see lots of personal information, and it's easy to make offhand remarks that could upset someone.
	Interviewer:	What kinds of things do you have to be careful about?
	Applicant:	Oh, even something as simple as a person's birthday. Most people wouldn't care, but some people might be offended if their birthdays got out. I've learned to be constantly on guard, to watch what I say. I'm a private person anyway, so that helps.

[This question explores the candidate's personal attitudes.]	**Interviewer:**	Monica, I've been asking you a lot of questions. Let me ask just one more; then it can be your turn. What are the factors that motivate you?

	Applicant:	Well, I like to be busy. If things aren't busy, I still work, but I like to be stimulated. I seem to get more work done when I'm busy than when there's plenty of time. It's crazy, but true. I'm also motivated by the chance to grow and take on as much responsibility as I can handle.
[Almost every employment interview includes a chance for the interviewee to ask questions.]	**Interviewer:**	Monica, what questions do you have for me? What can I tell you about the job or the company?
[The applicant wisely begins by asking about the company, not focusing on personal questions such as compensation.]	**Applicant:**	What kind of growth do you see for the company?
	Interviewer:	Well, we have 155 employees now. As I think you know, we're five years old, and we started with five employees. Our sales were up 14 percent last year, and it looks like we'll be expanding more.
	Applicant:	How many employees do you think will be added?
	Interviewer:	Well, we hired 20 new people last year, and we expect to hire almost the same number this year.
	Applicant:	And what's the turnover like?
	Interviewer:	That's a good question for a personnel person to ask! We've been growing so much, and people have been able to move into more responsible jobs, so they've been satisfied for the most part. Our turnover has been pretty low—about 15 percent annually.
[This question focuses on responsibilities of the job.]	**Applicant:**	Will the person you hire be involved in making policy?
	Interviewer:	Yes, definitely. We're still trying to catch up with ourselves after growing so fast. A big project for this year is to put together an employee handbook. Too many of our policies are verbal now, and that's not good. Developing that handbook would mean working directly with the president of the company, and that definitely involves developing policy.
[Finally, the applicant asks about compensation and benefits.]	**Applicant:**	Of course, I'm interested in learning about the benefits and salary.

	Interviewer:	Of course. Here's a copy of our benefits summary for you to study. We can talk about salary later. Right now I'd like you to meet a couple of our managers. After you've spoken with them, we can get back together to discuss salary and other matters.

[The interviewer appropriately defers a complete answer until the company has a clearer idea of the candidate's desirability.]

[The interviewer wraps up the conversation by describing when the hiring decision will be made.]

We will definitely be making our decision within the next 10 days, so I promise you you'll have an answer before the first of next month. It's been a real pleasure talking to you, Monica. You certainly express yourself well. I'll talk with you again soon.

Applicant: Thanks. I've enjoyed the talk, too. I'll look forward to hearing from you.

• Strategies for Performance Appraisal Interviewing

Performance appraisal interviews are a special kind of interview in which superiors and subordinates meet at regularly scheduled intervals (usually annually) to discuss the quality of the subordinate's performance. These interviews have several functions, including the following:

- *Letting the employee know where he or she stands.* This kind of feedback includes praising good work, communicating areas that need improvement, and conveying to the employee his or her prospects for advancement.
- *Developing employee skills.* The review can be a chance for the employee to learn new skills. Among their other roles, managers and supervisors should be teachers. The performance appraisal interview can be a chance to show an employee how to do a better job.
- *Improving employment relationship.* Performance reviews should improve superior–subordinate relationships and give employees a sense of participation in the job. Ideally, employees will leave the interview feeling better about themselves and the organization.
- *Helping management learn the employee's point of view.* A performance appraisal should include upward as well as downward communication. It provides a chance for subordinates to explain their perspective to managers.
- *Counseling the employee.* An appraisal interview provides the chance for managers to learn about personal problems that may be affecting an employee's performance and to offer advice and support.
- *Setting goals for the future.* One result of every performance appraisal interview should be a clear idea of how both the superior and the subordinate will behave in the future.

Even though performance appraisal interviews serve valuable functions, they aren't always a positive experience for employees or managers—especially when there are problems that must be addressed. As you learned in Chapter 5, receiving criticism can be a challenge. The interviewing strategies outlined in this section can help make sure a performance review meets the needs of both management and employees. While following these guidelines won't guarantee a successful performance review, it can increase the chances that the meeting will be genuinely constructive and serve the interests of both the superior and the subordinate.

Steps in the Appraisal Process

After an initial exchange of pleasantries—usually brief—the manager should provide a rationale for the interview, an outline of what information will be covered and how it will be used, and a preview of the interview's probable length. After the preliminaries, the body of an appraisal interview should go on to cover three areas: a review of the criteria established in past meetings, a discussion of the employee's performance, and a setting of goals for the future.

Review Progress   The first step in the body of any appraisal interview should be to identify the criteria by which the employee is being evaluated. Ideally, these criteria will already be clear to both the manager and the employee, but it is wise to restate them. A manager might say:

> Bill, as I'm sure you remember, we decided at our last meeting to focus on several targets. We agreed that if you could reach them, you'd be doing your present job very well and you'd be setting yourself up for an assistant sales manager's position. Here's the list of targets we developed last time [shows employee list]. So these are the areas we need to look at today.

Discuss Successes, Problems, and Needs   After the criteria have been defined, the discussion can focus on how well the employee has satisfied them. Discussion will be easiest when the goals are measurable: Are sales up 15 percent? Have jobs been completed on time? If the employee has explanations for why targets were not reached, it is the manager's job to consider these fairly. Some goals are subjective, so the evaluation of their performance will be a matter of judgment as well. Even seemingly vague goals like "being more patient with customers" can be at least partially clarified by turning them into simple behavioral descriptions such as "letting customers talk without interrupting them."

When evaluating past performance, it is important to maintain a balance among the points under consideration. Without meaning to let it happen, a manager and employee can become involved in discussing (or debating) a relatively unimportant point at length, throwing the overall look at the employee's performance out of perspective. A skillful interviewer will focus only on the most important criteria, usually dealing with no more than three areas that need work. Even the most demanding manager will realize upon reflection that changing old habits is difficult and it is unrealistic to expect dramatic improvement in too many areas within a short time.

Even when an appraisal is conducted with the best of intentions, its evaluative nature raises the odds of a defensive response. Feedback will be best received when it meets several criteria. Observing these guidelines can boost the chances of keeping the interview's tone constructive:

- *Feedback should be accurate.* Perhaps the worst mistake an evaluator can make is to get the facts wrong. Before you judge an employee, be sure you have an accurate picture of his or her performance and all the factors that affected it. A tell-and-listen approach can help the manager understand an employee's performance more fully.

- *Feedback should be relevant to the job.* For example, it may be legitimate to comment on an employee's appearance in a job that involves contact with the public, but it is out of line to be critical about the way he or she handles personal matters after business hours.

- *Feedback should include a balance of praise and constructive criticism.* Both everyday experience and research have demonstrated the power of positive reinforcement. But only mentioning the positives means forgoing the possibility for identifying areas for growth and improvement.

- *Feedback should be delivered in a way that protects people's dignity.* Sooner or later, even the most outstanding employee will need to hear criticism about his or her work. Delivering negative information is one of the biggest challenges a manager or supervisor can face. The guidelines in Chapter 5 (pp. 116–118) offer tips on how to offer negative feedback supportively. Handling critical situations well isn't just the boss's responsibility; the subordinate needs to behave responsibly too. The guidelines for coping nondefensively with criticism outlined on pp. 118–120 should be helpful when it is your turn to receive critical messages.

Table AI-1	Checklist for Performance Appraisal Interviewing

A. Interview covers key areas

   1. Orients employee

   2. Establishes positive climate

   3. Reviews past achievement of goals

   4. Identifies successes, problems, and needs in employee's area of responsibility

   5. Establishes new goals with employee

B. Feedback is delivered constructively

   1. Information is accurate

   2. Feedback is appropriate to critic's role

   3. There is a balance of praise and constructive criticism

C. Praise is delivered effectively

   1. Praise is sincere

   2. Specific behaviors identified

   3. Emphasis is on progress, not perfection

   4. Praise communicated by deeds as well as by words

D. Criticism is expressed constructively

   1. Criticism limited to key areas

   2. Criticism delivered in face-saving manner

   3. Criticism accompanied by offer to help

   4. Benefits of cooperating emphasized

E. Interview accomplishes all necessary functions

   1. Lets employee know where he or she stands

   2. Develops employee skills

   3. Improves communication climate and boosts morale

   4. Helps management understand employee's point of view

   5. Counsels employee as appropriate

   6. Sets goals for future

Set Goals   Once the employee and manager have discussed past successes, problems, and needs, the task becomes defining goals for the future. The goals should meet several criteria:

- They should focus on the most important aspects of the job. The tried-and-true 80:20 rule applies here: Changing 20 percent of a worker's behavior will usually solve 80 percent of the problems.
- They should be described as specifically as possible so both manager and employee will know what actions constitute the target.
- A time period should be stated for each target. People often work best when faced with a deadline, and setting dates lets both parties know when the results are due.
- The targets ought to provide some challenge to the worker, requiring effort yet being attainable. A manageable challenge will produce the greatest growth and leave workers and managers feeling pleased with the changes that occur.

Review and Respond to the Written Record   The appraisal process commonly has a written dimension in addition to the interview itself. Before the meeting, the manager often completes an evaluation form listing characteristics or behaviors important to the job. Ideally, the information on this form is taken from the goals set at the previous interview. In some organizations, the subordinate also completes a self-rating form covering similar areas. In most companies, a performance review is summarized and documented with a written evaluation. In most cases, the manager completes a final report that summarizes the results of the session. The employee usually has the option of adding his or her own response to the manager's report. This document then becomes part of the employee's records and is used as a basis for future evaluations and as a source of information for decisions about promotions.

• Sample Informative Presentation

The following presentation is typical of informative talks given every business day. The personnel specialist in a medium-sized company has gathered a group of staff members together to describe the features of a tax-reduction plan explaining employee benefits. Notice how the speaker uses most of the strategies covered in Chapters 9–12 to make her ideas clearer and to increase the attention of her audience.

The speaker's goal here is to help listeners decide whether they're interested enough in the benefits plan to attend a much longer meeting on the subject. She wisely chose this approach to avoid going into detail about the plan when some people might not be interested. By giving a short description of how the plan works, she can keep this introductory talk brief and simple.

[The promise of increasing take-home pay is a guaranteed attention-getter.]

I know you're busy, but I don't think you'll mind taking a few minutes away from work this morning. You see, I'm here today to show you a way that you can increase the amount of money you take home each month.

[This opening illustrates the persuasive element that is called for in many informative presentations.]

No, I'm not going to announce an across-the-board raise. But increasing your salary isn't the only way to boost your income. Another way that works just as well is to reduce your taxes. After all, every dollar less you pay in taxes is like having a dollar more in your pocket.

[An overall view of the plan is presented here.]

In the next few minutes, I'll explain the company's Flexible Benefits Plan. It's a perfectly legal option that lets you increase your real income by cutting the amount of taxes you pay, so that your income will grow even without a raise. I know this sounds too good to be true, but it really works! I've already signed up, and figure it will save me almost $2,000 a year. It can probably save you a lot, too.

[A brief transition alerts listeners to the first main point in the body of the presentation: the difference between before- and after-tax dollars.]

Before you can appreciate how the Flexible Benefits Plan works, you have to understand the difference between before-tax and after-tax dollars. *[The speaker shows Exhibit 1 here.]* Before-tax dollars are the amount that shows up every month in the "Gross Amount" box on our paychecks. But we don't get to spend our full salaries. There are several deductions: federal income tax withholding, Social Security (the amount in the "F.I.C.A." box), state tax withholding, and disability insurance premiums (the amount in the "S.D.I." box). What's left in the "Net Amount" box is our pay in after-tax dollars.

[The enlarged display of a familiar paycheck stub clarifies the unfamiliar concepts of before- and after-tax dollars.]

90-2176
1222

7209

PAY _____ One thousand four hundred twenty nine and 60/100 _____ DOLLARS

TIME WK'D	DATE	TO THE ORDER OF	GROSS AMOUNT	FED. W/H	F.I.C.A.	STATE W/H		S.D.I.		CREDIT UNION	NET AMOUNT
	7/31/13	J. Doe	1958.33	293.74	78.33	68.54		88.12			1429.60
					DESCRIPTION						

GU. Hinton

EXHIBIT 1   Paycheck Stub

[The speaker wisely avoids a complicated discussion of before- and after-tax dollars in different tax brackets.]

Once all those deductions are taken away from our pay, every before-tax dollar shrinks in value to about 73 cents. *[The speaker shows Exhibit 2 here.]* And that's in a low tax bracket. If your income is higher, then the difference between before- and after-tax dollars is even bigger. This means that it takes at least $136.33 in after-tax dollars to buy something that costs $100 in before-tax dollars.

[The visual display increases the clarity and impact of the difference between before- and after-tax dollars.]

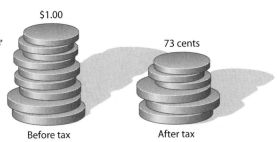

$1.00

73 cents

Before tax   After tax

EXHIBIT 2   Value of Before- and After-Tax Dollars

You can probably see now that it's better to buy things in before-tax dollars whenever you can. And that's what the Flexible Benefits Plan lets you do. Let me explain how it works.

The Flexible Benefits Plan is so great because it allows you to pay for some important items in before-tax dollars. The plan lets you set aside pay in two categories: medical costs and dependent care. Let's cover each of these in detail so you can see which expenses are covered.

A look at the chart entitled "Allowable Medical Expenses" shows which items you can use under the Flexible Benefits Plan. *[The speaker points to each item in Exhibit 3 as she discusses it.]* As I cover these expenses, think about how much you spend in each area.

- Health insurance deductibles
- Health insurance co-payments
- Drugs and prescriptions
- Vision care and equipment
- Psychologists and psychiatrists
- Dental care and orthodontia

EXHIBIT 3 Allowable Medical Expenses

First we'll talk about health-insurance deductibles and co-payments. Under our company's policy, you pay the first $300 of expenses for yourself and each dependent. You also make a $10 co-payment for each visit to a doctor. Let's say that you and one dependent have to pay the $300 deductible each year, and that you made five visits to the doctor. That's a total of $650 per year you could have covered under the plan.

Drugs and prescriptions include every kind of medicine you buy, even if you buy it over the counter without a prescription. And, don't forget, the plan covers payments you make for everyone you claim as a dependent: your kids, maybe your spouse, and maybe even an older parent whom you're caring for.

Here's an article from *Changing Times* magazine that says a family of three spends an average of $240 per year on drugs. Maybe you spend even more. Whatever you do spend on medicine can be included in the plan, which means you will pay less for it than if you used after-tax dollars.

[Examples of typical vision-care fees illustrate the potential costs in this area.]

Vision care and equipment include eyeglasses and contact lenses as well as any fees you or your dependents pay to optometrists or ophthalmologists. With a pair of reading glasses costing at least $45 and a new set of contact lenses costing more than $80, the money could really mount up.

Psychologists and psychiatrists are also covered, which means that any counseling you receive will cost a lot less.

Dental care and orthodontia are covered, too. If you or your dependents need major dental work, this can mean a lot. And if you're paying for your kids' braces, you can really save a bundle. We did some checking, and the average orthodontic treatment today runs about $3,500 over 3 years—or more than $1,000 per year.

[Comparing the unfamiliar benefits plan to the familiar notion of a discount helps make the advantages clear.]

Nobody likes to spend money for medical expenses like these, but paying for them with before-tax dollars under the Flexible Benefits Plan is like getting a discount of 20 percent or more—clearly, a great deal.

[The transition here uses signposting to mark a shift to the second type of expense covered by the plan.]

But medical costs aren't the only expenses you can include in the Flexible Benefits Plan. There's a second way you can boost your take-home pay: by including dependent care in the plan.

[The example of potential savings under the plan is a guaranteed attention-getter for working parents.]

For most people, dependents are children. Any costs of caring for your kids can be paid for in before-tax dollars, meaning you'll pay a lot less. You can include day care services, preschool fees, even in-home care for your child. We did some checking and found that keeping a child in preschool or day care in this area from 8:30 in the morning until 5 PM averages about $5,000 per year. By shifting this amount into the Flexible Benefits Plan, the real cost drops by more than $1,000. Not bad for filling out a few forms!

When you combine the savings on health care and dependents, the potential savings that come from joining the Flexible Benefits Plan are impressive. Let's take a look at a typical example of just how much money the Flexible Benefits Plan can save. Your personal situation probably won't be exactly like this one, but you can still get a feeling for how good the plan is. *[The speaker shows Exhibit 4.]*

[A restatement of the thesis is combined with the introduction of an example to support its claim.]

[The chart provides a visual outline of the example. Without the exhibit, the dollar amounts would be too confusing to follow.]

	WITHOUT PLAN	WITH PLAN
GROSS SALARY	$23,500	$23,500
SALARY REDUCTIONS		
Health Care	0	650
Prescriptions and Drugs	0	240
Vision Care	0	60
Dental Care	0	180
Dependent Care	0	1,800
	$23,500	$20,570
TAXES		
Federal Income Tax @ 15%	3,525	3,085
State Income Tax @ 3.5%	764	720
FICA and SDI @ 8.15%	1,915	1,676
	$6,204	$5,481
AFTER-TAX EXPENSES		
Health Care	650	0
Prescriptions and Drugs	240	0
Vision Care	60	0
Dental Care	180	0
Dependent Care	1,800	0
Net Pay	$14,366	$15,089
ANNUAL SAVINGS $723		

EXHIBIT 4 Savings with Flexible Benefits Plan

Let's suppose your salary is $23,500 and you have a spouse and one child. Let's say that your health and dependent expenses are pretty much like the ones we've been discussing here today. *[The speaker points to "Salary Reductions" section of chart.]* Your health insurance deductibles and co-payments amount to $650, and you spend $240 over the year on prescriptions and drugs. Let's say that one person in your family needs one set of eyeglasses. You all get dental checkups, and you don't even have cavities! You spend $1,800 on child care—not bad these days.

If we look at the top third of the chart, it might seem that following the plan costs you more. After all, your salary would be $23,500 without the plan but only $20,570 with your expenses deducted from the plan.

[As the speaker points to the "Annual Savings" line on the chart, the audience sees in real dollars the potential advantage of the plan.]

But look what happens once we start to figure taxes. *[The speaker points to "Taxes" section of chart.]* Since your pay with the plan is less, you pay less in taxes. A little subtraction shows that the difference between the $6,204 you'd pay without the plan and the $5,481 you'd pay with it amounts to a savings of $723.

This is just a small example of how much you can save. If your expenses are higher—if you have more medical costs, for example—the advantage is even greater. As your salary goes up and you move into a higher tax bracket, the advantages grow, too. And don't forget that the savings I've been talking about are just for 1 year. As time goes by, your earning power will grow even more.

[In a restatement of the thesis the speaker returns to the main advantage of the plan.]

Now you can see why we're so glad to offer the Flexible Benefits Plan. It can boost your take-home pay even before you get a raise. It costs you nothing.

[Listeners are told what to do next if they are interested in the plan.]

If you're interested in learning more, we encourage you to read the booklet I'll hand out in a moment. It contains a worksheet that will help you estimate how much you stand to save under the plan. If the idea still interests you, please attend the workshop we'll be holding next Friday during the lunch hour in the third-floor meeting room. At that time, we can answer your questions and make an appointment for each of you to sign up at the personnel office. In the meantime, I'll be happy to answer any questions you have now.

• Sample Sales Presentation

The following presentation (outlined in Figure A2.1) demonstrates most of the persuasive principles covered in Chapter 12 as well as the general guidelines about speaking to an audience introduced in Chapters 9 through 11. The purpose and approach are based on a sound audience analysis. As you will see, the talk has a clear thesis and a clear, logical organizational structure. A variety of verbal and visual supports add interest, clarity, and proof.

The speaker's company, Ablex Technologies, manufactures sophisticated electronic components. One of its best customers is BioMedical Instruments (BMI), which produces a wide variety of sophisticated medical diagnostic instruments. The company's biggest contracts with BMI are for kidney-dialysis and blood-analyzer parts, which total almost $1 million per year.

Under a much smaller and older contract, Ablex also supplies BMI with parts for an X-ray unit. BMI doesn't make the unit anymore but is committed to furnishing current users with replacement parts until the machines drop out of use, and Ablex is obliged to supply BMI. Producing these X-ray parts is usually a problem: Orders are small and sporadic, leading to delays and headaches for everyone concerned. The speaker is presenting a plan that offers a better way to handle replenishment of the X-ray parts.

The audience is Mary Ann Hirsch, the buyer at BMI, and two production engineers. Although the purchasing director and the chief project engineer are not at the presentation, they will rely on the information gathered by their subordinates and, ultimately, will be the ones to approve or reject this idea—so in a way, they're part of the audience, too.

Thesis: The proposed forecasting and purchasing agreement will allow both BMI and Ablex to better supply X-ray parts in a timely, affordable, and trouble-free manner.

Introduction
    I. Our basically positive relationship with BMI has only one problem: the X-ray parts.
    II. While a problem does exist, there is a solution
        A. The problem involves erratic orders for X-ray parts.
        B. Our solution has several benefits.

Body
    I. Supplying X-ray parts has been a continuing headache.
        A. Orders for X-ray parts are irregular and unpredictable. [*line graph*]
        B. These irregular orders make it tough to ship orders to BMI in a timely way. [*example*]
    II. Fortunately, there is a solution to the X-ray problem.
        A. Here's an outline of our plan.
        B. The plan has several advantages.
            1. Orders can be delivered more quickly. [*comparison chart*]
            2. Ordering is more flexible. [*examples*]
            3. Time can be saved in ordering and follow-up. [*example*]
            4. The unit cost is less than under current plan. [*column chart, comparison chart*]

Conclusion: By now you can see that there's a solution to the X-ray problem.
    I. The plan has advantages for everyone involved.
    II. We look forward to putting it into action soon.

FIGURE A2.1   Outline of Sample Presentation

[Introduction emphasizes the positive aspects of the relationship with the customer. Brief sketch of the problem establishes common ground. "We're in this together, and it's no good for either of us."]

We've been involved in a long, positive relationship with BMI. The only troubles we've ever encountered have come from the X-ray parts. Even though they are only a small part of our business with you, they seem to involve the greatest headaches for you and us. The timing of these orders is impossible for you to predict, which makes it hard for us to get parts from our suppliers and deliver the product to you quickly. This leads to all sorts of problems: unhappy customers who have to wait for the equipment they ordered and time spent by people at both of our companies keeping in touch.

[Preview lists the main advantages of the plan that will be proposed.]

We think there's a better way to handle the X-ray problem. It'll reduce frustration, cut costs, and let all of us spend our time on more productive parts of our jobs. But before we talk about this new plan, let me review why the present arrangement for handling X-ray orders is such a headache.

[Transition leads to the "problem" section of the presentation.]

The main problem we face is irregular orders. A look at the order history for the last year shows that there's no pattern—and no way to predict when customers will order replacement parts for their X-ray units. *[The speaker shows Exhibit 5 here.]*

[Visual exhibit clearly demonstrates the unpredictable nature of customer orders.]

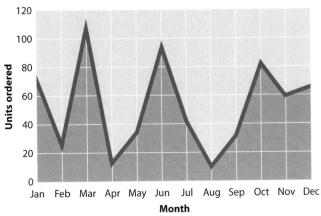

EXHIBIT 5   X-Ray Ordering Pattern

[Example shows the problems flowing from irregular orders.]

This unpredictable pattern makes it tough for us to serve you quickly. We have to order parts from our suppliers, which often can take a long time. For instance, in the February 17 order, it took 6 weeks for our suppliers to get us the parts we needed to manufacture the X-ray components you needed. Once we had the parts, it took us the usual 4 weeks to assemble them. As you said at the time, this delay kept your customer waiting almost 3 months for the components needed to get their equipment up and running, and that's poison for customer relations.

[Example highlights amount of time wasted.]

Delays like this aren't just bad for your relationship with customers, they also waste time—yours and ours. Mary Ann, do you remember how many phone calls and letters it took to keep track of that February order? In fact, every year we spend more time on these X-ray orders that involve a few thousand dollars than we do on the dialysis and blood-analyzer parts that involve around a million dollars annually. That's just not a good use of time.

[Transition leads to the second consequence of irregular orders: wasted time. "Solution" part of the presentation then introduced.]

So we clearly have a situation that's bad for everybody. Fortunately, we believe there's a better way—better for you, us, and your customers. The plan involves your giving us an annual purchasing forecast for X-ray parts. Instead of waiting for your customers to place individual orders, you'd estimate the total sales likely to occur in a year. Then we would acquire enough parts from our suppliers to assemble those items so that we could have them ready quickly as your customers place orders.

[Advantages of solution are previewed in the chart.]

This simple plan has several advantages. They're summarized on this chart, but let me explain them in a little more detail. *[The speaker shows Exhibit 6 here.]*

- Quicker delivery
- Flexible ordering
- Fewer problems
- Lower cost

EXHIBIT 6 Advantages of Annual Forecasting for X-Ray Parts

[Strongest advantage to listeners is introduced first to get positive impression early.]

The first advantage is that advance purchasing will speed up delivery of your orders. Instead of waiting for our suppliers to ship parts, we can begin to assemble your order as soon as you send it. You can get an idea of the time savings by looking at how much time this plan would have saved on the order you placed in February. *[The speaker shows Exhibit 7.]*

[Bar chart graphically demonstrates time saved.]

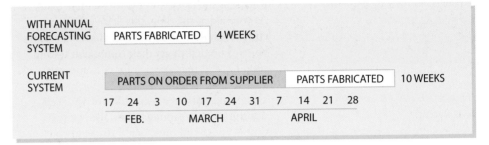

WITH ANNUAL FORECASTING SYSTEM	PARTS FABRICATED		4 WEEKS
CURRENT SYSTEM	PARTS ON ORDER FROM SUPPLIER	PARTS FABRICATED	10 WEEKS

17 24   3   10   17   24   31   7   14   21   28

FEB.   MARCH   APRIL

EXHIBIT 7   Annual Forecasting Speeds Delivery Time

[Transition leads to the second advantage of the plan: flexibility. Hypothetical example helps audience visualize this advantage.]

Besides being quick, the plan is flexible. If you wind up receiving more orders than you anticipated when you made your original forecast, you can update the plan every 6 months. That means we'll never run out of parts for the X-ray units. Suppose you projected 1,400 units in your original forecast. If you've already ordered 1,000 six months later, you could update your forecast at that point to 2,000 units and we'd have the parts on hand when you needed them.

[Transition leads to anticipation of a possible listener objection: What if orders decrease? Credible authority is cited to support this point.]

This semiannual revision of the forecast takes care of increases in orders, but you might be wondering about the opposite situation— what would happen if orders are less than you expected. The plan anticipates that possibility, too. We're willing to extend the date by which you're obliged to use your annual estimate of parts to 18 months. In other words, with this plan you'd have 18 months to use the parts you expected to use in 12. That's pretty safe, because Ted Forester [BMI's vice president of sales and marketing] predicts that the existing X-ray machines will be in use for at least the next 6 or 7 years before they're replaced with newer models.

[Internal review reminds listeners of previously introduced advantages and leads to identification of a third benefit: less wasted time.]

Flexibility and speed are two good advantages, but there are other benefits of the plan as well. It can save time for both you and us. You know how much time we spend on the phone every time there's a surprise X-ray order, and I imagine you have to deal with impatient customers, too. Talking about delays is certainly no fun, and with this annual purchasing plan it won't be necessary because we can guarantee delivery within 3 weeks of receiving your order. Think of the aggravation that will avoid!

[Second most important advantage is introduced last, where it is likely to be remembered by listeners.]

By now, you can see why we're excited about this plan. But there's one final benefit as well: The plan will save you money. When we order our parts in larger quantities, the unit price is less than the one we face with smaller orders. We're willing to pass along the savings to you, which means that you'll be paying less under this plan than you are now. Notice how ordering a year's supply of parts drops the unit price considerably. *[The speaker shows Exhibit 8.]*

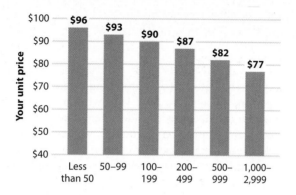

EXHIBIT 8   Annual Forecasting Reduces Unit Price

You can see that this plan is a real money saver. Compare the savings you could have realized on last year's order of 597 units if this plan had been in effect. *[The speaker shows Exhibit 9.]*

597 units at higher unit price	$55,506
597 units at volume unit price	45,969
First year savings	$ 9,537

EXHIBIT 9   One Year's Saving with Annual Forecasting Plan

[Conclusion reviews the plan's advantages and makes appeal to adopt it.]

So that's the plan. It's simple. It's risk-free. It's convenient. It's flexible. And along with all these advantages, it can cut your costs. We're prepared to start working with you immediately to put this plan into action. If we start soon, we'll never have to deal with X-ray headaches again. Then we can put our energy into the larger, more satisfying projects that are more rewarding for both of us.

appendix III
Business Writing

Entire books and academic courses are devoted to the study of business writing. This appendix is no substitute for a thorough study of this important topic. It does, however, provide some guidelines about creating the most common types of written business messages. Many organizations have their own styles, which may vary in one or more ways from these basic rules. When you are writing on behalf of an organization, you will want to learn and follow its conventions.

● Writing Well

Just as your style of dress and grooming create a first impression when you meet others in person, the appearance of your written messages makes a powerful statement to readers, who are likely to consider them a reflection of your other qualities. Besides creating a good impression of yourself, well designed and well executed business writing makes your message easier to understand. Likewise, a shabby e-mail, report, letter, or memo has the same effect as stained clothes, bad breath, mumbling, or rambling on disjointedly.

Adapt to Your Audience

Put yourself in the shoes of the person or people who will read your message, and write in a way that addresses their concerns, knowledge, and interests. Ask yourself: What do they want or need to know? How much detail is necessary? Why should they care about my topic? What will motivate them to do what I'm asking?

Once you have identified what your readers care about, write in a way that demonstrates your concern. Make the receiver's needs the subject of your first sentences. Instead of writing "We received your request for a refund and will begin working on it," write "You should receive your refund within 4 days." When responding to a complaint, don't say, "The long wait you experienced was due to a temporary staffing shortage." (The reader isn't likely to care about your staffing problems.) Instead, say, "You are absolutely right: Customers shouldn't have to wait for service."

Build Goodwill

The best way to build goodwill is to demonstrate you have the reader's best interests in mind.

- *Emphasize positive concepts rather than negative ones.* State what can be done rather than what can't be or hasn't been done. For example, when proposing a meeting, don't say you are busy next Tuesday. Instead, say, "I can meet anytime next Monday, Wednesday, Thursday, or Friday."

- *Adopt a helpful and respectful approach.* Blaming others and using "you" statements often create defensiveness. "You didn't turn in your time sheet before the June 1 deadline" is an accusatory "you" statement that blames the reader. You minimize the chance of a defensive reaction by saying the same thing just as clearly and less aggressively: "Because we received your time sheet on June 4, your check will be processed with others submitted that week and will be ready June 15."

Organize Carefully

First and foremost, business writing must be organized. Start by listing all of the items you need to cover and then group them into logical categories. Finally, arrange the categories into a clear organizational pattern according to your purpose. One general rule is to list items from most to least important. Another is to consider what the reader needs to know first in order to understand what comes next. The organizational patterns in Chapter 9 can also be used in many written messages.

Writing experts recommend putting good news first whenever possible: "Your order will be shipped today." If you are delivering bad news, begin by expressing agreement, appreciation, or explanation: "I was very pleased with the quality of your crew's work on the recent job. The only question I have is about the $250 listed as 'extra charges.'"

Your message will be clearest if you build coherence into each paragraph as well as into the overall design by using parallel structure and transitions as demonstrated in Chapter 9.

Be Accurate, Clear, and Professional

Whenever possible, use precise terms, describe in detail, and quantify facts rather than give opinion or evaluations. Use concrete statements rather than abstract ones and avoid jargon, slang, clichés, and idioms.

- *Proofread carefully.* Don't count on your spell-checker to catch your misspelling of *principle* when you meant *principal* or *it's* when you meant *its*. Spell-checking is no help with most names, so you will have to be sure the letter to Ms. MacGregor doesn't leave your desk addressed to Ms. McGregor.

- *Use precise terms that give specific details.* "We will contact you soon" leaves the reader asking, Who will contact me? How will contact be made? Letter, phone, in person? When will I be contacted? Next week? Next month? Instead, write "Our sales manager, Nahid Ravi, will phone you by June 6."

- *Use the active voice for more lively and direct writing.* "The memo was sent by the director" is written in the passive voice. "The director sent the memo" is written in active voice.

- *Use names and titles consistently.* If you are referring to everyone in a group by first and last name, don't add a title (Mrs. or Dr.) to only one person's name. If you are referring to everyone with a title and a last name, don't refer to lower-ranking, female, or minority participants by first name. Stay fair and consistent. Use "Ms." to refer to all women, unless you are certain someone has a personal preference for Mrs. or Miss.

- *Refer to an individual's age, race, or different ability only if necessary.* If you need to refer to ethnicity or race, use the term the group or the individual prefers (see discussion of ethnicities and disabilities in Chapter 2). Always refer to a person before a condition. Use "persons with HIV," not "HIV patients or victims." Use "persons who use wheelchairs," not "crippled persons" or "persons *confined* to wheelchairs." Don't label groups of people by a condition (epileptics, amputees). Use the additional guidelines for avoiding bias in your writing found at http://www.colby.edu/psychology/APA/Bias.pdf

- *Avoid jargon.* When writing for external audiences, avoid jargon and acronyms that your readers might not understand.

- *Avoid slang and pop culture terms.* Using slang ("dude," "awesome") will make you seem more adolescent than professional. Save informality for nonbusiness messages.

Be Concise

Time is precious for most businesspeople. There are several ways to tighten up your writing so your message can be read and understood quickly:

- *Omit needless words and phrases.* If one word will do, use it and eliminate the others. Some phrases are too cumbersome for business writing. For instance, "at the present time" can more succinctly be stated as "now." Other common phrases can be shortened:[1]

Lengthy Phrase	Shortened Version
The question as to whether	Whether
In the month of May	In May
We are in receipt of	We received
Please do not hesitate to call	Please call
Please be advised that I will arrive at 8:00.	I will arrive at 8:00.
A distance of 3 feet	3 feet

- *Eliminate "who is" and "that are."*[2] The sentence "Jeannette, who is the paralegal, declined to comment on the case" could be stated more simply: "Jeanette, the paralegal, declined to comment on the case."
- *Don't overuse intensifiers* ("really," "very," "so") *and superlatives* ("fantastic," "best"). Avoid excessive and unnecessary adverbs ("absolutely," "positively").
- *Avoid "fumblers."* Phrases like "what I mean is" and "what I'm trying to get at is" imply "I don't think I'm being clear" or "I don't think you can understand what I mean from what I wrote."[3]

Pay Attention to Appearance

The appearance of your message will determine the reaction it creates as much as its content. One consultant put it this way: "In memos and reports, intonation and body language aren't available to you. That's what formatting is for—to substitute for them."[4]

The first decision when formatting a business document is whether to type it or write it longhand. The culture of an organization usually offers clues about when handwritten notes are acceptable, so pay attention to how the successful people around you communicate.

Three occasions when handwritten notes are definitely appropriate—even preferable—are for thank-you notes and personal messages of congratulations or condolence. In addition, it may be acceptable to jot a quick note to a colleague or boss in longhand. In virtually every other situation, though, it's professional to type.

Documents should be laid out on the page or screen so they are easy to read and understand. One trick for making documents look professional is using "white space"—a term that refers to blank spaces on a page or screen. For instance, margins should be wide enough to keep the document from looking cramped—at least an inch all around on a printed page. Blank lines should be inserted between single-spaced paragraphs or between sections. Another trick for increasing readability is to left-align your documents. A ragged right edge is easier to read than a justified document that has a straight right margin.

For most documents, choose a font size between 10 and 12 points. The font you use also sends a message. In business documents, avoid shadow, script, outline, or radically different fonts because they can be difficult to read and may call more attention to the medium than the message. Keep fonts consistent for easier reading.

• Routine Business Messages

Along with the writing practices described so far, various forms of business writing each call for specific considerations.

E-mail Messages and Memos

Memos—e-mails and the printed variety—are the most common form of internal business correspondence. They range from short messages to longer documents. Regardless of their subject or length, the same considerations will shape these messages.

Paper or Electronic Format?   For centuries, paper was the only medium for memos. Now you can choose whether to deliver your message electronically, in hard copy, or both. Here are some factors to consider when deciding which format is most appropriate.

Choose e-mail when:

- The message is informal.
- You want the message delivered immediately.
- There are multiple recipients, especially when they are geographically distributed.
- You want a record that can be stored electronically and circulated easily.

Use paper when:

- You want to make a formal impression.
- Legal requirements demand a printed format.
- You want your message to stand out from a flood of e-mails.
- The recipient prefers hard copies.

The proper format for printed memos (like the one in Figure A3.1 on page 406) differs slightly from those sent as e-mails (see Figure 6.2, page 157).

Memo Tips

- Don't include a salutation ("Dear Joe") or complimentary close ("Sincerely,").
- Don't sign the memo at the bottom. You may write your initials next to your name on the "FROM" line.
- The body of a memo is single spaced, with blank lines separating paragraphs.

Style for Memos and E-mails   As the example in Figure A3.1 shows, how you express a message can be as important as the ideas behind it. Keep these factors in mind as you compose your thoughts.

- *Keep it short.* The most important stylistic guideline in crafting a useful e-mail message or memo is to make it as concise as you can. Whenever possible, limit your message to what can be expressed in two or three paragraphs—one screenful of text.
- *Make the essence of your message clear in the opening paragraph.* For example, "We need to decide on a logo for the new product within the next week," or "I'm writing to see whether you would be interested in serving on a community outreach committee."
- *Use formatting to make your points clear.* Single-space your message with a double space between paragraphs. Use bullets and numbered lists to make information more readable and accessible.

FIGURE A3.1   Memo Format

- *Be wary of using the informal style you might use outside of work.* Shortcuts ("wanna," "sorta"), emoticons, and chat acronyms (LOL for "laughing out loud") can create problems, especially with strangers. Don't use all capital letters as this creates the effect of shouting. All lowercase is unprofessional and inappropriate, too. Capitalization, grammar, and spelling are important. Profanity, off-color remarks, and gossip never belong in company e-mail.

Elements of E-mail Messages and Memos   Every e-mail and paper memo should include the date, your name, other people receiving the message (usually labeled "cc"), and a subject line. Beyond these basics, consider the following:

- Make your subject line brief and descriptive (e.g., "Agenda change for Friday's meeting") to help the receiver identify your topic. Messages with vague subject lines (e.g., "Update" or "Hi") run the risk of being ignored, misfiled, or deleted.

- If you need to correspond about several topics, consider separate messages for each one. This makes it easier for the recipient to keep track of and respond to each one.

- Consider sending a blind copy ("bcc") if you don't want the primary recipients to know that others are seeing the correspondence. This approach isn't necessarily devious. For example, you might send your boss a blind copy of your e-mail to an irate customer, saying, "This is how I resolved the problem we discussed last week."

Best Practices for E-mail Messages and Memos   When composing and sending memos and e-mails, follow this advice:

- *Don't use company channels for personal business.* Use your own personal e-mail account for private correspondence, chatting with friends, and other nonbusiness exchanges. One expert advised thinking of e-mails as "giant, moving billboards, exposing our every thought to the cyberworld."[5] Your personal e-mails most likely would not be the best advertising for your company.

- *Don't impose on others.* Most businesspeople are already overwhelmed with e-mail and paperwork, so only send messages on a "need-to-know" basis. Avoid the temptation to send unnecessary messages to others or forward ones the recipient won't appreciate.

- *Be cautious about putting delicate topics in writing.* Don't write about topics that would better be handled by phone or in person. Written channels usually aren't the best way to initiate difficult messages like negative appraisals, firings, and resignations. E-mail has the potential to be misunderstood, so avoid using it in a hurry or to convey sarcasm or humor if the receiver is likely to misunderstand.

- *Think before sending problematic messages.* Stop, think, and wait *before* you send a message if you are angry or frustrated. The scathing note you wrote in anger to one person may be forwarded to many colleagues. Once a message is sent, it is irretrievable and the impact on your career could be disastrous. Never send information you are not sure is accurate (e.g., canceled meetings, changed deadlines, budget figures).

- *Treat every message as a public, permanent document.* Despite what you might assume, e-mail is not private: It has the potential to be forwarded (purposely or accidently) without your permission or knowledge. Even if you delete a message, it can remain available to employers, other businesses, and courts for years. In fact, e-mail has the same weight as a letter or memo sent on company letterhead.[6]

- *Double-check your addressee list.* A misaddressed message can lead to embarrassment and humiliation.

- *Use "cc" when others need and expect copies and when you want the recipient to know you are sending them.* In reply to a customer's complaint, you might want that customer to see you are sending your response regarding safety to all technicians who were part of the problem.

- *Include relevant copy from earlier messages when you forward them or reply to the sender.* This provides all the relevant information in a single document.

- *Be mindful about using special formatting.* The fancy fonts and images you use may appear differently on your recipient's computer screen or portable device.

- *Honor the chain of command.* E-mail can be a way to level hierarchies and reach important people, expedite projects, and reduce time otherwise spent in meetings. Despite these advantages, it is often important to follow the regular chain of command. Pay attention to your organization's culture and your communication goals. Sending an e-mail to your CEO suggesting a new procedure for your division without first checking with your immediate supervisor could spell disaster for your career.

- *Consider using salutations.* Salutations ("Dear Mr. Nakayama," "Hi Gina") are an optional, but often useful, element of e-mail messages. As one expert pointed out, "Blunt is not businesslike."[7] (Salutations typically aren't used in printed memos.) Bulk or broadcast e-mails or those to groups can begin with salutations like "Good morning" or "Dear Computer Policy Committee Members."

- *Append a signature block.* You can set your e-mail program to append a signature block to the end of each e-mail message, which lists your name, title, organization, phone, fax, e-mail and physical addresses, and website link. This information allows others to reach you easily, regardless of where they are picking up your message. Cute quotations and graphics in your signature are not advisable for business, unless it is your company slogan or a tagline indicating the work you do.

Letters

Even in an age of electronic communication, there is still a place for traditional letters. They are used for formal occasions, when the correspondence may be displayed, when a signature on paper is a legal requirement, or when the recipient prefers to have a paper version.

Perhaps the most common layout for business letters is the block format. For an example, see Figure A3.2. As this name suggests, each element and paragraph is set flush with the left margin.

Heading	**TAMARA J. BUTTON** **1111 W. Stanton Rd.** **Andover, KS 67002** **(241) 264-1411 tjb@teacom.com**
Date *Don't abbreviate.*	March 11, 2013
Addressee *Unless writing a friend,* *include courtesy title* *(Mr., Ms., Dr., etc).*	Mr. Jacob Bruneau Franco-American Electrical Specialists 300 W. Burton Street Wichita, KS 67202
Salutation	Dear Mr. Bruneau:
Body of letter	
Set paragraphs flush *with left margin.*	After six years as an electrician in the U.S. Air Force, I am prepared to take the skills I developed in the military into the civilian sector. I hope you will find that the wide range of abilities and the work habits I developed in the military provide strong qualifications for the position of field manager that is currently posted on the Franco-American website.
Separate paragraphs *with a single* *vertical space.*	As the enclosed résumé indicates, I bring to the field manager's job a wide range of skills. I have worked on commercial, industrial, and residential projects. I learned the trade from the bottom up, starting as an apprentice and progressing until I supervised a crew of 40 subordinates on complex multimillion-dollar projects, both in the U.S. and abroad.
	My experience in the Air Force has also helped to develop the personal skills necessary to work in this demanding field. I have worked successfully with a wide range of "customers," including military commanders and civilian contractors. As I gained more responsibilities, I learned how to manage subordinates to get jobs done error-free and on schedule. I'm proud to say that, in my final assignment with the Air Force, I was recognized as "Noncommissioned Officer of the Year."
	I also bring to Franco-American a strong work ethic. I have tackled jobs under a variety of demanding conditions, ranging from the frozen arctic cold to triple-digit desert heat. Many of the jobs for which I was responsible required 24-hour availability.
	I would welcome the chance to meet with you in person to explore how I might help Franco-American Electric as a field manager. Thank you in advance for your time and consideration.
Complimentary close	Sincerely,
Signature	*Tamara J. Button*
Enclosure line	Enclosure: Résumé

FIGURE A3.2 Letter Format

Beyond the elements in Figure A3.2, some letters need to contain additional information. This might include status (e.g., Urgent, Confidential), attention line, list of recipients receiving copies, a postscript, and second page headers.

• Writing for Employment

Chapter 6 describes several paths to seeking employment. At some point most job seekers will send a job application letter and a résumé. The résumé remains a mainstay of the employment process, and now Internet options can enhance both the résumé process and product.

Résumés

A résumé is a marketing document—an advertisement in which you sell yourself to potential employers. A résumé summarizes your background and qualifications for employment. Résumés serve as a screening device, helping prospective employers decide which candidates' applications are worth further consideration.

A résumé won't get you hired, but it can put you on the short list of candidates to be considered or cause you to be dropped from the running. As you read in Chapter 6, in competitive hiring situations, screening candidates is a process of elimination as much as selection. The people doing the hiring have more applications than they can handle, so they naturally look for ways of narrowing down the pool of candidates to a manageable number. A good résumé can keep you in the running. A résumé can also be useful for presenting yourself to potential employers who might hire you for a job that hasn't yet been announced or even created.

Besides listing your qualifications, a résumé offers tangible clues about the type of person you are. Are you organized and thorough? How well can you present your ideas? Is your work accurate? After you have left the interview, your résumé will remain behind as a reminder of the way you tackle a job and of the kind of employee you are likely to be.

Résumé Fundamentals   No matter what the job or field, all good résumés follow the same fundamentals.

Customize to fit a particular position   You may keep a generic résumé on hand when a new networking contact unexpectedly asks for your résumé or to use as a template to adapt when specific openings occur, but the most effective résumés are tailored to the interests and needs of a particular position and employer. For example, a medical technician should stress laboratory skills when applying for a job in a lab; but when a job opening is in a clinic, the same technician should emphasize experience that involves working with people. A résumé that encourages job offers focuses on the employer's needs and how you can help the employer.

Be sure your résumé looks professional   Like every important business document, your résumé should be impeccable. Any mistakes or sloppiness here could cost you the job by raising doubts in an employer's mind. Even small errors can be fatal: According to the Society for Human Resource Management, more than 75 percent of employers reject applicants whose résumés contain spelling errors or are grammatically sloppy.[8]

Because the design of résumés can be complicated and the stakes are high, many candidates hire professional services to create them. Whether you create the résumé yourself or have it professionally done, the final product should reflect the professional image you want to create.

Although you want to make yourself stand out from the crowd, be cautious about using unusual fonts or paper. A novel approach may capture the fancy of a prospective boss, or it may be a turn-off. The more you know about the field and the organization itself, the better your decisions will be about the best approach.

In companies and positions looking for creativity, some novel ideas may work. A third place winner of an Enterprise Rent-A-Car creative résumé contest had submitted a pizza box résumé to a pizza corporation and her photo on a milk carton (to alert the company of its "missing" worker) to another.[9] And Internet startup company Intern Sushi has abandoned paper résumés altogether. Instead, applicants use digital media storytelling to showcase their creativity and credentials.[10] You may be remembered with a creative and unusual résumé, but these gimmicks won't work in most traditional employment situations. The résumé is a business document and needs to look professional.

Be positive, dynamic, and specific   Figures A3.3 and A3.4 illustrate several characteristics of effective résumés. Use the word "I" sparingly. The words "fired" and "unemployed" do not belong on your résumé.[11] Begin sentences with positive verbs (*created, developed, analyzed*), as in Table A3-1. And, of course, be absolutely honest about everything you include.

Be specific about accomplishments, including numbers whenever possible. For example, don't say "Designed training for large groups" when you can say "Designed training for groups of more than 100 employees." It's less effective to say "Helped cut costs" than to say "Reduced costs by 21 percent in 3 years."

Your résumé should almost never exceed two pages in length, and one is usually better. Employers are often unimpressed with longer résumés, which are hard to read and can seem padded, especially when they come from people with comparatively little job experience.

Résumé Elements   While résumés can be organized in more than one way, they almost always contain the same basic information. Résumés are not autobiographies: The purpose is to get an interview, not tell your life history. Personal information like age, height, weight, religion, race, marital status, and children does not belong in a résumé. The following elements appear in most, if not all, résumés.

Name and contact information   This usually includes your name, address, phone numbers, e-mail address, and website. Make sure the information allows an interested employer

Table A3-1	Dynamic Verbs in Résumés Demonstrate Accomplishments	
Communication/People Skills	**Technical Skills**	**Organizational Skills**
Collaborated	Assembled	Arranged
Communicated	Calculated	Compiled
Consulted	Constructed	Executed
Directed	Engineered	Maintained
Drafted	Fabricated	Monitored
Interviewed	Installed	Processed
Marketed	Maintained	Purchased
Moderated	Operated	Screened
Negotiated	Overhauled	Standardized
Presented	Programmed	Systematized
Publicized	Solved	Updated
Translated	Upgraded	Verified

Source: Sampled from Quintessential Careers. (n.d.). *Action verbs by skills categories*. Retrieved from http://www.quintcareers.com/action_skills.html. This website also lists action verbs to describe skills in each of these areas: creative, data/financial, helping, management/leadership, research, and teaching.

to reach you easily. Listing a personal e-mail address and home or cell phone number is preferable to listing a current employer's. Be certain to check these frequently and respond speedily. Be certain your voice mail message and e-mail address are not offensive or do not create an impression you wouldn't want. "Devilgirl" or "Lazyboy" does not convey the impression of a serious job candidate. You might set up a separate e-mail account expressly for seeking employment. If you will not be at your school or other current address long, list both a permanent home address and a school address. Indicate how long an address will be valid ("until May 31").

Objective or summary of qualifications   Some career advisors say a statement of your career objectives can help identify the fit between you and a job. An effective objective consists of two parts. The first part should announce your general goal and mention some important demonstrated skills—talents that will qualify you for the job. The second should detail one or more specific areas in which you want to work. For example:

> "A position in public relations using proven skills in writing, researching, and motivating. Special interests in radio and television programming."

An even more effective strategy is to begin your résumé with a summary of the assets you bring to a job. For example:

- Demonstrated skills as a self-starter who builds strong relationships with clients.
- Consistently met sales goals while working independently in satellite office.
- Had highest client retention rate of all sales representatives in Western Division.
- Earned "Certificate of Mastery" from TCE Institute while working full-time.

Although you will probably describe this information in the body of your résumé, leading with your strengths in a summary highlights them and motivates a prospective employer to examine the rest of your application more carefully.

Education   Employers are usually interested in learning about your post-high school education and training, degrees earned, major and minor fields of study, and dates of attendance and/or graduation. If you attended college, it is unnecessary to include high school. Begin with your most recent education and work backward. If the information is helpful and space permits, list notable courses you have taken. If your grade point average is impressive, include it. Finally, note any honors or awards you have earned. If they are numerous, list them in a separate "Awards and Honors" section.

Experience   Every employer wants to know what kinds of work you have performed. By using the general title "Work Experience" instead of the more limited "Employment History," you can highlight a summer internship, delete a dishwashing job, group minor or similar jobs together, and include volunteer work or club activities that taught you marketable skills.

Employers are more interested in the duties you performed than in job titles. They search for the answers to two questions: What can you do? What are your attributes as an employee? You can provide answers to these questions by accompanying your job title, name of employer, and city with a list of the duties you performed. There is no need to use complete sentences—phrases will do. Be sure to use very concrete language, including technical terminology, to describe the work you performed. Place this section either before or following the section on education, depending on which will be most important to an employer. For an extensive list of words that might help you accurately describe the transferable skills you have, see: http://owl.english.purdue.edu/handouts/pwp_skillinv.html.

Special interests and aptitudes   This is the place to showcase any unique talents or experiences you bring to the job. This section might include community service activities (cite offices you have held), languages you can write or speak, special equipment you can operate, relevant hobbies, and so on. The key here is to include only information the employer will find useful and that casts you in a favorable light.

Memberships　Include this section only if you belong to organizations related to the career field or position you are seeking. Include any offices or significant committee appointments you have held. Membership in service and civic groups is usually less important, so include it only if you have held a major office.

Certifications　If you are certified or licensed in any occupational field, either create a category in which to display that fact, or include it in the "Special Interests and Aptitudes" section described above. For instance, if you are a Microsoft Certified Systems Engineer, list your MCSE certification. If your Notary Public or CPR certification could benefit an employer, include it.

Reference list　Don't list references on a résumé unless specifically requested. Instead, create a reference list separate from your résumé and bring it to an interview. This list can include three to five persons (not family members) who know your work and character. Be certain you ask each potential reference in advance for permission to use his or her name.

Give each reference a copy of your résumé and keep each informed of the places and positions to which you are applying. You might remind a college professor of the term project you completed or remind a past employer of an accomplishment you'd like mentioned.

Types of Résumés　
There are two common approaches to organizing a résumé: chronological and functional. Each has its own advantages; the one you choose will probably depend on the specific job you are applying for and your past accomplishments.

Chronological résumés emphasize your education and work experience and are most effective when such experience clearly relates to the job you are seeking, when you have worked within the field. Within the categories "Education," "Work Experience," and "Related Experience" (if you have such a section), list entries in reverse order, beginning with your most recent experience. Under each position, describe your responsibilities and accomplishments, emphasizing ways in which they prepared you for the job you are now seeking. If you are a recent graduate, you may want to list your education first. (See Figure A3.3.)

Functional résumés feature the skills you bring to the job (organizer, researcher, manager, etc.), and as Figure A3.4 illustrates, they provide examples of the most significant experiences that demonstrate these abilities. This approach is especially appropriate in the following instances:

- When you are first entering the job market or reentering it after an absence.
- When you have held a variety of apparently unrelated jobs.
- When you are changing careers or specialties.
- When your work history has been interrupted.
- When your past job titles don't clearly show how you are qualified for the position you are seeking.

When you write a functional résumé, follow the "Skills" category immediately with a chronological "Work History" and a scaled-down "Education" section that lists only institutions, degrees, and dates. Either of the latter two categories may come first, depending on whether you gained most of your skills and experience in school or on the job.

Whatever format you choose, experts agree that strong résumés possess the same qualities:

- *They focus on the employer's needs.* If you understand what qualities (perseverance, innovation, ability to learn quickly) and skills (mastery of software, selling) an employer needs, you can focus your résumé to show how you fit the job.

ANTHONY TOLIVAR

e-mail: a.tolivar@connectnet.org | phone: 223-705-6596

Home address
1716 S. Hacienda Rd.
La Habra, CA 90631

University address
3211 Coit Rd.
Dallas, TX 75254

SUMMARY OF QUALIFICATIONS

- Academic background in political and economic dimensions of food policy
- Experience working in commercial and nonprofit organizations related to international food security
- Strong work ethic and ability to work independently as necessary

EDUCATION

Current: University of Texas at Dallas
Graduating (Bachelor of Science degree) in May 2014
Major in International Relations, Asian Studies emphasis

Fall 2011: Shanghai International Studies University (Rotary International Ambassadorial Scholar)
Mandarin language program, ethnographic study of contemporary Chinese culture.

RELATED EXPERIENCE

August 2012–January 2013: Undergraduate Research Fellow, University of Texas at Dallas
In Asia, analyzed the effectiveness of Rotary International programs in promoting international trade. Interviewed officials from municipal government, business, and nonprofit sectors in Philippines, Taiwan, Japan and China.

September 2012–February 2013: Correspondent, Food Policy blog (http://foodpolicy.org)
Published dispatches on insights gained from travels in East Asia for the award-winning Web site.

September 2010–present: Assistant Coordinator, International Food Security Treaty, Southwest Division
Assisted in coordinating media and fundraising events to educate public and recruited volunteers for this campaign to guarantee nutrition rights around the world.

May 2012–August 2012: International Trade Research Intern, Southern California World Trade Center
Conducted individualized, in-depth sales and marketing research for the Trade Center's members.

Fall 2011: Intern, The American Chamber of Commerce, Shanghai
Developed marketing materials, publications, and grant proposals to promote U.S. economic interests in China.

Summer 2010: Intern, Center for Food Safety, San Francisco, California
Conducted research to identify and remediate threats to food safety; helped develop funding proposals for major donors.

LANGUAGES

Fluency in Spanish
Competence in *biao zhun* (standard pronunciation) Mandarin Chinese

FIGURE A3.3 Chronological Résumé Featuring Education and Work Experience

- *They are concise.* A longwinded résumé sends the wrong message in a business environment where time is money and clarity is essential. Use simple, brief statements to describe yourself, and avoid verbose language.
- *They are honest.* Outright lies are obvious grounds for disqualification, of course. But getting caught exaggerating your qualifications will raise serious doubts about your honesty in other areas. As one expert put it, "Be aggressive, be bold, but be honest."[12]

Amy Matthews

Box C-23123
Cambridge, MA 02138
617-555-0392
amatthews@harvard.edu

OBJECTIVE	To contribute my education and health management skills in a position with a growing and dynamic firm.
EDUCATION	**BACHELOR OF SCIENCE** **Harvard University**, Cambridge, Massachusetts, May 2011 Major: Health Sciences Minor: Management
RELEVANT COURSES	• Human Anatomy & Physiology I • Human Anatomy & Physiology II • Health Policy • Organizational Analysis and Health Care • Health Care Management • Human Resource Management
Health Management Skills	• Served as Assistant to the Director of the Stacey G. Houndly Breast Cancer Foundation. • Functioned as Public Health Representative for the Cambridge Area Public Health Administration. • Coordinated, Harvard University Public Health Awareness Week, 2009, 2010.
Communications Skills	• Served as a phone-a-thon caller on several occasions, soliciting donations from Harvard alumni and parents for Harvard University. • Volunteered for a political campaign, distributing literature door to door, fielding questions and making phone calls to local constituents.
Management Skills	• Handled all back-office management functions, including employee relations and accounting. • Oversaw client relations, order processing and routine upkeep of the business. • Coordinated efforts between customer needs and group personnel. • Designed all market research analysis and projects for our client. • Delegated suggestions and duties to other team members. • Presented market research results to client with suggestions of implementation. • Participated in Youth Leadership Boston, a group dedicated to developing leadership skills through diverse programming.
Leadership Skills	• Served as formal/social coordinator for my sorority program council. • Elected Vice President of Risk Management for Panhellenic, a group that oversees and coordinates educational programming for Harvard's Greek system.
Systems Abilities	• Windows 8, Macintosh OS, and Linux operating systems • Microsoft Office (all applications and versions) • HTML/XML Web Publishing: Multiple authoring tools. Microsoft SQL, Oracle, and FileMaker Pro database management systems

FIGURE A3.4   Functional Résumé Focusing on Demonstrated Skills

Source: Adapted from Quintessential Careers. (n.d.). *Quintessential Careers functional resume sample.* Retrieved from http://www.quintcareers.com/resume_sample_1.html

Electronic Résumés   Electronic résumés are an increasingly widespread alternative to the paper-and-ink variety. Since many employers look for—and sometimes even require—applicants to submit information electronically, it is important to know how this part of the hiring system operates.

Strategies for electronic résumés   Résumé preparation and delivery are changing, but a basic principle holds: Adapt to your audience. Customize the content and method of transmission of your résumé for individual companies, positions, and, when possible, the people who will read it.

Compared to paper résumés, electronic ones have both advantages and drawbacks. When you send a paper résumé, the recipient sees exactly what you created, although receiving and forwarding it to others may take time. With electronic résumés, there is a greater risk that your reader may not be able to view the document for technical reasons or may not want to open the file because of the additional time it takes and the potential for a virus. Furthermore, some companies automatically delete unsolicited e-mails with attachments, so find out before you attach.

When you do submit a résumé electronically, follow these guidelines:[13]

- Don't bombard employers with résumés for positions that don't exist or for which you are not qualified.

- Do include a cover letter that tells the employer what position you are applying for. See the section below for more details on how to compose a cover letter.

- Do include key buzzwords. Many résumés are no longer read by a human. Instead, computers scan résumés for keywords related to specific jobs. For examples of skill keywords (by job categories) and personal trait keywords, see http://www.eresumes.com/eresumes.html. Use the *Occupational Outlook Handbook* (http://www.bls.gov/oco) and other career resources online for lists of keywords specific to your career field.

- Do consider the channels for submitting you résumé. The most common ways to submit electronic résumés are through e-mail attachments and Web-based interfaces.[14]

E-mail attachments   Submitting an e-mail résumé involves attaching a computer file of the résumé to an e-mail message and sending it to one or more prospective employers. You will probably create your résumé in a word processing format, but it is usually wise to convert and submit it in PDF format so it will look the way you want it to on any computer, and so it can't be modified. A résumé might also consist of a web page (HTML) file or, in some cases, even an audio or video format. The most important consideration when crafting a résumé you plan to submit as an e-mail attachment is to be sure the recipient will be able to open and read it after downloading.

Web-based interfaces   Web-based job banks are services where job seekers can post information about themselves for potential employers to review. Résumés posted on some job banks are open to anyone who wants to see them, while other banks allow you to store a résumé and send it to employers you select. More information on résumé banks is available at http://jobstar.org/internet/res-main.htm.

Web-based résumés have several advantages. Literally thousands of employers worldwide can access your materials as quickly as you post them. You can update and change your résumé readily. You can include portfolios with accessible graphics and sound that demonstrate your experience and showcase your expertise in displaying your work on the Internet.[15]

Despite these advantages, online résumés have a unique set of drawbacks. Once your résumé is posted on the Web, you may have no control over who sees it and where it is transferred. Many currently employed job-seekers have been chagrined to learn their current boss has found their postings in job banks. Check the privacy policies of sites before posting, but be aware those policies may change. The bottom line is that privacy is not assured once a résumé is posted. Be sure to date your résumé in case it becomes a permanent irretrievable fixture in cyberspace. For résumés posted online, you may choose to protect at least some of your privacy by listing only an e-mail address for contact. Before posting a résumé for a specific employer, check the employer's existence and legitimacy. You may want to leave out your current employer, listing only the type of position or the industry you are currently employed in so unscrupulous headhunters don't contact you at your present job. For more information on confidentiality and privacy online, go to http://featuredreports.monster.com/privacy/intro.

Employment-Seeking Letters

Letters give you the chance to present yourself to prospective employers in a favorable light. Here is advice about how to use this correspondence to your best advantage.

Cover Letters   Whenever you send your résumé to a prospective employer in print or electronically, accompany it with a cover letter that is personalized for the particular job you are applying for and the organization to which you are applying. As one expert put it, a cover letter is "an introduction, a sales pitch and a proposal for further action all in one."[16]

Cover letters should be sent to a specific individual. If you do not know the appropriate person, call the company and ask for the individual's name, being certain that you get the spelling and title correct.

As Figure A3.2 illustrates, cover letters include the following information:

- The first lines should let the reader know what position you are applying for, how you know of the position, and any connection you have to the company. If you are responding to an advertisement, mention the job title, number, and publication. You might be writing at the suggestion of a mutual acquaintance or as a result of your research.

- An introduction (or reintroduction) of yourself if the reader may not know (or remember) who you are.

- A brief description of the most impressive accomplishments that are relevant to the job at hand. Remember: Don't just say you can help the organization. Offer some evidence that backs up your claim. Show knowledge of the company through personal experience or positive news articles.

- A statement regarding the next step you hope to take—usually a request for an interview. Detail any information about limits on your availability, but keep these to an absolute minimum.

- A final, cordial expression of appreciation to the reader for considering you.

Follow-up Letters   Always follow up an interview by sending a thank-you to the interviewer(s). As with other correspondence, the decision about whether to convey it in print or via e-mail depends on the preferences of the person to whom you'll be writing. In any case, make sure your thank-you arrives within a day or two following your interview. Besides showing your good manners, a follow-up letter is an opportunity to remind the interviewer of your uniqueness and the strengths you will bring to the company.

Your follow-up letter should thank the interviewer for the opportunity to meet and the chance to have learned more about the position and the company. Also offer thanks for the chance to have met any other people to whom you were introduced. Use the letter to assert why you believe you are well qualified for the job, and how you can serve the company's needs. Address any concerns the interviewer may have had, and add information about yourself you did not have an opportunity to state during the interview.

Be certain the letter concludes on a positive note and expresses goodwill. Be absolutely positive you have correctly spelled every name you use and that your letter is free of any other mistakes. Errors are likely to raise doubts about the quality of work you might do after you are hired.

Thank-you letters are also appropriate for someone who has referred you to an employer, given a recommendation (phone or written) for you, or given job search information to you.

• Reports

Even once you get the job, you'll likely have a lot of writing to do. Reports are a part of business life. They vary in size and frequency from a half-page weekly memo on the number of new hires to a 20-page report complete with graphs, analysis, and recommendations on the feasibility of some new office space. The readers' needs and the corporate culture will determine the size, format, and frequency of reports.

Types of Reports

Reports, like presentations, may be informative or persuasive. Some reports present information, some may propose solutions to problems, and others analyze a problem and propose a course of action. Common reports include trip, progress, incident, and feasibility.

Trip   Trip reports often justify the money organizations spend on the trip. Know why the report is being written and for whom. Is it for your manager to justify the type of workshop you attended or for accounting to withstand an audit? Usually trip reports answer these questions: Where did you go? With whom? Why? When? What did you learn? Whom did you meet? State the name of the conference or meeting, city and location, and your purpose for attending.

In the body of your narrative, emphasize two or three key points. If your job is to report to all employees, select information employees need and will find interesting on safety, legal issues, or changes in policy. If your conference covered new products or new prices for old products, you may want to detail those. If your report goes only to your supervisor, you may want to include a section on needs or ideas for change that you learned on the trip.

Progress   Progress reports (also called periodic operating reports) occur at fixed intervals: weekly sales reports, monthly customer complaints, yearly safety reports. These reports may be largely statistical, but most will require some description of regular events and any unusual events (special sales, emergency closures, power outages). Answer the question, What is our status? If appropriate, indicate any hurdles you have overcome or have yet to overcome and then describe the next objective.

Incident   Incident reports (also called situational reports) report on nonroutine occurrences such as accidents or special events. They may be required in the form of memos. Some organizations have special forms for these reports with very precise requirements for legal or human resource concerns. Before beginning an incident report, be sure you know who is asking for the report and the level of detail required. Always ask if you aren't sure. When describing the incident, use precise facts such as numbers, dates, times, and quotations. Rather than report, "An employee fell on a staircase," write "Jane Winthrop, an employee in the Claims Department, reported that she fell on the north staircase inside the building at 4:00 PM, Tuesday, June 26, 2013."

Feasibility Reports   Feasibility reports address the questions of whether projects are possible, practical, advantageous, safe, or advisable. They use data to analyze the advantages and disadvantages of a particular project or to determine whether something can or should be done.

Begin by knowing what the main question is: How can we improve employee accessibility to supplies without loss of supplies? How can we improve training on new equipment in a timely manner to minimize repairs caused by improper use of new equipment? Then describe the problem or need, the criteria for comparing solutions, the possible solutions, and how well each solution meets the criteria. Tables, graphs, and other visuals are effective ways to add to this analysis section. Be certain you understand whether your assignment is to report information only or to draw conclusions and make recommendations. If the latter is part of your assignment, you'll want a section in which you give your recommendations.

Report Basics

Regardless of the report's contents and size, the following guidelines will help you produce a top-quality document on schedule.

Understand the Purpose   Begin by knowing the purpose of the report. A specific goal statement for reports should follow the same format for presentations explained in Chapter 9:

> "After reviewing this report, the Operations Manager will have a clear idea of how the cost of electricity has changed over the past three years, and how costs are likely to change in the next two years."
> "After reading this report, my boss will see that giving traveling staff laptop computers will increase their productivity enough to pay for the equipment."

You can define the purpose of a report by asking yourself what it will be used for, who will read it, and what amount of detail is required. A routine 1-page expense report isn't the place to present your ideas for reforming the company's accounting policy. By contrast, if you have been asked to analyze a problem of high employee turnover, simply presenting data without including your analysis of causes and proposing solutions would make the report incomplete. If you have any doubts about the purpose of the report, ask the person or people who have requested it for clarification.

Create a Schedule for a Longer Report   Once you understand the purpose of the report, list all of the tasks necessary to complete the report and devise a workable schedule. Allot time for researching (Internet, library visits, studies, surveys, interviews), outlining, writing a draft, getting any preliminary approvals needed, creating exhibits, and editing and writing the final copy.

Organize for Comprehension   Determine what organizational pattern will help readers understand your report. The organizational patterns discussed in Chapter 9 can also be used for written reports. Chronological patterns are often used for progress reports. Topical patterns work for reports that need to cover several areas. For example, a report on a possible location for a new factory might be organized by topics such as natural resources, transportation, workforce availability, and tax base. Another common organizational pattern for reports is by level of importance. A report on the growing loss of quality personnel might focus on the most important features first and move to less important ones. Create an outline to work from; it will help you clarify the organizational pattern.

Format for Readability   Break your report into logical divisions and indicate these with formatting: boldface, boxes, horizontal lines, headings, bullets, numbers, and white space. All of these can help the reader see what goes together and which are the important features. If it is permissible in your organization, use the templates for reports that are included in most word processing programs.

Document Carefully   The purpose of documentation is to give credit to your sources and allow the reader to identify and find the source if more information is needed. Citing your sources avoids plagiarism. In longer reports to scientific and academic organizations, use MLA or APA style. In business, use the style of documentation that is accepted within your organization or industry.

Determine the Preferred Medium   Some organizations prefer reports to be submitted eletronically, while others expect printed documents. Follow the protocol of the organization to which you'll be presenting the report.

Report Elements

Not every report should include all of the following elements. The amount of information covered, its nature, the conventions of the organization, and the needs of your readers will help you decide which parts to include.

Title Page   Every report needs a descriptive title. If the document is a long one, the first page should include the title; "Submitted by . . . " or "Prepared by . . . " with the author(s) name; and "Submitted to . . . " or "Prepared for . . . " with the name of the intended audience or person requesting the report. The last item on the page is the date of submission.

Letter of Transmittal   If the report is presented to persons inside the company, use a memo (instead of letter) of transmittal. The letter or memo will include a short history of the report (who assigned or authorized it and why), a brief summary of significant findings, conclusions, expression of thanks and acknowledgment of assistance from others, and clear instructions regarding how the reader is to respond. It is also appropriate to offer to answer questions and indicate how best to contact you.

Table of Contents   If the report is a long one with several sections, a table of contents will help readers locate material. Show the major sections of the report and the page each begins on.

Abstract or Executive Summary   This section provides readers with a quick overview of the report's key sections. In most cases the summary should be no longer than one page or 10 percent of the full report.

Exhibits and Appendixes   Many reports include tables, charts, graphs, and other visuals that illustrate points made in the body of the document. If there are several, a list of each exhibit and page number helps readers locate them. Depending on the accepted style in your field, these items can be listed as exhibits either within the body of the report or in appendixes at the back of the document.

Bibliography or References   Depending on the accepted practices in your occupation and the formality of the report, you might include only sources you cited or those you cited plus others you used but didn't cite. Some reports will include not only those sources cited and used but also additional sources of information.

glossary

Note: The number in parentheses at the end of each definition refers to the chapter in which the term is first introduced.

A

action-oriented listening style A listening style in which the listener's primary concern is understanding and organizing facts to accomplish a task or get a job done. *See also* Content-oriented listening style, People-oriented listening style, Time-oriented listening style. (3)

action items Specific tasks that were assigned during the course of a meeting. (8)

agenda A list of topics to be covered in a meeting. Agendas also usually note the meeting's time, length, location, and the members who will attend. Complete agendas provide background information and outcome goals. (8)

analytical listening A listening style that focuses on scrutinizing messages from a variety of perspectives. (3)

anchor A listener's preexisting position on an issue being advocated. (12)

asynchronous communication Communication that occurs with a delay between sending and receiving of a message; for example, text messaging or e-mail. (1)

audition interview A type of interview in which a prospective employer asks the candidate to demonstrate (rather than describe) his or her ability to perform a job-related task. (6)

authoritarian leadership style A leadership style in which the designated leader uses legitimate, coercive, and reward power to control members. (7)

authority rule A group decision-making method in which a designated leader makes a final decision, either with or without consulting group members. (8)

award presentation A type of presentation in which the speaker describes an award and explains the reasons the recipient is receiving it. (12)

B

Baby Boomers The generation born between 1946 and 1964 who shaped the 1960s social reforms and who value achievement, accuracy, and performance. (2)

bar chart A visual exhibit consisting of horizontal or vertical bars that depict the values of several items in comparative terms. (10)

behavioral interview An employment interview in which the candidate is asked to give concrete examples of past behaviors that show how he or she behaved in certain situations. (6)

benefits As used in a sales presentation, advantages the target audience will gain from the features of a product or service. (12)

biased language A statement that seems objective but actually conceals the speaker's attitude. (4)

bona fide occupational qualification (BFOQ) A job requirement deemed reasonably necessary for the performance of a particular job. In employment interviewing, only questions exploring BFOQs are lawful. (6)

brainstorming An approach to idea generation that encourages free thinking and minimizes conformity. (8)

briefing An informative presentation that succinctly informs listeners about a specific task at hand. (12)

bullying *See* Workplace bullying.

C

career research interview An informational interview to help a candidate define and achieve career goals. (6)

cause–effect pattern An organizational arrangement that shows that events happened or will happen as a result of certain circumstances. (9)

channel The method or medium used to deliver a message (e.g., face-to-face communication, blog, text message). (1)

chronological pattern An organizational arrangement that presents points according to their sequence in time. (9)

claim A statement asserting a fact or belief. (9)

closed question Question that restricts the interviewee's responses, usually to yes or no, a number, an item from preselected items, or an either–or response. (6)

co-culture A group that has a clear identity within the encompassing culture. (2)

coercive power The ability to influence others that arises because one can impose punishment or unpleasant consequences. (7)

cohesiveness The degree to which group members feel part of and want to remain with the group. (7)

collectivist culture A culture with a strong social framework in which members of a group are socialized to care for one another and for the group as a whole. (2)

column chart A visual exhibit consisting of vertical columns that depict the quantity of one or more items at different times. (10)

communication apprehension Anxiety about communicating. (11)

communication climate A metaphor used to describe the quality of relationships in an organization. (5)

communication networks Regular patterns or paths along which information flows in an organization. *See also* Formal communication networks, Informal communication networks. (1)

comparative advantages pattern An organizational strategy that puts several alternatives side by side and shows why one is the best. (9)

comparison A type of support in which the speaker shows how one idea is similar to another; may be figurative or literal. (10)

compromise An orientation toward negotiation that assumes each side needs to lose at least some of what it was seeking. (5)

confirming messages Messages that express value toward other persons. (5)

conflict phase The second of four group problem-solving phases; characterized by members taking strong stands that result in conflict within the group. *See also* Storming. (8)

connection power The ability to influence that arises because of one's connections and associations inside and outside the organization. (7)

consensus A decision-making method in which the group as a whole makes a decision that each member is willing to support. (8)

content messages The dimension of messages that focus on the topic under discussion. *See also* Relational messages. (1)

content-oriented listening style A listening style in which the listener hears details and analyzes and evaluates what is said. *See also* Action-oriented listening style, People-oriented listening style, Time-oriented listening style. (3)

context The environment of physical, social, chronological, and cultural variables that surrounds any process of communication. (1)

contingency approaches to leadership Leadership theories that assert the most effective leadership style is flexible, changing as needed with the context. (7)

counterfeit question Statement that appears to ask for information but actually offers advice or criticism. (3)

credibility The persuasive force that comes from the audience's belief in and respect for the speaker. (12)

criteria satisfaction pattern An organizational strategy that sets up standards (criteria) the audience accepts and then shows how the speaker's idea or product meets the criteria. (9)

critical incident question Interview question that asks the interviewee about a specific situation rather than a hypothetical one. (6)

critical listening A listening style of evaluating messages for accuracy and consistency. (3)

culture The set of values, beliefs, norms, customs, rules, and codes that leads people to define themselves as a distinct group, giving them a sense of commonality. (2)

D

decoding The process of attaching meaning to words, symbols, or behaviors. (1)

definition A form of support that explains the meaning of terms that are unfamiliar to an audience or are used in a specialized or uncommon way. (10)

democratic leadership style A leadership style in which the designated leader encourages members to share decision making. (7)

descriptive statement Statement that describe the speaker's perspective instead of evaluating the sender's behavior or motives. *See also* "I" language, "You" language. (5)

designated leader A leader whose title indicates a leadership role, either by appointment or by group selection. (7)

diagnostic interview An interview in which professionals (e.g., doctors and lawyers) gather information on their patients' or clients' needs. (6)

direct question (in a group) A question addressed (by name) to a particular individual. (8)

direct question (in an interview) Straightforward question that asks exactly what the interviewer wants to know. (6)

disconfirming messages Messages that show a lack of valuing for other persons. (5)

disfluencies Vocal disruptions such as stammers (uh, um) or filler words (ya know, like, OK) that distract audiences and interfere with understanding. (11)

downward communication Communication that flows from superiors to subordinates. (1)

E

emergence phase The third of four group problem-solving phases; characterized by an end to conflict and emergence of harmony within the group. *See also* Norming. (8)

emergent leader A leader chosen by the group, either officially or informally. (7)

emotional intelligence (EQ) Aptitude and skills needed for interacting well with others. Refers to interpersonal communication skills rather than cognitive or intellectual abilities. (5)

employment interview An interview designed to judge the candidate's qualifications and desirability for a job. (6)

encoding The intentional process of creating a message. (1)

equivocal terms Words with more than one generally accepted meaning. (4)

ethnocentrism The tendency to view life from the perspective of one's own culture and to judge one's own culture as superior to other cultures. (2)

example Brief illustration that backs up or explains a claim. (10)

exit interview An interview designed to discover why an employee is leaving an organization. (6)

expert opinion A decision-making method in which a single person perceived as an expert makes a decision for the group. (8)

expert power A decision-making method in which a single person perceived as an expert makes a decision for the group. (7)

extemporaneous presentation A type of delivery in which the major ideas are planned and rehearsed but the speech is given spontaneously from notes. (11)

F

factual question Question that asks for verifiable, factual information rather than opinion. (6)

fallacy An error in the logic of an argument. (12)

feasibility report A type of presentation that evaluates potential action steps and makes recommendations about how to proceed. (12)

features Qualities of a product or service that make it desirable and distinguish it from the competition. (12)

feedback The recognizable response to a message. (1)

feminine culture A culture in which gender roles are not highly differentiated and members value feelings, cooperation, and harmonic relationships. (2)

final report Report delivered upon completion of an undertaking. (12)

flip chart A large pad of paper, attached to an easel, that is used to create and/or display visuals. (10)

formal communication networks Officially designated paths of communication designed by management to indicate who should communicate with whom. (1)

forming A phase in problem-solving groups characterized by tentative statements and getting-acquainted types of communication. *See also* Orientation phase. (8)

functional roles Types of behavior that are necessary if a group is to do its job effectively. *See also* Relational roles, Task roles. (7)

G

gatekeeper A person, such as a personal assistant or a receptionist, who manages access to another person. (6)

genderlects Distinct and different styles of speaking that characterize masculine and feminine speech. (4)

general goal A broad indication of the purpose of a speech, generally to inform, persuade, or entertain. (9)

Generation X The generation born between 1965 and 1980 that is comfortable with technology, values work–life balance and creativity. (2)

Generation Y *See* Millennials.

goodwill speech A speech with the primary aim of creating a favorable image of the speaker's cause in the minds of the audience. (12)

graph A visual exhibit that shows the correlation between two quantities. (10)

groupthink A condition in which group members are unwilling to critically examine ideas because of their desire to maintain harmony. (7)

H

handout Document(s) distributed during or after a presentation. (10)

hidden agenda A group member's personal goal that is not made public. (7)

high-context culture A culture that relies heavily on the social and physical context and nonverbal cues to convey meaning and maintain social harmony. (2)

high-level abstractions Terms that cover a broad range of possible objects or events without much detail. (4)

highly structured interview An interview that consists of a standardized list of questions, sometimes in precise order and wording, as in research interviews. (6)

horizontal (lateral) communication Communication in which messages flow between members of an organization who have equal power or responsibility. (1)

hostile work environment A category of sexual harassment in which verbal and nonverbal behaviors have the intention or effect of interfering with someone's work or creating an environment that is intimidating, offensive, or hostile. (5)

hypothetical question Question that asks an interviewee how he or she might respond under certain circumstances. (6)

I

identity management The practice of presenting yourself in ways that produce a preferred image and distinctive sense of self. (1)

"I" language Language in which the communicator describes his or her feelings, needs, and behaviors without accusing others. (5)

immediacy Verbal and nonverbal behaviors that indicate closeness and liking. (4)

impromptu presentation A type of delivery in which the speaker has little or no preparation time before presenting his or her remarks. (11)

incivility The exchange of seemingly inconsequential, inconsiderate words and deeds that violate the conventional standards of workplace conduct. (5)

indirect question Question that gets at information the interviewer wants to know without asking for it directly. (6)

individualistic culture A culture whose members tend to put their own interests and personal choices ahead of social or group concerns. (2)

informal communication networks Patterns of interaction that are based on proximity, friendships, and shared interests. (1)

information power The ability to influence that arises because of one's access to otherwise obscure information. (7)

instrumental communication Messages designed to get a job done, to accomplish a mission. (1)

interview A two-party interaction in which at least one party has a specific, serious purpose and that usually involves the asking and answering of questions. (6)

investigative interview An interview designed to discover the causes of an incident or problem. (6)

J

jargon Specialized terminology used by members of a particular group. (4)

L

laissez-faire leadership style A leadership style in which the leader gives up power and transforms a group into a leaderless collection of equals. (7)

latitude of acceptance The range of positions or arguments a person would accept with little or no persuasion. (12)

latitude of noncommitment The range of positions or arguments a person neither accepts nor rejects. (12)

latitude of rejection The range of positions or arguments a person opposes. (12)

Leader–Member Exchange (LMX) A theory that views leadership as a collection of multiple relationships with members, each one unique. (7)

leading question Question that directs the interviewee to answer in a certain way, often by indicating the answer the interviewer wants to hear. (6)

life-cycle theory of leadership An approach to understanding leadership that suggests that a leader's attention to tasks and relationships should vary depending on the organizational maturity of subordinates. (7)

long-term orientation A cultural orientation that emphasizes long-lasting goals rather than short-term gratification. *See also* Short-term orientation. (2)

lose–lose approach An approach to negotiation in which one party's perceived loss leads to an outcome with negative consequences for the other parties. (5)

low-context culture A culture that employs language to express ideas and directions clearly and logically; members pay less attention to contextual clues for meaning. (2)

low-level abstractions Highly specific statements that refer to observable objects or events. (4)

M

majority vote A decision-making method in which a vote is taken and the item with the most votes is the one accepted. (8)

manuscript presentation A type of delivery in which the speaker reads word for word from prepared remarks. (11)

masculine culture A culture with highly differentiated gender roles in which members value performance, individual success, and advancement. (2)

meeting minutes A written record of the major discussions held, decisions made, and action items assigned. (8)

memorized presentation A type of delivery in which the speech is memorized and recited word for word from memory. (11)

message Any symbol or behavior from which others create meaning or that triggers a response. (1)

Millennials The generation born between1980 and 2000 who are technologically skilled, ethnically diverse, ambitious, and globally-focused in their worldview. (2)

mindful listening A style of listening in which one is fully present, focused, and attentive. (3)

mindless listening A manner of listening habitually or mechanically and without thoughtfulness. (3)

minority decision A decision-making method in which a few members make a decision for the whole group. (8)

moderately structured interview A flexible interview in which major topics, their order, questions, and probes are planned but not rigidly adhered to. (6)

monochronic time orientation A cultural orientation that values time, efficiency, promptness, and chronological order over personal relationships. *See also* Polychronic time orientation. (2, 4)

motion In a meeting conducted according to parliamentary procedure, a specific proposal for action that must be seconded in order to be discussed by the group. (8)

motivated sequence pattern An organizational strategy that presents a topic in terms of five sequential concepts: attention, need, satisfaction, visualization, and action. (9)

motivational speech A speech aimed primarily at generating enthusiasm for the topic being presented. (12)

N

negotiation Discussion of specific proposals for the purpose of finding a mutually acceptable agreement or settlement. (5)

networking The process of meeting people and maintaining contacts to give and receive information, advice, and job leads. (1)

noise Any factor that interferes with a message (also called *barriers* or *interference*). (1)

nominal group technique (NGT) A five-phase method for giving group members' ideas equal chance at consideration. (8)

nonstructured interview An interview that consists of a topical agenda but no planned, specific questions. (6)

nonverbal communication Communication by nonlinguistic means, whether visually, physically, or vocally. (4)

norming A phase in problem-solving groups characterized by an end to conflict and emergence of harmony within the group. *See also* Emergence phase. (8)

norms Informal rules about what behavior is appropriate in a group. Explicit norms are made clear by speaking about them or writing them out. Implicit norms are not openly discussed but are known and understood by group members. (7)

O

open question Question that invites a broad, detailed response. *See also* Closed question. (6)

opinion question Question that seeks the respondent's judgment about a topic. (6)

organizational chart A figure that displays hierarchical reporting relationships in an organization. (1)

organizational climate A relatively stable picture of an organization that is shared by its members. (5)

organizational culture A relatively constant and collective system of behaviors and values within an organization. (2)

orientation phase The first of four problem-solving phases of groups; characterized by tentative statements and getting-acquainted types of communication. *See also* Forming. (8)

overhead question A question directed at all members of a group, inviting a response from any member. (8)

P

panel interview An interview conducted by a group of questioners with whom the candidate will work, who are commonly from different levels within an organization. (6)

paralanguage Nonlinguistic vocal qualities such as rate, pitch, volume, and pauses. (4)

paraphrasing A response style in which the receiver restates the sender's content in his or her own words. (3)

parliamentary procedure An established set of rules that govern the process of conducting meetings. Codified in *Robert's Rules of Order.* (8)

people-oriented listening style A style of listening in which the listener is most concerned with creating and maintaining positive interpersonal relationships. *See also* Action-oriented listening style, Content-oriented listening style, Time-oriented listening style. (3)

performance appraisal interview An interview, usually conducted by a superior, in which the quality of a subordinate's work is discussed. (6)

performing A phase in problem-solving groups characterized by members' active endorsement of group decisions. *See also* Reinforcement phase. (8)

persuasion The act of motivating an audience, through communication, to voluntarily change a particular belief. (12)

pictogram A visual exhibit that employs an artistic or a pictorial variation of a bar, column, or pie chart. (10)

pie chart A round visual exhibit divided into segments to illustrate percentages of a whole. (10)

polychronic time orientation A cultural orientation in which people and personal relationships are more important than appointments and efficiency of time. *See also* Monochronic time orientation. (2, 4)

position power The ability to influence that comes from the position one holds. (7)

power distance A measure (high or low) of how comfortable a culture is with differences in distribution of authority. (2)

presentation software Computer software programs (e.g., PowerPoint, Keynote) that create displays used in presentations. Such programs typically include capabilities for creating special audio, visual, and transition effects, speaker notes, and handouts. (10)

primary question Interview question that introduces a new topic or a new area within a topic. *See also* Secondary question. (6)

problem-oriented message Message that aims to meet the needs of both the sender and the other party. (5)

problem–solution pattern An organizational arrangement in which the speaker first convinces the audience that a problem exists and then presents a plan to solve it. (9)

proposal A type of presentation that advocates for a particular position or action. (12)

Q

quid pro quo sexual harassment A form of sexual harassment that implies a job benefit or penalty is tied to an employee submitting to unwelcome sexual advances. (5)

quotation A form of support that uses the words of others who are authoritative or articulate to make a point more effectively than the speaker could on his or her own. (10)

R

rapport talk Language that creates connections, establishes goodwill, and builds community; more typically used by women. (4)

receiver Any person who perceives a message and attaches meaning to it, whether or not the message was intended for that person. (1)

referent power The ability to influence because one is respected or liked by the group. (7)

reflective-thinking sequence A seven-step problem-solving approach developed by John Dewey. (8)

reinforcement phase The fourth of four group problem-solving phases; characterized by members' active endorsement of group decisions. *See also* Performing. (8)

relational communication Messages that create and reflect the attitudes people have toward one another. (1)

relational listening An empathic listening style, primarily concerned with feelings. (3)

relational messages The dimension of messages that focus on how communicators feel about one another. *See also* Content messages. (1)

relational roles Functional roles that help facilitate smooth interaction among members. (7)

relative words Terms that only have meaning in relationship to other (unspecified) terms. (4)

relay question In groups, a question asked by one member that the leader then addresses to the entire group. (8)

relevancy challenge A request that asks a group member to explain how his or her seemingly off-track idea relates to the group task. (8)

report An informative presentation that describes the state of an operation. (12)

report talk Language that conveys information, facts, knowledge, and competence; more typically used by men. (4)

research interview An interview designed to gather data on which to base a decision. (6)

reverse question In groups, a question asked of the leader that the leader refers back to the person who asked it. (8)

reward power The ability to influence that arises because one can induce desirable consequences or rewards. (7)

rhetorical question A question with an obvious answer, which does not call for an overt response. (9)

risky shift A type of harmful conformity in which groups take positions that are more extreme (on the side of either caution or risk) than the positions of individual members. (7)

S

sales presentation A type of presentation aimed at persuading others to purchase a product or service. (12)

scannable résumé A résumé prepared in plain text format with clear keywords and phrases to be "read" and evaluated by software to screen potential job candidates. (6)

secondary question Interview question that seeks additional information about a topic under discussion. *See also* Primary questions. (6)

self-directed work teams Groups that manage their own behavior to accomplish a task. (7)

self-monitoring Paying close attention to one's own behavior and using these observations to shape the way one behaves. (4)

sender Someone who transmits a message, either intentionally or unintentionally. (1)

short-term orientation A cultural orientation that values quick payoffs over long-range goals. (2)

sincere question A genuine request for information, aimed at helping the receiver understand the sender's message. (3)

social intelligence The ability and skills of interacting well with other persons. *See also* Emotional intelligence. (5)

social orientation Cultural orientation that places a greater priority on personal relationships than on accomplishing tasks. *See also* Task orientation. (2)

spatial pattern An organizational arrangement that presents material according to its physical location. (9)

specific goal A concrete statement of what response a speaker is seeking as the result of his or her remarks. (9)

speech of introduction A type of presentation that prepares the audience to listen to another speaker by emphasizing the upcoming speaker's qualifications or importance of the topic. (12)

statistics Numbers used to represent an idea. (10)

status report The most common type of informative presentation; sometimes called a progress report. (12)

stories Detailed descriptions of incidents that illustrate a point; may be factual or hypothetical. (10)

storming A phase in problem-solving groups characterized by members taking strong stands that result in conflict within the group. *See also* Conflict phase. (8)

stress interview An employment interview in which the candidate is subjected to the pressures typically encountered on the job. (6)

structured interview An interview that consists of a standardized list of questions that allow only a limited range of answers with no follow-up. (6)

style approach to leadership An approach to studying leadership based on the assumption the designated leader's style of communication affects the group's effectiveness. (7)

supporting material Material that backs up claims in a presentation. (10)

survey interview An interview conducted with a number of people to gather information for conclusions, interpretations, or future action. (6)

synchronous communication Communication that occurs without a time lag between sending and receiving a message; for example, face-to-face communication. (1)

T

task orientation Cultural orientation that places a greater priority on accomplishing tasks than on managing personal relationships. *See also* Social orientation. (2)

task-oriented listening A listening style concerned with understanding information that will facilitate accomplishing the task at hand. (3)

task roles Functional roles needed to accomplish a group's mission. (7)

team A group that is especially cohesive and effective because of clear and inspiring goals, a results-driven structure, competent members, unified commitment, a collaborative climate, standards of excellence, external support and recognition, and principled leadership. (7)

teleconference A meeting or conference via telephone that enables participants in two or more locations to talk to each other. (8)

theory X Theory of human motivation that assumes employees are inherently lazy and will avoid work if they can. Organizations that operate on theory X typically have close supervision of workers and comprehensive systems of controls. *See also* Theory Y. (2)

theory Y Theory of human motivation that assumes employees, under optimal conditions, are self-motivated, eager to accept greater responsibility, and capable of self-control and self-direction. *See also* Theory X. (2)

thesis statement A single sentence that summarizes the central idea of a presentation. (9)

time-oriented listening style A listening style in which the listener thinks most about efficiency and prefers a fast pace. Such listeners often appear impatient. *See also* Action-oriented listening style, Content-oriented listening style, People-oriented listening style. (3)

toast A type of tribute that expresses appreciation and/or honors the accomplishments of an individual or a group. (12)

topical pattern An organizational arrangement in which ideas are grouped around logical themes or divisions of the subject. (9)

training An informative presentation that teaches listeners how to perform a task. (12)

trait approach to leadership An outdated leadership theory based on the belief all leaders possess common traits that make them effective. (7)

transition A statement used between parts of a presentation to help listeners understand the relationship of the parts to one another and to the thesis. (9)

tribute A type of special-occasion presentation that honors a person's or group's achievements or characteristics. (12)

trigger words Terms that have strong emotional associations that set off intense emotional reactions in certain listeners. (4)

U

uncertainty avoidance A measure of a culture's tolerance for ambiguity, lack of structure, and novelty. (2)

unstructured interview A flexible interview with a goal, and perhaps a few topical areas in mind, but no list of questions or follow-ups. (6)

upward communication Communication that flows from subordinates to superiors. (1)

V

videoconference A meeting or conference by means of audio and visual transmissions that enables two or more geographically separated persons to see, hear, and talk to each other. (8)

virtual team A team that conducts most or all of its work via electronic channels. (7)

W

welcoming remarks A type of special-occasion presentation in which the speaker welcomes an individual or group, indicating the significance of the visit and setting the tone for the occasion. (12)

win–lose approach An approach to negotiation that assumes any gain by one party is possible only at the expense of the other party. (5)

win–win approach A collaborative approach to negotiation that assumes solutions can be reached that meet the needs of all parties. (5)

work group A small, interdependent collection of people with a common identity who interact with one another, usually face-to-face over time, to reach a goal. (7)

workplace bullying Intense, malicious, ongoing, and damaging words or deeds that violate the conventional standards of workplace conduct. (5)

workplace dignity People's ability to gain a sense of self-respect and self-esteem from their jobs and to be treated respectfully by others. (5)

Y

"you" language Language that often begins with the word *you* and accuses or evaluates the other person. (5)

notes

Chapter 1

1. See, for example, Darling, A. L., & Dannels, D. P. (2003). Practicing engineers talk about the importance of talk: A report on the role of oral communication in the workplace. *Communication Education, 52*, 1–16.
2. Gray, E. F. (2010). Specific oral communication skills desired in new accountancy graduates. *Business Communication Quarterly, 73*, 40–67.
3. Ginsberg, S. (1997, May 5). So many messages and so little time. *Business Outlook,* p. C1.
4. See, for example, Petofi, A. (1988). The graphic revolution in computers. In. E. Cornish (Ed.), *Careers tomorrow: The outlook for work in a changing world* (pp. 62–66). Bethesda, MD: World Future Society.
5. Morreale, S. P., & Pearson, J. C. (2008). Why communication education is important: The centrality of the discipline in the 21st century. *Communication Education, 57*, 224–240.
6. Harper's index. (1994, December). *Harper's,* p. 13.
7. Mauksch, L. B., Dugdale, D. C., Dodson, S., & Epstein, R. (2008). Relationship, communication, and efficiency in the medical encounter. *Archives of Internal Medicine, 168*, 1387–1395; Holmes, F. (2007). If you listen, the patient will tell you the diagnosis. *International Journal of Listening, 21*, 156–161.
8. Joint Commission. (2006). *Sentinel event statistics.* Retrieved from http://www.jointcommission.org/SentinelEvents/Statistics
9. Joint Commission. (2004). *Sentinel event data: Root causes by event type.* Retrieved from http://www.jointcommission.org/assets/1/18/se_root_cause_event_type_2004_2Q2011.pdf
10. Levinson, W., Roter, D., & Mullooly, J. P. (1997). Physician-patient communication: The relationship with malpractice claims among primary care physicians and surgeons. *Journal of American Medical Association, 277*, 553–559. See also Rodriguez, H. P., Rodday, A. C., Marshall, R. E., Nelson, K. L., Rogers, W. H., & Safran, D. G. (2008). Relation of patients' experiences with individual physicians to malpractice risk. *International Journal for Quality in Health Care, 20*, 5–12.
11. Calandra, B. (2002, September 16). Toward a silver-tongued scientist. *The Scientist, 16,* 42.
12. Graduate Management Admissions Council. *Corporate recruiters survey 2006.* Retrieved from http://www.gmac.com/NR/rdonlyres/6838813E-4238-4B78-9C3D-F4AC11592BA6/0/CorpRecSurvey06Survey Report.pdf. See also Alsop, R. (2007, September 17). Recruiter's top schools. *Wall Street Journal* online.
13. *Santa Barbara News-Press.* (1999, August 22). p. J1.
14. Calandra, B. (2002, September 16). Toward a silver-tongued scientist. *The Scientist, 16,* p. 42.
15. National Association of Colleges and Employers. *Job outlook 2012.* Retrieved from http://www.naceweb.org/Research/Job_Outlook/Purchase_Job_Outlook_2012.aspx
16. Polk-Lepson Research Group. (2010). *Professionalism in the workplace.* Retrieved from http://www.ycp.edu/media/yorkwebsite/cpe/York-College-Professionalism-in-the-Workplace-Poll-2010.pdf
17. Watzlawick, P., Beavin, J. H., & Jackson, D. D. (1967). *Pragmatics of human communication.* New York, NY: Norton.
18. Watzlawick, P., Beavin, J. H., & Jackson, D. D. (1967). *Pragmatics of human communication.* New York, NY: Norton.
19. See, for example, Byron, K. (2008). Carrying too heavy a load? The communication and miscommunication of emotion by email. *Academy of Management Review, 33*, 309–327.
20. The earliest form of this model was created by Shannon, C. E., & Weaver, W. (1949). *The mathematical theory of communication.* Urbana: University of Illinois Press. The following discussion reflects changes in the theoretical understanding of communication. See, for example, Adler, R. B., Rosenfeld, L. B., & Proctor, R. F. (2012). *Interplay: The process of interpersonal communication.* New York, NY: Oxford University Press.
21. Powers, W. G., & Witt, P. L. (2008). Expanding the theoretical framework of communication fidelity. *Communication Quarterly, 56*, 247–267.
22. See, for example, Flaherty, L. M., Pearce, K. J., & Rubin, R. B. (1998). Internet and face-to-face communication: Not functional alternatives. *Communication Quarterly, 46,* 250–268; Sheer, V. C., & Chen, L. (2004). Improving media richness theory: A study of interaction goals, message valence, and task complexity in manager-subordinate communication. *Management Communication Quarterly, 18,* 76–93; and Turner, J. W., & Reinsch, N. L. (2007). The business communicator as presence allocator: Multicommunicating, equivocality, and status at work. *Journal of Business Communication, 44,* 36–58.
23. Byron, K. (2008). Carrying too heavy a load? The communication and miscommunication of emotion by email. *Academy of Management Review, 33*, 309–327.
24. Bryant, A. (2000, October 23). Fare rage. *Newsweek,* p. 46.
25. See, for example, Baxter, L. A. (1993). Talking things through and putting it in writing: Two codes of

communication in an academic institution. *Journal of Applied Communication Research, 21,* 313–323.

26. Leonardi, P. M., Treem, J. W., & Jackson, M. H. (2010). The connectivity paradox: Using technology to both decrease and increase perceptions of distance in distributed work arrangements. *Journal of Applied Communication Research, 38,* 85–105.

27. Mitchell, J. J. (1996, July 21). Why can't we all get along? E-mail vs. voice mail culture should provide a clue. *San Jose Mercury News,* p. 6E. For a discussion of the importance of personal contact in an increasingly technological world, see Herndon, S. R. (1997). Theory and practice: Implications for the implementation of communication technology in organizations. *Journal of Business Communication, 34,* 121–129.

28. Turner, J. W., Grube, J., Tinsley, C., Lee, C., & O'Pell, C. (2006). Exploring the dominant media: How does media use reflect organizational norms and affect performance? *Journal of Business Communication, 43,* 220–250.

29. Stephens, K. K., Sørnes, J. O., Rice, R. E., Browning, L. D., & Sætre, A. S. (2008). Discrete, sequential, and follow-up use of information and communication technology by experienced ICT users. *Management Communication Quarterly, 22,* 197–231.

30. Renischn, L., & Turner, J. W. (2006, July). Ari, r u there? Reorienting business communication for a technological era. *Journal of Business and Technical Communication, 20,* 339–356.

31. Lengel, R. J., & Daft, R. L. (1998). The selection of communication media as an executive skill. *Academy of Management Executive, 2,* 225–232.

32. Monge, P. R., & Contractor, N. S. (2003). *Theories of communication networks.* New York, NY: Oxford University Press.

33. Managers' shoptalk. (1985, February). *Working Woman,* p. 22.

34. Katz, D., & Kahn, R. (1978). *The social psychology of organizations* (2nd ed). New York, NY: Wiley.

35. Peters, T. J., & Waterman, R. H., Jr. (1982). *In search of excellence: Lessons from America's best-run companies.* New York, NY: Harper & Row.

36. Silverstein, S. (1999, January 10). Corporate communications gap keeps executives, lower ranks in the dark. *Los Angeles Times,* p. C5.

37. See, for example, Kassing, J. W. (2000). Investigating the relationship between superior-subordinate relationship quality and employee dissent. *Communication Research Reports, 17,* 58–70.

38. Schuster, L. (1982, April 20). Wal-Mart chief's enthusiastic approach infects employees, keeps retailer growing. *Wall Street Journal,* p. 21.

39. Rice, F. (1991, June 3). Champions of communication. *Fortune,* pp. 111–120.

40. Adapted from Katz, D., & Kahn, R. (1978). *The social psychology of organizations* (2nd ed). New York, NY: Wiley.

41. Kassing, J. W. (2000). Investigating the relationship between superior-subordinate relationship quality and employee dissent. *Communication Research Reports, 17,* 58–70.

42. Bennis, W. G. (1993). *An invented life: Reflections on leadership and change.* Reading, MA: Addison-Wesley.

43. Dansereau, F., & Markham, S. E. (1987). Superior-subordinate communication: Multiple levels of analysis. In F. M. Jablin, L. L. Putnam, K. H. Roberts, & L. W. Porter (Eds.), *Handbook of organizational communication* (pp. 343–388). Newbury Park, CA: Sage.

44. Bryant, A. (2011, June 27). A sitting duck can't catch a moving turkey. *New York Times.* Retrieved from http://www.nytimes.com/2011/06/26/business/26corner.html?_r=1&ref=exeloncorporation

45. Petzinger, T., Jr. (1996, September 27). Two executives cook up way to make Pillsbury listen. *Wall Street Journal,* p. B1.

46. Keil, M., Tiwana, M., Sainsbury, R., & Sneha, S. (2010). Toward a theory of whistleblowing intentions: A benefit-to-cost differential perspective. *Decision Sciences, 41,* 787–812.

47. Spillan, J. E., Mino, M., & Rowles. M. S. (2002). Sharing organizational messages through effective lateral communication. *Qualitative Research Reports in Communication, 3,* 96–104.

48. Goldhaber, G. (1993). *Organizational communication* (6th ed.). Dubuque, IA: William C. Brown.

49. Wilson, D. O. (1992). Diagonal communication links within organizations. *Journal of Business Communication, 29,* 129–143.

50. Mieszkowski, K. (1998, December). Change—Barbara Waugh. *Fast Company, 20,* pp. 146–154.

51. Adapted from Goldhaber, G. (1993). *Organizational communication* (6th ed.). Dubuque, IA: William C. Brown.

52. Ferguson, T. W. (1997, May 19). Who's mentoring whom? *Forbes,* p. 252.

53. See, for example, Doloff, P. G. (1999, February). Beyond the org chart. *Across the Board,* pp. 43–47.

54. Lukaszewski, J. E. (1997, August–September). You can become a verbal visionary. *Executive Speeches, 12,* 23–30.

55. Gregory, M. (2009). Inside the locker room: Male homosociability in the advertising industry. *Gender, Work & Organization, 16,* 323–347.

56. Bell, E. L. J. E., & Nkomo, S. M. (2001). *Our separate ways: Black and white women and the struggle for professional identity.* Boston, MA: Harvard Business School Press.

57. Did you hear it through the grapevine? (1994, October). *Training & Development,* p. 20.

58. See Cross, R., & Parker, A. (2004). *The hidden power of social networks: Understanding how work really gets done in organizations.* Boston, MA: Harvard Business School Press.

59. Deal, T. E., & Kennedy, A. A. (1982). *Corporate cultures: The rites and rituals of corporate life.* Reading, MA: Addison-Wesley.

60. Krackhardt, D., & Hanson, J. R. (1993, July). Informal networks: The company behind the chart. *Harvard Business Review, 71,* 104–111.

61. Kanter, R. M. (1989, November/December). The new managerial work. *Harvard Business Review, 67,* 85–92.

62. Bush J. B., Jr., & Frohman, A. L. (1991). Communication in a 'network' organization. *Organizational Dynamics, 20,* 23–36.

63. Eisenberg, E. M., & Goodall H. E., Jr. (1993). *Organizational communication: Balancing creativity and constraint.* New York: St. Martin's.

64. Murray, T. J. (1987, August). How to stay lean and mean. *Business Month,* pp. 29–32.

65. Jackson, M. (1998, January 7). Study shows workplace goofing off often pays off for the employer. *Santa Barbara News-Press,* p. B8.

66. For more advice on networking, see R. E. Kelley interviewed by Webber, A. M. (2000). Are you a star at work? In *Fast Company career guide* (pp. 46–50). New York, NY: Fast Company Media Group.

67. Seibert, S. E., Kraimer, M. L., & Liden, R. C. (2001). A social capital theory of career success. *Academy of Management Journal, 44,* 219–237.

68. Feely, T. H. (2000). Testing a communication network model of employee turnover based on centrality. *Journal of Applied Communication Research, 28,* 262–277. See also Network inside your organization. (2000). In *Fast Company career guide* (p. 13). New York, NY: Fast Company Media Group.

69. Dodds, P. S., Muhamad, R., & Watts, D. J. (2003). An experimental study of search in global social networks. *Science, 301,* 827–829.

70. Vanhonacker, W. R. (2004). *Guanxi* networks in China. *China Business Review, 31,* 48–53.

71. Zhang, Y., & Zhang, Z. (2006). Guanxi and organizational dynamics in China: A link between individual and organizational levels. *Journal of Business Ethics, 67,* 375–392.

72. Lyness, K. S., & Thompson, D. E. (2000). Climbing the corporate ladder: Do female and male executives follow the same route? *Journal of Applied Psychology, 85,* 86–101. See also Gregory, M. (2009). Inside the locker room: Male homosociality in the advertising industry. *Gender, Work & Organization, 16,* 323–347.

73. Kram, K. E. (1983). Phases of the mentoring relationship. *Academy of Management Journal, 12,* 608–625.

74. Gardenswartz, L., & Rowe, A. (1997, January). Starting a mentoring program? *Managing Diversity, 6,* 1–2. See also Advancing Women. (2006). *Mentoring process.* Retrieved from http://www.advancingwomen.com/wk_mentprocess.html

75. Driscoll, D. M. et al. (1997, June). Who says ethics are nice? *Across the Board, 34,* 47–50.

76. Montgomery, M. D., & Ramus, C. (2003, May). Corporate social responsibility reputation effects on MBA job choice. *Graduate School of Business Research Paper #1805,* Stanford, CA. Retrieved from https://gsbapps.stanford.edu/researchpapers/library/RP1805.pdf

77. Roberts, C. R. (2005, May 16). He argues for ethics. *Tacoma News Tribune.* Retrieved from http://elibrary.bigchalk.com

78. Velasquez, M., Ande, C., Shanks S. J. T., & Meyer, M. J. (2012). Thinking ethically: A framework for moral decision making. In J. E. Richardson (Ed.), *Business ethics 11/12* (pp. 2–4). New York, NY: McGraw-Hill.

79. O'Connor, P. J., & Godar, S. H. (1999). How not to make ethical decisions: Guidelines from management textbooks. *Teaching Business Ethics, 3,* 69–86. See also Tinsley, D. B. (2005). Ethics can be gauged by three rules. In J. E. Richardson (Ed.), *Business ethics 05/06* (pp. 11–12). Dubuque, IA: McGraw-Hill/Dushkin.

Chapter 2

1. While many Hispanics prefer to be identified with their country of origin and some prefer Latino or Latina to Hispanic, we generally use the term *Hispanic* while acknowledging the ongoing discussion. See Chong, N., & F. Baez, F. (2005). *Latino culture: A dynamic force in the changing American workplace.* Yarmouth, ME: Intercultural Press.

2. U.S. Census Bureau. (2011). *2005–2009 American community survey.* Retrieved from http://factfinder.census.gov

3. U.S. Census Bureau. (2004). Tripling of Hispanic and Asian populations in 50 years; Non-Hispanic whites may drop to half of total population. Retrieved from http://www.imdiversity.com/villages/asian/reference/census_2050_asian_projections.asp

4. Uniworld Business Publications. (2005). *Directory of foreign firms operating in the U.S.* (18th ed.). New York, NY: Uniworld Business Publications.

5. U.S. Census Bureau. (2001). *Population profile of the United States: 2000.* Retrieved from http://www.census.gov/population/www/pop-profile/files/2000/profile2000.pdf

6. Bureau of Labor Statistics. (2011, May 27). *Labor force characteristics of foreign-born workers summary.* Retrieved from http://www.bls.gov/news.release/forbrn.nr0.htm

7. Davies, A., Fidler, D., & Gorbis, M. (2011). *Future work skills: 2020.* Palo Alto, CA: Institute for the Future. Retrieved from http://cdn.theatlantic.com/static/front/docs/sponsored/phoenix/future_work_skills_2020.pdf

8. Hammonds, K. H. (2001, March). Fast forward. *Fast Company, 44,* 113–120.

9. DuPont advertisement, reprinted in Boone, L. E., Kurtz, D. L., & Block, J. R. (1996). *Contemporary business communication* (2nd ed.). Englewood Cliffs, NJ: Prentice-Hall.

10. Copeland, L. (1988, June). Making the most of cultural differences in the workplace. *Personnel,* p. 53.

11. Bartrum, N. (2003, July). Diversity for all. *Association Management,* p. 58.

12. Lustig, M. W., & Koester, J. (2003). *Intercultural competence: Interpersonal communication across cultures* (4th ed.). Boston, MA: Allyn & Bacon.

13. Hall, E. (1959). *The silent language.* Greenwich, CT: Fawcett.

14. Barker, J. A. (1992). *Future edge: Discovering the new paradigms of success.* New York, NY: William Morrow.

15. Barker, J. A. (1992). *Future edge: Discovering the new paradigms of success.* New York, NY: William Morrow.

16. Hansen, R. S. Uncovering a company's corporate culture is a critical task for job-seekers. Retrieved from http://www.quintcareers.com/employer_corporate_culture.html

17. Ravlin, E. C., & Adkins, C. L. (1989). A work values approach to corporate culture: A field test of the value of congruence process and its relationship to individual outcomes. *Journal of Applied Psychology, 74,* 424–433.

18. Kotter, J., & Heskett, J. (1992). *Corporate culture and performance.* New York, NY: Free Press.

19. Waldvogel, J. (2007). Greetings and closings in workplace email. *Journal of Computer-Mediated Communication, 12,* 456–477.

20. Orbe, M. P., & Harris, T. M. (2008). *Interracial communication: Theory into practice* (2nd ed.). Thousand Oaks, CA: Sage.

21. For a discussion of Greek and Israeli conflict styles see Hall, J. B. (2002). *Among cultures.* Fort Worth, TX: Harcourt College Publishers.

22. Lustig, M. W., & Koester, J. (2003). *Intercultural competence: Interpersonal communication across cultures* (4th ed.). Boston, MA: Allyn & Bacon.

23. Condon, E. C. (1976). Cross-cultural interferences affecting teacher–pupil communication in American schools. In F. L. Casmir (Ed.), *International and intercultural communication annual 3* (pp. 108–120). Falls Church, VA: Speech Communication Association.

24. Samovar, L. A., & Porter, R. (2004). *Communication between cultures* (5th ed.). Belmont, CA: Wadsworth.

25. Kohn, M. (1969). *Class and conformity: A study of values.* Homewood, IL: Dorsey Press.

26. Kim, Y. K., & Sax, L. J. (2009). Student–faculty interaction in research universities: Differences by student gender, race, social class, and first-generation status. *Research in Higher Education, 50,* 437–459.

27. Kaufman, P. (2003). Learning to not labor: How working-class individuals construct middle-class identities. *Sociological Quarterly, 44,* 481–504.

28. Lubrano, A. (2004). *Limbo: Blue-collar roots, white-collar dreams.* Hoboken, NJ: John Wiley; Lucas, K. (2011). The working class promise: A communicative account of mobility-based ambivalences. *Communication Monographs, 78,* 347–369. For a case study on social class mobility, see Lucas, K. (2010). Moving up: The challenges of communicating a new social class identity. In D. O. Braithwaite & J. T. Wood (Eds.), *Casing interpersonal communication: Case studies in personal and social relationships* (pp. 17–24). Dubuque, IA: Kendall-Hunt.

29. For information on generational differences, see Auby, K. (2008). *A Boomers guide to communicating with Gen X and Gen Y.* Retrieved from http://www.businessweek.com/magazine/content/08_34/b4097063805619.htm; Eisner, S. P. (2005). Managing Generation Y. *Advanced Management Journal, 70,* 13–17; Erickson, T. (2008, September 9). When Boomers work for Gen X and Gen Y. *Harvard Business Online.* Retrieved from http://www.businessweek.com/managing/content/sep2008/ca2008099_258565.htm. See also Lyons, S., Duxbury, L., & Higgins, C. (2005). Are gender differences in basic human values a generational phenomenon?" *Sex Roles: A Journal of Research, 53,* 763–779.

30. Howe, N., & Strauss, W. (2007, July). The next 20 years: How customers and workforce attitudes will evolve. *Harvard Business Review, 85,* 41–52.

31. Taylor, P., & Keeter, S. (2010). *The Millennials: Confident. Connected. Open to change.* Washington, DC: Pew Research Center. Retrieved from http://pewsocialtrends.org/files/2010/10/millennials-confident-connected-open-to-change.pdf

32. Zogby, J. (2008). *The way we'll be: The transformation of the American dream.* New York, NY: Random House; Zogby, J. (2008, October). The evolving American dream. *AARP Bulletin,* p. 37.

33. Myers, K. K., & Sadaghiani, K. (2010). Millennials in the workplace: A communication perspective on Millennials' organizational relationships and performance. *Journal of Business and Psychology, 25,* 225–238.

34. For a summary of research on this subject, see Bradac, J. J. (1990). Language attitudes and impression formation. In H. Giles & W. P. Robinson (Eds.), *The handbook of language and social psychology* (pp. 387–412). Chichester, UK: Wiley. See also Ng, S. H., & Bradac, J. (1993). *Power in language: Verbal communication and social influence.* Newbury Park, CA: Sage.

35. Bailey, R. W. (2003). Ideologies, attitudes, and perceptions. *American Speech, 88,* 115–142.

36. Frumkin, L. (2007). Influences of accent and ethnic background on perceptions of eyewitness testimony. *Psychology, Crime & Law, 13,* 317–331.

37. Gluszek, A., & Dovidio, J. F. (2010). Perceptions of bias, communication difficulties, and belonging in the United States. *Journal of Language & Social Psychology, 29,* 224–234.

38. Birdwhistell, R. L. (1970). *Kinesics and context.* Philadelphia, PA: University of Philadelphia Press.

39. Stone, K. G. (1995, February 19). Disability Act everyone's responsibility in America. *Albuquerque Journal,* p. H2.

40. Braithwaite, D. O., & Labrecque, D. (1994). Responding to the Americans with Disabilities Act: Contributions of interpersonal communication research and training. *Journal of Applied Communication Research, 22,* 285–294. See also Braithwaite, D. O. (1991). Just how much did that wheelchair cost?

Management of privacy boundaries by persons with disabilities. *Western Journal of Speech Communication, 55,* 254–275.

41. Communicating with people with disabilities. (1995, October 9). *Business First, 11,* p. 14B. See also Colvert, A. L., & Smith, J. (2000). What is reasonable? Workplace communication and people who are disabled. In D. O. Braithwaite & T. L. Thompson (Eds.), *Handbook of communication and people with disabilities: Research and application* (pp. 141–158). Mahwah, NJ: Erlbaum.

42. See, for example, Zhu, Y. (2001). Comparing English and Chinese persuasive strategies in trade fair invitations: A sociocognitive approach. *Document Design, 2*(1), 2–17.

43. Boone, L. E., Kurtz, D. L., & Block, J. R. (1997). *Contemporary Business Communication* (2nd ed.). Englewood Cliffs, NJ: Prentice Hall.

44. Williams, C. J. (1999, August 15). Not all ways Wal-Mart as chain takes on Germany. *Los Angeles Times,* p. C1.

45. Glover, K. M. (1990, August 13). Do's and taboos. *Business America, 111,* p. 5.

46. Katayama, F. H. (1989, November 13). How to act once you get there. *Fortune's Pacific Rim Guide,* pp. 87–90.

47. Falkoff, R. (2006). The karaoke business meeting. Retrieved from http://workabroad.monster.com/articles/karaoke/

48. UPS: From local startup to global titan. (2007, June 27). *Business Week.* Retrieved from http://www.businessweek.com/smallbiz/content/jun2007/sb20070627_827624.htm

49. Padgett, T., & Lee, C. S. (1994, September 19). Go south, young yanquis. *Newsweek,* p. 48.

50. Trompenaars, F. (1994). *Riding the waves of culture.* Burr Ridge, IL: Irwin.

51. Chen, M. (2003). *Inside Chinese business: A guide for managers worldwide.* Boston, MA: Harvard Business School Press.

52. Miller, M. (1992, August 15). A clash of corporate cultures. *Los Angeles Times,* pp. A1, A8.

53. Hall, E. (1959). *Beyond culture.* New York, NY: Doubleday.

54. Chen, M. (2003). *Inside Chinese business: A guide for managers worldwide.* Boston, MA: Harvard Business School Press.

55. Melymuka, K. (1997, April 28). Tips for teams. *Computerworld, 31,* p. 72.

56. Morris, M. (1981). *Saying and meaning in Puerto Rico: Some problems in the ethnology of discourse.* Oxford, UK: Pergamon.

57. Locke, D. (1992). *Increasing multicultural understanding: A comprehensive model.* Newbury Park, CA: Sage.

58. Hofstede, G. (1997). *Cultures and organizations: Software of the mind.* New York, NY: McGraw-Hill.

59. See, for example, Nishishiba, M., & Ritchie, L. D. (2000). The concept of trustworthiness: A cross-cultural comparison between Japanese and U.S. business people. *Journal of Applied Communication Research, 28,* 347–367. See also Witteborn, S. (2006, June 16). Conceptualization and study of collective identities: Implications for research in culture and communication. Paper presented at the International Communication Association annual meeting, Dresden, Germany.

60. Taub, D. (1996, December 16). Global recruiting: Richard Ferry helped take Korn/Ferry international from two-man office to world's no. 1 executive search firm. *Los Angeles Business Journal,* p. 1.

61. Formula for Success. (1992, December 8). *Financial World,* p. 40.

62. Hofstede, G. (1997). *Cultures and organizations: Software of the mind.* New York, NY: McGraw-Hill.

63. See Skelly, J. (1995, March/April.) The caux round table principles for business: The rise of international ethics. *Business Ethics,* pp. 2–5.

64. Buller, P. F., Kohls, J. J., & Anderson, K. S. (1997). A model for addressing cross-cultural ethical conflicts. *Business & Society, 36,* 169–193.

65. See Donaldson, T. (1996, September/October). Values in tension: Ethics away from home. *Harvard Business Review, 74,* 48–62.

66. See Donaldson, T. (1996, September/October). Values in tension: Ethics away from home. *Harvard Business Review, 74,* 48–62.

67. Kiboski, J. F. (1999). Effective communication in the performance appraisal interview: Face-to-face communication for public managers in the culturally diverse workplace. *Public Personnel Management, 28,* 301–323.

68. Marby, M. (1990, May 14). Pin a label on a manager—and watch what happens. *Newsweek,* p. 43.

69. Raymond, J. (2010, December 13). The cobra was ok; the duck tongue not so much. *New York Times,* p. B6.

70. Copeland, L. (1988, June). Making the most of cultural differences in the workplace. *Personnel,* p. 53.

71. Weiss, T. (1997). Reading culture: Professional communication as translation. *Journal of Business & Technical Communication, 11,* 321–338.

72. Gray, J. (1992). *Men are from Mars, women are from Venus: A practical guide for improving communication.* New York, NY: HarperCollins.

73. See, for example, Mulac, A. (2006). The gender-linked language effect: Do language differences really make a difference? In K. Dindia & D. J. Canary (Eds.), *Sex differences and similarities in communication: Critical essays and empirical investigations of sex and gender in interaction* (2nd ed., pp. 127–153). Mahwah, NJ: Erlbaum.

74. Tannen, D. (1990). *You just don't understand: Women and men in conversation.* New York, NY: Morrow.

75. Tannen, D. (1984). *Conversational style: Analysing talk among friends.* Norwood, NJ: Ablex.

76. Millhous, L. M. (1999). The experience of culture in multi-cultural groups. *Small Group Research, 30,* 280–308.

77. Pearson, J. C., Turner, L., & Todd-Mancillas, W. (1995). *Gender and communication* (3rd ed.). Madison, WI: Brown & Benchmark.

78. Dong, Q., Day, K. D., & Collaço, C. M. (2008). Overcoming ethnocentrism through developing intercultural communication sensitivity and multiculturalism. *Human Communication, 11*(1), 27–38.

79. Houston, M. (1994). When black woman talk with white women: Why dialogues are difficult. In A. Gonzalez, M. Houston, & V. Chen (Eds.), *Our voices: Essays in culture, ethnicity, and communication* (pp. 133–139). Los Angeles, CA: Roxbury.

80. Martin, J. M., & Nakayama, T. K. (2004). *Intercultural communication in contexts.* Boston, MA: McGraw-Hill.

81. Kelly, C. M. (1988). *The destructive achiever: Power and ethics in the American corporation.* Reading, MA: Addison-Wesley.

82. Cose, E. (1993). *The rage of a privileged class: Why are middle-class blacks so angry? Why should America care?* New York, NY: HarperCollins.

Chapter 3

1. Covey. S. (1989). *The seven habits of highly effective people.* New York, NY: Simon & Schuster.

2. Iacocca, L., & Novak, W. (1984). *Iacocca: An autobiography.* New York, NY: Bantam.

3. Franzen, J. (2003, October 6). The listener. *New Yorker,* p. 85.

4. Flynn, J., Valikoski, T., & Grau, J. (2008). Listening in the business context: Reviewing the state of research. *International Journal of Listening, 22,* 141–151.

5. Sweet, D. H. (1993). Successful job hunters are all ears. *Managing your career.* New York, NY: Dow Jones.

6. Sutcliffe, A. J. (1997). *First-job survival guide.* New York, NY: Henry Holt.

7. Winsor, J. L., Curtis, D. B., & Stephens, R. D. (1997). National preferences in business and communication education: An update. *Journal of the Association for Communication Administration, 3,* 170–179.

8. Gabric, D., & McFadden, K. L. (2001). Student and employer perceptions of desirable entry-level operations management skills. *Mid-American Journal of Business, 16*(1), 51–59; Landrum, R. E., & Harrold, R. (2003). What employers want from psychology graduates. *Teaching of Psychology, 30,* 131–133.

9. *U.S. News & World Report.* (1980, May 26). p. 65.

10. Drucker, P. F. (1974). *Management: Tasks, responsibilities, practices.* New York, NY: Harper & Row.

11. *Industrial Marketing.* (1982, April). p. 108.

12. McDaniel, S. H., Beckman, H. B., Morse, D. S., Silberman, J., Seaburn, D. B., & Epstein, R. M. (2007). Physician self-disclosure in primary care visits: Enough about you, what about me? *Archives of Internal Medicine, 167,* 1321–1326.

13. Cooper, E. (2001, July). Are you in the listening zone? Most times, it's not what you say that makes the sale—it's how you listen. *On Wall Street, 11*(7).

14. Peterson, S. (1995, January 1). Managing your communication. *Vital Speeches of the Day, 61,* 188–191.

15. Brownell, J. (1990). Perceptions of effective listeners: A management study. *Journal of Business Communication, 27,* 401–415.

16. Wolvin, A. D., & Coakley, C. G. (1991). A survey of the status of listening training in some Fortune 500 companies. *Communication Education, 40,* 152–165.

17. Spitzberg, B. H. (1994). The dark side of incompetence. In W. R. Cupach & B. H. Spitzberg (Eds.), *The dark side of interpersonal communication* (pp. 25–50). Hillsdale, NJ: Erlbaum.

18. Nichols, R. G. (1957). *Are you listening?* New York, NY: McGraw-Hill.

19. Turner, J. W., & Reinsch, N. L. (2007). The business communicator as presence allocator: Multicommunicating, equivocality, and status at work. *Journal of Business Communication, 44,* 36–58.

20. Tannen, D. (1990). *You just don't understand: Women and men in conversation.* New York, NY: Morrow.

21. Booth-Butterfield, M. (1984). She hears…he hears: What they hear and why. *Personnel Journal, 63,* 36–43.

22. Arsenault, A. (2007, May). *Too much information? Gatekeeping and information dissemination in a networked world.* Paper presented at the International Communication Association annual meeting, San Francisco, CA.

23. Hamilton, J. (2008, October 16). Bad at multitasking? Blame your brain. *National Public Radio.* Retrieved from http://www.npr.org/templates/story/story. php?storyId=95784052

24. Vangelisti, A., Knapp, M. L., & Daly, J. A. (1990). Conversational narcissism. *Communication Monographs, 57,* 251–274.

25. Thomlison, T. D. (1997). Intercultural listening. In D. Borisoff & M. Purdy (Eds.), *Listening in everyday life: A personal and professional approach* (pp. 79–120). Lanham, MD: University Press of America.

26. Lusting, M. L., & Koester, J. (1999). *Intercultural competence: Interpersonal communication across cultures* (3rd ed). New York, NY: Longman.

27. Mare, L. D. (1990). Ma and Japan. *Southern Speech Communication Journal, 55,* 319–328.

28. Peters, T. (1987). *Thriving on chaos: Handbook for a management revolution.* New York, NY: Knopf.

29. Langer, E. (1990). *Mindfulness.* Reading, MA: Addison-Wesley; Hajek, C., & Giles, H. (2003). New directions in intercultural communication competence: The process model. In J. O. Greene & B. R. Burleson (Eds.), *Handbook of communication and social interaction skills* (pp. 935–958). Mahwah, NJ: Lawrence Erlbaum.

30. Burgoon, J. K., Berger, C. R., & Waldron, V. R. (2000). Mindfulness and interpersonal communication. *Journal of Social Issues, 56,* 105–127.

31. Miller, A. (2008, September). The mindful society. *Shambhala Sun,* pp. 56–62, 106. Retrieved from http://www.shambhalasun.com/index.php?option=com_content&task=view&id=3253&Itemid=244

32. Covey. S. (1989). *The seven habits of highly effective people.* New York, NY: Simon & Schuster.

33. Dollinger, T. (2004, March 29). Listen using the 20/80 rule. *Listening Leader* [newsletter].

34. Carnoy, D. (1998, October). Rick Pitino. *Success, 45,* 68–71.

35. Borisoff, D., & Victor, D. A. (1989). *Conflict management: A communication skills approach.* Englewood Cliffs, NJ: Prentice-Hall.

36. Wyer R. S., Jr., & Adaval, R. (2003). Message reception skills in social communication. In J. O. Greene & B. R. Burleson (Eds.), *Handbook of communication and social interaction skills* (pp. 291–355). Mahwah, NJ: Lawrence Erlbaum.

37. Marquardt, M. J. (2005). *Leading with questions: How leaders find the right solutions by knowing what to ask.* Hoboken, NJ: Jossey-Bass.

Chapter 4

1. Keysar, B., & Henly, A. S. (2003). Speakers' overestimation of their effectiveness. *Psychological Science, 13,* 207–212. See also Wyer, R. S., & Adaval, R. (2003). Message reception skills in social communication. In J. O. Greene & B. R. Burleson (Eds.), *Handbook of communication and social interaction skills* (pp. 291–355). Mahwah, NJ: Lawrence Erlbaum.

2. Bello, R. (2000). Determinants of equivocation. *Communication Research, 27,* 161–194.

3. Meyer, M., & Fleming, C. (1994, August 15). Silicon screenings: The marriage of Hollywood and Silicon Valley gets off to a rocky start. *Newsweek,* p. 63.

4. Miller, M. (1992, August 15). A clash of corporate cultures. *Los Angeles Times,* pp. A1, A8.

5. Armstrong, J. S. (1980). Unintelligible management research and academic prestige. *Interfaces, 10,* 80–86.

6. Eisenberg, E. M. (1984). Ambiguity as strategy in organizational communication. *Communication Monographs, 51,* 227–242.

7. Legard, D. (2003, June 17). IT vendors worst for jargon, Deloitte says. *IDG News Service.* Retrieved from http://www.idg.net/idgns/2003/06/17/ITVendorsWorstForJargon Deloitte.shtml

8. Simmons, T. (2003, April). Are you a buzzword abuser? *Presentations,* pp. 31–34.

9. Terez, T. (2002, February). Eager for a paradigm shift? Not so fast!" *Workforce,* p. 26.

10. Quinn, C. (2007, September 1). Lose the office jargon, it may sunset you. *The Age.* Retrieved from http://www.theage.com.au/news/in-depth/bjobsb-lose-the-office-jargon-it-may-sunset-your-career/2007/08/31/1188067363016.html

11. Weiss, T. (1995). Translation in a borderless world. *Technical Communication Quarterly, 4,* 407–425.

12. See, for example, Bavelas, J. B., Black, A., Chovil, N., & Mullett, J. (1990). *Equivocal communication.* Newbury Park, CA: Sage; Eisenberg, E. M., Goodall, H. L., Jr., & Tretheway, A. (2007). *Organizational communication: Balancing creativity and constraint* (6th ed.). New York, NY: Bedford/St. Martin's.

13. Schneider, A. (2000, June 30). Why you can't trust letters of recommendation. *The Chronicle of Higher Education, 46,* pp. A14–A16. Retrieved from http://chronicle.com/article/Why-You-Can-t-Trust-Letters/2132; Conrad, C., & Poole, M. S. (2005). *Strategic organizational communication in a global economy* (6th ed). Belmont, CA: Thomson Wadsworth.

14. Litigation-proof letters of recommendation. (n.d.). Retrieved from http://www.wildcowpublishing.com/other/letter.html

15. Rubin, R. (2003, May 1) Doctor-patient language gap isn't healthy. *USA Today,* p. 9D.

16. Jay, T., & Janschewitz, K. (2008). The pragmatics of swearing. *Journal of Politeness Research: Language, Behavior, Culture, 4,* 267–288.

17. The F word means you're fired! (2008). *The Ladders.* Retrieved from http://marketing.theladders.com/press-releases/fired-survey-common-causes-2008-4-28

18. *Reeves v. C. H. Robinson Worldwide, Inc.* (11th, 2010). Retrieved from http://www.ca11.uscourts.gov/opinions/ops/200710270op2.pdf

19. Johnson, D. I., & Lewis, N. (2010). Perceptions of swearing in the work setting: An expectancy violations theory perspective. *Communication Reports, 23,* 106–118.

20. Sutton, R. I. (2010, June 18). Is it sometimes useful to cuss when you are at work? The strategic use of swear words. *Psychology Today.* Retrieved from http://www.psychologytoday.com/blog/work-matters/201006/is-it-sometimes-useful-cuss-when-you-are-work

21. Bradac, J. J., Wiemann, J. M., & Schaefer, K. (1994). The language of control in interpersonal communication. In J. A. Daly & J. M. Wiemann (Eds.), *Strategic interpersonal communication* (pp. 102–104). Hillsdale, NJ: Erlbaum. See also Ng, S. H., & Bradac, J. J. (1993). *Power in language: Verbal communication and social influence.* Newbury Park, CA: Sage.

22. Hosman, L. A. (1989). The evaluative consequences of hedges, hesitations, and intensifiers: Powerful and powerless speech styles. *Human Communication Research, 15,* 383–406.

23. Tannen, D. (1995). *Talking from 9 to 5: Women and men in the workplace.* New York, NY: Morrow.

24. Bradac, J. J. (1983). The language of lovers, flovers, and friends: Communicating in social and personal relationships. *Journal of Language and Social Psychology, 2,* 141–162.

25. Geddes, D. (1992). Sex roles in management: The impact of varying power of speech style on union members' perception of satisfaction and effectiveness. *Journal of Psychology, 126,* 589–607.

26. Hitchens, C. (2010, January 13). The other L-word. *Vanity Fair.* Retrieved from http://www.vanityfair.com/culture/features/2010/01/hitchens-like-201001

27. Dziedzic, S. (2011). 6 filler words that, like, won't get you hired, you know? *Brand-Yourself.com.* Retrieved from http://blog.brand-yourself.com/personal-brand/6-filler-words-that-wont-get-you-hired/

28. Tannen, D. (1990). *You just don't understand: Women and men in conversation.* New York, NY: Morrow. For a detailed summary of masculine and feminine language, see Canary, D., & Emmers-Sommer, T. (1997). *Sex and gender differences in personal relationships.* New York, NY: Guilford; Tannen, D. (1994). *Talking from 9 to 5: How women's and men's conversational styles affect who gets heard, who gets credit, and what get done at work.* New York, NY: Morrow; Wood, J. T. (2011). *Gendered lives: Communication, gender, and culture* (9th ed.). Boston, MA: Cengage.

29. Tannen, D. (1994). *Talking from 9 to 5: How women's and men's conversational styles affect who gets heard, who gets credit, and what get done at work.* New York, NY: Morrow.

30. Mullany, L. (2007). *Gendered discourse in the professional workplace.* Houndmills, UK: Palgrave Macmillan.

31. Byron, K. (2007). Male and female managers' ability to read emotions: Relationships with supervisor's performance ratings and subordinates' satisfaction ratings. *Journal of Occupational and Organizational Psychology, 80,* 713–733.

32. Mell, M. R., Vazire, S., Ramirez-Esparza, N., Slatcher, R. B., & Pennebaker, J. W. (2007, July). Are women really more talkative than men? *Science, 317,* 82. See also Tannen, D. (2007, July 15). Who does the talking here? *The Washington Post,* p. B07. Retrieved from http://www9.georgetown.edu/faculty/tannend/post071507.htm

33. Mullany, L. (2007). *Gendered discourse in the professional workplace.* Houndmills, UK: Palgrave Macmillan.

34. For example, see Geddes, D. (1992). Sex roles in management: The impact of varying power of speech style on union members' perception of satisfaction and effectiveness. *Journal of Psychology, 126,* 589–607.

35. For a discussion of the principle "You can't not communicate nonverbally," see Clevenger, T., Jr. (1991). Can one not communicate? A conflict of models. *Communication Studies, 42,* 340–353.

36. Kalman, Y. M., Ravid, G., Raban, D. R., & Rafaeli, S. (2006). Pauses and response latencies: A chronemic analysis of asynchronous CMC. *Journal of Computer-Mediated Communication, 12,* 1–23.

37. McCoy, L. (1996, September/October). First impressions. *Canadian Banker,* pp. 32–36.

38. Stiff, J. B., Hale, J. L., Garlick, R., & Rogan, R. G. (1990). Effect of cue incongruence and social normative influences on individual judgments of honesty and deceit. *Southern Speech Communication Journal, 55,* 206–229.

39. Friedman, H. S. (2001). Paradoxes of nonverbal detection, expression, and responding: Points to ponder. In J. A. Hall & F. J. Bernieri (Eds.), *Interpersonal sensitivity: Theory and measurement* (pp. 351–362). Mahwah, NJ: Erlbaum.

40. Byron, K., Terranova, S., & Nowicki, S. (2007). Nonverbal emotion recognition and salespersons: Linking ability to perceived and actual success. *Journal of Applied Social Psychology, 37,* 2600–2619.

41. Baron, R. A., & Markman, G. D. (2003). Beyond social capital: The role of entrepreneurs' social competence in their financial success. *Journal of Business Venturing, 18,* 41–60.

42. Byron, K. (2007). Male and female managers' ability to read emotions: Relationships with supervisor's performance ratings and subordinates' satisfaction ratings. *Journal of Occupational and Organizational Psychology, 80,* 713–733.

43. Ekman, P. (1973). Cross-cultural studies of facial expression. In P. Ekman (Ed.), *Darwin and facial expression* (pp. 169–122). New York, NY: Academic Press.

44. Sussman, N., & Rosenfeld, H. (1982). Influence of culture, language and sex on conversational distance. *Journal of Personality and Social Psychology, 42,* 67–74.

45. Ambady, N., LaPlante, D., Nguyen, T., Rosenthal, R., Chaumeton, N., & Levinson, W. (2002). Surgeons' tone of voice: A clue to malpractice history. *Surgery, 132,* 5–9.

46. Word up. (2001, September 21). *The Guardian.* Retrieved from http://www.guardian.co.uk/g2/story/0,3604,555379,00.html

47. See, for example, Burgoon, J. K., Birk, T., & Pfau, M. (1990). Nonverbal behaviors, persuasion, and credibility. *Human Communication Research, 17,* 140–169.

48. See Rothwell, J. D. (1998). *In mixed company* (3rd ed.). Ft. Worth, TX: Harcourt Brace Jovanovich.

49. Roan, S. (1990, December 18). Overweight and under pressure. *Los Angeles Times,* pp. E1, E4.

50. Philip Condit, CEO, Boeing/McDonnell Douglas: A true listening leader. (1997, November 24). *Listening Leader.* Retrieved from http://www.listencoach.com/SiteFrameSet.html

51. Matthews, J. (1994, January 31). In offices across America, attire is changing. *Washington Post,* p. 26.

52. Hammonds, K. H. (2003, July). All the right moves: Meanwhile, back at the office. *Fast Company, 72,* p. 70. Retrieved from http://www.fastcompany.com/magazine/72/backattheoffice.html

53. Laabs, J. H. (2000). Mixing business with passion. *Workforce, 79*(3), 80–85.

54. Amiel, I. (1999). A nationwide survey on business casual conducted by a team of AICI professionals.

Association of Image Consultants International. Retrieved from http://www.aici.org/dec99p5.html

55. Amiel, I. (1999). A nationwide survey on business casual conducted by a team of AICI professionals. *Association of Image Consultants International.* Retrieved from http://www.aici.org/dec99p5.html

56. Marchetti, M. (2003, May 1). Barbarians at the buffet. *Successful Meetings.* Retrieved from http://www.successfulmeetings.com/article.aspx?id=1719

57. Cullen, L. T. (2008, May 29). What (not) to wear to work. *Time,* p. 49.

58. Lorenz, K. (2007, August 24). Too much skin: 10 taboos for office attire. *CareerBuilder.com.* Retrieved from http://www.careerbuilder.com/Article/CB-666-The-Workplace-Too-Much-Skin-10-Taboos-for-Office-Attire/?pf=true

59. Glick, P., Larsen, S., Johnson, C., & Branstiter, H. (2005). Evaluations of sexy women in low- and high-status jobs. *Psychology of Women Quarterly, 29,* 389–395; and Wookey, M. L., Graves, N. A., & Butler, J. C. (2009). Effects of a sexy appearance on perceived competence of women. *Journal of Social Psychology, 149,* 116–118.

60. Wells, W., & Siegel, B. (1961). Stereotyped somatypes. *Psychological Reports, 8,* 1175–1178.

61. Reitman, V. (1999, February 22). Learning to grin—and bear it. *Los Angeles Times,* p. A1.

62. Hunter, B. (1982, March 8). Are you ready to face 60 Minutes? *Industry Week,* p. 74.

63. Memos. (1982, January 11). *Industry Week,* p. 11.

64. Mehrabian, A. (1980). *Silent messages: Implicit communication of emotions and attitudes* (2nd ed.). Belmont, CA: Wadsworth.

65. Borisoff, D., & Merrill, L. (1992). *The power to communicate: Gender differences as barriers* (2nd ed.). Prospect Heights, IL: Waveland Press.

66. Hall, E. (1969). *The hidden dimension.* New York, NY: Doubleday.

67. Gueguen, N., & Vion, M. (2009). The effect of a practitioner's touch on a patient's medication compliance. *Psychology, Health & Medicine, 14,* 689–694.

68. J. Hornik, J. (1992). Effects of physical contact on customers' shopping time and behavior. *Marketing Letters, 3,* 49–55.

69. Smith, D. E., Gier, J. A., & Willis, F. N. (1982). Interpersonal touch and compliance with a marketing request. *Basic and Applied Social Psychology, 3,* 35–38.

70. Kraus, M. W., Huang, C., & Keltner, D. (2010). Tactile communication, cooperation, and performance: An ethological study of the NBA. *Emotion, 10,* 745–749.

71. Knapp, M., L., & Hall, J. A. (1992). *Nonverbal behavior in human interaction* (3rd ed.). Ft. Worth, TX: Harcourt Brace Jovanovich.

72. Knapp, M., L., & Hall, J. A. (1992). *Nonverbal behavior in human interaction* (3rd ed.). Ft. Worth, TX: Harcourt Brace Jovanovich.

73. Mehrabian, A. (1980). *Silent messages: Implicit communication of emotions and attitudes* (2nd ed.). Belmont, CA: Wadsworth.

74. Ogilvy, D. (1968). *Principles of management.* New York, NY: Ogilvy & Mather.

75. Allen, T. (1969, November). Meeting the technical information needs of research and development projects. M.I.T. Industrial Liaison Program Report No. 13-314, Cambridge, MA.

76. Manning, P. (1965). *Office design: A study of environment.* Liverpool, UK: Pilkington Research Unit.

77. Andersen, P. A., & Bowman, L. L. (1999). Positions of power: Nonverbal influence in organizational communication. In L. K. Guerrero, J. A. DeVito, & M. L. Hecht (Eds.), *The nonverbal communication reader: Classic and contemporary readings* (2nd ed., pp. 317–334). Prospect Heights, IL: Waveland Press.

78. Steele, F. (1973). *Physical settings and organizational development.* Reading, MA: Addison-Wesley.

79. McGrath, J. E., & Kelly, J. R. (1989). *Time and human interaction.* New York, NY: Guilford. See also Ballard, D. I., & Seibold, D. R. (2000). Time orientation and temporal variation across work groups: Implications for group and organizational communication. *Western Journal of Communication, 64,* 218–242.

80. Are you really ready to change jobs? (1986, September 28). *Fall Job Market, Washington Post* [advertising supplement], p. 22.

81. Hamachek, D. E. (1987). *Encounters with the self* (2nd ed.). Ft. Worth, TX: Holt, Rinehart and Winston. See also Daly, J. A., Vangelisti, A. L., & Daughton, S. M. (1987). The nature and correlates of conversational sensitivity. *Human Communication Research, 14,* 167–202.

82. Dunning, D. A., & Kruger, J. (1999). Unskilled and unaware of it: How difficulties in recognizing one's own incompetence lead to inflated self-assessments. *Journal of Personality and Social Psychology, 77,* 1121–1134.

83. Mehrabian, A. (1972). *Nonverbal communication.* Chicago, IL: Aldine/Atherton.

84. Research summarized by Richmond, V. P., & McCroskey, J. C. (2004). *Nonverbal behavior in interpersonal relations* (5th ed.). Boston, MA: Allyn & Bacon.

85. Friedman, H. S., Riggio, R. E., & Casella, D. F. (1988). Nonverbal skill, personal charisma, and initial attraction. *Personality & Social Psychology Bulletin, 14,* 203–211.

86. See Griffin, E. (2012). Expectancy violations theory. In *A first look at communication theory* (8th ed., pp. 84–97). New York, NY: McGraw-Hill.

Chapter 5

1. Curtis, D. B., Winsor, J. L., & Stephens, R. D. (1989). National preferences in business and communication education. *Communication Education, 38,* 6–14.

2. Goodspeed, L. (1999, April 23). 'People skills' stressed over experience for tech CEOs. *Boston Business Journal, 19,* p. 46.

3. Hersh, R. H. (1997). Intentions and perceptions: A national survey of public attitudes toward liberal arts education. *Change, 29,* 16–23. For more information on the importance of communication skills for managers, see St. John, D. (1996, March). Forget the global communication climate for a minute: How's the weather inside your own organization? *Communication World, 12,* p. 24.

4. See, for example, Bellinger, R. (1999, August 30). It takes more than tech. *Electronic Engineering Times,* pp. 91–96; Napolitano, J. M. (2000, March/April). Learning to really communicate. *Journal of Property Management,* p. 12. See also Mauksch, L. B., Dugdale, D. C., Dodson, S., & Epstein, R. (2008). Relationship, communication, and efficiency in the medical encounter: Creating a clinical model from a literature review. *Archives of Internal Medicine, 168,* 1387–1395.

5. Goleman, D. (1995). *Emotional intelligence: Why it can matter more than I.Q.* New York, NY: Bantam. See also Weisinger, H. (1997). *Emotional intelligence at work: The untapped edge for success.* San Francisco, CA: Jossey-Bass; Goleman, D. (2006). *Social intelligence: The new science of human relationships.* New York, NY: Random House.

6. Goleman, D. (2000). *Working with emotional intelligence.* New York, NY: Bantam. See also Suliman, A. M., & Al-Shaikh, F. N. (2007). Emotional intelligence at work: Links to conflict and innovation. *Employee Relations, 29,* 208–220.

7. Dilenschneider, R. L. (1997, March). Social intelligence. *Executive Excellence, 14,* p. 8.

8. Lucas, K. (2011, May). Communicating workplace dignity: An exploratory study. Paper presented at the International Communication Association annual conference, Boston, MA.

9. Hodson, R. (2001). *Dignity at work.* Cambridge, UK: Cambridge University Press.

10. Hodson, R., & Roscigno, V. J. (2004). Organizational success and worker dignity: Complementary or contradictory? *American Journal of Sociology, 110,* 672–708.

11. Lucas, K. (2012, May). Toward a conceptual understanding of communicating workplace dignity. Paper presented at International Communication Association annual conference, Phoenix, AZ.

12. Sutton, R. I. (2007). *The no asshole rule: Building a civilized workplace and surviving one that isn't.* New York, NY: Warner Business Books; Wood, M. S., & Karau, S. J. (2009). Preserving employee dignity during the termination interview: An empirical examination. *Journal of Business Ethics, 86,* 519–534; Hodson, R. (2001). *Dignity at work.* Cambridge, UK: Cambridge University Press.

13. Lucas, K. (2012, May). Toward a conceptual understanding of communicating workplace dignity. Paper presented at International Communication Association annual conference, Phoenix, AZ.

14. Kassing, J. W. (2008). Consider this: A comparison of factors contributing to employees' expressions of dissent. *Communication Quarterly, 56,* 342–355.

15. Bell, S. J., Mengüç, B., & Widing II, R. E. (2010). Salesperson learning, organizational learning, and retail store performance. *Journal of the Academy of Marketing Science, 38,* 187–201; Evans, K. R., Landry, T. D., Po-Chien, L., & Shaoming, Z. (2007). How sales controls affect job-related outcomes: the role of organizational sales-related psychological climate perceptions. *Journal of the Academy Of Marketing Science, 35,* 445–459.

16. Verbeke, W., Franses, P., le Blanc, A., & van Ruiten, N. (2008). Finding the keys to creativity in ad agencies. *Journal of Advertising, 37,* 121–130.

17. Kowalski, C., Nitzsche, A., Scheibler, F., Steffen, P., Albert, U., & Pfaff, H. (2009). Breast cancer patients' trust in physicians: The impact of patients' perception of physicians' communication behaviors and hospital organizational climate. *Patient Education & Counseling, 77,* 344–348.

18. Gibb, J. R. (1961). Defensive communication. *Journal of Communication, 11,* 141–148.

19. Fisher, R., & Brown, S. (1988). *Getting together: Building relationships as we negotiate.* Boston, MA: Houghton Mifflin.

20. "Nineteen eighty-nine turkeys of the year." (1989, November 23). *San Jose Mercury News,* p. 1D.

21. Patterson, K. (2005, July 20). Mutual respect: The continuance condition of safety. [e-newsletter]. *VitalSmarts.* Retrieved from http://www.vitalsmarts.com/jul202005.aspx

22. Patterson, K. (2005, October 5). Talk tentatively. [e-newsletter]. *VitalSmarts.* Retrieved from http://www.vitalsmarts.com/oct052005.aspx

23. Carson, C., & Cupach, W. R. (2000). Facing corrections in the workplace: The influence of perceived face threat on the consequences of managerial reproaches. *Journal of Applied Communication Research, 28,* 215–234.

24. Wittenberg, P. M. (1995). Discipline with dignity: A positive approach for managers. *Federal Probation, 59*(3), 40–42.

25. Korobkin, R., & Guthrie, C. (1994). Psychological barriers to litigation settlement and experimental approach. *Michigan Law Review, 107,* 107–192.

26. Anderson, K. (2000). Handling criticism with honesty and grace. *Public Management, 82,* 30–34.

27. Andersson, L. M., & Pearson, C. M. (1999). Tit for tat? The spiraling effect of incivility in the workplace. *Academy of Management Review, 24,* 452–471.

28. Jayson, S. (2011, August 9). Incivility a growing problem at work, psychologists say. *USA Today.* Retrieved from http://yourlife.usatoday.com/parenting-family/story/2011/08/Incivility-a-growing-problem-at-work-psychologists-say/49854130/1

Paper presented at International Communication Association annual conference, Phoenix, AZ.

29. Sypher, B. D. (2004). Reclaiming civil discourse in the workplace. *Southern Communication Journal, 69,* 257–269.

30. Pearson, C. M., & Porath, C. L. (2009). *The cost of bad behavior: How incivility is damaging your business and what to do about it.* New York, NY: Portfolio.

31. Pearson, C. M., Andersson, L., & Porath, C. L. (2000). Assessing and attacking workplace incivility. *Organizational Dynamics, 29,* 123–137.

32. Lutgen-Sandvik, P. (2003). The communicative cycle of employee emotional abuse: Generation and regeneration of workplace mistreatment. *Management Communication Quarterly, 16,* 471–501.

33. Namie, G., & Namie, R. (2009). *The bully at work: What you can do to stop the hurt and reclaim your dignity on the job.* Naperville, IL: Sourcebooks.

34. Lutgen-Sandvik, P. (2003). The communicative cycle of employee emotional abuse: Generation and regeneration of workplace mistreatment. *Management Communication Quarterly, 16,* 471–501.

35. Pearson, C. M., & Porath, C. L. (2009). *The cost of bad behavior: How incivility is damaging your business and what to do about it.* New York, NY: Portfolio.

36. Jansma, L. (2000). Sexual harassment research: Integration, reformulation, and implications for mitigation efforts. In M. E. Roloff (Ed.), *Communication yearbook 23* (pp. 163–225). Thousand Oaks, CA: Sage.

37. Dougherty, D. S. (2009). Sexual harassment as destructive organizational process. In B. D. Sypher & P. Lutgen-Sandvik (Eds.), *Destructive organizational communication: Processes, consequences, and constructive ways of organizing* (pp. 203–225). New York, NY: Routledge.

38. From http://www.de.psu.edu/harassment/legal

39. U.S. Equal Opportunity Employment Commission. (2011). *Sexual harassment charges: EEOC & FEPAs combined: FY 1997–FY 2010.* Retrieved from http://www.eeoc.gov/eeoc/statistics/enforcement/sexual_harassment.cfm

40. Dougherty, D. S. (2009). Sexual harassment as destructive organizational process. In B. D. Sypher & P. Lutgen-Sandvik (Eds.), *Destructive organizational communication: Processes, consequences, and constructive ways of organizing* (pp. 203–225). New York, NY: Routledge.

41. New Mexico Commission on the Status of Women. (2002). *Dealing with sexual harassment.* Retrieved from www.state.nm.us/womens-commission/Publications/sexhbrochre.pdf

42. For more information about this survey, see Zupek, R. (2009, December 17). Fight the good fight: Six tips to managing workplace conflict. *CareerBuilder.com.* Retrieved from http://msn.careerbuilder.com/custom/msn/careeradvice/viewarticle.aspx?articleid=1202&SiteId=cbmsnhp41202&sc_extcmp=JS_1202_home&GT1=10563&cbRecursionCnt=1&cbsid=ee90ae37f14e40e8b4ae5ad806a33652-250077808-JT-5

43. Slaton, J. (1996, November 25). Hoteliers say hiring is their toughest job. *New Orleans City Business.*

44. Berglos, S. (1995, May). Harmony is death: Let conflict reign. *Inc.,* pp. 56–58.

45. Coser, L. (1956). *The functions of social conflict.* New York, NY: Free Press.

46. For a detailed account of these conflict types, see Wilmot, W. W., & Hocker, J. L. (2007). *Interpersonal conflict* (7th ed.). New York, NY: McGraw-Hill.

47. Folger, J. P., Poole, M. S., & Sturtman, R. K. (2004). *Working through conflict: Strategies for relationships, groups, and organizations* (5th ed.). Boston, MA: Allyn & Bacon.

48. For more detailed descriptions of the approaches to conflict discussed in the text, see Wilmot, W. W., & Hocker, J. L. (2007). *Interpersonal conflict* (7th ed.). New York, NY: McGraw-Hill.

49. Starkey, D. (1998, February 20). Finding common ground. *Sacramento Business Journal,* pp. 12–13.

50. McCormack, M. H. (1984). *What they don't teach you at Harvard Business School.* New York, NY: Bantam.

51. Pavitt, C., & Kemp, B. (1999). Contextual and relational factors in interpersonal negotiation strategy choice. *Communication Quarterly, 47,* 133–150. See also Friedman, S. D., Christensen, P., & DeGroot, J. (1998, November/December). Work and life: The end of the zero-sum game. *Harvard Business Review, 76,* 119–129.

52. Burke, R. J. (1970). Methods of resolving superior–subordinate conflict: The constructive use of subordinate differences and disagreements. *Organizational Behavior and Human Performance, 5,* 393–411.

53. Fisher, R., & Ury, W. (1981). *Getting to yes: Negotiating agreement without giving in.* Boston, MA: Houghton Mifflin.

Chapter 6

1. Stewart, C. J., & Cash, W. B., Jr. (2011). *Interviewing: Principles and practices* (13th ed.). Boston, MA: McGraw-Hill.

2. Stewart, C. J., & Cash, W. B., Jr. (2011). *Interviewing: Principles and practices* (13th ed.). Boston, MA: McGraw-Hill.

3. Stewart, C. J., & Cash, W. B., Jr. (2011). *Interviewing: Principles and practices* (13th ed.). Boston, MA: McGraw-Hill.

4. McCormack, M. H. (1984). *What they don't teach you at Harvard Business School.* New York, NY: Bantam.

5. Shepherd, S. J. (1986, March). How to get that job in 60 minutes or less. *Working Woman, 10,* p. 118.

6. Walton, S., & Huey, J. (1993). *Made in America.* New York, NY: Bantam.

7. Granovetter, M. (1995). *Getting a job: A study of contacts and careers* (2nd ed.). Chicago, IL: University of Chicago Press.

8. Bolles, R. N. (2012). *What color is your parachute? A practical manual for job-hunters and career-changers.* Berkeley, CA: Ten Speed Press.

9. Baker, W. (2000). *Achieving success through social capital.* San Francisco, CA: Jossey-Bass.

10. Tugend, A. (2008, December 19). Readers weigh in with tips on jobs and money. *New York Times.* Retrieved from http://www.nytimes.com/2008/12/20/your-money/20shortcuts.html?pagewanted=all

11. Rogers, E. M. (1983). *Diffusion of innovations* (3rd ed.). New York, NY: Free Press.

12. Dobbs, K. (2001, April). Knowing how to keep the best and brightest. *Workforce, 80*(4), 57–60.

13. Peterson, M. S. (1997). Personnel interviewers' perceptions of the importance and adequacy of applicants' communication skills. *Communication Education, 46,* 287–291.

14. Tschirgi, H. D. (1973). What do recruiters really look for in candidates? *Journal of College Placement, 34,* 75–79.

15. For an assessment of interview effectiveness, see Kirkwood, W. G., & Ralston, S. M. (1999). Inviting meaningful applicant performance in employment interviews. *Journal of Business Communication, 66,* 55–76.

16. Ricklefs, R. (1979, September 19). The hidden hurdle: Executive recruiters say firms tend to hire 'our kind of person.' *Wall Street Journal,* p. 1.

17. Bolles, R. N. (2012). *What color is your parachute? A practical manual for job-hunters and career-changers.* Berkeley, CA: Ten Speed Press.

18. Bolles, R. N. (1997). *What color is your parachute? A practical manual for job-hunters and career-changers.* Berkeley, CA: Ten Speed Press.

19. Bolles, R. N. (2012). *What color is your parachute? A practical manual for job-hunters and career-changers* (Kindle ed.). Berkeley, CA: Ten Speed Press.

20. Berkelaar, B. (2008, May). *Cyber-vetting (potential) employees: An emerging area of study for organizational communication.* Paper presented at the International Communication Association annual meeting, Montreal, QC.

21. Rosen. J. (2010, July 25). The web means the end of forgetting. *New York Times Magazine, 114,* pp. 30–35.

22. Murphy, S. (1999, December 19). The second interview. *Santa Barbara News Press,* p. E1.

23. Richtel, M. (2000, February 6). Online revolution's latest twist: Job interviews with a computer. *New York Times,* p. E1.Retrieved from http://query.nytimes.com/gst/fullpage.html?res=9C04E2DC1F3FF935A35751C0A669C8B63&sec=&spon=&emc=eta1

24. Ace your audition interview. (2001). Retrieved from http://www.wetfeet.com/asp/article.asp?aid562

25. Trotsky, J. (2001, January). Oh, will you behave? *Computerworld, 35*(2), 42–43.

26. Farmery, P. (2000). Recruiters offer a new view of the job interview. In *Job choices: Diversity edition* (pp. 61–64). Bethlehem, PA: National Association of Colleges and Employers.

27. Ayres, J., Keereetaweep, T., Chen, P., & Edwards, P. A. (1998). Communication apprehension and employment interviews. *Communication Education, 47,* 1–17.

28. Goodall, D. B., & Goodall, H. L., Jr., (1982). The employment interview: A selective review of the literature with implications for communications research. *Communication Quarterly, 30,* 116–122.

29. Eder, R. W., & Ferris, G. R. (Eds.). (1989). *The employment interview: Theory, research, and practice.* Newbury Park, CA: Sage.

30. Medley, H. A. (1978). *Sweaty palms: The neglected art of being interviewed.* Belmont, CA: Wadsworth.

31. Medley, H. A. (1978). *Sweaty palms: The neglected art of being interviewed.* Belmont, CA: Wadsworth.

32. Caggiano, C. (1998, October). 'What were you in for?' and other great job-interview questions of our time. *Inc., 20*(14), p. 117.

33. Cooper, C. L. (1993, May/June). No more stupid questions. *Psychology Today, 26*(3), 14–15.

34. Martz, G. (1996). *How to survive without your parents' money.* New York, NY: Villiard.

35. Brandt, G. (2011, April 27). Executive recruiters agree there are only three true job interview questions. *Forbes.* Retrieved from http://www.forbes.com/sites/georgebradt/2011/04/27/top-executive-recruiters-agree-there-are-only-three-key-job-interview-questions

36. Bolles, R. N. (2012). *What color is your parachute? A practical manual for job-hunters and career-changers.* Berkeley, CA: Ten Speed Press.

37. Ralston, S. M., & Kirkwood, W. (1999). The trouble with applicant impression management. *Journal of Business and Technical Communication, 13,* 190–207. See also Ralston, S. M. (2000). The 'veil of ignorance': Exploring ethical issues in the employment interview. *Business Communication Quarterly, 63,* 50–52.

38. Rosenfeld, P. (1997). Impression management, fairness and the employment interview. *Journal of Business Ethics, 16,* 801–808.

39. Beatty, R. H. (2003). *The interview kit* (3rd ed.). Hoboken, NJ: John Wiley & Sons.

40. Silverstein, S., & Brooks, N. R. (1993, March 1). And be sure to mention your favorite subject: You. *Los Angeles Times,* p. D3.

41. Quoted in Kleiman, C. (2003, February 16). Passion play. *The Salt Lake Tribune and the Deseret News,* p. F1.

42. Chen, H. (2009). Can this interview be saved? Maybe with a proper thank you note and follow up. *Vault.* Retrieved from http://www.vault.com/nr/main_article_detail.jsp?article_id=8801822&cat_id=0&ht_type=10

43. Medley, H. A. (1978). *Sweaty palms: The neglected art of being interviewed.* Belmont, CA: Wadsworth.

44. Dickson, M. B. (1993). *Supervising employees with disabilities: Beyond ADA compliance.* Menlo Park, CA: Crisp.

45. Sincoff, M. Z., & Goyer, R. S. (1984). *Interviewing.* New York, NY: Macmillan. See also Washington, T. (2001). Advice on answering illegal interview questions: Reply candidly or tactfully decline. *Wall*

Street Journal Career Journal. Retrieved from http://www.careerjournal.com/emailfriend/sendmail1.asp?txtTargetPage5http%3A//www.careerjournal.com/jobhunting/interviewing/19971231-washington.html

46. Springston, J. K., & Keyton, J. (1988). So tell me, are you married? When the interviewee knows you're asking an illegal question. In J. W. Robinson (Ed.), *Proceedings of the 1988 Annual National Conference of the Council of Employee Responsibilities and Rights* (pp. 177–186). Virginia Beach, VA.

47. Woo, J. (1992, March 11). Job interviews pose risk to employers. *Wall Street Journal,* pp. B1, B5.

48. McShulskis, E. (1997, June). Be aware of illegal interview questions. *HR Magazine, 42*(6), pp. 22–23.

49. Fry, R. (2002). *Your first interview* (4th ed.). Franklin Lakes, NJ: Career Press.

50. Adapted from Wilson, G. L., & Goodall, H. L., Jr. (1991). *Interviewing in context.* New York, NY: McGraw-Hill.

Chapter 7

1. Reich, R. (1987). *Tales of a new America.* New York, NY: Time Books.

2. Devine, D. J., Clayton, L. D., Phillips, J. L., Dunford, B. B. & Melner, S. B. (1999). Teams in organizations: Prevalence, characteristics, and effectiveness. *Small Group Research, 30,* 678–711.

3. Redmond, M. V. (1986). A plan for the successful use of teams in design education. *Journal of Architectural Education, 17*(4), 27–49.

4. Jones, B. (2009). The burden of knowledge and the death of the renaissance man: Is innovation getting harder? *Review of Economic Studies, 76,* 283–317.

5. Gawande, A. (2011, May 26). *Cowboys and pit crews.* Commencement address at Harvard Medical School. Retrieved from http://www.newyorker.com/online/blogs/newsdesk/2011/05/atul-gawande-harvard-medical-school-commencement-address.html

6. Professional occupations in multimedia. (1995). In *California occupational guide,* No. 2006. Sacramento, CA: California State Employment Division. See also North Valley Private Industry Council. (1997). *A labor market analysis of the interactive digital media industry: Opportunities in multimedia.* San Francisco, CA: Reagan & Associates.

7. Lazzareschi, C. (1994, September 12). Being part of the team at work. *Los Angeles Times,* p. 13.

8. For a more detailed discussion of the advantages and drawbacks of working in groups, see Forsutj, D. R. (2010). *Group dynamics.* Boston, MA: Cengage.

9. Rachman, D. J., & Mescon, M. H. (1990). *Profile kit for business today* (4th ed.). New York, NY: Random House.

10. Basic types of virtual teams. (2009). *Free Management Library.* Retrieved from http:// http://managementhelp.org/groups/virtual/defined.pdf

11. For example see, Katzenbach, J. R., & Smith, D. K. (1993, March/April). The discipline of teams. *Harvard Business Review, 86*(2), 111–120.

12. Peters, T. J., & Waterman, R. H., Jr. (1982). *In search of excellence: Lessons from America's best run companies.* New York, NY: Harper & Row.

13. Bormann, E. (1990). *Small group communication: Theory and practice.* New York, NY: Harper & Row.

14. Is your team too big? Too small? What's the right number? (2006, June 14). Retrieved from http://knowledge.wharton.upenn.edu/article.cfm?articleid=1501

15. Gribas, J. (1999). Organizational sports metaphors: Reconsidering gender bias in the team concept. *Communication Research Reports, 16,* 55–64.

16. Brounstein, M. (n.d.). *Differences between work groups and teams.* Retrieved from http://www.dummies.com/how-to/content/differences-between-work-groups-and-teams.html; see also Michelman, P. (2004). *How will you make your team a team?* Cambridge, MA: Harvard Management Press.

17. LaFasto, F., & Larson, C. (2001). *When teams work best: 6,000 team members and leaders tell what it takes to succeed.* Thousand Oaks, CA: Sage.

18 Hirokawa, R. Y., Cathcart, R. S., Samovar, L. A., & Henman, L. D. (Eds.). (2003). *Small group communication: Theory & practice.* Los Angeles, CA: Roxbury.

19. Fisher, K. (2000). *Leading self-directed work teams: A guide to developing new team leadership skills.* New York, NY: McGraw-Hill.

20. Melymuka, K. (1997, April 28). Tips for teams. *Computerworld, 31*(17), 70–72.

21. Alge, B. J., Wiethoff, C., & Klein, H. J. (2003). When does the medium matter? Knowledge-building experiences and opportunities in decision-making teams. *Organizational Behavior and Human Decision Processes, 91,* 26–37.

22. Montoya-Weiss, M. M., Massey, A. P., & Song, M. (2001). Getting it together: Temporal coordination and conflict management in global virtual teams. *Academy of Management Journal, 44,* 1251–1262.

23. Wigglesworth, D. C. (1997, July). Bookshelf. *HR Magazine, 42*(7), pp. 133–134.

24. Herndon, S. L. (1997). Theory and practice: Implications for the implementation of communication technology in organizations. *Journal of Business Communication, 34,* 121–129.

25. Mohta, P. (1996, Winter). Virtual networking via the internet. *Computer Technology Review, 16*(1), 12–13.

26. Max, S. (2011, October 11). Employees alone together. *Wall Street Journal Online.* Retrieved from http://online.wsj.com/article/SB10001424052970204524604576611262007838444.html

27. Rothwell, J. D. (2013). *In mixed company: Small group communication* (8th ed.). Boston, MA: Cengage.

28. Lewin, K., Lippitt, R., & White, R. K. (1939). Patterns of aggressive behavior in experimentally created social climates. *Journal of Social Psychology, 10,* 271–299.

29. Foels, R., Driskell, J. E., Mullen, B., & Salas, E. (2000). The effects of democratic leadership on group member satisfaction. *Small Group Research, 20,* 676–701.

30. Rosenbaum, L. L., & Rosenbaum, W. B. (1971). Morale and productivity consequences of group leadership style, stress, and type of task. *Journal of Applied Psychology, 55,* 343–358.

31. Blake, R. R., & Mouton, J. S. (1985). *The new managerial grid.* Houston, TX: Gulf.

32. Fiedler, F. E. (1967). *A theory of leadership effectiveness.* New York: McGraw-Hill.

33. Hersey, P., & Blanchard, K. (1982). *Management of organizational behavior* (4th ed.). Englewood Cliffs, NJ: Prentice-Hall; Blanchard, K. (1988, September). Selecting a leadership style that works. *Today's Office, 23,* p. 14.

34. Graen, G. B., & Scandura, T. A. (1987). Toward psychology of dyadic organizing. In B. M. Staw & L. L. Cummings (Eds.), *Research in organizational behavior* (Vol. 9, pp. 175–208). Greenwich, CT: JAI Press.

35. Becker, J. A. H., Halbesleben, J. R. B., & O'Hair, D. H. (2005). Defensive communication and burnout in the workplace: The mediating role of leader-member exchange. *Communication Research Reports, 22,* 143–150; Fairhurst, G. T. (1993). The leader-member exchange patterns of women leaders in industry: A discourse analysis. *Communication Monographs, 60,* 321–351 ; Lamude, K. C., Scudder, J., Simmons, D., & Torres, P. (2004). Organizational newcomers: Temporary and regular employees, same-sex and mixed-sex superior-subordinate dyads, supervisor influence techniques, subordinates communication satisfaction, and leader-member exchange. *Communication Research Reports, 21,* 60–67.

36. Mueller B, & Lee J. (2002). Leader-member exchange and organizational communication satisfaction in multiple contexts. *Journal of Business Communication, 39,* 220–244.

37. Madlock, P. E., Martin, M. M., Bogdan, L., & Ervin, M. (2007). The impact of communication traits on leader-member exchange. *Human Communication, 10,* 451–464.

38. Abu Bakar, H., Dilbeck, K. E., & McCroskey, J. C. (2010). Mediating role of supervisory communication practices on relations between leader-member exchange and perceived employee commitment to workgroup. *Communication Monographs, 77,* 637–656. See also Graen, G. B., & Uhl-Bien, M. (1991). The transformation of professionals into self-managing and partially self-designing contributors: Towards a theory of leadership making. *Journal of Management Systems, 3,* 33–48.

39. Bormann, E. (1990). *Small group communication: Theory and practice.* New York, NY: Harper & Row. For a succinct description of Bormann's findings, see Rothwell, J. D. (2013). *In mixed company: Small group communication* (8th ed.). Boston, MA: Cengage.

40. Fisher, R., & Sharp, A. (1998). *Getting it done: How to lead when you're not in charge.* New York, NY: Harper Business.

41. Wellins, R. S., Byham, W. C., & Wilson, J. M. (1991). *Empowered teams: Creating self-directed work groups that improve quality, productivity, and participation.* San Francisco, CA: Jossey-Bass.

42. Chansler, P. A., Swamidass, P. M., & Canmann, C. (2003). Self-managing teams: An empirical study of group cohesiveness in 'natural work groups' at a Harley-Davidson motor company plant. *Small Group Research, 34,* 101–120.

43. The discussion of the first five types of power is adapted from the work of French, J. R. P., & Raven, B. (1959). The bases of social power. In D. Cartwright (Ed.), *Studies in social power* (pp. 150–167). Ann Arbor: University of Michigan Institute for Social Research. Information power was introduced by Raven, B., & Kruglanski, W. (1975). Conflict and power. In P. G. Swingle (Ed.), *The structure of conflict* (pp. 177–219). New York, NY: Academic Press. Connection power was introduced by Hersey, P., & Blanchard, K. (1982). *Management of organizational behavior* (4th ed.). Englewood Cliffs, NJ: Prentice-Hall.

44. Pescosolido, A. T. (2001). Informal leaders and the development of group efficacy. *Small Group Research, 32,* 74–93.

45. Loh, S. T. (1993, March 1). You say the boss is how old? *Los Angeles Times,* pp. 9–10.

46. For a discussion of relational roles, see Keyton, J. (1999). Relational communication in groups. In L. R. Frey (Ed.), *Handbook of group communication theory and research* (pp. 192–222). Thousand Oaks, CA: Sage.

47. Matson, E. (1996, April). The seven sins of deadly meetings. *Fast Times, 2,* pp. 122–125.

48. See, for example, Mayer, M. E. (1998). Behaviors leading to more effective decisions in small groups embedded in organizations. *Communication Reports, 11,* 123–132.

49. Heckman, F. (2001, May). A purpose and a place: Harmonizing elements to create an organization with rhythm. *News for a Change, 5*(5), 1–3.

50. Heckman, F. (2001, May). A purpose and a place: Harmonizing elements to create an organization with rhythm. *News for a Change, 5*(5), 1–3.

51. For a discussion of how norms develop, see Anderson, C. M., Riddle, B. L., & Martin, M. M. (1999). Socialization processes in groups. In L. R. Frey (Ed.), *Handbook of group communication theory and research* (pp. 139–163). Thousand Oaks, CA: Sage.

52. Eisenberg, E. M., Goodall, H. L., & Trethwey, A. (2010). *Organizational communication: Balancing creativity and constraint* (6th ed.). New York, NY: Bedford/St. Martin's.

53. Browning, L. (1992, May). *Reasons for success at Motorola.* Paper presented at the International Communication Association annual meeting, Miami, FL.

54. For example see, Mulvey, P. W., Bowes-Sperry, L., & Klein, H. J. (1998). The effects of perceived loafing and defensive impression management on group effectiveness. *Small Group Research, 29,* 394–415.

55. Oetzel, J. G., Burtis, T. E., Chew Sanchez, M. I., & Perez, F. G. (2001). Investigating the role of communication in culturally diverse work groups: A review and synthesis. In W. B. Gudykunst (Ed.), *Communication yearbook 25* (pp. 237–269). New York, NY: Routledge.

56. Some sequences of escalating penalties for nonconformity have been described in the literature. For example, see Wenberg, J. R., & Wilmot, W. (1973). *The personal communication process*. New York, NY: Wiley; Daniels, T. D., & Spiker, B. K. (1997). *Perspectives on organizational communication* (4th ed.). Dubuque, IA: Wm. C. Brown.

57. Melymuka, K. (1997). Tips for teams. *Computerworld, 31*(17), 70–72.

58. Janis, I. L. (1972). *Victims of groupthink*. Boston, MA: Houghton Mifflin.

59. Gammage, K. L., Carron, A. V., & Estabrooks, P. A. (2001). Team cohesion and individual productivity. *Small Group Research, 32*, 3–18.

60. Adapted from Bormann, E. G. (1975). *Discussion and group methods* (2nd ed.). New York, NY: Harper & Row. See also Adler, P., & Adler, P. (1988). Intense loyalty in organizations: A case study of college athletics. *Administrative Science Quarterly, 33*, 401–418.

61. Janis, I. L. (1972). *Victims of groupthink*. Boston, MA: Houghton Mifflin. See also Ross, J. A. (2008). *Team camaraderie: Can you have too much?* Retrieved from http://blogs.hbr.org/hmu/2008/02/team-camaraderie-can-you-have-1.html

62. Goby, V. (2007). Business communication needs. *Journal of Business and Technical Communication, 21*, 425–437. See also Sharon, A. (2008, February 5). The death of groupthink. *Business Week*. Retrieved from http://www.businessweek.com/print/managing/content/feb2008/ca2008025_687188.htm

63. Myers, D. G., & Lamm, H. (1976). The group polarization phenomenon. *Psychological Bulletin, 83*, 602–627. For a more detailed discussion of how the risky shift operates, see BarNir, A. (1998). Can group- and issue-related factors predict choice shift? *Small Group Research, 29*, 308–338.

64. Robbins, S. P. (1990). *Organizational behavior: Concepts, controversies, and applications* (4th ed.). Englewood Cliffs, NJ: Prentice-Hall.

Chapter 8

1. NFO Worldwide. (1998). *Meetings in America: A study of trends, costs, and attitudes toward business travel and teleconferencing, and their impact on productivity*. Greenwich, CT: Infocom.

2. Tuck, L. (1995, May). Meeting madness. *Presentations, 9*(5), 20–25.

3. Microsoft. (2005, March 12). *Survey finds workers average only three productive days per week*. Retrieved from http://www.microsoft.com/presspass/press/2005/mar05/03-15threeproductivedayspr.mspx

4. Rogelberg, S. G., Leach, D. J., Warr, P. B., & Burnfield, J. L. (2006). 'Not another meeting!' Are meeting time demands related to employee well-being? *Journal of Applied Psychology, 91*, 83–96.

5. Rogelberg, S. G., Scott, C., & Kello, J. (2007, Winter). The science and fiction of meetings. *MIT Sloan Management Review, 48*, 18–21.

6. Rogelberg, S. G., Leach, D. J., Warr, P. B., & Burnfield, J. L. (2006). 'Not another meeting!' Are meeting time demands related to employee well-being? *Journal of Applied Psychology, 91*, 83–96.

7. Microsoft. (2005, March 12). *Survey finds workers average only three productive days per week*. Retrieved from http://www.microsoft.com/presspass/press/2005/mar05/03-15threeproductivedayspr.mspx

8. Smith, S. M. (1991). Managing your meeting for a "bottom line payoff." In R. A. Swanson & B. O. Knapp (Eds.), *Innovative Meeting Management*. Austin, TX: Minnesota Mining and Manufacturing.

9. Matson, E. (1996, April). The seven sins of deadly meetings. *Fast Company, 2*, pp. 122–125.

10. Williams, F. (1983). *Executive communication power: Basic skills for management success*. Englewood Cliffs, NJ: Prentice-Hall.

11. Hill, J. (2002, November). Random access. *Presentations, 16*(11), 13–18.

12. Adapted from Collins, S. D. (2003). *Communication in a virtual organization*. Cincinnati, OH: Thomson.; International Listening Leaders Institute. (2004, December 8). *Listening leader tip of the week: Ten listening leader strategies to enhance conference calls* [electronic newsletter]. Retrieved from http://ezines.webvalence.com/sites/ListeningLeader/Broadcast.D20041208.html

13. Tuck, L. (1996, September). Brave new meetings. *Presentations, 10*(9), 28–36.

14. Stone, F. (1997, February). We've got to stop meeting like this. *Getting results… For the hands-on manager, 42*(5), p. 5.

15. Luong, A., & Rogelberg, S. G. (2005). Meetings and more meetings: The relationship between meeting load and the daily well-being of employees. *Group Dynamics, 9*, 58–67.

16. 3M. (199-). *Six secrets to improve your future business meetings*. Austin, TX: 3M Visual Systems; Farivar, C. (2007, April 9). *How to run an effective meeting*. Retrieved from http://www.cbsnews.com/8301-505125_162-51061211/how-to-run-an-effective-meeting/; DeWine, S. (1994). *The consultant's craft: Improving organizational communication*. New York, NY: St. Martin's; Lippincott, S. M. (1999). *Meetings: Do's, don'ts, and donuts* (2nd ed.). Pittsburgh, PA: Lighthouse Point Press.

17. For example see, Cook, J. M. (1997, August). 7 tips for planning an effective meeting. *Presentations, 11*(8), 26.

18. Allard, C. (1992, August). Trust and teamwork: More than just buzzwords. *En Route Technology*, p. 41.

19. 3M Meeting Network. (2003). *Building great agendas.* Retrieved from http://www.3m.com/meeting network/readingroom/meetingguide_building.html

20. 3M Meeting Network. (2003). *Building great agendas.* Retrieved from http://www.3m.com/meeting network/readingroom/meetingguide_building.html

21. Olofson, C. (1998, September). The Ritz puts on stand-up meetings. *Fast Company, 17,* p. 62.

22. Steele, C. O. (1994, March). Make your meetings more productive. *Black Enterprise, 24*(8), 76.

23. De Wine, S. (1994). *The consultant's craft: Improving organizational communication.* New York, NY: St. Martin's.

24. Xerox Learning Systems. (n.d.). *Leading meetings.* Great Neck, NY: Xerox Learning Systems.

25. For a summary of the rules of parliamentary procedure, see Introduction to Robert's Rules of Order. Retrieved from http://www.robertsrules.org/rulesintro.htm

26. Tannen, D. (1994). *Talking from 9 to 5: How women's and men's conversational styles affect who gets heard, who gets credit, and what gets done at work.* New York, NY: Morrow. For an overview of the subject, see Bonito, J. A., & Hollingshead, A. B. (1997). Participation in small groups. In B. R. Burleson (Ed.), *Communication yearbook 20* (pp. 227–261). Newbury Park, CA: Sage.

27. Faure, C. (2004). Beyond brainstorming: Effects of different group procedures on selection of ideas and satisfaction with the process. *Journal of Creative Behavior, 8*(1), 13–34.

28. Xerox Learning Systems. (n.d.). *Leading meetings.* Great Neck, NY: Xerox Learning Systems.

29. 3M Management Institute. (1992, June). Meeting quality: A chicken-egg question? *Meeting Management News, 4,* pp. 2–3.

30. Allard, C. (1992, August). Trust and teamwork: More than just buzzwords. *En Route Technology,* p. 41.

31. Xerox Learning Systems. (n.d.). *Leading meetings.* Great Neck, NY: Xerox Learning Systems.

32. Fisher, B. A. (1970). Decision emergence: Phases in group decision making. *Speech Monographs, 37,* 53–66. See also Poole, M. S., & Roth, J. (1989). Decision development in small groups, IV: A typology of group decision paths. *Human Communication Research, 15,* 232–256.

33. Tuckman, B. W. (1965). Developmental sequence in small groups. *Psychological Bulletin, 63,* 384–399. The terms *forming, storming, norming,* and *performing* originate from this article.

34. Kuhn, T. (2000). Do conflict management styles affect group decision making? *Human Communication Research, 26,* 558–590. See also Nemeth, C. J., & Nemeth-Brown, B. (2003). Better than individuals? The potential benefits of dissent and diversity for group creativity. In P. Paulus & B. Nijstad (Eds.), *Group creativity.* Oxford, UK: Oxford University Press; Nemeth, C. J., & Ormiston, M. (2007). Creative idea generation: Harmony versus stimulation. *European Journal of Experimental Social Psychology, 37,* 524–535.

35. Buzaglo, G., & Wheelan, S. A. (1999). Facilitating work team effectiveness. *Small Group Research, 30,* 108–129.

36. Poole, M. S., & Roth, J. (1989). Decision development in small groups, V: Test of a contingency model. *Human Communication Research, 15,* 549–589.

37. For example see, Catmull, E. (2008, September). How Pixar fosters collective creativity. *Harvard Business Review, 86*(9), 64–78.

38. Rae-Dupree, J. (2008, December 7). For innovators, there is brainpower in numbers. *New York Times,* p. BU 3.

39. Osborn, A. (1959). *Applied imagination.* New York, NY: Scribner's. See also Hurt, F. (1994, November). Better brainstorming. *Training & Development, 48*(11), 57–59.

40. *New World Encyclopedia.* Retrieved from http://www.newworldencyclopedia.org/entry/Linus_Pauling

41. Thompson, K. (2008). *Six ways to kill a brainstorm.* Retrieved from http://www.masternewmedia.org/news/2008/04/23/how_not_to_brainstorm_your.htm

42. DeRosa, D. M., Smith, C. L., & Hantula, D. A. (2007). The medium matters: Mining the long-promised merit of group interaction in creative idea generation tasks in a meta-analysis of the electronic group brainstorming literature. *Computers in Human Behavior, 23,* 1549–1581.

43. Rietzschel, E. F., Nijstad, B. A., & Stroebe, W. (2006). Productivity is not enough: A comparison of interactive and nominal groups in idea generation and selection. *Journal of Experimental Social Psychology, 42,* 244–251.

44. Zey, M. (Ed.). (1992). *Decision making: Alternatives to rational choice models.* Newbury Park, CA: Sage.

45. See Hirokawa, R. Y. (1983). Group communication and problem-solving effectiveness: An investigation of group phases. *Human Communication Research, 9,* 291–305; Marby, E. R., & Barnes, R. E. (1980). *The dynamics of small group communication.* Englewood Cliffs, NJ: Prentice-Hall; Maier, N. R. F., & Maier, R. A. (1957). An experimental test of the effects of 'developmental' vs. 'free' discussions on the quality of group decisions. *Journal of Applied Psychology, 41,* 320–323; Bayless, O. L. (1967). An alternative model for problem-solving discussion. *Journal of Communication, 17,* 188–197.

46. For a more current version of the reflective-thinking model, see Gouran, D., Hirokawa, R., Julian, K., & Leatham, G. (1993). The evolution and current status of the functional perspective on communication decision-making and problem-solving groups. In S. A. Deetz (Ed.), *Communication yearbook 16* (pp. 573–600). Newbury Park, CA: Sage.

47. Mayer, M. E. (1998). Behaviors leading to more effective decisions in small groups embedded in organizations. *Communication Reports, 11,* 123–132.

48. Baum, J. A. C. (2003). *Running an effective team meeting.* Retrieved from http://www.rotman.utoronto.ca/~baum/mgt2003/meetings.html

49. Day, B. (1990, October 6). The art of conducting international business. *Advertising Age, 61*(42), p. 46.

50. Crucial Skills. (2008, May 14). Crucial tip: Using consult decisions. *Crucial Skills Newsletter, 6*(20), p. 1

Chapter 9

1. Meilach, D. Z. (1994). Even the odds with visual presentations. *Presentations, 8*(11), SS1–SS6.

2. Tuck, L. (1992). Profiling the presentation professional. *Presentation Products, 6*(11), 35–42.

3. Lannon, J. M. (2003). *Technical communication* (9th ed). New York, NY: Longman.

4. Wright, J. P. (1979). *On a clear day you can see General Motors.* New York, NY: Avon.

5. Boettinger, H. M. (1969). *Moving mountains, or the art of letting others see things your way.* New York, NY: Collier.

6. Conference Board. (1987). *Across the Board, 24*(8), 7.

7. Toastmasters International. (2012). *Toastmasters International—About us.* Retrieved from http://www.toastmasters.org/Members/MembersFunctionalCategories/AboutTI.aspx

8. For example, see Carrell, L. (2009). Communication training for clergy: Exploring impact on the transformative quality of sermon communication. *Communication Education, 58*, 15–34; Siebold, D. R., Kudsi, S., & Rude, M. (1993). Does communication training make a difference? Evidence for the effectiveness of a presentation skills program. *Journal of Applied Communication Research, 21*, 111–129.

9. Zelazny, G. (2006). *Say it with presentations.* New York, NY: McGraw-Hill.

10. Iacocca, L., & Novak, W. (1984). *Iacocca: An autobiography.* New York, NY: Bantam.

11. Molloy, J. T. (1985). *Molloy's live for success.* New York, NY: Bantam.

12. Vasilion, S. (1997, September 24). Personal communication.

13. Naguib, R. (2009). *International Audiences.* Retrieved from http://www.toastmasters.org/MainMenuCategories/FreeResources/NeedHelpGivingaSpeech/BusinessPresentations/SpeakingGlobally_1/InternationalAudiences.aspx

14. Williams, C. J. (2008, September 29). Jury duty? You may want to edit your online profile. *Los Angeles Times,* p. A6.

15. *Thud and blunder in the news rooms.* (1995, March 5). *The Independent.* Retrieved from http://www.independent.co.uk/opinion/thud-and-blunder-in-the-news-rooms-1610069.html

16. Bradley, B. E. (1991). *Fundamentals of speech communication: The credibility of ideas* (6th ed.). Dubuque, IA: Wm. C. Brown.

17. Meilach, D. Z. (1994). Even the odds with visual presentations. *Presentations, 8*(11), SS1–SS6.

18. The gray flannel sideshow. (1993). *Presentations, 7*(11), 50.

19. Marsh, H. L. (1983, May). *Summary membership remarks.* Presentation at New York Chapter of the Institute of Internal Auditors meeting. New York, NY.

20. Linver, S. & Mengert, J. (1994). *Speak and get results: The complete guide to speeches and presentations that work in any business situation* (Rev. ed.). New York, NY: Fireside.

21. Windsor, J. (2010, July 31). Smart presentations: Will you pass the two-word test for ultimate presentations? *Sales and Marketing Management.* Retrieved from http://www.salesandmarketing.com/article/smart-presentations-will-you-pass-two-word-test-ultimate-presentations

22. For a discussion of research supporting the value of organization, see Lucas, S. E. (2009). *The art of public speaking* (10th ed.). New York, NY: McGraw-Hill. Also see Faylor, N. R., Beebe, S. A., Houser, M. L., & Mottet, T. P. (2008). Perceived differences in instructional communication behaviors between effective and ineffective corporate trainers. *Human Communication, 11*, 145–156.

23. Adapted from Bovée, C. L., & Thill, J. T. (1989). *Business communication today* (2nd ed.). New York, NY: Random House. Student examples of moving from what audiences know to what they don't know are found in DeVito, J. A. (2000). *The elements of public speaking* (7th ed.). New York, NY: Longman.

24. The White House. (2005). *President discusses strengthening social security in Florida.* Retrieved from http://www.whitehouse.gov/news/releases/2005/02/20050204-13.html

25. For a discussion of nonlinear organizing patterns, see Jaffe, C. (2001). *Public speaking: Concepts and skills for a diverse society* (3rd ed.). Belmont, CA: Wadsworth; Lustig M. W., & Koester J. (2003). *Intercultural competence: Interpersonal communication across culture* (4th ed.). New York, NY: Allyn & Bacon.

26. Presentation planning: Draw a logic tree. (1993). *Meeting Management News, 1*, 1–2.

27. Hybels, S., & Weaver, R. L., Jr. (2001). *Communicating effectively* (6th ed.). Boston, MA: McGraw-Hill; Osborn, M., & Osborn, S. (2000). *Public speaking* (5th ed.). Boston, MA: Houghton Mifflin.

28. The uppermost limit of items people can usually recall from their short-term memory is seven. For oral presentations, however, limiting the number of main points to five increases the odds that listeners will retain them. See Katt, J., Murdock, J., Butler, J., & Pryor, B. (2008). Establishing best practices for the use of PowerPoint™ as a presentation aid. *Human Communication, 11*, 193–200.

29. Zielinski, D. (2003, June 4). Perfect practice. *Presentations.* Retrieved from http://www.cttnewsletter.com/article/perfect-practice-0

30. Moran, R. T. (1989). Tips on making speeches to international audiences. *International Management, 44*, 74.

31. Schulz, K. (2011, March). *On being wrong.* Speech delivered at TED annual conference, Long Beach, CA. Retrieved from http://www.ted.com/talks/kathryn_schulz_on_being_wrong.html

32. Meyer, P. (2011, July). *How to spot a liar.* Speech delivered at TED global conference, Eidenburg, Scotland. Retrieved from http://www.ted.com/talks/pamela_meyer_how_to_spot_a_liar.html

33. Robinson, J. W. (1987). *Winning them over.* Rocklin, CA: Prima.

34. U.S. Department of Justice. (2009). Remarks as prepared for delivery by U.S. Attorney General Eric Holder at the Department of Justice African American history month program. Retrieved from http://www.usdoj.gov/ag/speeches/2009/ag-speech-090218.html

35. U.S. Department of Justice. (2009). Remarks as prepared for delivery by U.S. Attorney General Eric Holder at the Department of Justice African American history month program. Retrieved from http://www.usdoj.gov/ag/speeches/2009/ag-speech-090218.html

36. Unknown. (1993). *Executive Speechwriter Newsletter, 8,* 3.

37. Carter, J. (2003). *Camp David 25th anniversary forum special conference series.* Woodrow Wilson International Center for Scholars: Washington, D.C.

38. Advanced Public Speaking Institute. (2003). *How to close a speech.* Retrieved from http://www.public-speaking.org/public-speaking-closings-article.htm

Chapter 10

1. Poole, L. (1984, February). A tour of the Mac desktop. *Mac World, 1*(2), 16–27.

2. Spangenberg, C. (1977). Basic values and the techniques of persuasion. *Litigation, 3*(3), 13–18.

3. Anderson, H. (1989, May 21). Day care: Big hit at the office. *Los Angeles Times,* pp. 30–33.

4. Slow Down Fast. (2007). *Company perks: Do they assist with life balance?* Retrieved from http://www.slowdownfast.com/company-perks-do-they-assist-with-life-balance/

5. Applegate, J. (1994, April 12). Best, worst small-business names of 1994. *Los Angeles Times,* p. D3.

6. Applegate, J. (1994, April 12). Best, worst small-business names of 1994. *Los Angeles Times,* p. D3.

7. Poundsford, M. (2007). Using storytelling, conversation and coaching to engage. *Strategic Communication Management, 11,* 32–35.

8. Gallo, C. (2008, September 12). *Use storytelling to strengthen your presentations.* Retrieved from http://www.businessweek.com/smallbiz/content/sep2008/sb20080912_141650.htm

9. Gallo, C. (2008, September 12). Use storytelling to strengthen your presentations. Retrieved from http://www.businessweek.com/smallbiz/content/sep2008/sb20080912_141650.htm

10. Small, D. A., Loewenstein, G., & Slovic, P. (2007). Sympathy and callousness: The impact of deliberative thought on donations to identifiable and statistical victims. *Organizational Behavior and Human Decision Processes, 102,* 143–153.

11. Adapted from Daly, J. A., & Englebert, I. N. (2001). *Presentations in everyday life.* Boston, MA: Houghton Mifflin.

12. Rooney, A. (1989). Sales vs. service. *Executive Speechwriter Newsletter, 14,* 5.

13. Slan, J. (1998). *Using stories and humor: Grab your audience!* Boston, MA: Allyn & Bacon.

14. Lukaszewski, J. E. (1997).You can become a verbal visionary. *Executive Speeches, 12*(1), 23–30.

15. Lindsey, L. L., & Yun, K. A. (2003). Examining the persuasive effect of statistical messages: A test of mediating relationships. *Communication Studies, 54,* 306–321.

16. Jolie, A. (2012). Remember the refugees…who are dying at this very moment. *Vital Speeches International, 4*(2), 38–39.

17. Small Business Report. (1987, March). Making time and money real. *Executive Communication Report 3.*

18. Diamond, S. J. (1991, June 13). Some airlines' ads mislead without lying. *Los Angeles Times,* p. E1.

19. Romans, C. (2009, February 4). *Numb and number: Is trillion the new billion?* Retrieved from http://www.cnn.com/2009/LIVING/02/04/trillion.dollars/index.html?eref=rss_topstories

20. Miners deserve better. (2006, January 5). *Los Angeles Times,* p. B12.

21. Anderson, K. (December 29, 2011). *Craft an attention-grabbing message.* Retrieved from http://blogs.hbr.org/cs/2011/12/craft_an_attention-grabbing_me.html

22. The quotes in this section were accessed from Woopidoo Quotations. (n.d.). *Business quotes by business leaders.* Retrieved from http://www.woopidoo.com/business_quotes

23. Paper work is avoidable (if you call the shots). (1977, June 17). *Wall Street Journal,* p. 24.

24. Vogel, D. R., Dickson, G. W., & Lehman, J. A. (1986). Driving the audience action response. *Computer Graphics World, 5*(6), 25–28. See also Vogel, D. R., Dickson, G. W., & Lehman, J. A. (1986). *Persuasion and the role of visual presentation support: The UM/3M Study.* Austin, TX: 3M Corporation.

25. Molina, D. (2011, October 2). Conquering my fear of speaking in public. *New York Times,* p. B8.

26. For more suggestions on how to use handouts, see Pike, R. W. (1994). Handouts: A little charity to your audience goes a long way. *Presentations, 8*(5), 31–35.

27. For a discussion of PowerPoint's limitations, see Ganzel, R. (2000). Power pointless. *Presentations, 14*(2), 54–57.

28. Tufte, E. R. (2003). *The cognitive style of PowerPoint.* Cheshire, CT: Graphics Press.

29. Parker, I. (2001, May 28). Absolute PowerPoint. *New Yorker,* pp. 76-87. See also Simons, T. (2004). Does PowerPoint make you stupid? *Presentations, 18*(3), 25–31.

30. Jaffe, G. (2000, April 26). What's your point, lieutenant? Just cut to the pie charts. *Wall Street Journal,* p. A1.

31. For more information on using visual aids effectively, see Kosslyn, S. M., & Chabris, C. (1993). The mind is not a camera, the brain is not a VCR: Some psychological guidelines for designing charts and graphs. *Aldus Magazine, 4*(6), 33–36.

32. Medaris, K. (2008, October 6). *Purdue expert gives do's and don'ts of visual presentations.* Retrieved from http://news.uns.purdue.edu/x/2008b/081006T-SmithPower.html

33. Tuck, L. (1994). Improving your image with LCD panels. *Presentations, 8*(1), 32.

34. Pearson, L. (1993). The medium speaks. *Presentation Products, 7*(6), 55–56.

35. For example, see Tuck, L. (1994). Using type intelligently. *Presentations, 8*(4), 30–32; Hinkin, S. (1995). Not just another pretty face: 10 tips for the most effective use of type. *Presentations, 9*(1), 34–36.

36. Terberg, J. (2005). Font choices play a crucial role in presentation design. *Presentations,19*(4). Retrieved from www.presentations.com/presentations/creation/article_display.jsp?vnu_content_id=1000875169

Chapter 11

1. Ailes, R., & Kraushar, J. (1988). *You are the message.* New York, NY: Doubleday.

2. Locker, K. O. (2000). *Business and administrative communication* (5th ed.). Boston, MA: McGraw-Hill/Irwin.

3. Landis, M. (1980, Spring). Taking the butterflies out of speechmaking. *Creative Living, 9,* 19.

4. Zielinski, D. (2003, June 4). Perfect practice. *Presentations.* Retrieved from http://www.cttnewsletter.com/article/perfect-practice-0

5. Adapted from Fletcher, L. (1990). *How to design and deliver a speech* (4th ed.). New York, NY: Harper & Row.

6. Grossman, J. (1983, March). Resurrecting auto graveyards. *Inc., 5*(3), 73–80.

7. Haynes, W. L. (1990). Public speaking pedagogy in the media age. *Communication Education, 38,* 89–102.

8. Ailes, R., & Kraushar, J. (1988). *You are the message.* New York, NY: Doubleday.

9. Stella, P. J. (1994, November). Are there any questions? *Presentations, 8*(11), 12–13.

10. Cleveland, K. E. (2003). *Agree for maximum impact.* Retrieved from http://www.pertinent.com/articles/persuasion/kenrickP2.asp

11. Wallace I., & Wallechinsky, D. (1977). *Book of lists.* New York, NY: Bantam.

12. The speaker may look calm but survey confirms jitters. (1981, September 13). *Los Angeles Times,* p. 13.

13. Stein, M. B., Walker J. R., Jr., & Forde, D. R. (1996). Public-speaking fears in a community sample: Prevalence, impact on functioning, and diagnostic classification. *Archives of General Psychiatry, 53,* 169–174. See also Addressing fears. (1996, June). *Psychology Today, 29*(3), 11.

14. Watson, A. K. (1995). Taking the sweat out of communication anxiety. *Personnel Journal, 74,* 111–117.

15. For example, see Behnke, R. R., Sawyer, C. R., & King, P. E. (1987). The communication of public speaking anxiety. *Communication Education, 36,* 138–141; Burgoon, J., Pfau, M., Birk, T., & Manusov, V. (1987). Nonverbal communication performance and perceptions associated with reticence. *Communication Education, 36,* 119–130; McEwan, K. L., & Devins, G. (1983). Increased arousal in emotional anxiety noticed by others. *Journal of Abnormal Psychology, 92,* 417–421.

16. Humes, J. C. (1980). *Talk your way to the top.* New York, NY: McGraw-Hill.

17. Sawyer, C. R., & Behnke, R. R. (1999). State anxiety patterns for public speaking and the behavior inhibition system. *Communication Reports, 12,* 33–41.

18. Finn, A. N., Sawyer, C. R., & Schrodt, P. (2009). Examining the effect of exposure therapy on public speaking state anxiety. *Communication Education, 58,* 92–109.

19. Pogue, D. (1995, January). Panic on the podium. *Mac World, 12,* pp. 97–98.

20. Smith, T. E., & Bainbridge, A. (2006). Get real: Does practicing speeches before an audience improve performance? *Communication Quarterly, 54,* 111–125.

21. Zielinski, D. (2003, June 4). Perfect practice. *Presentations.* Retrieved from http://www.cttnewsletter.com/article/perfect-practice-0

22. Daly, J. A., Vangelisti, A. L., & Weber, D. J. (1995). Speech anxiety affects how people prepare speeches: A protocol analysis of the preparation processes of speakers. *Communication Monographs, 62,* 383–397.

23. For example see, Ellis, A. (1977). *A new guide to rational living.* North Hollywood, CA: Wilshire Books; Beck, A. (1976). *Cognitive therapy and the emotional disorders.* New York, NY: International Universities Press.

24. Baskerville, D. (1994, May). Public speaking rule #1: Have no fear. *Black Enterprise, 24*(10), 76–81.

25. Ayres, J., Hopf, T., & Peterson, E. (2000). A test of communication orientation motivation (COM) therapy. *Communication Reports, 13,* 35–44.

Chapter 12

1. Meister, J. C. (1998). *Corporate universities* (Rev. ed.). New York, NY: McGraw-Hill.

2. American Society for Training & Development. (2011). *The 2011 state of the industry: Increased commitment to workplace learning.* Retrieved from http://www.astd.org/TD/Archives/2011/Nov/Free/Nov_11_Feature_State_of_the_Industry.htm

3. Bingham, T., & Galagan, P. (2011). *Committed to innovation.* Retrieved from http://www.astd.org/TD/Archives/2011/Jul/Free/

4. Lowenstein, M., & Spletzer, J. (1994). *Informal training: A review of existing data and some new evidence,* Report NLS 94–20. Retrieved from http://www.bls.gov/ore/pdf/nL940050.pdf

5. Molenda, M., Pershing, J. A., & Reigluth, C. M. (1996). Designing instructional systems. In R. L. Craig (Ed.), *The ASTD training and development handbook* (pp. 266–293). New York, NY: McGraw-Hill.

6. Blanchard, K. (1987). Managers must learn to teach. *Today's Office, 22,* 8–9.

7. How Lever's 'hands-on' demos ignited rep enthusiasm. (1993). *Business Marketing Digest, 18*(3), 29–32.

8. Bocher, D. (2003). *Speak with confidence: Powerful presentations that inform, inspire and persuade.* New York, NY: McGraw-Hill.

9. Research summarized in Leahey, T. H., & Harris, R. J. (1989). *Human learning* (2nd ed.) Englewood Cliffs, NJ: Prentice-Hall.

10. Lukaszewski, J. E. (1997). You can become a verbal visionary. *Executive Speeches, 12*(1)*,* 23–30.

11. Singer, B. (2001). *$ales dogs.* New York, NY: Warner Books.

12. Fisher, A. (1996, November 11). Willy Loman couldn't cut it. *Fortune, 134,* p. 210.

13. Alonzo, V. (2000, October). 5 steps to bigger sales. *Incentive, 174*(10), 117–119.

14. Toastmasters. (1992). *Specialty speeches.* Mission Viejo, CA: Toastmasters International.

15. Quoted in Rackham, N. *(1988). Spin selling.* New York, NY: McGraw-Hill.

16. Adapted from Adler, R. B., & Rodman, G. (2003). *Understanding human communication* (8th ed.). New York, NY: Oxford University Press.

17. Burgoon. M., & Miller, M. D. (1990). Communication and influence. In G. L. Dahnke & G. W. Clatterbuck (Eds.), *Human communication: Theory and research* (pp. 229–258). Belmont, CA: Wadsworth.

18. Petty, R. E., & Cacioppo, J. T. (1990). Involvement and persuasion: Tradition versus integration. *Psychological Bulletin, 107,* 367–374.

19. For a detailed review of credibility, see Gass, R. H., & Seiter, J. S. (1999). *Persuasion, social influence and compliance-gaining.* Boston, MA: Allyn & Bacon; Lucas, S. E. (2009). *The art of public speaking* (10th ed.). New York, NY: McGraw-Hill.

20. This discussion of fallacies is adapted from Adler, R. B., & Rodman, G. (2009). *Understanding human communication* (10th ed.). New York, NY: Oxford University Press.

21. Sprague, J., Stuart, D., & Bodary, D. (2012). *The speaker's handbook* (10th ed.). Boston, MA: Cengage.

22. At Lanier a better mousetrap isn't quite enough. (1979, February 26). *Fortune, 105,* pp. 74–76.

23. O'Keefe, D. J. (1990). *Persuasion: Theory and research.* Newbury Park, CA: Sage. See also Griffin, E. M. (2009). *A first look at communication theory* (7th ed.). New York, NY: McGraw-Hill.

24. Griffin, E. M. (2009). *A first look at communication theory* (7th ed.). New York, NY: McGraw-Hill.

25. Burgoon, M., & Burgoon, J. K. (1975). Message strategies in influence attempts. In G. J. Hanneman & W. J. McEwen (Eds.),*Communication and behavior* (pp. 149–165). Reading, MA: Addison-Wesley.

26. Allen, M. (1993). Determining the persuasiveness of message sidedness: A prudent note about utilizing research summaries. *Western Journal of Communication, 57,* 98–103. See also Allen, M., & Hale, J. (1990). Testing a model of message sidedness: Three replications. *Communication Monographs, 57,* 275–291.

27. For more information on cultural differences in styles of persuasion, see Lustig, M. L., & Koester, J. (2006). *Intercultural competence: Interpersonal communication across cultures* (5th ed.). Boston, MA: Pearson Education; Lieberman, D. A. (1994). *Public speaking in the multicultural environment.* Englewood Cliffs, NJ: Prentice-Hall.

28. Adapted from Daly, J. A., & Eisenberg, I. N. (2001). *Presentations in everyday life.* Boston, MA: Houghton Mifflin.

29. Osgood, C. (1988). *Osgood on speaking: How to think on your feet without falling on your face.* New York, NY: Morrow.

30. Adapted from Gard, G. C. (1988, November). Accepting an award: How to be gracious and effective in 30 seconds. *Toastmaster,* p. 20.

Appendix III

1. The economy of plain English. (1995, January). *American Salesman, 40*(1), 15; Five phrases to eliminate from your business writing. (2000, September). *Manager's Intelligence Report,* p. 1.

2. Bugeja, M. (2000, October). Say what you mean. *Successful Meetings, 49*(11), 135.

3. Trim the fat from your business writing with these ideas. (2000, January). *Manager's Intelligence Report,* p. 4.

4. Lewis, B. (1999, November 22). Make sure you actually communicate rather than simply offer information. *InfoWorld,* p. 80.

5. Baldrige, L., & O'Brien, G. (2000). Netiquette. *Kinko's Impress,* pp. 20–21.

6. Lucrezio, P. (2000, February 2). Companies must develop, enforce email usage policies. *Capital District Business Review,* p. 37.

7. Humphries, A. (2000, September 29). *Email for careerists: Care enough to send the very best.* Retrieved from http://archives.cnn.com/2000/CAREER/corporateclass/09/29/email.protocol/index.html

8. Hsu, T. (2009, March 29). Crafting a resume that will grab recruiters. *Los Angeles Times.* Retrieved from http://www.latimes.com/business/la-fi--cover29-2009mar29,0,4601180.story?page=3

9. Bass, C. D. (2000, June 18). Unusual résumé may net that job. *Albuquerque Journal,* p. I-1.

10. Zax, D. (2012, March 6). Fast talk: How Intern Sushi wants to skewer the resume. *Fast Company.* Retrieved from http://www.fastcompany.com/1822643/fast-talk-how-intern-sushi-wants-to-skewer-the-resume

11. Bureau of Economic Research and Analysis. (2000). *The job hunters guide.* Albuquerque, NM: New Mexico Department of Labor.

12. Enelow, W. S. (n.d.). *What do employers really want in a résumé?* Retrieved from http://www.jobweb.com/catapult/enelow-r.html

13. Hansen, K. (n.d.). Common sense steps can prevent employer backlash against online resumes. *Quintessential Careers.* Retrieved from http://www.quintcareers.com/online_resume_guide.html

14. Smith, R. (2001). *eResumes 101: Choosing your best electronic resume format.* Retrieved from http://www.eresumes.com/tut_eresume.html

15. Gerson, S. J., & Gerson, S. M. (2000). *Technical writing: Process and product* (3rd ed.) Upper Saddle River, NJ: Prentice-Hall.

16. Tullier, M. (2002). *The art and science of writing cover letters: The best way to make a first impression.* Retrieved from http://resume.monster.com/coverletter/coverletters

credits

Text

Chapter 1:   **Page 7:** Reprinted from *Job Outlook 2011—Student Version*, from JobWeb (www.jobweb.com), with permission of the National Association of Colleges and Employers, copyright holder; **p. 19:** Adapted from Mark P. Orbe, and Carol J. Bruess, CONTEMPORARY ISSUES INTERPERSONAL COMMUNICATION (Los Angeles: Roxbury, 2005), p. 309. Reprinted by permission of Oxford University Press.

Chapter 2:   **Page 32:** Passel, J. S. and Cohn, D. *U.S. Population Projections: 2005–2050.* Washington, D.C.: Pew Research Center, 2008. Reprinted by permission; **p. 41:** F. Trompenaars, RIDING THE WAVES OF CULTURE (New York: McGraw-Hill/Irwin, 1994), p. 70. Reprinted by permission of The McGraw-Hill Companies; **p. 42:** Earley, P. C., & Mosakowski, E. (2004, October). Cultural intelligence. *Harvard Business Review, 82(10) 139–146;* **p. 43:** Reprinted by permission of Harvard Business School Press. From *Inside Chinese Business: A Guide for Managers Worldwide* by Ming-Jer Chen. Boston, MA 2001, p. 136. Copyright © 2001 by the Harvard Business School Publishing Corporation; all rights reserved; **p. 47:** Texas Instruments, Inc. (2011). *Corporate social responsibility: The TI ethics quick test.* Retrieved from http://www.ti.com/corp/docs/company/citizen/ethics/quicktest.shtml. Courtesy of Texas Instruments; **p. 49:** "Difference as Advantage: Maximize the Benefits of Your Cultural Identity on the Job" by Chandra Prasad from www.imdiversity.com. Chandra Prasad is the author *of On Borrowed Wings: A Novel* and the editor of *Mixed: An Anthology of Short Fiction on the Multiracial Experience.* You can read about her work at www.chandraprasad.com; **p. 51:** From Philip R. Harris and Robert T. Moran, *Managing Cultural Differences*, 2/e, pp. 245–247. Copyright © 2007. Reprinted by permission of Elsevier.

Chapter 3:   **Page 63:** A. D. Wolvin and C. G. Coakley, PERSPECTIVES ON LISTENING (Norwood, NJ: Ablex, 1993), p. 115. Used by permission. **p. 67:** Adapted from Bodie, G. (2011). The listening styles profile-revised (LSP-R): A scale revision and validation. Used with permission of the author.

Chapter 5:   **Page 117:** J. Brownell, LISTENING: ATTITUDES, PRINCIPLES, AND SKILLS, 3rd Ed. (Boston, Pearson Education, Inc., 2006), p. 23. Used by permission.

Chapter 6:   **Page 163:** Careerbuilder.com (2012, February 22.). *Hiring managers share the most memorable interview mistakes in annual CareerBuilder Survey.* Retrieved from http://www.careerbuilder.com/share/aboutus/pressreleasesdetail.aspx?id=pr680&sd=2%2f22%2f2012&ed=12%2f31%2f2012&siteid=cbpr&sc_cmp1=cb_pr680_

Chapter 7:   **Page 193:** From *Leadership Dilemmas—Grid Solutions* by Robert R. Blake and Anne Adams McCanse (formerly the *Managerial Grid* by Robert R. Blake and Jane S. Mouton). Houston: Gulf Publishing Company, p. 29. Copyright 1991 by Scientific Methods, Inc. Reproduced by permission of Grid International Inc.; **p. 195:** Reprinted by permission of Waveland Press, Inc., from Hackman, M. A., & Johnson, C. E. (2004). *Leadership: A communication perspective.* Long Grove, IL: Waveland Press, Inc. All rights reserved.

Chapter 8:	**Page 220:** John E. Tropman, "The Agenda Bell." Copyright © John E. Tropman. Used with permission.
Chapter 10:	**Page 307:** The McChrystal Afghanistan PowerPoint slide: Can you do any better? From http://www.guardian.co.uk/news/datablog/2010/apr/29/mcchrystal-afghanistan-powerpoint-slide
Chapter 12:	**Page 346:** Reprinted by permission of NTL® Institute for Behavioral Sciences.

Photos

Chapter 1:	**Page 2:** © Ingram Publishing RF; **p. 4:** © James Hardy/PhotoAlto/Corbis RF; **p. 7:** Yellow Dog Productions/Getty Images; **p. 18:** Sydney Shaffer/Getty Images RF.
Chapter 2:	**Page 30:** flickr RF/Getty Images RF; **p. 36:** Panoramic Images/Getty Images; **p. 40:** Ryan McVay/Getty Images RF; **p. 44:** © Daniel Adler.
Chapter 3:	**Page 56:** © mediacolor's/Alamy; **p. 58:** © The McGraw-Hill Companies, Inc./Mark Dierker, photographer; **p. 65:** © Graham Bell/Corbis RF; **p. 70:** © Juice Images/Corbis RF.
Chapter 4:	**Page 76:** Juice Images/Getty Images RF; **p. 86:** © Daniel Adler; **p. 90:** Michael Goldman/Getty Images RF; **p. 94:** © Ocean/Corbis RF.
Chapter 5:	**Page 108:** Leland Bobbe/Getty Images; **p. 112:** © Jose Luis Pelaez Inc/Blend Images LLC RF; **p. 122:** chamferbox/photos.com RF; **p. 124:** Jack Star/PhotoLink/Getty Images RF; **p. 126:** Burke/Triolo Productions/Getty Images RF.
Chapter 6:	**Page 140:** © Josef Lindau/Corbis; **p. 143:** © Ocean/Corbis RF; **p. 147:** Apostrophe Productions/Getty Images; **p. 150:** Antonio M. Rosario/Getty Images RF.
Chapter 7:	**Page 182:** © Tim Pannell/Corbis RF; **p. 184:** Flying Colours Ltd/Getty Images RF; **p. 186:** Ira Block/Getty Images; **p. 191:** © Daniel Adler; **p. 205:** © Ingram Publishing RF.
Chapter 8:	**Page 210:** © Beau Lark/Corbis RF; **p. 222:** Peter Dazeley/Getty Images; **p. 235:** Gary S. Chapman/Getty Images RF; **p. 238:** © Glow Images/Getty Images RF.
Chapter 9:	**Page 244:** David Ball/Getty Images; **p. 246:** © Jon Feingersh Photography Inc./Blend Images/Corbis RF; **p. 253:** © Daniel Adler; **p. 260:** © Kreber/Corbis RF; **p. 265:** © McGraw-Hill Companies/Mark Dierker, photographer.
Chapter 10:	**Page 286:** Kutay Tanir/Getty Images RF.
Chapter 11:	**Page 314:** © Ocean/Corbis RF; **p. 317:** © Randy Faris/Corbis; **p. 324:** © SuperStock/SuperStock.
Chapter 12:	**Page 338:** © Simon Jarratt/Corbis RF; **p. 340:** © Peter Turnley/Corbis; **p. 359:** Walter B. McKenzie/Getty Images; **p. 363:** © RTimages/Alamy RF; **p. 367:** Jetta Productions/Getty Images; **p. 373:** © Blend Images/Alamy RF.

index

COMM 1010 REQUIRED ASSIGNMENTS
TABLE OF CONTENTS

NOTES TO INSTRUCTORS:

1. No student may earn a grade of C or higher unless they submit all four of these term projects.
2. Please consult the departmental COMM 1010 website for additional materials, including samples of student work.
3. All of the assignments shown this appendix are required. The order of units may be changed to fit the individual instructor's scheduling preference.

Assignments to Accompany Interviewing Skills Unit

[Each student submits BOTH parts. Interviewee must be a professional who is not a close friend or relative.]

Assignments to Accompany Interpersonal Skills Unit

[Assign only ONE of these proposals, to be completed by each individual student.]

Assignments to Accompany Teamwork Communication Skills Unit

[Complete ALL parts of this project as a team. Each team will submit ONE copy of each of the following documents: FOUR weekly meeting reports and ONE formal written report, including three attachments. This assignment does not require an oral presentation, though groups could deliver 5-minute presentations as an optional in-class activity.]

Assignments to Accompany Oral Presentation Skills Unit

[Each student submits all three parts. Speeches shall be delivered by each individual student in front of the entire class, accompanied by their PowerPoint and using their Key Word Outline as speaking notes.]

Assignments to Accompany Wrap-Up

CAREER RESEARCH INTERVIEW ASSIGNMENT

Learning Objectives: This assignment gives you an opportunity to
- apply the communication strategies you've learned as you conduct an information-seeking interview
- learn about a career you're interested in
- analyze yourself as an interviewer
- use memo format in reporting what you learned from the interview
- write a formal letter of thanks

Brief Description: Conduct a 30 minute career research interview with a professional in a field of your choice. Create an interview plan. Write an analysis of outcomes.

Two-Step Assignment: This assignment is submitted in two steps: (1) preparation and (2) results.

****

CAREER RESEARCH INTERVIEW PART 1: INTERVIEW PREPARATION

A. Reading Assignment:
1. Read Chapter 6 in your text.
2. Read Appendix II "Business Writing," the sections about "Memos" and "Formal Letters."

B. Preliminary Research:
Choose a profession, job, or volunteer activity you'd like to learn about. Prepare for your interview by conducting background research.
1. In the library:
   -Consult your reference librarian. Most libraries have abundant career research resources.
   -Page through a copy of the Occupational Outlook Handbook.
2. On the web:
   -www.bls.gov/oco/ provides a searchable version of the Occupational Outlook Handbook. In exchange for using this free site, you may be asked to complete a short customer satisfaction survey which will help them improve the site for future users.
   -www.careergames.com provides a free self-assessment tool.
   -wetfeet.com describes various careers and gives information about projected future demand for these careers
   -www.jobweb.com offers links to job choice guides focused on liberal arts, science, and diversity.
3. Networking: Use your personal network to investigate potential careers (see Ch 1 Self-Assessment).

C. Choose the "Right" Interviewee:
Use your personal network to locate a professional who is employed in your field of interest.
1. This person should be a **stranger**. An interview is a formal occasion; you won't experience a realistic formal atmosphere with a friend or relative.
2. Choose a local interviewee so you can conduct the interview **in person**. A face-to-face interview includes a nonverbal dimension that is integral to this assignment.
3. Contact your potential interviewee right away to set up a time and place for your interview. Allow plenty of lead time. Choose a time and place that are convenient for the interviewee.
4. Before you contact your potential interviewee, plan a gracious self-introduction. Refer to Figure 6-1 (Request for Informational Interview) for ideas. Since time is short, it's fine for this assignment to contact them by phone or email, rather than writing a formal letter.
5. It's highly recommended that you re-confirm your appointment a few days ahead of time. At that point, tell them the three or four specific topics you'll be asking about.

D. Prepare Your Interview Topics and Questions

1. Your interview plan should include an opening, a body, and a closing (see student sample).
2. In the body of your interview, focus your investigation around two to four topics, such as
   -a description of typical daily tasks, activities , and schedule in this profession
   - what your interviewee likes and dislikes about their profession
   - what types of training and education they would recommend to prepare for this profession
   - what the prospects for future employment are in this profession
   - any other advice they would like to add
3. Plan a number of primary questions for each of your topics. Use mostly open (rather than closed) and neutral (rather than leading) questions. Consult Chapter 6 and "Writing Interview Questions."
    1. Write questions that sound conversational. If you use long, "stuffy"-sounding questions, you may feel robotic when you ask them.
    2. Plan some secondary questions (probes) to ask in case you don't get full answers to your primary questions.

E. Materials To Submit For Part 1:
Submit a word-processed, spell-checked plan with two headings: 'Preliminary Research' and 'Interview Plan'

E.1. Preliminary Research:
1. **The Interviewee**: Explain who you chose to interview, why you chose them, how you contacted them, where you will interview them, and why you chose that place.
2. **Career Research**: Describe the results of your background research. What type of work are you investigating? What is the nature of the work? What types of daily activities are involved? What education does this career typically require? What is a typical pay scale? What is a typical mission statement?
3. **Cite the research references** you used to gather this information, right within this paragraph, linked to the information you gained from that reference.

E.2. Interview Plan:
1. **Opening**: Write out the exact words you'll use to open the interview. In your actual interview, you won't read this word for word, but stick to the spirit of the script. Include all the elements of an interview opening (see Chapter 6).

2. **Body**: Outline your questions, using your three or four topics as headings.
   - Under each topic, write several primary questions. Label them as open or closed.
   - Under each primary question, write at least one secondary question. You might not have time to ask all these questions, but it's best to be prepared. Leave room to jot down a few handwritten notes --- just a few words--- under each question.
   - *Add a final topic titled **"Clearinghouse Questions**." Under this topic, ask a couple of wide-open questions such as "Is there anything else you can think of that you'd like to share?" and "Who else would you recommend that I talk to?". Sometimes, you'll get the most important information of the interview in the clearinghouse stage. You might learn about some aspect of the career that hadn't even dawned on you to ask about. These questions also signal that the interview is coming to a close, so it will seem less abrupt when you announce that you're done.

3. **Closing**: Outline the exact words you might use to close the interview. Don't READ these words at the time of the interview, but think through what you'll say, so the closing won't sound awkward. Remind your interviewee to complete the evaluation form.

TIPS FOR WRITING INTERVIEW QUESTIONS

1. **Open versus closed questions**: For an information-gathering interview, use mostly open-ended questions, which are worded to encourage interviewees to expand on their answers. Use few closed questions, unless you are seeking a specific fact. Compare the following examples of open versus closed questions:

OPEN QUESTIONS	CLOSED or BIPOLAR QUESTIONS
(encourage interviewee to expand on answer)	*(seek a short answer or yes/answer)*
Tell me about the education I'd need for this job.	Would I have to get a college degree to qualify for this job?
Describe some of your favorite activities.	Do you like your job?
How lucrative is this career?	How much money do you make?
What kinds of opportunities for advancement does this field offer?	Is it easy to get promotions?

2. **Primary and secondary questions**: For each topic in your interview, write a series of follow up questions, which you can use if the interviewee doesn't tell you all you want to know about the question you've asked. You can skip these secondary questions if the interviewee has already answered them. Some of your secondary questions will probably be closed questions.

For example, suppose you ask: "Describe a typical day on your job. " (Primary; Open)
In case your interviewee doesn't say much, be prepared with several secondary Qs such as:
>   -How flexible is the schedule? (Secondary; Open)
>   -How rapid is the pace of the work? (Secondary; Open)
>   -What are the customers' personalities like? (Secondary; Open)
>   -Which tasks tend to take the most time? (Secondary; Closed)
>   -What is your least favorite activity? Secondary; Closed)

3. **Questions that show research**: The best interview questions are specific to the job you're investigating. Compare (Set A) generic, vague questions with (Set B) specific, detailed questions that show the interviewer has spent some time researching the topic::

>   Set A. **Generic, vague questions (avoid these)**
>   >   -How did you get into teaching?
>   >   >   Do you like it?
>   >   -What school did you attend?
>   >   >   Was it a good school?
>   >   -What is your schedule like?
>   >   >   Can you take a lot of time off?

>   Set B. **Specific, detailed questions (ask this type of question)**
>   >   -What does your job as Director of Lab Services entail?
>   >   -Describe your background in technical work?
>   >   >   How important is that background?
>   >   -What's the most common prosthesis you supply to patients?
>   >   >   What's the most unusual one you've made?
>   >   >   Have you ever been uncertain about how to go about making just the right kind of prosthetic that will work in a certain situation?
>   >   -Do many of your patients have lowered cognitive function?
>   >   >   How do you work with patients who have trouble understanding you?
>   >   -Tell me an example of an illness that could result in amputation.
>   >   >   What special challenges are there when you work with diabetics?
>   >   -What changes do you see on the horizon for the prosthetics field?
>   >   >   How will you keep up with your training?

4. *Asking Questions about Your Interviewee's "Personal Life"*
Some of you would like to ask whether the person has a family, whether they can spend time with family, whether they can support a family on their income, and the like. If you were asking these personal questions of applicants in a job interview, the questions would be considered illegal questions. Such questions aren't illegal in information-gathering interviews, but they might be considered "nosy." If you choose to ask personal questions, allow the person the freedom not to answer. You might start with a disclaimer such as "I'm curious about the effects of this job on family life." See what their response is before you ask specifically about their own personal life. You might want to be cautious about asking their exact income, too! You could ask for a typical range.

Grading Criteria	Score and Comments
Background Research: **Interviewee** • Identifies an interviewee who is a qualified professional in the field you wish to research • Provides name of interviewee, organization, and job title • Selects an interviewee who is not a relative or close friend • Explains why you chose this interviewee and how you contacted them • Pinpoints date, time, and location of interview **Career Research** • Identifies sources consulted • Links sources clearly to the information derived from each source • Describes nature of this type of work • Explains education required; pay scale; mission statement, and the like	(up to 10 points)
Format & Professionalism • Submitted by due date • Follows assigned format • Arranged under appropriate topic headings • Includes primary & secondary questions • Labels questions as open vs. closed; • Includes "clearinghouse" questions • Exhibits impeccable spelling, punctuation, grammar	(up to 10 points)
Body of Interview - Quality of Questions • Questions are specific and indicate student has done background research • Sufficient questions to fill 30 minutes of lively conversation • Questions show originality of thought • Questions relate to the topic	(up to 10 points)
Opening and Closing of Interview **Opening:** • Greeting • Orientation: reason for interview, goals, preview **Closing:** • Review—summary of the interview • Future action • Closing pleasantries	(up to 10 points)
Total Points (out of 40 possible)	

CAREER RESEARCH INTERVIEW ASSIGNMENT_PART 2: RESULTS

A. Reconfirm Your Appointment: Contact your interviewee a few days before the appointed date. Give your interviewee on overview of the topics you'll be asking about so they can think about their answers ahead of time.

B. Rehearse: To conduct an effective interview, ask questions in a natural, conversational style. Look up from your outline. Glance at your outline enough to keep yourself on track, but don't keep your eyes glued to it.

Rehearse your interview out loud until you're familiar with your opening, closing, and questions. Practice asking the questions out loud. Practice making good eye contact by rehearsing with a friend or by looking at yourself in a mirror while you ask the questions. Check that you aren't playing with your hair, slouching, or tapping your foot.

Realize that your interviewee may answer some of your later questions while responding to your earlier questions, so you might need to revise your questions on the fly. You might also think of additional secondary questions during the interview. In case this happens, be ready to go with the flow.

C. Print Your Evaluation Form; Address (to your instructor) & Stamp a Business-Sized Envelope:
Print a copy of the evaluation form (posted on this site). Print your name on it. Take it with you for your interviewee to complete. Provide a stamped envelope addressed to your instructor. Ask your interviewee to send the evaluation directly to the instructor. Ask the interviewee to attach their business card if they have one. Your instructor will return the form with your graded assignment.

D. Conduct Your Interview
1. Dress professionally.
2. Arrive a little early. Allow extra travel time in case you get lost or traffic gets jammed. (Leave a time cushion after the interview as well, so you can complete your notes, as explained below.)
3. Greet your interviewee with a warm handshake and a pleasant smile.
4. During the opening moments of your interview, express appreciation that the interviewee is willing to help you. Overview the topics you'll be asking about (even though you will have already given the interviewee this information when you confirmed the interview). Remind the interviewee that your assignment specifies a 30 minute interview. Giving the interviewee this reminder will make it easier to close the interview graciously when you've reached the time limit. If you do extend past 30 minutes, be absolutely sure the interviewee is not pressed for time and truly wants to talk longer.
5. Remind the interviewee that they'll be evaluating your performance as an interviewer. Explain that you won't get credit for the assignment until the instructor receives the completed evaluation form; however, the content of the evaluation will not affect your grade. Its purpose is to help you learn more.
6. If you plan to record the interview, you must ask the interviewee's permission first. Don't put the recorder in a location that will be distracting. Have it all cued up and ready to go so you don't waste their time setting it up.
7. Maintain good eye contact during the interview, especially while the interviewee is answering your questions. Look interested!! It's next to impossible to maintain eye contact and a smoothly-flowing conversation if you are taking notes. Moreover, most interviewees will stop talking and wait while you write. This tends to break the train of thought and wasting your interviewee's time. So... use the **brief delay** method. During the interview, jot down only numbers or very brief specific details. **Within five minutes** after the interview ends, write out a longer version of your notes. You should be able to remember most important material if you wait no longer than five minutes. You can sit in your car or in a lobby to do this.
8. As interviewer, you are responsible for regulating the flow of the interview. This is an art. You need to direct the interview, yet let the interviewee expand on areas they are interested in. A good information-gathering interviewer lets the interviewee take the lead. However, use your judgment. If the interviewee rambles, goes off topic, or talks way too long regarding one of your questions, **politely** interrupt them and move on to the next question. If they don't talk long enough, that's why you have written secondary questions. Keep asking open-ended questions to get more information.
9. End the interview with a gracious closing. Summarize what you've learned and truthfully explain how it will help you. Don't exaggerate. Thank the interviewee for their time.
10. Before you leave, be sure you have the interviewee's postal address so you can send them a formal, typed letter of thanks. Give your interviewee the evaluation form, along with a stamped envelope addressed to your instructor. If possible, the interviewee should attach a business card. It's in your best interest to remind them that you will not receive credit for your assignment until the instructor receives the completed and signed evaluation form.

E. Send a Letter of Thanks

Within a day or two, send your interviewee by postal mail a formal, word-processed letter of thanks. Although it's often fine to send a hand-written note, for this class please use block letter format (illustrated in your text).

Your letter should contain at least three paragraphs. In the first paragraph, express your sincere thanks; target one or two specific concepts you learned. In the second paragraph, expand on those concepts. Explain exactly how the information will help you. In the closing paragraph, reiterate your appreciation, without using the phrase "thank you" again. If overused, that lovely phrase can sound insincere. End on a positive note.

F. Complete Your Formal Written Interview Analysis

Compose a **memo** that **analyzes what you learned** from the interview and **suggests how you might improve**.

F.1. Memo Format: Memos are a form of workplace writing that follows a specific format. They are briefer than other types of documents, and are often arranged under headings. Although memos are brief, they are often packed with detail. The tone is more formal than spoken conversation. Spelling, grammar, and punctuation ARE important, even when you send a memo via e-mail.

- o The heading includes four required lines (To; From; Subject; Date) and may include optional lines (CC; Attachments).
- o Below the heading, open with a short overview paragraph describing the purpose of the memo. Your opening paragraph will NOT have a heading.
- o Continue with the rest of the material arranged under headings.
- o The closing paragraph often summarizes the key points of the memo. It ends with a concluding statement that re-clarifies the purpose of the memo.
- o Refer to Appendix II, Business Writing, "Routine Business Messages."

F.2. Content for this Analysis Memo

1. Create one heading **for each** of the topics of your interview. Under each of these two to four topic headings, write a paragraph or two explaining what you learned about the topic.
   - Write in first person ('I') when you are reporting what YOU learned from your interviewee.
   - Write in third person ('he' or 'she') when you explain what the interviewee did or said (unless you are writing a direct quote). Don't use more than two direct quotes. If you do use a quote (not required) each must be no longer than twelve words.
2. Add two more headings: **"Analysis of .... as my Career Choice"** and **"Analysis of my Interview Process."**
   - Under the heading, **"Analysis of .... as my Career Choice"**, explain how the information you learned has affected your interest in this career field. Use specific information you learned in the interview and explain how it has impacted your career plans.
   - Under the heading, **"Analysis of my Interview Process"**, describe what you've learned about interviewing. Assess your strengths and weaknesses. Propose what you'll do differently in future interviews.
3. Draw your memo to a close with a concluding summary paragraph.

Materials To Submit For Part 2: Be sure your instructor receives all four of these items:
- an updated copy of your interview outline, incorporating any revisions you made after receiving feedback on Part 1
- your analysis memo
- a copy of the formal letter of thanks (in block style) you sent to your interviewee
- a completed evaluation form, sent to your instructor by your interviewee

INTERVIEW EVALUATION QUESTIONNAIRE

Student's Name:_____ Location of Interview_____Date of Interview____

1. What are your frank reactions to the manner in which the student initiated the interview? (Did s/he give a clear explanation of the type of information s/he was seeking and <u>why</u> s/he was seeking it?)

2. What is your reaction to the student's self-presentation? What specific behaviors were effective or not effective (e.g. confidence, eye contact, vocabulary, tone of voice, dress, level of interest, etc.)?

3. What is your reaction to the student's organization of the interview as a whole? Did the questions elicit information that you feel is important? Did s/he skip from topic to topic too quickly? Did s/he allow you enough time to answer?

4. What specific suggestions can you give this student to help improve her/his performance in interviewing?

Signature of Interviewee_____ Name of Firm_____

Position_____ Business Address_____ Business Email _____

THANK YOU FOR CONTRIBUTING TO THIS STUDENT'S EDUCATION!

[up to 60 points possible]

> The following two items are not awarded points, but must be submitted with this assignment before you can earn any points at all:
> • a copy of your revised interview outline
> • the evaluation form, filled out by your professional interviewee

Grading Criteria	Score and Comments
Professionalism • Demonstrates impeccable spelling, grammar, punctuation, sentence structure • Tone of writing is professional (not overly casual; not overly "stiff") • Adheres to assignment instructions • Nonverbal appearance of documents communicates attention to detail	(up to 10 points)
Opening Paragraph • Begins without a heading. • Presents overview of the entire memo • Written in a way that encourages reader to keep reading.	(up to 5 points)
Summaries of Interview Topics • Headings address each interview topic, including clearinghouse questions. • Each paragraph begins with topic sentence that summarizes, in your own words, the main point of this section. • Each topic sentence is supported with several specific examples. • Written in 1st person when you're discussing what you did or learned; written in 3rd person when you describe what the interviewee said.	(up to 10 points)
Analysis of Career Choice • Starts with a heading • Each paragraph begins with topic sentence that summarizes, in your own words, what you learned. • Explains how this material relates to you personally • Demonstrates depth of thought • Describes what you have learned from the experience.	(up to 10 points)
Self-Analysis of Your Own Interview Process • Starts with a heading • Each paragraph begins with topic sentence • Demonstrates depth of thought • Invokes concepts and strategies from the text • Sets forth a plan for future improvement	(up to 10 points)
Concluding Paragraph • Summary restates major points of paper, using different wording • Closes with a statement about what you have learned, how you will apply this information, and/or what your next steps will be.	(up to 5 points)
Letter of Thanks • Uses block style business letter format • Each element of the block style (heading; greeting; closing; etc) follows standard convention • Contains three paragraphs of adequate length • Targets one or two concrete, specific learning points • Expands on these points in the middle paragraph • Expressed in a sincere, gracious tone • Avoids overusing the word "thanks" or "thank you"	(up to 10 points)
Total Points (out of 60 possible)	

PROPOSAL FOR IMPROVING COMMUNICATION

Proposals are a typical form of workplace communication. Your instructor will assign one of the three following options for the proposal assignment.

■■

OPTION A: INTERPERSONAL COMMUNICATION IMPROVEMENT PROPOSAL

Learning Objectives: Your underlying task is to demonstrate that you understand communication concepts taught in this course. To this end, you'll define and explain appropriate communication terminology and propose how you can implement these concepts to improve your own communication. This assignment offers you an opportunity to

- apply your understanding of communication theory toward improving your communication competence
- write a professional proposal

Assignment Description: Submit a word-processed individual proposal (approximately 1500 words) in which you (a) analyze your use of a communication concept of your own choosing and (b) propose one or two concepts from the text you can apply to improve this aspect of your communication. Both the problem and solution must involve communication concepts taught in your COMM 1010 class. You may use the text Self-Assessment tools for ideas.

How to Prepare:
1. Think of one specific unwanted communication habit you are currently using but would like to improve upon. Please note: it is only your OWN ways of interacting that you can change; **do not expect or attempt to change another person's communication habits. Examples:**
      -improve your communication in a team project (Chapters 7 & 8)
      -monitor your own nonverbal messages during performance appraisals (Chapter 6)
      -listen more attentively in your classes (Chapter 3)
      -interact more productively with an uncooperative co-worker (Chapter 5)
      -negotiate rather than act combatively during conflicts (Chapter 5)
      -deliver less ambiguous instructions to co-workers (Chapter 1)
      -respond more constructively when you receive critique from your instructors (Chapter 5)
      -organize your oral presentations more clearly (Chapter 9)
      -manage your anxiety of public speaking (Chapter 11)
      -work more effectively with a classmate from another culture (Chapter 2)

2. Now identify one or two of the specific communication concepts we've studied in this course that might help you improve your communication competency. It will be easier to write your proposal if you choose a narrowly focused concept (e.g., use of the communication model; listening; nonbiased language; unequivocal messages; upward, downward or horizontal communication; formal or informal networks; organizational culture; clarity of messages; listening; nonverbal expression).

3. Review the course material regarding your chosen concept. Mark the pages where you found this material; you'll need to cite specific pages from the text in your proposal.

4. View the sample student proposal.

Audience Analysis: The purpose of a proposal is to persuade your reader (in this case, your instructor) that your proposal will bring about positive, lasting results. Consider the following so you can adapt this proposal to your reader's interests.

Your proposal makes a statement about who you are. Write so it reflects the best you can be. Aim for ZERO errors in grammar, punctuation, and spelling. If your proposal is sloppily written, your reader may assume you are a careless person. The reader will be less likely to value the recommendations in your proposal. A flawless proposal builds your credibility, so your reader is more likely to accept your ideas. To "sell" your proposal, you'll need to supply convincing evidence that

- your plan is feasible, is cost effective, can actually be implemented, and will produce results (citations from your text are an effective form of evidence).
- you have a strong grasp of communication knowledge (i.e., evidence that you know what you're talking about). You can do this by including vocabulary and principles you've learned in class and by describing specific examples of how you can apply these principles.
- you can communicate effectively via written language. Grammar, spelling, neatness, and format will add to or detract from your credibility (see Adler & Elmhorst, Appendix II, Business Writing, 'Writing Well').

Content and Format for this Proposal: Your proposal should be arranged under several headings, as follows. Use a heading for each section except the title page.

Title Page: On the title page, center the following information. Each item should be on a separate line, single-spaced: title of the report; (skip two lines); Submitted by [your name]; college name; class and section; date submitted.

Overview: Start the overview on a new page. This section serves as a preview of the contents of your report. This section should only consist of about six to ten sentences.

Your goal in the overview is to convince the reader that your proposal is worth reading. One effective approach is to briefly summarize the problem, then briefly state how your proposal will solve that problem. End with a strong constructive statement about the value your recommendations will bring to the organization, team, class, friendship, or family. In the overview, be very brief and get right to the point. Reserve the details about your proposal for later. Use powerful language (recall Chapter 4), but be very sincere... don't oversimplify or exaggerate your claims. It wouldn't be realistic to claim that you evolve to instant, perfect communication overnight. Communication habits take a LONG time to change.

Description of Problem: Convince your reader that a communication weakness exists that needs to be managed. Be specific. Integrate terminology from the text as you identify what is wrong. Include page references from the text. Provide one or two specific examples of the weakness. It might be helpful to include quotations of words you've said that were problematic and a description of the ways others have reacted to your communication. Consider how these drawbacks impact the organization, team, friendship, or family as a whole.

Resources and Constraints: This section will be probably be shorter than the problem description and recommendations sections. Take stock of the current situation. What resources can you identify that could help you improve your communication? The text is one example. Excellent role models might be another resource. How can you use these resources to help you improve your communication? Describe any constraints that are likely to impede your progress in improving your communication habits. For example, if you are working three jobs and taking a full-time class load, your ability to put time and effort into this project is likely to be curtailed. (If this were the case, you might realize that improving your communication habits can bring lifelong benefits, so you might suggest in your recommendations that you will drop one job or not take as many classes at a time, to enable you to work on your life skills.)

Recommendations: This is the most crucial section of your proposal. This will be the longest section of your entire document. Propose how you plan to improve the communication weakness. Describe exactly what you plan to accomplish. Detail the specific steps you will take to achieve your objectives. Be realistic. Be specific. If you quoted examples of detrimental language in your problem description, it would be helpful to include here some examples of effective phrases you could substitute. Explain why your plan is desirable for the organization, team, relationship, and for you. Show why your plan is feasible. Your recommendations should demonstrate that you are personally "engaging" with the concepts learned in this class. You don't need to quote directly from the text, but include page references so the reader can look up the concepts easily.

Summary: Summarize the problem and the recommendations. Explain how these recommendations, if adopted, would improve communication. Be as specific as possible. End with a strong, constructive message about the importance of this proposal. Add a gracious closing statement (e.g., you are looking forward to implementing the plan; you are expecting constructive results; etc.).

Works Cited: You're required to integrate several references from your communication text. Identify your source in two places.
   -Use **parenthetical citations** within the body of your paper when you refer to information from your readings. Here's an example: (Adler & Elmhorst, p. 23).

   - At the end of your report, include a section titled **Works Cited**. Cite your text in APA or MLA style.
      Adler, R & Elmhorst, J .(2013). Communicating at work: SLCC custom text (2nd ed). Boston: McGraw Hill.

   -You're only required to cite your text. If you include optional additional sources, list them in a recognized format (such as APA or MLA) in alphabetical order, according to authors' last names.

Grading Criteria: Refer to the Scoring Guide for this assignment.

PROPOSAL FOR IMPROVING COMMUNICATION
OPTION B: ORGANIZATIONAL COMMUNICATION IMPROVEMENT PROPOSAL

Learning Objectives: For this assignment you'll assume the role of organizational consultant. You'll submit a proposal for improving a communication process in a bona fide organization. Your underlying task is to demonstrate that you understand the concepts of communication taught in this course. You'll define and explain appropriate communication terminology and propose how you can implement these concepts to improve communication within an organizational setting. This assignment offers you an opportunity to

- apply your understanding of communication theory in solving an organizational problem
- write a professional proposal

Assignment Description: Submit a word-processed individual proposal (approximately 1500 words) in which you (a) analyze an organization's use of a communication concept and (b) propose one or two specific communication concepts from the text you could apply to improve this aspect of the organization's communication. Both the problem and solution must involve communication concepts taught in your COMM 1010 class.

How to Prepare:

1. Think of one specific communication problem you've experienced in an organizational context. Choose ONE specific problem (e.g. an uncooperative co-worker; a supervisor who doesn't listen well; a conflict between workers of different ethnic backgrounds; receiving ambiguous instructions; information overload; a defensive climate). Don't try to solve all your organization's problems at once!

2. Identify one or two of the **communication concepts** we've studied in this course that might help explain or **solve** that problem (e.g., use of the communication model; listening; verbal or nonverbal messages; ambiguity; upward, downward or horizontal communication; formal or informal networks; organizational culture; communicating across diversity; conflict, etc.). Note that both the problem and solution must involve **communication concepts**. A proposal to send your office on a vacation to Italy would not be appropriate for this assignment.

3. Review all portions of your text and class notes related to the communication concept you've chosen; you'll need to cite specific pages from the text in your proposal.

4. View the sample student proposal.

5. Write a proposal in which you recommend a plan for remedying this one communication problem. Your proposal should be specific, concrete, and realistic. Proposing that all employees should take a class in communication is not specific. You could, however, detail the step-by-step contents of a one-hour training session. Proposing that your supervisor should be fired is not realistic. (Do you have the power to make this happen?) You could, however, develop a word-by-word role play of how you would explain to your supervisor (or the supervisor's manager) that you need more specific feedback about your performance.

Audience Analysis:
The purpose of a proposal is to persuade your reader (in this case, your instructor) to accept your plan (i.e., to hire you for the consultant job). You may assume that your instructor is the person in your organization who is vested with the authority to decide whether to adopt your plan or not. Consider the following as you adapt your proposal to your reader's interests.

Your proposal makes a statement about who you are, so be sure it reflects the best you can be. Aim for ZERO errors in grammar, punctuation, and spelling If your proposal is sloppily written, your reader may assume you are a careless person. The reader will be less likely to value the recommendations in your proposal. A flawless proposal builds your credibility, so your reader is more likely to accept your ideas. To "sell" your proposal, you'll need to supply convincing evidence that

- your plan is feasible, is cost effective, can actually be implemented, and will produce results (citations from your text are an effective form of evidence).
- you have a strong grasp of communication knowledge (i.e., evidence that you know what you're talking about). You can do this by including vocabulary and principles you've learned in class and by describing specific examples of how you can apply these principles.

- You can communicate effectively via written language. Grammar, spelling, neatness, and format will add to or detract from your credibility (see Adler & Elmhorst, Appendix II, Business Writing, Writing Well).

Content and Format for this Proposal: Typically, each company has its own preferred format for proposals. For this class, please use the following format. Include a heading for each section except the title page.

Title Page: On the title page, center the following information. Each item should be on a separate line, single-spaced: title of the report; (skip two lines); Submitted by [your name]; college name; class and section; date submitted.

Overview: Start the overview on a new page. This section serves as a preview of the contents of your report. This section should only consist of about six to ten sentences. Your goal in the overview is to convince your reader (instructor or CEO) that your proposal is worth reading. Briefly summarize the problem, then briefly state how your proposal will solve that problem. End with a strong constructive statement about the value of your recommendations.

Use positive language, but be sincere... don't oversimplify or exaggerate your claims. It wouldn't be realistic to claim that your organization will evolve to instant, perfect communication overnight. Communication habits take a LONG time to change.

Description of Problem: Pack this section with specific, concrete details. Convince your reader that a communication weakness exists that needs to be managed. Identify the weakness, using terminology from the text. Cite the page reference. Provide one or two specific examples of the detrimental communication. When possible, include quotations of words that were problematic and a description of the ways others have reacted to those words. Explain consequences (how this communication pattern negatively impacts the organization or team as a whole).

Resources and Constraints: This section will be shorter than the problem description and recommendations sections. Take stock of the current situation. What resources can you identify that could help improve the organization's communication? The text is one example. Excellent role models might be another resource. How can you use these resources to help you improve communication? Describe any constraints that are likely to impede progress in improving communication.

Recommendations: This is the most crucial section of your proposal. This will be the longest section of your proposal. Explain your solution precisely. What do you plan to accomplish? How will you implement it? Include VERY SPECIFIC steps and examples. Use information from the text. Cite the page reference. Explain why your plan is desirable for the organization, and show why it is feasible.

Summary: Summarize the problem and the recommendations. Explain how your recommendations, if adopted, would improve communication in the organization. End with a strong, constructive message about the importance of this proposal. Add a gracious closing statement (e.g., you are looking forward to implementing the plan; or you are expecting constructive results).

Works Cited: You're required to integrate several references from your communication text. Identify your source two ways.

-Use **parenthetical citations** within the body of your paper when you refer to information from your readings. Here's an example: (Adler & Elmhorst, p. 23).

- At the end of your report, include a section titled **Works Cited**. Cite your text in APA or MLA style.
   Adler, R & Elmhorst, J. (2013). Communicating at work: SLCC custom text (2nd ed.). Boston: McGraw Hill.

-You're only required to cite your text. If you include optional additional sources, list them in APA or MLA format in alphabetical order, according to authors' last names.

Grading Criteria: Refer to the Scoring Guide for this assignment.

COMMUNICATION IMPROVEMENT PROPOSAL: Scoring Guide for Options A & B

[up to 50 points possible]

Grading Criteria	Score & Comments
I. Professionalism • Written in formal proposal format; arranged under assigned headings • Submitted on time • Each heading is supported by two or three substantive paragraphs • Each paragraph starts with a clear topic sentence • Demonstrates impeccable spelling, grammar, punctuation, sentence structure • Tone of writing is appropriate for a business/professional audience (not overly casual; not overly "stiff")	(up to 5 points)
II. Title Page and Overview • Title Page follows the assigned format • Overview concisely summarizes the problem • Overview convinces reader that suggested solution is realistic and will work • Overview entices reader to continue reading	(up to 5 points)
III. Description of Problem • Integrates concepts and terminology from the text • Links page references from the text to the concepts used • Identifies a meaningful communication problem • Provides specific examples • Demonstrates knowledge of communication concepts • Considers impact of your personal communication on your professional and personal success • Statements are realistic, not overly exaggerated	(up to 10 points)
IV. Assets and Constraints • Integrates concepts and terminology from the text • Links page references from the text to the concepts used • Identifies useful assets • Recognizes actual constraints • Provides specific examples • Demonstrates knowledge of communication concepts • Statements are realistic, not overly exaggerated	(up to 5 points)
IV. Recommendations • Recommendations are useful • Recommendations are feasible • Recommendations are not overly simplified • Recommendations are not exaggerated • Integrates terminology from the text • Demonstrates knowledge of communication concepts • Provides specific examples • Considers impact of your personal communication on your professional and personal success	(up to 20 points)
V. Summary and Works Cited • Conclusion briefly summarizes entire proposal • Conclusion convinces reader that the proposal is worthy • Conclusion ends with a gracious statement • References are cited within the body of text (parenthetical citations) • References are listed in correct format in Works Cited section at end of report	(up to 5 points)
Total Score	

PROPOSAL FOR IMPROVING COMMUNICATION
OPTION C: TEAM COMMUNICATION IMPROVEMENT PROPOSAL

Learning Objectives: Your underlying task is to demonstrate that you understand communication concepts taught in this course. To this end, you'll define and explain appropriate communication terminology and propose how you can implement these concepts to improve team communication. This assignment offers you an opportunity to

- apply your understanding of communication theory toward improving team communication competence
- write a professional proposal

Assignment Description: You'll submit a word-processed individual proposal (approximately 1500 words) in which you (a) analyze your team's communication processes during the team project from this class and (b) propose one or two specific communication changes you would make the next time you are involved in a group project. Both the problem and solution must involve communication concepts taught in your COMM 1010 class.

How to Prepare:

1. Think of two specific communication strengths and two specific weaknesses your team experienced during your class decision-making project. Because this project has been a learning situation, there will be some concepts you have applied well, and others that still need improvement. Please write an honest assessment.

2. Identify one or two of the **communication concepts** from this course that help explain your successes and might help improve your weaknesses. Note that both the problem and solution must involve **communication concepts**. A proposal to disband the team and work individually would not be appropriate for this assignment.

3. Review all portions of your text and class notes related to the communication concepts you've chosen; you'll need to cite specific pages from the text in your proposal.

4. View the sample student proposal.

5. Write a proposal that is specific, concrete, and realistic. Proposing that all teammates should take another class in communication is not specific. You could, however, detail the step-by-step contents of a one-hour training session. Proposing that one of your teammates should be removed from the group is not realistic. (Do you have the power to make this happen?) You could, however, develop a word-by-word role play of how you would talk to that teammate.

Audience Analysis: The purpose of a proposal is to persuade your reader (in this case, your instructor) that your plan is feasible. A potential secondary audience might be other students.

Your proposal makes a statement about who you are, so be sure it reflects the best you can be. Aim for ZERO errors in grammar, punctuation, and spelling. If your proposal is sloppily written, your reader may assume you are a careless person. The reader will be less likely to value the recommendations in your proposal. A flawless proposal builds your credibility, so your reader is more likely to accept your ideas. To "sell" your proposal, you'll need to supply convincing evidence that

- you have participated actively in the group decision-making project
- you have learned some new concepts of small group communication in this class
- you understand the material taught in this class about effective group work
- you have thoughtfully evaluated your own group's process
- you have integrated concepts from the course in your recommendations for improving your performance in future teamwork assignments
- your proposal includes all the required content, including specific examples of your own group's performance
- you can communicate effectively via written language. Grammar, spelling, neatness, and format will add to or detract from your credibility (see Adler & Elmhorst, Appendix II, Business Writing, 'Writing Well').

Format for the Proposal:
Typically, each company has its own preferred format for proposals. For this class, please use the following format. Include a heading for each section except the title page.

Title Page: On the title page, center the following information. Each item should be on a separate line, single-spaced: title of the report; (skip two lines); Submitted by [your name]; college name; class and section; date submitted.

Overview: This section serves as a preview of the contents of your report. Your goal is to convince the reader that your proposal is worthwhile. One effective approach is to briefly introduce your group's purpose, method, and end-product. Next, briefly identify your group's assets and limitations. Clarify how your recommendations will help reduce the limitations. End with a strong constructive statement about the value of your recommendations.

Group Assets: Describe two strengths your group exhibited. Each strength should correspond to a communication concept or a critical thinking concept you've learned in this class. In this section,
- Define and describe each concept (include a page reference from the text) in some depth. Explain why this concept contributes to effective team work. Prove to your reader that you know what this concept means. Think of this as a take-home essay exam.
- Then explain how your group illustrated this concept. Be specific. That is, if you claim that your group avoided groupthink, include specific examples of devil's advocate questions your group members asked.

Group Limitations: Describe two weaknesses your group exhibited. Each weakness should correspond to a group communication concept or a critical thinking concept you've learned in this class. In this section,
- Define and describe each concept (include a reference from the text). As in the section about assets, provide an in-depth description of what the concept means and why it's important in group work.
- Then explain how your group did not demonstrate this concept. Be specific. That is, if you claim that your group did not respect each others' viewpoints, include examples of exact statements that demonstrated disconfirming messages.

Recommendations: This is the most crucial section of your proposal. This will be the longest section of your document.
- Propose what you would do to improve your team's communication, if you could do this project over again. For example, you might suggest a different way to organize your group or a better method of assigning roles. Integrate explanations and references from the text.
- Now, explain how you will apply these recommendations in future group situations you may participate in. Be as specific as possible. Your recommendations should demonstrate that you are personally "engaging" with the concepts of group communication learned in this class.

Conclusion: Summarize your objectives, assets, limitations, and recommendations. End with a strong, constructive message about the importance of this proposal.

Works Cited: You're required to integrate several references from your communication text. Identify your source two ways.

-Use **parenthetical citations** within the body of your paper when you refer to information from your readings. Here's an example: (Adler & Elmhorst, p. 23).

- At the end of your report, include a section titled **Works Cited**. Cite your text in APA or MLA style.
Adler, R & Elmhorst, J. (2013). Communicating at work: SLCC custom text (2nd ed.). Boston: McGraw Hill.

-You're only required to cite your text. If you include optional additional sources, list them in APA or MLA format in alphabetical order, according to authors' last names.

Grading Criteria: Refer to the Scoring Guide for this assignment.

COMMUNICATION IMPROVEMENT PROPOSAL: Scoring Guide for Option C

[up to 50 points possible]

Grading Criteria	Score & Comments
I. Professionalism • Written in formal proposal format; arranged under assigned headings • Submitted on time • Each heading is supported by two or three substantive paragraphs • Each paragraph starts with a clear topic sentence • Demonstrates impeccable spelling, grammar, punctuation, sentence structure • Tone of writing is appropriate for a business/professional audience (not overly casual; not overly "stiff")	(up to 5 points)
II. Title Page, Overview • Title Page follows the assigned format • Overview concisely summarizes the group assignment, assets, and limitations • Overview convinces reader that suggested solution is realistic and will work • Overview entices reader to continue reading	(up to 5 points)
III. Description of Group Assets • Integrates concepts and terminology from the text • Links page references from the text to the concepts used • Identifies useful assets • Provides specific examples • Demonstrates knowledge of communication concepts • Statements are realistic, not overly exaggerated	(up to 5 points)
IV. Description of Group Limitations • Integrates concepts and terminology from the text • Links page references from the text to the concepts used • Recognizes actual constraints • Provides specific examples • Shares responsibility for limitations • Demonstrates knowledge of communication concepts • Statements are realistic, not overly exaggerated	(up to 10 points)
IV. Recommendations • Recommendations are useful • Recommendations are feasible • Recommendations are not overly simplified • Recommendations are not exaggerated • Integrates terminology from the text • Demonstrates knowledge of communication concepts • Provides specific examples • Considers impact of your personal communication on your professional and personal success	(up to 20 points)
V. Summary and Works Cited • Conclusion briefly summarizes entire proposal • Conclusion convinces reader that the proposal is worthy • Conclusion ends with a gracious statement • References are cited within the body of text (parenthetical citations) • References are listed in correct format in Works Cited section at end of report	(up to 5 points)
Total Score	

TEAM DECISION-MAKING ASSIGNMENT

Learning Outcomes: Making decisions and writing reports are typical workplace tasks. If you remember only one strategy from this class, we hope you will remember and use this process for making well-reasoned decisions and for solving problems effectively. When you apply this process properly, it can reduce the chance that you'll make decisions you later regret. This project provides an opportunity for you to
- try out the group communication skills you're learning as you apply the reflective decision-making protocol to make a realistic decision
- improve your writing skills as your team submits your results in a formal written report

The Reflective-Thinking Sequence was first proposed by John Dewey over 80 years ago. Dewey is known as the father of American educational philosophy. Dewey created a curriculum that encouraged students to be curious and to learn to love learning. Dewey's decision-making protocol is a well-researched and effective strategy that combines left-brain and right-brain thinking. Once you learn this protocol, you'll be able to use it
- in your personal life as you make your own important decisions
- in the workplace as you work individually or with teams to solve problems

Assignment Description: You'll collaborate with a team of classmates, using the Reflective Thinking Process, to make a well-reasoned decision. Students often dread academic teamwork because it sometimes seems like pulling teeth to get other group members to contribute. There is often too much "social loafing" (sitting back and sliding while others do most the work). However, if you and your team members follow instructions carefully and promptly, this group project should run smoothly and won't require too much time. In fact, many groups end up really enjoying this project!

Your team will work through the steps of the Reflective-Thinking Sequence in four meetings. If your team stays on task, each meeting should only require 30 to 45 minutes. Adhere to the specific instructions for each meeting. Use one of the case studies as your topic, or attempt to make a real-life decision relevant to the lives of one of your group members.

How to Prepare
1. Read the description of "Systematic Problem Solving" in Chapter 8 of your text.
2. Peruse the Decision-Making Grid instructions for each meeting.
3. Look at the Sample Decision-Making Report.

Assignment Steps: (1) work through the decision-making protocol during several team meetings; then (2) report your results in a formal written report (submit one report per group).

****

TEAM DECISION-MAKING PROJECT PART 1: TEAM MEETING INSTRUCTIONS
With your team, work through each step of the reflective sequence in order. Don't skip any steps. At the discretion of your instructor, you'll be allowed time for four in-class meetings.

TEAM MEETING #1: During your FIRST group meeting, create your Team Contract AND work on steps I and II. Submit your completed **Meeting 1 Chart** to your instructor after this meeting for comments and points (one copy per group).

1. Prepare your Team Contract: Effective teams attend to team relations BEFORE attempting to solve the task at hand. Set a good working environment by agreeing, as a team, on your norms and roles.

A. **Group Norms.** Norms are the ground rules that all members agree to adhere to. Develop at least five norms that all team members are willing to support. Include both task norms and relational norms. Be realistic! If there's a chance someone might be late to one meeting, do NOT write "We will all be on time to every meeting." Instead, you could write, "We will attempt to arrive on time. If we must be late, we will email our contributions to the group facilitator so they arrive well before the meeting begins."
Examples:
Relational norms:
- Listen to each other's ideas without interrupting or one-upping anyone.
- Invite quite persons to participate.
- Refrain from whining.

Task norms
- Keep our meetings to 90 minutes or less.
- Read all assigned material in the text and class Web site before the meeting begins.
- Stay on task.

B. **Group Roles.** Roles are actions that individual team players fill. Many of your roles will help you achieve the norms you set above. Identify at least three task roles and three relational roles that your team members should attend to. Assign each person at least two roles. Roles should be flexible. Usually you will have more than one person assigned to each role, to be sure it gets done. Each person should fill several roles. You may rotate roles.

Examples:

Relational roles:
- gatekeeper (be sure each member gets equal time to express ideas)
- harmonizer (if competition develops between members, help them worth through it)

Task roles:
- facilitator (make sure all tasks are done on time; submit weekly reports to instructor)
- time keeper
- procedural monitor (be sure team is correctly following each step of the assigned project)
- devil's advocate (be sure each idea --- except during brainstorming sessions --- is thoroughly questioned)
- proofreader
- information agent (inputs facts and relevant resources to support ideas)
- initiator (suggests new ideas and insights)

After you have agreed on the contents of your Team Contract, list each member's name in alphabetical order. Add your email addresses and phone numbers where team members can reach each other. Email a copy to me. Keep a copy in your files. You will submit a copy of your contract as an attachment to your final report.

Now, you may begin work on the problem. The "PAC_BOY" acronym represents the order of these decision-making steps.

Step I: State the problem as a question. [P = Problem]

1. Choose one of the case studies or select your own decision to make.
2. You may use the suggested question wording from the case study, or you may modify the wording.
3. Recall that the question should have the following characteristics:
    1. one single question
    2. open-ended (not a yes/no answer).
       That is, don't ask "Should I fire all the employees?" or "Is it a good idea to fire the employer" or Can we fire the employer" because a yes/no question limits your possibilities to only two choices. Instead, you might ask "What is the best way to improve communication between managers and employees at ABC, Inc.?"
    3. Don't state the solution in the question. That is, don't ask "How can we get our friend arrested for using marijuana?" because that type of question also limits your possibilities too much. You already have a solution in mind. Be open to many possibilities. Instead, you might ask "How can we best respond to our friend's marijuana habit?"
    4. The project must be small scale and realistic ... something that your group can actually solve within one month. Please do NOT select topics about which you are not experts. For example, you do not have the expertise to end a war or change the federal food stamp program. You DO have the expertise to help a local organization recruit more volunteers or to help a study group find a better method for improving their grades.

Step II: Study your problem [A = Analysis]
1. You need to understand exactly what is wrong before you can do much good trying to solve anything.
2. This step will require some research. Talk to people who could help you with your solution. Find out what resources are available to you. Because these are hypothetical problems, in some cases you will need to suppose the answers.
3. Investigate the following aspects of your problem situation, and write a brief paragraph about each aspect:
    1. Characteristics:
        1. what aspects of the problem do you observe?
        2. why is this a problem?
        3. what future effects might it create?
    2. Stakeholders (people affected by the problem)
        1. Who does this problem affect, and how? (It will probably affect several different sets of people)
        2. What are the attitudes and expectations of the people affected?
    3. History: This step is important. Find out what other people with similar problems have done, so you don't have to reinvent the wheel.
        1. When and how did this problem begin?
        2. What, if any, attempts have already been made to try to fix the problem?
        3. Why haven't past attempts to manage the problem worked?
    4. Policies and politics:
        1. What federal or state laws affect the problem or your solution?
        2. What organizational policies might affect the problem?
        3. Are there any ethical concerns you should take into account?
    5. Resources available to help you tackle the problem

1. How much money is available?
2. How much time is available?
3. What sources of knowledge can you consult to get ideas about how to solve this problem?
    1. (Sources could include SLCC student officers, campus police, faculty members, books, web sites, anyone who has tried to deal with a similar problem in the past)
    2. Include your text and class lectures for this course as potential sources. They contain many useful ideas about ethics, effective communication, and group interactions.

TEAM MEETING #2: During your SECOND meeting, complete Steps II and III. Submit your completed <u>Meeting 2 Chart</u> to your instructor after this meeting for comments and points (one copy per group).

Step III: Criteria [NOTE: Criterion = singular (one criterion); Criteria = plural (more than one)] [C = Criteria]

1. Before you start proposing solutions, you need to decide what a good solution would accomplish.
2. First, write a general goal.
3. Next, identify seven to twelve "criteria" that you will use later, when you will be judging the merits of each of your proposed solutions.
4. Don't mix up solutions in your criteria list.
5. Use the text to help you think of criteria that illustrate sound communication principles. Write down the page number next to the criterion.
6. Here are some examples of criteria. You will need to develop more of your own:
    o costs less than $200
    o requires no more than two hours per person
    o complies with Utah State safety standards
    o is acceptable to our manager
    o does not overburden one individual more than another
    o respects the personal privacy of every individual
    o applies communication principles we've learned in this class
        ▪ Document these concepts by including **references** from the text

TEAM MEETING #3: During your THIRD group meeting, work on Steps IV-VI. Submit your completed <u>Meeting 3 Chart</u> to your instructor after this meeting for comments and points (one copy per group).

Step IV: Brainstorm possible solutions to your problem [B = Brainstorm]

- It's difficult to brainstorm correctly, but please try to do so. Follow the text guidelines for brainstorming.
- When you brainstorm, stimulate creative thinking by writing down as many ideas as you can, as quickly as you can. At this point, it's OK if the suggestions are silly, impractical, or unreasonable. For this task, you want quantity, not quality.
- DO NOT EVALUATE solutions at this time. Anything goes. Just list as many ideas as you can think of. Don't worry whether they might work or not. The judgment stage will come later.
- Some of your proposed solutions should be based on material you've learned in this class. In your report, include these **references** ....write down the appropriate page numbers.

Step V: Evaluate your proposed solutions. [O = Organize and assess]

- Narrow down your brainstormed list to your top four or five solutions.
- Create a comparison chart. List your solutions as column headings and your criteria as row headings.
- If some criteria seem very important, use a 10 point scale instead of a 5 point scale (see Criterion 1 below).
- Discuss each solution in turn, and rate each solution according to each criterion.
- Keep this chart. You will submit it as part of your group report.

Sample Chart
Solutions
Established

	Solution 1	Solution 2	Solution 3	Solution 4	Solution 5
Criterion 1	9	7	2	6	8
Criterion 2	2	4	5	5	3
Criterion 3	4	5	3	1	5
Criterion 4	4	5	4	3	5
Criterion 5	2	5	5	5	3
TOTALS	21	26	19	20	24

Evaluating According to Criteria

Step VI: Select the best solution   {Y = Yes, we can find a solution]

    1.   Here's where your right-brain thinking comes into play. Based on your chart and discussion, produce a final recommendation aimed at remedying the problem. You are not obliged to choose the solution that had the highest score, since some criteria may be more important than others. You may want to combine parts of different solutions to reach your final recommendation.

TEAM MEETING #4: During your FOURTH group meeting, complete Step VI and begin Step VII. Submit your completed <u>Meeting 4 Chart</u> to your instructor after this meeting for comments and points (one copy per group).

Step VI: Select the best solution (continued)

    2.   **Hold a second chance discussion: double-check your recommendation**.
        1.   Often in the heat of creativity, potential negatives don't occur to us. If you've ever made a decision, then had second thoughts the next morning, you will understand my point.
        2.   It's best to schedule this second chance meeting at least 24 hours after Step V, to give your subconscious time to surface any doubts you may have.
        3.   List any potential negative consequences that might occur if you implement this solution.
        4.   Modify your recommendation accordingly.
    3.   Be sure your report is well-documented (includes references).
    4.   Write out, in some depth, your answer to the question: "How does this solution excel over the other solutions that you proposed?"

Step VII: Plan how you would implement the solution.

    1.   Assign individuals to write up each part of the final report.
    2.   **Don't forget your bibliography** and your analysis chart.

TEAM MEETING #5: During your FIFTH group meeting, proofread and revise your formal written report. Distribute participation points.

    1.   Proofread all parts of your report and revise as necessary.
    2.   Check the required format to be sure you have followed directions precisely.
    3.   As a team, decide how you will distribute participation points.
    4.   Your entire team must be present for this activity. That way, each person will have a chance to explain why they qualify for points.
    5.   Do NOT assign points to a student who has contributed to less than 30% of your project.
    6.   Compile all the parts of your report and submit.

In this project, you'll make a decision or solve a problem, using the Reflective Thinking Process. This process combines your right-brain, intuitive thinking with your left-brain analytical thinking. As you work through each step in order, notice how you switch back and forth between intuition and logic.

Fill in this chart during your first meeting. At the completion of your meeting, submit a copy of your completed chart to your instructor to receive feedback, and to earn up to 10 team points for a well-executed Progress Chart. Each member **who participated in this meeting** earns the same number of points on this assignment.

Meeting #1 Date, Time, Location:	
Members Present (include last & first name, telephone number, and an email address that you read frequently)	Members Not Present (include last and first name, telephone number, and email address)

In your first meeting, you will write your Team Contract and complete the first step of the PAC – BOY acronym. P = Problem: agree on the Problem to be solved and write it as an open-ended question.

Task 1: Team Contract	
Develop Relational Norms (3 or more) (see Table 7-5)	1. Example: We commit to putting group goals above personal goals, so we will each MAKE the time to participate fully in each step of this project.
Develop Task Norms (3 or more) (see Table 7-5)	1. Example: If we have to miss a meeting, we will email our info to all members at least one day in advance. .
Assign Relational Roles (see Table7-5) You may assign multiple roles to members.	1. Example: Participation Encouragers – Frank N. Stein & Ima Goner 2. 3. 4. 5.
Assign Task Roles (see Table 7-5) You may assign a leader [recommended] or rotate leadership.	1. Example: Devil's Advocate - Gil Bates 2. 3. 4. 5.

A22

Team Contract Analysis:	Leader: list here the initials of all members who agree to abide by this contract.
• Are your norms and roles realistic? • Is EVERY member really willing & able to abide by them? • Have you set up a way to enforce these norms and roles? • If not, revise them NOW.	

Task 2: Define the Problem (logic)

With your group, select one of the problems from the "Problem-solving Scenarios" handout OR choose a workplace problem that one of your group members is currently attempting to solve (or a major decision one of your group members is involved in). **Describe your problem or decision here:**	**Tips:** 1. Keep the scope of your problem manageable. It must be something you can actually complete in four weeks. For example, it's not likely you can end world hunger or create world peace in four weeks. 2. Choose a problem/decision you have the authority to do something about. You might want to fire your boss or end all tests in college, but that's probably not within your power.
State your problem as an open-ended question:	**Tips:** Don't write a question that already states your solution. For example, **"How can we make our curfew later" is not a probing question because you already know what you want.** You could rephrase it as "What is the best way to satisfy our parents' wish to keep us safe, yet still allow us to attend school play practices at night?"
Analyze your problem question: Can your group answer YES to each of the following? Our problem statement • addresses one SINGLE issue • is an open-ended question (can't be answered by yes, no, or maybe) • does not contain an expected solution If you answered NO to any of these, revise your Problem Statement again.	Leader: list here the initials of all members who agree that this problem is stated as an open-ended question AND are willing to work with the group to find a satisfactory solution to this problem.

Task 3: Begin Analysis of Your Problem (logic)

Assign members to find information about each of the following characteristics of your problem. Members are responsible for bringing the information to your next established meeting. Do NOT sign up for a task unless you are willing to commit to bringing the needed information on time.

Group members should help each other think of places to go to find the assigned information. You may want to briefly discuss elements of analysis at the first meeting, but most of your discussion should be held AFTER members have completed their research.

List assignments here:	Member(s) responsible:
1. Characteristics: What are the symptoms of the problem? Include positive as well as negative aspects of the current situation.	1.

2. Stakeholders: What groups are affected? How does this problem impact each group? What are each group's goals? (Think outside the box. Include as many different sets of stakeholders as you can think of.)	2.
3. History: What solutions have been tried in the past to solve similar problems? How well have these solutions worked? Whom have these solutions helped? Whom have they hindered? How do you know?	3.
4. Policies and politics: What regulations, professional requirements, political considerations, and/or ethical expectations might impact your solution?	4.
5. Resources: What references can you consult to get ideas for good solutions? (You are required to use your communication text as one of your references.) Who else can you talk to? How much time and money are you willing to commit?	5.
6. Other: Assign other tasks as needed?	6.
Follow up: Assign the following follow-up tasks: 1. Who will submit this chart? 2. Who will contact each member before the next meeting to be sure they have completed their task? 3. How (and how often) will you communicate between meetings to answer questions and share comments?	1. 2. 3.

Planning for Meeting 2:	
• When and where will your next meeting be? • All members need to read instructions for Meeting 2 before the next meeting. • Agree to come prepared with the material you signed up to bring. If you can't attend Meeting 2 for some reason, email your materials well ahead of time to all group members.	All members who have agreed to prepare for and attend Meeting #2 initial here:

Fill in this chart during your 2nd meeting. At the completion of your meeting, submit this chart to your instructor to receive feedback and up to 10 team points for a well-executed Progress Chart. Each member **who participated in this meeting** earns the same number of points on this assignment.

Meeting 2 Date, Time, Location:	
Members Present:	Members Not Present:

In your second meeting, you will complete the first half of the PAC – BOY acronym. Start by reviewing "P" (State the Problem). Next, discuss thoroughly "A" (Analysis of the Problem) and "C" (Criteria; e.g., requirements for an effective solution).

Task 1: Problem, stated as an open-ended question (logic)
Re-read your problem question.   Do you still agree that it meets the characteristics of an effective "problem question"? Discuss and revise again as needed. You may wish to incorporate suggestions that other class members sent your group.

Task 2: Analysis of Your Problem: (logic)
Write detailed notes about each element of your analysis in this chart.
7.   Characteristics: What are the symptoms of the problem? Include positive as well as negative aspects of the current situation.
8.   Stakeholders: What persons or groups of persons are affected by this problem? How does this problem impact each group? What are each group's goals? (Think outside the box. Include as many different sets of stakeholders as you can think of.)

9. History: What solutions have been tried in the past to solve similar problems? How well have these solutions worked? Whom have these solutions helped? Whom have they hindered? How do you know?

10. Policies and politics: What regulations, professional requirements, political considerations, and/or ethical expectations might impact your solution?

11. Resources: What references did you consult to get ideas for good solutions? (You are required to use your communication text as one of your references.) Who else did you talk to? What did you learn from these references? How much time and money are you willing to commit?

12. Other:

Now that you've discussed many ramifications of your problem, you are ready for the "C" step. C = Criteria.

SPELLING NOTE: If there is just one, it's a **criterion**. If there are more than one (plural form), they are **criteria**.

This step of setting criteria is probably the most important step of the entire process. It is tempting at this point to start suggesting solutions, but an effective problem-solver will hold her horses and focus ONLY on criteria at this point. Criteria are requirements that a good solution must meet. The first three criteria, which are required, already filled in.

Task 3: Criteria – Develop at least seven strong criteria that a good solution will meet. (logic)
Our solution will …..

1. apply principles of effective communication that we are learning in the class.
2. be achievable within our four week time frame.
3. cost less than _____ .
4. –

5. –

6. –

7. –

8. –

9. –

10. -

   .

Analysis: Reread your list of criteria. Be sure these are all **criteria, not solutions**. Remove any solutions from the list. If you feel confused, contact your instructor for an explanation.

Now it's time to digest all this information. Take a break and ponder your problem during the next week. As you reflect, it's likely that you will think of additional points to add to the analysis or to the list of criteria. Bring them to the next meeting. You might also gain suggestions from class members.

Planning for Meeting 3:	
1. When and where will your next meeting be? 2. Who will submit your meeting 2 results? Each member needs to complete the following before the next meeting: 3. bring additional ideas to add to steps 2 and 3 that you completed during this meeting. 4. read instructions for Meeting 3. 5. review Chapter 8, "Encourage Creativity." 6. read the requirements for the group's final written report 7. send during the week a private email to your leader. Comment about how well you think the group process is going. Are all members following the norms? Are all members filling their roles? Does the group need to make any changes to ensure that it acts as a highly functional team, not just a random herd of cats or sheep? Avoid GROUPTHINK.	All members who have agreed to prepare for and attend Meeting #3 initial here:

COMM 1010: TEAM DECISION-MAKING PROJECT PROGRESS CHART   MEETING #3

Score: /10

Fill in this chart during your 3rd meeting. At the completion of your meeting, submit this chart to your instructor to receive feedback and up to 10 team points for a well-executed Progress Chart. Each member **who participated in this meeting** earns the same number of points for this assignment.

Meeting 3 Date, Time, Location:	
Members Present	Members Not Present

Begin with a discussion of the group process.

Task #1: Group Process Discussion	
The leader will anonymously share emails s/he has received from members during the week regarding how well the group is working together. As a group, recommend solutions to any challenges. If necessary, you may consult your instructor for advice.	**Tip:** Review your group contract. Are all members abiding by the terms of the contract? If not, why not? Revise the contract if needed.

Task #2: Review Steps 1, 2, & 3
Review your notes from previous meetings. Make revisions or additions based on ideas you've come up with during the past week.

In your third meeting, you will complete the second half of the PAC – BOY acronym. B = **B**rainstorm possible solutions. O = **O**rganize your ideas into a chart in which you evaluate each solution in terms of how well it meets your criteria. Y = **Y**es!!! Based on your chart, you will develop the best possible solution.

Task #3: Brainstorm Possible Solutions (right-brain, creative, intuitive thinking)	
As a group, review the text guidelines for brainstorming (see "Encourage Creativity" in Chapter 8). **Brainstorming tips:** • Suggest as many possible solutions to your problem as you can think of. • Write down all the ideas, even if they repeat each other. • Encourage wild and crazy ideas (e.g., "go to the moon for a vacation"), just to get your creativity flowing. • Don't react to any ideas, either positively ("Oh, I like that one" or negatively "That would never work.") • Think outside the box. Stretch your imaginations. • Don't stop until you have brainstormed **at least** a dozen possible solutions.	
Self-analysis: • How well were you able to complete this brainstorming session without evaluating any solutions? • Did you succeed in thinking outside the box? • What was the most "creative" solution?	
Choose the best: 1. 2. 3. 4. 5. 6.	**Tip: (apply left-brain, logical analysis)** • As a group, eliminate any brainstormed solutions that are not feasible. • Eliminate any duplication. • Combine similar ideas. • From the remaining solutions, choose your top five or six.

A28

Now, move on to O = **O**rganize your ideas into a chart in which you evaluate each solution in terms of how well it meets your criteria.

Task #4: organize your criteria and solutions into a chart. (logic)
1. Create a table with solutions listed across the top and criteria listed on the left. Discuss and rate each solution in terms of each criterion using a scale of 0 (does not meet this criterion at all) to 5 (meets this criterion exceedingly well). If a criterion is very important, use a scale of 1 to 10. Total the score for each solution on the bottom row. (See example below.) 2. When you submit your final report, attach a copy of this chart as an appendix to the report.

Here is an example:

	Solution 1	Solution 2	Solution 3	Solution 4	Solution 5	Solution 6	Totals
Criterion 1	0	2	5	5	3	1	
Criterion 2	4	4	2	5	5	4	
Criterion 3	1	0	2	2	3	3	
Criterion 4	4	0	0	0	2	1	
Criterion 5	5	5	5	2	3	4	
Totals:	14	11	14	14	16	13	

Now, move on to Y = **Y**es!!! Based on your chart, develop the best possible solution.

Task #5: Yes, we can develop a good strategy. (combine left-brain logic and right-brain creativity)	
Using the chart from the Organize step as a springboard, develop your optimal solution. Record your solution here:	**Tips:** • Don't be tied down by the chart. The totals might be misleading because some criteria might be more important than others. Just use this chart as a guide. • If you find strong elements from several different solutions, you might be able to combine them into your final strategy. • Be creative!

Design specific steps you would follow if you were actually implementing your solution. Each step should include a person responsible for implementing it, as well as a due date. (You are not required to actually implement the solution, but some groups have done so and have found the results to be rewarding.)

Step	Due Date	Person Assigned

Take a break and ponder your solution during the next week. This incubation time is critical, because we rarely think of everything on the spot. Try to think of any contingencies that might prevent this solution from working as you want it to. Bring these ideas to the next meeting. You'll have a "second-chance" to make final revisions.

Follow up: Prepare to write your group report.

As a group, analyze the "occasion" and "audience" for your report.	Summarize here the results of your audience analysis.
• What conventions (style, format, tone, headings) are appropriate for a formal business report? • Who is your intended audience? • What are the goals of the intended reader? • How can you best meet those goals?	
Assign members to write up a draft for each section of your formal report. • Title Page - • Table of Contents – • Executive Summary - • Project Description - • Methods - • Conclusion - • Works Cited – • Appendices A & B -	**Tip:** As you assign each task, discuss **as a group** the content you would like to see in each element of the report. This is a group project, not a collection of individual essays.

Planning for Meeting 4:	
Who will submit your meeting 3 results? _____ When and where will your next meeting be? Before your next meeting, each member needs to 8. read the Meeting 3 reports that will be posted online by other groups. 9. reply to at least one other group's report with suggestions, comments, or questions. 10. read instructions for Meeting 4. 11. review the requirements for the group's final report. 12. bring at least two possible contingencies (things that could go wrong with your solution). You'll have a chance to edit your solution and suggest how to handle any contingencies that might arise. 13. read the requirements for distributing participation points. You'll be working this out as a group at your next meeting.	All members who have agreed to prepare for and attend Meeting #4 initial here:

Score: __/10

Fill in this chart during your 4th meeting. This week, you don't need to post your results online. Instead, your team will submit your formal Report. At the completion of your meeting, submit a copy of your completed chart to receive feedback and points from your instructor.

Meeting 4 Date, Time, Location:	
Members Present	Members Not Present

Task #1: Hold a "second-chance" analysis of your chosen solution. (combines right & left brain)
Each member was assigned to think of two "contingencies" – things that might go wrong and interfere with your solution working as you intended it to work. List here at least four contingencies: 1. 2. 3. 4.
How would you cope with each of these contingences? 1. 2. 3. 4.
Based on this discussion, revise your solution and implementation plan as needed.

Task #2: Assess the occasion and audience for your report	
What conventions are appropriate for a "business report"? (Refer to Appendix 2, "Writing Well" and "Reports.") Summarize your discussion here:	
Assess your audience: • Who will be reading your report? • What will your reader be looking for?	Tip: Your report is a representation of all the work you've put into this project. Plan carefully so you will end up

A31

• How can you meet your reader's needs?	with a report that represents your very best work. Consider the advice in your text appendix about careful organization, concise writing, professional style, and goodwill.

Task #3: Fine-tune your report

Each member should have brought a draft of their assigned sections of the report, so all you need to do now is some responsible editing. As a group, consider each element of the report, one at a time.

Questions to consider:

- Does the content of this section accurately capture our group findings?
- Are the vocabulary, style, tone, and presentation appropriate? Does the style of this section match the style of the other sections?
- Are the grammar, punctuation, and spelling impeccable? (Use tools such as Spell Check and Grammar Check to help you. However, these are not foolproof, so use your own judgment as well.)
- Are references cited parenthetically within the body of your text and also cited in a separate Works Cited section? (Use the Bibliography tool to help you cite your sources correctly.)

After all revisions are completed, select a Report template or format and prepare a final version of your report.

- Who will compile this final version?
- Who will submit this final version, along with the three required attachments (A: team contract; B: solution comparison chart: and C: participation points)?

Task #4: Distribute participation points

Instructions:

1. Your team will have a total of __x___ participation points to distribute among team members. (X = number of members who participated in at least 1/3 of the meetings and group work.) For example, if your group has five members, you will have a total of fifty points to distribute.

2. The allocation must be decided by the group as a whole, not just by one or two powerful individuals.

3. Not all points need to be distributed. The points are not free "gifts"; they must have been honestly earned.

4. Base your allocation on objective criteria such as attendance, follow-through on tasks, initiative, and contribution of ideas. Hopefully the idea of using "criteria" sounds familiar to all of you by now! Make a ranking chart if you wish.

5. Along with each member's name and points they earned, include a brief justification of why you assigned them that number of points.

6. Submit this information to your instructor, attached as an appendix to your report.

List your criteria here:

-
-
-
-
-
-
-

TEAM DECISION-MAKING PROJECT_PART 2: FORMAL REPORT

After your team reaches its final decision, convey your results in ONE formal written report. This is a TEAM product. Collaborate on content, format, and professional appearance. Aim for a seamless document that showcases a similar tone, writing style, and format throughout. Each member should proofread the entire document and suggest revisions before your appointed team representative submits it.

A. Assess Occasion and Audience: Assess and adapt to the expectations of the occasion and of the audience you're writing for. Attend to the following:

Occasion: This report requires a professional style of writing. You're expected to follow a specific format, with a professional appearance. Your document should have a consistent tone throughout, so proofread each team member's work carefully. The document you submit makes a statement about who you are, so be sure your document reflects the best you can be. Use appropriate business language. Your report should explain academic concepts in a style that is clear, concise, and easy to read. Grammar, punctuation, and spelling should be flawless. A sloppy style suggests to your audience that it's not worth reading any farther than the Executive Summary.

Audience: For this assignment, your primary audience (intended reader) is your instructor. A potential secondary audience might be other students. In the workplace, your audience would be your customer or your manager. Impress these readers favorably by furnishing evidence that

- you have successfully completed all the steps of the reflective thinking problem solving sequence
- your problem analysis was conducted thoughtfully, using effective critical thinking and analysis
- your proposed solution is achievable and will solve the problem adequately
- your report includes all the required content
- your report follows the required format

B. Format for the Final Report: Typically, each organization has its own preferred format for proposals. For this class, please use the following format. Type a **heading** for each section except the Title Page.

Title Page: On the title page, center the following information. Each item should be on a separate line, single-spaced: a short title for the problem your group selected; (skip two lines); submitted by [list all actively participating group members, in alphabetical order by LAST name]; (skip one line); college name; class and section; date submitted.

Table of Contents: List each section in order (flush left). List the page number for each section on the right side of the page. Review this page at the end to be sure any edits haven't changed the numbering.

Executive Summary: This summary may seem like overkill to you, but it is an essential element of a business report. It allows a busy executive to quickly determine whether the report is worth reading. Don't let the title of this section intimidate you. This section is actually just a preview of the contents of your report. Place the Executive Summary on a page by itself. This summary should be no longer than one or two paragraphs, and does not use internal headings. It needs to include one or two sentences regarding each section of your report. These sentences will state why the section is important or will outline the outcomes of that section.

Project Description: Write a two paragraph description of what your group set out to accomplish. This is NOT the same as the Executive Summary. This section tells the reader what your assignment was. After you have explained he nature of your assignment, identify the decision you chose to focus on. Describe your group's purpose and why it's important to come to a decision about this issue. Since you will have come to your decision by the time your write this report, briefly explain why your outcome is effective.

Methods: Begin this section with an introductory paragraph, explaining that your team used the reflective thinking process to arrive at a solution. Clarify the purpose of the reflective thinking process (in general, not as applied to your project). Then explain that you will describe each step your group took in accomplishing your purpose (e.g., what your group did at each meeting), and will provide a brief description of your group's end-product.

For each step in the Reflective-Thinking Sequence create a subheading. Under each subheading include a detailed description of your team's findings. Remember to discuss (in the section explaining your final solution) potential limitations of the solution (which you uncovered when you discussed what could possibly go wrong with your solution) and how you will manage them if they occur. (Refer to "Review of Steps" at the end of this document for a quick review of the steps to cover.)

Conclusion: Your conclusion will include a brief recap of your main points, along with an explication of why your solution is excellent.

Works Cited: Include a complete bibliographical reference for <u>the text</u> and any other materials you've cited in your report.

Appendices: You'll attach three appendices. Each appendix should have its own title at the top of the page.
1. a copy of your Team Contract
2. a copy of your comparison chart which you used to analyze your potential solutions
3. the participation points you assigned to each member, with an explanation of why you assigned those points. Arrange in alphabetical order: last name, first name

C. Submit Your Final Report: Designate one individual to submit the final polished version of your report on time.

REVIEW OF STEPS TO ADDRESS IN <u>THE METHODS SECTION OF YOUR FORMAL REPORT:</u>
COVER EACH OF THESE STEPS IN-DEPTH

The "PAC_BOY" acronym represents the order of these decision-making steps.

- **Part I: [P= Problem]**
  State your problem question
  - "What is the best way .... "

- **Part II: [A = Analyze the problem]**
  Describe your research about the problem. Summarize what you learned about each of the following:
  1. Characteristics of the problem
  2. Stakeholders
  3. History
  4. Policies/politics
  5. Resources available

- **Part III: [C=Criteria] List the criteria you'll use to evaluate your proposed solutions.**
  - What is your general goal?
  - List at least seven realistic criteria that your solution needs to conform to
    - Some of these criteria should include references from class materials

- **Part IV: [B=Brainstorm]**
  Brainstorm possible solutions
  - List all the solutions you brainstormed
    - Some of these solutions should include references from class materials

- **Part V: [O = Organize and assess]**
  Organize your solutions into a chart that will help you choose the best.
  - Explain how you narrowed your solutions to your top five to seven
  - Explain the chart you used for analyzing the solutions. You may either insert the chart here or include it in the attachments section.
  - Answer the question: "How does this solution excel over the other solutions that you proposed?"
  - Hold a <u>Second Chance Meeting</u>: Discuss potential negative consequences and how you could minimize them.
  - Revise your solution if necessary.

- **Part VI: [Y = Yes we can!]**
  Implementation
  - Describe how you plan to implement the solution.
  - This plan must be realistic (something that you as students could actually do in the available time frame).

TEAM MEMBER EVALUATION GUIDELINES
TO ACCOMPANY TEAM DECISION-MAKING PROJECT

Compute the number of participation points your team may distribute among yourselves by multiplying the number of members by 10. For example, if your team has seven active members, you will have a total of 70 points to distribute. If any member contributed less than 30% of the final product, don't award them any points. Reduce the total number of points available to your group by 10.

As a team, decide how to award the points equitably among all members. This decision MUST be made by the group as a whole (that is, all members who are present at the final meeting when you make this important decision).

Not all points need to be distributed. Participation points are not gifts. They are designed to reward students who put in the most effort on the project. Be honest with yourself and your classmates.

RULES:

1. You may not award every group member the same number of points. Some members will receive more than ten points and some members will receive fewer than ten points, based upon their participation. If your team is convinced that each member should receive the same number of points, discuss this ahead of time with your instructor.

2. Use the decision-making protocol to make your decision about participation points. Base your decision on criteria such as
   - **Attendance:** Did this person attend all the group meetings? Were they on time?
   - **Quantity:** Did this participant contribute frequently to the team effort?
   - **Quality:** What was the quality of this member's contributions?
   - **Follow-through:** Did this person complete assignments on time? Were they well prepared for each meeting?
   - **Cooperation:** Did this person enhance the supportive climate of the group? Did they encourage others to participate? Were they an active listener as well as a contributor?
   - **Attitude:** Did they maintain a cheerful 'can-do' demeanor or did they whine and gripe?
   - **General interest in the project and the team:** Did they seem to take the assignment seriously? Did they seem interested in producing a **quality** product, rather than just getting it over with?

3. List team members alphabetically (Last name _ First Name). After each name, identify the number of points awarded. Write an explanation for EACH MEMBER, justifying the number of points awarded.

4. Submit your points as Appendix C of your Team Formal Written Report.

REMEMBER: You may not award all members the same number of points!

TEAM DECISION-MAKING REPORT: Scoring Guide for Formal Report
[up to 60 points possible]

Grading Criteria	Score and Comments
I. Professionalism • Written in formal report format • Report is submitted on time • Report is arranged under the assigned headings • Methods section is arranged under subheadings • Each heading / subheading is supported by at least two paragraphs. • Each paragraph starts with a clear topic sentence • Report demonstrates impeccable spelling, grammar, punctuation, sentence structure • Entire report is written in one unified "voice" throughout; no abrupt changes in style from one section to the next • Tone of writing is appropriate for a business/professional audience (not overly casual; not overly "stiff")	**(up to 10 points)**
II. Title Page, Table of Contents, Works Cited • These pages follow the assigned format • These pages include all required material (see specifications) • Page numbers are correctly indicated in the Table of Contents • References are cited within the body of the text (parenthetical citations) • References are listed in correct format in the Works Cited section at end of report	**(up to 5 points)**
III. Executive Summary and Project Description **Executive Summary:** • Each paragraph begins with topic sentence • Provides overview of entire project • Is concisely written • Addresses each section of the report • Entices reader to continue reading **Project Description:** • Summarizes what the group set out to accomplish. • Identifies the problem. • Describes group's purpose • Explains why it's important to find a solution to the problem.	**(up to 10 points)**
IV. Methods: Steps 1-2 Methods section begins with an overall description of the Reflective-Thinking Sequence **Step 1:** • identifies the problem question • problem question is open-ended' • problem question does not tell us the desired answer • the problem is of a manageable scope for your group to solve in your allotted time period	**(up to 10 points)**

Step 2:	
<ul><li>Sets forth what the team learned about five different areas of background research</li><li>Shows that your group has done sufficient investigation to understand the problem</li><li>Uncovers resources available to your group for help in solving the problem</li></ul>	
V. Methods: Step 3 **Step 3:**<ul><li>Demonstrates that you understand what a criterion is</li><li>Explains why criteria are important and how they are used</li><li>Criteria are realistic</li><li>Criteria are appropriate</li><li>Criteria are helpful in determining the best solution</li><li>Some criteria involve communication concepts from this class</li></ul>	(up to 5 points)
VI. Methods: Steps 4-5 **Step 4**<ul><li>Describes process of brainstorming</li><li>Explains why brainstorming solutions is important</li><li>Identifies a number of brainstormed solutions</li><li>Some possible solutions show creativity & thinking outside the box</li><li>Some possible solutions are feasible</li></ul>**Step 5:**<ul><li>Explains process of narrowing solutions</li><li>Refers to solution ranking chart</li><li>Describes why chosen solution excels over others</li><li>Chosen solution is realistic</li><li>**Explores possible negative consequences** of solution</li><li>Suggests how to manage these unintended consequences if they should occur</li></ul>	(up to 10 points)
VII. Methods: Step 6 **Step 6:**<ul><li>Sets forth a detailed implementation plan</li><li>Assigns tasks to specific individuals</li><li>Includes a time line</li></ul>	(up to 5 points)
VIII. Conclusion and Appendices **Conclusion:**<ul><li>recaps main points</li><li>explains why chosen solution excels over others</li></ul>**Appendices:**<ul><li>Each Appendix is clearly labeled</li><li>Team Contract contains all required material</li><li>Comparison chart shows at least five possible solutions, rated according to at least seven criteria</li><li>Participation points are awarded to each team member</li><li>Participation point ratings are clearly justified</li></ul>	(up to 5 points)
Total score (out of 60)	

INFORMATIVE ORAL PRESENTATION ASSIGNMENT

Learning Outcomes: For this assignment, you'll deliver a five-minute, extemporaneous, informative oral presentation, using a key-word outline (NOT a word-for-word script), to an audience of at least ten adults. You'll show a PowerPoint presentation along with your speech. Your task is to demonstrate the principles of extemporaneous speaking you've been learning about in this course. This assignment offers you an opportunity to

- apply your understanding of the principles of extemporaneous speaking and
- practice delivering a professional presentation

About Anxiety: Every semester, some students enroll in this class who experience speech anxiety or panic disorder. If you fall into this category, start working with your instructor ahead of time. With patience and persistence, it IS POSSIBLE to overcome this challenge. If you take some first steps in this class toward overcoming anxiety, you'll be better off for the rest of your life.

The speech counts for a significant number of points out of your grade. Even if you don't think you'll do well, turn in your materials, show up for your delivery session, and make an attempt to deliver your speech. You're likely to earn at last 60% of the points toward Part 3 of this assignment if you attempt to complete your delivery. If you don't show up, you forfeit all the points for speech delivery. If you don't complete this assignment, the highest grade you can earn in this class is a C-. Don't ignore this very important assignment, even if it terrifies you. Your instructor is supporting you. Your instructor wants you to succeed. Your instructor will work with you.

Three-Step Assignment: This assignment is divided into three steps: the outline, the PowerPoint, and the final delivery. You'll get plenty of feedback after you submit the first two steps. You can revise and resubmit Parts 1 & 2 if you wish. You can ask questions at any time. Thus, when you finally stand up and present your ideas orally to the audience, you should be so well prepared and so familiar with your speech that you'll have a pleasant and rewarding experience.
****

INFORMATIVE ORAL PRESENTATION ASSIGNMENT *PART 1: DRAFT OF OUTLINE*

A. How to Prepare:
1. Read Chapters 9 – 11 and the section about Informative Presentations from Chapter 12.
2. View the student examples for the outline, PowerPoint, and speech delivery.

B. Select your topic. The criteria for your topic are (1) expertise, (2) narrow focus, (3) intellectual stimulation, and (4) informative approach.
  Expertise: Choose a topic you have a lot of knowledge about. Research has shown that credibility (competence in your subject matter) is the most important determinant of whether your speech is successful or not. Few people are invited to speak about a topic they're not an "expert" on.

  Teach the audience something you've learned at school or at work or through a hobby. You'll be more comfortable talking about a topic you're very familiar with (e.g., how to select a pair of hiking boots that fit well; the effect of sugar on our metabolism; typical causes of earthquakes; tips for creating an artistic scrapbook; guide dogs for the blind) than a topic you know little about. You'll be able to make your speech interesting if you have prior experience with the topic; you can liven it up by including brief personal experiences.

  Narrow focus: Choose a very specific focus for your speech. Avoid broad issues such as political topics, gun control, abortion, and the like. Try writing one preliminary draft of an outline; then discard all your main points except ONE. Start over, using the one main point you've selected as the topic of your speech. Your audience can understand and enjoy the speech much more if you narrow your topic. This will allow you ample time to make each point "come alive" for your audience by integrating a variety of statistics, quotes, examples, and personal stories.

  Intellectual stimulation: Avoid frivolous topics such as "the value of procrastinating," "101 uses for duct tape," or "how to make a peanut butter sandwich." Teach something of informative value for your audience. The audience should leave your speech thinking, "I'm really glad I learned about that!" Don't waste the time of your classmates. Since time is money, you're figuratively stealing when you waste another person's time.

  You may choose a topic the audience already has some knowledge about (e.g. the value of exercise). If you do so, however, teach something **new** about the topic. It isn't enough to say generic statements such as "exercise is good for you." To add depth to this topic, you might explain step-by-step the physiological process through which exercise affects our heart. Display a diagram and explain a few basic physiological terms.

  Informative: Aim for a "teaching" approach rather than a "preaching" approach. Master principles of informative speaking before you venture forth into the arena of persuasion. Effective persuasion is difficult; save your persuasive speech until you take COMM 1020 - Public Speaking.

C. Write a specific purpose statement. After you've selected your topic, consider your audience. What specific knowledge about your topic would you like them to walk away with? Express this as a purpose statement that begins with the words: "My audience will ...." This goal is for planning purposes only. You won't say this out loud to your audience. Examples:

My audience will realize they can start saving for tax-free retirement now by opening a Roth IRA.
My audience will understand how they can benefit their children by reading out loud to them.

D. Write a thesis statement. Write a sentence that clearly summarizes this one key idea. Unlike in written compositions, the thesis of a speech should not be a complex sentence. Keep it simple, focused, and easy to understand. You'll say this sentence out loud in your introduction so your audience will know from the start what your speech is about. Examples:

You can start saving for retirement today by opening a Roth IRA.
You can give your child a great gift by reading out loud.

E. Select two or three main points. Write out these points as complete sentences in your outline. The points must be logically related to each other. Examples:

After you put money into a Roth IRA, you won't have to pay taxes on it again.
In an emergency, you can withdraw your Roth contributions without penalty.

F. Develop your supporting material. For each main point, locate at least three specific items that provide strong verbal support for that point. Refer to Table 10-1 in your text. Use a variety of types of support (definition; example; story; statistics; comparisons; quotations).

Keep good records of the sources of your information. Help your audience link this information to its source by naming your references (at least three authoritative references) **out loud** in your speech, <u>immediately before</u> you tell us the information you obtained from that source.

In addition to material from at least three authoritative references, include a mini-story, example, or advice, in which you tell us about your own experience with this topic. This should be a brief, but lively narrative. Your audience will connect to it! You'll be more credible if you share your own expertise.

G. Choose your pattern of organization. Select one of the informative patterns of organization described in your text (chronological; spatial; topical; or cause-effect). In some cases, you might be able to use a problem-solution pattern, as long as you are describing, not persuading.

H. Arrange all the pieces into a key-word outline. Follow the format of the sample student outline. First, develop the body of your speech. Then write an introduction and conclusion. Insert transitions between your main points.

Key-word outline: This outline will become your speaking notes. Except for your thesis and your main points, avoid writing complete sentences in your speaking notes. If you used complete sentences, you'd be tempted to read your sentences. Reading from your outline is not the same as speaking dynamically to an audience. If you read, you lose eye contact with your audience, and your voice lacks natural expressiveness.

Background Information: Above your outline, identify your specific goal; intended audience; pattern of organization; your experience with the topic; and the number of references you will cite out loud (at least three are required).

Introduction: The introduction should be short ... less than 5% of your total speaking time. Start your speech introduction with a "hook" (AKA "attention-getter"). Next, clearly state your thesis. Third, preview your main points. This helps the audience understand the structure and purpose of your speech. Your preview will be clearer if you enumerate each of your main points. Enumeration helps the listeners understand what they should listen for. Here's an example: "First, I'll explain what keratoconus is. Then, I'll tell you how to prevent it." Chapter 9 includes additional examples.

Body: Write each main point as a sentence. Under each main point, arrange the details in outline format, showing key words only. Refer to the student example.

Transitions: Insert transitions between your main points to help your audience follow your line of development. Transitions are sentences that help us segue from one main point to the next (e.g., "Now that I've explained what keratoconus is, I'd like to tell you how to prevent it.")

Conclusion: The conclusion should be short ... less than 5% of your total speaking time. Your conclusion should echo your thesis and main points (using different wording). This helps reinforce the key idea you want your audience to remember. Then add a memorable statement that brings your speech to a clear end. Refer to examples in Chapter 9. Beware .... don't add any new information in your conclusion. All new information should be stated within the body of the speech.

Works Cited: Include your complete Works Cited list at the bottom of the outline. You must include at least three respectable references (not counting yourself -- you are not a reference). References contribute to your credibility as a speaker. Use a recognized format such as MLA or APA.

I. Submit your draft outline to your instructor for feedback and points. After you receive feedback on your draft outline, rework and revise your outline. Then practice, practice, practice for your delivery session. Convert your word-processed key-word outline to very large font with lots of empty space on the page. Use this version as your speaking notes.

INFORMATIVE ORAL PRESENTATION ASSIGNMENT *PART 1:* A GUIDE FOR OUTLINING YOUR SPEECH

Part A: AUDIENCE AND OCCASION ANALYSIS:
(This information is for your instructor; you will not SAY this out loud in your speech)

Specific Goal: My audience will _____ (explain what you expect your audience to experience, feel, or learn).

Pattern Of Organization: I've chosen the [chronological; spatial; topical; or cause-effect] pattern of organization because
_____ .

Audience Analysis: Explain briefly how you will present your topic in a way that is interesting to your specific audience of students. Discuss here what "value added" (new knowledge) you will give to your classmates. It is unethical to waste their time by telling them information that they already know.

Occasion Analysis: Explain how your speech is appropriate to the specific circumstances and location where it will be given (in this case, an academic/ professional/informative occasion).

Part B: SPEECH OUTLINE:
(Use this outline as your speaking notes when you deliver your speech.)
You must cite at least one expert reference out loud as part of the support for EACH main point,
for a total of at least three authoritative references.

Speech Title: _____

Introduction:

    I. Hook (attention-getter): Cite an incident, tell a story, or use an example that will interest the audience in your topic.

    II. Indicate your expertise with this topic (could be moved to your first main point).

    III. Thesis: This sentence summarizes your "teaching point" (central message) for your audience.

    IV. Preview: List your main points here in very brief form (no more than 5 words per point).

        First, …

        Second, …

        Third, …

[**Transition:** Write here a transition from the preview to the body: ….]

Body:

I. **First major point** (write as a complete sentence)

    [Under one of the pieces of evidence supporting this point, include a reference.]

    A. evidence to explain or support this point (short phrase only)

        1. detail about this evidence (short phrase only)

        2. another detail about this evidence (short phrase only)

        3. A third detail about this evidence (short phrase only)

        4.-5. Fourth and fifth details, as needed.

    B. another piece of evidence to explain or support this point (short phrase only)

        1. detail (short phrase only)

        2. detail (short phrase only)

        3. detail (short phrase only)

    C. a third piece of evidence to explain or support this point (short phrase only)

        1. detail (short phrase only)

        2. detail (short phrase only)

        3. detail (short phrase only)

    D. one or two more pieces of evidence, as needed.

[**Transition**: Write here a transition from point 1 to point 2. Use a complete sentence.]

II. **Second major point** (write as a complete sentence)
Follow the same pattern as for Point I above.
> [Under one of the pieces of evidence supporting this point, include a reference.]

>> A. evidence to explain or support this point (short phrase only)
>>> 1. detail about this evidence (short phrase only)
>>> 2. – 5. Additional details (short phrases only)

>> B. - D. additional pieces of evidence to explain or support this point (short phrase only), with details, in the same format shown above.

[**Transition**: Write your transition from point 2 to point 3. Use a complete sentence.]

III. **Third major point**   (You may add a third main point, developed in outline form, as above.)

Conclusion: Write down the words you will say as you conclude your speech. You may use complete sentences here, but do not read your conclusion from your notes when you deliver your speech.

> I. Summary of key points.
> II. Review of thesis.
> III. Memorable message.

TIP: In the conclusion, echo your thesis and preview, using different words than you used in your Introduction. Then draw the speech to a close with a brief memorable message. Do NOT introduce any new material in the conclusion. Practice your ending until it feels "final." Don't be tempted to weaken a fine speech by adding a lame "that's it" at the end.

Works Cited: Include a list of authoritative references (at least three) that you used to gather facts for your speech. List references in alphabetical order by authors' last names. Include dates and places of publication. For Web references, include the author or sponsoring company, common name of the Web site, and URL (available at www. ....)

Example Citation:

> Adler, R & Elmhorst, J. (2013). Communicating at work: SLCC custom text (2nd ed.). Boston: McGraw Hill.

INFORMATIVE ORAL PRESENTATION
SCORING GUIDE FOR PART 1: DRAFT OF SPEECH OUTLINE
[up to 20 points total]

Grading Criteria	Score and Comments
Background Information • specific goal has single, narrow focus • speech is appropriate for audience identified • pattern of organization correctly identified • explains speaker's expertise • plans to cite at least 3 references	(up to 3 pts)
Outline- Introduction • hook captures audience attention • hook leads directly into thesis • speaker's expertise is clarified • thesis has same single, narrow focus as specific goal • clear preview of two or three main points	(up to 2 pts)
Outline- Main Points • main points correspond to preview • each main point focuses on one single idea • each main point is meaningfully related to thesis • main points flow logically • effective transitions between main points	(up to 3 pts)
Outline- Academic Rigor **Ethos:** • at least 3 references integrated into body of outline • references are authoritative **Logos:** • each main point is well supported (researched fact, statistics, academic studies, examples, charts) • information probes beyond common knowledge **Pathos:** • each main point is brought home to audience (brief story, comparison, personalized comments, vivid word pictures)	(up to 5 pts)
Conclusion • reviews major points • reflects back to thesis • ends with memorable message	(up to 2 pts)
Works Cited • cites at least three authoritative references • references show academic rigor • references written in correct format	(up to 5 pts)
Total points (out of 20 possible)	

INFORMATIVE ORAL PRESENTATION ASSIGNMENT
PART 2: DRAFT OF POWERPOINT DISPLAY

A. Prepare
- Review the section of your text titled Visual Aids in Chapter 10.
- Read the document titled "Effective PowerPoint Design" distributed by your instructor
- View the student example of a PowerPoint display distributed by your instructor.

B. Create a draft of the PowerPoint slides you'll show as you deliver your speech
- Create a maximum of six slides (obtain instructor approval for any exceptions): Title Slide, Preview Slide, Main Point Slides, and Conclusion. Content will correspond to the outline you submitted in Part 1.
  - ✓ one title slide that includes a title and your name
  - ✓ a preview slide that summarizes as key-word bullet points your two or three main points from your outline
  - ✓ one slide for each main point (limit = two or three main points); use the main point as the title of your slide, with bullet points for the subheadings you'll cover as you discuss this point.
  - ✓ one conclusion slide

- Check the characteristics of effective slides
  - ✓ simple and brief (avoid animations and busy backgrounds)
  - ✓ spacious (maximum 25 words per line; maximum 6 lines per slide; **no block quotes**; key words only, not complete sentences), so audience can gather the info with a quick glance)
  - ✓ very large font size (easy to read from the back of the room; for each 10' to the back of the room, add one inch to the screen height of your letters).
  - ✓ consistent (same color scheme and capitalization scheme throughout; avoid all caps)
  - ✓ correct spelling and grammar
  - ✓ graphics and photos are clearly labeled and relevant to the point you're making (as you deliver the speech, you'll need to explain the meaning of any graphics or photos)

- Spend less time on your PowerPoint than on your outline and delivery practice. The slides are only a side-kick. YOU and your oral presentation are the main attraction.

Submit your PowerPoint draft
Based on feedback from your instructor, rework and revise your slides before you deliver your speech.

- Practice using these slides as you practice delivering your speech. Practice at least three times all the way through, standing up and out loud. Practice is the best antidote to anxiety.

- Bring your revised version with you on the day you deliver your speech, stored on a USB compatible thumb drive.

- Print out a one-page summary showing thumbnails of your slides to submit to your instructor.

Grading Criteria	Score and Comments
Organization • topic is narrow • title slide • preview slide lists all main points as brief phrases • 2 to 4 main point slides correspond to points listed in preview • points proceed in logical order • one conclusion slide • photos, tables, charts (if used) are clearly labeled	**(up to 5 pts)**
Simplicity • slides appear spacious • uses large font • bulleted lists are left aligned • few animations • key words only; **no complete sentences** • no more than 7 lines per slide • no more than 7 words per line (<30 characters) • no block quotes	**(up to 5 pts)**
Consistency remains consistent throughout entire slide show: • one color scheme • one background style or theme • one font style	**(up to 5 pts)**
Correctness • assignment is submitted on time • correct grammar, spelling & capitalization; • factual correctness • content is relevant to speech thesis	**(up to 5 pts)**
Total points (out of 20 possible)	

INFORMATIVE ORAL PRESENTATION ASSIGNMENT
PART 3: EXTEMPORANEOUS DELIVERY OF YOUR INFORMATIVE SPEECH

A. How to Prepare:

1. Review text Chapter 11: Delivering the Presentation.

2. Watch the student video example. Notice the following:
    -**Conversational flow of speaking**. This demonstrates "extemporaneous" speaking... using an outline for your speaking notes, yet speaking naturally. This is the delivery style you should be aiming for: well-organized, but not memorized, and not reading word-for-word.
    -**In-depth explanations**. Discuss advantages, disadvantages, what might go wrong. Use examples and metaphors.
    -**References**. Tell us where you got your information. Add insights from experts.
    -**Personal commentary**. Personalize the speech by explaining your interest in the topic. Add you own brief story or your own personal observations. This will help you "connect" with the audience.

3. Sign up for a specific day and time to deliver your speech. Consider this to be a contract. If you miss your time slot, it's highly likely you won't get a second chance to deliver for reduced points, because most class schedules are tightly organized.

4. Print out a word-processed, single-sided KEY WORD outline for your speech on 8.5 x 11 paper.
    -If you submitted a sentence outline in Step 1, convert to a key-word outline.
    -If you submitted a key word outline in Step 1, prepare a more spacious version.
    -Print a copy with enlarged type and lots of white space so you can easily glance down and find your place when the paper is set on a lectern.
    - Mark up your outline to emphasize key points, references, pauses, and other reminders.
    -Use this outline, not a word-for-word manuscript, when you practice and deliver your speech.
    -Avoid relying on note cards. Holding a set of note cards in your hand can be distracting to both the speaker and the listener. Professionals rarely use note cards. Learn to speak from a printed outline.

5. Practice pays off. Practice is the #1 remedy for nervousness.
    -**Use a conversational style**: Practice until you' can deliver your speech in a way that sounds natural, not robotic. Omit teen talk and fillers ("well," "like," "just," "kind of," "and that," " yeah", "and stuff"). Practice pronouncing unfamiliar words until they roll easily off your tongue. Stumbling on words reduces your credibility.

    -**Stand up and speak out loud.** Speaking is a motor skill, and must be learned through bodily action. (Similarly, you can't learn to ski by just imagining in your mind what you would do; you have to get out there and do it.) Practice in front of a mirror, your favorite pet, or an audience of friends. Practice until you're sounding confident and enthusiastic! Then you'll actually enjoy this opportunity to share your knowledge with others.

    -**Practice from your key word outline.** Practice speaking extemporaneously without reading directly from your notes. Aim to look at your notes about 10% of the time, so you won't lose your place. Look at your audience the remaining 90% of the time.

    -**Practice advancing your slides.** Practice advancing your slides as you say your speech. This isn't as easy as it sounds. You'll need to look at the audience and your notes, yet remember to advance your slides.

    -**Practice stating your references orally**. Practice stating your 3 or more references out loud right during the speech, at the moment when you tell us the information from them. (These are called oral footnotes.) Don't just read a list of references at the beginning or end of your speech.

Here 's an example of how you can state a reference in your speech: "Verderber suggests in his book 'The Challenge of Effective Speaking' that we should spend as much time (or more) practicing our speech out loud as we spent planning and researching its content."

-Practice staying within your time limit. Your speech needs to last 5 minutes, with a 45 second grace period on either side of the time limit. Practice until you're confident you can present your speech smoothly in that time frame without rushing or stalling. If your speech is shorter than 4 ½ minutes, add another specific example. Examples add interest to your speech. If your speech runs longer than 5 ½ minutes, consider narrowing your topic. Select one of your main points and turn that into your new speech. A narrow topic will make your job easier.

B. Oral Presentation: On your assigned date, you'll present your 5 minute informative speech to the class, accompanied by PowerPoint technology. Deliver your speech extemporaneously … don't read it or memorize it.
- **If you read from your notes, you'll sacrifice many points, no matter how good the content is.**
- **By the same token, if you wing your speech without preparing a substantive outline, you'll sacrifice even more points.**

C. Written Materials: On the day of your speech, submit:
1. revised word-processed key-word outline
2. on the bottom of the last page of your outline, type a bibliography <u>of at least 3 references</u> that you'll also <u>cite out loud</u> in the body of speech (not at the beginning or end)
3. thumbnails of your PowerPoint slides, consolidated onto one page of paper
4. three blank evaluation forms
   -one professor evaluation form
   -two peer evaluation forms
   -write your name and the title of your speech on the top line of each form
   -leave the remainder of the forms blank for evaluator use

D. Criteria for Grading: To receive an "A," your presentation must:
1. be delivered extemporaneously (**without reading**) from a word-processed key-word outline
2. have a narrow focus
3. be arranged according to one of the <u>informative</u> organizational patterns from Chapter 9 or 12.
4. start with an introduction that includes a hook, thesis, and brief preview of main points that clearly support the thesis
5. in the body, support each of these main points with a variety of in-depth evidence (facts, stories, examples, statistics, definitions, quotes from experts, etc.)
6. relate facts to the audience in an interesting, intellectually stimulating, and understandable manner, using metaphors, examples, and/or illustrations
7. incorporate adequate research (at least 3 credible references), stated orally in the speech and written in the bibliography on your outline
8. conclude with a summary of your main points and an informative (not persuasive) memorable message that relates back to the thesis
9. be accompanied by a set of PowerPoint slides based on effective principles of design

Speech Part 3 - Delivery Scoring Guide   [Total Score= _____ out of 60 pts]

Speaker's Name: _____ Speech Title: _____ Speech Duration: _____

Criteria for Evaluating Speech	Rating	Detailed Explanation of Ratings
ORGANIZATION: [0 - 10 points]		
Attention-getter captures audience interest and leads appropriately into thesis		
Thesis is clearly indicated; thesis clarifies a single meaningful central theme		
Preview lists main points as key words only		
Transitions signpost movement between main points		
Main points are logically organized; each point relates back to thesis		
Conclusion ties back to thesis, summarizes main points, ends w/ memorable message		
ETHOS AND REFERENCES: [0-10 points]		
Speaker demonstrates expertise in this topic		
Information is accurate and is adapted to interests & knowledge of THIS audience		
3 or more expert references cited out loud within speech body		
References clearly linked in speech body to the information they represent		
References are of academic quality		
Works Cited lists at least 3 references, arranged alphabetically, in APA or MLA format		
SUPPORTING MATERIAL: [0-20 points]		
Narrow focus (post-hole speech); content goes beyond common knowledge		
Speech is intellectually stimulating (audience learns something useful)		
Variety of types of supporting material are used (definition; facts; statistics; research studies; examples; quotes; comparisons; mini-stories; demonstrations; word pictures)		
Speaker interprets material to make it meaningful for this specific audience		
DELIVERY: [0–10 points]		
Speech adheres to time limit		
Eye contact (90%; all audience members); extemporaneous style (not reading)		
Oral speaking style (personal pronouns; contractions; non-complex sentences; personalized interjections; conversational tone)		
Vocal & facial variety; energy; enthusiasm		
Fluency; pronunciation; articulation; grammar; free from "fillers" or "teen talk"		
Non-distracting gestures; stance; body movement		
Attire is professional (or appropriate for topic)		
REVISED VERSION OF POWER POINT: [0 – 5 points]		
Follows progression of speech (title slide; preview; one slide per main point; conclusion)		
Can be easily read (spacious; large font; 7x7 rule)		
Consistent color, theme, and font throughout		
Correct grammar, spelling; punctuation		
Slides displayed so all can see; speaker looks at audience, not at slides		
REVISED VERSION OF SPEECH OUTLINE: [0 – 5 points]		
Speaking notes typed on 8.5 x 11 paper		
Speaking notes arranged in outline format using key words (PHRASES, not sentences)		
Introduction shows clear thesis and preview		
Main points worded as meaningful statements; transitions lead from one main point to the next		

EVALUATION SCALE:
Enter a <u>numeric score</u> for each uppercase topic.
Rate each criterion within topic areas using +, √, -, or 0.
     + = EXCEEDS EXPECTATIONS;   √ = MEETS EXPECTATIONS;   - = NEEDS IMPROVEMENT   0= DOES NOT MEET EXPECTATIONS

COMM 1010: ePORTFOLIO ASSIGNMENT

SLCC now requires students to add a submission to your ePortfolio for every General Education class you take. These portfolios can be helpful in applying for jobs, or in showing family and friends what you've accomplished.

Outline for your ePortfolio

Arrange your ePortfolio website under the following tabs:

Welcome
Goals and Outcomes
Coursework - with three subsections: General Education; My Major; Electives
Learning Outside the Classroom
Resume

Content to include for your COMM 1010 entry

Create a separate page for COMM 1010 under the General Education subsection. Label this page according to the role COMM 1010 fills in your General Education, such as Student Choice (for A.S. degrees) or Communication (for A.A.S. degrees). If you're not sure what label to use, ask your advisor.

Include two parts in your COMM 1010 ePortfolio page:

(1) a self-reflection: Write a paragraph or two describing how you can apply what you've learned in this class to other classes, to the workplace, and/or to other areas of your life. Please be sincere. Don't over-inflate your claims.
(2) your favorite assignment. This can be one of the papers you've submitted in this class or the PowerPoint, outline, or video of your speech. Don't submit the group report however; this should be an example of your individual work.

Where to post

If you haven't yet started your ePortfolio, you'll need to open your own site. Use the FREE option at one of the sites listed below. You do NOT need to pay for this site. Yola is probably the easiest to use. Weebly is more powerful. Wordpress is set up like a blog, in case you want others to submit comments to you.

http://www.yola.com/
http://www.weebly.com/
http://wordpress.com/

How to get help setting up your ePortfolio

SLCC has set up a web page and manual to help guide you through this process (see links below). If you have additional questions, you can contact Kati.Lewis@slcc.edu.

General information about your ePortfolio: http://www.slcc.edu/gened/eportfolio/Students.asp
Access SLCC ePortfolio Manual: http://www.slcc.edu/gened/eportfolio/docs/EPortfolioManual.pdf